Hal R. Broswell

THE

TREASURY OF DAVID.

THE

TREASURY OF DAVID:

CONTAINING

AN ORIGINAL EXPOSITION OF THE BOOK OF PSALMS;

A COLLECTION OF ILLUSTRATIVE EXTRACTS FROM THE WHOLE
RANGE OF LITERATURE;

A SERIES OF HOMILETICAL HINTS UPON ALMOST EVERY
VERSE;

AND LISTS OF WRITERS UPON EACH PSALM.

BY

C. H. SPURGEON.

VOL. I.

PSALM I. TO XXVI.

NEW YORK:

I. K. FUNK & CO., 10 AND 12 DEY STREET.

1882.

AUTHORIZATION.

"Messrs. I. K. Funk & Co. have entered into an arrangement with me to reprint THE TREASURY OF DAVID *in the United States. I have every confidence in them that they will issue it correctly and worthily. It has been the great literary work of my life, and I trust it will be as kindly received in America as in England. I wish for Messrs. Funk success in a venture which must involve a great risk, and much outlay."*

Dec. 8, 1881.   C. H. SPURGEON.

PREFACE.

MY Preface shall at least possess the virtue of brevity, as I find it difficult to impart to it any other.

The delightful study of the Psalms has yielded me boundless profit and ever-growing pleasure ; common gratitude constrains me to communicate to others a portion of the benefit, with the prayer that it may induce them to search further for themselves. That I have nothing better of my own to offer upon this peerless book is to me matter of deepest regret ; that I have anything whatever to present is subject for devout gratitude to the Lord of grace. I have done my best, but, conscious of many defects, I heartily wish I could have done far better.

The Exposition here given is my own. I consulted a few authors before penning it, to aid me in interpretation and arouse my thoughts ; but, still I can claim originality for my comments, at least so I honestly think. Whether they are better or worse for that, I know not ; at least I know I have sought heavenly guidance while writing them, and therefore I look for a blessing on the printing of them.

The collection of quotations was an after-thought. In fact, matter grew upon me which I thought too good to throw away. It seemed to me that it might prove serviceable to others, if I reserved portions of my reading upon the various Psalms ; those reserves soon acquired considerable bulk, so much so that even in this volume only specimens are given and not the bulk.

One thing the reader will please clearly to understand, and I beg him to bear it in mind ; *I am far from endorsing all I have quoted.* I am neither responsible for the scholarship or ortho-doxy of the writers. The names are given that each author may bear his own burden ; and a variety of writers have been quoted that the thoughts of many minds might be before the reader. Still I trust nothing evil has been admitted ; if it be so it is an oversight.

The research expended on this volume would have occupied far too much of my time, had not my friend and amanuensis Mr. John L. Keys, most diligently aided me in investigations at the British Museum, Dr. Williams's Library, and other treasuries of theological lore. With his help I have ransacked books by the hundred, often without finding a memorable line as a reward, but at other times with the most satisfactory result. Readers little know how great labour the finding of but one pertinent extract may involve ; labour certainly I have not spared : my earnest prayer is that some measure of good may come of it to my brethren in the ministry and to the church at large.

The Hints to the Village Preacher are very simple, and an apology is due to my ministerial readers for inserting them, but I humbly hope they may render assistance to those for whom alone they are designed, viz., lay preachers whose time is much occupied, and whose attainments are slender.

Should this first volume meet with the approbation of the judicious, I shall hope by God's grace to continue the work as rapidly as I can consistently with the research demanded and my incessant pastoral duties. Another volume will follow in all probability in twelve months' time, if life be spared and strength be given.

It may be added, that although the comments were the work of my health, the rest of the volume is the product of my sickness. When protracted illness and weakness laid me aside from daily preaching, I resorted to my pen as an available means of doing good. I would have preached had I been able, but as my Master denied me the privilege of thus serving him, I gladly availed myself of the other method of bearing testimony for his name. O that he may give me fruit in this field also, and his shall be all the praise.

C. H. Spurgeon

Clapham, December, 1869.

INDEX

OF AUTHORS QUOTED OR REFERRED TO.

EXPOSITIONS OF THE PSALMS.

PSALM I.

TITLE.—*This Psalm may be regarded as* THE PREFACE PSALM, *having in it a notification of the contents of the entire Book. It is the psalmist's desire to teach us the way to blessedness, and to warn us of the sure destruction of sinners. This, then, is the matter of the first Psalm, which may be looked upon, in some respects, as the text upon which the whole of the Psalms make up a divine sermon.*

DIVISION.—*This Psalm consists of two parts : in the first (from verse 1 to the end of the 3rd) David sets out wherein the felicity and blessedness of a godly man consisteth, what his exercises are, and what blessings he shall receive from the Lord. In the second part (from verse 4 to the end) he contrasts the state and character of the ungodly, reveals the future, and describes, in telling language, his ultimate doom.*

EXPOSITION.

BLESSED *is* the man that walketh not in the counsel of the ungodly, nor standeth in the way of sinners, nor sitteth in the seat of the scornful.

2 But his delight *is* in the law of the LORD ; and in his law doth he meditate day and night.

" BLESSED "—see how this Book of Psalms opens with a benediction, even as did the famous Sermon of our Lord upon the Mount ! The word translated " blessed " is a very expressive one. The original word is plural, and it is a controverted matter whether it is an adjective or a substantive. Hence we may learn the multiplicity of the blessings which shall rest upon the man whom God hath justified, and the perfection and greatness of the blessedness he shall enjoy. We might read it, " Oh, the blessednesses ! " and we may well regard it (as Ainsworth does) as a joyful acclamation of the gracious man's felicity. May the like benediction rest on us !

Here the gracious man is described both negatively (verse 1) and positively (verse 2). He is a man *who does not walk in the counsel of the ungodly*. He takes wiser counsel, and walks in the commandments of the Lord his God. To him the ways of piety are paths of peace and pleasantness. His footsteps are ordered by the Word of God, and not by the cunning and wicked devices of carnal men. It is a rich sign of inward grace when the outward walk is changed, and when ungodliness is put far from our actions. Note next, *he standeth not in the way of sinners*. His company is of a choicer sort than it was. Although a sinner himself, he is now a blood-washed sinner, quickened by the Holy Spirit, and renewed in heart. Standing by the rich grace of God in the congregation of the righteous, he dares not herd with the multitude that do evil. Again it is said, " *nor sitteth in the seat of the scornful.*" He finds no rest in the atheist's scoffings. Let others make a mock of sin, of eternity, of hell and heaven, and of the Eternal God ; this man has learned better philosophy than that of the infidel, and has too much sense of God's presence to endure to hear his name blasphemed. The seat of the scorner may be very lofty, but it is very near to the gate of hell ; let us flee from it, for it shall soon be empty, and destruction shall swallow up the man who sits therein. Mark the gradation in the first verse :

He walketh not in the counsel of the ungodly,
Nor *standeth*   in the *way*   of   *sinners,*
Nor SITTETH   in the SEAT   of   SCORNFUL.

When men are living in sin they go from bad to worse. At first they merely *walk* in the counsel of the careless and *ungodly*, who forget God—the evil is rather practical than habitual—but after that, they become habituated to evil, and they *stand* in the way of open *sinners* who wilfully violate God's commandments ; and if let alone, they go one step further, and become themselves pestilent teachers and tempters of others, and thus they *sit in the seat of the scornful.*

They have taken their degree in vice, and as true Doctors of Damnation they are installed, and are looked up to by others as Masters in Belial. But the blessed man, the man to whom all the blessings of God belong, can hold no communion with such characters as these. He keeps himself pure from these lepers; he puts away evil things from him as garments spotted by the flesh; he comes out from among the wicked, and goes without the camp, bearing the reproach of Christ. O for grace to be thus separate from sinners.

And now mark his positive character. "*His delight is in the law of the Lord.*" He is not *under* the law as a curse and condemnation, but he is *in* it, and he delights to be in it as his rule of life; he delights, moreover, to *meditate* in it, to read it *by day*, and think upon it *by night*. He takes a text and carries it with him all day long; and in the night-watches, when sleep forsakes his eyelids, he museth upon the Word of God. In the *day* of his prosperity he sings *psalms* out of the Word of God, and in the *night* of his affliction he comforts himself with *promises* out of the same book. "The law of the Lord" is the daily bread of the true believer. And yet, in David's day, how small was the volume of inspiration, for they had scarcely anything save the first five books of Moses! How much more, then, should we prize the whole written Word which it is our privilege to have in all our houses! But, alas, what ill-treatment is given to this angel from heaven! We are not all Berean searchers of the Scriptures. How few among us can lay claim to the benediction of the text! Perhaps some of you can claim a sort of negative purity, because you do not walk in the way of the ungodly; but let me ask you—Is your delight in the law of God? Do you study God's Word? Do you make it the man of your right hand—your best companion and hourly guide? If not, this blessing belongeth not to you.

3 And he shall be like a tree planted by the rivers of water, that bringeth forth his fruit in his season; his leaf also shall not wither; and whatsoever he doeth shall prosper.

"*And he shall be like a tree planted;*" not a wild tree, but "a tree *planted,*" chosen, considered as property, cultivated and secured from the last terrible uprooting, for "every plant, which my heavenly Father hath not planted, shall be rooted up:" Matthew xv. 13. "*By the rivers of water;*" so that even if one river should fail, he hath another. The rivers of pardon and the rivers of grace, the rivers of the promise and the rivers of communion with Christ, are never-failing sources of supply. He is "like a tree planted by the rivers of water, *that bringeth forth his fruit in his season;*" not unseasonable graces, like untimely figs, which are never full-flavored. But the man who delights in God's Word, being taught by it, bringeth forth patience in the time of suffering, faith in the day of trial, and holy joy in the hour of prosperity. Fruitfulness is an essential quality of a gracious man, and that fruitfulness should be seasonable. "*His leaf also shall not wither;*" his faintest word shall be everlasting; his little deeds of love shall be had in remembrance. Not simply shall his fruit be preserved, but *his leaf* also. He shall neither lose his beauty nor his fruitfulness. "*And whatsoever he doeth shall prosper.*" Blessed is the man who hath such a promise as this. But we must not always estimate the fulfilment of a promise by our own eye-sight. How often, my brethren, if we judge by feeble sense, may we come to the mournful conclusion of Jacob, "All these things are against me!" For though we know our interest in the promise, yet are we so tried and troubled, that sight sees the very reverse of what that promise foretells. But to the eye of faith this word is sure, and by it we perceive that our works are prospered, even when everything seems to go against us. It is not outward prosperity which the Christian most desires and values; it is soul prosperity which he longs for. We often, like Jehoshaphat, make ships to go to Tarshish for gold, but they are broken at Ezion-geber; but even here there is a true prospering, for it is often for the soul's health that we should be poor, bereaved, and persecuted. Our worst things are often our best things. As there is a curse wrapped up in the wicked man's mercies, so there is a blessing concealed in the righteous man's crosses, losses, and sorrows. The trials of the saint are a divine husbandry, by which he grows and brings forth abundant fruit.

4 The ungoldy *are* not so : but *are* like the chaff which the wind driveth away.

We have now come to the second head of the Psalm. In this verse the contrast of the ill estate of the wicked is employed to heighten the coloring of that fair and pleasant picture which precedes it. The more forcible translation of the Vulgate and of the Septuagint version is—"*Not so the ungodly, not so.*" And we are hereby to understand that whatever good thing is said of the righteous is not true in the case of the ungodly. Oh ! how terrible is it to have a double negative put upon the promises ! and yet this is just the condition of the ungodly. Mark the use of the term " *ungodly*," for, as we have seen in the opening of the Psalm, these are the beginners in evil, and are the least offensive of sinners. Oh ! if such is the sad state of those who quietly continue in their morality, and neglect their God, what must be the condition of open sinners and shameless infidels ? The first sentence is a negative description of the ungodly, and the second is the positive picture. Here is their *character*—" they are like chaff," intrinsically worthless, dead, unserviceable, without substance, and easily carried away. Here, also, mark their *doom*,—" *the wind driveth away ;*" death shall hurry them with its terrible blast into the fire in which they shall be utterly consumed.

5 Therefore the ungodly shall not stand in the judgment, nor sinners in the congregation of the righteous.

They shall stand there to be judged, but not to be acquitted. Fear shall lay hold upon them there ; they shall not stand their ground ; they shall flee away ; they shall not stand in their own defence ; for they shall blush and be covered with eternal contempt.

Well may the saints long for heaven, for no evil men shall dwell there, "*nor sinners in the congregation of the righteous.*" All our congregations upon earth are mixed. Every Church hath one devil in it. The tares grow in the same furrows as the wheat. There is no floor which is as yet thoroughly purged from chaff. Sinners mix with saints, as dross mingles with gold. God's precious diamonds still lie in the same field with pebbles. Righteous Lots are this side heaven continually vexed by the men of Sodom. Let us rejoice then, that in " the general assembly and church of the firstborn" above, there shall by no means be admitted a single unrenewed soul. Sinners cannot live in heaven. They would be out of their element. Sooner could a fish live upon a tree than the wicked in Paradise. Heaven would be an intolerable hell to an impenitent man, even if he could be allowed to enter ; but such a privilege shall never be granted to the man who perseveres in his iniquities. May God grant that we may have a name and a place in his courts above !

6 For the LORD knoweth the way of the righteous : but the way of the ungodly shall perish.

Or, as the Hebrew hath it yet more fully, " The Lord is *knowing* the way of the righteous." He is constantly looking on their way, and though it may be often in mist and darkness, yet the Lord knoweth it. If it be in the clouds and tempest of affliction, he understandeth it. He numbereth the hairs of our head ; he will not suffer any evil to befall us. " He knoweth the way that I take : when he hath tried me, I shall come forth as gold. (Job xxiii. 10.) " *But the way of the ungodly shall perish.*" Not only shall *they* perish themselves, but *their way* shall perish too. The righteous carves his name upon the rock, but the wicked writes his remembrance in the sand. The righteous man ploughs the furrows of earth, and sows a harvest here, which shall never be fully reaped till he enters the enjoyments of eternity ; but as for the wicked, he ploughs the sea, and though there may seem to be a shining trail behind his keel, yet the waves shall pass over it, and the place that knew him shall know him no more for ever. The very "way" of the ungodly shall perish. If it exist in remembrance, it shall be in the remembrance of the bad ; for the Lord will cause the name of the wicked to rot, to become a stench in the nostrils of the good, and to be only known to the wicked themselves by its putridity.

May the Lord cleanse our hearts and our ways, that we may escape the doom of the ungodly, and enjoy the blessedness of the righteous !

EXPLANATORY NOTES AND QUAINT SAYINGS.

Whole Psalm.—As the book of the Canticles is called the Song of Songs by a Hebraism, it being the most excellent, so this Psalm may not unfitly be entitled, the Psalm of Psalms, for it contains in it the very pith and quintessence of Christianity. What Jerome saith on St. Paul's epistles, the same may I say of this Psalm ; it is short as to the composure, but full of length and strength as to the matter. This Psalm carries blessedness in the frontispiece ; it begins where we all hope to end : it may well be called a Christian's Guide, for it discovers the quicksands where the wicked sink down in perdition, and the firm ground on which the saints tread. to glory.—*Thomas Watson's Saints' Spiritual Delight*, 1660.

This whole Psalm offers itself to be drawn into these two opposite propositions : a godly man is blessed, a wicked man is miserable ; which seem to stand as two challenges, made by the prophet : one, that he will maintain a godly man against all comers, to be the only Jason for winning the golden fleece of blessedness ; the other, that albeit the ungodly make a show in the world of being happy, yet they of all men are most miserable.—*Sir Richard Baker*, 1640.

I have been induced to embrace the opinion of some among the ancient interpreters (Augustine, Jerome, etc.), who conceive that the first Psalm is intended to be descriptive of the character and reward of the JUST ONE, *i.e.* the Lord Jesus.—*John Fry*, B.A., 1842.

Verse 1.—The psalmist saith more to the point about true happiness in this short Psalm than any one of the philosophers, or all of them put together ; they did but beat the bush, God hath here put the bird into our hand.—*John Trapp*, 1660.

Verse 1.—Where the word *blessed* is hung out as a sign, we may be sure that we shall find a godly man within.—*Sir Richard Baker*.

Verse 1.—The seat of the drunkard is the seat of the scornful.—*Matthew Henry*, 1662—1714.

Verse 1.—"*Walketh* NOT . . . . . NOR *standeth* . . . . . NOR *sitteth*," etc. Negative precepts are in some cases more absolute and peremptory than affirmatives ; for to say, "that hath walked in the counsel of the godly," might not be sufficient ; for, he might walk in the counsel of the godly, and yet walk in the counsel of the ungodly too ; not both indeed at once, but both at several times ; where now, this negative clears him at all times.—*Sir Richard Baker*.

Verse 1.—The word הָאִישׁ *haish* is emphatic, *that man ;* that one among a thousand who lives for the accomplishment of the end for which God created him.—*Adam Clarke*, 1844.

Verse 1.—"*That walketh not in the counsel of the ungodly.*" Mark certain circumstances of their differing characters and conduct. I. The *ungodly man* has his *counsel.* II. The *sinner* has his *way ;* and III. The *scorner* has his *seat.* The *ungodly man* is unconcerned about religion ; he is neither zealous for his own salvation nor for that of others ; and he *counsels* and *advises* those with whom he converses to adopt his plan, and not trouble themselves about praying, reading, repentance. etc., etc. ; "there is no need for such things ; live an honest life, make no fuss about religion, and you will fare well enough at last." Now "blessed is the man who walks not in this man's counsel," who does not come into his measures, nor act according to his plan.

The *sinner* has his particular *way* of transgressing ; one is a *drunkard*, another *dishonest*, another *unclean*. Few are given to every species of vice. There are many *covetous* men who abhor *drunkenness*, many *drunkards* who abhor *covetousness;* and so of others. *Each has his easily besetting sin;* therefore, says the prophet, "*Let the wicked* forsake HIS WAY." Now, *blessed is he who stands not in such a man's* WAY.

The *scorner* has brought, in reference to himself, all religion and moral feeling to an end. He has *sat down*—is utterly confirmed in impiety, and makes a mock at sin. His conscience is seared, and he is a believer in all unbelief. Now, *blessed is the man who sits not down in his* SEAT.—*Adam Clarke.*

Verse 1.—In the Hebrew, the word "*blessed*" is a plural noun, *ashrey (blessednesses),* that is, all blessednesses are the portion of that man who has not gone away, etc. ; as though it were said, "All things are well with that man who," etc. Why do you hold any dispute ? Why draw vain conclusions ? If a man has found that pearl of great price, to love the law of God and to be separate from the ungodly, all blessednesses belong to that man ; but, if he does not find this jewel, he will seek for all blessednesses but will never find one ! For as all things are pure unto the pure, so all things are lovely unto the loving, all things good unto the good ; and, universally, such as thou art thyself, such is God himself unto thee, though he is not a creature. He is perverse unto the perverse, and holy unto the holy. Hence nothing can be good or saving unto him who is evil ; nothing sweet unto him unto whom the law of God is not sweet. The word "*counsel*" is without doubt here to be received as signifying decrees and doctrines, seeing that no society of men exists without being formed and preserved by decrees and laws. David, however, by this term strikes at the pride and reprobate temerity of the ungodly. First, because they will not humble themselves so far as to walk in the law of the Lord, but rule themselves by their own counsel. And then he calls it their " counsel," because it is their prudence, and the way that seems to them to be without error. For this is the destruction of the ungodly—their being prudent in their own eyes and in their own esteem, and clothing their errors in the garb of prudence and of the right way. For if they came to men in the open garb of error, it would not be so distinguishing a mark of blessedness not to walk with them. But David does not here say, " in the folly of the ungodly," or " in the error of the ungodly ;" and therefore he admonishes us to guard with all diligence against the appearance of what is right, that the devil transformed into an angel of light do not seduce us by his craftiness. And he contrasts the counsel of the wicked with the law of the Lord, that we may learn to beware of wolves in sheep's clothing, who are always already to give counsel to all, to teach all, and to offer assistance unto all, when they are of all men the least qualified to do so. The term " *stood* " descriptively represents their obstinacy, and stiff-neckedness, wherein they harden themselves and make their excuses in words of malice, having become incorrigible in their ungodliness. For " to stand," in the figurative manner of Scripture expression, signifies to be firm and fixed : as in Rom. xiv. 4, " To his own master he standeth or falleth : yea, he shall be holden up, for God is able to make him stand." Hence the word " column " is by the Hebrew derived from their verb " to stand," as is the word statue among the Latins. For this is the very self-excuse and self-hardening of the ungodly—their appearing to themselves to live rightly, and to shine in the eternal show of works above all others. With respect to the term " *seat,*" to sit in the seat, is to teach, to act the instructor and teacher ; as in Matt. xxiii. 2, " The scribes sit in Moses' chair." *They* sit in the seat of pestilence, who fill the church with the opinions of philosophers, with the traditions of men, and with the counsels of their own brain, and oppress miserable consciences, setting aside, all the

while, the word of God, by which alone the soul is fed, lives, and is preserved.—
Martin Luther, 1536—1546.

Verse 1.—" *The scornful.*" *Peccator cum in profundum venerit contemnet*—
when a wicked man comes to the depth and worst of sin, he despiseth. Then
the Hebrew will despise Moses (Exodus ii. 14), " Who made thee a prince and
a judge over us ?" Then Ahab will quarrel with Micaiah (1 Kings xxii. 18),
because he doth not prophesy good unto him. Every child in Bethel will mock
Elisha (2 Kings ii. 23), and be bold to call him " bald pate." Here is an original
drop of venom swollen to a main ocean of poison : as one drop of some serpents'
poison, lighting on the hand, gets into the veins, and so spreads itself over all
the body till it hath stifled the vital spirits. God shall " laugh you to scorn,"
(Psalm ii. 4), for laughing him to scorn ; and at last despise you that have
despised him in us. That which a man spits against heaven, shall fall back on
his own face. Your indignities done to your spiritual physicians shall sleep in
the dust with your ashes, but stand up against your souls in judgment.—*Thomas
Adams,* 1614.

Verse 2.—" *But his will is in the law of the Lord.*" The " will," which is
here signified, is that delight of heart, and that certain pleasure, in the law,
which does not look at what the law promises, nor at what it threatens, but at
this only ; that " the law is holy, and just, and good." Hence it is not only a
love of the law, but that loving delight in the law which no prosperity, nor
adversity, nor the world, nor the prince of it, can either take away or destroy ;
for it victoriously bursts its way through poverty, evil report, the cross, death,
and hell, and in the midst of adversities, shines the brightest.—*Martin Luther.*

Verse 2. —" *His delight is in the law of the Lord.*"—This *delight* which the prophet here speaks of is the only delight that neither blushes nor looks pale ; the
only delight that gives a repast without an after reckoning ; the only delight
that stands in construction with all tenses ; and like Æneas Anchyses, carries
his parents upon his back.—*Sir Richard Baker.*

Verse 2.—" *In his law doth he meditate.*" In the plainest text there is a world
of holiness and spirituality ; and if we in prayer and dependence upon God did
sit down and study it, we should behold much more than appears to us. It may
be, at once reading or looking, we see little or nothing ; as Elijah's servant went
once, and saw nothing ; therefore he was commanded to look seven times.
What now ? says the prophet, " I see a cloud rising, like a man's hand ;" and
by-and-by, the whole surface of the heavens was covered with clouds. So you
may look lightly upon a Scripture and see nothing ; *meditate often upon it,* and
there you shall see a light, like the light of the sun.—*Joseph Caryl,* 1647.

Verse 2.—" *In his law doth he meditate day and night.*"—The good man doth
meditate on the law of God day and night. The pontificians beat off the common
people from this common treasury, by objecting this supposed difficulty. Oh,
the Scriptures are hard to be understood, do not you trouble your heads about
them ; we will tell you the meaning of them. They might as well say, heaven
is a blessed place, but it is a hard way to it ; do not trouble yourselves, we will
go thither for you. Thus in the great day of trial, when they should be saved
by their book, alas ! they have no book to save them. Instead of the Scriptures they can present images ; these are the laymen's books ; as if they were
to be tried by a jury of carvers and painters, and not by the twelve apostles.
Be not you so cheated ; but study the gospel as you look for comfort by the
gospel. He that hopes for the inheritance, will make much of the conveyance.
Thomas Adams.

Verse 2.—To " *meditate,*" as it is generally understood, signifies to discuss, to
dispute ; and its meaning is always confined to a being employed in words, as
in Psalm xxxii. 30, " The mouth of the righteous shall meditate wisdom." Hence
Augustine has, in his translation, " chatter ;" and a beautiful metaphor it is—
as chattering is the employment of birds, so a continual conversing in the law
of the Lord (for talking is peculiar to man), ought to be the employment of

man. But I cannot worthily and fully set forth the gracious meaning and force of this word ; for this "meditating" consists first in an intent observing of the words of the law, and then in a comparing of the different Scriptures ; which is a certain delightful hunting, nay, rather a playing with stags in a forest, where the Lord furnishes us with the stags, and opens to us their secret coverts. And from this kind of employment, there comes forth at length a man well instructed in the law of the Lord to speak unto the people.—*Martin Luther.*

Verse 2.—"*In his law doth he meditate day and night.*" The godly man will read the Word by *day*, that men, seeing his good works, may glorify his Father who is in heaven ; he will do it in the *night*, that he may not be seen of men : by *day*, to show that he is not one of those who dread the light ; by *night*, to show that he is one who can shine in the shade : by *day*, for that is the time for working—work whilst it is day ; by *night*, lest his Master should come as a thief, and find him idle.—*Sir Richard Baker.*

Verse 2.—I have no rest, but in a nook, with *the book.*—*Thomas à Kempis,* 1380—1471.

Verse 2.—"*Meditate.*" Meditation doth discriminate and characterise a man ; by this he may take a measure of his heart, whether it be good or bad ; let me allude to that ; "For as he thinketh in his heart, so is he." Prov. xxiii. 7. As the meditation is, such is the man. Meditation is the touchstone of a Christian ; it shows what metal he is made of. It is a spiritual index ; the index shows what is in the book, so meditation shows what is in the heart.—*Thomas Watson's Saints' Spiritual Delight.*

Meditation chews the cud, and gets the sweetness and nutritive virtue of the Word into the heart and life : this is the way the godly bring forth much fruit. *Bartholomew Ashwood's Heavenly Trade,* 1688.

The naturalists observe that to uphold and accommodate bodily life, there are divers sorts of faculties communicated, and these among the rest : 1. An attractive faculty, to assume and draw in the food ; 2. A retentive faculty, to retain it when taken in ; 3. An assimilating faculty, to concoct the nourishment ; 4. An augmenting faculty, for drawing to perfection. Meditation is all these. It helps judgment, wisdom, and faith to ponder, discern, and credit the things which reading and hearing supply and furnish. It assists the memory to lock up the jewels of divine truth in her sure treasury. It has a digesting power, and turns special truth into spiritual nourishment ; and lastly, it helps the renewed heart to grow upward and increase its power to know the things which are freely given to us of God.—*Condensed from Nathaniel Ranew,* 1670.

Verse 3.—"*A tree.*"—There is one tree, only to be found in the valley of the Jordan, but too beautiful to be entirely passed over ; the oleander, with its bright blossoms and dark green leaves, giving the aspect of a rich garden to any spot where it grows. It is rarely if ever alluded to in the Scriptures. But it may be the tree planted by the streams of water which bringeth forth his fruit in due season, and "whose leaf shall not wither."—*A. P. Stanley, D.D., in "Sinai and Palestine."*

Verse 3.—"*A tree planted by the rivers of water.*"—This is an allusion to the Eastern method of cultivation, by which rivulets of water are made to flow between the rows of trees, and thus, by artificial means, the trees receive a constant supply of moisture.

Verse 3.—"*His fruit in his season.*"—In such a case expectation is never disappointed. Fruit is expected, fruit is borne, and it comes also in the time in which it should come. A godly education, under the influences of the divine Spirit, which can never be withheld where they are earnestly sought, is sure to produce the fruits of righteousness ; and he who reads, prays, and meditates, will ever *see* the *work* which God has given him to do ; the *power* by which he is to perform it ; and the *times, places,* and *opportunities* for doing those things by which God can obtain most glory, his own soul most good, and his neighbour most edification.—*Adam Clarke.*

Verse 3.—" In his season." The Lord reckons the times which pass over us, and puts them to our account : let us, therefore, improve them, and, with the impotent persons at the pool of Bethesda, step in when the angel stirs the water. Now the church is afflicted, it is a season of prayer and learning ; now the church is enlarged, it is a season of praise ; I am now at a sermon, I will hear what God will say ; now in the company of a learned and wise man, I will draw some knowledge and counsel from him ; I am under a temptation, now is a fit time to lean on the name of the Lord ; I am in a place of dignity and power, let me consider what it is that God requireth of me in such a time as this. And thus as the tree of life bringeth fruit every month, so a wise Christian, as a wise husbandman, hath his distinct employments for every month, bringing forth his fruit in his season.—*John Spencer's Things New and Old,* 1658.

Verse 3.—" In his season." Oh, golden and admirable word ! by which is asserted the liberty of Christian righteousness. The ungodly have their stated days, stated times, certain works, and certain places ; to which they stick so closely, that if their neighbours were perishing with hunger, they could not be torn from them. But this blessed man, being free at all times, in all places, for every work, and to every person, will serve you whenever an opportunity is offered him ; whatsoever comes into his hands to do, he does it. He is neither a Jew, nor a Gentile, nor a Greek, nor a barbarian, nor of any other particular person. He gives his fruit in his season, so often as either God or man requires his work. Therefore his fruits have no name, and his times have no name.—*Martin Luther.*

Verse 3.—" His leaf also shall not wither." He describes the fruit before he does the leaf. The Holy Spirit himself always teaches every faithful preacher in the church to know that the kingdom of God does not stand in word but in power. 1 Cor. iv. 20. Again, "Jesus began both to do and to teach." Acts i. 1. And again, "Which was a prophet mighty in deed and word." Luke xxiv. 19. And thus, let him who professes the word of doctrine, first put forth the fruits of life, if he would not have his fruit to wither, for Christ cursed the fig tree which bore no fruit. And, as Gregory saith, that man whose life is despised is condemned by his doctrine, for he preaches to others, and is himself reprobated.—*Martin Luther.*

Verse 3.—" His leaf also shall not wither." The Lord's trees are all ever-greens. No winter's cold can destroy their verdure ; and yet, unlike evergreens in our country, they are all fruit bearers.—*C. H. S.*

Verse 3.—" And whatsoever he doeth, [or, *maketh or taketh in hand] shall prosper."* And with regard to this "prospering," take heed that thou understandest not a carnal prosperity. This prosperity is hidden prosperity, and lies entirely secret in spirit ; and therefore if thou hast not this prosperity that is by faith, thou shouldst rather judge thy prosperity to be the greatest adversity. For as the devil bitterly hates this leaf and the word of God, so does he also those who teach and hear it, and he persecutes such, aided by all the powers of the world. Therefore thou hearest of a miracle the greatest of all miracles, when thou hearest that all things prosper which a blessed man doeth.—*Martin Luther.*

*Verse 3.—*A critical journal has shown that instead of "*Whatsoever it doeth shall prosper,*" the rendering might be, "*Whatsoever it produceth shall come to maturity.*" This makes the figure entire, and is sanctioned by some MSS. and ancient versions.

*Verse 3 (last clause).—*Outward prosperity, if it follow close walking with God, is very sweet ; as the cipher, when it follows a figure, adds to the number, though it be nothing in itself.—*John Trapp.*

Verse 4.—" Chaff." Here, by the way, we may let the wicked know they have a thanks to give they little think of ; that they may thank the godly for all the good days they live upon the earth, seeing it is for their sakes and not for their own that they enjoy them. For as the chaff while it is united and keeps close to the wheat, enjoys some privileges for the wheat's sake, and is laid up carefully in the barn ; but as soon as it is divided, and parted from the wheat, it is cast out and scattered by the wind ; so the wicked, whilst the godly are in company and live amongst them, partake for their sake of some blessedness promised to the godly ; but if the godly forsake them or be taken from them, then either a deluge of water comes suddenly upon them, as it did upon the old world when Noah left it ; or a deluge of fire, as it did upon Sodom, when Lot left it, and went out of the city.—*Sir Richard Baker.*

Verse 4.—" *Driveth away,*" or tosseth away ; the Chaldee translateth for " wind," " whirlwind."—*Henry Ainsworth,* 1639.

This shows the vehement tempest of death, which sweeps away the soul of the ungodly.

Verse 5.—" *Therefore the ungodly shall not stand in the judgment,*" etc. And may not a reason also be conceived thus, why the ungodly can never come to be of the congregation of the righteous : the righteous go a way that God knows, and the wicked go a way that God destroys ; and seeing that these ways can never meet, how should the men meet that go these ways ? And to make sure work that they shall never meet indeed, the prophet expresseth the way of the righteous by the first link of the chain of God's goodness, which is his *knowledge ;* but expresseth the way of the wicked by the last link of God's justice, which is his *destroying ;* and though God's justice and his mercy do often meet, and are contiguous one to another, yet the first link of his mercy and the last link of his justice can never meet, for it never comes to destroying till God be heard to say *Nescio vos,* " *I know you not,*" and *nescio vos* in God, and God's knowledge, can certainly never possibly meet together.—*Sir Richard Baker.*

Verse 5.—The Irish air will sooner brook a toad, or a snake, than heaven a sinner.—*John Trapp.*

Verse 6.—" *For the Lord knoweth the way of the righteous : but the way of the ungodly shall perish.*" Behold how David here terrifies us away from all prosperous appearances, and commends to us various temptations and adversities. For this " way" of the righteous all men utterly reprobate ; thinking also, that God knoweth nothing about any such way. But this is the wisdom of the cross. Therefore, it is God alone that knoweth the way of the righteous, so hidden is it to the righteous themselves. For his right hand leads them on in a wonderful manner, seeing that it is a way, not of sense, nor of reason, but of faith only ; even of that faith that sees in darkness, and beholds things that are invisible.—*Martin Luther.*

Verse 6.—" *The righteous.*" They that endeavour righteous living in themselves and have Christ's righteousness imputed to them.—*Thomas Wilcocks,* 1586.

HINTS TO THE VILLAGE PREACHER.

Verse 1.—May furnish an excellent text upon " Progress in Sin," or " The Purity of the Christian," or " The Blessedness of the Righteous." Upon the last subject speak of the believer as BLESSED—1. By God ; 2. In Christ ; 3. With all blessings ; 4. In all circumstances ; 5. Through time and eternity ; 6. To the highest degree.

Verse 1.—Teaches a godly man to beware, (1) of the opinions, (2) of the practical life, and (3) of the company and association of sinful men. Show how meditation upon the Word will assist us in keeping aloof from these three evils.

The insinuating and progressive nature of sin.—*J. Morison.*

Verse 1, *in connection with the whole Psalm.* The wide difference between the righteous and the wicked.

Verse 2.—THE WORD OF GOD. 1. The believer's delight in it. 2. The believer's acquaintance with it. We long to be in the company of those we love.

Verse 2.—I. What is meant by "the law of the Lord." II. What there is in it for the believer to delight in. III. How he shows his delight, thinks of it, reads much, speaks of it, obeys it, does not delight in evil.

Verse 2 (*last clause*).—The benefits, helps, and hindrances of meditation.

Verse 3.—"*The fruitful tree.*" I. Where it grows. II. How it came there. III. What it yields. IV. How to be like it.

Verse 3.—"*Planted by the rivers of water.*" I. The origination of Christian life, "*planted.*" II. The streams which support it. III. The fruit expected from it.

Verse 3.—Influence of religion upon prosperity.—*Blair.*

The nature, causes, signs, and results of true prosperity.

"*Fruit in his season ;*" virtues to be exhibited at certain seasons—patience in affliction ; gratitude in prosperity ; zeal in opportunity, etc.

"*His leaf also shall not wither ;*" the blessing of retaining an unwithered profession.

Verses 3, 4.—See No. 280 of "Spurgeon's Sermons."—"The Chaff Driven Away."

Sin puts a negative on every blessing.

Verse 5.—The sinner's double doom. 1. Condemned at the judgment-bar. 2. Separated from the saints. Reasonableness of these penalties, "therefore," and the way to escape them.

"*The congregation of the righteous*" viewed as the church of the first-born above. This may furnish a noble topic.

Verse 6 (*first sentence*).—A sweet encouragement to the tried people of God. The knowledge here meant. 1. *Its character.*—It is a knowledge of observation and approbation. 2. *Its source.*—It is caused by omniscience and infinite love. 3. *Its results.*—Support, deliverance, acceptance, and glory at last.

Verse 6 (*last clause*).—His way of pleasure, of pride, of unbelief, of profanity, of persecution, of procrastinating, of self-deception, etc. : all these shall come to an end.

WORKS UPON THE FIRST PSALM.

The Way to Blessedness: a Commentary on the First Psalm. By PHINEAS FLETCHER. 4to., London. 1632.

A Discourse about the State of True Happiness, delivered in certain Sermons in Oxford, and at Paul's Cross. By ROBERT BOLTON. London. 1625.

David's Blessed Man ; or, a Short Exposition on the First Psalm, directing a Man to True Happiness. By SAMUEL SMITH, preacher of the Word at Prittlewell in Essex. 1635. [Reprinted in Nichol's Series of Commentaries.]

Meditations and Disquisitions upon the First Psalm of David.—Blessed is the Man.—By Sir RICHARD BAKER, Knight. London. 1640. [The same volume contains Meditations upon "Seven Consolatorie Psalms of David," namely, 23, 27, 30, 84, 103, and 116.]

The Christian on the Mount ; or, a Treatise concerning Meditation ; wherein the necessity, usefulness, and excellency of Meditation, are at large discussed. By THOMAS WATSON. 1660.

PSALM II.

TITLE.—*We shall not greatly err in our summary of this sublime Psalm if we call it* THE PSALM OF MESSIAH THE PRINCE ; *for it sets forth, as in a wondrous vision, the tumult of the people against the Lord's anointed, the determinate purpose of God to exalt his own Son, and the ultimate reign of that Son over all his enemies. Let us read it with the eye of faith, beholding, as in a glass, the final triumph of our Lord Jesus Christ over all his enemies. Lowth has the following remarks upon this Psalm :* " *The establishment of David upon his throne, notwithstanding the opposition made to it by his enemies, is the subject of the Psalm. David sustains in it a twofold character, literal and allegorical. If we read over the Psalm, first with an eye to the literal David, the meaning is obvious, and put beyond all dispute by the sacred history. There is indeed an uncommon glow in the expression and sublimity in the figures, and the diction is now and then exaggerated, as it were on purpose to intimate, and lead us to the contemplation of higher and more important matters concealed within. In compliance with this admonition, if we take another survey of the Psalm as relative to the person and concerns of the spiritual David, a noble series of events immediately rises to view, and the meaning becomes more evident, as well as more exalted. The colouring which may perhaps seem too bold and glaring for the king of Israel, will no longer appear so when laid upon his great Antitype. After we have thus attentively considered the subjects apart, let us look at them together, and we shall behold the full beauty and majesty of this most charming poem. We shall perceive the two senses very distinct from each other, yet conspiring in perfect harmony, and bearing a wonderful resemblance in every feature and lineament, while the analogy between them is so exactly preserved, that either may pass for the original from whence the other was copied. New light is continually cast upon the phraseology, fresh weight and dignity are added to the sentiments, till, gradually ascending from things below to things above, from human affairs to those that are Divine, they bear the great important theme upwards with them, and at length place it in the height and brightness of heaven.*"

DIVISION.—*This Psalm will be best understood if it be viewed as a four-fold picture. (In verses* 1, 2, 3) *the Nations are raging ;* (4 to 6) *the Lord in heaven derides them ;* (7 to 9) *the Son proclaims the decree ; and (from* 10 *to end) advice is given to the kings to yield obedience to the Lord's anointed. This division is not only suggested by the sense, but is warranted by the poetic form of the Psalm, which naturally falls into four stanzas of three verses each.*

EXPOSITION.

WHY do the heathen rage, and the people imagine a vain thing ?

2 The kings of the earth set themselves, and the rulers take counsel together, against the LORD, and against his anointed, *saying,*

3 Let us break their bands asunder, and cast away their cords from us.

We have, in these first three verses, a description of the hatred of human nature against the Christ of God. No better comment is needed upon it than the apostolic song in Acts iv. 27, 28 : " For of a truth against thy holy child Jesus, whom thou hast anointed, both Herod, and Pontius Pilate, with the Gentiles, and the people of Israel, were gathered together, for to do whatsoever thy hand and thy counsel determined before to be done." The Psalm begins abruptly with an angry interrogation ; and well it may : it is surely but little to be wondered at, that the sight of creatures in arms against their God should amaze the psalmist's mind. We see the *heathen raging,* roaring like the sea, tossed to and fro with restless waves, as the ocean in a storm ; and then we mark the people in their hearts *imagining a vain thing* against God. Where there is much rage there is generally some folly, and in this case there is an excess of it. Note, that the commotion is not caused by the people only, but their leaders foment the rebellion. " *The kings of the earth set themselves.*" In determined malice they arrayed themselves in opposition against God. It was not temporary rage, but deep-seated hate, for they *set themselves* resolutely to withstand the Prince of Peace. " *And the rulers take counsel together.*" They go about their warfare craftily, not with foolish haste, but deliberately. They use all the skill which art can give. Like Pharaoh, they cry, " Let us deal wisely with them." O that men were half as careful in God's service to serve him wisely, as his enemies are to attack his kingdom craftily. Sinners have their wits about them, and yet saints are dull. But what say they ? what is the meaning of this commotion ? " *Let us break their bands asunder.*" Let us be free to commit all manner of abomination. Let us be our own gods. Let us rid ourselves of all restraint." Gathering impudence by the traitorous proposition of rebellion, they add— " *let us cast away ;*" as if it were an easy matter,—" let us fling off " *their cords from us.*'" What ! O ye kings, do ye think yourselves Samsons ? and are the bands of Omnipotence but as green withs before you ? Do you dream that you shall snap to pieces and destroy the mandates of God—the decrees of the Most High—as if they were but tow ? And do ye say, " Let us cast away their cords from us ?" Yes ! There are monarchs who have spoken thus, and there are still rebels upon thrones. However mad the resolution to revolt from God, it is one in which man has persevered ever since his creation, and he continues in it to this very day. The glorious reign of Jesus in the latter day will not be consummated, until a terrible struggle has convulsed the nations. His coming will be as a refiner's fire, and like fuller's soap, and the day thereof shall burn as an oven. Earth loves not her rightful monarch, but clings to the usurper's sway : the terrible conflicts of the last days will illustrate both the world's love of sin and Jehovah's power to give the kingdom to his only Begotten. To a graceless neck the yoke of Christ is intolerable, but to the saved sinner it is easy and light. We may judge ourselves by this, do we love that yoke, or do we wish to cast it from us ?

4 He that sitteth in the heavens shall laugh : the Lord shall have them in derision.

Let us now turn our eyes from the wicked council-chamber and raging tumult of man, to the secret place of the majesty of the Most High. What doth God say ? What will the King do unto the men who reject his only-begotten Son, the Heir of all things ?

Mark the quiet dignity of the Omnipotent One, and the contempt which he pours upon the princes and their raging people. He has not taken the trouble to rise up and do battle with them—he despises them, he knows how absurd, how irrational, how futile are their attempts against him—he therefore *laughs* at them.

5 Then shall he speak unto them in his wrath, and vex them in his sore displeasure.

6 Yet have I set my king upon my holy hill of Zion.

After he has laughed he shall *speak ;* he needs not smite ; the breath of his lips is enough. At the moment when their power is at its height, and their fury most violent, *then* shall his Word go forth against them. And what is it that he says ?—it is a very galling sentence—" *Yet,*" says he, " despite your malice, despite your tumultuous gatherings, despite the wisdom of your counsels, despite the craft of your lawgivers, ' *yet have I set my king upon my holy hill of Zion.*'" Is not that a grand exclamation ! He has already done that which the enemy seeks to prevent. While they are proposing, he has disposed the matter. Jehovah's will is done, and man's will frets and raves in vain. God's Anointed is appointed, and shall not be disappointed. Look back through all the ages of infidelity, hearken to the high and hard things which men have spoken against the Most High, listen to the rolling thunder of earth's volleys against the Majesty of heaven, and then think that God is saying all the while, " Yet have I set my king upon my holy hill of Zion." Yet Jesus reigns, yet he sees of the travail of his soul, and " his unsuffering kingdom yet shall come" when he shall take unto himself his great power, and reign from the river unto the ends of the earth. Even now he reigns in Zion, and our glad lips sound forth the praises of the Prince of Peace. Greater conflicts may here be foretold, but we may be confident that victory will be given to our Lord and King. Glorious triumphs are yet to come ; hasten them, we pray thee, O Lord ! It is Zion's glory and joy that her King is in her, guarding her from foes, and filling her with good things. Jesus sits upon the throne of grace, and the throne of power in the midst of his church. In him is Zion's best safeguard ; let her citizens be glad in him.

> " Thy walls are strength, and at thy gates
> A guard of heavenly warriors waits;
> Nor shall thy deep foundations move,
> Fixed on his counsels and his love.
>
> Thy foes in vain designs engage ;
> Against his throne in vain they rage,
> Like rising waves, with angry roar,
> That dash and die upon the shore."

7 I will declare the decree : the LORD hath said unto me, Thou *art* my son ; this day have I begotten thee.

8 Ask of me, and I shall give *thee* the heathen *for* thine inheritance, and the uttermost parts of the earth *for* thy possession.

9 Thou shalt break them with a rod of iron ; thou shalt dash them in pieces like a potter's vessel.

This Psalm wears something of a dramatic form, for now another person is introduced as speaking. We have looked into the council-chamber of the wicked, and to the throne of God, and now we behold the Anointed declaring his rights of sovereignty, and warning the traitors of their doom.

God has laughed at the counsel and ravings of the wicked, and now Christ the Anointed himself comes forward, as the Risen Redeemer, " declared to be the Son of God with power, according to the spirit of holiness, by the resurrection from the dead." Rom. i. 4. Looking into the angry faces of the rebellious kings, the Anointed One seems to say, " If this sufficeth not to make you silent, ' *I will declare the decree.* '" Now this decree is directly in conflict with the device of man, for its tenour is the establishment of the very dominion against which the nations are raving. " *Thou art my Son.*" Here is a noble proof of the glorious Divinity of our Immanuel. " For unto which of the angels said he at any time, Thou art my Son, this day have I begotten thee ?" What a mercy to have a Divine Redeemer in whom to rest our confidence ! " *This day have I begotten thee.*" If this refers to the Godhead of our Lord, let us not attempt to fathom it, for it is a great truth, a truth reverently to be received, but not irreverently to be scanned. It may be added, that if this relates to the Begotten One in his human nature, we must here also rejoice in the mystery, but not attempt to violate its sanctity by intrusive prying into the secrets of the Eternal God. The things which are revealed are enough, without venturing into vain speculations. In attempting to define the Trinity, or unveil the essence of Divinity, many men have lost themselves : here great ships have foundered. What have we to do in such a sea with our frail skiffs ?

" *Ask of me.*" It was a custom among great kings, to give to favoured ones whatever they might ask. (See Esther v. 6 ; Matt. xiv. 7.) So Jesus hath but to ask and have. Here he declares that his very enemies are his inheritance. To their face he declares this decree, and " Lo ! here," cries the Anointed One, as he holds aloft in that once pierced hand the sceptre of his power, " He hath given me this, not only the right to be a king, but the power to conquer." Yes ! Jehovah hath given to his Anointed a rod of iron with which he shall break rebellious nations in pieces, and, despite their imperial strength, they shall be but as potters' vessels, easily dashed into shivers, when the rod of iron is in the hand of the omnipotent Son of God. Those who will not bend must break. Potters' vessels are not to be restored if dashed in pieces, and the ruin of sinners will be hopeless if Jesus shall smite them.

> " Ye sinners seek his grace,
> Whose wrath ye cannot bear;
> Fly to the shelter of his cross,
> And find salvation there."

10 Be wise now therefore, O ye kings : be instructed, ye judges of the earth.

11 Serve the LORD with fear, and rejoice with trembling.

12 Kiss the Son, lest he be angry, and ye perish *from* the way, when his wrath is kindled but a little.   Blessed *are* all they that put their trust in him.

The scene again changes, and counsel is given to those who have taken counsel to rebel. They are exhorted to obey, and give the kiss of homage and affection to him whom they have hated.

" *Be wise.*"—It is always wise to be willing to be instructed, especially when such instruction tends to the salvation of the soul. " Be wise *now, therefore;*" delay no longer, but let good reason weigh with you. Your warfare cannot succeed, therefore desist and yield cheerfully to him who will make you bow if you refuse his yoke. O how wise, how infinitely wise is obedience to Jesus, and how dreadful is the folly of those who continue to be his enemies ! " *Serve the Lord with fear ;*" let reverence and humility be mingled with your service. He is a great God, and ye are but puny creatures ; bend ye, therefore, in lowly worship, and let a filial fear mingle with all your obedience to the great Father of the Ages. " *Rejoice with trembling.*"—There must ever be a holy fear mixed with the Christian's joy. This is a sacred compound, yielding a sweet smell, and we must see to it that we burn no other upon the altar. Fear, without joy, is torment ; and joy, without holy fear, would be presumption. Mark the solemn argument for reconciliation and obedience. It is an awful thing to *perish* in the midst of sin, in the very *way* of rebellion ; and yet how easily could *his wrath* destroy us suddenly. It needs not that his anger should be heated seven times hotter ; let the fuel kindle *but a little,* and we are consumed. O sinner ! Take heed of the terrors of the Lord ; for " our God is a consuming fire." Note the benediction with which the Psalm closes :—" *Blessed are all they that put their trust in him.*" Have we a share in this blessedness ? Do we trust in *him ?* Our faith may be slender as a spider's thread ; but if it be real, we are in our measure blessed. The more we trust, the more fully shall we know this blessedness. We may therefore close the Psalm with the prayer of the apostles :—" Lord, increase our faith."

The first Psalm was a contrast between the righteous man and the sinner ; the second Psalm is a contrast between the tumultuous disobedience of the ungodly world and the sure exaltation of the righteous Son of God. In the first Psalm, we saw the wicked driven away like chaff ; in the second Psalm, we see them broken in pieces like a potter's vessel. In the first Psalm, we beheld the righteous like a tree planted by the rivers of water ; and here, we contemplate Christ the Covenant Head of the righteous, made better than a tree planted by the rivers of water, for *he* is made king of all the islands, and all the heathen bow before him and kiss the dust ; while he himself gives a blessing to all those who put their trust in him. The two Psalms are worthy of the very deepest attention ; they are, in fact, the preface to the entire Book of Psalms, and were by some of the ancients, joined into one. They are, however, two Psalms ; for Paul speaks of this as the second Psalm. (Acts xiii. 33.) The first shows us the character and lot of the righteous ; and the next teaches us that the Psalms are Messianic, and speak of Christ the Messiah—the Prince who shall reign from the river even unto the ends of the earth. That they have both a far-reaching prophetic outlook we are well assured, but we do not feel competent to open up that matter, and must leave it to abler hands.

EXPLANATORY NOTES AND QUAINT SAYINGS.

Verse 1.—" *Why do nations make a noise,*" tumultuate, or rage ? The Hebrew verb is not expressive of an internal feeling, but of the outward agitation which denotes it. There may be an allusion to the rolling and roaring of the sea, often used as an emblem of popular commotion, both in the Scriptures and the classics. The past tense of this verb (*why have they raged ?*) refers to the commotion as already begun, while the future in the next clause expresses its continuance.—*J. A. Alexander, D.D.*, 1850.

Verse 1.—" *Rage.*" The word with which Paul renders this in the Greek denotes rage, pride, and restiveness, as of horses that neigh, and rush into the battle. Ἐφρύαξαν, from Φρυάσσω, to snort or neigh, properly applied to a high-mettled horse. See Acts iv. 25.

Verse 1.—" *A vain thing.*" A medal was struck by Diocletian, which still remains, bearing the inscription, " The name of Christians being extinguished." And in Spain, two monumental pillars were raised, on which were written :— I. " Diocletian Jovian Maximian Herculeus Cæsares Augusti, for having extended the Roman Empire in the east and the west, and for having extinguished the name of Christians, who brought the Republic to ruin." II. " Diocletian Jovian Maximian Herculeus Cæsares Augusti, for having adopted Galerius in the east, for having everywhere abolished the superstition of Christ, for having extended the worship of the gods." As a modern writer has elegantly observed : " We have here a monument raised by Paganism, over the grave of its vanquished foe. But in this, ' the people imagined a vain thing ; ' so far from being deceased, Christianity was on the eve of its final and permanent triumph, and the stone guarded a sepulchre empty as the urn which Electra washed with her tears. Neither in Spain, nor elsewhere, can be pointed out the burial place of Christianity ; it is not, for the living have no tomb.' "

Verses 1—4.—Herod, the fox, plotted against Christ, to hinder the course of his ministry and mediatorship, but he could not perform his enterprise ; 'tis so all along, therefore it is said, " *Why do the heathen imagine a vain thing ?*" A vain thing, because a thing successless, their hands could not perform it. It was vain, not only because there was no true ground of reason why they should imagine or do such a thing, but vain also because they laboured in vain, they could not do it, and therefore it follows, " *He that sitteth in the heavens shall laugh : the Lord shall have them in derision.*" The Lord sees what fools they are, and men (yea, themselves) shall see it. The prophet gives us an elegant description to this purpose. Isaiah lix. 5, 6. " *They weave the spider's web. . . . Their webs shall not become garments, neither shall they cover themselves with their works.*" As if he had said, they have been devising and setting things in a goodly frame to catch flies ; they have been spinning a fine thread out of their brains, as the spider doth out of her bowels ; such is their web, but when they have their web they cannot cut it out, or make it up into a garment. They shall go naked and cold, notwithstanding all their spinning and weaving, all their plotting and devising. The next broom that comes will sweep away all their webs and the spiders too, except they creep apace. God loves and delights to cross worldly proverbs and worldly craft.—*Joseph Caryl,* 1647.

Verse 2.—The *many* had done their part, and now the *mighty* show themselves.—*John Trapp.*

Verse 2.—"*They banded themselves against the Lord, and against his Anointed.*" But why did they band themselves against the Lord, or against his Anointed? What was their desire of him? To have his goods? No, he had none for himself; but they were richer than he. To have his liberty? Nay, that would not suffice them, for they had bound him before. To bring the people unto dislike of him? Nay, that would not serve them, for they had done so already, until even his disciples were fled from him. What would they have, then? his blood? Yea, "they took counsel," saith Matthew, "to put him to death." They had the devil's mind, which is not satisfied but with death. And how do they contrive it? He saith, "they took counsel about it."—*Henry Smith,* 1578.

Verse 2.—"*Against Jehovah and against his Anointed.*" What an honour it was to David to be thus publicly associated with Jehovah! And, because he was HIS anointed, to be an object of hatred and scorn to the ungodly world! If this very circumstance fearfully augmented the guilt, and sealed the doom of these infatuated heathen, surely it was that which above everything else would preserve the mind of David calm and serene, yea, peaceful and joyful notwithstanding the proud and boastful vauntiness of his enemies. . . . . . . When writing this Psalm David was like a man in a storm, who hears only the roaring of the tempest, or sees nothing but the raging billows threatening destruction on every side of him. And yet his faith enabled him to say, "*The people imagine a vain thing.*" They cannot succeed. They cannot defeat the counsels of heaven. They cannot injure the Lord's Anointed.—*David Pitcairn,* 1851.

Verse 3.—Resolved they were to run riot, as lawless, and aweless, and therefore they slander the sweet laws of Christ's kingdom as bonds and thick cords, which are signs of slavery. Jer. xxvii. 2, 6, 7. But what saith our Saviour? "My yoke is easy, and my burden is light." It is no more burden to a regenerate man than wings to a bird. The law of Christ is no more as bands and cords, but as girdles and garters which gird up his loins and expedite his course.—*John Trapp.*

Verse 4.—"*He that sitteth in the heavens.*" Hereby it is clearly intimated, (1) that the Lord is far above all their malice and power, (2) that he seeth all their plots, looking down on all; (3) that he is of omnipotent power, and so can do with his enemies as he lists. "Our God is in the heavens: he hath done whatsoever he pleased." Psalm cxv. 3.—*Arthur Jackson,* 1643.

Verse 4.—"*He that sitteth in the heavens shall laugh,*" etc. Sinners' follies are the just sport of God's infinite wisdom and power; and those attempts of the kingdom of Satan, which in our eyes are formidable, in his are despicable. *Matthew Henry.*

Verse 4.—"*He that sitteth in the heavens shall laugh.*" They scoff at us, God laughs at them. Laugh? This seems a hard word at the first view: are the injuries of his saints, the cruelties of their enemies, the derision, the persecution of all that are round about us, no more but matter of laughter? Severe Cato thought that laughter did not become the gravity of Roman consuls; that it is a diminution of states, as another told princes; and is it attributed to the Majesty of heaven? According to our capacities, the prophet describes God, as ourselves would be in a merry disposition, deriding vain attempts. He laughs, but it is in scorn; he scorns, but it is with vengeance. Pharaoh imagined that by drowning the Israelite males, he had found a way to root their name from the earth ; but when at the same time, his own daughter, in his own court gave princely education to Moses, their deliverer, did not God laugh ?

Short is the joy of the wicked. Is Dagon put up to his place again ? God's smile shall take off his head and his hands, and leave him neither wit to guide nor power to subsist. . . . . . We may not judge of God's works until the fifth act : the case, deplorable and desperate in outward appearance, may with one smile from heaven find a blessed issue. He permitted his temple to be sacked and rifled, the holy vessels to be profaned and caroused in ; but did not God's smile make Belshazzar to tremble at the handwriting on the wall ? Oh, what are his frowns, if his smiles be so terrible !—*Thomas Adams.*

Verse 4.—The expression, "*He that sitteth in the heavens*," at once fixes our thoughts on a being infinitely exalted above man, who is of the earth, earthy. And when it is said, "HE shall *laugh*," this word is designed to convey to our minds the idea, that the greatest confederacies amongst kings and peoples, and their most extensive and vigorous preparations, to defeat HIS purposes or to injure HIS servants, are in HIS sight altogether insignificant and worthless. HE looks upon their poor and puny efforts, not only without uneasiness or fear, but HE laughs at their folly ; HE treats their impotency with derision. He knows how HE can crush them like a moth when HE pleases, or consume them in a moment with the breath of HIS mouth. How profitable is it for us to be reminded of truths such as these ! Ah ! it is indeed "*a vain thing*" for the potsherds of the earth to strive with the glorious Majesty of Heaven.—*David Pitcairn.*

Verse 4.—"*The Lord*," in Hebrew, Adonai, mystically signifieth my stays, or my sustainers—my pillars. Our English word "Lord" hath much the same force, being contracted of the old Saxon word "Llaford," or "Hlafford," which cometh from "Laef," to sustain, refresh, cherish.—*Henry Ainsworth.*

Verse 4.—"*He that sitteth in the heavens shall laugh at them : the Lord shall have them in derision.*" This tautology or repetition of the same thing, which is frequent in the Scriptures, is a sign of the thing being established : according to the authority of the patriarch Joseph (Gen. xli. 32), where, having interpreted the dreams of Pharaoh, he said, "And for that the dream was doubled unto Pharaoh twice ; it is because the thing is established by God, and God will shortly bring it to pass." And therefore, here also, "*shall laugh at them,*" and "*shall have them in derision,*" is a repetition to show that there is not a doubt to be entertained that all these things will most surely come to pass. And the gracious Spirit does all this for our comfort and consolation, that we may not faint under temptation, but lift up our heads with the most certain hope ; because "he that shall come will come, and will not tarry." Hebrews x. 37.—*Martin Luther.*

Verse 5.—"*Vex them ;*" either by horror of conscience, or corporal plagues ; one way or the other he will have his pennyworths of them, as he always has had of the persecutors of his people.—*John Trapp.*

Verses 5, 9.—It is easy for God to destroy his foes. . . . Behold Pharaoh, his wise men, his hosts, and his horses plouting and plunging, and sinking like lead in the Red sea. Here is the end of one of the greatest plots ever formed against God's chosen. Of thirty Roman emperors, governors of provinces, and others high in office, who distinguished themselves by their zeal and bitterness in persecuting the early Christians, one became speedily deranged after some atrocious cruelty, one was slain by his own son, one became blind, the eyes of one started out of his head, one was drowned, one was strangled, one died in a miserable captivity, one fell dead in a manner that will not bear recital, one died of so loathsome a disease that several of his physicians were put to death because they could not abide the stench that filled his room, two committed suicide, a third attempted it, but had to call for help to finish the work, five were assassinated by their own people or servants, five others died the most miserable and excruciating deaths, several of them having an untold complication of diseases, and eight were killed in battle, or after being taken prisoners. Among these was Julian the apostate. In the days of his prosperity he is said to have pointed his dagger to heaven defying the Son of God, whom he commonly called the Galilean. But when he was wounded in battle, he saw that all was over with him, and he gathered up his clotted blood, and threw it into the air, exclaiming, "Thou hast conquered, O thou Galilean." Voltaire has told us of the agonies of Charles IX. of France, which drove the blood through the pores of the skin of that miserable monarch, after his cruelties and treachery to the Huguenots. *William S. Plumer, D.D., LL.D.*, 1867.

Verse 6.—"*Yet have I set my King.*" Notice—1. The royal office and character of our glorious Redeemer: he is a King, "This name he hath on his vesture and on his thigh." Rev. xix. 16. 2. The authority by which he reigns; he is "*my King,*" says God the Father, and I have set him up from everlasting: "The Father judgeth no man; but hath committed all judgment unto the Son." The world disowns his authority, but I own it; I have set him, I have "given him to be head over all things to the church." 3. His particular kingdom over which he rules; it is over "*my holy hill of Zion*"—an eminent type of the gospel church. The temple was built upon Mount Zion and therefore called a *holy hill.* Christ's throne is in his church, it is his head-quarters, and the place of his peculiar residence. Notice the firmness of the divine purpose with respect unto this matter. "*Yet have I set*" him "*King;*" *i.e.,* whatever be the plots of hell and earth to the contrary, he reigns by his Father's ordination. *Stephen Charnock*, 1628—1680.

Verse 6.—"*Yet have I set my* KING," etc.—Jesus Christ is a threefold King. *First*, his enemies' King; *secondly*, his saints' King; *thirdly*, his Father's King.

First, Christ is his enemies' King, that is, he is King over his enemies. Christ is a King above all kings. What are all the mighty men, the great, the honourable men of the earth to Jesus Christ? They are but like a little bubble in the water; for if all the nations, in comparison to God, be but as the drop of the bucket, or the dust of the balance, as the prophet speaks in Isaiah xl. 15, how little then must be the kings of the earth! Nay, beloved, Christ Jesus is not only higher than kings, but he is higher than the angels; yea, he is the head of angels; and, therefore, all the angels in heaven are commanded to worship him. Col. ii. 12; Heb. i. 6. . . . . . He is King over all kingdoms, over all nations, over all governments, over all powers, over all people. Dan. vii. 14. . . . . . The very heathen are given to Christ, and the uttermost parts of the earth for his possession. Psalm ii. 8.

Secondly. Jesus Christ is his saints' King. He is King of the bad, and of the good; but as for the wicked, he rules over them by his power and might; but the saints, he rules in them by his Spirit and graces. Oh! this is Christ's spiritual kingdom, and here he rules in the hearts of his people, here he rules over their consciences, over their wills, over their affections, over their judgments and understandings, and nobody hath anything to do here but Christ. Christ is not only the King of nations, but the King of saints; the one he rules over, the other he rules in.

Thirdly. Jesus Christ is his Father's King too, and so his Father calls him: "*I have set my King upon my holy hill of Zion.*" Well may he be our King, when he is God's King. But you may say, how is Christ the Father's King? Because he rules for his Father. There is a twofold kingdom of God committed to Jesus Christ; *first*, a spiritual kingdom, by which he rules in the hearts of his people, and so is King of saints; and, *secondly*, a providential kingdom, by which he rules the affairs of this world, and so is King of nations.—*Condensed from William Dyer's Christ's Famous Titles*, 1665.

Verse 6.—"*Zion.*" The *name* "Zion" signifies a "distant view" (*speculam*). And the church is called "a distant view" (*specula*), not only because it views God and heavenly things by faith (that is, afar off), being wise unto the things that are above, not unto those that are on the earth; but also, because there are within her true viewers, or seers, and watchmen in the spirit, whose office is to take charge of the people under them, and to watch against the snares of enemies and sins ; and such are called in the Greek bishops (ʼεπίσκοποι), that is, spyers or seers ; and you may for the same reason give them, from the Hebrew, the appellation of Zionians or Zioners.—*Martin Luther.*

Verse 7.—The dispute concerning the eternal filiation of our Lord betrays more of presumptuous curiosity than of reverent faith. It is an attempt to explain where it is far better to adore. We could give rival expositions of this verse, but we forbear. The controversy is one of the most unprofitable which ever engaged the pens of theologians.—*C. H. S.*

Verse 8.—"*Ask of me.*" The priesthood doth not appear to be settled upon Christ by any other expression than this, "*Ask of me.*" The Psalm speaks of his investiture in his kingly office ; the apostle refers this to his priesthood, his commission for both took date at the same time ; both bestowed, both confirmed by the same authority. The office of asking is grounded upon the same authority as the honour of king. Ruling belonged to his royal office, asking to his priestly. After his resurrection, the Father gives him a power and command of asking.—*Stephen Charnock.*

Verse 8.—As the limner looks on the person whose picture he would take, and draws his lines to answer him with the nearest similitude that he can, so God looks on Christ as the archetype to which he will conform the saint, in suffering, in grace, in glory ; yet so that Christ hath the pre-eminence in all. Every saint must suffer, because Christ suffered : Christ must not have a delicate body under a crucified head ; yet never any suffered, or could, what he endured. Christ is holy, and therefore so shall every saint be, but in an inferior degree ; an image cut in clay cannot be so exact as that engraved on gold. Now, our conformity to Christ appears, that as the promises made to him were performed upon his prayers to his Father, his promises made to his saints are given to them in the same way of prayer : "*Ask of me,*" saith God to his Son, "*and I shall give thee.*" And the apostle tells us, "Ye have not, because ye ask not." God hath promised support to Christ in all his conflicts. Isaiah xlii. 1. "Behold my servant, whom I uphold ;" yet he prayed "with strong cries and tears," when his feet stood within the shadow of death. A seed is promised to him, and victory over his enemies, yet for both these he prays. Christ towards us acts as a king, but towards his Father as a priest. All he speaks to God is by prayer and intercession. So the saints, the promise makes them kings over their lusts, conquerors over their enemies ; but it makes them priests towards God, by prayer humbly to sue out those great things given in the promise.—*William Gurnall,* 1617—1679.

Verse 8.—It will be observed in our Bible that two words of verse eight are in italics, intimating that they are not translations of the Hebrew, but additions made for the purpose of elucidating the meaning. Now if the "*thee*" and the "*for*" are left out, the verse will read thus, "Ask of me, and I shall give the heathen, thine inheritance, and thy possession, the uttermost parts of the earth." And this reading is decidedly preferable to the other. It implies that by some previous arrangement on the part of God, he had already assigned an inheritance of the heathen, and the possession of the earth, to the person of whom he says, "Thou art my Son." And when God says, "I will give," etc., he reveals to his Anointed, not so much in what the inheritance consisted, and what was the extent of possession destined for him, as the promise of his readiness to bestow it. The heathen were already "the inheritance," and the ends of the earth "the possession," which God had *purposed* to give to his Anointed. Now he says to him, "Ask of me," and he *promises* to fulfil his purpose. This is the idea involved in the words of the text, and the importance of it will become more apparent, when we consider its application to the *spiritual* David, to the true Son of God, "whom he hath appointed the heir of all things."

Verse 9.—The " *rod* " has a variety of meanings in Scripture. It might be of different materials, as it was employed for different purposes. At an early period, a wooden rod came into use as one of the insignia of royalty, under the name of sceptre. By degrees the sceptre grew in importance, and was regarded as characteristic of an empire, or of the reign of some particular king. A golden sceptre denoted wealth and pomp. The right, or straight sceptre, of which we read in Psalm xlv. 6, is expressive of the justice and uprightness, the truth and equity, which shall distinguish Messiah's reign, after his kingdom on earth has been established. But when it is said in Rev. xix. 15, that he, " whose name is called the Word of God," will smite the nations, and " rule them with a rod of iron," if the rod signifies " his sceptre," then the " iron" of which it is made must be designed to express the severity of the judgments which this omnipotent " King of kings" will inflict on all who resist his authority. But to me it appears doubtful whether the " rod of iron" symbolises the royal sceptre of the Son of God at his second advent. It is mentioned in connection with " a sharp sword," which leads me to prefer the opinion that it also ought to be regarded as a weapon of war ; at all events, the " rod of iron" mentioned in the Psalm we are endeavouring to explain, is evidently not the emblem of sovereign power, although represented as in the hands of a king, but an instrument of correction and punishment. In this sense the word " rod " is often used . . . . When the correcting rod, which usually was a wand or cane, is represented as in this second Psalm, to be of " iron," it only indicates how weighty, how severe, how effectual the threatened chastisement will be—it will not merely bruise, but it will break. " *Thou shalt break them with a rod of iron.*"

Now it is just such a complete breaking as would not readily be effected excepting by *an iron rod*, that is more fully expressed in the following clause of the verse, " Thou shalt dash them in pieces like a potter's vessel." The completeness of the destruction, however, depends on two things. Even an iron rod, if gently used, or used against a hard and firm substance, might cause little injury ; but, in the case before us, it is supposed to be applied with great force, " Thou shalt *dash* them ;" and it is applied to what will prove as brittle and frangible as " *a potter's vessel* "—" Thou shalt dash them *in pieces.*" . . . .
Here, as in other respects, we must feel that the predictions and promises of this Psalm were but very partially fulfilled in the history of the literal David. Their real accomplishment, their awful completion, abides the day when the spiritual David shall come in glory and in majesty as Zion's King, with a rod of iron to dash in pieces the great antichristian confederacy of kings and peoples, and to take possession of his long-promised and dearly-purchased inheritance. And the signs of the times seem to indicate that the coming of the Lord draws nigh.—*David Pitcairn.*

Verse 10.—" *Be wise now, therefore, O ye kings,*" etc. As Jesus is King of kings and Judge of judges, so the gospel is the teacher of the greatest and wisest. If any are so great as to spurn its admonitions, God will make little of them ; and if they are so wise as to despise its teachings, their fancied wisdom shall make fools of them. The gospel takes a high tone before the rulers of the earth, and they who preach it should, like Knox and Melvill, magnify their office by bold rebukes and manly utterances even in the royal presence. A clerical sycophant is only fit to be a scullion in the devil's kitchen.—*C. H. S.*

Verse 11.—" *Serve the Lord with fear.*" This fear of God qualifies our joy. If you abstract fear from joy, joy will become light and wanton ; and if you abstract joy from fear, fear then will become slavish.—*William Bates, D.D., 1625—1699.*
Verse 11.—" *Serve the Lord with fear, and rejoice with trembling.*" There are two kinds of serving and rejoicing in God. First, a serving in security, and a rejoicing in the Lord without fear ; these are peculiar to hypocrites, who are

secure, who please themselves, and who appear to themselves to be not unuseful servants, and to have great merit on their side, concerning whom it is said (Psalm x. 5), "Thy judgments are far above out of his sight;" and also afterwards (Psalm xxxvi. 1), "There is no fear of God before his eyes." These do righteousness without judgment at all times; and permit not Christ to be the Judge to be feared by all, in whose sight no man living is justified. Secondly, a serving with fear and a rejoicing with trembling; these are peculiar to the righteous who do righteousness at all times, and always rightly attemper both; never being without judgments, on the one hand, by which they are terrified and brought to despair of themselves and of all their own works; nor without that righteousness, on the other, on which they rest, and in which they rejoice in the mercy of God. It is the work of the whole lives of these characters to accuse themselves in all things, and in all things to justify and praise God. And thus they fulfil that word of Proverbs, "Blessed is the man that feareth alway" (xxviii. 14); and also that of Philip. iv. 4, "Rejoice in the Lord alway." Thus, between the upper and nether mill-stone (Deut. xxiv. 6), they are broken in pieces and humbled, and the husks being thus bruised off, they come forth the all-pure wheat of Christ.—*Martin Luther.*

Verse 11.—The fear of God promotes spiritual joy; it is the morning star which ushers in the sunlight of comfort. "Walking in the fear of God, and in the comfort of the Holy Ghost." God mingles joy with fear, that fear may not be slavish.—*Thomas Watson,* 1660.

Verse 12.—"*Kiss,*" a sign of love among equals: Gen. xxxiii. 4; 1 Sam. xx. 41; Rom. xvi. 16; 1 Cor. xvi. 20. Of subjection in inferiors: 1 Sam. x. 1. Of religious adoration in worshippers: 1 Kings xix. 18; Job xxxi. 27.—*John Richardson, Bishop of Ardagh,* 1655.

Verse 12.—"*Kiss the Son, lest he be angry.*" From the Person, *the Son,* we shall pass to the act (*Osculamini, kiss the Son*); in which we shall see, that since this is an act which licentious men have depraved (carnal men do it, and treacherous men do it—*Judas* betrayed his Master by a kiss), and yet God commands this, and expresses love in this; everything that hath, or may be abused, must not therefore be abandoned; the turning of a thing out of the way, is not a taking of that thing away, but good things deflected to ill uses by some, may be by others reduced to their first goodness. Then let us consider and magnify the goodness of God, that hath brought us into this distance, that we may *kiss the Son,* that the expressing of this love lies in our hands, and that, whereas the love of the church, in the Old Testament, even in the Canticle, went no farther but to the *Osculatur me* (*O that he would kiss me with the kisses of his mouth!* Cant. i. 1), now, in the Christian church, and in the visitation of a Christian soul, he hath invited us, enabled us to kiss him, for he is presentially amongst us. This leads us to give an earnest persuasion and exhortation *to kiss the Son,* with all those affections, which we shall there find to be expressed in the Scriptures, in that testimony of true love, *a holy kiss.* But then, lest that persuasion by love should not be effectual and powerful enough to us, we shall descend from that duty, to the danger, from love, to fear, "*lest he be angry;*" and therein see first, that God, who is love, can be angry; and then, that this God who is angry here, is the Son of God, he that hath done so much for us, and therefore in justice may be angry; he that is our Judge, and therefore in reason we are to fear his anger: and then, in a third branch, we shall see how easily this anger departs—a kiss removes it.

Verse 12.—"*Kiss the Son.*" That is, embrace him, depend upon him all these ways: as thy kinsman, as thy sovereign; at thy going, at thy coming; at thy reconciliation, in the truth of religion in thyself, in a peaceable unity with the church, in a reverent estimation of those men, and those means, whom he sends. Kiss him, and be not ashamed of kissing him; it is that which the spouse desired, "*I would kiss thee, and not be despised.*" Cant. vii. 1. If thou be despised for loving Christ in his gospel, remember that when David was thought base, for dancing before the ark, his way was to be more base. If thou be thought frivolous for thrusting in at service, in the forenoon, be more frivolous, and come again in the afternoon : " *Tanto major requies, quanto ab amore Jesu nulla requies ;*"* " The more thou troublest thyself, or art troubled by others for Christ, the more peace thou hast in Christ." . . . . " *Lest he be angry.*" Anger, as it is a passion that troubles, and disorders, and discomposes a man, so it is not in God ; but anger, as it is a sensible discerning of foes from friends, and of things that conduce, or disconduce to his glory, so it is in God. In a word, Hilary hath expressed it well : " *Pœna patientis, ira decernentis ;*" " Man's suffering is God's anger." When God inflicts such punishments as a king justly incensed would do, then God is thus angry. Now here, our case is heavier ; it is not this great, and almighty, and majestical God, that may be angry—that is like enough ; but even the *Son*, whom we must *kiss*, may be *angry ;* it is not a person whom we consider merely as God, but as man ; nay not as man neither, but *a worm, and no man*, and he may be angry, and angry to our ruin. . . . . " *Kiss the Son*," and he will not *be angry ;* if he be, kiss the rod, and he will be angry no longer—love him lest he be : fear him when he is angry : the preservative is easy, and so is the restorative too : the balsamum of this kiss is all, to suck spiritual milk out of the left breast, as well as out of the right, to find mercy in his judgments, reparation in his ruins, feasts in his lents, joy in his anger.—*From Sermons of John Donne, D.D., Dean of St. Paul's.* 1621--1631.

Verse 12.—" *Kiss the Son.*" To make peace with the Father, kiss the Son. " Let him kiss me," was the church's prayer. Cant. i. 2. Let us kiss him—that be our endeavour. Indeed, the Son must first kiss us by his mercy, before we can kiss him by our piety. Lord, grant in these mutual kisses and interchangeable embraces now, that we may come to the plenary wedding supper hereafter ; when the choir of heaven, even the voices of angels, shall sing epithalamiums, nuptial songs, at the bridal of the spouse of the Lamb.—*Thomas Adams.*

Verse 12.—" *If his wrath be kindled but a little ;*" the Hebrew is, if his nose or nostril be kindled but a little ; the nostril, being an organ of the body in which wrath shows itself, is put for wrath itself. Paleness and snuffling of the nose are symptoms of anger. In our proverbials, to take a thing in snuff, is to take it in anger.—*Joseph Caryl.*

Verse 12.—" *His wrath.*" Unspeakable must the wrath of God be when it is kindled fully, since perdition may come upon the *kindling of it but a little.*— *John Newton.*

HINTS TO THE VILLAGE PREACHER.

Whole Psalm.—Shows us the nature of sin, and the terrible results of it if it could reign.

Verse 1.—*Nothing is more irrational than irreligion.* A weighty theme.

The reasons why sinners rebel against God, stated, refuted, lamented, and repented of.

The crowning display of human sin in man's hatred of the Mediator.

Verses 1 *and* 2.—Opposition to the gospel, unreasonable and ineffectual.—*Two sermons by John Newton.*

Verses 1 *and* 2.—These verses show that all trust in man in the service of God is vain. Inasmuch as men oppose Christ, it is not good to hang our trust upon *the multitude* for their number, *the earnest* for their zeal, *the mighty* for their countenance, or *the wise* for their counsel, since all these are far oftener against Christ than for him.

---

* Gregory.

Verse 2.—" Spurgeon's Sermons," No. 495, " The Greatest Trial on Record."

Verse 3.—The true reason of the opposition of sinners to Christ's truth, viz. : their hatred of the restraints of godliness.

Verse 4.—God's derision of the rebellious, both now and hereafter.

Verse 5.—*The voice of wrath.* One of a series of sermons upon the voices of the divine attributes.

Verse 6.—*Christ's sovereignty.* 1. The opposition to it : " *yet.*" 2. The certainty of its existence : " *Yet have I set.*" 3. The power which maintains it : " *have I set.*" 4. The place of its manifestation : " *my holy hill of Zion.*" 5. The blessings flowing from it.

Verse 7.—The divine decree concerning Christ, in connection with the decrees of election and providence. The Sonship of Jesus.

This verse teacheth us faithfully to declare, and humbly to claim, the gifts and calling that God hath bestowed upon us.—*Thomas Wilcocks.*

Verse 8.—Christ's inheritance.—*William Jay.*

Prayer indispensable.—*Jesus must ask.*

Verse 9.—*The ruin of the wicked.* Certain, irresistible, terrible, complete, irretrievable, " like a potter's vessel."

The destruction of systems of error and oppression to be expected. The gospel an iron rod quite able to break mere pots of man's making.

Verse 10.—True wisdom, fit for kings and judges, lies in obeying Christ.

The gospel, a school for those who would learn how to rule and judge well. They may consider its principles, its exemplar, its spirit, etc.

Verse 11.—*Mingled experience.* See the case of the women returning from the sepulchre. Matt. xxviii. 8. This may be rendered a very comforting subject, if the Holy Spirit direct the mind of the preacher.

True religion, a compound of many virtues and emotions.

Verse 12.—*An earnest invitation.* 1. *The command.* 2. *The argument.* 3. *The benediction* upon the obedient.—" Spurgeon's Sermons," No. 260.

Last clause.—Nature, object, and blessedness of saving faith.

WORK UPON THE SECOND PSALM.

Zion's King : the Second Psalm expounded in the Light of History and Prophecy. By the Rev. DAVID PITCAIRN. 1851.

PSALM III.

TITLE.—"A Psalm of David, when he fled from Absalom his Son." *You will re-member the sad story of David's flight from his own palace, when, in the dead of the night, he forded the brook Kedron, and went with a few faithful followers to hide himself for awhile from the fury of his rebellious son. Remember that David in this was a type of the Lord Jesus Christ. He, too, fled; he, too, passed over the brook Kedron when his own people were in rebellion against him, and with a feeble band of followers he went to the garden of Geth-semane. He, too, drank of the brook by the way, and therefore doth he lift up the head. By very many expositors this is entitled* THE MORNING HYMN. *May we ever wake with holy confidence in our hearts, and a song upon our lips!*

DIVISION.—*This Psalm may be divided into four parts of two verses each. Indeed, many of the Psalms cannot be well understood unless we attentively regard the parts into which they should be divided. They are not continuous descriptions of one scene, but a set of pictures of many kindred subjects. As in our modern sermons, we divide our discourse into different heads, so is it in these Psalms. There is always unity, but it is the unity of a bundle of ar-rows, and not of a single solitary shaft. Let us now look at the Psalm before us. In the first two verses you have David making a complaint to God concerning his enemies; he then declares his confidence in the Lord (3, 4), sings of his safety in sleep (5, 6), and strengthens himself for future conflict (7, 8).*

EXPOSITION.

L ORD, how are they increased that trouble me! many *are* they that rise up against me.

2 Many *there be* which say of my soul, *There is* no help for him in God. Selah.

The poor broken-hearted father complains of the multitude of his enemies : and if you turn to 2 Samuel xv. 12, you will find it written that "the conspiracy was strong ; for the people increased continually with Absalom," while the troops of David constantly diminished! *"Lord, how are they increased that trouble me!"* Here is a note of exclamation to express the wonder of woe which amazed and perplexed the fugitive father. Alas! I see no limit to my misery, for my troubles are enlarged! There was enough at first to sink me very low ; but lo! my enemies multiply. When Absalom, my darling, is in rebellion against me, it is enough to break my heart ; but lo! Ahithophel hath forsaken me, my faithful counsellors have turned their backs on me ; lo! my generals and soldiers have deserted my standard. "How are they increased that trouble me!" Troubles always come in flocks. Sorrow hath a numerous family.

"*Many are they that rise up against me.*" Their hosts are far superior to mine! Their numbers are too great for my reckoning!

Let us here recall to our memory the innumerable hosts which beset our Divine Redeemer. The legions of our sins, the armies of fiends, the crowd of bodily pains, the host of spiritual sorrows, and all the allies of death and hell, set themselves in battle against the Son of Man. O how precious to know and believe that he has routed their hosts, and trodden them down in his anger! They who would have troubled us he has removed into captivity, and those who would have risen up against us he has laid low. The dragon lost his sting when he dashed it into the soul of Jesus.

David complains before his loving God of the worst weapon of his enemies' attacks, and the bitterest drop of his distresses. "Oh!" saith David, " *many there be that say of my soul, There is no help for him in God.*" Some of his distrustful friends said this sorrowfully, but his enemies exultingly boasted of it, and longed to see their words proved by his total destruction. This was the unkindest cut of all, when they declared that his God had forsaken him. Yet David knew in his own conscience that he had given them some ground for this exclamation, for he had committed sin against God in the very light of day. Then they flung his crime with Bathsheba into his face, and they said, "Go up, thou bloody man ; God hath forsaken thee and left thee." Shimei cursed him, and swore at him to his very face, for he was bold because of his backers, since multitudes of the men of Belial thought of David in like fashion. Doubtless, David felt this infernal suggestion to be staggering to his faith. If all the trials which come from heaven, all the temptations which ascend from hell, and all the crosses which arise from earth, could be mixed and pressed together, they would not make a trial so terrible as that which is contained in this verse. It is the most bitter of all afflictions to be lead to fear that there is no help for us in God. And yet remember our most blessed Saviour had to endure this in the deepest degree when he cried, "My God, my God, why hast thou forsaken me ?" He knew full well what it was to walk in darkness and to see no light. This was the curse of the curse. This was the wormwood mingled with the gall. To be deserted of his Father was worse than to be the despised of men. Surely we should love him who suffered this bitterest of temptations and trials for our sake. It will be a delightful and instructive exercise for the loving heart to mark the Lord in his agonies as here pourtrayed, for there is here, and in very many other Psalms, far more of David's Lord than of David himself.

"*Selah.*" This is a musical pause ; the precise meaning of which is not known. Some think it simply a rest, a pause in the music ; others say it means, "Lift up the strain—sing more loudly—pitch the tune upon a higher key—there is nobler matter to come, therefore retune your harps." Harp-strings soon get out of order and need to be screwed up again to their proper tightness, and certainly our heart-strings are evermore getting out of tune. Let "Selah" teach us to pray

> "O may my heart in tune be found
> Like David's harp of solemn sound."

At least, we may learn that wherever we see "Selah," we should look upon it as a note of observation. Let us read the passage which precedes and succeeds it with greater earnestness, for surely there is always something excellent where we are required to rest and pause and meditate, or when we are required to lift up our hearts in grateful song. "Selah."

3 But thou, O LORD, *art* a shield for me ; my glory, and the lifter up of mine head.

4 I cried unto the LORD with my voice, and he heard me out of his holy hill. Selah.

Here David avows his confidence in God. "*Thou, O Lord, art a shield for me.*" The word in the original signifies more than a shield ; it means a buckler round about, a protection which shall surround a man entirely, a shield above, beneath, around, without and within. Oh ! what a shield is God for his people ! He wards off the fiery darts of Satan from beneath, and the storms of trials from above, while, at the same instant, he speaks peace to the tempest within the breast. Thou art "*my glory.*" David knew that though he was driven from his capital in contempt and scorn, he should yet return in triumph, and by faith he looks upon God as honouring and glorifying him. O for grace to see our future glory amid present shame ! Indeed, there is a present glory in our afflictions, if we could but discern it ; for it is no mean thing to have fellowship with Christ in his sufferings. David was honoured when he made the ascent of Olivet, weeping, with his head covered ; for he was in all this made like unto his Lord. May we learn, in this respect, to glory in tribulations also ! "*And the lifter up of mine head*"—thou shalt yet exalt me. Though I hang my head in sorrow, I shall very soon lift it up in joy and thanksgiving. What a divine trio of mercies is contained in this verse !—defence for the defenceless, glory for the despised, and joy for the comfortless. Verily we may well say, " there is none like the God of Jeshurun."

"*I cried unto the Lord with my voice.*" Why doth he say, " with my voice?" Surely, silent prayers are heard. Yes, but good men often find that, even in secret, they pray better aloud than they do when they utter no vocal sound. Perhaps, moreover, David would think thus :—" My cruel enemies clamour against me ; *they* lift up their voices, and, behold, *I* lift up mine, and my cry outsoars them all. They clamour, but the cry of my voice in great distress pierces the very skies, and is louder and stronger than all their tumult ; for there is one in the sanctuary who hearkens to me from the seventh heaven, and he hath ' *heard me out of his holy hill.*' " Answers to prayers are sweet cordials for the soul. We need not fear a frowning world while we rejoice in a prayer-hearing God.

Here stands another *Selah*. Rest awhile, O tried believer, and change the strain to a softer air.

5 I laid me down and slept ; I awaked ; for the LORD sustained me.

6 I will not be afraid of ten thousands of people, that have set *themselves* against me round about.

David's faith enabled him to *lie down ;* anxiety would certainly have kept him on tiptoe, watching for an enemy. Yea, he was able to sleep, *to sleep* in the midst of trouble, surrounded by foes. " So he giveth his beloved sleep." There is a sleep of presumption ; God deliver us from it ! There is a sleep of holy confidence ; God help us so to close our eyes ! But David says he *awaked* also. Some sleep the sleep of death ; but he, though exposed to many enemies, reclined his head on the bosom of his God, slept happily beneath the wing of Providence in sweet security, and then awoke in safety. " *For the Lord sustained me.*" The sweet influence of the Pleiades of promise shone upon the sleeper, and he awoke conscious that the Lord had preserved him. An excellent divine has well remarked—" This quietude of a man's heart by faith in God, is a higher sort of work than the natural resolution of manly courage, for it is the gracious operation of God's Holy Spirit upholding a man above nature, and therefore the Lord must have all the glory of it."

Buckling on his harness for the day's battle, our hero sings, "*I will not be afraid of ten thousands of people, that have set themselves against me round about.*" Observe that he does not attempt to under-estimate the number or wisdom of his enemies. He reckons them at tens of thousands, and he views them as cunning huntsmen chasing him with cruel skill. Yet he trembles not, but looking his foeman in the face he is ready for the battle. There may be no way of escape ; they may hem me in as the deer are surrounded by a circle of hunters ; they may surround me on every side, but in the name of God I will dash through them ; or, if I remain in the midst of them, yet shall they not hurt me ; I shall be free in my very prison.

But David is too wise to venture to the battle without prayer ; he therefore betakes himself to his knees, and cries aloud to Jehovah.

7 Arise, O LORD ; save me, O my God : for thou hast smitten all mine enemies *upon* the cheek bone ; thou hast broken the teeth of the ungodly.

His only hope is in his God, but that is so strong a confidence, that he feels the Lord hath but to *arise* and he is saved. It is enough for the Lord to stand up, and all is well. He compares his enemies to wild beasts, and he declares that God hath broken their jaws, so that they could not injure him ; " *Thou hast broken the teeth of the ungodly.*" Or else he alludes to the peculiar temptations to which he was then exposed. They had spoken against him ; God, therefore, has smitten them upon the cheek bone. They seemed as if they would devour him with their mouths ; God hath broken their teeth, and let them say what they will, their toothless jaws shall not be able to devour him. Rejoice, O believer, thou hast to do with a dragon whose head is broken, and with enemies whose teeth are dashed from their jaws !

8 Salvation *belongeth* unto the LORD : thy blessing *is* upon thy people. Selah.

This verse contains the sum and substance of Calvinistic doctrine. Search Scripture through, and you must, if you read it with a candid mind, be persuaded that the doctrine of salvation by grace alone is the great doctrine of the word of God : " *Salvation belongeth unto the Lord.*" This is a point concerning which we are daily fighting. Our opponents say, " Salvation belongeth to the free will of man ; if not to man's merit, yet at least to man's will ;" but we hold and teach that salvation from first to last, in every iota of it, belongs to the Most High God. It is God that chooses his people. *He* calls them by his grace ; *he* quickens them by his Spirit, and keeps them by his power. It is not of man, neither by man ; " not of him that willeth, nor of him that runneth, but of God that showeth mercy." May we all learn this truth experimentally, for our proud flesh and blood will never permit us to learn it in any other way. In the last sentence the peculiarity and speciality of salvation are plainly stated : " *Thy blessing is upon thy people.* Neither upon Egypt, nor upon Tyre, nor upon Nineveh ; thy blessing is upon thy chosen, thy blood-bought, thine everlastingly-beloved people. " *Selah :*" lift up your hearts, and pause, and meditate upon this doctrine. " Thy blessing is upon thy people." Divine, discriminating, distinguishing, eternal, infinite, immutable love, is a subject for constant adoration. Pause, my soul, at this *Selah,* and consider thine own interest in the salvation of God ; and if by humble faith thou art enabled to see Jesus as thine by his own free gift of himself to thee, if this greatest of all blessings be upon thee, rise up and sing—

> " Rise, my soul ! adore and wonder !
> Ask, ' O why such love to me ?'
> Grace hath put me in the number
> Of the Saviour's family :
> Hallelujah !
> Thanks, eternal thanks, to thee !"

EXPLANATORY NOTES AND QUAINT SAYINGS.

Title.—With regard to the authority of the TITLES, it becomes us to speak with diffidence, considering the very opposite opinions which have been offered upon this subject by scholars of equal excellence. In the present day, it is too much the custom to slight or omit them altogether, as though added, nobody knows when or by whom, and as, in many instances, inconsistent with the subject-matter of the Psalm itself : while Augustine, Theodoret, and various other early writers of the Christian church, regard them as a part of the inspired text ; and the Jews still continue to make them a part of their chant, and their rabbins to comment upon them.

It is certainly unknown who invented or placed them where they are ; but it is unquestionable that they have been so placed from time immemorial ; they occur in the Septuagint, which contains also in a few instances titles to Psalms that are without any in the Hebrew ; and they have been copied after the Septuagint by Jerome. So far as the present writer has been able to penetrate the obscurity that occasionally hangs over them, they are a direct and most valuable key to the general history or subject of the Psalms to which they are prefixed ; and, excepting where they have been evidently misunderstood or misinterpreted, he has never met with a single instance in which the drift of the title and its respective Psalm do not exactly coincide. Many of them were, doubtless, composed by Ezra at the time of editing his own collection, at which period some critics suppose the whole to have been written ; but the rest appear rather to be coeval, or nearly so, with the respective Psalms themselves, and to have been written about the period of their production.—*John Mason Good, M.D., F.R.S.*, 1854.

See title. Here we have the first use of the word *Psalm.* In Hebrew, *Mizmor,* which hath the signification of pruning, or cutting off superfluous twigs, and is applied to songs made of short sentences, where many superfluous words are put away.—*Henry Ainsworth.*

Upon this note an old writer remarks, "Let us learn from this, that in times of sore trouble men will not fetch a compass and use fine words in prayer, but will offer a prayer which is pruned of all luxuriance of wordy speeches."

Whole Psalm.—Thus you may plainly see how God hath wrought in his church in old time, and therefore should not discourage yourselves for any sudden change ; but with David, acknowledge your sins to God, declare unto him how many there be that vex you and rise up against you, naming you Huguenots, Lutherans, Heretics, Puritans, and the children of Belial, as they named David. Let the wicked idolaters brag that they will prevail against you and overcome you, and that God hath given you over, and will be no more your God. Let them put their trust in Absalom, with his large golden locks ; and in the wisdom of Ahithophel, the wise counsellor ; yet say you, with David, " *Thou, O Lord, art my defender, and the lifter up of my head.*" Persuade yourselves, with David, that the Lord is your defender, who hath compassed you round about, and is, as it were, a " *shield* " that doth cover you on every side. It is he only that may and will compass you about with glory and honour. It is he that will thrust down those proud hypocrites from their seat, and exalt the lowly and meek. It is he which will " *smite*" your " enemies on *the cheek bone,*" and burst all their teeth in sunder. He will hang up Absalom by his own long hairs ; and Ahithophel through desperation shall hang himself. The bands shall be broken, and you delivered ; for this belongeth unto the Lord, to save his from their enemies, and to bless his people, that they may safely proceed in their pilgrimage to heaven without fear.—*Thomas Tymme's* "*Silver Watch Bell,*" 1634.

Verse 1.—Absalom's faction, like a snowball, strangely gathered in its motion. David speaks of it as one amazed ; and well he might, that a people he had so many ways obliged, should almost generally revolt from him, and rebel against him, and choose for their head such a silly, giddy young fellow as Absalom was. How slippery and deceitful are the many ! And how little fidelity and constancy is to be found among men ! David had had the hearts of his subjects as much as ever any king had, and yet now of a sudden he had lost them ! As people must not trust too much to princes (Psalm cxlvi. 3), so princes must not build too much upon their interest in the people. Christ the Son of David had many enemies, when a great multitude came to seize him, when the crowd cried, " Crucify him, crucify him," how were they then increased that troubled him ! Even good people must not think it strange if the stream be against them, and the powers that threaten them grow more and more formidable.—*Matthew Henry.*

Verse 2.—When the believer questions the power of God, or his interest in it, his joy gusheth out as blood out of a broken vein. This verse is a sore stab indeed.—*William Gurnall.*

Verse 2.—A child of God startles at the very thought of despairing of help in God ; you cannot vex him with anything so much as if you offer to persuade him, " *There is no help for him in God.*" David comes to God, and tells him what his enemies said of him, as Hezekiah spread Rabshakeh's blasphemous letter before the Lord ; they say, " *There is no help for me in thee ;*" but, Lord, if it be so, I am undone. They say to my soul, " *There is no salvation*" (for so the word is) "*for him in God ;*" but, Lord, do thou say unto my soul, " *I am thy salvation*" (Psalm xxxv. 3), and that shall satisfy me, and in due time silence them.—*Matthew Henry.*

Verses 2, 4, 8.—" *Selah.*" סֶלָה. Much has been written on this word, and still its meaning does not appear to be wholly determined. It is rendered in the Targum or Chaldee paraphrase, לְעָלְמִין, *lealmin, for ever,* or *to eternity.* In the Latin Vulgate, it is omitted, as if it were no part of the text. In the Septuagint it is rendered Διαψαλμα, supposed to refer to some variation or modulation of the voice in singing. Schleusner, *Lex.* The word occurs seventy-three times in the Psalms, and three times in the book of Habakkuk (iii. 3, 9, 13). It is never translated in our version, but in all these places the original word *Selah* is retained. It occurs only in poetry, and is supposed to have had some reference to the singing or cantillation of the poetry, and to be probably a musical term. In general, also, it indicates a pause in the sense, as well as in the musical performance. Gesenius (*Lex.*) supposes that the most probable meaning of this musical term or note is *silence* or *pause,* and that its use was, in chanting the words of the Psalm, to direct the singer *to be silent, to pause a little,* while the instruments played an interlude or harmony. Perhaps this is all that can now be known of the meaning of the word, and this is enough to satisfy every reasonable enquiry. It is probable, if this was the use of the term, that it would commonly correspond with the sense of the passage, and be inserted where the sense made a pause suitable ; and this will doubtless be found usually to be the fact. But any one acquainted at all with the character of musical notation, will perceive at once that we are not to suppose that this would be invariably or necessarily the fact, for the musical pauses by no means always correspond with pauses in the sense. This word, therefore, can furnish very little assistance in determining the meaning of the passages where it is found. Ewald supposes, differing from this view, that it rather indicates that in the places where it occurs the voice is to be raised, and that it is synonymous with *up, higher, loud,* or *distinct,* from סָל, *sal,* סָלַל, *saïal, to ascend.* Those who are disposed to enquire further respecting its meaning, and the uses of musical pauses in general, may be referred to Ugolin, " Thesau. Antiq. Sacr.," tom. xxii. —*Albert Barnes,* 1868.

Verses 2, 4, 8.—*Selah,* סֶלָה, is found seventy-three times in the Psalms, generally at the end of a sentence or paragraph ; but in Psalm lv. 19 and lvii. 3, it stands in the middle of the verse. While most authors have agreed in considering this word as somehow relating to the *music,* their conjectures about its precise meaning have varied greatly. But at present these two opinions chiefly obtain. Some, including Herder, De Wette, Ewald (*Poet. Bücher,* i. 179), and Delitzsch, derive it from סָלָה, or סָלַל, *to raise,* and understand an *elevation* of the voice or music ; others, after Gesenius, in *Thesaurus,* derive it from סָלָה, *to be still* or *silent,* and understand a pause in the singing. So Rosenmüller, Hengstenberg, and Tholuck. Probably *selah* was used to direct the singer to be silent, or to pause a little, while the instruments played an interlude (so Sept., *διάψαλμα*) or symphony. In Psalm ix. 16, it occurs in the expression *higgaion selah,* which Gesenius, with much probability, renders *instrumental music, pause ; i.e.,* let the instruments strike up a symphony, and let the singer pause. By Tholuck and Hengstenberg, however, the two words are rendered *meditation, pause ; i.e.*, let the singer meditate while the music stops. *Benjamin Davies, Ph. D., LL.D., article Psalms, in Kitto's Cyclopædia of Biblical Literature.*

Verse 3.—"*Lifter up of my head.*" God will have the body partake with the soul—as in matters of grief, so in matters of joy ; the lanthorn shines in the light of the candle within.—*Richard Sibbs*, 1639.

There is a lifting up of the head by elevation to office, as with Pharaoh's butler ; this we trace to the divine appointment. There is a lifting up in honour after shame, in health after sickness, in gladness after sorrow, in restoration after a fall, in victory after a temporary defeat ; in all these respects the Lord is the lifter up of our head.—*C. H. S.*

Verse 4.—When prayer leads the van, in due time deliverance brings up the rear.—*Thomas Watson.*

Verse 4.—"*He heard me.*" I have often heard persons say in prayer, "Thou art a prayer-hearing and a prayer-answering God," but the expression contains a superfluity, since for God to hear is, according to Scripture, the same thing as to answer.—*C. H. S.*

Verse 5.—"*I laid me down and slept ; I awaked ; for the Lord sustained me.*" The title of the Psalm tells us when David had this sweet night's rest ; not when he lay on his bed of down in his stately palace at Jerusalem, but when he fled for his life from his unnatural son Absalom, and possibly was forced to lie in the open field under the canopy of heaven. Truly it must be a soft pillow indeed that could make him forget his danger, who then had such a disloyal army at his back hunting of him ; yea, so transcendent is the influence of this peace, that it can make the creature lie down as cheerfully to sleep in the grave, as on the softest bed. You will say that child is willing that calls to be put to bed ; some of the saints have desired God to lay them at rest in their beds of dust, and that not in a pet and discontent with their present trouble, as Job did, but from a sweet sense of this peace in their bosoms. "Now let thy servant depart in peace, for mine eyes have seen thy salvation," was the swan-like song of old Simeon. He speaks like a merchant that had got all his goods on ship-board, and now desires the master of the ship to hoist sail, and be gone homewards. Indeed, what should a Christian, that is but a foreigner here, desire to stay any longer for in the world, but to get his full lading in for heaven ? And when hath he that, if not when he is assured of his peace with God ? This peace of the gospel, and sense of the love of God in the soul, doth so admirably conduce to the enabling of a person in all difficulties, and temptations, and troubles, that ordinarily, before he calls his saints to any hard service, or hot work, he gives them a draught of this cordial wine next their hearts, to cheer them up and embolden them in the conflict.—*William Gurnall.*

Verse 5.—Gurnall, who wrote when there were houses on old London Bridge, has quaintly said, "Do you not think that they sleep as soundly who dwell on London Bridge as they who live at Whitehall or Cheapside ? for they know that the waves which rush under them cannot hurt them. Even so may the saints rest quietly over the floods of trouble or death, and fear no ill."

Verse 5.—Xerxes, the Persian, when he destroyed all the temples in Greece, caused the temple of Diana to be preserved for its beautiful structure : that soul which hath the beauty of holiness shining in it, shall be preserved for the glory of the structure ; God will not suffer his own temple to be destroyed. Would you be secured in evil times ? Get grace and fortify this garrison ; a good conscience is a Christian's fort-royal. David's enemies lay round about him ; yet, saith he, "*I laid me down and slept.*" A good conscience can sleep in the mouth of a cannon ; grace is a Christian's coat of mail, which fears not the arrow or bullet. True grace may be shot at, but can never be shot through ; grace puts the soul into Christ, and there it is safe, as the bee in the hive, as the dove in the ark. "There is no condemnation to them which are in Christ Jesus." Rom. viii. 1.—*Thomas Watson.*

Verse 5.—"*The Lord sustained me.*" It would not be unprofitable to consider the sustaining power manifested in us while we lie asleep. In the flowing of the blood, heaving of the lung, etc., in the body, and the continuance of mental faculties while the image of death is upon us.—*C. H. S.*

Verse 6.—"*I will not be afraid of ten thousands of people, that have set themselves against me round about.*" The psalmist will trust, *despite appearances.* He will not be afraid though ten thousands of people have set themselves against him round about. Let us here limit our thoughts to this one idea, "despite appearances." What could look worse to human sight than this array of ten thousands of people? Ruin seemed to stare him in the face; wherever he looked an enemy was to be seen. What was one against ten thousand? It often happens that God's people come into circumstances like this; they say, "All these things are against me;" they seem scarce able to count their troubles; they cannot see a loophole through which to escape; things look very black indeed; it is great faith and trust which says under these circumstances, "I will not be afraid."

These were the circumstances under which Luther was placed, as he journeyed towards Worms. His friend Spalatin heard it said, by the enemies of the Reformation, that the safe conduct of a heretic ought not to be respected, and became alarmed for the reformer. "At the moment when the latter was approaching the city, a messenger appeared before him with this advice from the chaplain, 'Do not enter Worms!' And this from his best friend, the elector's confidant, from Spalatin himself! . . . But Luther, undismayed, turned his eyes upon the messenger, and replied, 'Go and tell your master, that even should there be as many devils in Worms as tiles upon the housetops, still I would enter it.' The messenger returned to Worms, with this astounding answer: 'I was then undaunted,' said Luther, a few days before his death, 'I feared nothing.'"

At such seasons as these, the reasonable men of the world, those who walk by sight and not by faith, will think it reasonable enough that the Christian should be afraid; they themselves would be very low if they were in such a predicament. Weak believers are now ready to make excuses for us, and we are only too ready to make them for ourselves; instead of rising above the weakness of the flesh, we take refuge under it, and use it as an excuse. But let us think prayerfully for a little while, and we shall see that it should not be thus with us. To trust only when appearances are favourable, is to sail only with the wind and tide, to believe only when we can see. Oh! let us follow the example of the psalmist, and seek that unreservedness of faith which will enable us to trust God, come what will, and to say as he said, "*I will not be afraid of ten thousands of people, that have set themselves against me round about.*"—*Philip Bennett Power's 'I wills' of the Psalms,* 1862.

Verse 6.—"*I will not be afraid,*" etc. It makes no matter what our enemies be, though for number, legions; for power, principalities; for subtlety, serpents; for cruelty, dragons; for vantage of place, a prince of the air; for maliciousness, spiritual wickedness; stronger is he that is in us, than they who are against us; nothing is able to separate us from the love of God. In Christ Jesus our Lord, we shall be more than conquerors.—*William Cowper,* 1612.

Verse 7.—"*Arise, O Lord,*" Jehovah! This is a common scriptural mode of calling upon God to manifest his presence and his power, either in wrath or favour. By a natural anthropomorphism, it describes the intervals of such manifestation as periods of inaction or of slumber, out of which he is besought to rouse himself. "*Save me,*" even me, of whom they say there is no help for him in God. "*Save me, O my God,*" mine by covenant and mutual engagement, to whom I therefore have a right to look for deliverance and protection. This confidence is warranted, moreover, by experience. "*For thou hast,*" in former exigencies, *"smitten all mine enemies,"* without exception *" (on the) cheek "* or *jaw*, an act at once violent and insulting.—*J. A. Alexander, D.D.*

Verse 7.—*" Upon the cheek bone."*—The language seems to be taken from a comparison of his enemies with wild beasts. The cheek bone denotes the bone in which the teeth are placed, and to break that is to disarm the animal. *Albert Barnes, in loc.*

Verse 7.—When God takes vengeance upon the ungodly, he will smite in such a manner as to make them feel his almightiness in every stroke. All his power shall be exercised in punishing and none in pitying. O that every obstinate sinner would think of this, and consider his unmeasurable boldness in thinking himself able to grapple with Omnipotence !—*Stephen Charnock.*

Verse 8.—*" Salvation belongeth unto the Lord:"* parallel passage in Jonah ii. 9, *" Salvation is of the Lord."* The mariners might have written upon their ship, instead of Castor and Pollux, or the like device, *Salvation is the Lord's ;* the Ninevites might have written upon their gates, *Salvation is the Lord's ;* and whole mankind, whose cause is pitted and pleaded by God against the hardness of Jonah's heart, in the last, might have written on the palms of their hands, *Salvation is the Lord's.* It is the argument of both the Testaments, the staff and supportation of heaven and earth. They would both sink, and all their joints be severed, if the salvation of the Lord were not. The birds in the air sing no other notes, the beasts in the field give no other voice, than *Salus Jehovæ*, Salvation is the Lord's. The walls and fortresses to our country's gates, to our cities and towns, bars to our houses, a surer cover to our heads than a helmet of steel, a better receipt to our bodies than the confection of apothecaries, a better receipt to our souls than the pardons of Rome, is *Salus Jehovæ*, the salvation of the Lord. The salvation of the Lord blesseth, preserveth, upholdeth all that we have ; our basket and our store, the oil in our cruses, our presses, the sheep in our folds, our stalls, the children in the womb, at our tables, the corn in our fields, our stores, our garners ; it is not the virtue of the stars, nor nature of all things themselves, that giveth being and continuance to any of these blessings. And, *" What shall I more say ?"* as the apostle asked (Heb. xi.) when he had spoken much, and there was much more behind, but time failed him. Rather, what should I not say ? for the world is my theatre at this time, and I neither think nor can feign to myself anything that hath not dependence upon this acclamation, *Salvation is the Lord's.* Plutarch writeth, that the Amphictions in Greece, a famous council assembled of twelve sundry people, wrote upon the temple of Apollo Pythius, instead of the Iliads of Homer, or songs of Pindarus (large and tiring discourses), short sentences and memoratives, as, *Know thyself, Use moderation, Beware of suretyship,* and the like ; and doubtless though every creature in the world, whereof we have use, be a treatise and narration unto us of the goodness of God, and we might weary our flesh, and spend our days in writing books of that inexplicable subject, yet this short apothegm of Jonah comprehendeth all the rest, and standeth at the end of the song, as the altars and stones that the patriarch set up at the parting of the ways, to give knowledge to the after-world by what means he was delivered. I would it were daily preached in our temples, sung in our streets, written upon our door-posts, painted upon our walls, or rather cut with an adamant claw upon the tables of our hearts, that we might never forget salvation to be the Lord's. We have need of such remembrances to keep us in practice of revolving the mercies of God. For nothing decayeth sooner than love ; *nihil facilius quam amor putrescit.* And of all the powers of the soul, memory is most delicate, tender, and brittle, and first waxeth old, *memoria delicata, tenera, fragilis, in quam primum senectus incurrit ;* and of all the apprehensions of memory, first benefit, *primum senescit beneficium.*—*John King's Commentary on Jonah,* 1594.

Verse 8.—*" Thy blessing is upon thy people."* The saints are not only blessed when they are comprehensors, but while they are viators. They are blessed before they are crowned. This seems a paradox to flesh and blood : what, reproached and maligned, yet blessed ! A man that looks upon the children of God with a carnal eye, and sees how they are afflicted, and like the ship in the gospel, which was covered with waves (Matt. viii. 24), would think they were far from blessedness. Paul brings a catalogue of his sufferings (2 Cor. xi. 24—26), "Thrice was I beaten with rods, once was I stoned, thrice I suffered shipwreck," etc. And those Christians of the first magnitude, of whom the world was not worthy, "Had trials of cruel mockings and scourgings, they were sawn asunder, they were slain with the sword." Heb. xi. 36, 37. What ! and were all these during the time of their sufferings blessed ? A carnal man would think, if this be to be blessed, God deliver him from it. But, however sense would give their vote, our Saviour Christ pronounceth the godly man blessed ; though a mourner, though a martyr, yet blessed. Job on the dunghill was blessed Job. The saints are blessed when they are cursed. Shimei did curse David (2 Samuel xvi. 5), "He came forth and cursed him ;" yet when he was cursed David he was blessed David. The saints though they are bruised, yet they are blessed. Not only they shall be blessed, but they are so. Psalm cxix. 1. "Blessed are the undefiled." Psalm iii. 8. "*Thy blessing is upon thy people.*"—*Thomas Watson.*

As a curious instance of Luther's dogmatical interpretations, we give very considerable extracts from his rendering of this Psalm without in any degree endorsing them.—C. H. S.

Whole Psalm.—That the meaning of this Psalm is not historical, is manifest from many particulars, which militate against its being so understood. And first of all, there is this which the blessed Augustine has remarked ; that the words, "I laid me down to sleep and took my rest," seem to be the words of Christ rising from the dead. And then that there is at the end the blessing of God pronounced upon the people, which manifestly belongs to the whole church. Hence, the blessed Augustine interprets the Psalm in a threefold way : first, concerning Christ the head ; secondly, concerning the whole of Christ, that is, Christ and his church, the head and the body ; and thirdly, figuratively, concerning any private Christian. Let each have his own interpretation. I, in the meantime, will interpret it concerning Christ ; being moved so to do by the same argument that moved Augustine—that the fifth verse does not seem appropriately to apply to any other but Christ. First, because, "Flying down" and "sleeping," signify in this place altogether a natural death, not a natural sleep. Which may be collected from this—because it then follows, "and rose again." Whereas if David had spoken concerning the sleep of the body, he would have said, "and awoke ;" though this does not make so forcibly for the interpretation of which we are speaking, if the Hebrew word be closely examined. But again, what new thing would he advance by declaring that he laid him down and slept ? Why did he not say also that he walked, ate, drank, laboured, or was in necessity, or mention particularly some other work of the body ? And moreover, it seems an absurdity under so great a tribulation, to boast of nothing else but the sleep of the body ; for that tribulation would rather force him to a privation from sleep, and to be in peril and distress ; especially since those two expressions, "I laid me down," and "I slept," signify the quiet repose of one lying down in his place, which is not the state of one who falls asleep from exhausture through sorrow. But this consideration makes the more forcibly for us—that he therefore glories in his rising up again because it was the Lord that sustained him, who raised him up while sleeping, and did not leave him in sleep. How can such a glorying agree, and what new kind of religion can make it agree, with any particular sleep of the body ? (for

3

in that case, would it not apply to the daily sleep also ?) and especially, when this sustaining of God indicates at the same time an utterly forsaken state in the person sleeping, which is not the case in corporal sleep ; for there the person sleeping may be protected even by men being his guards ; but this sustaining being altogether of God, implies, not a sleep, but a heavy conflict. And lastly, the word HEKIZOTHI itself favours such an interpretation ; which, being here put absolutely and transitively, signifies, "I caused to arise or awake." As if he had said, "I caused myself to awake, I roused myself." Which certainly more aptly agrees with the resurrection of Christ than with the sleep of the body ; both because those who are asleep are accustomed to be roused and awaked, and because it is no wonderful matter, nor a matter worthy of so important a declaration, for any one to awake of himself, seeing that it is what takes place every day. But this matter being introduced by the Spirit as a something new and singular, is certainly different from all that which attends common sleeping and waking.

Verse 2.—"*There is no help for him in his God.*" In the Hebrew the expression is simply, "in God," without the pronoun "*his*," which seems to me to give clearness and force to the expression. As if he had said, They say of me that I am not only deserted and oppressed by all creatures, but that even God, who is present with all things, and preserves all things, and protects all things, forsakes me as the only thing out of the whole universe that he does not preserve. Which kind of temptation Job seems also to have tasted where he says, "Why hast thou set me as a mark against thee ?" vii. 20. For there is no temptation, no, not of the whole world together, nor of all hell combined in one, equal unto that wherein God stands contrary to a man, which temptation Jeremiah prays against (xvii. 17), "Be not a terror unto me ; thou art my hope in the day of evil ;" and concerning which also the sixth Psalm following saith, "O Lord, rebuke me not in thine anger ;" and we find the same petitions throughout the psaltery. This temptation is wholly unsupportable, and is truly hell itself ; as it is said in the same sixth Psalm, "for in death there is no remembrance of thee," etc. In a word, if you have never experienced it, you can never form any idea of it whatever.

Verse 3.—"*For thou, O Lord, art my helper, my glory, and the lifter up of my head.*" David here contrasts three things with three ; helper, with many troubling ; glory, with many rising up ; and the lifter up of the head, with the blaspheming and insulting. Therefore, the person here represented is indeed alone in the estimation of man, and even according to his own feelings also ; but in the sight of God, and in a spiritual view, he is by no means alone ; but protected with the greatest abundance of help ; as Christ saith (John xvi. 32), "Behold, the hour cometh when ye shall leave me alone ; and yet I am not alone, because the Father is with me." . . . . The words contained in this verse are not the words of nature, but of grace ; not of free-will, but of the spirit of strong faith ; which, even though seeing God, as in the darkness of the storm of death and hell, a deserting God, acknowledges him a sustaining God ; when seeing him as a persecuting God, acknowledges him a helping God ; when seeing him as a condemner, acknowledges him a Saviour. Thus this faith does not judge of things according as they seem to be, or are felt, like a horse or mule which have no understanding ; but it understands things which are not seen, for "hope that is seen is not hope : for what a man seeth, why doth he yet hope for ?" Romans viii. 24.

Verse 4.—"*I cried unto the Lord with my voice, and he heard me out of his holy hill.*" In the Hebrew, the verb is in the future, and is, as Hieronymus translates it, "I will cry," and, "he shall hear ;" and this pleases me better than the perfect tense ; for they are the words of one triumphing in, and praising and glorifying God, and giving thanks unto him who sustained, preserved, and lifted him up, according as he had hoped in the preceding verse. For it is usual with those that triumph and rejoice, to speak of those things which they have done and suffered, and to sing a song of praise unto their helper and deliverer ; as in Psalm lxvi. 16, "Come, then, all ye that fear God, and I will declare what he hath done for my soul. I cried unto him with my mouth, and he was extolled with my tongue." And also Psalm lxxxi. 1,"Sing aloud unto God our strength." And so again, Exodus xv. 1, "Let us sing unto the Lord, for he hath triumphed gloriously." And so here, being filled with an overflowing sense of gratitude and joy, he sings of his being dead, of his having slept and rose up again, of his enemies being smitten, and of the teeth of the ungodly being broken. This it is which causes the change ; for he who hitherto had been addressing God in the second person, changes on a sudden his address to others concerning God, in the third person, saying, "*and he heard me,*" not "and thou heardest me ;" and also, "*I cried unto the Lord,*" not "I cried unto thee," for he wants to make all know what benefits God has heaped upon him ; which is peculiar to a grateful mind.

Verse 5.—"*I laid me down and slept ; I awaked ; for the Lord sustained me.*" Christ, by the words of this verse, signifies his death and burial. . . . . . . For it is not to be supposed that he would have spoken so importantly concerning mere natural rest and sleep ; especially since that which precedes, and that which follows, compel us to understand him as speaking of a deep conflict and a glorious victory over his enemies. By all which things he stirs us up and animates us to faith in God, and commends unto us the power and grace of God ; that he is able to raise us up from the dead ; an example of which he sets before us, and proclaims it unto us as wrought in himself. . . . . And this is shown also farther in his using gentle words, and such as tend wonderfully to lessen the terror of death. "*I laid me down* (saith he), *and slept.*" He does not say, I died and was buried ; for death and the tomb had lost both their name and their power. And now death is not death, but a sleep ; and the tomb not a tomb, but a bed and resting place ; which was the reason why the words of this prophecy were put somewhat obscurely and doubtfully, that it might by that means render death most lovely in our eyes (or rather most contemptible), as being that state from which, as from the sweet rest of sleep, an undoubted arising and awaking are promised. For who is not most sure of an awaking and arising, who lies down to rest in a sweet sleep (where death does not prevent) ? This person, however, does not say that he died, but that he laid him down to sleep, and that therefore he awaked. And more-over, as sleep is useful and necessary for a better renewal of the powers of the body (as Ambrosius says in his hymn), and as sleep relieves the weary limbs, so is death also equally useful, and ordained for the arriving at a better life. And this is what David says in the following Psalm, "I will lay me down in peace, and take my rest, for thou, Lord, in a singular manner hast formed me in hope." Therefore, in considering death, we are not so much to consider death itself, as that most certain life and resurrection which are sure to those who are in Christ ; that those words (John viii. 51) might be fulfilled, "If a man keep my say-ing, he shall never see death." But how is it that he shall never see it ? Shall he not feel it ? Shall he not die ? No ! he shall only see sleep, for, having the eyes of his faith fixed upon the resurrection, he so glides through death, that he does not even see death ; for death, as I have said, is to him no death at all. And hence, there is that also of John xi. 25, "He that believeth in me, though he were dead, yet shall he live."

Verse 7.—"*For thou hast smitten all mine enemies upon the cheek bone ; thou hast broken the teeth of the ungodly.*" Hieronymus uses this metaphor of "*cheek bones,*" and "*teeth,*" to represent cutting words, detractions, calumnies, and other injuries of the same kind, by which the innocent are oppressed : according to that of Proverbs xxx. 14, "There is a generation whose teeth are as swords, and their jaw-teeth as knives. to devour the poor from off the earth, and the needy from among men." It was by these that Christ was devoured, when, before Pilate, he was condemned to the cross by the voices and accusations of his enemies. And hence it is that the apostle saith (Gal. v. 15), "But if ye bite and devour one another, take heed that ye be not consumed one of another."

Verse 8.—"*Salvation is of the Lord, and thy blessing is upon thy people.*" A most beautiful conclusion this, and, as it were, the sum of all the feelings spoken of. The sense is, it is the Lord alone that saves and blesses : and even though the whole mass of all evils should be gathered together in one against a man, still, it is the Lord who saves : salvation and blessing are in his hands. What then shall I fear ? What shall I not promise myself ? When I know that no one can be destroyed, no one reviled, without the permission of God, even though all should rise up to curse and to destroy ; and that no one of them can be blessed and saved without the permission of God, how much soever they may bless and strive to save themselves. And as Gregory Nazianzen says, "Where God gives, envy can avail nothing ; and where God does not give, labour can avail nothing." And in the same way also Paul saith (Rom. viii. 31), "If God be for us, who can be against us ?" And so, on the contrary, if God be against them, who can be for them ? And why ? Because "*salvation is of the Lord,*" and not of them, nor of us, for "vain is the help of man."—*Martin Luther.*

HINTS TO THE VILLAGE PREACHER.

Verse 1.—*The saint telling his griefs to his God.* (1) His right to do so. (2) The proper manner of telling them. (3) The fair results of such holy communications with the Lord.

When may we expect increased troubles ? Why are they sent ? What is our wisdom in reference to them ?

Verse 2.—The lie against the saint and the libel upon his God.

Verse 3.—The threefold blessing which God affords to his suffering ones—Defence, Honour, Joy. Show how all these may be enjoyed by faith, even in our worst estate.

Verse 4.—(1) In dangers we should pray. (2) God will graciously hear. (3) We should record his answers of grace. (4) We may strengthen ourselves for the future by remembering the deliverances of the past.

Verse 5.—(1) Describe sweet sleeping. (2) Describe happy waking. (3) Show how both are to be enjoyed, "*for the Lord sustained me.*"

Verse 6.—Faith surrounded by enemies and yet triumphant.

Verse 7.—(1) Describe the Lord's past dealing with his enemies ; "thou hast." (2) Show that the Lord should be our constant resort, "O Lord," "O my God." (3) Enlarge upon the fact that the Lord is to be stirred up : "Arise." (4) Urge believers to use the Lord's past victories as an argument with which to prevail with him.

Verse 7 (*last clause*).—Our enemies vanquished foes, toothless lions.

Verse 8 (*first clause*).—Salvation of God from first to last. (See the exposition.)

Verse 8 (*last clause*).—They were blessed *in* Christ, *through* Christ, and shall be blessed *with* Christ. The blessing rests upon their persons, comforts, trials, labours, families, etc. It flows from grace, is enjoyed by faith, and is insured by oath, etc.—*James Smith's Portions,* 1802—1862.

PSALM IV.

TITLE.—*This Psalm is apparently intended to accompany the third, and make a pair with it. If the last may be entitled* THE MORNING PSALM, *this from its matter is equally deserving of the title of* THE EVENING HYMN. *May the choice words of the 8th verse be our sweet song of rest as we retire to our repose!*

> "Thus with my thoughts composed to peace,
> I'll give mine eyes to sleep;
> Thy hand in safety keeps my days,
> And will my slumbers keep."

The Inspired title runs thus: " To the chief Musician on Neginoth, a Psalm of David." *The chief musician was the master or director of the sacred music of the sanctuary. Concerning this person carefully read* 1 *Chron.* vi. 31, 32 ; xv. 16—22 ; xxv. 1, 7. *In these passages will be found much that is interesting to the lover of sacred song, and very much that will throw a light upon the mode of praising God in the temple. Some of the titles of the Psalms are, we doubt not, derived from the names of certain renowned singers, who composed the music to which they were set.*

On Neginoth, that is, on stringed instruments, or hand instruments, which were played on with the hand alone, as harps and cymbals. The joy of the Jewish church was so great that they needed music to set forth the delightful feelings of their souls. Our holy mirth is none the less overflowing because we prefer to express it in a more spiritual manner, as becometh a more spiritual dispensation. In allusion to these instruments to be played on with the hand, Nazianzen says, " Lord, I am an instrument for thee to touch." *Let us lay ourselves open to the Spirit's touch, so shall we make melody. May we be full of faith and love, and we shall be living instruments of music.*

Hawker says: " The Septuagint read the word which we have rendered in our translation chief musician Lamenetz, instead of Lamenetzoth, the meaning of which is unto the end. From whence the Greek and Latin fathers imagined, that all psalms which bear this inscription refer to the Messiah, the great end. If so, this Psalm is addressed to Christ; and well it may, for it is all of Christ, and spoken by Christ, and hath respect only to his people as being one with Christ. The Lord the Spirit give the reader to see this, and he will find it most blessed.*

DIVISION.—*In the first verse David pleads with God for help. In the second he expostulates with his enemies, and continues to address them to the end of verse 5. Then from verse 6 to the close he delightfully contrasts his own satisfaction and safety with the disquietude of the ungodly in their best estate. The Psalm was most probably written upon the same occasion as the preceding, and is another choice flower from the garden of affliction. Happy is it for us that David was tried, or probably we should never have heard these sweet sonnets of faith.*

EXPOSITION.

HEAR me when I call, O God of my righteousness : thou hast enlarged me *when I was* in distress ; have mercy upon me, and hear my prayer.

This is another instance of David's common habit of pleading past mercies as a ground for present favour. Here he reviews his Ebenezers and takes comfort from them. It is not to be imagined that he who has helped us in six troubles will leave us in the seventh. God does nothing by halves, and he will never cease to help us until we cease to need. The manna shall fall every morning until we cross the Jordan.

Observe, that David speaks first to God and then to men. Surely we should all speak the more boldly to men if we had more constant converse with God. He who dares to face his Maker will not tremble before the sons of men.

The name by which the Lord is here addressed, " *God of my righteousness,*" deserves notice, since it is not used in any other part of Scripture. It means,

Thou art the author, the witness, the maintainer, the judge, and the rewarder of my righteousness ; to thee I appeal from the calumnies and harsh judgments of men. Herein is wisdom, let us imitate it and always take our suit, not to the petty courts of human opinion, but into the superior court, the King's Bench of heaven.

" *Thou hast enlarged me when I was in distress.*" A figure taken from an army enclosed in a defile, and hardly pressed by the surrounding enemy. God hath dashed down the rocks and given me room ; he hath broken the barriers and set me in a large place. Or, we may understand it thus :—" God hath enlarged my heart with joy and comfort, when I was like a man imprisoned by grief and sorrow." God is a never-failing comforter.

" *Have mercy upon me.*" Though thou mayest justly permit my enemies to destroy me, on account of my many and great sins, yet I flee to thy mercy, and I beseech thee *hear my prayer*, and bring thy servant out of his troubles. The best of men need mercy as truly as the worst of men. All the deliverances of saints, as well as the pardons of sinners, are the free gifts of heavenly grace.

2 O ye sons of men, how long *will ye turn* my glory into shame ? *how long* will ye love vanity, *and* seek after leasing ? Selah.

In this second division of the Psalm, we are led from the closet of prayer into the field of conflict. Remark the undaunted courage of the man of God. He allows that his enemies are great men (for such is the import of the Hebrew words translated—*sons of men*), but still he believes them to be foolish men, and therefore chides them, as though they were but children. He tells them that they *love vanity, and seek after leasing*, that is, lying, empty fancies, vain conceits, wicked fabrications. He asks them *how long* they mean to make his honour a jest, and his fame a mockery ? A little of such mirth is too much, why need they continue to indulge in it ? Had they not been long enough upon the watch for his halting ? Had not repeated disappointments convinced them that the Lord's anointed was not to be overcome by all their calumnies ? Did they mean to jest their souls into hell, and go on with their laughter until swift vengeance should turn their merriment into howling ? In the contemplation of their perverse continuance in their vain and lying pursuits, the Psalmist solemnly pauses and inserts a *Selah*. Surely we too may stop awhile, and meditate upon the deep-seated folly of the wicked, their continuance in evil, and their sure destruction ; and we may learn to admire that grace which has made us to differ, and taught us to *love* truth, and *seek* after righteousness.

3 But know that the LORD hath set apart him that is godly for himself ; the LORD will hear when I call unto him.

" *But know.*" Fools will not learn, and therefore they must again and again be told the same thing, especially when it is such a bitter truth which is to be taught them, viz. :—the fact that the godly are the chosen of God, and are, by distinguishing grace, set apart and separated from among men. Election is a doctrine which unrenewed men cannot endure, but nevertheless, it is a glorious and well-attested truth, and one which should comfort the tempted believer. Election is the guarantee of complete salvation, and an argument for success at the throne of grace. HE who chose us for himself will surely hear our prayers. The Lord's elect shall not be condemned, nor shall their cry be unheard. David was king by divine decree, and we are the Lord's people in the same manner ; let us tell our enemies to their faces, that they fight against God and destiny, when they strive to overthrow our souls. O beloved, when you are on your knees, the fact of your being *set apart* as God's own peculiar treasure, should give you courage and inspire you with fervency and faith. " Shall not God avenge his own elect, which cry day and night unto him ?" Since he chose to love us he cannot but choose to hear us.

4 Stand in awe, and sin not : commune with your own heart upon your bed, and be still. Selah.

" *Tremble and sin not.*" How many reverse this counsel and sin but tremble not. O that men would take the advice of this verse and *commune with their own hearts.* Surely a want of thought must be one reason why men are so mad as to despite Christ and hate their own mercies. O that for once their passions would be quiet and let them *be still*, that so in solemn silence they might review the past, and meditate upon their inevitable doom. Surely a thinking man might have enough sense to discover the vanity of sin and the worthlessness of the world. Stay, rash sinner, stay, ere thou take the last leap. Go to *thy bed* and think upon thy ways. Ask counsel of thy pillow, and let the quietude of night instruct thee! Throw not away thy soul for nought! Let reason speak! Let the clamorous world be still awhile, and let thy poor soul plead with thee to bethink thyself before thou seal its fate, and ruin it for ever! *Selah.* O sinner! pause while I question thee awhile in the words of a sacred poet,—

> " Sinner, is thy heart at rest ?
> Is thy bosom void of fear ?
> Art thou not by guilt oppress'd ?
> Speaks not conscience in thine ear ?
>
> Can this world afford thee bliss ?
> Can it chase away thy gloom ?
> Flattering, false, and vain it is ;
> Tremble at the worldling's doom !
>
> Think, O sinner, on thy end,
> See the judgment-day appear,
> Thither must thy spirit wend,
> There thy righteous sentence hear.
>
> Wretched, ruin'd, helpless soul,
> To a Saviour's blood apply ;
> He alone can make thee whole,
> Fly to Jesus, sinner, fly !"

5 Offer the sacrifices of righteousness, and put your trust in the LORD.

Provided that the rebels had obeyed the voice of the last verse, they would now be crying,—" What shall we do to be saved ?" And in the present verse, they are pointed to the *sacrifice*, and exhorted to *trust in the Lord.* When the Jew offered sacrifice righteously, that is, in a spiritual manner, he thereby set forth the Redeemer, the great sin-atoning Lamb ; there is, therefore, the full gospel in this exhortation of the Psalmist. O sinners, flee ye to the sacrifice of Calvary, and there put your whole confidence and *trust*, for he who died for men is the LORD JEHOVAH.

6 *There be* many that say, Who will shew us *any* good ? LORD, lift thou up the light of thy countenance upon us.

We have now entered upon the third division of the Psalm, in which the faith of the afflicted one finds utterance in sweet expressions of contentment and peace.

There were many, even among David's own followers, who wanted to *see* rather than to believe. Alas ! this is the tendency of us all ! Even the regenerate sometimes groan after the sense and sight of prosperity, and are sad when darkness covers all good from view. As for worldlings, this is their unceasing cry. " *Who will shew us any good?*" Never satisfied, their gaping mouths are turned in every direction, their empty hearts are ready to drink in any fine delusion which impostors may invent ; and when these fail, they soon yield to despair, and declare that there is no good thing in either heaven or earth. The true believer is a man of a very different mould. His face is not downward like the beasts', but upward like the angels'. He drinks not from the muddy pools of Mammon, but from the fountain of life above. The light of God's countenance is enough for him. This is his riches, his honour, his health, his ambition, his ease. Give him this, and he will ask no more. This is joy unspeakable, and full of glory. Oh, for more of the indwelling of the Holy Spirit, that our fellowship with the Father and with his Son Jesus Christ may be constant and abiding !

7 Thou hast put gladness in my heart, more than in the time *that* their corn and their wine increased.

"It is better," said one, "to feel God's favour one hour in our repenting souls, than to sit whole ages under the warmest sunshine that this world affordeth." Christ in the heart is better than corn in the barn, or wine in the vat. Corn and wine are but fruits of the world, but the light of God's countenance is the ripe fruit of heaven. "Thou art with me," is a far more blessed cry than "Harvest home." Let my granary be empty, I am yet full of blessings if Jesus Christ smiles upon me ; but if I have all the world, I am poor without Him.

We should not fail to remark that this verse is the *saying* of the righteous man, in opposition to the saying of the many. How quickly doth the tongue betray the character ! "*Speak*, that I may see thee !" said Socrates to a fair boy. The metal of a bell is best known by its sound. Birds reveal their nature by their song. Owls cannot sing the carol of the lark, nor can the nightingale hoot like the owl. Let us, then, weigh and watch our words, lest our speech should prove us to be foreigners, and aliens from the commonwealth of Israel.

8 I will both lay me down in peace, and sleep : for thou, LORD, only makest me dwell in safety.

Sweet Evening Hymn ! I shall not sit up to watch through fear, but I will *lie down ;* and then I will not lie awake listening to every rustling sound, but I will lie down *in peace and sleep*, for I have nought to fear. He that hath the wings of God above him needs no other curtain. Better than bolts or bars is the protection of the Lord. Armed men kept the bed of Solomon, but we do not believe that he slept more soundly than his father, whose bed was the hard ground, and who was haunted by blood-thirsty foes. Note the word "*only*," which means that God alone was his keeper, and that though alone, without man's help, he was even then in good keeping, for he was "alone with God." A quiet conscience is a good bedfellow. How many of our sleepless hours might be traced to our untrusting and disordered minds. They slumber sweetly whom faith rocks to sleep. No pillow so soft as a promise ; no coverlet so warm as an assured interest in Christ.

O Lord, give us this calm repose on thee, that like David we may lie down in peace, and sleep each night while we live ; and joyfully may we lie down in the appointed season, to sleep in death, to rest in God !

Dr. Hawker's reflection upon this Psalm is worthy to be prayed over and fed upon with sacred delight. We cannot help transcribing it.

"Reader ! let us never lose sight of the Lord Jesus while reading this psalm. He is the Lord our righteousness ; and therefore, in all our approaches to the mercy seat, let us go there in a language corresponding to this which calls Jesus the Lord our righteousness. While men of the world, from the world are seeking their chief good, let us desire his favour which infinitely transcends corn and wine, and all the good things which perish in the using. Yes, Lord, *thy favour is better than life itself*. Thou causest them that love thee to inherit substance, and fillest all their treasure.

"Oh ! thou gracious God and Father, hast thou in such a wonderful manner set apart one in our nature for thyself ? Hast thou indeed chosen one out of the people ? Hast thou beheld him in the purity of his nature,—as one in every point Godly ? Hast thou given him as the covenant of the people ?

And hast thou declared thyself well pleased in him? Oh! then, well may my soul be well pleased in him also. Now do I know that my God and Father will hear me when I call upon him in Jesus' name, and when I look up to him for acceptance for Jesus' sake! Yes, my heart is fixed, O Lord, my heart is fixed; Jesus is my hope and righteousness; the Lord will hear me when I call. And henceforth will I both lay me down in peace and sleep securely in Jesus, accepted in the Beloved; for *this is the rest wherewith the Lord causeth the weary to rest, and this is the refreshing.*"

EXPLANATORY NOTES AND QUAINT SAYINGS.

Verse 1.—"*Hear me when I call,*" etc. Faith is a good orator and a noble disputer in a strait; it can reason from God's readiness to hear: "*Hear me when I call, O God.*" And from the everlasting righteousness given to the man in the justification of his person: "*O God of my righteousness.*" And from God's constant justice in defending the righteousness of his servant's cause: "*O God of my righteousness.*" And from both present distresses and those that are by-past, wherein he hath been, and from by-gone mercies received: "*Thou hast enlarged me when I was in distress.*" And from God's grace, which is able to answer all objections from the man's unworthiness or ill-deserving: "*Have mercy upon me, and hear my prayer.*"—*David Dickson*, 1653.

Verse 1.—"*Hear me.*" The great Author of nature and of all things does nothing in vain. He instituted not this law, and, if I may so express it, art of praying, as a vain and insufficient thing, but endows it with wonderful efficacy for producing the greatest and happiest consequences. He would have it to be the key by which all the treasures of heaven should be opened. He has constructed it as a powerful machine, by which we may, with easy and pleasant labour, remove from us the most dire and unhappy machinations of our enemy, and may with equal ease draw to ourselves what is most propitious and advantageous. Heaven and earth, and all the elements, obey and minister to the hands which are often lifted up to heaven in earnest prayer. Yea, all works, and, which is yet more and greater, all the words of God obey it. Well known in the sacred Scriptures are the examples of Moses and Joshua, and that which James (v. 17) particularly mentions of Elijah, whom he expressly calls ὁμοιοπαθὴς, *a man subject to like infirmities* with ourselves, that he might illustrate the admirable force of prayer, by the common and human weakness of the person by whom it was offered. And that Christian legion under Antoninus is well known and justly celebrated, which, for the singular ardour and efficacy of its prayers, obtained the name of κεραυνοβόλος, *the thundering legion.*—*Robert Leighton, D.D., Archbishop of Glasgow,* 1611—1684.

Verse 2.—"*O ye sons of men, how long will ye turn my glory into shame? how long will ye love vanity, and seek after leasing? Selah.*" Prayer soars above the violence and impiety of men, and with a swift wing commits itself to heaven, with happy omen, if I may allude to what the learned tell us of the augury of the ancients, which I shall not minutely discuss. Fervent prayers stretch forth a strong, wide-extended wing, and while the birds of night hover beneath, they mount aloft, and point out, as it were, the proper seats to which we should aspire. For certainly there is nothing that cuts the air so swiftly, nothing that takes so sublime, so happy, and so auspicious a flight as prayer, which bears the soul on its pinions, and leaves far behind all the dangers, and even the delights of this low world of ours. Behold this holy man, who just before was crying to God in the midst of distress, and with urgent importunity entreating that he might be heard, now, as if he were already possessed of all he had asked, taking upon him boldly to rebuke his enemies, how highly soever they were exalted, and how potent soever they might be even in the royal palace. *Robert Leighton, D.D.*

Verse 2.—" *O ye sons of men, how long will ye turn my glory into shame ?*" etc. We might imagine every syllable of this precious Psalm used by our Master some evening, when about to leave the temple for the day, and retiring to his wonted rest at Bethany (v. 8), after another fruitless expostulation with the men of Israel. And we may read it still as the very utterance of his heart, longing over man, and delighting in God. But, further, not only is this the utterance of the Head, it is also the language of one of his members in full sympathy with him in holy feeling. This is a Psalm with which the righteous may make their dwellings resound, morning and evening, as they cast a sad look over a world that rejects God's grace. They may sing it while they cling more and more every day to Jehovah, as their all-sufficient heritage, now and in the age to come. They may sing it, too, in the happy confidence of faith and hope, when the evening of the world's day is coming, and may then fall asleep in the certainty of what shall greet their eyes on the resurrection morning—

" Sleeping embosomed in his grace,
Till morning-shadows flee."

Andrew A. Bonar, 1859.

Verse 2.—" *Love Vanity.*" They that love sin, love *vanity ;* they chase a bubble, they lean upon a reed, their hope is as a spider's web.

" *Leasing.*" This is an old Saxon word signifying falsehood.

Verse 2.—" *How long will ye love vanity, and seek after leasing?*" " Vanity of vanities, and all is vanity." This our first parents found, and therefore named their second son Abel, or vanity. Solomon, that had tried these things, and could best tell the vanity of them, he preacheth this sermon over again and again, " Vanity of vanities, and all is vanity." It is sad to think how many thousands there be that can say with the preacher, " Vanity of vanities, all is vanity ;" nay, swear it, and yet follow after these things as if there were no other glory, nor felicity, but what is to be found in these things they call vanity. Such men will sell Christ, heaven, and their souls, for a trifle, that call these things vanity, but do not cordially believe them to be vanity, but set their hearts upon them as if they were their crown, the top of all their royalty and glory. Oh ! let your souls dwell upon the vanity of all things here below, till your hearts be so thoroughly convinced and persuaded of the vanity of them, as to trample upon them, and make them a footstool for Christ to get up, and ride in a holy triumph in your hearts.

Gilemex, king of Vandals, led in triumph by Belisarius, cried out, " Vanity of vanities, all is vanity." The fancy of Lucian, who placeth Charon on the top of a high hill, viewing all the affairs of men living, and looking on their greatest cities as little birds' nests, is very pleasant. Oh, the imperfection, the ingratitude, the levity, the inconstancy, the perfidiousness of those creatures we most servilely affect ! Ah, did we but weigh man's pain with his payment, his crosses with his mercies, his miseries with his pleasures, we should then see that there is nothing got by the bargain, and conclude, " Vanity of vanities, all is vanity." Chrysostom said once, " That if he were the fittest in the world to preach a sermon to the whole world, gathered together in one congregation, and had some high mountain for his pulpit, from whence he might have a prospect of all the world in his view, and were furnished with a voice of brass, a voice as loud as the trumpets of the archangel, that all the world might hear him, he would choose to preach upon no other text than that in the Psalms, O mortal men, ' *How long will ye love vanity, and follow after leasing ?* ' "—*Thomas Brooks,* 1608—1680.

Verse 2.—" *Love vanity.*" Men's affections are according to their principles ; and every one loves that most *without him* which is most suitable to somewhat *within him : liking* is founded in *likeness,* and has therefore that word put upon it. It is so in whatsoever we can imagine ; whether in temporals or spirituals, as to the things of this life, or of a better. Men's love is according to some working and impression upon their own spirits. And so it is here in the point of vanity ; those which are vain persons, they delight in vain things ; as children, they love such matters as are most agreeable to their childish dispositions, and as do suit them in that particular. Out of the heart comes all kind of evil.—*Thomas Horton*, 1675.

Verse 3.—" *The Lord hath set apart him that is godly for himself.*" When God chooseth a man, he chooseth him for himself ; for himself to converse with, to communicate himself unto him as a friend, a companion, and his delight. Now, it is holiness that makes us fit to live with the holy God for ever, since without it we cannot see him (Heb. xii. 14), which is God's main aim, and more than our being his children : as one must be supposed a man, one of mankind, having a soul reasonable, ere we can suppose him capable of adoption, or to be another man's heir. As therefore it was the main first design in God's eye, before the consideration of our happiness, let it be so in ours.—*Thomas Goodwin*, 1600—1679.

Verse 3.—What rare persons the godly are : " The righteous is more excellent than his neighbour." Prov. xii. 26. As the flower of the sun, as the wine of Lebanon, as the sparkling upon Aaron's breastplate, such is the orient splendour of a person embellished with godliness. . . . . The godly are precious, therefore they are set apart for God, " *Know that the Lord hath set apart him that is godly for himself.*" We set apart things that are precious ; the godly are set apart as God's peculiar treasure (Psalm cxxxv. 4) ; as his garden of delight (Cant. iv. 12) ; as his royal diadem (Isaiah xliii. 3) ; the godly are the excellent of the earth (Psalm xvi. 3) ; comparable to fine gold (Lam. iv. 2) ; double refined. Zech. xiii. 9. They are the glory of the creation. Isaiah xlvi. 13. Origen compares the saints to sapphires and crystals : God calls them jewels. Mal. iii. 17. *Thomas Watson.*

Verse 3.—" *The Lord will hear when I call unto him.*" Let us remember that the experience of one of the saints concerning the verity of God's promises, and of the certainty of the written privileges of the Lord's people, is a sufficient proof of the right which all his children have to the same mercies, and a ground of hope that they also shall partake of them in their times of need. *David Dickson*, 1653.

Verse 4.—" *Stand in awe and sin not.*" Jehovah is a name of great power and efficacy, a name that hath in it five vowels, without which no language can be expressed ; a name that hath in it also three syllables, to signify the Trinity of persons, the eternity of God, One in Three and Three in One ; a name of such dread and reverence amongst the Jews, that they tremble to name it, and therefore they use the name *Adonai (Lord)* in all their devotions. And thus ought every one to " *stand in awe, and sin not,*" by taking the name of God in vain ; but to sing praise, and honour, to remember, ro declare, to exalt, to praise and bless it ; for holy and reverend, only worthy and excellent is his name.—*Rayment*, 1630.

Verse 4.—" *Commune with your own heart.*" The language is similar to that which we use when we say, " Consult your better judgment," or " Take counsel of your own good sense."—*Albert Barnes, in loc.*

Verse 4.—If thou wouldst exercise thyself to godliness in solitude, accustom thyself to soliloquies, I mean to conference with thyself. He needs never be idle that hath so much business to do with his own soul. It was a famous answer which Antisthenes gave when he was asked what fruit he reaped by all his studies. By them, saith he, I have learned both to live and talk with myself. Soliloquies are the best disputes ; every good man is best company for himself of all the creatures. Holy David enjoineth this to others, " *Commune with your own hearts upon your bed, and be still.*" " *Commune with your own hearts ;*" when ye have none to speak with, talk to yourselves. Ask yourselves for what end ye were made, what lives ye have led, what times ye have lost, what love ye have abused, what wrath ye have deserved. Call yourselves to a reckoning, how ye have improved your talents, how true or false ye have been to your trust, what provision ye have laid in for an hour of death, what preparation ye have made for a great day of account. "*Upon your beds.*" Secrecy is the best opportunity for this duty. The silent night is a good time for this speech. When we have no outward objects to disturb us, and to call our eyes, as the fools' eyes are always, to the ends of the earth ; then our eyes, as the eyes of the wise, may be in our heads ; and then our minds, like the windows in Solomon's temple, may be broad inwards. The most successful searches have been made in the night season ; the soul is then wholly shut up in the earthly house of the body, and hath no visits from strangers to disquiet its thoughts. Physicians have judged dreams a probable sign whereby they might find out the distempers of the body. Surely, then, the bed is no bad place to examine and search into the state of the soul. "*And be still.*" Self-communion will much help to curb your headstrong, ungodly passions. Serious consideration, like the casting up of earth amongst bees, will allay inordinate affections when they are full of fury, and make such a hideous noise. Though sensual appetites and unruly desires are, as the people of Ephesus, in an uproar, pleading for their former privilege, and expecting their wonted provision, as in the days of their predominancy, if conscience use its authority, commanding them in God's name, whose officer it is, to keep the king's peace, and argue it with them, as the town-clerk of Ephesus, " We are in danger to be called in question for this day's uproar, there being no cause whereby we may give an account of this day's concourse ;" all is frequently by this means hushed, and the tumult appeased without any further mischief.—*George Swinnock*, 1627—1673.

Verse 4.—"*Commune with your own heart upon your bed, and be still.*" When we are most retired from the world, then we are most fit to have, and usually have, most communion with God. If a man would but abridge himself of sleep, and wake with holy thoughts, when deep sleep falleth upon sorrowful labouring men, he might be entertained with visions from God, though not such visions as Eliphaz and others of the saints have had, yet visions he might have. Every time God communicates himself to the soul, there is a vision of love, or mercy, or power, somewhat of God in his nature, or in his will, is showed unto us. David shows us divine work when we go to rest. The bed is not all for sleep : " *Commune with your own heart upon your bed, and be still.*" Be still or quiet, and then commune with your hearts ; and if *you* will commune with your hearts, God will come and commune with your hearts too, his Spirit will give you a loving visit and visions of his love.—*Joseph Caryl.*

Verse 4.—"*Stand in awe.*"

With sacred *awe* pronounce his name,
Whom words nor thoughts can reach.

John Needham, 1768.

Verse 6.—Where Christ reveals himself there is satisfaction in the slenderest portion, and without Christ there is emptiness in the greatest fulness.—*Alexander Grosse, on enjoying Christ,* 1632.

Verse 6.—"*Many,*" said David, "*ask who will shew us any good ?*" meaning riches, and honour, and pleasure, which are not good. But when he came to godliness itself, he leaves out "*many,*" and prayeth in his own person, " *Lord, lift thou up the light of thy countenance upon us ;*" as if none would join with him. *Henry Smith.*

Verse 6.—"*Who will shew us any good ?*" This is not a fair translation. The word *any* is not in the text, nor anything equivalent to it ; and not a few have quoted *it*, and preached upon the text, placing the principal emphasis upon this illegitimate. The place is sufficiently emphatic. There are *multitudes who say, Who will shew us good ?* Man wants *good ;* he hates *evil* as evil, because he has *pain, suffering,* and *death* through it ; and he wishes to find that *supreme good* which will content his heart, and save him from evil. But men mistake this good. They look for a good that is to gratify their *passions ;* they have no notion of any happiness that does not come to them through the *medium of their senses.* Therefore they reject *spiritual good,* and they reject the supreme God, by whom alone all the powers of the soul of man can be gratified.—*Adam Clarke.*

Verse 6.—" *Lift thou up,*" etc. This was the blessing of the high priest and is the heritage of all the saints. It includes reconciliation, assurance, communion, benediction, in a word, the fulness of God. Oh, to be filled therewith ! *C. H. S.*

Verses 6, 7.—Lest riches should be accounted evil in themselves, God sometimes gives them to the righteous ; and lest they should be considered as the *chief good,* he frequently bestows them on the wicked. But they are more generally the portion of his enemies than his friends Alas ! what is it to receive and not to be received ? to have none other dews of blessing than such as shall be followed by showers of brimstone ? We may compass ourselves with sparks of security, and afterwards be secured in eternal misery. This world is a floating island, and so sure as we cast anchor *upon* it, we shall be carried away *by* it. God, and all that he has made, is not more than God without anything that he has made. He can never want treasure who has such a golden mine. *He* is enough without the creature, but the *creature* is not anything without him. It is, therefore, better to enjoy him without anything else, than to enjoy everything else without him. It is better to be a wooden vessel filled with wine, than a golden one filled with water.—*William Secker's Nonsuch Professor,* 1660.

Verse 7.—What madness and folly is it that the favourites of heaven should envy the men of the world, who at best do but feed upon the scraps that come from God's table ! Temporals are the bones ; spirituals are the marrow. Is it below a man to envy the dogs, because of the bones ? And is it not much more below a Christian to envy others for temporals, when himself enjoys spirituals ? *Thomas Brooks.*

Verse 7.—" *Thou hast put gladness in my heart.*" The comforts which God reserves for his mourners are filling comforts (Rom. xv. 13) ; " The God of hope fill you with joy" (John xvi. 24) ; " Ask that your joy may be full." When God pours in the joys of heaven they fill the heart, and make it run over (2 Cor. vii. 4) ; " I am exceeding joyful ;" the Greek is, I overflow with joy, as a cup that is filled with wine till it runs over. Outward comforts can no more fill the heart than a triangle can fill a circle. Spiritual joys are satisfying (Psalm lxiii. 5) ; " My heart shall be satisfied as with marrow and fatness ; and my mouth shall praise thee with joyful lips ;" " *Thou hast put gladness in my heart.*" Worldly joys do put gladness into the face, but the spirit of God puts gladness into the heart ; divine joys are heart joys (Zech. x. 7 ; John xvi. 22) ; " Your heart shall rejoice" (Luke i. 47) ; " My spirit rejoiced in God." And to show how filling these comforts are, which are of a heavenly extraction, the psalmist says they create greater joy than when " *corn and wine increase.*" Wine and oil may delight but not satisfy ; they have their vacuity and indigence. We may say, as Zech. x. 2, " They comfort in vain ;" outward comforts do sooner cloy than cheer, and sooner weary than fill. Xerxes offered great rewards to him that could find out a new pleasure ; but the comforts of the Spirit are satisfactory, they recruit the heart (Psalm xciv. 19), " Thy comforts delight my soul." There is as much difference between heavenly comforts and earthly, as between a banquet that is eaten, and one that is painted on the wall.—*Thomas Watson.*

Verse 8.—It is said of the husbandman, that having cast his seed into the ground, he sleeps and riseth day and night, and the seed springs and grows he knoweth not how. Mark iv. 26, 27. So a good man having by faith and prayer cast his care upon God, he resteth night and day, and is very easy, leaving it to his God to perform all things for him according to his holy will.— *Matthew Henry.*

Verse 8.—When you have walked with God from morning until night, it
remaineth that you *conclude* the day well, when you would give yourself to rest
at night. Wherefore, first, look back and take a strict view of your whole
carriage that *day past.* Reform what you find amiss ; and rejoice, or be grieved,
as you find you have done well or ill, as you have advanced or declined in grace
that day. Secondly, since you cannot sleep in safety if God, who is your *keeper*
(Psalm cxxi. 4, 5), do not *wake and watch for you* (Psalm cxxvii. 1) ; and
though you have *God* to watch when you sleep, you cannot be safe, if he that
watcheth be your *enemy.* Wherefore it is very convenient that at night you
renew and confirm your peace with God by faith and prayer, commending and
committing yourself to God's tuition by prayer (Psalm iii. 4, 5 ; Psalm xcii. 2),
with thanksgiving before you go to bed. Then shall you *lie down in safety,*
Psalm iv. 8. All this being done, yet while you are *putting off* your apparel,
when you are *lying down,* and when you are *in bed,* before you sleep, it is good
that *you commune with* your *own heart.* Psalm iv. 4. If possibly you can fall
asleep with *some heavenly meditation,* then will your sleep be *more sweet*
(Prov. iii. 21, 24, 25) ; and *more secure* (Prov. vi. 22) ; your *dreams* fewer,
or more *comfortable ;* your head will be fuller of good thoughts (Prov. vi. 22),
and your heart will be in a *better frame* when you *awake,* whether in the night
or in the morning.—*Condensed from Henry Scudder's Daily Walk,* 1633.

Verse 8.—"*I will both,*" etc. We have now to retire for a moment from the
strife of tongues and the open hostility of foes, into the stillness and privacy of
the chamber of sleep. Here, also, we find the "I will" of trust. "*I will
both lay me down in peace, and sleep ; for thou, Lord, only makest me dwell in safety.*"
God is here revealed to us as exercising *personal care in the still chamber.* And
there is something here which should be inexpressibly sweet to the believer, for
this shows the minuteness of God's care, the individuality of his love ; how it
condescends and stoops, and acts, not only in great, but also in little spheres ;
not only where glory might be procured from great results, but where nought
is to be had save the gratitude and love of a poor feeble creature, whose life has
been protected and preserved, in a period of helplessness and sleep. How blessed
would it be if we made a larger recognition of God in the still chamber ; if we
thought of him as being there in all hours of illness, of weariness, and pain ; if
we believed that his interest and care are as much concentrated upon the feeble
believer there as upon his people when in the wider battle field of the strife of
tongues. There is something inexpressibly touching in this "lying down" of
the Psalmist. In thus lying down he voluntarily gave up any guardianship of
himself ; he resigned himself into the hands of another ; he did so completely, for
in the absence of all care he slept ; there was here a perfect trust. Many a
believer lies down, but it is not to sleep. Perhaps he feels safe enough so far
as his body is concerned, but cares and anxieties invade the privacy of his
chamber ; they come to try his faith and trust ; they threaten, they frighten, and
alas ! prove too strong for trust. Many a poor believer might say, "I will lay
me down, but not to sleep." The author met with a touching instance of this,
in the case of an aged minister whom he visited in severe illness. This worthy
man's circumstances were narrow, and his family trials were great ; he said, "The
doctor wants me to sleep, but how can I sleep with care sitting on my pillow ?"
It is the experience of some of the Lord's people, that although equal to an
emergency or a continued pressure, a re-action sets in afterwards ; and when
they come to be alone their spirits sink, and they do not realise that strength
from God, or feel that confidence in him which they felt while the pressure was
exerting its force. . . . . There is a trial in stillness ; and oftentimes the
still chamber makes a larger demand upon loving trust than the battle field.
O that we could trust God more and more with personal things ! O that
he were the God of our chamber, as well as of our temples and houses ! O
that we could bring him more and more into the minutiæ of daily life ! If we
did thus, we should experience a measure of rest to which we are, perhaps,
strangers now ; we should have less dread of the sick chamber ; we should have

that unharassed mind which conduces most to repose, in body and soul ; we should be able to say, " I will lie down and sleep, *and leave to-morrow with God !*" Ridley's brother offered to remain with him during the night preceding his martyrdom, but the bishop declined, saying, that " he meant to go to bed, and sleep as quietly as ever he did in his life."—*Philip Bennett Power's 'I Wills' of the Psalms.*

Verse 8.—Due observation of Providence will both beget and secure inward tranquillity in your minds amidst the vicissitudes and revolutions of things in this unstable vain world. " *I will both lay me down in peace, and sleep ; for the Lord only maketh me dwell in safety.*" He resolves that sinful fears of events shall not rob him of his inward quiet, nor torture his thoughts with anxious presages ; he will commit all his concerns into that faithful fatherly hand that had hitherto wrought all things for him ; and he means not to lose the comfort of one night's rest, nor bring the evil of to-morrow upon the day ; but knowing in whose hand he was, wisely enjoys the sweet felicity of a resigned will. Now this tranquillity of our minds is as much begotten and preserved by a due consideration of providence as by anything whatsoever.—*John Flavel,* 1627—1691.

Verse 8.—Happy is the Christian, who having nightly with this verse, committed himself to his bed as to his grave, shall at last, with the same words, resign himself to his grave as to his bed, from which he expects in due time to arise, and sing a morning hymn with the children of the resurrection.—*George Horne, D.D.,* 1776.

Verse 9.—" *Sleep.*"

" How blessed was that *sleep*
The sinless Saviour knew !
In vain the storm-winds blew,
Till he awoke to others' woes,
And hushed the billows to repose.

How beautiful is *sleep*—
The *sleep* that Christians know !
Ye mourners ! cease your woe,
While soft upon his Saviour's breast,
The righteous sinks to endless rest."

Mrs. M' Cartree.

HINTS TO THE VILLAGE PREACHER.

Verse 1.—Is full of matter for a sermon upon, *past mercies a plea for present help.* The first sentence shows that believers desire, expect, and believe in a God that heareth prayer. The title—*God of my righteousness,* may furnish a text (see exposition), and the last sentence may suggest a sermon upon, " The best of saints must still appeal to God's mercy and sovereign grace."

Verse 2.—*Depravity of man* as evinced (1) by continuance in despising Christ, (2) loving vanity in his heart, and (3) seeking lies in his daily life.

Verse 2.—The length of the sinner's sin. " How long ?" May be bounded by repentance, shall be by death, and yet shall continue in eternity.

Verse 3.—*Election.*—Its aspects towards God, our enemies, and ourselves.

Verse 3.—" *The Lord will hear when I call unto him.*" Answers to prayer certain to special persons. Mark out those who can claim the favour.

Verse 3.—*The gracious Separatist.* Who is he ? Who separated him ? With what end ? How to make men know it ?

Verse 4.—The sinner directed to review himself, that he may be convinced of sin.—*Andrew Fuller,* 1754—1815.

Verse 4.—" *Be still.*" Advice—good, practical, but hard to follow. Times when seasonable. Graces needed to enable one to be still. Results of quietness. Persons who most need the advice. Instances of its practice. Here is much material for a sermon.

Verse 5.—The nature of those sacrifices of righteousness which the Lord's people are expected to offer.—*William Ford Vance,* 1827.

Verse 6.—The cry of the world and the church contrasted. *Vox populi* not always *Vox Dei.*

Verse 6.—The cravings of the soul all satisfied in God.

Verses 6, 7.—An assurance of the Saviour's love, the source of unrivalled joy.

Verse. 7.—The believer's joys. (1) Their source, " *Thou ;*" (2) their season —even now—" *Thou hast ;*" (3) their position, " *in my heart ;*" (4) their excellence, " *more than in the time that their corn and their wine increased.*"

Another excellent theme suggests itself—" The superiority of the joys of grace to the joys of earth ;" or, " Two sorts of prosperity—which is to be the more desired ?"

Verse 8.—The peace and safety of the good man.—*Joseph Lathrop, D.D.,* 1805.

Verse 8.—A bedchamber for believers, a vesper song to sing in it, and a guard to keep the door.

Verse 8. —The Christian's good-night.

Verses 2 *to* 8.—The means which a believer should use to win the ungodly to Christ. (1.) Expostulation, verse 2. (2.) Instruction, verse 3. (3.) Exhortation, verses 4, 5. (4.) Testimony to the blessedness of true religion, as in verses 6, 7. (5.) Exemplification of that testimony by the peace of faith, verse 8.

WORKS UPON THE FOURTH PSALM.

Choice and Practical Expositions on four select Psalms : namely, the Fourth Psalm, in eight Sermons, etc. By THOMAS HORTON, D.D. 1675.

Meditations, Critical and Practical, on Psalm IV., in Archbishop Leighton's Works.

PSALM V.

TITLE.—"To the Chief Musician upon Nehiloth, a Psalm of David." *The Hebrew word Nehiloth is taken from another word, signifying "to perforate," "to bore through," whence it comes to mean a pipe or a flute; so that this song was probably intended to be sung with an accompaniment of wind instruments, such as the horn, the trumpet, flute, or cornet. However, it is proper to remark that we are not sure of the interpretation of these ancient titles, for the Septuagint translates it, "For him who shall obtain inheritance," and Aben Ezra thinks it denotes some old and well known melody to which this Psalm was to be played. The best scholars confess that great darkness hangs over the precise interpretation of the title; nor is this much to be regretted, for it furnishes an internal evidence of the great antiquity of the Book. Throughout the first, second, third, and fourth Psalms, you will have noticed that the subject is a contrast between the position, the character, and the prospects of the righteous and of the wicked. In this Psalm you will note the same. The Psalmist carries out a contrast between himself made righteous by God's grace, and the wicked who opposed him. To the devout mind there is here presented a precious view of the Lord Jesus, of whom it is said that in the days of his flesh, he offered up prayers and supplication with strong crying and tears.*

DIVISION.—*The Psalm should be divided into two parts, from the first to the seventh verse, and then from the eighth to the twelfth. In the first part of the Psalm David most vehemently beseeches the Lord to hearken to his prayer, and in the second part he retraces the same ground.*

EXPOSITION.

GIVE ear to my words, O LORD, consider my meditation.

There are two sorts of prayers—those expressed in words, and the unuttered longings which abide as silent meditations. Words are not the essence but the garments of prayer. Moses at the Red Sea cried to God, though he said nothing. Yet the use of language may prevent distraction of mind, may assist the powers of the soul, and may excite devotion. David, we observe, uses both modes of prayer, and craves for the one a hearing, and for the other a *consideration*. What an expressive word! "*Consider my meditation.*" If I have asked that which is right, give it to me; if I have omitted to ask that which I most needed, fill up the vacancy in my prayer. "Consider my meditation." Let thy holy soul *consider* it as presented through my all-glorious Mediator: then regard thou it in thy wisdom, weigh it in the scales, judge thou of my sincerity, and of the true state of my necessities, and answer me in due time for thy mercy's sake! There may be prevailing intercession where there are no words; and alas! there may be words where there is no true supplication. Let us cultivate the *spirit* of prayer which is even better than the *habit* of prayer. There may be seeming prayer where there is little devotion. We should begin to pray before we kneel down, and we should not cease when we rise up.

2 Hearken unto the voice of my cry, my King, and my God : for unto thee will I pray.

"*The voice of my cry.*" In another Psalm we find the expression, "The voice of my weeping." Weeping has a voice—a melting, plaintive tone, an ear-piercing shrillness, which reaches the very heart of God; and *crying* hath a voice—a soul-moving eloquence; coming from *our* heart it reaches *God's* heart. Ah! my brothers and sisters, sometimes we cannot put our prayers into words: they are nothing but a *cry*: but the Lord can comprehend the meaning, for he hears a voice in our cry. To a loving father his children's cries are music, and they have a magic influence which his heart cannot resist. "*My*

4

King, and my God.'' Observe carefully these little pronouns, ''*my* King, and *my* God.'' They are the pith and marrow of the plea. Here is a grand argument why God should answer prayer—because he is *our* King and *our* God. We are not aliens to him : he is the King of our country. Kings are expected to hear the appeals of their own people. We are not strangers to him ; we are his worshippers, and he is our God : ours by covenant, by promise, by oath, by blood.

" *For unto thee will I pray.*'' Here David expresses his declaration that he will seek to God, and to God alone. God is to be *the only object of worship : the only resource of our soul in times of need. Leave broken cisterns to the godless, and let the godly drink from the Divine fountain alone. " Unto thee will I pray.'' He makes a resolution, that as long as he lived he would pray. He would never cease to supplicate, even though the answer should not come.

3 My voice shalt thou hear in the morning, O LORD ; in the morning will I direct *my prayer* unto thee, and will look up.

Observe, this is not so much a prayer as a resolution, " ' *My voice shalt thou hear ;* ' I will not be dumb, I will not be silent, I will not withhold my speech, I *will* cry to thee, for the fire that dwells within compels me to pray.'' We can sooner die than live without prayer. None of God's children are possessed with a dumb devil.

" *In the morning.*'' This is the fittest time for intercourse with God. An hour in the morning is worth two in the evening. While the dew is on the grass, let grace drop upon the soul. Let us give to God the mornings of our days and the morning of our lives. Prayer should be the key of the day and the lock of the night. Devotion should be both the morning star and the evening star.

If we merely read our English version, and want an explanation of these two sentences, we find it in the figure of an archer, " *I will direct my prayer unto thee,*'' I will put my prayer upon the bow, I will direct it towards heaven, and then when I have shot up my arrow, *I will look up* to see where it has gone. But the Hebrew has a still fuller meaning than this—'' I will *direct* my prayer.'' It is the word that is used for the laying in order of the wood and the pieces of the victim upon the altar, and it is used also for the putting of the shewbread upon the table. It means just this : '' I will arrange my prayer before thee ;'' I will lay it out upon the altar in the morning, just as the priest lays out the morning sacrifice. I will *arrange* my prayer ; or, as old Master Trapp has it, '' I will marshal up my prayers,'' I will put them in order, call up all my powers, and bid them stand in their proper places, that I may pray with all my might, and pray acceptably.

" *And will look up,*'' or, as the Hebrew might better be translated, '' ' I will look out,' I will look out for the answer ; after I have prayed, I will expect that the blessing shall come.'' It is a word that is used in another place where we read of those who watched for the morning. So will I watch for thine answer, O my Lord ! I will spread out my prayer like the victim on the altar, and I will look up, and expect to receive the answer by fire from heaven to consume the sacrifice.

Two questions are suggested by the last part of this verse. Do we not miss very much of the sweetness and efficacy of prayer by a want of careful meditation before it, and of hopeful expectation after it ? We too often rush into the presence of God without forethought or humility. We are like men who present themselves before a king without a petition, and what wonder is it that we often miss the end of prayer ? We should be careful to keep the stream of meditation always running ; for this is the water to drive the mill of prayer. It is idle to pull up the flood-gates of a dry brook, and then hope to see the wheel revolve. Prayer without fervency is like hunting with a dead dog, and prayer without preparation is hawking with a blind falcon. Prayer is the work of the

Holy Spirit, but he works by means. God made man, but he used the dust of the earth as a material : the Holy Ghost is the author of prayer, but he employs the thoughts of a fervent soul as the gold with which to fashion the vessel. Let not our prayers and praises be the flashes of a hot and hasty brain, but the steady burning of a well-kindled fire.

But, furthermore, do we not forget to watch the result of our supplications ? We are like the ostrich, which lays her eggs and looks not for her young. We sow the seed, and are too idle to seek a harvest. How can we expect the Lord to open the windows of his grace, and pour us out a blessing, if we will not open the windows of expectation and look up for the promised favour ? Let holy preparation link hands with patient expectation, and we shall have far larger answers to our prayers.

4 For thou *art* not a God that hath pleasure in wickedness : neither shall evil dwell with thee.

5 The foolish shall not stand in thy sight : thou hatest all workers of iniquity.

6 Thou shalt destroy them that speak leasing : the LORD will abhor the bloody and deceitful man.

And now the Psalmist having thus expressed his resolution to pray, you hear him putting up his prayer. He is pleading against his cruel and wicked enemies. He uses a most mighty argument. He begs of God to put them away from him, because they were displeasing to God himself. "*For thou art not a God that hath pleasure in wickedness: neither shall evil dwell with thee.*" "When I pray against my tempters," says David, "I pray against the very things which thou thyself abhorrest." *Thou* hatest evil : Lord, I beseech thee, deliver *me* from it ! Let us learn here the solemn truth of the hatred which a righteous God must bear towards sin. *He has no pleasure in wickedness,* however wittily, grandly, and proudly it may array itself. Its glitter has no charm for him. Men may bow before successful villainy, and forget the wickedness of the battle in the gaudiness of the triumph, but the Lord of Holiness is not such-an-one as we are. "*Neither shall evil dwell with thee.*" He will not afford it the meanest shelter. Neither on earth nor in heaven shall evil share the mansion of God. Oh, how foolish are we if we attempt to entertain two guests so hostile to one another as Christ Jesus and the devil ! Rest assured, Christ will not live in the parlour of our hearts if we entertain the devil in the cellar of our thoughts. "*The foolish shall not stand in thy sight.*" Sinners are fools written large. A little sin is a great folly, and the greatest of all folly is great sin. Such sinful fools as these must be banished from the court of heaven. Earthly kings were wont to have fools in their trains, but the only wise God will have no fools in his palace above. "*Thou hatest all workers of iniquity.*" It is not a little dislike, but a thorough hatred which God bears to workers of iniquity. To be hated of God is an awful thing. O let us be very faithful in warning the wicked around us, for it will be a terrible thing for them to fall into the hands of an angry God ! Observe, that evil speakers must be punished as well as evil workers, for "*thou shalt destroy them that speak leasing.*" All liars shall have their portion in the lake which burneth with fire and brimstone. A man may lie without danger of the law of man, but he will not escape the law of God. Liars have short wings, their flight shall soon be over, and they shall fall into the fiery floods of destruction. "*The Lord will abhor the bloody and deceitful man.*" Bloody men shall be made drunk with their own blood, and they who began by deceiving others shall end with being deceived themselves. Our old proverb saith, "Bloody and deceitful men dig their own graves." The voice of the people is in this instance the voice of God. How forcible is the word *abhor !* Does it not show us how powerful and deep-seated is the hatred of the Lord against the workers of iniquity ?

7 But as for me, I will come *into* thy house in the multitude of thy mercy : *and* in thy fear will I worship toward thy holy temple.

With this verse the first part of the Psalm ends. The Psalmist has bent his knee in prayer ; he has described before God, as an argument for his deliverance, the character and the fate of the wicked ; and now he contrasts this with the condition of the righteous. " *But as for me, I will come into thy house.*" I will not stand at a distance, I will come into thy sanctuary, just as a child comes into his father's house. But I will not come there by my own merits ; no, I have a multitude of sins, and therefore I will come *in the multitude of thy mercy.* I will approach thee with confidence because of thy immeasurable grace. God's judgments are all numbered, but his mercies are innumerable ; he gives his wrath by weight, but without weight his mercy. " *And in thy fear will I worship toward thy holy temple,*"—towards the temple of thy holiness. The temple was not built on earth at that time ; it was but a tabernacle ; but David was wont to turn his eyes spiritually to that temple of God's holiness where between the wings of the Cherubim Jehovah dwells in light ineffable. Daniel opened his window towards Jerusalem, but we open our hearts towards heaven.

8 Lead me, O LORD, in thy righteousness because of mine enemies ; make thy way straight before my face.

Now we come to the second part, in which the Psalmist repeats his arguments, and goes over the same ground again.

" *Lead me, O Lord,*" as a little child is led by its father, as a blind man is guided by his friend. It is safe and pleasant walking when God leads the way. " *In thy righteousness,*" not in *my* righteousness, for that is imperfect, but in *thine,* for thou art righteousness itself. " *Make thy way,*" not *my* way, " *straight before my face.*" Brethren, when we have learned to give up our own way, and long to walk in God's way, it is a happy sign of grace ; and it is no small mercy to see the way of God with clear vision straight before our face. Errors about duty may lead us into a sea of sins, before we know where we are.

9 For *there is* no faithfulness in their mouth ; their inward part *is* very wickedness ; their throat *is* an open sepulchre ; they flatter with their tongue.

This description of depraved man has been copied by the Apostle Paul, and, together with some other quotations, he has placed it in the second chapter of Romans, as being an accurate description of the whole human race, not of David's enemies only, but of all men by nature. Note that remarkable figure, " *Their throat is an open sepulchre,*" a *sepulchre* full of loathsomeness, of miasma, of pestilence and death. But, worse than that, it is an *open* sepulchre, with all its evil gases issuing forth, to spread death and destruction all around. So, with the throat of the wicked, it would be a great mercy if it could always be closed. If we could seal in continual silence the mouth of the wicked it would be like a sepulchre shut up, and would not produce much mischief. But " their throat is an *open* sepulchre," consequently all the wickedness of their heart exhales, and comes forth. How dangerous is an open sepulchre ; men in their journeys might easily stumble therein, and find themselves among the dead. Ah ! take heed of the wicked man, for there is nothing that he will not say to ruin you ; he will long to destroy your character, and bury you in the hideous sepulchre of his own wicked throat. One sweet thought here, however. At the resurrection there will be a resurrection not only of bodies, but characters. This should be a great comfort to a man who has been abused and slandered. " Then shall the righteous shine forth as the sun." The world may think you vile, and bury your character ; but if you have been upright, in the day when the graves shall give up their dead, this open sepulchre of the sinner's throat shall be compelled to give up your heavenly character, and you shall come forth and be honoured in the sight of men. " *They flatter with their tongue.*" Or, as we might read it, " They have an oily tongue, a smooth tongue." A smooth tongue is a great evil ; many have been bewitched by it. There be many human ant-eaters that with their long tongues covered with oily words entice and entrap the unwary and make their gain thereby. When the wolf licks the lamb, he is preparing to wet his teeth in its blood.

10 Destroy thou them, O God ; let them fall by their own counsels ; cast them out in the multitude of their transgressions ; for they have rebelled against thee.

" *Against thee :*" not against *me*. If they were *my* enemies I would forgive them, but I cannot forgive *thine*. We are to forgive *our* enemies, but God's enemies it is not in our power to forgive. These expressions have often been noticed by men of over refinement as being harsh, and grating on the ear. " Oh !" say they, " they are vindictive and revengeful." Let us remember that they might be translated as prophecies, not as wishes ; but we do not care to avail ourselves of this method of escape. We have never heard of a reader of the Bible who, after perusing these passages, was made revengeful by reading them, and it is but fair to test the nature of a writing by its effects. When we hear a judge condemning a murderer, however severe his sentence, we do not feel that we should be justified in condemning others for any private injury done to us. The Psalmist here speaks as a judge, *ex officio ;* he speaks as God's mouth, and in condemning the wicked he gives us no excuse whatever for uttering anything in the way of malediction upon those who have caused us personal offence. The most shameful way of cursing another is by pretending to bless him. We were all somewhat amused by noticing the toothless malice of that wretched old priest of Rome when he foolishly cursed the Emperor of France with his blessing. He was blessing him in form and cursing him in reality. Now, in direct contrast we put this healthy commination of David, which is intended to be a blessing by warning the sinner of the impending curse. O impenitent man, be it known unto thee that all thy godly friends will give their solemn assent to the awful sentence of the Lord, which he shall pronounce upon thee in the day of doom ! Our verdict shall applaud the condemning curse which the Judge of all the earth shall thunder against the godless.

In the following verse we once more find the contrast which has marked the preceding Psalms.

11 But let all those that put their trust in thee rejoice : let them ever shout for joy, because thou defendest them : let them also that love thy name be joyful in thee.

Joy is the privilege of the believer. When sinners are destroyed our rejoicing shall be full. They laugh first and weep ever after ; we weep now, but shall rejoice eternally. When they howl we shall *shout,* and as they must groan for ever, so shall we *ever shout* for joy. This holy bliss of ours has a firm foundation, for, O Lord, we are *joyful in thee.* The eternal God is the well-spring of our bliss. We love God, and therefore we delight in him. Our heart is at ease in our God. We fare sumptuously every day because we feed on him. We have music in the house, music in the heart, and music in heaven, for the Lord Jehovah is our strength and our song ; he also is become our salvation.

12 For thou, LORD, wilt bless the righteous ; with favour wilt thou compass him as *with* a shield.

Jehovah has ordained his people the heirs of blessedness, and nothing shall rob them of their inheritance. With all the fulness of his power he will bless them, and all his attributes shall unite to satiate them with divine contentment. Nor is this merely for the present, but the blessing reaches into the long and unknown future. *"Thou, Lord, wilt bless the righteous."* This is a promise of infinite length, of unbounded breadth, and of unutterable preciousness.

As for the defence which the believer needs in this land of battles, it is here promised to him in the fullest measure. There were vast shields used by the ancients as extensive as a man's whole person, which would surround him entirely. So says David, *"With favour wilt thou compass him as with a shield."* According to Ainsworth there is here also the idea of being crowned, so that we wear a royal helmet, which is at once our glory and defence. O Lord, ever give to us this gracious coronation !

EXPLANATORY NOTES AND QUAINT SAYINGS.

Verse 1.—*" Give ear to my words, O Lord, consider my meditation."* It is certain that the greater part of men, as they babble out vain, languid, and inefficacious prayers, most unworthy the ear of the blessed God, so they seem in some degree to set a just estimate upon them, neither hoping for any success from them, nor indeed seeming to be at all solicitous about it, but committing them to the wind as vain words, which in truth they are. But far be it from a wise and pious man, that he should so foolishly and coldly trifle in so serious an affair ; his prayer has a certain tendency and scope, at which he aims with assiduous and repeated desires, and doth not only pray that he may pray, but that he may obtain an answer ; and as he firmly believes that it may be obtained, so he firmly, and constantly, and eagerly urges his petition, that he may not flatter himself with an empty hope.—*Robert Leighton, D.D.*

Verses 1, 2.—Observe the order and force of the words, *" my cry,"* *" the voice of my prayer ;"* and also, *" give ear,"* *" consider,"* *" hearken."* These expressions all evince the urgency and energy of David's feelings and petitions. First, we have, *" give ear ;"* that is, hear me. But it is of little service for the words to be heard, unless the *" cry,"* or the roaring, or the meditation, be *considered.* As if he had said, in a common way of expression, I speak with deep anxiety and concern, but with a failing utterance ; and I cannot express myself, nor make myself understood as I wish. Do thou, therefore, understand from my feelings more than I am able to express in words. And, therefore, I add my *" cry ;"* that what I cannot express in words for thee to hear, I may by my *" cry"* signify to thine understanding. And when thou hast understood me, then, O Lord, *" Hearken unto the voice of my prayer,"* and despise not what thou hast thus heard and understood. We are not, however, to understand that hearing, understanding, and hearkening, are all different acts in God, in the same way as they are in us ; but that our feelings towards God are to be thus varied and increased ; that is, that we are first to desire to be heard, and then, that our prayers which are heard may be understood ; and then, that being understood, they may be hearkened unto, that is, not disregarded.—*Martin Luther.*

Verse 1.—*" Meditation"* fits the soul for supplication ; meditation fills the soul with good liquor, and then prayer broaches it, and sets it a-running. David first mused, and then spake with his tongue, *" Lord, make me to know mine end."* Psalm xxxix. 3, 4. Nay, to assure us that meditation was the mother which bred and brought forth prayer, he calls the child by its parent's name, *" Give ear to my words, O Lord, consider my meditation."* Meditation is like the charging of a piece, and prayer the discharging of it. *" Isaac went into the field to meditate."* Genesis xxiv. 63. The Septuagint, the Geneva translation, and Tremellius, in his marginal notes on it, read it to *" pray ;"* and the Hebrew word הָגָה used there signifieth both to *pray* and *meditate ;* whereby we may learn they are very near akin ; like twins, they be in the same womb, in the same

word. Meditation is the best beginning of prayer, and prayer is the best conclusion of meditation. When the Christian, like Daniel, hath first opened the
windows of his soul by contemplation, then he may kneel down to prayer.—
George Swinnock.

Verse 3.—" *My voice shalt thou hear in the morning, O Lord.*"

> When first thy eyes unveil, give thy soul leave
>   To do the like; our bodies but forerun
> The spirit's duty ; true hearts spread and heave
>   Unto their God, as flowers do to the sun;
> Give him thy first thoughts, then, so shalt thou keep
> Him company all day, and in him sleep.
>
> Yet never sleep the sun up; prayer should
>   Dawn with the day, there are set awful hours
> 'Twixt heaven and us ; the manna was not good
>   After sun-rising, for day sullies flowers.
> Rise to prevent the sun; sleep doth sins glut,
> And heaven's gate opens when the world's is shut.
>
> Walk with thy fellow-creatures ; note the hush
>   And whisperings amongst them. Not a spring
> Or leaf but hath his *morning* hymn ; each bush
>   And oak doth know I AM—canst thou not sing?
> O leave thy cares and follies ! Go this way,
> And thou art sure to prosper all the day.
>   *Henry Vaughan,* 1621—1695.

Verse 3.—" *My voice shalt thou hear in the morning.*" " *In the morning shall
my prayer prevent thee,*" said Heman. That is the fittest time for devotion,
you being then fresh in your spirits, and freest from distractions. Which opportunity for holy duties may fitly be called *the wings of the morning.—Edward
Reyner,* 1658.

Verse 3.—" *In the morning.*" " In the days of our fathers," says Bishop
Burnet, " when a person came early to the door of his neighbour, and desired to
speak with the master of the house, it was as common a thing for the servants
to tell him with freedom—' My master is at prayer,' as it now is to say, ' My
master is not up.' "

Verse 3.—" *In the morning I will direct my prayer unto thee, and will look up,*"
or, *I will marshal my prayer,* I will bring up petition after petition, pleading
after pleading, even till I become like Jacob, a prince with God, till I have won
the field and got the day. Thus the word is applied by a metaphor both to
disputations with men and supplications to God. Further, we may take the
meaning plainly without any strain of rhetoric, *Set thy words in order before me.*
Method is good in everything, either an express or covert method. Sometimes
it is the best of art to cover it ; in speaking there is a special use of method, for
though, as one said very well (speaking of those who are more curious about
method than serious about matter), " *Method never converted any man;*" yet
method and the ordering of words is very useful. Our speeches should not be
heaps of words, but words bound up ; not a throng of words, but words set in
array, or, as it were, in rank and file.—*Joseph Caryl.*

Verse 3.—" *I will direct my prayer unto thee and will look up.*" In the words
you may observe two things : first, David's posture in prayer ; secondly, his practice after prayer. First, his posture in prayer, " *I will direct my prayer unto thee.*"
Secondly, his practice after prayer, " *And I will look up.*" The prophet in these
words, makes use of two military words. First, he would not only pray, but
marshal up his prayers, he would put them in battle array ; so much the Hebrew
word עָרַךְ imports. Secondly, when he had done this, then he would be as
a spy upon his watch-tower, to see whether he prevailed, whether he got the
day or no ; and so much the Hebrew word צָפָה imports. When David had set
his prayers, his petitions, in rank and file, in good array, then he was resolved
he would look abroad, he would look about him to see at what door God would

send in an answer of prayer. He is either a fool or a madman, he is either very weak or very wicked, that prays and prays, but never looks after his prayers ; that shoots many an arrow towards heaven, but never minds where his arrows alight.— *Thomas Brooks.*

Verse 3.—David would *direct his prayer to God and look up ;* not down to the world, down to corruption, but up to God what he would speak. Psalm lxxxv. 8. "I will hear what God the Lord will speak," Let the resolution of the prophet be thine, "I will look unto the Lord ; I will wait for the God of my salvation : my God will hear me." Micah vii. 7.— *William Greenhill,* 1650.

Verse 3.—"*I will direct my prayer to thee, and will look up,*" that is, I will trade, I will send out my spiritual commodities, and expect a gainful return ; I will make my prayers, and not give them for lost, but look up for an answer. God will bring man home by a way contrary to that by which he wandered from him. Man fell from God by distrust, by having God in suspicion ; God will bring him back by trust, by having good thoughts of him. Oh, how richly laden might the vessel which thou sendest out come home, wouldst thou but long and look for its return !— *George Swinnock.*

Verse 3.—Faith hath a supporting act after prayer ; it supports the soul to expect a gracious answer : "*I will direct my prayer unto thee, and will look up,*" or I will look ; for what, but for a return ? An unbelieving heart shoots at random, and never minds where his arrow lights, or what comes of his praying ; but faith fills the soul with expectation. As a merchant, when he casts up his estate, he counts what he hath sent beyond sea, as well as what he hath in hand ; so doth faith reckon upon what he hath sent to heaven in prayer and not received, as well as those mercies which he hath received, and are in hand at present. Now this expectation which faith raiseth in the soul after prayer, appears in the power that it hath to quiet and compose the soul in the interim between the sending forth, as I may say, the ship of prayer, and its return home with its rich lading it goes for, and it is more or less, according as faith's strength is. Sometimes faith comes from prayer in triumph, and cries, *Victoria.* It gives such a being and existence to the mercy prayed for in the Christian's soul before any likelihood of it appears to sense and reason, that the Christian can silence all his troubled thoughts with the expectation of its coming. Yea, it will make the Christian disburse his praises for the mercy long before it is received. . . . . . . For want of looking up many a prayer is lost. If you do not believe, why do you pray ? And if you believe, why do you not expect ? By praying you seem to depend on God ; by not expecting, you again renounce your confidence. What is this, but to take his name in vain ? O Christian, stand to your prayer in a holy expectation of what you have begged upon the credit of the promise. . . . Mordecai, no doubt, had put up many prayers for Esther, and therefore he waits at the king's gate, looking what answer God would in his providence give thereunto. Do thou likewise.— *William Gurnall.*

Verse 4.—"*Thou art not a God that hath pleasure in wickedness.*" As a man that cutteth with a dull knife is the cause of cutting, but not of the ill-cutting and hacking of the knife—the knife is the cause of that ; or if a man strike upon an instrument that is out of tune, he is the cause of the sound, but not of the jarring sound—that is the fault of the untuned strings ; or, as a man riding upon a lame horse, stirs him—the man is the cause of the motion, but the horse himself of the halting motion : thus God is the author of every action, but not of the evil of that action—that is from man. He that makes instruments and tools of iron or other metal, he maketh not the rust and canker which corrupteth them, that is from another cause ; nor doth that heavenly workman, God Almighty, bring in sin and iniquity ; nor can he be justly blamed if his creatures do soil and besmear themselves with the foulness of sin, for he made them good.— *Spencer's Things New and Old.*

Verses 4—6.—Here the Lord's alienation from the wicked is set forth gradually, and seems to rise by six steps. First, *he hath no pleasure in them ;*

secondly, *they shall not dwell with him;* thirdly, he casteth them forth, *they shall not stand in his sight;* fourthly, his heart turns from them, *thou hatest all the workers of iniquity;* fifthly, his hand is turned upon them, *thou shalt destroy them that speak leasing;* sixthly, his spirit riseth against them, and is alienated from them, *the Lord will abhor the bloody man.* This estrangement is indeed a *strange* (yet a certain) *punishment to "the workers of iniquity."* These words, "*the workers of iniquity,*" may be considered two ways. First, as intending (not all degrees of sinners, or sinners of every degree, but) the highest degree of sinners, great, and gross sinners, resolved and wilful sinners. Such as sin industriously, and, as it were, artificially, with skill and care to get themselves a name, as if they had an ambition to be accounted *workmen* that need not be ashamed in doing that whereof all ought to be ashamed ; these, in strictness of Scripture sense, are "*workers of iniquity.*" Hence note, *notorious sinners make sin their business, or their trade.* Though every sin be *a work of iniquity,* yet only some sinners are "*workers of iniquity;*" and they who are called so, make it their calling to sin. We read of some *who love and make a lie.* Rev. xxii. 15. A lie may be told by those who neither love nor make it ; but there are lie-makers, and they, sure enough, are lovers of a lie. Such craftsmen in sinning are also described in Psalm lviii. 2—" Yea, in heart ye work wickedness ; ye weigh the violence of your hands in the earth." The psalmist doth not say, they had wickedness in their heart, but they did work it there ; *the heart is a shop within, an underground shop;* there they did closely contrive, forge, and hammer out their wicked purposes, and fit them into actions.—*Joseph Caryl.*

Verse 5.—What an astonishing thing is sin, which maketh the God of love and Father of mercies an enemy to his creatures, and which could only be purged by the blood of the Son of God ! Though all must believe this who believe the Bible, yet the exceeding sinfulness of sin is but weakly apprehended by those who have the deepest sense of it, and will never be fully known in this world.—*Thomas Adam's Private Thoughts,* 1701—1784.

Verse 5 (last clause).—"*Thou hatest all workers of iniquity.*" For what God thinks of sin, see Deut. vii. 22 ; Prov. vi. 16 ; Rev. ii. 6, 15 ; where he expresseth his detestation and hatred of it, from which hatred proceeds all those direful plagues and judgments thundered from the fiery mouth of his most holy law against it ; nay, not only the work, but *worker* also of iniquity becomes the object of his hatred.—*William Gurnall.*

Verse 5 (last clause).—"*Thou hatest all workers of iniquity.*" If God's hatred be against the workers of iniquity, how great is it against iniquity itself ! If a man hate a poisonous creature, he hates poison much more. The strength of God's hatred is against sin, and so should we hate sin, and hate it with strength ; it is an abomination unto God, let it be so unto us. Prov. vi. 16—19, " These six things doth the Lord hate ; yea, seven are an abomination unto him ; a proud look, a lying tongue, and hands that shed innocent blood, an heart that deviseth wicked imaginations, feet that be swift in running to mischief, a false witness that speaketh lies, and he that soweth discord among brethren."—*William Greenhill.*

Verse 5 (last clause).—Those whom the Lord hates must perish. But he hates impenitent sinners, "*Thou hatest all workers of iniquity.*" Now, who are so properly workers of iniquity as those who are so eager at it that they will not leave this work, though they be in danger to perish for it ? Christ puts it out of doubt. The workers of iniquity must perish. Luke xiii. 27. Those whom the Lord will tear in his wrath must perish with a witness ; but those whom he hates, he tears, &c. Job xvi. 8. What more due to such impenitent sinners than hatred ! What more proper than wrath, since they treasure up wrath ? Rom. ii. Will he entertain those in the bosom of love whom his soul hates ? No ; destruction is their portion. Prov. xxi. 15. If all the curses of the law, all the threatenings of the gospel, all judgments in earth or in hell, will be the ruin of him, he must perish. If the Lord's arm be strong enough to wound him dead, he must die. Psalm lxviii. 21. . . . . Avoid all that Christ hates. If you love, approve, entertain that which is hateful to Christ, how can he love you? What is that which Christ hates? The psalmist (Psalm xlv. 7) tells us, making it one of Christ's attributes, to hate wickedness. . . . . As Christ hates iniquity, so the *"workers of iniquity."* You must not love them, so as to be intimate with them, delight in the company of evil doers, openly profane, scorners of godliness, obstructors of the power of it. 2 Cor. vi. 14—18. If you love so near relations to wicked men, Christ will have no relation to you. If you would have communion with Christ in sweet acts of love, you must have no fellowship with the unfruitful works of darkness, nor those that act them.—*David Clarkson, B.D.*, 1621—1686.

Verse 6.—" *Thou shalt destroy them that speak leasing,*" whether in jest or earnest. Those that lie in jest will (without repentance) go to hell in earnest. *John Trapp.*

Verse 6.—" *Thou shalt destroy them that speak leasing,*" etc. In the same field wherein Absalom raised battle against his father, stood the oak that was his gibbet. The mule whereon he rode was his hangman, for the mule carried him to the tree, and the hair wherein he gloried served for a rope to hang. Little know the wicked how everything which now they have shall be a snare to trap them when God begins to punish them.—*William Cowper*, 1612.

Verse 7.—"*In thy fear will I worship.*" As natural fear makes the spirits retire from the outward parts of the body to the heart, so a holy fear of miscarrying in so solemn a duty would be a means to call thy thoughts from all exterior carnal objects, and fix them upon the duty in hand. As the sculpture is on the seal, so will the print on the wax be ; if the fear of God be deeply engraven on thy heart, there is no doubt but it will make a suitable impression on the duty thou performest.—*William Gurnall.*

Verse 7.—David saith, "*In thy fear will I worship toward thy holy temple.*" The temple did shadow forth the body of our Lord Christ, the Mediator, in whom only our prayers and services are accepted with the Father which Solomon respected in looking towards the temple.—*Thomas Manton, D.D.*, 1620—1677.

Verse 7.—"*But as for me,*" etc. A blessed verse this ! a blessed saying ! The words and the sense itself, carry with them a powerful contrast. For there are two things with which this life is exercised, HOPE and FEAR, which are, as it were, those two springs of Judges i. 15, the one from above, the other from beneath. *Fear* comes from beholding the threats and fearful judgments of God ; as being a God in whose sight no one is clean, every one is a sinner, every one is damnable. But *hope* comes from beholding the promises, and the all-sweet mercies of God ; as it is written (Psalm xxv. 6), " Remember, O Lord, thy loving kindnesses, and thy tender mercies which have been ever of old." Between these two, as between the upper and nether millstone, we must always be ground and kept, that we never turn either to the right hand or to the left. For this turning is the state peculiar to hypocrites, who are exercised with the two contrary things, security and presumption.—*Martin Luther.*

Verse 9.—If the whole soul be infected with such a desperate disease, what a great and difficult work is it to regenerate, to restore men again to spiritual life and vigour, when every part of them is seized by such a mortal distemper ! How great a cure doth the Spirit of God effect in restoring a soul by sanctifying it ! To heal but the lungs or the liver, if corrupted, is counted a great cure, though performed but upon one part of thee ; but all thy inward parts are very rottenness. " *For there is no faithfulness in their mouth ; their inward part is very wickedness ; their throat is an open sepulchre ; they flatter with their tongue.*" How great a cure is it then to heal thee ! Such as is only in the skill and power of God to do.—*Thomas Goodwin.*

Verse 9.—" *Their throat is an open sepulchre.*" This figure graphically portrays the filthy conversation of the wicked. Nothing can be more abominable to the senses than an open sepulchre, when a dead body beginning to putrefy steams forth its tainted exhalations. What proceeds out of their mouth is infected and putrid ; and as the exhalation from a sepulchre proves the corruption within, so it is with the corrupt conversation of sinners.—*Robert Haldane's " Expositions of the Epistle to the Romans,"* 1835.

Verse 9.—*" Their throat is an open sepulchre."* This doth admonish us, (1) that the speeches of natural unregenerate men are unsavory, rotten, and hurtful to others ; for, as a sepulchre doth send out noisome savours and filthy smells, so evil men do utter rotten and filthy words. (2) As a sepulchre doth consume and devour bodies cast into it, so wicked men do with their cruel words destroy others ; they are like a gulf to destroy others. (3) As a sepulchre, having devoured many corpses, is still ready to consume more, being never satisfied, so wicked men, having overthrown many with their words, do proceed in their outrage, seeking whom they may devour.—*Thomas Wilson,* 1653.

Verse 9.—*" Their inward part,"* etc. Their hearts are storehouses for the devil.—*John Trapp.*

Verse 10.—All those portions where we find apparently prayers that breathe revenge, are never to be thought of as anything else than the *breathed assent of righteous souls* to the justice of their God, who taketh vengeance on sin. When taken as the words of Christ himself, they are no other than an echo of the Intercessor's acquiescence at last in the sentence on the barren fig-tree. It is as if he cried aloud, " Hew it down now, I will intercede no longer, the doom is righteous, *destroy them, O God ; cast them out in* (or, for) *the multitude of their transgressions, for they have rebelled against thee."* And in the same moment he may be supposed to invite his saints to sympathise in his decision ; just as in Rev. xviii. 20, " Rejoice over her, thou heaven, and ye holy apostles and prophets." In like manner, when one of Christ's members, in entire sympathy with his Head, views the barren fig-tree from the same point of observation, and sees the glory of God concerned in inflicting the blow, he too can cry, " Let the axe smite !" Had Abraham stood beside the angel who destroyed Sodom, and seen how Jehovah's name required the ruin of these impenitent rebels, he would have cried out, " Let the shower descend ; let the fire and brimstone come down !" not in any spirit of revenge ; not from want of tender love to souls, but from intense earnestness of concern for the glory of his God. We consider this explanation to be the real key that opens all the difficult passages in this book, where curses seem to be called for on the head of the ungodly. They are no more than a carrying out of Deut. xxvii. 15—26, " Let all the people say, Amen," and an entering into the Lord's holy abhorrence of sin, and delight in acts of justice expressed in the " Amen, hallelujah," of Rev. xix. 3.—*Andrew A. Bonar,* 1859.

Verse 10.—*(Or imprecatory passages generally.)* Lord, when in my daily service I read David's Psalms, give me to alter the accent of my soul according to their several subjects. In such Psalms wherein he confesseth his sins, or requesteth thy pardon, or praiseth for former, or prayeth for future favours, in all these give me to raise my soul to as high a pitch as may be. But when I come to such Psalms wherein he curseth his enemies, O there let me bring my soul down to a lower note. For those words were made only to fit David's mouth. I have the like breath, but not the same spirit to pronounce them. Nor let me flatter myself, that it is lawful for me, with David, to curse thine enemies, lest my deceitful heart entitle mine enemies to be thine, and so what was religion in David, prove malice in me, whilst I act revenge under the pretence of piety.—*Thomas Fuller, D.D.,* 1608—1661.

Verse 12.—When the strong man armed comes against us, when he darts his fiery darts, what can hurt us, if God compass us about with *his lovingkindness as with a shield ?* He can disarm the tempter and restrain his malice, and tread him under our feet. If God be not with us, if he do not give us sufficient grace, so subtle, so powerful, so politic an enemy, will be too hard for us. How surely are we foiled, and get the worse, when we pretend to grapple with him in our own strength ! How many falls, and how many bruises by those falls have we got, by relying too much on our own skill ? How often have we had the help of God when we have humbly asked it ! And how sure are we to get the victory, *if Christ pray for us that we do not fail!* Luke xxii. 31. Where can we go for shelter but unto God our Maker ! When this lion of the forest does begin to roar, how will he terrify and vex us, till he that permits him for awhile to trouble us, be pleased to chain him up again !—*Timothy Rogers,* 1691.

Verse 12.—*"As with a shield."* Luther, when making his way into the presence of Cardinal Cajetan, who had summoned him to answer for his heretical opinions at Augsburg, was asked by one of the Cardinal's minions, where he should find a shelter, if his patron, the Elector of Saxony, should desert him ? " Under the shield of heaven !" was the reply. The silenced minion turned round, and went his way.

Verse 12.—*" With favour will thou compass him as with a shield."* The shield is not for the defence of any particular part of the body, as almost all the other pieces are : helmet, fitted for the head ; plate, designed for the breast ; and so others, they have their several parts, which they are fastened to ; but the shield is a piece that is intended for the defence of the whole body. It was used therefore to be made very large ; for its broadness, called a gate or door, because so long and large, as in a manner to cover the whole body. And if the shield were not large enough at once to cover every part, yet being a movable piece of armour, the skilful soldier might turn it this way or that way, to catch the blow or arrow from lighting on any part they were directed to. And this indeed doth excellently well set forth the universal use that faith is of to the Christian. It defends the whole man : every part of the Christian by it is preserved. . . . The shield doth not only defend the whole body, but it is a defence to the soldier's armour also ; it keeps the arrow from the helmet as well as head, from the breast and breastplate also. Thus faith, it is armour upon armour, a grace that preserves all the other graces.—*William Gurnall.*

HINTS TO THE VILLAGE PREACHER.

Verses 1, 2.—Prayer in its threefold form. " *Words, meditation, cry.*" Showing how utterance is of no avail without heart, but that fervent longings and silent desires are accepted, even when unexpressed.

Verse 3.—The excellence of morning devotion.

Verse 3 (*last two clauses*).—1. Prayer directed. 2. Answers expected.

Verse 4.—God's hatred of sin an example to his people.

Verse 5.—" *The foolish.*" Show why sinners are justly called fools.

Verse 7.—" *Multitude of thy mercy.*" Dwell upon the varied grace and goodness of God.

Verse 7.—The devout resolution.

Verse 7.—I. Observe the *singularity* of the resolution. II. Mark the *object* of the resolution. It regards the service of God in the sanctuary. " I will come into thine *house.* . . . in thy fear will I *worship* towards thy *holy temple.*" III. The *manner* in which he would accomplish the resolution. (1) Impressed with a sense of the divine goodness : " I will come into thy house in *the multitude of thy mercy.*" (2) Filled with holy veneration : " And *in thy fear* will I worship." *William Jay,* 1842.

Verse 8.—God's guidance needed always, and especially when enemies are watching us.

Verse 10.—Viewed as a threatening. The sentence, "Cast them out in the multitude of their transgressions," is specially fitted to be the groundwork of a very solemn discourse.

Verse 11.—I. The character of the righteous : *faith and love.* II. The privileges of the righteous. (1) *Joy*—great, pure, satisfying, triumphant, (*shout*) constant (*ever*). (2) *Defence*—by power, providence, angels, grace, etc.

Verse 11.—Joy in the Lord both a duty and a privilege.

Verse 12 (*first clause*).—*The divine blessing upon the righteous.* It is ancient, effectual, constant, extensive, irreversible, surpassing, eternal, infinite.

Verse 12 (*second clause*).—A sense of divine favour a defence to the soul.

PSALM VI.

TITLE.—*This Psalm is commonly known as the first of* THE PENITENTIAL PSALMS,* *and certainly its language well becomes the lip of a penitent, for it expresses at once the sorrow, (verses 3, 6, 7), the humiliation (verses 2 and 4), and the hatred of sin (verse 8), which are the unfailing marks of the contrite spirit when it turns to God. O Holy Spirit, beget in us the true repentance which needeth not to be repented of. The title of this Psalm is, "To the chief Musician on Neginoth upon Sheminith,† A Psalm of David," that is, to the chief musician with stringed instruments, upon the eighth, probably the octave. Some think it refers to the bass or tenor key, which would certainly be well adapted to this mournful ode. But we are not able to understand these old musical terms, and even the term "Selah," still remains untranslated. This, however, should be no difficulty in our way. We probably lose but very little by our ignorance, and it may serve to confirm our faith. It is a proof of the high antiquity of these Psalms that they contain words, the meaning of which is lost even to the best scholars of the Hebrew language. Surely these are but incidental (accidental I might almost say, if I did not believe them to be designed by God), proofs of their being, what they profess to be, the ancient writings of King David of olden times.*

DIVISION.—*You will observe that the Psalm is readily divided into two parts. First, there is the Psalmist's plea in his great distress, reaching from the first to the end of the seventh verse. Then you have, from the eighth to the end, quite a different theme. The Psalmist has changed his note. He leaves the minor key, and betakes himself to sublimer strains. He tunes his note to the high key of confidence, and declares that God hath heard his prayer, and hath delivered him out of all his troubles.*

EXPOSITION.

O LORD, rebuke me not in thine anger, neither chasten me in thy hot displeasure.

2 Have mercy upon me, O LORD; for I *am* weak: O LORD, heal me; for my bones are vexed.

3 My soul is also sore vexed: but thou, O LORD, how long?

4 Return, O LORD, deliver my soul: oh save me for thy mercies' sake.

5 For in death *there is* no remembrance of thee: in the grave who shall give thee thanks?

6 I am weary with my groaning; all the night make I my bed to swim; I water my couch with my tears.

7 Mine eye is consumed because of grief; it waxeth old because of all mine enemies.

Having read through the first division, in order to see it as a whole, we will now look at it verse by verse. "*O Lord, rebuke me not in thine anger.*" The Psalmist is very conscious that he deserves to be rebuked, and he feels, moreover, that the rebuke in some form or other must come upon him, if not for condemnation, yet for conviction and sanctification. "Corn is cleaned with wind, and the soul with chastenings." It were folly to pray against the golden hand which enriches us by its blows. He does not ask that the rebuke may be totally withheld, for he might thus lose a blessing in disguise; but, "Lord, rebuke me not *in thine anger*." If thou remindest me of my sin, it is good; but, oh, remind me not of it as one incensed against me, lest thy servant's heart should sink in

---

despair. Thus saith Jeremiah, " O Lord, correct me, but with judgment ; not in thine anger, lest thou bring me to nothing." I know that I must be chastened, and though I shrink from the rod yet do I feel that it will be for my benefit ; but, oh, my God, " *chasten me not in thy hot displeasure*," lest the rod become a sword, and lest in smiting, thou shouldest also kill. So may we pray that the chastisements of our gracious God, if they may not be entirely removed, may at least be sweetened by the consciousness that they are " not in anger, but in his dear covenant love."

2, 3. "*Have mercy upon me, O Lord ; for I am weak.*" Though I deserve destruction, yet let thy mercy pity my frailty. This is the right way to plead with God if we would prevail. Urge not your goodness or your greatness, but plead your sin and your littleness. Cry, "*I am weak*," therefore, O Lord, give me strength and crush me not. Send not forth the fury of thy tempest against so weak a vessel. Temper the wind to the shorn lamb. Be tender and pitiful to a poor withering flower, and break it not from its stem. Surely this is the plea that a sick man would urge to move the pity of his fellow if he were striving with him, " Deal gently with me, ' for I am weak.' " A sense of sin had so spoiled the Psalmist's pride, so taken away his vaunted strength, that he found himself weak to obey the law, weak through the sorrow that was in him, too weak, perhaps, to lay hold on the promise. "*I am weak.*" The original may be read, " I am one who droops," or withered like a blighted plant. Ah ! beloved, we know what this means, for we, too, have seen our glory stained, and our beauty like a faded flower.

" *O Lord, heal me ; for my bones are vexed.*" Here he prays for *healing*, not merely the mitigation of the ills he endured, but their entire removal, and the curing of the wounds which had arisen therefrom. His bones were " *shaken*," as the Hebrew has it. His terror had become so great that his very bones shook ; not only did his flesh quiver, but the bones, the solid pillars of the house of manhood, were made to tremble. " My bones are shaken." Ah, when the soul has a sense of sin, it is enough to make the bones shake ; it is enough to make a man's hair stand up on end to see the flames of hell beneath him, an angry God above him, and danger and doubt surrounding him. Well might he say, " My bones are shaken." Lest, however, we should imagine that it was merely bodily sickness—although bodily sickness might be the outward sign—the Psalmist goes on to say, " *My soul is also sore vexed.*" Soul-trouble is the very soul of trouble. It matters not that the bones shake if the soul be firm, but when the soul itself is also sore vexed this is agony indeed. "*But thou, O Lord, how long?*" This sentence ends abruptly, for words failed, and grief drowned the little comfort which dawned upon him. The Psalmist had still, however, some hope ; but that hope was only in his God. He therefore cries, " O Lord, how long ?" The coming of Christ into the soul in his priestly robes of grace is the grand hope of the penitent soul ; and, indeed, in some form or other, Christ's appearance is, and ever has been, the hope of the saints.

Calvin's favourite exclamation was, " Domine usquequo"—"*O Lord, how long?*" Nor could his sharpest pains, during a life of anguish, force from him any other word. Surely this is the cry of the saints under the altar, " O Lord, how long ?" And this should be the cry of the saints waiting for the millennial glories, " Why are his chariots so long in coming ; Lord, how long ?" Those of us who have passed through conviction of sin knew what it was to count our minutes hours, and our hours years, while mercy delayed its coming. We watched for the dawn of grace, as they that watch for the morning. Earnestly did our anxious spirits ask, " O Lord, how long ?"

4. " *Return, O Lord ; deliver my soul.*" As God's absence was the main cause of his misery, so his return would be enough to deliver him from his trouble. " *Oh save me for thy mercies' sake.*" He knows where to look, and what arm to lay hold upon. He does not lay hold on God's left hand of justice, but on his right hand of mercy. He knew his iniquity too well to think of merit, or appeal to anything but the grace of God.

"*For thy mercies' sake.*" What a plea that is! How prevalent it is with God! If we turn to justice, what plea can we urge? but if we turn to mercy we may still cry, notwithstanding the greatness of our guilt, "Save me for thy mercies' sake."

Observe how frequently David here pleads the name of Jehovah, which is always intended where the word Lord is given in capitals. Five times in four verses we here meet with it. Is not this a proof that the glorious name is full of consolation to the tempted saint? Eternity, Infinity, Immutability, Self-existence, are all in the name Jehovah, and all are full of comfort.

5. And now David was in great fear of death—death temporal, and perhaps death eternal. Read the passage as you will, the following verse is full of power. "*For in death there is no remembrance of thee; in the grave who shall give thee thanks?*" Churchyards are silent places; the vaults of the sepulchre echo not with songs. Damp earth covers dumb mouths. "O Lord!" saith he, "if thou wilt spare me I will praise thee. If I die, then must my mortal praise at least be suspended; and if I perish in hell, then thou wilt never have any thanksgiving from me. Songs of gratitude cannot rise from the flaming pit of hell. True, thou wilt doubtless be glorified, even in my eternal condemnation, but then, O Lord, I cannot glorify thee voluntarily; and among the sons of men, there will be one heart the less to bless thee." Ah! poor trembling sinners, may the Lord help you to use this forcible argument! It is for God's glory that a sinner should be saved. When we seek pardon, we are not asking God to do that which will stain his banner, or put a blot on his escutcheon. He delighteth in mercy. It is his peculiar, darling attribute. Mercy honours God. Do not we ourselves say, "Mercy blesseth him that gives, and him that takes?" And surely, in some diviner sense, this is true of God, who, when he gives mercy, glorifies himself.

6, 7. The Psalmist gives a fearful description of his long agony: "*I am weary with my groaning.*" He had groaned till his throat was hoarse; he had cried for mercy till prayer became a labour. God's people may groan, but they may not grumble. Yea, they must groan, being burdened, or they will never shout in the day of deliverance. The next sentence, we think, is not accurately translated. It should be, "*I shall make my bed to swim every night*" (when nature needs rest, and when I am most alone with my God). That is to say, my grief is fearful even now, but if God do not soon save me, it will not stay of itself, but will increase, until my tears will be so many, that my bed itself shall swim. A description rather of what he feared would be, than of what had actually taken place. May not our forebodings of future woe become arguments which faith may urge when seeking present mercy? "*I water my couch with my tears. Mine eye is consumed because of grief; it waxeth old because of all mine enemies.*" As an old man's eye grows dim with years, so, says David, my eye is grown red and feeble through weeping. Conviction sometimes has such an effect upon the body, that even the outward organs are made to suffer. May not this explain some of the convulsions and hysterical attacks which have been experienced under convictions in the revivals in Ireland. Is it surprising that some should be smitten to the earth, and begin to cry aloud; when we find that David himself made his bed to swim, and grew old while he was under the heavy hand of God? Ah! brethren, it is no light matter to feel one's self a sinner, condemned at the bar of God. The language of this Psalm is not strained and forced, but perfectly natural to one in so sad a plight.

8 Depart from me, all ye workers of iniquity; for the Lord hath heard the voice of my weeping.

9 The Lord hath heard my supplication; the Lord will receive my prayer.

10 Let all mine enemies be ashamed and sore vexed: let them return *and* be ashamed suddenly.

8. Hitherto, all has been mournful and disconsolate, but now—

> "Your harps, ye trembling saints,
>   Down from the willows take."

Ye must have your times of weeping, but let them be short. Get ye up, get ye up, from your dunghills! Cast aside your sackcloth and ashes! Weeping may endure for a night, but joy cometh in the morning.

David has found peace, and rising from his knees he begins to sweep his house of the wicked. "*Depart from me, all ye workers of iniquity.*" The best remedy for us against an evil man is a long space between us both. "Get ye gone; I can have no fellowship with you." Repentance is a practical thing. It is not enough to bemoan the desecration of the temple of the heart, we must scourge out the buyers and sellers, and overturn the tables of the money changers. A pardoned sinner *will hate the sins* which cost the Saviour his blood. Grace and sin are quarrelsome neighbours, and one or the other must go to the wall.

"*For the Lord hath heard the voice of my weeping.*" What a fine Hebraism, and what grand poetry it is in English! "He hath heard the voice of my weeping." Is there a voice in weeping? Does weeping speak? In what language doth it utter its meaning? Why, in that universal tongue which is known and understood in all the earth, and even in heaven above. When a man weeps, whether he be a Jew or Gentile, Barbarian, Scythian, bond or free, it has the same meaning in it. Weeping is the eloquence of sorrow. It is an unstammering orator, needing no interpreter, but understood of all. Is it not sweet to believe that our tears are understood even when words fail? Let us learn to think of tears as liquid prayers, and of weeping as a constant dropping of importunate intercession which will wear its way right surely into the very heart of mercy, despite the stony difficulties which obstruct the way. My God, I will "weep" when I cannot plead, for thou hearest the voice of my weeping.

9. "*The Lord hath heard my supplication.*" The Holy Spirit had wrought into the Psalmist's mind the confidence that his prayer was heard. This is frequently the privilege of the saints. Praying the prayer of faith, they are often infallibly assured that they have prevailed with God. We read of Luther that, having on one occasion wrestled hard with God in prayer, he came leaping out of his closet crying, "*Vicimus, vicimus;*" that is, "We have conquered, we have prevailed with God." Assured confidence is no idle dream, for when the Holy Ghost bestows it upon us, we know its reality, and could not doubt it, even though all men should deride our boldness. "*The Lord will receive my prayer.*" Here is past experience used for future encouragement. *He hath, he will.* Note this, O believer, and imitate its reasoning.

10. "*Let all mine enemies be ashamed and sore vexed.*" This is rather a prophecy than an imprecation, it may be read in the future, "All my enemies shall be ashamed and sore vexed." *They shall return and be ashamed instantaneously,*—in a moment;—their doom shall come upon them suddenly. Death's day is doom's day, and both are sure and may be sudden. The Romans were wont to say, "The feet of the avenging Deity are shod with wool." With noiseless footsteps vengeance nears its victim, and sudden and overwhelming shall be its destroying stroke. If this were an imprecation, we must remember that the language of the old dispensation is not that of the new. We pray *for* our enemies, not *against* them. God have mercy on them, and bring them into the right way.

Thus the Psalm, like those which precede it, shews the different estates of the godly and the wicked. O Lord, let us be numbered *with* thy people, both now and for ever!

EXPLANATORY NOTES AND QUAINT SAYINGS.

Whole Psalm.—David was a man that was often exercised with sickness and troubles from enemies, and in all the instances almost that we meet with in the Psalms of these his afflictions, we may observe the outward occasions of trouble brought him under the suspicion of God's wrath and his own iniquity ; so that he was seldom sick, or persecuted, but this called on the disquiet of conscience, and brought his sin to remembrance ; as in this Psalm, which was made on the occasion of his sickness, as appears from verse eight, wherein he expresseth the vexation of his soul under the apprehension of God's anger ; all his other griefs running into this channel, as little brooks, losing themselves in a great river, change their name and nature. He that was at first only concerned for his sickness, is now wholly concerned with sorrow and smart under the fear and hazard of his soul's condition ; the like we may see in Psalm xxxviii. and many places more.—*Richard Gilpin*, 1677.

Verse 1.—"*Rebuke me not.*" God hath two means by which he reduceth his children to obedience ; his word, by which he rebukes them ; and his rod, by which he chastiseth them. The word precedes, admonishing them by his servants whom he hath sent in all ages to call sinners to repentance : of the which David himself saith, "Let the righteous rebuke me ;" and as a father doth first rebuke his disordered child, so doth the Lord speak to them. But when men neglect the warnings of his word, then God, as a good father, takes up the rod and beats them. Our Saviour wakened the three disciples in the garden three times, but seeing that served not, he told them that Judas and his band were coming to awaken them whom his own voice could not waken.—*A. Symson*, 1638.

Verse 1.—"*Jehovah, rebuke me not in thine anger,*" etc. He does not altogether refuse punishment, for that would be unreasonable ; and to be without it, he judged would be more hurtful than beneficial to him ; but what he is afraid of is the wrath of God, which threatens sinners with ruin and perdition. To anger and indignation David tacitly opposes fatherly and gentle chastisement, and this last he was willing to bear.—*John Calvin*, 1509—1564.

Verse 1.—"*O Lord, rebuke me not in thine anger.*"

> The anger of the Lord ? Oh, dreadful thought !
> How can a creature frail as man endure
> The tempest of his wrath ? Ah, whither flee
> To 'scape the punishment he well deserves ?
> Flee to the cross ! the great atonement there
> Will shield the sinner, if he supplicate
> For pardon with repentance true and deep,
> And faith that questions not. Then will the frown
> Of anger pass from off the face of God,
> Like a black tempest cloud that hides the sun.　　　*Anon.*

Verse 1.—"*Lord, rebuke me not in thine anger,*" etc. ; that is, do not lay upon me that thou hast threatened in thy law ; where anger is not put for the decree, nor the execution, but for the denouncing. So (Matt. iii. 11, and so Hos. xi. 9), "I will not execute the fierceness of mine anger," that is, I will not execute my wrath as I have declared it. Again, it is said, he executes punishment on the wicked ; he declares it not only, but executeth it, so anger is put for the execution of anger.—*Richard Stock*, 1641.

Verse 1.—"*Neither chasten me in thine hot displeasure.*"

> O keep up life and peace within,
> If I must feel thy chastening rod !
> Yet kill not me, but kill my sin,
> And let me know thou art my God.
> O give my soul some sweet foretaste
> Of that which I shall shortly see !
> Let faith and love cry to the last,
> "Come, Lord, I trust myself with thee !"
> 　　　　　　　*Richard Baxter*, 1615—1691.

Verse 2.—"*Have mercy upon me, O Lord.*" To fly and escape the anger of God, David sees no means in heaven or in earth, and therefore retires himself to God, even to him who wounded him that he might heal him. He flies not with Adam to the bush, nor with Saul to the witch, nor with Jonah to Tarshish ; but he appeals from an angry and just God to a merciful God, and from himself to himself. The woman who was condemned by King Philip, appealed from Philip being drunken to Philip being sober. But David appeals from one virtue, justice, to another, mercy. There may be appellation from the tribunal of man to the justice-seat of God ; but when thou art indicted before God's justice-seat, whither or to whom wilt thou go but to himself and his mercy-seat, which is the highest and last place of appellation ? "I have none in heaven but thee, nor in earth besides thee." . . . . . David, under the name of *mercy*, includeth all things, according to that of Jacob to his brother Esau, "I have gotten mercy, and therefore I have gotten all things." Desirest thou any thing at God's hands ? Cry for *mercy*, out of which fountain all good things will spring to thee.—*Archibald Symson.*

Verse 2.—"*For I am weak.*" Behold what rhetoric he useth to move God to cure him, "*I am weak*," an argument taken from his weakness, which indeed were a weak argument to move any man to show his favour, but is a strong argument to prevail with God. If a diseased person would come to a physician, and only lament the heaviness of his sickness, he would say, God help thee ; or an oppressed person come to a lawyer, and show him the estate of his action and ask his advice, that is a golden question ; or to a merchant to crave raiment, he will either have present money or a surety ; or a courtier favour, you must have your reward ready in your hand. But coming before God, the most forcible argument that ye can use is your necessity, poverty, tears, misery, unworthiness, and confessing them to him, it shall be an open door to furnish you with all things that he hath. . . . . The tears of our misery are forcible arrows to pierce the heart of our heavenly Father, to deliver us and pity our hard case. The beggars lay open their sores to the view of the world, that the more they may move men to pity them. So let us deplore our miseries to God, that he, with the pitiful Samaritan, at the sight of our wounds, may help us in due time.—*Archibald Symson.*

Verse 2.—"*Heal me,*" etc. David comes not to take physic upon wantonness, but because the disease is violent, because the accidents are vehement ; so vehement, so violent, as that it hath pierced *ad ossa*, and *ad animam*, "*My bones are vexed, and my soul is sore troubled,*" therefore "*heal me ;*" which is the reason upon which he grounds this second petition, "*Heal me, because my bones are vexed,*" etc.—*John Donne.*

Verse 2.—"*My bones are vexed.*" The Lord can make the strongest and most insensible part of man's body sensible of his wrath when he pleaseth to touch him, for here David's bones are vexed.—*David Dickson.*

Verse 2.—The term "*bones*" frequently occurs in the Psalms, and if we examine we shall find it used in three different senses. (1.) It is sometimes applied literally to our blessed Lord's human body, to the body which hung upon the cross, as, "They pierced my hands and my feet ; I may tell all my bones." (2.) It has sometimes also a further reference to his mystical body the church. And then it denotes all the members of Christ's body that stand firm in the faith, that cannot be moved by persecutions, or temptations, however severe, as, "All my bones shall say, Lord, who is like unto thee ?" (3.) In some passages the term bones is applied to the soul, and not to the body, to the inner man of the individual Christian. Then it implies the strength and fortitude of the soul, the determined courage which faith in God gives to the righteous. This is the sense in which it is used in the second verse of Psalm vi., "O Lord, heal me ; for my bones are vexed."—*Augustine, Ambrose, and Chrysostom ; quoted by F. H. Dunwell, B.A., in "Parochial Lectures on the Psalms,"* 1855.

Verse 3.—"*My soul.*" Yokefellows in sin are yokefellows in pain ; the soul is punished for informing, the body for performing, and as both the informer and performer, the cause and the instrument, so shall the stirrer up of sin and the executor of it be punished.—*John Donne.*

Verse 3.—"*O Lord, how long?*" Out of this we have three things to observe ; first, that there is an appointed time which God hath measured for the crosses of all his children, before which time they shall not be delivered, and for which they must patiently attend, not thinking to prescribe time to God for their delivery, or limit the Holy One of Israel. The Israelites remained in Egypt till the complete number of four hundred and thirty years were accomplished. Joseph was three years and more in the prison till the appointed time of his delivery came. The Jews remained seventy years in Babylon. So that as the physician appointeth certain times to the patient, both wherein he must fast, and be dieted, and wherein he must take recreation, so God knoweth the convenient times both of our humiliation and exaltation. Next, see the impatiency of our nature in our miseries, our flesh still rebelling against the Spirit, which oftentimes forgetteth itself so far, that it will enter into reasoning with God, and quarrelling with him, as we may read of Job, Jonas, etc., and here also of David. Thirdly, albeit the Lord delay his coming to relieve his saints, yet hath he great cause if we could ponder it ; for when we were in the heat of our sins, many times he cried by the mouth of his prophets and servants, "O fools, how long will you continue in your folly?" And we would not hear ; and therefore when we are in the heat of our pains, thinking long, yea, every day a year till we be delivered, no wonder it is if God will not hear ; let us consider with ourselves the just dealing of God with us ; that as he cried and we would not hear, so now we cry, and he will not hear.—*A. Symson.*

Verse 3.—"*O Lord, how long?*" As the saints in heaven have their *usque quo*, how long, Lord, holy and true, before thou begin to execute judgment ? So, the saints on earth have their *usque quo.* How long, Lord, before thou take off the execution of this judgment upon us ? For, our deprecatory prayers are not mandatory, they are not directory, they appoint not God his ways, nor his times ; but as our postulatory prayers are, they also are submitted to the will of God, and have all in them that ingredient, that herb of grace, which Christ put into his own prayer, that *veruntamen, yet not my will, but thy will be fulfilled ;* and they have that ingredient which Christ put into our prayer, *fiat voluntas, thy will be done in earth as it is in heaven ;* in heaven there is no resisting of his will ; yet in heaven there is a soliciting, a hastening, an accelerating of the judgment, and the glory of the resurrection ; so though we resist not his corrections here upon earth, we may humbly present to God the sense which we have of his displeasure, for this sense and apprehension of his corrections is one of the principal reasons why he sends them ; he corrects us therefore that we might be sensible of his corrections ; that when we, being humbled under his hand, have said with his prophet, "*I will bear the wrath of the Lord because I have sinned against him*" (Mic. vii. 9), he may be pleased to say to his correcting angel, as he did to his destroying angel, *This is enough*, and so burn his rod now, as he put up his sword then.—*John Donne.*

Verse 4.—"*Return, O Lord, deliver my soul*," etc. In this his besieging of God, he brings up his works from afar off, closer ; he begins in this Psalm, at a deprecatory prayer ; he asks nothing, but that God would do nothing, that he would forbear him—*rebuke me not, correct me not.* Now, it costs the king less to give a pardon than to give a pension, and less to give a reprieve than to give a pardon, and less to connive, not to call in question, than either reprieve, pardon, or pension ; to forbear is not much. But then as the mathematician said, that he could make an engine, a screw, that should move the whole frame of the world, if he could have a place assigned him to fix that engine, that screw upon, that so it might work upon the world ; so prayer, when one petition hath taken hold upon God, works upon God, moves God, prevails with God, entirely for all. David then having got this ground, this footing in God, he brings his works closer ; he comes from the deprecatory to a postulatory prayer ; not only that God would do nothing against him, but that he would do something for him. God hath suffered man to see *Arcana imperii*, the secrets of his state, how he governs—he governs by precedent ; by precedents of his predecessors, he cannot, he hath none ; by precedents of other gods he cannot, there are none ; and yet he proceeds by precedents, by his own precedents, he does as he did before, *habenti dat*, to him that hath received he gives more, and is willing to be wrought and prevailed upon, and pressed with his own example. And, as though his doing good were but to learn how to do good better, still he writes after his own copy, and *nulla dies sine linea*. He writes something to us, that is, he doth something for us every day. And then, that which is not often seen in other masters, his copies are better than the originals ; his latter mercies larger than his former ; and in this postulatory prayer, larger than the deprecatory, enters our text, " *Return, O Lord ; deliver my soul : O save me,*" etc.—*John Donne.*

Verse 5.—" *For in death there is no remembrance of thee, in the grave who will give thee thanks ?*" Lord, be thou pacified and reconciled to me . . . . for shouldst thou now proceed to take away my life, as it were a most direful condition for me to die before I have propitiated thee, so I may well demand what increase of glory or honour will it bring unto thee ? Will it not be infinitely more glorious for thee to spare me, till by true contrition I may regain thy favour ?—and then I may live to praise and magnify thy mercy and thy grace : thy mercy in pardoning so great a sinner, and then confess thee by vital actions of all holy obedience for the future, and so demonstrate the power of thy grace which hath wrought this change in me ; neither of which will be done by destroying me, but only thy just judgments manifested in thy vengeance on sinners.—*Henry Hammond, D.D.*, 1659.

Verse 6.—" *I fainted in my mourning.*" It may seem a marvellous change in David, being a man of such magnitude of mind, to be thus dejected and cast down. Prevailed he not against Goliath, against the lion and the bear, through fortitude and magnanimity ? But now he is sobbing, sighing, and weeping as a child ! The answer is easy ; the diverse persons with whom he hath to do occasioneth the same. When men and beasts are his opposites, then he is more than a conqueror ; but when he hath to do with God against whom he sinned, then he is less than nothing.

Verse 6.—" *I caused my bed to swim.*" . . . . . . Showers be better than dews, yet it is sufficient if God at least hath bedewed our hearts, and hath given us some sign of a penitent heart. If we have not rivers of waters to pour forth with David, neither fountains flowing with Mary Magdalen, nor as Jeremy, desire to have a fountain in our head to weep day and night, nor with Peter weep bitterly ; yet if we lament that we cannot lament, and mourn that we cannot mourn : yea, if we have the smallest sobs of sorrow and tears of compunction, if they be true and not counterfeit, they will make us acceptable to God ; for as the woman with the bloody issue that touched the hem of Christ's garment, was no less welcome to Christ than Thomas, who put his fingers in the print of the nails ; so, God looketh not at the quantity, but the sincerity of our repentance.

Verse 6.—" *My bed.*" The place of his sin is the place of his repentance, and so it should be ; yea, when we behold the place where we have offended, we should be pricked in the heart, and there again crave him pardon. As Adam sinned in the garden, and Christ sweat bloody tears in the garden. " Examine your hearts upon your beds, and convert unto the Lord ;" and whereas ye have stretched forth yourselves upon your bed to devise evil things, repent there and make them sanctuaries to God. Sanctify by your tears every place which ye have polluted by sin. And let us seek Christ Jesus on our own bed, with the spouse in the Canticles, who saith, "By night on my bed I sought him whom my soul loveth."—*Archibald Symson.*

Verse 6.—"*I water my couch with tears.*" Not only I *wash*, but also I *water.* The faithful sheep of the great Shepherd go up from the *washing* place, every one bringeth forth twins, and none barren among them. Cant. iv. 2. For so Jacob's sheep, having conceived at the watering troughs, brought forth strong and party-coloured lambs. David likewise, who before had erred and strayed like a lost sheep making here his bed a washing-place, by so much the less is barren in obedience, by how much the more he is fruitful in repentance. In Solomon's temple stood the caldrons of brass, to wash the flesh of those beasts which were to be sacrificed on the altar. Solomon's father maketh a water of his tears, a caldron of his bed, an altar of his heart, a sacrifice, not of the flesh of unreasonable beasts, but of his own body, a living sacrifice, which is his reasonable serving of God. Now the Hebrew word here used signifies properly, to cause to swim, which is more than simply to wash. And thus the Geneva translation readeth it, I cause my bed every night to swim. So that as the priests used to swim in the molten sea, that they might be pure and clean, against they performed the holy rites and services of the temple, in like manner the princely prophet washeth his bed, yea, he swimmeth in his bed, or rather he causeth his bed to swim in tears, as in a sea of grief and penitent sorrow for his sin.—*Thomas Playfere,* 1604.

Verse 6.—"*I water my couch with my tears.*" Let us water our bed every night with our tears. Do not only blow upon it with intermissive blasts, for then like fire, it will resurge and flame the more. Sin is like a stinking candle newly put out, it is soon lighted again. It may receive a wound, but like a dog it will easily lick itself whole ; a little forbearance multiplies it like Hydra's heads. Therefore, whatsoever aspersion the sin of the day has brought upon us, let the tears of the night wash away.—*Thomas Adams.*

Verses 6, 7.—Soul-trouble is attended usually with great pain of body too, and so a man is wounded and distressed in every part. There is no soundness in my flesh, because of thine anger, says David. "The arrows of the Almighty are within me, the poison whereof drinketh up my spirit." Job vi. 4. Sorrow of heart contracts the natural spirits, making all their motions slow and feeble ; and the poor afflicted body does usually decline and waste away ; and, therefore, saith Heman, "My soul is full of troubles, and my life draweth nigh unto the grave." In this inward distress we find our strength decay and melt, even as wax before the fire ; for sorrow darkeneth the spirits, obscures the judgment, blinds the memory, as to all pleasant things, and beclouds the lucid part of the mind, causing the lamp of life to burn weakly. In this troubled condition the person cannot be without a countenance that is pale, and wan, and dejected, like one that is seized with strong fear and consternation ; all his motions are sluggish, and no sprightliness nor activity remains. A merry heart doth good, like a medicine ; but a broken spirit drieth the bones. Hence come those frequent complaints in Scripture : My moisture is turned into the drought of the summer : I am like a bottle in the smoke ; my soul cleaveth unto the dust : my face is foul with weeping, and on my eyelid is the shadow of death. Job. xvi. 16, xxx. 17, 18—19. My bones are pierced in me, in the night season, and my sinews take no rest ; by the great force of my disease is my garment changed. He hath cast me into the mire, and I am become like dust and ashes. Many times indeed the trouble of the soul does begin from the weakness and indisposition of the body. Long affliction, without any prospect of remedy, does, in process of time, begin to distress the soul itself. David was a man often exercised with sickness and the rage of enemies ; and in all the instances almost that we meet with in the Psalms, we may observe that the outward occasions of trouble brought him under an apprehension of the wrath of God for his sin. (Psalm vi. 1, 2 ; and the reasons given, verses 5 and 6.) All his griefs running into this most terrible thought, that God was his enemy. As little brooks lose themselves in a great river, and change their name and nature, it most frequently happens, that when our pain is long and sharp, and helpless and unavoidable, we begin to question the sincerity of our estate towards God, though at its first assault we had few doubts or fears about it. Long weakness of body makes the soul more susceptible of trouble, and uneasy thoughts.— *Timothy Rogers on Trouble of Mind.*

Verse 7.—" *Mine eye is consumed.*" Many make those eyes which God hath given them, as it were two lighted candles to let them see to go to hell ; and for this God in justice requiteth them, that seeing their minds are blinded by the lust of the eyes, the lust of the flesh, and the pride of life, God, I say, sendeth sickness to debilitate their eyes which were so sharp-sighted in the devil's service, and their lust now causeth them to want the necessary sight of their body.

Verse 7.—" *Mine enemies.*" The pirates seeing an empty bark, pass by it ; but if she be loaded with precious wares, then they will assault her. So, if a man have no grace within him, Satan passeth by him as not a convenient prey for him ; but being loaded with graces, as the love of God, his fear, and such other spiritual virtues, let him be persuaded that according as he knows what stuff is in him, so will he not fail to rob him of them, if in any case he may. *Archibald Symson.*

Verse 7.—That eye of his that had looked and lusted after his neighbour's wife is now dimmed and darkened with grief and indignation. He had wept himself almost blind.—*John Trapp.*

Verse 8.—" *Depart from me,*" etc., *i.e.,* you may now go your way ; for that which you look for, namely, my death, you shall not have at this present ; *for the Lord hath heard the voice of my weeping, i.e.,* has graciously granted me that which with tears I asked of him.—*Thomas Wilcocks.*

Verse 8.—" *Depart from me, all ye workers of iniquity.*" May not too much familiarity with profane wretches be justly charged upon church members ? I know man is a sociable creature, but that will not excuse saints as to their carelessness of the choice of their company. The very fowls of the air, and beasts of the field, love not heterogeneous company. " Birds of a feather flock together." I have been afraid that many who would be thought eminent, of a high stature in grace and godliness, yet see not the vast difference there is between nature and regeneration, sin and grace, the old and the new man, seeing all company is alike unto them.—*Lewis Stuckley's* " *Gospel Glass,*" 1667.

Verse 8.—" *The voice of my weeping.*" Weeping hath a voice, and as music upon the water sounds farther and more harmoniously than upon the land, so prayers, joined with tears, cry louder in God's ears, and make sweeter music than when tears are absent. When Antipater had written a large letter against Alexander's mother unto Alexander, the king answered him, " One tear from my mother will wash away all her faults." So it is with God. A penitent tear is an undeniable ambassador, and never returns from the throne of grace unsatisfied.—*Spencer's Things New and Old.*

Verse 8.—The wicked are called " *workers of iniquity,*" because they are free and ready to sin, they have a strong tide and bent of spirit to do evil, and they do it not to halves but thoroughly ; they do not only begin or nibble at the bait a little (as a good man often doth), but greedily swallow it down, hook and all ; they are fully in it, and do it fully ; they make a work of it, and so are " *workers of iniquity.*"—*Joseph Caryl.*

Verse 8.—Some may say, " My constitution is such that I cannot weep ; I may as well go to squeeze a rock, as think to get a tear." But if thou canst not weep for sin, canst thou grieve ? Intellectual mourning is best ; there may be sorrow where there are no tears, the vessel may be full though it wants vent ; it is not so much the weeping eye God respects as the broken heart ; yet I would be loath to stop their tears who can weep. God stood looking on Hezekiah's tears (Isaiah xxxviii. 5), " I have seen thy tears." David's tears made music in God's ears, " The Lord hath heard the voice of my weeping." It is a sight fit for angels to behold, tears as pearls dropping from a penitent eye.—*T. Watson.*

Verse 8.—" *The Lord hath heard the voice of my weeping.*" God hears the voice of our looks, God hears the voice of our tears sometimes better than the voice of our words ; for it is the Spirit itself that makes intercession for us. Rom. viii. 26. *Gemitibus inenarrabilibus,* in those *groans,* and so in those *tears,* which we *cannot utter ; ineloquacibus,* as Tertullian reads that place, devout, and simple tears, which cannot speak, speak aloud in the ears of God ; nay, tears which we cannot utter ; not only not utter the force of the tears, but not utter the very tears themselves. As God sees the water in the spring in the veins of the earth before it bubble upon the face of the earth, so God sees tears in the heart of a man before they blubber his face ; God hears the tears of that sorrowful soul, which for sorrow cannot shed tears. From this casting up of the eyes, and pouring out the sorrow of the heart at the eyes, at least opening God a window through which he may see a wet heart through a dry eye ; from these overtures of repentance, which are as those imperfect sounds of words, which parents delight in, in their children, before they speak plain, a penitent sinner comes to a verbal and a more express prayer. To these prayers, these vocal and verbal prayers from David, God had given ear, and from this hearing of those prayers was David come to this thankful confidence, " *The Lord hath heard, the Lord will hear.*"—*John Donne.*

Verse 8.—What a strange change is here all on a sudden ! Well might Luther say, "Prayer is the leech of the soul, that sucks out the venom and swelling thereof." " Prayer," saith another, " is an exorcist with God, and an exorcist against sin and misery." Bernard saith, " How oft hath prayer found me despairing almost, but left me triumphing, and well assured of pardon !" The same in effect saith David here, " Depart from me, all ye workers of iniquity ; for the Lord hath heard the voice of my weeping." What a word is that to his insulting enemies ! Avaunt ! come out ! vanish ! These be words used to devils and dogs, but good enough for a Doeg or a Shimei. And the Son of David shall say the same to his enemies when he comes to judgment.—*John Trapp.*

Verse 9.—" *The Lord hath heard my supplication,*" etc. The psalmist three times expresses his confidence of his prayers being heard and received, which may be either in reference to his having prayed so many times for help, as the apostle Paul did (2 Cor. xii. 8) ; and as Christ his antitype did (Matt. xxvi. 39, 42, 44) ; or to express the certainty of it, the strength of his faith in it, and the exuberance of his joy on account of it.—*John Gill, D.D.,* 1697—1771.

Verse 10.—" *Let all mine enemies be ashamed,*" etc. If this were an imprecation, a malediction, yet it was medicinal, and had *rationem boni,* a charitable tincture and nature in it ; he wished the men no harm as men. But it is rather *prædictorium,* a prophetical vehemence, that if they will take no knowledge of God's declaring himself in the protection of his servants, if they would not consider that God had heard, and would hear, had rescued, and would rescue his children, but would continue their opposition against him, heavy judgments would certainly fall upon them ; their punishment should be certain, but the effect should be uncertain ; for God only knows whether his correction shall work upon his enemies to their mollifying, or to their obduration. **.** . . . In the second word, " *Let them be sore vexed,*" he wishes his enemies no worse than himself had been, for he had used the same word of himself before, *Ossa turbata, My bones are vexed ;* and, *Anima turbata, My soul is vexed ;* and considering that David had found this vexation to be his way to God, it was no malicious imprecation to wish that enemy the same physic that he had taken, who was more sick of the same disease than he was. For this is like a troubled sea after a tempest ; the danger is past, but yet the billow is great still ; the danger was in the calm, in the security, or in the tempest, by misinterpreting God's corrections to our obduration, and to a remorseless stupefaction ; but when a man is come to this holy vexation, to be troubled, to be shaken with the sense of the indignation of God, the storm is past, and the indignation of God is blown over. That soul is in a fair and near way of being restored to a calmness, and to reposed security of conscience that is come to this holy vexation.—*John Donne.*

Verse 10.—"*Let all mine enemies* [or *all mine enemies shall*] *be ashamed, and sore vexed,*" etc. Many of the mournful Psalms end in this manner, to instruct the believer that he is continually to look forward, and solace himself with beholding that day, when his warfare shall be accomplished ; when sin and sorrow shall be no more ; when sudden and everlasting confusion shall cover the enemies of righteousness ; when the sackcloth of the penitent shall be exchanged for a robe of glory, and every tear become a sparkling gem in his crown ; when to sighs and groans shall succeed the songs of heaven, set to angelic harps, and faith shall be resolved into the vision of the Almighty.—*George Horne.*

HINTS TO THE VILLAGE PREACHER.

Verse 1.—*A sermon for afflicted souls.* I. God's twofold dealings. (1) *Rebuke,* by a telling sermon, a judgment on another, a slight trial in our own person, or a solemn monition in our conscience by the Spirit. (2) *Chastening.* This follows the other when the first is disregarded. Pain, losses, bereavements, melancholy, and other trials. II. The evils in them to be most dreaded, anger and hot displeasure. III. The means to avert these ills. Humiliation, confession, amendment, faith in the Lord, etc.

Verse 1.—The believer's greatest dread, the anger of God. What this fact reveals in the heart ? Why it is so ? What removes the fear ?

Verse 2.—The *argumentum ad misericordiam.*

Verse 2.—First sentence—*Divine healing.* 1. What precedes it, *my bones are vexed.* 2. How it is wrought. 3. What succeeds it.

Verse 3.—The impatience of sorrow ; its sins, mischief, and cure.

Verse 3.—A fruitful topic may be found in considering the question, How long will God continue afflictions to the righteous ?

Verse 4.—"*Return, O Lord.*" A prayer suggested by a sense of the Lord's absence, excited by grace, attended with heart searching and repentance, backed by pressing danger, guaranteed as to its answer, and containing a request for all mercies.

Verse 4.—The prayer of the deserted saint. 1. *His state :* his soul is evidently in bondage and danger ; 2. *His hope :* it is in the Lord's *return.* 3. *His plea :* mercy only.

Verse 5.—The final suspension of earthly service considered in various practical aspects.

Verse 5.—The duty of praising God while we live.

Verse 6.—Saints' tears in quality, abundance, influence, assuagement, and final end.

Verse 7.—The voice of weeping. What it is.

Verse 8.—The pardoned sinner forsaking his bad companions.

Verse 9.—Past answers the ground of present confidence. He *hath,* he *will.*

Verse 10.—The shame reserved for the wicked.

WORKS UPON THE SIXTH PSALM.

A Godly and Fruitfull Exposition on the Sixt Psalme, the First of the Peni-tentials; in a sacred Septenarie; or, a Godly and Fruitfull Exposition on the Seven Psalmes of Repentance. By MR. ARCHIBALD SYMSON, late Pastor of the Church at Dalkeeth in Scotland. 1638.

Sermons on the Penitential Psalms, in "The Works of John Donne, D.D., Dean of St. Paul's," 1621—1631. Edited by HENRY ALFORD, M.A. In six volumes. 1839.

On Verse 6. The Sick Man's Couch; a Sermon preached before the most noble Prince Henry, at Greenwich, Mar. 12., ann. 1604. By THOMAS PLAYFERE, &c., in Playfere's Sermons.

PSALM VII.

TITLE.—"Shiggaion of David, which he sang unto the Lord, concerning the words of Cush the Benjamite."—"*Shiggaion of David.*" *As far as we can gather from the observations of learned men, and from a comparison of this Psalm with the only other Shiggaion in the Word of God, (Hab. iii.,) this title seems to mean "variable songs," with which also the idea of solace and pleasure is associated. Truly our life-psalm is composed of variable verses; one stanza rolls along with the sublime metre of triumph, but another limps with the broken rhythm of complaint. There is much bass in the saint's music here below. Our experience is as variable as the weather in England.*

From the title we learn the occasion of the composition of this song. It appears probable that Cush the Benjamite had accused David to Saul of treasonable conspiracy against his royal authority. This the king would be ready enough to credit, both from his jealousy of David, and from the relation which most probably existed between himself, the son of Kish, and this Cush, or Kish, the Benjamite. He who is near the throne can do more injury to a subject than an ordinary slanderer.

This may be called the SONG OF THE SLANDERED SAINT. *Even this sorest of evils may furnish occasion for a Psalm. What a blessing would it be if we could turn even the most disastrous event into a theme for song, and so turn the tables upon our great enemy. Let us learn a lesson from Luther, who once said, "David made Psalms; we also will make Psalms, and sing them as well as we can to the honour of our Lord, and to spite and mock the devil."*

DIVISION.—*In the first and second verses the danger is stated, and prayer offered. Then the Psalmist most solemnly avows his innocence. (3, 4, 5.) The Lord is pleaded with to arise to judgment (6, 7). The Lord, sitting upon his throne, hears the renewed appeal of the Slandered Supplicant (8, 9). The Lord clears his servant, and threatens the wicked (10, 11, 12, 13). The slanderer is seen in vision bringing a curse upon his own head, (14, 15, 16,) while David retires from trial singing a hymn of praise to his righteous God. We have here a noble sermon upon that text: "No weapon that is formed against thee shall prosper, and every tongue that riseth against thee in judgment thou shalt condemn."*

EXPOSITION.

O LORD my God, in thee do I put my trust : save me from all them that persecute me, and deliver me :

2 Lest he tear my soul like a lion, rending *it* in pieces, while *there is* none to deliver.

David appears before God to plead with him against the Accuser, who had charged him with treason and treachery. The case is here opened with an avowal of confidence in God. Whatever may be the emergency of our condition we shall never find it amiss to retain our reliance upon our God. "*O Lord my God,*" mine by a special covenant, sealed by Jesus' blood, and ratified in my own soul by a sense of union to thee ; "*in thee,*" and in thee only, "*do I put my trust,*" even now in my sore distress. I shake, but my rock moves not. It is never right to distrust God, and never vain to trust him. And now, with both divine relationship and holy trust to strengthen him, David utters the burden of his desire—"*save me from all them that persecute me.*" His pursuers were very many, and any one of them cruel enough to devour him ; he cries, therefore, for salvation from them *all*. We should never think our prayers complete until we *ask* for preservation from *all* sin, and all enemies. "*And deliver me,*" extricate me from their snares, acquit me of their accusations, give a true and just deliverance in this trial of my injured character. See how clearly his case is stated ; let us see to it, that we know what we would have when we are come to the throne of mercy. Pause a little while before you pray, that you may not offer the sacrifice of fools. Get a distinct idea of your need, and then you can pray with the more fluency of fervency.

"*Lest he tear my soul.*" Here is the plea of fear co-working with the plea of faith. There was one among David's foes mightier than the rest, who had both dignity, strength, and ferocity, and was, therefore, "*like a lion.*" From this foe he urgently seeks deliverance. Perhaps this was Saul, his royal enemy ; but in our own case there is one who goes about like a lion, seeking whom he may devour, concerning whom we should ever cry, "Deliver us from the Evil One." Notice the vigour of the description—"*rending it in pieces, while there is none to deliver.*" It is a picture from the shepherd-life of David. When the fierce lion had pounced upon the defenceless lamb, and had made it his prey, he would rend the victim in pieces, break all the bones, and devour all, because no shepherd was near to protect the lamb or rescue it from the ravenous beast. This is a soul-moving portrait of a saint delivered over to the will of Satan. This will make the bowels of Jehovah yearn. A father cannot be silent when a child is in such peril. No, he will not endure the thought of his darling in the jaws of a lion, he will arise and deliver his persecuted one. Our God is very pitiful, and he will surely rescue his people from so desperate a destruction. It will be well for us here to remember that this is a description of the danger to which the Psalmist was exposed from slanderous tongues. Verily this is not an over-drawn picture, for the wounds of a sword will heal, but the wounds of the tongue cut deeper than the flesh, and are not soon cured. Slander leaves a slur, even if it be wholly disproved. Common fame, although notoriously a common liar, has very many believers. Once let an ill word get into men's mouths, and it is not easy to get it fully out again. The Italians say that good repute is like the cypress, once cut, it never puts forth leaf again ; this is not true if our character be cut by a stranger's hand, but even then it will not soon regain its former verdure. Oh, 'tis a meanness most detestable to stab a good man in his reputation, but diabolical hatred observes no nobility in its mode of warfare. We must be ready for this trial, for it will surely come upon us. If God was slandered in Eden, we shall surely be maligned in this land of sinners. Gird up your loins, ye children of the resurrection, for this fiery trial awaits you all.

3 O LORD my God, if I have done this ; if there be iniquity in my hands ;

4 If I have rewarded evil unto him that was at peace with me ; (yea, I have delivered him that without cause is mine enemy :)

5 Let the enemy persecute my soul, and take *it ;* yea, let him tread down my life upon the earth, and lay mine honour in the dust. Selah.

The second part of this wandering hymn contains a protestation of innocence, and an invocation of wrath upon his own head, if he were not clear from the evil imputed to him. So far from hiding treasonable intentions in his hands, or ungratefully requiting the peaceful deeds of a friend, he had even suffered his enemy to escape when he had him completely in his power. Twice had he spared Saul's life ; once in the cave of Adullam, and again when he found him sleeping in the midst of his slumbering camp : he could, therefore, with a clear conscience, make his appeal to heaven. He needs not fear the curse whose soul is clear of guilt. Yet is the imprecation a most solemn one, and only justifiable through the extremity of the occasion, and the nature of the dispensation under which the Psalmist lived. *We* are commanded by our Lord Jesus to let our yea be yea, and our nay, nay ; "for whatsoever is more than this cometh of evil." If we cannot be believed on our word, we are surely not to be trusted on our oath ; for to a true Christian his simple word is as binding as another man's oath. Especially beware, O unconverted men ! of trifling with solemn imprecations. Remember the woman at Devizes, who wished she might die if she had not paid her share in a joint purchase, and who fell dead there and then with the money in her hand.

Selah. David enhances the solemnity of this appeal to the dread tribunal of God by the use of the usual pause.

From these verses we may learn that no innocence can shield a man from the calumnies of the wicked. David had been scrupulously careful to avoid any appearance of rebellion against Saul, whom he constantly styled "the Lord's anointed;" but all this could not protect him from lying tongues. As the shadow follows the substance, so envy pursues goodness. It is only at the tree laden with fruit that men throw stones. If we would live without being slandered we must wait till we get to heaven. Let us be very heedful not to believe the flying rumours which are always harassing gracious men. If there are no believers in lies there will be but a dull market in falsehood, and good men's characters will be safe. Ill-will never spoke well. Sinners have an ill-will to saints, and therefore, be sure they will not speak well of them.

6 Arise, O LORD, in thine anger, lift up thyself because of the rage of mine enemies : and awake for me *to* the judgment *that* thou hast commanded.

7 So shall the congregation of the people compass thee about : for their sakes therefore return thou on high.

We now listen to a fresh prayer, based upon the avowal which he has just made. We cannot pray too often, and when our heart is true, we shall turn to God in prayer as naturally as the needle to its pole.

"*Arise, O Lord, in thine anger.*" His sorrow makes him view the Lord as a judge who had left the judgment-seat and retired into his rest. Faith would move the Lord to avenge the quarrel of his saints. "*Lift up thyself because of the rage of mine enemies*"—a still stronger figure to express his anxiety that the Lord would assume his authority and mount the throne. Stand up, O God, rise thou above them all, and let thy justice tower above their villainies. "*Awake for me to the judgment that thou hast commanded.*" This is a bolder utterance still, for it implies sleep as well as inactivity, and can only be applied to God in a very limited sense. He never slumbers, yet doth he often seem to do so ; for the wicked prevail, and the saints are trodden in the dust. God's silence is the patience of longsuffering, and if wearisome to the saints, they should bear it cheerfully in the hope that sinners may thereby be led to repentance.

"*So shall the congregation of the people compass thee about.*" Thy saints shall crowd to thy tribunal with their complaints, or shall surround it with their solemn homage : "*for their sakes therefore return thou on high.*" As when a judge travels at the assizes, all men take their cases to his court that they may be heard, so will the righteous gather to their Lord. Here he fortifies himself in prayer by pleading that if the Lord will mount the throne of judgment, multitudes of the saints would be blessed as well as himself. If I be too base to be remembered, yet "*for their sakes,*" for the love thou bearest to thy chosen people, come forth from thy secret pavilion, and sit in the gate dispensing justice among the people. When my suit includes the desires of all the righteous it shall surely speed, for " shall not God avenge his own elect ?"

8 The LORD shall judge the people : judge me, O LORD, according to my righteousness, and according to mine integrity *that* is in me.

9 Oh let the wickedness of the wicked come to an end ; but establish the just : for the righteous God trieth the hearts and reins.

If I am not mistaken, David has now seen in the eye of his mind the Lord ascending to his judgment-seat, and beholding him seated there in royal state, he draws near to him to urge his suit anew. In the last two verses he besought Jehovah to arise, and now that he is arisen, he prepares to mingle with "the congregation of the people" who compass the Lord about. The royal heralds proclaim the opening of the court with the solemn words, " *The Lord shall judge the people.*" Our petitioner rises at once, and cries with earnestness and humility, " *Judge me, O Lord, according to my righteousness, and according to mine integrity that is in me.*" His hand is on an honest heart, and his cry is to a righteous Judge. He sees a smile of complacency upon the face of the King, and in the name of all the assembled congregation he cries aloud, " *Oh let the wickedness of the wicked come to an end ; but establish the just.*" Is not this the universal longing of the whole company of the elect ? When shall we be delivered from the filthy conversation of these men of Sodom ? When shall we escape from the filthiness of Mesech and the blackness of the tents of Kedar ?

What a solemn and weighty truth is contained in the last sentence of the ninth verse ! How deep is the divine knowledge !—" *he trieth.*" How strict, how accurate, how intimate his search !—" *he trieth the hearts,*" the secret thoughts, " *and reins,*" the inward affections. " All things are naked and opened to the eyes of him with whom we have to do."

10 My defence *is* of God, which saveth the upright in heart.

11 God judgeth the righteous, and God is angry *with the wicked* every day.

12 If he turn not, he will whet his sword ; he hath bent his bow, and made it ready.

13 He hath also prepared for him the instruments of death ; he ordaineth his arrows against the persecutors.

The judge has heard the cause, has cleared the guiltless, and uttered his voice against the persecutors. Let us draw near, and learn the results of the great assize. Yonder is the slandered one with his harp in hand, hymning the justice of his Lord, and rejoicing aloud in his own deliverance. " *My defence is of God, which saveth the upright in heart.*" Oh, how good to have a true and *upright* heart. Crooked sinners, with all their craftiness, are foiled by the upright in heart. God defends the right. Filth will not long abide on the pure white garments of the saints, but shall be brushed off by divine providence, to the vexation of the men by whose base hands it was thrown upon the godly. When God shall try our cause, our sun has risen, and the sun of the wicked is set for ever. Truth, like oil, is ever above, no power of our enemies can drown it ; we shall refute their slanders in the day when the trumpet wakes the dead, and we shall shine in honour when lying lips are put to silence. O believer, fear not all that thy foes can do or say against thee, for the tree which God plants no winds can hurt. " *God judgeth the righteous,*" he hath not given thee up to be condemned by the lips of persecutors. Thine enemies cannot sit on God's throne, nor blot thy name out of his book. Let them alone, then, for God will find time for his revenges.

" *God is angry with the wicked every day.*" He not only detests sin, but is angry with those who continue to indulge in it. We have no insensible and stolid God to deal with ; he can be angry, nay, he is angry to-day and every day with you, ye ungodly and impenitent sinners. The best day that ever dawns on a sinner brings a curse with it. Sinners may have many feast days, but no safe days. From the beginning of the year even to its ending, there is not an hour in which God's oven is not hot, and burning in readiness for the wicked, who shall be as stubble.

" *If he turn not, he will whet his sword.*" What blows are those which will be dealt by that long uplifted arm ! God's sword has been sharpening upon the revolving stone of our daily wickedness, and if we will not repent, it will speedily cut us in pieces. Turn or burn is the sinner's only alternative. " *He hath bent his bow and made it ready.*" Even now the thirsty arrow longs to wet itself with the blood of the *persecutor.* The bow is bent, the aim is taken, the arrow is fitted to the string, and what, O sinner, if the arrow should be let fly at thee even now! Remember, God's arrows never miss the mark, and are, every one of them, "instruments of death." Judgment may tarry, but it will not come too late. The Greek proverb saith, "The mill of God grinds late, but grinds to powder."

14 Behold, he travaileth with iniquity, and hath conceived mischief, and brought forth falsehood.

15 He made a pit, and digged it, and is fallen into the ditch *which* he made.

16 His mischief shall return upon his own head, and his violent dealing shall come down upon his own pate.

In three graphic pictures we see the slanderer's history. A woman in travail furnishes the first metaphor. "*He travaileth with iniquity.*" He is full of it, pained until he can carry it out, he longs to work his will, he is full of pangs until his evil intent is executed. "*He hath conceived mischief.*" This is the original of his base design. The devil has had doings with him, and the virus of evil is in him. And now behold the progeny of this unhallowed conception. The child is worthy of its father, his name of old was "the father of lies," and the birth doth not belie the parent, for *he brought forth falsehood.* Thus, one figure is carried out to perfection ; the Psalmist now illustrates his meaning by another, taken from the stratagems of the hunter. "*He made a pit, and digged it.*" He was cunning in his plans, and industrious in his labours. He stooped to the dirty work of digging. He did not fear to soil his own hands, he was willing to work in *a ditch* if others might fall therein. What mean things men will do to wreak revenge on the godly. They hunt for good men, as if they were brute beasts ; nay, they will not give them the fair chase afforded to the hare or the fox, but must secretly entrap them, because they can neither run them down nor shoot them down. Our enemies will not meet us to the face, for they fear us as much as they pretend to despise us. But let us look on to the end of the scene. The verse says, he "*is fallen into the ditch which he made.*" Ah! there he is, let us laugh at his disappointment. Lo! he is himself the beast, he has hunted his own soul, and the chase has brought him a goodly victim. Aha, aha, so should it ever be. Come hither and make merry with this entrapped hunter, this biter who has bitten himself. Give him no pity, for it will be wasted on such a wretch. He is but rightly and richly rewarded by being paid in his own coin. He cast forth evil from his mouth, and it has fallen into his bosom. He has set his own house on fire with the torch which he lit to burn a neighbour. He sent forth a foul bird, and it has come back to its nest. The rod which he lifted on high, has smitten his own back. He shot an arrow upward, and it has "*returned upon his own head.*" He hurled a stone at another, and it has "*come down upon his own pate.*" Curses are like young chickens, they always come home to roost. Ashes always fly back in the face of him that throws them. "As he loved cursing, so let it come unto him." (Ps. cix. 17.) How often has this been the case in the histories of both ancient and modern times. Men have burned their own fingers when they were hoping to brand their neighbour. And if this does not happen now, it will hereafter. The Lord has caused dogs to lick the blood of Ahab in the midst of the vineyard of Naboth. Sooner or later the evil deeds of persecutors have always leaped back into their arms. So will it be in the last great day, when Satan's fiery darts shall all be quivered in his own heart, and all his followers shall reap the harvest which they themselves have sown.

17 I will praise the LORD according to his righteousness : and will sing praise to the name of the LORD most high.

We conclude with the joyful contrast. In this all these Psalms are agreed ; they all exhibit the blessedness of the righteous, and make its colours the more glowing by contrast with the miseries of the wicked. The bright jewel sparkles in a black foil. *Praise* is the occupation of the godly, their eternal work, and their present pleasure. *Singing* is the fitting embodiment for praise, and therefore do the saints make melody before the Lord Most High. The slandered one is now a singer : his harp was unstrung for a very little season, and now we leave him sweeping its harmonious chords, and flying on their music to the third heaven of adoring praise.

EXPLANATORY NOTES AND QUAINT SAYINGS.

Title.—" Shiggaion," though some have attempted to fix on it a reference to the moral aspect of the world as depicted in this Psalm, is in all probability to be taken as expressing the *nature of the composition.* It conveys the idea of something *erratic* (שָׁגָה, to wander) in the style ; something not so calm as other Psalms ; and hence *Ewald* suggests, that it might be rendered, " a confused ode," a Dithyramb. This characteristic of excitement in the style, and a kind of disorder in the sense, suits Habakkuk iii. 1, the only other place where the word occurs.—*Andrew A. Bonar.*

Whole Psalm.—Whatever might be the occasion of the Psalm, the real subject seems to be the Messiah's appeal to God against the false accusations of his enemies ; and the predictions which it contains of the final conversion of the whole world, and of the future judgment, are clear and explicit.—*Samuel Horsley, LL.D.,* 1733—1806.

Verse 1.—" *O Lord, my God, in thee do I put my trust.*" This is the first instance in the Psalms where David addresses the Almighty by the united names Jehovah and my God. No more suitable words can be placed at the beginning of any act of prayer or praise. These names show the ground of the confidence afterwards expressed. They " denote at once supreme reverence and the most endearing confidence. They convey a recognition of God's infinite perfections, and of his covenanted and gracious relations."—*William S. Plumer.*

Verse 2.—" *Lest he tear my soul like a lion,*" etc. It is reported of tigers, that they enter into a rage upon the scent of fragrant spices ; so do ungodly men at the blessed savour of godliness. I have read of some barbarous nations, who, when the sun shines hot upon them, they shoot up their arrows against it ; so do wicked men at the light and heat of godliness. There is a natural antipathy between the spirits of godly men and the wicked. Genesis iii. 15. " I will put enmity between thy seed and her seed."—*Jeremiah Burroughs,* 1660.

Verse 3.—" *O Lord, my God, if I have done this, if there be iniquity in my hands.*" In the primitive times the people of God were then a people under great reproach. What strange things does Tertullian tell us they reproached them withal ; as that in their meetings they made Thyestes suppers, who invited his brother to a supper, and presented him with a dish of his own flesh. They charged them with uncleanness because they met in the night (for they durst not meet in the day), and said, they blew out the candles when they were together, and committed filthiness. They reproached them for ignorance, saying, they were all unlearned ; and therefore the heathens in Tertullian's time used to paint the God of the Christians with an ass's head, and a book in his hand, to signify that though they pretended learning, yet they were an unlearned, silly people, rude and ignorant. Bishop Jewel in his sermon upon

Luke xi. 5, cites this out of Tertullian, and applies it to his time :—"Do not our adversaries do the like," saith he, "at this day, against all those that profess the gospel of Christ? Oh, say they, who are they that favour this way? they are none but shoemakers, tailors, weavers, and such as were never at the university ;" they are the bishop's own words. He cites likewise Tertullian a little after, saying, that the Christians were accounted the public enemies of the State. And Josephus tells us of Apollinaris, speaking concerning the Jews and Christians, that they were more foolish than any barbarian. And Paulus Fagius reports a story of an Egyptian, concerning the Christians, who said, "They were a gathering together of a most filthy, lecherous people ;" and for the keeping of the Sabbath, he says, "they had a disease that was upon them, and they were fain to rest the seventh day because of that disease." And so in Augustine's time, he hath this expression, "Any one that begins to be godly, presently he must prepare to suffer reproach from the tongues of adversaries ;" and this was their usual manner of reproach, "What shall we have of you, an Elias? a Jeremy?" And Nazianzen, in one of his orations says, "It is ordinary to reproach, that I cannot think to go free myself." And so Athanasius, they called him Sathanasius, because he was a special instrument against the Arians. And Cyprian, they called him Coprian, one that gathers up dung, as if all the excellent things that he had gathered in his works were but dung.—*Jeremiah Burroughs.*

Verse 3.—"*If I have done this ; if there be iniquity in my hands.*" I deny not but you may, and ought to be sensible of the wrong done to your name, for as "a good name is a precious ointment" (Cant. i. 3), so to have an evil name is a great judgment; and therefore you ought not to be insensible of the wrong done to your name by slanders and reproaches, saying, "Let men speak of me what they please, I care not, so long as I know mine own innocency," for though the testimony of your own innocency be a ground of comfort unto you, yet your care must be not only to approve yourselves unto God, but also unto men, to be as careful of your good names as possibly ye can ; but yet you are not to manifest any distemper or passion upon the reproachful speeches of others against you.—*Thomas Gouge,* 1660.

Verse 3.—It is a sign that there is some good in thee if a wicked world abuse thee. "*Quid mali feci ?*" said Socrates, what evil have I done that this bad man commends me ? The applause of the wicked usually denotes some evil, and their censure imports some good.—*Thomas Watson.*

Verse 3.—"*If there be iniquity in my hands.*" Injustice is ascribed to the *hand*, not because injustice is always, though usually it be, done by the hand. With the hand men take away, and with that men detain the right of others. David speaks thus (1 Chron. xii. 17), "Seeing there is no wrong in mine hands ;" that is, I have done no wrong.—*Joseph Caryl.*

Verses 3, 4.—A good conscience is a flowing spring of assurance. "For our rejoicing is this, the testimony of our conscience, that in simplicity and godly sincerity, not with fleshly wisdom, but by the grace of God, we have had our conversation in the world, and more abundantly to you-ward." 2 Cor. i. 12. "Beloved, if our heart condemn us not, then have we confidence towards God." 1 John iii. 21. A good conscience has sure confidence. He who has it sits in the midst of all combustions and distractions, Noah-like, all sincerity and serenity, uprightness and boldness. What the probationer disciple said to our Saviour, "Master, I will follow thee whithersoever thou goest," that a good conscience says to the believing soul ; I will stand by thee ; I will strengthen thee ; I will uphold thee ; I will be a comfort to thee in life, and a friend to thee in death. "Though all should leave thee, yet will I never forsake thee."—*Thomas Brooks.*

Verse 4.—"*Yea, I have delivered him that without cause is mine enemy.*" Meaning Saul, whose life he twice preserved, once in Engedi, and again when he slept on the plain.—*John Gill.*

6

Verse 4.—"*If I have rewarded evil unto him that was at peace with me.*" To do evil for good, is human corruption ; to do good for good, is civil retribution ; but to do good for evil, is Christian perfection. Though this be not the grace of nature, yet it is the nature of grace.—*William Secker.*

Verse 4.—Then is grace victorious, and then hath a man a noble and brave spirit, not when he is overcome by evil (for that argueth weakness), but when he can overcome evil. And it is God's way to shame the party that did the wrong, and to overcome him too ; it is the best way to get the victory over him. When David had Saul at an advantage in the cave, and cut off the lap of his garment, and did forbear any act of revenge against him, Saul was melted, and said to David, "Thou art more righteous than I." 1 Sam. xxiv. 17. Though he had such a hostile mind against him, and chased and pursued him up and down, yet when David forebore revenge when it was in his power, it overcame him, and he falls a-weeping.—*Thomas Manton.*

Verse 5.—"*Let him tread down my life upon the earth.*" The allusion here is to the manner in which the vanquished were often treated in battle, when they were rode over by horses, or trampled by men in the dust. The idea of David is, that if he was guilty he would be willing that his enemy should triumph over him, should subdue him, should treat him with the utmost indignity and scorn.—*Albert Barnes, in loc.*

Verse 5.—"*Mine honour in the dust.*" When Achilles dragged the body of Hector in the dust around the walls of Troy, he did but carry out the usual manners of those barbarous ages. David dares in his conscious innocence to imprecate such an ignominious fate upon himself if indeed the accusation of the black Benjamite be true. He had need have a golden character who dares to challenge such an ordeal.—*C. H. S.*

Verse 6.—"*The judgment which thou hast ordained.*" In the end of the verse he shows that he asks nothing but what is according to the appointment of God. And this is the rule which ought to be observed by us in our prayers ; we should in everything conform our requests to the divine will, as John also instructs us. 1 John iv. 14. And, indeed, we can never pray in faith unless we attend, in the first place, to what God commands, that our minds may not rashly and at random start aside in desiring more than we are permitted to desire and pray for. David, therefore, in order to pray aright, reposes himself on the word and promise of God ; and the import of his exercise is this : Lord, I am not led by ambition, or foolish headstrong passion, or depraved desire, inconsiderately to ask from thee whatever is pleasing to my flesh ; but it is the clear light of thy word which directs me, and upon it I securely depend.—*John Calvin.*

Verse 7.—"*The congregation of the people:*" either, 1. A great number of all sorts of people, who shall observe thy justice, and holiness, and goodness in pleading my righteous cause against my cruel and implacable oppressor. Or rather, 2. The whole body of thy people Israel, by whom both these Hebrew words are commonly ascribed in Holy Scripture. "*Compass thee about ;*" they will, and I, as their king and ruler in thy stead, will take care that they shall come from all parts and meet together to worship thee, which in Saul's time they have grossly neglected, and been permitted to neglect, and to offer to thee praises and sacrifices for thy favour to me, and for the manifold benefits which they shall enjoy by my means, and under my government. "*For their sakes ;*" or, *for its sake, i.e.,* for the sake of thy congregation, which now is woefully dissipated and oppressed, and has in a great measure lost all administration of justice, and exercise of religion. "*Return thou on high,*" or, *return to thy high place, i.e.* to thy tribunal, to sit there and judge my cause. An allusion to earthly tribunals, which generally are set up on high above the people. 1 Kings x. 19.—*Matthew Pool,* 1624—1679.

Verse 8.—Believers ! let not the terror of that day dispirit you when you meditate upon it ; let those who have slighted the Judge, and continue enemies to him and the way of holiness, droop and hang down their heads when they think of his coming ; but lift ye up your heads with joy, for the last day will be your best day. The Judge is your Head and Husband, your Redeemer, and your Advocate. Ye must appear before the judgment-seat ; but ye shall not come into condemnation. His coming will not be against you, but for you. It is otherwise with unbelievers, a *neglected Saviour* will be a *severe Judge.—Thomas Boston*, 1676—1732.

Verse 9.—" *The righteous God trieth the hearts and reins.*" As common experience shows that the workings of the mind, particularly the passions of joy, grief, and fear, have a very remarkable effect on the *reins* or *kidneys* (see Prov. xxiii. 16 ; Psalm lxxiii. 21), so from their retired situation in the body, and their being hid in fat, they are often used to denote the most secret workings and affections of the soul. And to " see or examine the *reins*," is to see or examine those most secret thoughts or desires of the soul.—*John Parkhurst*, 1762.

Verse 9 (*last clause*).—" *The righteous God trieth the hearts and reins.*"

" I that alone am infinite, can try
How deep within itself thine heart doth lie.
Thy seamen's plummet can but reach the ground,
I find that which thine heart itself ne'er found."

Francis Quarles, 1592—1644.

Verse 9.—" *The heart*," may signify the cogitations, and the " *reins*" the affections.—*Henry Ainsworth.*

Verse 10.—" *My defence is of God.*" Literally, " *My shield is upon God,*" like Psalm lxii. 8, " My salvation is *upon God.*" The idea may be taken from the armour-bearer, ever ready at hand to give the needed weapon to the warrior. *Andrew A. Bonar.*

Verse 11.—" *God judgeth the righteous,*" etc. Many learned disputes have arisen as to the meaning of this verse ; and it must be confessed that its real import is by no means easily determined : without the words written in italics, which are not in the original, it will read thus, " God judgeth the righteous, and God is angry every day." The question still will be, is this a good rendering ? To this question it may be replied, that there is strong evidence for a contrary one. AINSWORTH translates it, " God *is* a just judge ; and God angrily threateneth every day." With this corresponds the reading of COVERDALE's Bible, " God is a righteous judge, and God is ever threatening." In King Edward's Bible, of 1549, the reading is the same. But there is another class of critics who adopt quite a different view of the text, and apparently with much colour of argument. BISHOP HORSLEY reads the verse, " God is a righteous judge, although he is not angry every day." In this rendering he seems to have followed most of the ancient versions. The VULGATE reads it, " God is a judge, righteous, strong, and patient ; will he be angry every day ?" The SEPTUAGINT reads it, " God is a righteous judge, strong, and longsuffering ; not bringing forth his anger every day." The SYRIAC has it, " God is the judge of righteousness ; he is not angry every day." In this view of the text Dr. A. Clarke agrees, and expresses it as his opinion that the text was first corrupted by the CHALDEE. This learned divine proposes to restore the text thus, " אֵל, *el*, with the vowel point *tseri*, signifies God ; אַל, *al*, the same letters, with the point *pathach*, signifies *not.*" There is by this view of the original no repetition of the divine name in the verse, so that it will simply read, as thus restored, " God is a righteous judge, and is NOT angry every day." The text at large, as is intimated in the VULGATE, SEPTUAGINT, and some other ancient versions, conveys a strong intimation of the longsuffering of God, whose hatred of sin is unchangeable, but whose anger against transgressors is marked by infinite patience, and does not burst forth in vengeance every day.—*John Morison, in " An Exposition of the Book of Psalms,"* 1829.

Verse 11.—" *God is angry.*" The original expression here is very forcible. The true idea of it appears to be, to *froth* or *foam at the mouth* with indignation. *Richard Mant, D.D.,* 1824.

Verses 11, 12.—God hath set up his royal standard in defiance of all the sons and daughters of apostate Adam, who from his own mouth are proclaimed rebels and traitors to his crown and dignity ; and as against such he hath taken the field, as with fire and sword, to be avenged on them. Yea, he gives the world sufficient testimony of his incensed wrath, by that of it which is revealed from heaven daily in the judgments executed upon sinners, and those many but of a span long, before they can show what nature they have by actual sin, yet crushed to death by God's righteous foot, only for the viperous kind of which they come. At every door where sin sets its foot, there the wrath of God meets us. Every faculty of soul, and member of body, are used as a weapon of unrighteousness against God ; so every one hath its portion of wrath, even to the tip of the tongue. As man is sinful all over, so is he cursed all over. Inside and outside, soul and body, is written all with woes and curses, so close and full, that there is not room for another to interline, or add to what God hath written.— *William Gurnall.*

Verses 11—13.—The idea of God's righteousness must have possessed great vigour to render such a representation possible. There are some excellent remarks upon the ground of it in Luther, who, however, too much overlooks the fact, that the psalmist presents before his eyes this form of an angry and avenging God, primarily with the view of strengthening by its consideration his own hope, and pays too little regard to the distinction between the psalmist, who only indirectly teaches what he described as part of his own inward experience, and the prophet : "The prophet takes a lesson from a coarse human similitude, in order that he might inspire terror unto the ungodly. For he speaks against stupid and hardened people, who would not apprehend the reality of a divine judgment, of which he had just spoken ; but they might possibly be brought to consider this by greater earnestness on the part of man. Now, the prophet is not satisfied with thinking of the sword, but he adds thereto the bow ; even this does not satisfy him, but he describes how it is already stretched, and aim is taken, and the arrows are applied to it as here follows. So hard, stiff-necked, and unabashed are the ungodly, that however many threatenings may be urged against them, they will still remain unmoved. But in these words he forcibly describes how God's anger presses hard upon the ungodly, though they will never understand this until they actually experience it. It is also to be remarked here, that we have had so frightful a threatening and indignation against the ungodly in no Psalm before this ; neither has the Spirit of God attacked them with so many words. Then in the following verses, he also recounts their plans and purposes, shows how these shall not be in vain, but shall return again upon their own head. So that it clearly and manifestly appears to all those who suffer wrong and reproach, as a matter of consolation, that God hates such revilers and slanderers above all other characters."—*E. W. Hengstenberg, in loc.,* 1845.

Verse 12.—" *If he turn not,*" etc. How few do believe what a quarrel God hath with wicked men ? And that not only with the loose, but the formal and hypocritical also ? If we did we would tremble as much to be among them as to be in a house that is falling ; we would endeavour to " save" ourselves " from this untoward generation." The apostle would not so have adjured them, so charged, so entreated them, had he not known the danger of wicked company. " *God is angry with the wicked every day ;*" *his bow is bent, the arrows are on the string ;* the instruments for their ruin are all prepared. And is it safe to be there where the arrows of God are ready to fly about our ears ?

How was the apostle afraid to be in the bath with Cerinthus! "Depart," saith God by Moses, "from the tents of Korah, Dathan, and Abiram, lest ye be consumed in all their sins." How have the baskets of good figs suffered with the bad! Is it not prejudicial to the gold to be with the dross? Lot had been ruined by his neighbourhood to the Sodomites if God had not wrought wonderfully for his deliverance. Will you put God to work miracles to save you from your ungodly company? It is dangerous being in the road with thieves whilst God's hue and cry of vengeance is at their backs. "A companion of fools shall be destroyed." The very beasts may instruct you to consult better for your security: the very deer are afraid of a wounded chased deer, and therefore for their preservation thrust him out of their company.—*Lewis Stuckley.*

Verse 12.—"*If he turn not, he will whet his sword,*" etc. The whetting of the sword is but to give a keener edge that it may cut the deeper. God is silent as long as the sinner will let him; but when the sword is whet, it is to cut; and when the bow is bent, it is to kill; and woe be to that man who is the butt.—*William Secker.*

Verse 13.—"*He hath also prepared for him the instruments of death; he ordaineth his arrows against the persecutors.*" It is said that God hath ordained his arrows against the persecutors; the word signifies such as burn in anger and malice against the godly; and the word translated *ordained,* signifies God hath wrought his arrows; he doth not shoot them at random, but he works them against the wicked. Illiricus hath a story which may well be a commentary upon this text in both the parts of it. One Felix, Earl of Wartenberg, one of the captains of the Emperor Charles V., swore in the presence of divers at supper, that before he died he would ride up to the spurs in the blood of the Lutherans. Here was one that burned in malice, but behold how God works his arrows against him; that very night the hand of God so struck him, that he was strangled and choked in his own blood; so he rode not, but bathed himself, not up to the spurs, but up to the throat, not in the blood of the Lutherans, but in his own blood before he died.—*Jeremiah Burroughs.*

Verse 13.—"*He ordaineth his arrows.*" This might more exactly be rendered, "He maketh his arrows burning." This image would seem to be deduced from the use of fiery arrows.—*John Kitto,* 1804—1854.

Verse 14.—"*Behold he travaileth with iniquity,*" etc. The words express the *conception, birth, carriage* and *miscarriage,* of a *plot* against David. In which you may consider:—(1.) What his *enemies* did. (2.) What *God* did. (3.) What *we all* should do: his enemies' *intention,* God's *prevention,* and our *duty;* his enemies' intention, *he travaileth with iniquity, and conceiveth mischief;* God's prevention, *he brought forth a lie;* our duty, *Behold* . . . . . Observe the aggravation of the sin, *he conceiveth.* He was not put upon it, or forced into it: it was voluntary. The more liberty we have not to sin, makes our sin the greater. He did not this in passion, but in cold blood. The less will, less sin.—*Richard Silbs.*

Verse 14.—"*He travaileth with iniquity, and hath conceived mischief.*" All note that conceiving is before travailing, but here travailing, as a woman in labour, goeth first; the reason whereof is, that the wicked are so hotly set upon the evil which they maliciously intend, that they would be immediately acting of it if they could tell how, even before they have conceived by what means; but in fine they bring forth but a lie, that is, they find that their own hearts lied to them, when they promised good success, but they had evil. For their haste to perpetrate mischief is intimated in the word rendered "*persecutors*" (verse 13), which properly signifieth *ardentes, burning;* that is, with a desire to do mischief—and this admits of no delay. A notable common-place, both setting forth the evil case of the wicked, especially attempting anything against the righteous, to move them to repentance—for thou hast God for thine enemy warring against thee, whose force thou canst not resist—and the greedy desire of the wicked to be evil, but their conception shall all prove abortive.—*J. Mayer, in loc.*

Verse 14.—" *And hath brought forth falsehood.*" Every sin is a lie.—*Augustine.*

Verse 14.　　　" Earth's entertainments are like those of Jael,
　　　　　　　Her left hand brings me milk, her right, a nail."

　　　　　　　　　　　　　　　　　　　　　　Thomas Fuller.

Verses 14, 15.·—" *They have digged a pit for us*"—and that low, unto hell—
" *and are fallen into it themselves.*"
　　　　　　" No juster law can be devised or made,
　　　　　　　Than that sin's agents fall by their own trade."

The order of hell proceeds with the same degrees ; though it give a greater
portion, yet still a just proportion, of torment.　These wretched guests were
too busy with the waters of sin ; behold, now they are in the depth of a pit,
" where no water is."　Dives, that wasted so many tuns of wine, cannot now
procure water, not a pot of water, not a handful of water, not a drop of water,
to cool his tongue.　*Desideravit guttam, qui non dedit micam.* A just recompense !　He would not give a crumb ; he shall not have a drop.　Bread
hath no smaller fragment than a crumb, water no less fraction than a drop.　As
he denied the least comfort to Lazarus living, so Lazarus shall not bring him
the least comfort dead.　Thus the pain for sin answers the pleasure of sin. . . .
Thus damnable sins shall have semblable punishments ; and as Augustine of the
tongue, so we may say of any member . . . . . If it will not serve God in
action, it shall serve him in passion.—*Thomas Adams.*

Verse 15.—" *He made a pit, and digged it.*"　The practice of making pitfalls was
anciently not only employed for ensnaring wild beasts, but was also a stratagem
used against men by the enemy, in time of war.　The idea, therefore, refers to a
man who, having made such a pit, whether for man or beast, and covered it
over so as completely to disguise the danger, did himself inadvertently tread on
his own trap, and fall into the pit he had prepared for another.—*Pictorial Bible.*

Verse 16.—That most witty of commentators, Old Master Trapp, tells the
following notable anecdote, in illustration of this verse :—That was a very
remarkable instance of Dr. Story, who, escaping out of prison in Queen Elizabeth's days, got to Antwerp, and there thinking himself out of the reach of
God's rod, he got commission under the Duke of Alva to search all ships coming
thither for English books.　But one Parker, an English merchant, trading to
Antwerp, laid his snare fair (saith our chronicler), to catch this foul bird, causing
secret notice to be given to Story, that in his ship were stores of heretical
books, with other intelligence that might stand him in stead.　The Canonist
conceiving that all was quite sure, hasted to the ship, where, with looks very
big upon the poor mariners, each cabin, chest, and corner above-board were
searched, and some things found to draw him further on : so that the hatches
must be opened, which seemed to be unwillingly done, and great signs of fear
were showed by their faces.　This drew on the Doctor to descend into the
hold, where now in the trap the mouse might well gnaw, but could not get out,
for the hatches were down, and the sails hoisted up, which, with a merry gale,
were blown into England, where ere long he was arraigned, and condemned of
high treason, and accordingly executed at Tyburn, as he had well deserven.

Verse 16.—The story of Phalaris's bull, invented for the torment of others,
and serving afterwards for himself, is notorious in heathen story. . . . . . .
It was a voluntary judgment which Archbishop Cranmer inflicted on himself
when he thrust that very hand into the fire, and burnt it, with which he had
signed to the popish articles, crying out, " *Oh, my unworthy right hand !*"
but who will deny that the hand of the Almighty was also concerned in it ?—
William Turner in " *Divine Judgments by way of Retaliation,*" 1697.

Verse 17.—To bless God for mercies is the way to increase them ; to bless him
for miseries is the way to remove them : no good lives so long as that which is
thankfully improved ; no evil dies so soon as that which is patiently endured.—
William Dyer.

---

* Aug. Hom. 7.

HINTS TO THE VILLAGE PREACHER.

Verse 1.—The necessity of faith when we address ourselves to God. Show the worthlessness of prayer without trust in the Lord.

Verses 1, 2.—Viewed as a prayer for deliverance from all enemies, especially Satan the lion.

Verse 3.—Self-vindication before men. When possible, judicious, or service-able. With remarks upon the spirit in which it should be attempted.

Verse 4.—" *The best revenge.*" Evil for good is devil-like, evil for evil is beast-like, good for good is man-like, good for evil is God-like.

Verse 6.—How and in what sense divine anger may become the hope of the righteous.

Fire fought by fire, or man's anger overcome by God's anger.

Verse 7.—" *The congregation of the people.*" 1. Who they are. 2. Why they congregate together with one another. 3. Where they congregate. 4. Why they choose such a person to be the centre of their congregation.

Verse 7.—The gathering of the saints around the Lord Jesus.

Verse 7 (*last clause*).—The coming of Christ to judgment for the good of his saints.

Verse 8.—The character of the Judge before whom we all must stand.

Verse 9 (*first clause*).—(1) By changing their hearts ; or (2) by restraining their wills, (3) or depriving them of power, (4) or removing them. Show the times when, the reasons why, such a prayer should be offered, and how, in the first sense, we may labour for its accomplishment.

Verse 9.—This verse contains two grand prayers, and a noble proof that the Lord can grant them.

Verse 9.—The period of sin, and the perpetuity of the righteous.—*Matthew Henry.*

Verse 9.—" *Establish the just.*" By what means and in what sense the just are established, or, the true established church.

Verse 9 (*last clause*).—God's trial of men's hearts.

Verse 10.—" *Upright in heart.*" Explain the character.

Verse 10.—The believer's trust in God, and God's care over him. Show the action of faith in procuring defence and protection, and of that defence upon our faith by strengthening it, etc.

Verse 11.—The Judge, and the two persons upon their trial.

Verse 11 (*second clause*).—God's present, daily, constant, and vehement anger, against the wicked.

Verse 12.—See " Spurgeon's Sermons," No. 106. " Turn or Burn."

Verses 14, 15, 16.—Illustrate by three figures the devices and defeat of perse-cutors.

Verse 17.—The excellent duty of praise.

Verse 17.—View the verse in connection with the subject of the Psalm, and show how the deliverance of the righteous, and the destruction of the wicked are themes for song.

PSALM VIII.

TITLE.—"To the Chief Musician upon Gittith, a Psalm of David." *We are not clear upon the meaning of the word Gittith. Some think it refers to Gath, and may refer to a tune commonly sung there, or an instrument of music there invented, or a song of Obededom the Gittite, in whose house the ark rested, or, better still, a song sung over Goliath of Gath. Others, tracing the Hebrew to its root, conceive it to mean a song for the winepress, a joyful hymn for the treaders of grapes. The term Gittith is applied to two other Psalms, (lxxxi. and lxxxiv.) both of which, being of a joyous character, it may be concluded, that where we find that word in the title, we may look for a hymn of delight.*

We may style this Psalm the Song of the Astronomer: let us go abroad and sing it beneath the starry heavens at eventide, for it is very probable that in such a position, it first occurred to the poet's mind. Dr. Chalmers says, " There is much in the scenery of a nocturnal sky, to lift the soul to pious contemplation. That moon, and these stars, what are they? They are detached from the world, and they lift us above it. We feel withdrawn from the earth, and rise in lofty abstraction from this little theatre of human passions and human anxieties. The mind abandons itself to reverie, and is transferred in the ecstasy of its thought to distant and unexplored regions. It sees nature in the simplicity of her great elements, and it sees the God of nature invested with the high attributes of wisdom and majesty."

DIVISION.—*The first and last verses are a sweet song of admiration, in which the excellence of the name of God is extolled. The intermediate verses are made up of holy wonder at the Lord's greatness in creation, and at his condescension towards man. Poole, in his annotations, has well said, " It is a great question among interpreters, whether this Psalm speaks of man in general, and of the honour which God puts upon him in his creation; or only of the man Christ Jesus. Possibly both may be reconciled and put together, and the controversy, if rightly stated, may be ended, for the scope and business of this Psalm seems plainly to be this: to display and celebrate the great love and kindness of God to mankind, not only in his creation, but especially in his redemption by Jesus Christ, whom, as he was man, he advanced to the honour and dominion here mentioned, that he might carry on his great and glorious work. So Christ is the principal subject of this Psalm, and it is interpreted of him, both by our Lord himself (Matt. xxi. 16), and by his holy apostle (1 Cor. xv. 27 ; Heb. ii. 6, 7).*

EXPOSITION.

O LORD our Lord, how excellent *is* thy name in all the earth ! who hast set thy glory above the heavens.

Unable to express the glory of God, the Psalmist utters a note of exclamation. O Jehovah our Lord ! We need not wonder at this, for no heart can measure, no tongue can utter, the half of the greatness of Jehovah. The whole creation is full of his glory and radiant with the excellency of his power ; his goodness and his wisdom are manifested on every hand. The countless myriads of terrestrial beings, from man the head, to the creeping worm at the foot, are all supported and nourished by the Divine bounty. The solid fabric of the universe leans upon his eternal arm. Universally is he present, and everywhere is his name excellent. God worketh ever and everywhere. There is no *place* where God is not. The miracles of his power await us on all sides. Traverse the silent valleys where the rocks enclose you on either side, rising like the battlements of heaven till you can see but a strip of the blue sky far overhead ; you may be the only traveller who has passed through that glen ; the bird may start up affrighted, and the moss may tremble beneath the first tread of human foot ; but God is there in a thousand wonders, upholding yon rocky barriers, filling the flowercups with their perfume, and refreshing the lonely pines with the breath of his mouth. Descend, if you will, into the lowest depths of the ocean, where undisturbed the water sleeps, and the very sand is motionless in unbroken quiet, but the glory of the Lord is there, revealing its excellence in the silent palace of the sea. Borrow the wings of the morning and fly to the uttermost parts of the sea, but God is there. Mount to the highest heaven, or dive into the deepest hell, and God is in both hymned in everlasting song, or justified in terrible vengeance. Everywhere, and in every place, God dwells and is manifestly at work. Nor on earth alone is Jehovah extolled, for his brightness shines forth in the firmament above the earth. His glory exceeds the glory of the starry heavens ; above the region of the stars he hath set fast his everlasting throne, and there he dwells in light ineffable. Let us adore him "who alone spreadeth out the heavens, and treadeth upon the waves of the sea ; who maketh Arcturus, Orion, and Pleiades, and the chambers of the south." (Job ix. 8, 9.) We can scarcely find more fitting words than those of Nehemiah, "Thou, even thou, art Lord alone ; thou hast made heaven, the heaven of heavens, with all their host, the earth, and all things that are therein, the seas, and all that is therein, and thou preservest them all ; and the host of heaven worshippeth thee." Returning to the text we are led to observe that this psalm is addressed to God, because none but the Lord himself can fully know his own glory. The believing heart is ravished with what it sees, but God only knows the glory of God. What a sweetness lies in the little word _our,_ how much is God's glory endeared to us when we consider our interest in him as our Lord. _How excellent is thy name!_ no words can express that excellency ; and therefore it is left as a note of exclamation. The very _name_ of Jehovah is excellent, what must his person be. Note the fact that even the heavens cannot contain his glory, it is set _above the heavens,_ since it is and ever must be too great for the creature to express. When wandering amid the Alps, we felt that the Lord was infinitely greater than all his grandest works, and under that feeling we roughly wrote these few lines :—

Yet in all these how great soe'er they be,
We see not Him. The glass is all too dense
And dark, or else our earthborn eyes too dim.

Yon Alps, that lift their heads above the clouds
And hold familiar converse with the stars,
Are dust, at which the balance trembleth not,
Compared with His divine immensity.
The snow-crown'd summits fail to set Him forth,
Who dwelleth in Eternity, and bears
Alone, the name of High and Lofty One.
Depths unfathomed are too shallow to express
The wisdom and the knowledge of the Lord.
The mirror of the creatures has no space
To bear the image of the Infinite.
'Tis true the Lord hath fairly writ his name,
And set his seal upon creation's brow.
But as the skilful potter much excels
The vessel which he fashions on the wheel,
E'en so, but in proportion greater far,
Jehovah's self transcends his noblest works.
Earth's ponderous wheels would break, her axles snap,
If freighted with the load of Deity.
Space is too narrow for the Eternal's rest,
And time too short a footstool for his throne.
E'en avalanche and thunder lack a voice,
To utter the full volume of his praise.
How then can I declare him ? Where are words
With which my glowing tongue may speak his name ?
Silent I bow, and humbly I adore.

2 Out of the mouth of babes and sucklings hast thou ordained strength because of thine enemies, that thou mightest still the enemy and the avenger.

Nor only in the heavens above is the Lord seen, but the earth beneath is telling forth his majesty. In the sky, the massive orbs, rolling in their stupendous grandeur, are witnesses of his power in great things, while here below, the lisping utterances of babes are the manifestations of his strength in little ones. How often will children tell us of a God whom we have forgotten! How doth their simple prattle refute those learned fools who deny the being of God! Many men have been made to hold their tongues, while sucklings have borne witness to the glory of the God of heaven. It is singular how clearly the history of the church expounds this verse. Did not the children cry "Hosannah!" in the temple, when proud Pharisees were silent and contemptuous? and did not the Saviour quote these very words as a justification of their infantile cries? Early church history records many amazing instances of the testimony of children for the truth of God, but perhaps more modern instances will be the most interesting. Fox tells us, in the Book of Martyrs, that when Mr. Lawrence was burnt in Colchester, he was carried to the fire in a chair, because, through the cruelty of the Papists, he could not stand upright, several young children came about the fire, and cried, as well as they could speak, "Lord, strengthen thy servant, and keep thy promise." God answered their prayer, for Mr. Lawrence died as firmly and calmly as any one could wish to breathe his last. When one of the Popish chaplains told Mr. Wishart, the great Scotch martyr, that he had a devil in him, a child that stood by cried out, "A devil cannot speak such words as yonder man speaketh." One more instance is still nearer to our time. In a postscript to one of his letters, in which he details his persecution when first preaching in Moorfields, Whitfield says, "I cannot help adding that several little boys and girls, who were fond of sitting round me on the pulpit while I preached, and handed to me people's notes—though they were often pelted with eggs, dirt, &c., thrown at me—never once gave way; but on the contrary, every time I was struck, turned up their little weeping eyes, and seemed to wish they could receive the blows for me. God make them, in their growing years, great and living martyrs for him who, out of the mouths of babes and sucklings, perfects praise!" He who delights in the songs of angels is pleased to honour himself in the eyes of his enemies by the praises of little children. What a contrast between the glory above the heavens, and the mouths of babes and sucklings! yet by both the name of God is made excellent.

3 When I consider thy heavens, the work of thy fingers, the moon and the stars, which thou hast ordained;
4 What is man, that thou art mindful of him? and the son of man, that thou visitest him?

At the close of that excellent little manual entitled "The Solar System," written by Dr. Dick, we find an eloquent passage which beautifully expounds the text:—A survey of the solar system has a tendency to moderate the pride of man and to promote humility. Pride is one of the distinguishing characteristics of puny man, and has been one of the chief causes of all the contentions, wars, devastations, systems of slavery, and ambitious projects which have desolated and demoralized our sinful world. Yet there is no disposition more incongruous to the character and circumstances of man. Perhaps there are no rational beings throughout the universe among whom pride would appear more unseemly or incompatible than in man, considering the situation in which he is placed. He is exposed to numerous degradations and calamities, to the rage of storms and tempests, the devastations of earthquakes and volcanoes, the fury of whirlwinds, and the tempestuous billows of the ocean, to the ravages of the sword, famine, pestilence, and numerous diseases; and at length he must sink into the grave, and his body must become the companion of worms! The most dignified and haughty of the sons of men are liable to these and similar degradations as well as the meanest of the human family. Yet, in such circumstances, man—that puny worm of the dust, whose knowledge is so limited, and whose follies are so numerous and glaring—has the effrontery to strut in all the haughtiness of pride, and to glory in his shame.

When other arguments and motives produce little effect on certain minds, no considerations seem likely to have a more powerful tendency to counteract this deplorable propensity in human beings, than those which are borrowed from the objects connected with astronomy. They show us what an insignificant being— what a mere atom, indeed, man appears amidst the immensity of creation! Though he is an object of the paternal care and mercy of the Most High, yet he is but as a grain of sand to the whole earth, when compared to the countless myriads of beings that people the amplitudes of creation. What is the whole of this globe on which we dwell compared with the solar system, which contains a mass of matter ten thousand times greater? What is it in comparison of the hundred millions of suns and worlds which by the telescope have been descried throughout the starry regions? What, then, is a kingdom, a province, or a baronial territory, of which we are as proud as if we were the lords of the universe and for which we engage in so much devastation and carnage? What are they, when set in competition with the glories of the sky? Could we take our station on the lofty pinnacles of heaven, and look down on this scarcely distinguishable speck of earth, we should be ready to exclaim with Seneca, "Is it to this little spot that the great designs and vast desires of men are confined? Is it for this there is so much disturbance of nations, so much carnage, and so many ruinous wars? Oh, the folly of deceived men, to imagine great kingdoms in the compass of an atom, to raise armies to decide a point of earth with the sword!" Dr. Chalmers, in his Astronomical Discourses, very truthfully says, "We gave you but a feeble image of our comparative insignificance, when we said that the glories of an extended forest would suffer no more from the fall of a single leaf, than the glories of this extended universe would suffer though the globe we tread upon, 'and all that it inherits, should dissolve.'"

5 For thou hast made him a little lower than the angels, and hast crowned him with glory and honour.

6 Thou madest him to have dominion over the works of thy hands; thou hast put all *things* under his feet:

7 All sheep and oxen, yea, and the beasts of the field;

8 The fowl of the air, and the fish of the sea, *and whatsoever* passeth through the paths of the sea.

These verses may set forth man's position among the creatures before he fell; but as they are, by the apostle Paul, appropriated to man as represented by the Lord Jesus, it is best to give most weight to that meaning. In order of dignity, man stood next to the angels, and a little lower than they; in the Lord Jesus this was accomplished, for he was made a little lower than the angels by the suffering of death. Man in Eden had the full command of all creatures, and they came before him to receive their names as an act of homage to him as the vicegerent of God to them. Jesus in his glory, is now Lord, not only of all living, but of all created things, and, with the exception of him who put all things under him, Jesus is Lord of all, and his elect, in him, are raised to a dominion wider than that of the first Adam, as shall be more clearly seen at his coming. Well might the Psalmist wonder at the singular exaltation of man in the scale of being, when he marked his utter nothingness in comparison with the starry universe.

Thou madest him a little lower than the angels—a little lower in nature, since they are immortal, and but a little, because time is short; and when that is over, saints are no longer lower than the angels. The margin reads it, "A little while inferior to." *Thou crownest him.* The dominion that God has bestowed on man is a great *glory and honour* to him ; for all dominion is honour, and the highest is that which wears the crown. A full list is given of the subjugated creatures, to show that all the dominion lost by sin is restored in Christ Jesus. Let none of us permit the possession of any earthly creature to be a snare to us, but let us remember that we are to reign over them, and not to allow them to reign over us. Under our feet we must keep the world, and we must shun that base spirit which is content to let worldly cares and pleasures sway the empire of the immortal soul.

9 O LORD our Lord, how excellent is thy name in all the earth !

Here, like a good composer, the poet returns to his key-note, falling back, as it were, into his first state of wondering adoration. What he started with as a proposition in the first verse, he closes with as a well proven conclusion, with a sort of *quod erat demonstrandum.* O for grace to walk worthy of that excellent name which has been named upon us, and which we are pledged to magnify !

EXPLANATORY NOTES AND QUAINT SAYINGS.

Title.—" *Gittith,*" was probably a musical instrument used at their rejoicings after the vintage. The vintage closed the civil year of the Jews, and this Psalm directs us to the latter-day glory, when the Lord shall be King over all the earth, having subdued all his enemies. It is very evident that the vintage was adopted as a figurative representation of the final destruction of all God's enemies. · Isaiah lxiii. 1—6 ; Rev. xix. 18—20. The ancient Jewish interpreters so understood this Psalm, and apply it to the mystic vintage. We may then consider this interesting composition as a prophetic anticipation of the kingdom of Christ, to be established in glory and honour in the " world to come," the habitable world. Heb. ii. 5. We see not yet all things put under his feet, but we are sure that the Word of God shall be fulfilled, and every enemy, Satan, death, and hell, shall be for ever subdued and destroyed, and creation itself delivered from the bondage of corruption into the glorious liberty of the children of God. Rom. viii. 17—23. In the use of this Psalm, then, we anticipate that victory, and in the praise we thus celebrate, we go on from strength to strength, till, with him who is our glorious Head, we appear in Zion before God.—*W. Wilson, D.D., in loc.*

Whole Psalm.—Now, consider but the scope of the Psalm, as the apostle quoteth it to prove the world to come. Heb. ii. Any one that reads the Psalm would think that the psalmist doth but set forth old Adam in his kingdom, in his paradise, made a little lower than the angels—for we have spirits wrapped up in flesh and blood, whereas they are spirits simply—a degree lower, as if they were dukes, and we marquises ; one would think, I say, that this were all his meaning, and that it is applied to Christ but by way of allusion. But the truth is, the apostle bringeth it in to prove and to convince these Hebrews, to whom he wrote, that that Psalm was meant of Christ, of that man whom they expected to be the Messiah, the Man Christ Jesus. And that he doth it, I prove by the sixth verse— it is the observation that Beza hath—" One in a certain place," quoting David, διεμαρτύρατο, hath testified ; so we may translate it, hath testified it, *etiam atque etiam,* testified most expressly ; he bringeth an express proof for it that it was meant of the Man Christ Jesus ; therefore it is not an allusion. And indeed it was Beza that did first begin that interpretation that I read of, and himself therefore doth excuse it and make an apology for it, that he diverteth out of the common road, though since many others have followed him.

Now the scope of the Psalm is plainly this : in Rom. v. 14, you read that Adam was a type of him that was to come. Now in Psalm viii., you find there Adam's world, the type of a world to come ; he was the first Adam, and had a world, so the second Adam hath a world also appointed for him ; there is his oxen and his sheep, and the fowls of the air, whereby are meant other things, devils perhaps, and wicked men, the prince of the air ; as by the heavens there, the angels, or the apostles rather—" the heavens declare the glory of God ;" that is applied to the apostles, that were preachers of the gospel.

To make this plain to you, that that Psalm where the phrase is used, " All things under his feet," and quoted by the apostle in Eph. i. 22—therefore it is proper—was not meant of man in innocency, but of the Messiah, the Lord Jesus Christ ; and therefore, answerably, that the world there is not this world, but a world on purpose made for this Messiah, as the other was for Adam.

First, it was not meant of man in innocency properly and principally. Why ? Because in the first verse he saith, " Out of the mouths of babes and suck-lings hast thou ordained strength." There were no babes in the time of Adam's innocency, he fell before there were any. Secondly, he addeth, " That thou mightest still the enemy and the avenger ;" the devil that is, for he showed him-self the enemy there, to be a manslayer from the beginning. God would use man to still him ; alas ! he overcame Adam presently. It must be meant of another therefore, one that is able to still this enemy and avenger.

Then he saith, " How excellent is thy name in all the earth ! who hast set thy glory above the heavens." Adam had but paradise, he never propagated God's name over all the earth ; he did not continue so long before he fell as to beget sons ; much less did he found it in the heavens.

Again, verse 4, " What is man, and the son of man ?" Adam, though he was man, yet he was not the son of man ; he is called indeed, " the son of God " (Luke iii. 38), but he was not *filius hominis.* I remember Ribera urgeth that.

But take an argument the apostle himself useth to prove it. This man, saith he, must have all subject to him ; all but God, saith he ; he must have the angels subject to him, for he hath put all principalities and powers under his feet, saith he. This could not be Adam, it could not be the man that had this world in a state of innocency ; much less had Adam all under his feet. No, my brethren, it was too great a vassalage for Adam to have the creatures thus bow to him. But they are thus to Jesus Christ, angels and all ; they are all under his feet, he is far above them.

Secondly, it is not meant of man fallen, that is as plain ; the apostle himself saith so. " We see not," saith he, " all things subject unto him." Some think that it is meant as an objection that the apostle answereth ; but it is indeed to prove that man fallen cannot be meant in Psalm viii. Why ? Because, saith he, we do not see anything, all things at least, subject unto him ; you have not any one man, or the whole race of man, to whom all things have been subject ; the creatures are sometimes injurious to him. We do not see him, saith he ; that is, the nature of man in general considered. Take all the monarchs in the world, they never conquered the whole world ; there was never any one man that was a sinner that had all subject to him. " But we see," saith he—mark the opposition—"but we see Jesus," that Man, " crowned with glory and honour;" therefore, it is this Man, and no man else ; the opposition implieth it." . . . . So now it remaineth, then, that it is only Christ, God-man, that is meant in Psalm viii. And indeed, and in truth, Christ himself interpreteth the Psalm of himself ; you have two witnesses to confirm it, Christ himself and the apostle. Matt. xxi. 16. When they cried hosanna to Christ, or " save now," and made him the Saviour of the world, the Pharisees were angry, our Saviour confuteth them by this very Psalm : " Have ye not read," saith he, " out of the mouths of babes and sucklings thou hast perfected praise ?" He quoteth this very Psalm which speaks of himself ; and Paul, by his warrant, and perhaps from that hint, doth thus argue out of it, and convince the Jews by it.—*Thomas Goodwin.*

Verse 1.—"*How excellent is thy name in all the earth !*" How illustrious is the name of Jesus throughout the world ! His incarnation, birth, humble and obscure life, preaching, miracles, passion, death, resurrection, and ascension, are celebrated through the whole world. His religion, the gifts and graces of his Spirit, his people—Christians, his gospel, and the preachers of it, are everywhere spoken of. No name is so universal, no power and influence so generally felt, as those of the Saviour of mankind. Amen.—*Adam Clarke.*

Verse 1.—"*Above the heavens ;*" not in the heavens, but "*above the heavens ;*" even greater, beyond, and higher than they ; "angels, principalities, and powers, being made subject unto him." As Paul says, he hath "ascended up far above all heavens." And with this his glory above the heavens is connected, his sending forth his name upon earth through his Holy Spirit. As the apostle adds in this passage, "He hath ascended up far above all heavens ; and he gave some apostles." And thus here : "Thy name excellent in all the world ;" "Thy glory above the heavens."—*Isaac Williams.*

Verse 2.—"*Out of the mouth of babes and sucklings hast thou ordained strength,*" etc. In a prophetical manner, speaking of that which was to be done by children many hundreds of years after, for the asserting of his infinite mercy in sending his Son Jesus Christ into the world to save us from our sins. For so the Lord applieth their crying, "Hosannah to the Son of David" in the temple. And thus both Basil and other ancients, and some new writers also understand it. But Calvin will have it meant of God's wonderful providing for them, by turning their mothers' blood into milk, and giving them the faculty to suck, thus nourishing and preserving them, which sufficiently convinceth all gainsayers of God's wonderful providence towards the weakest and most shiftless of all creatures.—*John Mayer,* 1653.

Verse 2.—Who are these "*babes and sucklings*" ? 1. Man in general, who springeth from so weak and poor a beginning as that of babes and sucklings, yet is at length advanced to such power as to grapple with, and overcome the enemy and the avenger. 2. David in particular, who being but a ruddy youth, God used him as an instrument to discomfit Goliath of Gath. 3. More especially our Lord Jesus Christ, who assuming our nature and all the sinless infirmities of it, and submitting to the weakness of an infant, and after dying is gone in the same nature to reign in heaven, till he hath brought all his enemies under his feet. Psalm cx. 1., and 1 Cor. xv. 27. Then was our human nature exalted above all other creatures, when the Son of God was made of a woman, carried in the womb. 4. The apostles, who to outward appearance were despicable, in a manner children and sucklings in comparison of the great ones of the world ; poor despised creatures, yet principal instruments of God's service and glory. Therefore 'tis notable, that when Christ glorifieth his Father for the wise and free dispensation of his saving grace (Matt. xi. 25), he saith, "I thank thee, O Father, Lord of heaven and earth, because thou hast hid these things from the wise and prudent, and hast revealed them unto babes," so called from the meanness of their condition. . . . And you shall see it was spoken when the disciples were sent abroad, and had power given them over unclean spirits. "In that hour Jesus rejoiced in spirit, and said, I thank thee, O Father, Lord of heaven and earth, that thou hast hid these things from the wise and prudent, and hast revealed them unto babes." This he acknowledged to be an act of infinite condescension in God. 5. Those children that cried *Hosanna* to Christ, make up part of the sense, for Christ defendeth their practice by this Scripture. . . . 6. Not only the apostles, but all those that fight under Christ's banner, and are listed into his confederacy, may be called babes and sucklings ; first, because of their condition ; secondly, their disposition. . . .

1. Because of their condition. . . . . God in the government of the world is pleased to subdue the enemies of his kingdom by weak and despised instruments. 2. Because of their disposition : they are most humble spirited. We are told (Matt. xviii. 3), " Except ye be converted, and become as little children," etc. As if he had said, you strive for pre-eminence and worldly greatness in my kingdom ; I tell you my kingdom is a kingdom of babes, and containeth none but the humble, and such as are little in their own eyes, and are contented to be small and despised in the eyes of others, and so do not seek after great matters in the world. A young child knoweth not what striving or state meaneth, and therefore by an emblem and visible representation of a child set in the midst of them, Christ would take them off from the expectation of a carnal kingdom.—*Thomas Manton*, 1620—1677.

Verse 2.—" *That thou mightest still the enemy and the avenger.*" This very confusion and revenge upon Satan, who was the cause of man's fall, was aimed at by God at first ; therefore is the first promise and preaching of the gospel to Adam brought in rather in sentencing him than in speaking to Adam, that the seed of the woman should break the serpent's head, it being in God's aim as much to confound him as to save poor man.—*Thomas Goodwin.*

Verse 2.—The work that is done in love loses half its tedium and difficulty. It is as with a stone, which in the air and on the dry ground we strain at but cannot stir. Flood the field where it lies, bury the block beneath the rising water ; and now, when its head is submerged, bend to the work. Put your strength to it. Ah ! it moves, rises from its bed, rolls on before your arm. So, when under the heavenly influences of grace the tide of love rises, and goes swelling over our duties and difficulties, a child can do a man's work, and a man can do a giant's. Let love be present in the heart, and " *out of the mouths of babes and sucklings* God ordaineth strength."—*Thomas Guthrie, D.D.*

Verse 2.—" *Out of the mouth of babes and sucklings,*" etc. That poor martyr, Alice Driver, in the presence of many hundreds, did so silence Popish bishops, that she and all blessed God that the proudest of them could not resist the spirit in a silly woman ; so I say to thee, " *Out of the mouth of babes and suck-lings*" God will be honoured. Even thou, silly worm, shalt honour him, when it shall appear what God hath done for thee, what lusts he hath mortified, and what graces he hath granted thee. The Lord can yet do greater things for thee if thou wilt trust him. He can carry thee upon eagles' wings, enable thee to bear and suffer strong affliction for him, to persevere to the end, to live by faith, and to finish thy course with joy. Oh ! in that he hath made thee low in heart, thy other lowness shall be so much the more honour to thee. Do not all as much and more wonder at God's rare workmanship in the ant, the poorest bug that creeps, as in the biggest elephant ? That so many parts and limbs should be united in such a little space ; that so poor a creature should provide in the summer-time her winter food ? Who sees not as much of God in a bee as in a greater creature ? Alas ! in a great body we look for great abilities and wonder not. Therefore, to conclude, seeing God hath clothed thy uncomely parts with the more honour, bless God, and bear thy baseness more equally ; thy greatest glory is yet to come, that when the wise of the world have rejected the counsel of God, thou hast (with those poor publicans and soldiers), magni-fied the ministry of the gospel. Surely the Lord will also be admired in thee (1 Thess. i.), a poor silly creature, that even thou wert made wise to salvation and believest in that day. Be still poor in thine own eyes, and the Lord will make thy proudest scornful enemies to worship at thy feet, to confess God hath done much for thee, and wish thy portion when God shall visit them.—*Daniel Rogers*, 1642.

Verse 3.—" *When I consider.*" Meditation fits for humiliation. When David had been contemplating the works of creation, their splendour, harmony, motion, influence, he lets the plumes of pride fall, and begins to have self-abasing thoughts. " *When I consider thy heavens, the work of thy fingers, the moon and the stars which thou hast ordained, what is man that thou art mindful of him?"—Thomas Watson.*

Verse 3.—"*When I consider thy heavens,*" etc. David surveying the firmament, broke forth into this consideration : "*When I consider thy heavens, the work of thy fingers, the moon and the stars, which thou hast created, what is man?*" etc. How cometh he to mention the moon and stars, and omit the sun ? the other being but his pensioners, shining with that exhibition of light which the bounty of the sun allots them. It is answered, this was David's night meditation, when the sun, departing to the other world, left the lesser lights only visible in heaven ; and as the sky is best beheld by day in the glory thereof, so too it is best surveyed by night in the variety of the same. Night was made for man to rest in. But when I cannot sleep, may I, with the psalmist, entertain my waking with good thoughts. Not to use them as opium, to invite my corrupt nature to slumber, but to bolt out bad thoughts, which otherwise would possess my soul.—*Thomas Fuller*, 1608—1661.

Verse 3.—"*Thy heavens.*" The carnal mind sees God in nothing, not even in spiritual things, his word and ordinances. The spiritual mind sees him in everything, even in natural things, in looking on the heavens and the earth and all the creatures—"THY *heavens;*" sees all in that notion, in their relation to God as his work, and in them his glory appearing ; stands in awe, fearing to abuse his creatures and his favours to his dishonour. "*The day is thine, and the night also is thine ;*" therefore ought not I to forget thee through the day, nor in the night.—*Robert Leighton, D.D.*

Verse 3.—"*The stars.*" I cannot say that it is chiefly the contemplation of their infinitude, and the immeasurable space they occupy, that enraptures me in the stars. These conditions rather tend to confuse the mind ; and in this view of countless numbers and unlimited space there lies, moreover, much that belongs rather to a temporary and human than to an eternally abiding consideration. Still less do I regard them absolutely with reference to the life after this. But the mere thought they are so far beyond and above everything terrestrial—the feeling, that before them everything earthly so utterly vanishes to nothing—that the single man is so infinitely insignificant in the comparison with these worlds strewn over all space—that his destinies, his enjoyments, and sacrifices, to which he attaches such a minute importance—how all these fade like nothing before such immense objects ; then, that the constellations bind together all the races of man, and all the eras of the earth, that they have beheld all that has passed since the beginning of time, and will see all that passes until its end ; in thoughts like these I can always lose myself with a silent delight in the view of the starry firmament. It is, in very truth, a spectacle of the highest solemnity, when, in the stillness of night, in a heaven quite clear, the stars, like a choir of worlds, arise and descend, while existence, as it were, falls asunder into two separate parts ; the one, belonging to earth, grows dumb in the utter silence of night, and thereupon the other mounts upward in all its elevation, splendour, and majesty. And, when contemplated from this point of view, the starry heavens have truly a moral influence on the mind.—*Alexander Von Humboldt*, 1850.

Verse 3.—"*When I consider thy heavens,*" etc. Could we transport ourselves above the moon, could we reach the highest star above our heads, we should instantly discover new skies, new stars, new suns, new systems, and perhaps more magnificently adorned. But even there, the vast dominions of our great Creator would not terminate ; we should then find, to our astonishment, that we had only arrived at the borders of the works of God. It is but little that we can know of his works, but that little should teach us to be humble, and to admire the divine power and goodness. How great must that Being be who produced these immense globes out of nothing, who regulates their courses, and whose mighty hand directs and supports them all ! What is the clod of earth which we inhabit, with all the magnificent scenes it presents to us, in comparison of those innumerable worlds ? Were this earth annihilated, its absence would no more be observed than that of a grain of sand from the sea shore. What then are provinces and kingdoms when compared with those worlds? They are but atoms dancing in the air, which are discovered to us by the sunbeams. What then am I, when reckoned among the infinite number of God's creatures? I am lost in mine own nothingness! But little as I appear in this respect, I find myself great in others. There is great beauty in this starry firmament which God has chosen for his throne! How admirable are those celestial bodies! I am dazzled with their splendour, and enchanted with their beauty! But notwithstanding this, however beautiful, and however richly adorned, yet this sky is void of intelligence. It is a stranger to its own beauty, while I, who am mere clay, moulded by a divine hand, am endowed with sense and reason. I can contemplate the beauty of these shining worlds; nay, more, I am already, to a certain degree, acquainted with their sublime Author; and by faith I see some small rays of his divine glory. O may I be more and more acquainted with his works, and make the study of them my employ, till by a glorious change I rise to dwell with him above the starry regions.—*Christopher Christian Sturm's "Reflections,"* 1750—1786.

Verse 3.—*" Work of God's fingers."* That is most elaborate and accurate: a metaphor from embroiderers, or from them that make tapestry.—*John Trapp.*

Verse 3.—*" When I consider thy heavens,"* etc. It is truly a most Christian exercise to extract a sentiment of piety from the works and the appearances of nature. It has the authority of the sacred writers upon its side, and even our Saviour himself gives it the weight and the solemnity of his example. "Behold the lilies of the field; they toil not, neither do they spin, yet your heavenly Father careth for them." He expatiates on the beauty of a single flower, and draws from it the delightful argument of confidence in God. He gives us to see that taste may be combined with piety, and that the same heart may be occupied with all that is serious in the contemplations of religion, and be at the same time alive to the charms and the loveliness of nature. The psalmist takes a still loftier flight. He leaves the world, and lifts his imagination to that mighty expanse which spreads above it and around it. He wings his way through space, and wanders in thought over its immeasurable regions. Instead of a dark and unpeopled solitude, he sees it crowded with splendour, and filled with the energy of the divine presence. Creation rises in its immensity before him, and the world, with all which it inherits, shrinks into littleness at a contemplation so vast and so overpowering. He wonders that he is not overlooked amid the grandeur and the variety which are on every side of him; and, passing upward from the majesty of nature to the majesty of nature's Architect, he exclaims, "What is man, that thou art mindful of him, or the son of man that thou shouldest deign to visit him?" It is not for us to say whether inspiration revealed to the psalmist the wonders of the modern astronomy. But, even though the mind be a perfect stranger to the science of these enlightened times, the heavens present a great and an elevating spectacle, an immense concave reposing upon the circular boundary of the world, and the innumerable lights which are suspended from on high, moving with solemn regularity along its surface. It seems to have been at night that the piety of the psalmist was awakened by this contemplation; when the moon and the stars were visible, and not when the sun had risen in his strength and thrown a splendour around him, which bore down and eclipsed all the lesser glories of the firmament.—*Thomas Chalmers, D.D.,* 1817.

Verse 3.—*" Thy heavens"* :—

> This prospect vast, what is it?—weigh'd aright,
> 'Tis nature's system of divinity,
> And every student of the night inspires.
> 'Tis elder Scripture, writ by God's own hand:
> Scripture authentic! uncorrupt by man.   *Edward Young.*

Verse 3.—*" The stars."* When I gazed into these stars, have they not looked down on me as if with pity from their serene spaces, like eyes glistening with heavenly tears over the little lot of man!—*Thomas Carlyle.*

Verses 3, 4.—*" When I consider thy heavens,"* etc. Draw spiritual inferences

7

from occasional objects. David did but wisely consider the heavens, and he breaks out into self-abasement and humble admirations of God. Glean matter of instruction to yourselves, and praise to your Maker from everything you see ; it will be a degree of restoration to a state of innocency, since this was Adam's task in paradise. Dwell not upon any created object only as a *virtuoso*, to gratify your rational curiosity, but as a Christian, call religion to the feast, and make a spiritual improvement. No creature can meet our eyes but affords us lessons worthy of our thoughts, besides the general notices of the power and wisdom of the Creator. Thus may the sheep read us a lesson of patience, the dove of innocence, the ant and bee raise blushes in us for our sluggishness, and the stupid ox and dull ass correct and shame our ungrateful ignorance. . . . . . He whose eyes are open cannot want an instructor, unless he wants a heart.—*Stephen Charnock.*

Verse 4.—" *What is man that thou art mindful of him ?*" etc. My readers must be careful to mark the design of the psalmist, which is to enhance, by this comparison, the infinite goodness of God ; for it is, indeed, a wonderful thing that the Creator of heaven, whose glory is so surpassingly great as to ravish us with the highest admiration, condescends so far as graciously to take upon him the care of the human race. That the psalmist makes this contrast may be inferred from the Hebrew word אֱנוֹשׁ, *enosh*, which we have rendered *man*, and which expresses the frailty of man rather than any strength or power which he possesses. . . . . . Almost all interpreters render פָּקַד, *pakad,* the last word of this verse, *to visit ;* and I am unwilling to differ from them, since this sense suits the passage very well. But as it sometimes signifies *to remember,* and as we will often find in the Psalms the repetition of the same thought in different words, it may here be very properly translated *to remember ;* as if David had said, " This is a marvellous thing, that God thinks upon men, and remembers them continually."—*John Calvin, 1509—1564.*

Verse 4.—" *What is man ?*" But, O God, what a little lord hast thou made over this great world ! The least corn of sand is not so small to the whole earth, as man is to the heaven. When I see the heavens, the sun, the moon, and stars, O God, what is man ? Who would think thou shouldst make all these creatures for one, and that one well-near the least of all ? Yet none but he can see what thou hast done ; none but he can admire and adore thee in what he seeth : how had he need to do nothing but this, since he alone must do it ! Certainly the price and value of things consist not in the quantity ; one diamond is worth more than many quarries of stone ; one loadstone hath more virtue than mountains of earth. It is lawful for us to praise thee in ourselves. All thy creation hath not more wonder in it than one of us : other creatures thou madest by a simple command ; MAN, not without a divine consultation : others at once ; man thou didst form, then inspire : others in several shapes, like to none but themselves ; man, after thine own image : others with qualities fit for service ; man, for dominion. Man had his name from thee ; they had their names from man. How should we be consecrated to thee above all others, since thou hast bestowed more cost on us than other !—*Joseph Hall, D.D., Bishop of Norwich, 1574—1656.*

Verse 4.—" *What is man, that thou art mindful of him ? or the son of man, that thou shouldst visit him ?*" And (Job vii. 17, 18) " What is man, that thou shouldst magnify him ? and that thou shouldst set thy heart upon him ? and that thou shouldst visit him every morning ?" Man, in the pride of his heart, seeth no such great matter in it ; but a humble soul is filled with astonishment. " Thus saith the high and lofty One that inhabiteth eternity, whose name is Holy ; I dwell in the high and holy place, with him also that is of a contrite and humble spirit, to revive the spirit of the humble, and to revive the heart of the contrite ones." Isaiah lvii. 15. Oh, saith the humble soul, will the Lord have respect unto such a vile worm as I am ? Will the Lord acquaint himself with such a sinful wretch as I am ? Will the Lord open his arms, his bosom, his heart to me ? Shall such a loathsome creature as I find favour in his eyes ? In Ezek. xvi. 1—5, we have a relation of the wonderful condescension of God to man, who is there resembled to a wretched infant cast out in the day of its birth, in its blood and filthiness, no eye pitying it ; such loathsome creatures are we before God ; and yet when he passed by, and saw us polluted in our blood, he said unto us, "Live." It is doubled because of the strength of its nature ; it was "the time of love" (verse 8). This was love indeed, that God should take a filthy, wretched thing, and spread his skirts over it, and cover its nakedness and swear unto it, and enter into a covenant with it, and make it his ; that is, that he should espouse this loathsome thing to himself, that he would be a husband to it ; this is love unfathomable, love inconceivable, self-principle love ; this is the love of God to man, for God is love. Oh, the depth of the riches of the bounty and goodness of God ! How is his love wonderful, and his grace past finding out ! How do you find and feel your hearts affected upon the report of these things ? Do you not see matter of admiration and cause of wonder ? Are you not as it were launched forth into an ocean of goodness, where you can see no shore, nor feel no bottom ? Ye may make a judgment of yourselves by the motions and affections that ye feel in yourselves at the mention of this. For thus Christ judged of the faith of the centurion that said unto him, "Lord, I am not worthy that thou shouldst come under my roof. When Jesus heard this, he marvelled, and said to them that followed him, I say unto you, I have not found so great faith, no, not in Israel." Matthew viii. 8—10. If, then, you feel not your souls mightily affected with this condescension of God, say thus unto your souls, What aileth thee, O my soul, that thou art no more affected with the goodness of God ? Art thou dead, that thou canst not feel ? Or art thou blind, that thou canst not see thyself compassed about with astonishing goodness ? Behold the King of glory descending from the habitation of his majesty, and coming to visit thee ! Hearest not thou his voice, saying, "Open to me, my sister : behold, I stand at the door and knock. Lift up yourselves, O ye gates, and be ye lifted up, ye everlasting doors, that the King of glory may come in " ? Behold, O my soul, how he waits still while thou hast refused to open to him ! Oh, the wonder of his goodness ! Oh, the condescension of his love, to visit me, to sue unto me, to wait upon me, to be acquainted with me ! Thus work up your souls into an astonishment at the condescension of God.—*James Janeway*, 1674.

Verse 4.—Man, in Hebrew—infirm or miserable man—by which it is apparent that he speaks of man not according to the state of his creation, but as fallen into a state of sin, and misery, and mortality. *Art mindful of him, i.e.*, carest for him, and conferrest such high favours upon him. *The son of man*, Heb., *the son of Adam*, that great apostate from and rebel against God ; the sinful son of a sinful father—his son by likeness of disposition and manners, no less than by procreation ; all which tends to magnify the divine mercy. *That thou visitest him*—not in anger, as that word is sometimes used, but with thy grace and mercy, as it is taken in Gen. xxi. 1 ; Ex. iv. 31 ; Psalm lxv. 9 ; cvi. 4 ; cxliv. 3.

Verse 4.—" What is man ?" The Scripture gives many answers to this question. Ask the prophet Isaiah, " *What is man ?*" and he answers (xl. 6), man is " grass"—" All flesh is grass, and all the goodliness thereof is as the flower of the field." Ask David, " *What is man ?*" He answers (Psalm lxii. 9), man is " *a lie*," not a liar only, or a deceiver, but " *a lie*," and a deceit. All the answers the Holy Ghost gives concerning man, are to humble man : man is ready to flatter himself, and one man to flatter another, but God tells us plainly what we are. . . . . It is a wonder that God should vouchsafe a gracious look upon such a creature as man ; it is wonderful, considering the distance between God and man, as man is a creature and God the creator. " *What is man*," that God should take notice of him ? Is he not a clod of earth, a piece of clay ? But consider him as a sinful and an unclean creature, and we may wonder to amazement : what is an unclean creature that God should magnify

him ? Will the Lord indeed put value upon filthiness, and fix his approving
eye upon an impure thing ? One step further ; what is rebellious man, man
an enemy to God, that God should magnify him ! what admiration can answer
this question ? Will God prefer his enemies, and magnify those who would
cast him down ? Will a prince exalt a traitor, or give him honour who attempts
to take away his life ? The sinful nature of man is an enemy to the nature of
God, and would pull God out of heaven ; yet God even at that time is raising
man to heaven : sin would lessen the great God, and yet God greatens sinful
man.—*Joseph Caryl.*

Verse 4.—" *What is man ?* " Oh, the grandeur and littleness, the excellence
and the corruption, the majesty and meanness of man !—*Pascal,* 1623—1662.

Verse 4.—" *Thou visitest him.* " To visit is, first, to afflict, to chasten, yea, to
punish ; the highest judgments in Scripture come under the notions of visitations. " Visiting the iniquity of the fathers upon the children" (Ex. xxxiv. 7),
that is, punishing them. . . . And it is a common speech with us when a
house hath the plague, which is one of the highest strokes of temporal affliction,
we use to say, " Such a house is visited." Observe then, afflictions are visitations. . . . Secondly, to visit, in a good sense, signifies to show mercy, and to
refresh, to deliver and to bless ; " Naomi heard how that the Lord had visited
his people in giving them bread." Ruth i. 6. " The Lord visited Sarah," etc. Gen.
xxi. 1, 2. That greatest mercy and deliverance that ever the children of men had,
is thus expressed, " The Lord hath visited and redeemed his people." Luke i. 68.
Mercies are visitations ; when God comes in kindness and love to do us good, he
visiteth us. And these mercies are called visitations in two respects : 1. Because
God comes near to us when he doth us good ; mercy is a drawing near to a soul,
a drawing near to a place. As when God sends a judgment, or afflicts, he is
said to depart and go away from that place ; so when he doth us good, he comes
near, and as it were applies himself in favour to our persons and habitations.
2. They are called a visitation because of *the freeness of them.* A visit is one
of the freest things in the world ; there is no obligation but that of love to
make a visit ; because such a man is my friend and I love him, therefore I visit
him. Hence, that greatest act of free grace in redeeming the world is called a
visitation, because it was as freely done as ever any friend made a visit to see
his friend, and with infinite more freedom. There was no obligation on man's
side at all, many unkindnesses and neglects there were ; God in love came to
redeem man. Thirdly, to visit imports an act of care and inspection, of tutor-
age and direction. The pastor's office over the flock is expressed by this act
(Zech. x. 3 ; Acts xv. 36) ; and the care we ought to have of the fatherless and
widows is expressed by visiting them. " Pure religion." saith the apostle James,
" is this, To visit the fatherless and widows in their affliction" (chap. i. 27) ; and
in Matt. xxv. 34, Christ pronounceth the blessing on them who, when he was in
prison, visited him, which was not a bare seeing, or asking ' how do you,' but it
was care of Christ in his imprisonment, and helpfulness and provision for him in his
afflicted members. That sense also agrees well with this place, Job vii. 17, 18,
" *What is man, that thou shouldst visit him ?* "—*Joseph Caryl.*

Verse 4.—" *What is man, that thou art mindful of him ? or the son of man,
that thou visitest him ?* "

Lord, what is man that thou
So mindful art of him ? Or what's the son
Of man, that thou the highest heaven didst bow,
    And to his aide didst runne ?

Man's but a piece of clay
That's animated by thy heavenly breath,
And when that breath thou tak'st away,
    Hee's clay again by death.
He is not worthy of the least
    Of all Thy mercies at the best.

Baser than clay is he,
For sin hath made him like the beasts that perish,
Though next the angels he was in degree ;
　　Yet this beast thou dost cherish.
Hee is not worthy of the least,
Of all thy mercies, hee's a beast.

Worse than a beast is man,
Who after thine own image made at first,
Became the divel's sonne by sin.　And can
　　A thing be more accurst?
Yet thou thy greatest mercy hast
On this accursed creature cast.

Thou didst thyself abase,
And put off all thy robes of majesty,
Taking his nature to give him thy grace,
　　To save his life didst dye.
He is not worthy of the least
Of all thy mercies ; one's a feast.

　Lo ! man is made now even
With the blest angels, yea, superiour farre,
Since Christ sat down at God's right hand in 'heaven,
　　And God and man one are.
Thus all thy mercies man inherits,
Though not the least of them he merits.
　　　　　　　　　　Thomas Washbourne, D.D., 1654.

Verse 4.—" What is man ?"—

How poor, how rich, how abject, how august,
How complicate, how wonderful is man !
How passing wonder HE who made him such !
Who centred in our make such strange extremes !
From different natures marvellously mix'd,
Connexion exquisite of distant worlds !
Distinguish'd link in being's endless chain !
Midway from nothing to the Deity !
A beam ethereal, sullied and absorb'd,
Though sullied and dishonour'd, still divine !
Dim miniature of greatness absolute !
An heir of glory ! a frail child of dust !
Helpless, immortal ! insect *infinite!*
A worm ! a god ! I tremble at myself,
And in myself am lost.　　　*Edward Young,* 1681—1775.

Verses 4.—8—" What is man," etc. :

　　—— Man is ev'ry thing,
And more : he is a tree, yet bears no fruit ;
　A beast, yet is, or should be more :
　Reason and speech we onely bring.
Parrats may thank us, if they are not mute,
　　They go upon the score.

Man is all symmetrie,
Full of proportions, one limbe to another,
　And all to all the world besides :
　Each part may call the farthest, brother.
For head with foot hath private amitie,
　　And both with moons and tides.

Nothing hath got so farre,
But man hath caught and kept it, as his prey.
　His eyes dismount the highest starre :
　He is in little all the sphere.
Herbs gladly cure our flesh, because that they
　　Finde their acquaintance there.

For us the windes do blow ;
The earth doth rest, heav'n move, and fountains flow.
　Nothing we see, but means our good,
　As our *delight,* or as our *treasure:*
The whole is, either our cupboard of *food,*
　　Or cabinet of *pleasure.*

The starres have us to bed :
Night draws the curtain, which the sun withdraws :
    Musick and light attend our head.
All things unto our *flesh* are kinde
In their *descent* and *being ;* to our *minde*
    In their *ascent* and *cause.*

Each thing is full of dutie :
Waters united are our navigation ;
    Distinguished, our habitation ;
    Below, our drink ; above, our meat :
Both are our cleanlinesse.   Hath one such beautie ?
    Then how are all things neat !

More servants wait on man,
Than he'l take notice of : in ev'ry path
    He treads down that which doth befriend him,
    When sicknesse makes him pale and wan,
Oh, mightie love ! Man is one world, and hath
    Another to attend him.

George Herbert, 1593.

Verse 5.—" *Thou hast made him a little lower than the angels.*"   Perhaps it was not so much in nature as in position that man, as first formed, was inferior to the angels.   At all events, we can be sure that nothing higher could be affirmed of the angels, than that they were made in the image of God.   If, then, they had originally superiority over man, it must have been in the degree of resemblance.   The angel was made immortal, intellectual, holy, powerful, glorious, and in these properties lay their likeness to the Creator.   But were not these properties given also to man ?   Was not man made immortal, intellectual, holy, powerful, glorious ?   And if the angel excelled the man, it was not, we may believe, in the possession of properties which had no counterpart in the man ; both bore God's image, and both therefore had lineaments of the attributes which centre in Deity.   Whether or not these lineaments were more strongly marked in the angel than in the man, it were presumptuous to attempt to decide ; but it is sufficient for our present purpose that the same properties must have been common to both, since both were modelled after the same divine image ; and whatever originally the relative positions of the angel and the man, we cannot question that since the fall man has been fearfully inferior to the angels. The effect of transgression has been to debase all his powers, and so bring him down from his high rank in the scale of creation ; but, however degraded and sunken, he still retains the capacities of his original formation, and since these capacities could have differed in nothing but degree from the capacities of the angel, it must be clear that they may be so purged and enlarged as to produce, if we may not say to restore, the equality. . . . . . Oh ! it may be, we again say, that an erroneous estimate is formed, when we separate by an immense space the angel and the man, and bring down the human race to a low station in the scale of creation.   If I search through the records of science, I may indeed find that, for the furtherance of magnificent purposes, God hath made man " a little lower than the angels ;" and I cannot close my eyes to the melancholy fact, that as a consequence upon apostacy there has been a weakening and a rifling of those splendid endowments which Adam might have transmitted unimpaired to his children.   And yet the Bible teems with notices, that so far from being by nature higher than men, angels even now possess not an importance which belongs to our race.   It is a mysterious thing, and one to which we scarcely dare allude, that there has arisen a Redeemer of fallen men, but not of fallen angels.   We would build no theory on so awful and inscrutable a truth ; but is it too much to say, that the interference on the behalf of man and the non-interference on the behalf of angels, gives ground for the persuasion, that men occupy at least not a lower place than angels in the love and the solicitude of their Maker ?   Besides, are not angels represented as " ministering spirits, sent forth to minister to the heirs of salvation ?'' And what is the idea conveyed by such a representation, if it be not that believers, being attended and waited on by angels, are as children of God marching forwards to a splendid throne, and so elevated amongst creatures, that those who have the wind in their wings, and are brilliant as a flame of fire, delight to do them honour ? And, moreover, does not the repentance of a single sinner minister gladness to a whole throng of angels ? And who shall say that this sending of a new wave of rapture throughout the hierarchy of heaven does not betoken such immense sympathy with men as goes far towards proving him the occupant of an immense space in the scale of existence ? We may add, also, that angels learn of men ; inasmuch as Paul declares to the Ephesians, that "now unto the principalities and powers in heavenly places is made known by the church, the manifold wisdom of God." And when we further remember, that in one of those august visions with which the Evangelist John was favoured, he beheld the representatives of the church placed immediately before the eternal throne, whilst angels, standing at a greater distance, thronged the outer circle, we seem to have accumulated proof that men are not to be considered as naturally inferior to angels—that however they may have cast themselves down from eminence, and sullied the lustre and sapped the strength of their first estate, they are still capable of the very loftiest elevation, and require nothing but the being restored to their forfeited position, and the obtaining room for the development of their powers, in order to their shining forth as the illustrious ones of the creation, the breathing, burning images of the Godhead. . . . . The Redeemer is represented as submitting to be humbled—"made a little lower than the angels," for the sake or with a view to the glory that was to be the recompense of his sufferings. This is a very important representation—one that should be most attentively considered ; and from it may be drawn, we think, a strong and clear argument for the divinity of Christ.

We could never see how it could be humility in any creature, whatever the dignity of his condition, to assume the office of a Mediator and to work out our reconciliation. We do not forget to how extreme degradation a Mediator must consent to be reduced, and through what suffering and ignominy he could alone achieve our redemption ; but neither do we forget the unmeasured exaltation which was to be the Mediator's reward, and which, if Scripture be true, was to make him far higher than the highest of principalities and powers ; and we know not where would have been the amazing humility, where the unparalleled condescension, had any mere creature consented to take the office on the prospect of such a recompense. A being who knew that he should be immeasurably elevated if he did a certain thing, can hardly be commended for the greatness of his humility in doing that thing. The nobleman who should become a slave, knowing that in consequence he should be made a king, does not seem to us to afford any pattern of condescension. He must be the king already, incapable of obtaining any accession to his greatness, ere his entering the state of slavery can furnish an example of humility. And, in like manner, we can never perceive that any being but a divine Being can justly be said to have given a model of condescension in becoming our Redeemer. . . . . . If he could not lay aside the perfections, he could lay aside the glories of Deity ; without ceasing to be God he could appear to be man ; and herein we believe was the humiliation— herein that self-emptying which Scripture identifies with our Lord's having been "made a little lower than the angels." In place of manifesting himself in the form of God, and thereby centering on himself the delighted and reverential regards of all unfallen orders of intelligences, he must conceal himself in the form of a servant, and no longer gathering that rich tribute of homage, which had flowed from every quarter of his unlimited empire, produced by his power, sustained by his providence, he had the same essential glory, the same real dignity, which he had ever had. These belonged necessarily to his nature, and could no more be parted with, even for a time, than could that nature itself. But every outward mark of majesty and of greatness might be laid aside ; and Deity, in place of coming down with such dazzling manifestations of supremacy as would have compelled the world he visited to fall prostrate and adore, might so veil his splendours, and so hide himself in an ignoble form, that when men saw him there should be no "beauty that they should desire him." And this was what Christ did, in consenting to be "made a little lower than the angels;" and in doing this he emptied himself, or "made himself of no reputation." The very being who in the form of God had given its light and magnificence to heaven, appeared upon earth in the form of a servant; and not merely so—for every creature is God's servant, and therefore the form of a servant would have been assumed, had he appeared as an angel or an archangel—but in the form of the lowest of these servants, being "made in the likeness of men"—of men the degraded, the apostate, the perishing.—*Henry Melvill, B.D.*, 1854.

Verses 5, 6.—God magnifies man in the work of creation. The third verse shows us what it was that raised the psalmist to this admiration of the goodness of God to man: "*When I consider thy heavens, the work of thy fingers, the moon and the stars, which thou hast ordained; Lord, what is man?*" God in the work of creation made all these things serviceable and instrumental for the good of man. What is man, that he should have a sun, moon, and stars, planted in the firmament for him? What creature is this? When great preparations are made in any place, much provisions laid in, and the house adorned with richest furnitures, we say, "*What is this man that comes to such a house?*" When such a goodly fabric was raised up, the goodly house of the world adorned and furnished, we have reason admiringly to say, What is this man that must be the tenant or inhabitant of this house? There is yet a higher exaltation of man in the creation; man was magnified with the stamp of God's image, one part whereof the psalmist describes in the sixth verse, "*Thou madest him to have dominion over the works of thy hands; thou hast put all things under his feet,*" etc. Thus man was magnified in creation. What was man that he should have the rule of the world given him? That he should be lord over the fish of the sea, and over the beasts of the field, and over the fowls of the air? Again, man was magnified in creation, in that God set him in the next degree to the angels; "*Thou hast made him a little lower than the angels;*" there is the first part of the answer to this question, man was magnified in being made so excellent a creature, and in having so many excellent creatures made for him. All which may be understood of man as created in God's image; but since the transgression it is peculiar to Christ, as the apostle applies it (Heb. ii. 6), and if those who have their blood and dignity restored by the work of redemption, which is the next part of man's exaltation.—*Joseph Caryl.*

Verses 5—8.—Augustine having allegorised much about the wine-presses in the title of this Psalm, upon these words, "What is man, or the son of man," the one being called אֱנוֹשׁ, from *misery*, the other בֶּן־אָדָם, the *Son of Adam*, or *man*, saith, that by the first is meant man in the state of sin and corruption; by the other, man regenerated by grace, yet called the son of man because made more excellent by the change of his mind and life, from old corruption to newness, and from an old to a new man; whereas he that is still carnal is miserable; and then ascending from the body to the head, Christ, he extols his glory as being set over all things, even the angels, and heavens, and the whole world as is elsewhere showed that he is. Eph. i. 21. And then leaving the highest things he descended to "*sheep and oxen;*" whereby we may understand *sanctified men* and *preachers*, for to *sheep* are the *faithful* often compared, and *preachers* to *oxen*. 1 Cor. ix. "Thou shalt not muzzle the mouth of the ox that treadeth out the corn." "*The beasts of the field*" set forth the *voluptuous* that live at large, going in the broad way: *the fowls of the air*, the *lifted up by pride:* "*the fishes of the sea*," such as through a covetous desire of riches pierce into the lower parts of the 'earth, as the fishes dive to the bottom of the sea. And because men pass the seas again and again for riches, he addeth, "*that passeth through the way of the sea*," and to that of diving to the bottom of the waters may be applied (1 Tim. vi. 9), "They that will be rich, fall into many noisome lusts, that drown the soul in perdition." And hereby seem to be set forth the three things of the world of which it is said, "they that love them, the love of the Father is not in them." "The lust of the heart" being sensuality ; "the lust of the eyes," covetousness ; to which is added, "the pride of life." Above all these Christ was set, because without all sin ; neither could any of the devil's three temptations, which may be referred hereunto, prevail with him. And all these, as well as "sheep and oxen," are in the church, for which it is said, that into the ark came all manner of beasts, both clean and unclean, and fowls ; and all manner of fishes, good and bad, came into the net, as it is in the parable. All which I have set down, as of which good use may be made by the discreet reader.—*John Mayer*.

Verse 6.—"*Thou hast put all things under his feet.*" Hermodius, a nobleman born, upbraided the valiant captain Iphicrates for that he was but a shoemaker's son. "My blood," saith Iphicrates, "taketh beginning at me ; and thy blood, at thee now taketh her farewell ;" intimating that he, not honouring his house with the glory of his virtues, as the house had honoured him with the title of nobility, was but as a wooden knife put into an empty sheath to fill up the place ; but for himself, he, by his valorous achievements was now beginning to be the raiser of his family. Thus, in the matter of spirituality, he is the best gentleman that is the best Christian. The men of Berea, who received the word with all readiness, were more noble than those of Thessalonica. The burgesses of God's city be not of base lineage, but truly noble ; they boast not of their generation, but their regeneration, which is far better ; for, by their second birth they are the sons of God, and the church is their mother, and Christ their elder brother, the Holy Ghost their tutor, angels their attendants, and all other creatures their subjects, the whole world their inn, and heaven their home.—*John Spencer's "Things New and Old."*

Verse 6.—"*Thou madest him to have dominion over the works of thy hands,*" etc. For thy help against wandering thoughts in prayer . . . . labour to keep thy distance to the world, and that sovereignty which God hath given thee over it in its profits and pleasures, or whatever else may prove a snare to thee. While the father and master know their place, and keep their distance, so long children and servants will keep theirs by being dutiful and officious ; but when they forget this, the father grows fond of the one, and the master too familiar with the other, then they begin to lose their authority and the others to grow saucy and under no command ; bid them go, and it may be they will not stir ; set them a task, and they will bid you do it yourself. Truly, thus it fares with the Christian ; all the creatures are his servants, and so long as he keeps his heart at a holy distance from them, and maintains his lordship over them, not laying them in his bosom, which God hath put "*under his feet,*" all is well ; he marches to the duties of God's worship in a goodly order. He can be private with God, and these not be bold to crowd in to disturb him.—*William Gurnall*.

Verses 7, 8.—He who rules over the material world, is Lord also of the intellectual or spiritual creation represented thereby. The souls of the faithful, lowly and harmless, are the sheep of his pasture ; those who, like oxen, are strong to labour in the church, and who, by expounding the Word of Life, tread out the corn for the nourishment of the people, own him for their kind and beneficent Master ; nay, tempers fierce and untractable as the beasts of the desert, are yet subject to his will ; spirits of the angelic kind, that, like the birds of the air, traverse freely the superior region, move at his command ; and those evil ones whose habitation is in the deep abyss, even to the great leviathan himself, all are put under the feet of King Messiah.—*George Horne, D.D.*

Verse 8.—Every dish of fish and fowl that comes to our table, is an instance of this dominion man has over the works of God's hands, and it is a reason of our subjection to God our chief Lord, and to his dominion over us.

HINTS TO THE VILLAGE PREACHER.

Verse 1.—" *O Lord, our Lord.*"—Personal appropriation of the Lord as ours. The privilege of holding such a portion.

" *How excellent,*" etc.   The excellence of the name and nature of God in all places, and under all circumstances.

Sermon or lecture upon the glory of God in creation and providence.

" *In all the earth.*"   The universal revelation of God in nature and its excellency.

" *Thy glory above the heavens.*"   The incomprehensible and infinite glory of God.

" *Above the heavens.*"   The glory of God outsoaring the intellect of angels, and the splendour of heaven.

Verse 2.—Infant piety, its possibility, potency, " strength," and influence, " that thou mightest still," etc.

The strength of the gospel not the result of eloquence or wisdom in the speaker.

Great results from small causes when the Lord ordains to work.

Great things which can be said and claimed by babes in grace.

The stilling of the powers of evil by the testimony of feeble believers.

The stilling of the Great Enemy by the conquests of grace.

Verse 4.—Man's insignificance.   God's mindfulness of man.   Divine visits. The question, " What is man ?"   Each of these themes may suffice for a discourse, or they may be handled in one sermon.

Verse 5.—Man's relation to the angels.

The position which Jesus assumed for our sakes.

Manhood's crown—the glory of our nature in the person of the Lord Jesus.

Verses 5, 6, 7, 8.—The universal providential dominion of our Lord Jesus.

Verse 6.—Man's rights and responsibilities towards the lower animals.

Verse 6.—Man's dominion over the lower animals, and how he should exercise it.

Verse 6 (second clause).—The proper place for all worldly things, " *under his feet.*"

Verse 9.—The wanderer in many climes enjoying the sweetness of his Lord's name in every condition.

PSALM IX.

TITLE.—To the Chief Musician upon Muth-labben, a Psalm of David. *The meaning of this title is very doubtful. It may refer to the tune to which the Psalm was to be sung, so Wilcocks and others think; or it may refer to a musical instrument now unknown, but common in those days; or it may have a reference to Ben, who is mentioned in 1 Chron. xv. 18, as one of the Levitical singers. If either of these conjectures should be correct, the title of Muth-labben has no teaching for us, except it is meant to show us how careful David was that in the worship of God all things should be done according to due order. From a considerable company of learned witnesses we gather that the title will bear a meaning far more instructive, without being fancifully forced: it signifies a Psalm concerning the death of the Son. The Chaldee has, "concerning the death of the Champion who went out between the camps," referring to Goliath of Gath, or some other Philistine, on account of whose death many suppose this Psalm to have been written in after years by David. Believing that out of a thousand guesses this is at least as consistent with the sense of the Psalm as any other, we prefer it; and the more especially so because it enables us to refer it mystically to the victory of the Son of God over the champion of evil, even the enemy of souls (verse 6). We have here before us most evidently a triumphal hymn; may it strengthen the faith of the militant believer and stimulate the courage of the timid saint, as he sees here* THE CONQUEROR, *on whose vesture and thigh is the name written, King of kings and Lord of lords.*

ORDER.—*Bonar remarks, "The position of the Psalms in their relation to each other is often remarkable. It is questioned whether the present arrangement of them was the order in which they were given forth to Israel, or whether some later compiler, perhaps Ezra, was inspired to attend to this matter, as well as to other points connected with the canon. Without attempting to decide this point, it is enough to remark that we have proof that the order of the Psalms is as ancient as the completing of the canon, and if so, it seems obvious that the Holy Spirit wished this book to come down to us in its present order. We make these remarks, in order to invite attention to the fact, that as the eighth caught up the last line of the seventh, this ninth Psalm opens with an apparent reference to the eighth:—*

> "I will praise thee, O Lord, with my whole heart;
> I will shew forth all thy marvellous works.
> I will be glad and rejoice in thee. (Comp. Song i. 4; Rev. xix. 7.)
> I will sing to THY NAME, O thou Most High." *Verses* 1, 2.

As if "The Name," so highly praised in the former Psalm, were still ringing in the ear of the sweet singer of Israel. And in verse 10, he returns to it, celebrating their confidence who "know" that "name" as if its fragrance still breathed in the atmosphere around.

DIVISION.—*The strain so continually changes, that it is difficult to give an outline of it methodically arranged: we give the best we can make. From verses 1 to 6 is a song of jubilant thanksgiving; from 7 to 12, there is a continued declaration of faith as to the future. Prayer closes the first great division of the Psalm in verses 13 and 14. The second portion of this triumphal ode, although much shorter, is parallel in all its parts to the first portion, and is a sort of rehearsal of it. Observe the song for past judgments, verses 15, 16; the declaration of trust in future justice, 17, 18; and the closing prayer, 19, 20. Let us celebrate the conquests of the Redeemer as we read this Psalm, and it cannot but be a delightful task if the Holy Ghost be with us.*

EXPOSITION.

I WILL praise *thee*, O LORD, with my whole heart; I will shew forth all thy marvellous works.

2 I will be glad and rejoice in thee: I will sing praise to thy name, O thou most High.

3 When mine enemies are turned back, they shall fall and perish at thy presence.

For thou hast maintained my right and my cause ; thou satest in the throne judging right.

5 Thou hast rebuked the heathen, thou hast destroyed the wicked, thou hast put out their name for ever and ever.

6 O thou enemy, destructions are come to a perpetual end : and thou hast destroyed cities ; their memorial is perished with them.

1. With a holy resolution the songster begins his hymn ; *I will praise thee, O Lord.* It sometimes needs all our determination to face the foe, and bless the Lord in the teeth of his enemies ; vowing that whoever else may be silent *we* will bless his name ; here, however, the overthrow of the foe is viewed as complete, and the song flows with sacred fulness of delight. It is our duty to praise the Lord ; let us perform it as a privilege. Observe that David's praise is all given to the Lord. Praise is to be offered to God alone ; we may be grateful to the intermediate agent, but our thanks must have long wings and mount aloft to heaven. *With my whole heart.* Half heart is no heart. *I will show forth.* There is true praise in the thankful telling forth to others of our heavenly Father's dealings with us ; this is one of the themes upon which the godly should speak often to one another, and it will not be casting pearls before swine if we make even the ungodly hear of the loving-kindness of the Lord to us. *All thy marvellous works.* Gratitude for one mercy refreshes the memory as to thousands of others. One silver link in the chain draws up a long series of tender remembrances. Here is eternal work for us, for there can be no end to the showing forth of *all* his deeds of love. If we consider our own sinfulness and nothingness, we must feel that every work of preservation, forgiveness, conversion, deliverance, sanctification, &c., which the Lord has wrought for us, or in us is a *marvellous* work. Even in heaven, divine loving-kindness will doubtless be as much a theme of surprise as of rapture.

2. Gladness and joy are the appropriate spirit in which to praise the goodness of the Lord. Birds extol the Creator in notes of overflowing joy, the cattle low forth his praise with tumult of happiness, and the fish leap up in his worship with excess of delight. Moloch may be worshipped with shrieks of pain, and Juggernaut may be honoured by dying groans and inhuman yells, but he whose name is Love is best pleased with the holy mirth, and sanctified gladness of his people. Daily rejoicing is an ornament to the Christian character, and a suitable robe for God's choristers to wear. God loveth a *cheerful* giver, whether it be the gold of his purse or the gold of his mouth which he presents upon his altar. *I will sing praise to thy name, O thou most High.* Songs are the fitting expressions of inward thankfulness, and it were well if we indulged ourselves and honoured our Lord with more of them. Mr. B. P. Power has well said, "The sailors give a cheery cry as they weigh anchor, the ploughman whistles in the morning as he drives his team ; the milkmaid sings her rustic song as she sets about her early task ; when soldiers are leaving friends behind them, they do not march out to the tune of the ' Dead March in Saul,' but to the quick notes of some lively air. A praising spirit would do for us all that their songs and music do for them ; and if only we could determine to praise the Lord, we should surmount many a difficulty which our low spirits never would have been equal to, and we should do double the work which can be done if the heart be languid in its beating, if we be crushed and trodden down in soul. As the evil spirit in Saul yielded in the olden time to the influence of the harp of the son of Jesse, so would the spirit of melancholy often take flight from us, if only we would take up the song of praise."

3. God's presence is evermore sufficient to work the defeat of our most furious foes, and their ruin is so complete when the Lord takes them in hand, that even flight cannot save them, they fall to rise no more when he pursues them. We

must be careful, like David, to give all the glory to him whose presence gives the victory. If we have here the exultings of our conquering Captain, let us make the triumphs of the Redeemer the triumphs of the redeemed, and rejoice with him at the total discomfiture of all his foes.

4. One of our nobility has for his motto, "I will maintain it;" but the Christian has a better and more humble one, "Thou hast maintained it." "God and my right," are united by my faith : while God lives my right shall never be taken from me. If we seek to maintain the cause and honour of our Lord we may suffer reproach and misrepresentation, but it is a rich comfort to remember that he who sits in the throne knows our hearts, and will not leave us to the ignorant and ungenerous judgment of erring man.

5. God rebukes before he destroys, but when he once comes to blows with the wicked he ceases not until he has dashed them in pieces so small that their very name is forgotten, and like a noisome snuff their remembrance is put out for ever and ever. How often the word "thou" occurs in this and the former verse, to show us that the grateful strain mounts up directly to the Lord as doth the smoke from the altar when the air is still. My soul send up all the music of all thy powers to him who has been and is thy sure deliverance.

6. Here the Psalmist exults over the fallen foe. He bends as it were, over his prostrate form, and insults his once vaunted strength. He plucks the boaster's song out of his mouth, and sings it for him in derision. After this fashion doth our Glorious Redeemer ask of death, "Where is thy sting?" and of the grave, "Where is thy victory?" The spoiler is spoiled, and he who made captive is led into captivity himself. Let the daughters of Jerusalem go forth to meet their King, and praise him with timbrel and harp.

7 But the LORD shall endure for ever : he hath prepared his throne for judgment.

8 And he shall judge the world in righteousness, he shall minister judgment to the people in uprightness.

9 The LORD also will be a refuge for the oppressed, a refuge in times of trouble.

10 And they that know thy name will put their trust in thee : for thou, LORD, hast not forsaken them that seek thee.

11 Sing praises to the LORD, which dwelleth in Zion : declare among the people his doings.

12 When he maketh inquisition for blood, he remembereth them : he forgetteth not the cry of the humble.

In the light of the past the future is not doubtful. Since the same Almighty God fills the throne of power, we can with unhesitating confidence, exult in our security for all time to come.

7. The enduring existence and unchanging dominion of our Jehovah, are the firm foundations of our joy. The enemy and his destructions shall come to a perpetual end, but God and his throne shall *endure for ever*. The eternity of divine sovereignty yields unfailing consolation. By the throne being *prepared for judgment*, are we not to understand the swiftness of divine justice. In heaven's court suitors are not worn out with long delays. Term-time lasts all the year round in the court of King's Bench above. Thousands may come at once to the throne of the Judge of all the earth, but neither plaintiff nor defendant shall have to complain that he is not prepared to give their cause a fair hearing.

8. Whatever earthly courts may do, heaven's throne ministers judgment in uprightness. Partiality and respect of persons are things unknown in the dealings of the Holy One of Israel. How the prospect of appearing before the impartial tribunal of the Great King should act as a check to us when tempted to sin, and as a comfort when we are slandered or oppressed.

9. He who gives no quarter to the wicked in the day of judgment, is the defence and refuge of his saints in the day of trouble. There are many forms of oppression ; both from man and from Satan oppression comes to us ; and for all its forms, a refuge is provided in the Lord Jehovah. There were cities of refuge under the law, God is our refuge-city under the gospel. As the ships when vexed with tempest make for harbour, so do the oppressed hasten to the wings of a just and gracious God. He is a high tower so impregnable, that the hosts of hell cannot carry it by storm, and from its lofty heights faith looks down with scorn upon her enemies.

10. Ignorance is worst when it amounts to ignorance of God, and knowledge is best when it exercises itself upon *the name* of God. This most excellent knowledge leads to the most excellent grace of faith. O, to learn more of the attributes and character of God. Unbelief, that hooting nightbird, cannot live in the light of divine knowledge, it flies before the sun of God's great and gracious name. If we read this verse literally, there is, no doubt, a glorious fulness of assurance in the names of God. We have recounted them in the " Hints for Preachers," and would direct the reader's attention to them. By knowing his name is also meant an experimental acquaintance with the attributes of God, which are everyone of them anchors to hold the soul from drifting in seasons of peril. The Lord may hide his face for a season from his people, but he never has utterly, finally, really, or angrily, *forsaken them that seek him.* Let the poor seekers draw comfort from this fact, and let the finders rejoice yet more exceedingly, for what must be the Lord's faithfulness to those who find if he is so gracious to those who seek.

"O hope of every contrite heart,
    O joy of all the meek,
To those who fall how kind thou art,
    How good to those who seek.

"But what to those who find, ah, this
    Nor tongue nor pen can show
The love of Jesus what it is,
    None but his loved ones know."

11. Being full of gratitude himself, our inspired author is eager to excite others to join the strain, and praise God in the same manner as he had himself vowed to do in the first and second verses. The heavenly spirit of praise is gloriously contagious, and he that hath it is never content unless he can excite all who surround him to unite in his sweet employ. Singing and preaching, as means of glorifying God, are here joined together, and it is remarkable that, connected with all revivals of gospel ministry, there has been a sudden outburst of the spirit of song. Luther's Psalms and Hymns were in all men's mouths, and in the modern revival under Wesley and Whitefield, the strains of Charles Wesley, Cennick, Berridge, Toplady, Hart, Newton, and many others, were the outgrowth of restored piety. The singing of the birds of praise fitly accompanies the return of the gracious spring of divine visitation through the proclamation of the truth. Sing on brethren, and preach on, and these shall both be a token that the Lord still dwelleth in Zion. It will be well for us when coming up to Zion, to remember that the Lord dwells among his saints, and is to be had in peculiar reverence of all those that are about him.

12. When an inquest is held concerning the blood of the oppressed, the martyred saints will have the first remembrance ; he will avenge his own elect. Those saints who are living shall also be heard ; they shall be exonerated from blame, and kept from destruction, even when the Lord's most terrible work is going on ; the man with the inkhorn by his side shall mark them all for safety, before the slaughtermen are permitted to smite the Lord's enemies. The humble cry of the poorest saints shall neither be drowned by the voice of thundering justice nor by the shrieks of the condemned.

13 Have mercy upon me, O LORD ; consider my trouble *which I suffer* of them that hate me, thou that liftest me up from the gates of death :

14 That I may shew forth all thy praise in the gates of the daughter of Zion : I will rejoice in thy salvation.

Memories of the past and confidences concerning the future conducted the man of God to the mercy seat to plead for the needs of the present. Between praising and praying he divided all his time. How could he have spent it more profitably ? His first prayer is one suitable for all persons and occasions, it breathes a humble spirit, indicates self-knowledge, appeals to the proper attributes, and to the fitting person. *Have mercy upon me, O Lord.* Just as Luther used to call some texts little bibles, so we may call this sentence a little prayer-book ; for it has in it the soul and marrow of prayer. It is multum in parvo, and like the angelic sword turns every way. The ladder looks to be short, but it reaches from earth to heaven. What a noble title is here given to the Most High. *Thou that liftest me up from the gates of death!* What a glorious lift ! In sickness, in sin, in despair, in temptation, we have been brought very low, and the gloomy portal has seemed as if it would open to imprison us, but, underneath us were the everlasting arms, and, therefore, we have been uplifted even to the gates of heaven. Trapp quaintly says, " He commonly reserveth his hand for a dead lift, and rescueth those who were even talking of their graves." We must not overlook David's object in desiring mercy, it is God's glory : " *that I may show forth all thy praise.*" Saints are not so selfish as to look only to self ; they desire mercy's diamond that they may let others see it flash and sparkle, and may admire Him who gives such priceless gems to his beloved. The contrast between the gates of death and the gates of the New Jerusalem is very striking ; let our songs be excited to the highest and most rapturous pitch by the double consideration of whence we are taken, and to what we have been advanced, and let our prayers for mercy be made more energetic and agonizing by a sense of the grace which such a salvation implies. When David speaks of his showing forth *all* God's praise, he means that, in his deliverance grace in all its heights and depths would be magnified. Just as our hymn puts it :—

> " O the length and breadth of love !
> Jesus, Saviour, can it be ?
> All thy mercy's height I prove,
> All the depth is seen in me."

Here ends the first part of this instructive psalm, and in pausing awhile we feel bound to confess that our exposition has only flitted over its surface and has not digged into the depths. The verses are singularly full of teaching, and if the Holy Spirit shall bless the reader, he may go over this Psalm, as the writer has done scores of times, and see on each occasion fresh beauties.

15 The heathen are sunk down in the pit *that* they made : in the net which they hid is their own foot taken.

16 The LORD is known *by* the judgment *which* he executeth : the wicked is snared in the work of his own hands. Higgaion. Selah.

In considering this terrible picture of the Lord's overwhelming judgments of his enemies, we are called upon to ponder and meditate upon it with deep seriousness by the two untranslated words, Higgaion, Selah. Meditate, pause. Consider, and tune your instrument. Bethink yourselves and solemnly adjust your hearts to the solemnity which is so well becoming the subject. Let us in a humble spirit approach these verses, and notice, first, that the character of God requires the punishment of sin. *Jehovah is known by the judgment which he executeth;* his holiness and abhorrence of sin is thus displayed. A ruler who winked at evil would soon be known by all his subjects to be evil himself, and he, on the other hand, who is severely just in judgment reveals his own nature thereby. So long as our God is God, he will not, he cannot spare the guilty ; except through that one glorious way in which he is just, and yet the justifier of him that believeth in Jesus. We must notice, secondly, that the manner of his judgment is singularly wise, and indisputably just. He makes the wicked become their own executioners. "The heathen are sunk down in the pit that they made," &c. Like cunning hunters they prepared a pitfall for the godly and fell into it themselves : the foot of the victim escaped their crafty snares, but the toils surrounded themselves : the cruel snare was laboriously manufactured, and it proved its efficacy by snaring its own maker. Persecutors and oppressors are often ruined by their own malicious projects. "Drunkards kill themselves ; prodigals beggar themselves ;" the contentious are involved in ruinous costs ; the vicious are devoured with fierce diseases ; the envious eat their own hearts ; and blasphemers curse their own souls. Thus, men may read their sin in their punishment. They sowed the seed of sin, and the ripe fruit of damnation is the natural result.

17 The wicked shall be turned into hell, *and* all the nations that forget God.

18 For the needy shall not alway be forgotten : the expectation of the poor shall *not* perish for ever.

17. The justice which has punished the wicked, and preserved the righteous, remains the same, and therefore in days to come, retribution will surely be meted out. How solemn is the seventeenth verse, especially in its warning to forgetters of God. The moral who are not devout, the honest who are not prayerful, the benevolent who are not believing, the amiable who are not converted, these must all have their portion with the openly wicked in the hell which is prepared for the devil and his angels. There are whole nations of such ; the forgetters of God are far more numerous than the profane or profligate, and according to the very forceful expression of the Hebrew, the nethermost hell will be the place into which all of them shall be hurled headlong. Forgetfulness seems a small sin, but it brings eternal wrath upon the man who lives and dies in it.

18. Mercy is as ready to her work as ever justice can be. Needy souls fear that they are forgotten ; well, if it be so, let them rejoice that they *shall not alway* be so. Satan tells poor tremblers that their hope shall perish, but they have here the divine assurance that *their expectation shall not perish for ever.* "The Lord's people are a humbled people, afflicted, emptied, sensible of need, driven to a daily attendance on God, daily begging of him, and living upon the hope of what is promised ;" such persons may have to wait, but they shall find that they do not wait in vain.

19 Arise, O LORD ; let not man prevail : let the heathen be judged in thy sight.

20 Put them in fear, O LORD : *that* the nations may know themselves *to be but* men. Selah.

19. Prayers are the believer's weapons of war. When the battle is too hard for us, we call in our great ally, who, as it were, lies in ambush until faith gives the signal by crying out, "Arise, O Lord." Although our cause be all but lost, it shall be soon won again if the Almighty doth but bestir himself. He will not suffer man to prevail over God, but with swift judgments will confound their gloryings. In the very sight of God the wicked will be punished, and he who is now all tenderness will have no bowels of compassion for them, since they had no tears of repentance while their day of grace endured.

20. One would think that men would not grow so vain as to deny themselves to be but men, but it appears to be a lesson which only a divine schoolmaster can teach to some proud spirits. Crowns leave their wearers *but men*, degrees of eminent learning make their owners not more than *men*, valour and conquest cannot elevate beyond the dead level of " *but men ;*" and all the wealth of Crœsus, the wisdom of Solon, the power of Alexander, the eloquence of Demosthenes, if added together, would leave the possessor but a man. May we ever remember this, lest like those in the text, we should be *put in fear*.

Before leaving this Psalm, it will be very profitable if the student will peruse it again as the triumphal hymn of the Redeemer, as he devoutly brings the glory of his victories and lays it down at his Father's feet. Let us joy in his joy, and our joy shall be full.

EXPLANATORY NOTES AND QUAINT SAYINGS.

Whole Psalm.—We are to consider this song of praise, as I conceive, to be the language of our great Advocate and Mediator, " in the midst of the church giving thanks unto God," and teaching us to anticipate by faith his great and final victory over all the adversaries of our peace temporal and spiritual, with especial reference to his assertion of his royal dignity on Zion, his holy mountain. The victory over the enemy, we find by the fourth verse, is again ascribed to the decision of divine justice, and the award of a righteous judge, who has at length resumed his tribunal. This renders it certain, that the claim preferred to the throne of the Almighty, could proceed from the lips of none but our MELCHIZEDEC.—*John Fry, B.A.*, 1842.

Verse 1.—" *I will praise thee, O Lord, with my whole heart.*" As a vessel by the scent thereof tells what liquor is in it, so should our mouths smell continually of that mercy wherewith our hearts have been refreshed : for we are called vessels of mercy.—*William Cowper*, 1612.

Verse 1.—" *I will praise the Lord with my whole heart, I will shew forth all thy marvellous works.*" The words, " *With my whole heart,*" serve at once to show the greatness of the deliverances wrought for the psalmist, and to distinguish him from the hypocrites—the coarser, who praise the Lord for his goodness merely with the lips ; and the more refined, who praise him with just half their heart, while they secretly ascribe the deliverance more to themselves than to him. " *All thy wonders,*" the marvellous tokens of thy grace. The psalmist shows by this term, that he recognized them in all their greatness. Where this is done, there the Lord is also praised with the whole heart. *Half-heartedness*, and the depreciation of divine grace, go hand in hand. The ב is the ב *instrum.* The heart is the instrument of praise, the mouth only its organ.—*E. W. Hengstenberg.*

Verse 1 (second clause).—When we have received any special good thing from the Lord, it is well, according as we have opportunities, to tell others of it. When the woman who had lost one of her ten pieces of silver, found the missing portion of her money, she gathered her neighbours and her friends together, saying, " Rejoice with me, for I have found the piece which I had lost." We may do the same ; we may tell friends and relations that we have received such-and-such a blessing, and that we trace it directly to the hand of God. Why have we not already done this ? Is there a lurking unbelief as to whether it really came from God ; or are we ashamed to own it before those who are perhaps accustomed to laugh at such things ? Who knows so much of the marvellous works of God as his own people ; if they be silent, how can we expect the world to see what he has done? Let us not be ashamed to glorify God, by telling what we know and feel he has done; let us watch our opportunity to bring out distinctly the fact of his acting; let us feel delighted at having an opportunity, from our own experience, of telling what must turn to his praise; and them that honour God, God will honour in turn; if we be willing to talk of his deeds, he will give us enough to talk about.—*P. B. Power, in ' I Wills' of the Psalms.*

Verses 1, 2.—"*I will confess unto thee, O Lord, with my whole heart,*" etc. Behold, with what a flood of the most sweet affections he says that he "*will confess,*" "*show forth,*" "*rejoice,*" "*be glad,*" and "*sing,*" being filled with ecstasy! He does not simply say, "*I will confess,*" but, "*with my heart,*" and "*with my whole heart.*" Nor does he propose to speak simply of "*works,*" but of the "*marvellous works*" of God, and of "*all*" those "*works.*" Thus his spirit (like John in the womb) exults and rejoices in God his Saviour, who has done great things for him, and those marvellous things which follow. In which words are opened the subject of this Psalm: that is, that he therein sings the marvellous works of God. And these works are wonderful, because he converts, by those who are nothing, those who have all things, and, by the ALMUTH who live in hidden faith, and are dead to the world, he humbles those who flourish in glory, and are looked upon in the world. Thus accomplishing such mighty things without force, without arms, without labour, by the cross only and blood. But how will his saying, that he will show forth "*all*" his marvellous works, agree with that of Job ix. 10, "which doeth great things past finding out; yea, and wonders without number"? For, who can show forth all the marvellous works of God? We may say, therefore, that these things are spoken in that excess of feeling in which he said (Psalm vi. 6), "I will water my couch with my tears." That is, he hath such an ardent desire to speak of the wonderful works of God, that, as far as his wishes are concerned, he *would* set the "*all*" forth, though he *could* not do it, for love has neither bounds nor end: and, as Paul saith (1 Cor. xiii. 7), "Love beareth all things, believeth all things, hopeth all things;" hence it can do all things, and does do all things, for God looketh at the heart and spirit.—*Martin Luther.*

Verse 3.—"*When mine enemies are turned back,*" etc. *Were turned back,* repulsed, and put to flight. To render this in the present time, as our translators did, is certainly improper; it destroys the coherence, and introduces obscurity. Ainsworth saw this, and rendered in the past, "When mine enemies turned backward." "*At thy presence.*" That is, by thine anger. For as God's presence or face denotes his favour to such as fear and serve him, so it denotes his anger towards the wicked. "The face of Jehovah is against them that do evil."—*B. Boothroyd,* 1824.

Verse 3.—"*They shall fall and perish.*" It refers to those that either faint in a march, or are wounded in a battle, or especially that in flight meet with galling haps in their way, and so are galled and lamed, rendered unable to go forward, and so fall, and become liable to all the chances of pursuits, and as here, are overtaken and perish in the fall.—*Henry Hammond, D.D.*

Verse 5.—"*Thou hast rebuked the heathen,*" etc.—Augustine applieth all this mystically, as is intimated (verse 1) that it should be applied, for, "I will speak," saith he, "of all thy wonderful works;" and what so wonderful as the turning of the spiritual enemy backward, whether the devil, as when he said, "Get thee behind me, Satan;" or the old man, which is turned backward when he is put off, and the new man put on?—*John Mayer.*

Verse 8.—"*He shall judge the world in righteousness.*" In this judgment tears will not prevail, prayers will not be heard, promises will not be admitted, repentance will be too late; and as for riches, honourable titles, sceptres, and diadems, these will profit much less; and the inquisition shall be so curious and diligent, that not one light thought nor one idle word (not repented of in the life past), shall be forgotten. For truth itself hath said, not in jest, but in earnest, "Of every idle word which men have spoken, they shall give an account in the day of judgment." Oh, how many which now sin with great delight, yea, even with greediness (as if we served a god of wood or of stone, which seeth nothing, or can do nothing), will be then astonished, ashamed, and silent! Then shall the days of thy mirth be ended, and thou shalt be overwhelmed with everlasting darkness; and instead of thy pleasures, thou shalt have everlasting torments.—*Thomas Tymme.*

Verse 8.—"*He shall judge the world in righteousness.*" Even Paul, in his great address on Mars' Hill, a thousand years after, could find no better words in which to teach the Athenians the doctrine of the judgment-day than the Septuagint rendering of this clause.—*William S. Plumer.*

Verse 8.—The guilty conscience cannot abide this day. The silly sheep, when she is taken, will not bleat, but you may carry her and do what you will with her, and she will be subject; but the swine, if she be once taken, she will roar and cry, and thinks she is never taken but to be slain. So of all things the guilty conscience cannot abide to hear of this day, for they know that when they hear of it, they hear of their own condemnation. I think if there were a general collection made through the whole world that there might be no judgment-day, then God would be so rich that the world would go a-begging and be a waste wilderness. Then the covetous judge would bring forth his bribes; then the crafty lawyer would fetch out his bags; the usurer would give his gain, and a double thereof. But all the money in the world will not serve for our sin, but the judge must answer his bribes, he that hath money must answer how he came by it, and just condemnation must come upon every soul of them; then shall the sinner be ever dying and never dead, like the salamander, that is ever in the fire and never consumed.—*Henry Smith.*

Verse 9.—It is reported of the Egyptians that, living in the fens, and being vexed with gnats, they used to sleep in high towers, whereby, those creatures not being able to soar so high, they are delivered from the biting of them: so would it be with us when bitten with cares and fear, did we but run to God for refuge, and rest confident of his help.—*John Trapp.*

Verse 10.—"*They that know thy name will put their trust in thee.*" Faith is an intelligent grace; though there can be knowledge without faith, yet there can be no faith without knowledge. One calls it quicksighted faith. Knowledge must carry the torch before faith. 2 Tim. i. 12. "For I know whom I have believed." As in Paul's conversion a light from heaven "shined round about him" (Acts ix. 3), so before faith be wrought, God shines in with a light upon the understanding. A blind faith is as bad as a dead faith: that eye may as well be said to be a good eye which is without sight, as that faith is good without knowledge. Devout ignorance damns; which condemns the church of Rome, that think it a piece of their religion to be kept in ignorance; these set up an altar to an unknown God. They say ignorance is the mother of devotion; but sure where the sun is set in the understanding, it must needs be night in the affections. So necessary is knowledge to the being of faith, that the Scriptures do sometimes baptise faith with the name of knowledge. Isa. liii. 11. "By his knowledge shall my righteous servant justify many." Knowledge is put there for faith.—*Thomas Watson.*

Verse 10.—"*They that know thy name will put their trust in thee: for thou, Lord, hast not forsaken them that seek thee.*" The mother of unbelief is ignorance of God, his faithfulness, mercy, and power. *They that know thee, will trust in thee.* This confirmed Paul, Abraham, Sarah, in the faith. "I know whom I have believed, and am persuaded that he is able to keep that which I have committed unto him against that day." 2 Tim. i. 12. "He is faithful that promised," and "able also to perform." Heb. x. 23, and xi. 11; Rom.

iv. 21. The free promises of the Lord are all certain, his commandments right and good, the recompense of reward inestimably to be valued above thousands of gold and silver ; trust therefore in the Lord, O my soul, and follow hard after him. Thou hast his free promise, who never failed, who hath promised more than possibly thou couldst ask or think, who hath done more for thee than ever he promised, who is good and bountiful to the wicked and ungodly ; thou doest his work, who is able and assuredly will bear thee out. There is a crown of glory proposed unto thee above all conceit of merit ; stick fast unto his word, and suffer nothing to divide thee from it. Rest upon his promises though he seem to kill thee ; cleave unto his statutes though the flesh lust, the world allure, the devil tempt by flatteries or threatenings to the contrary.—*John Ball*, 1632.

Verse 10.—" *They that know thy name will put their trust in thee.*" They can do no otherwise who savingly know God's sweet attributes, and noble acts for his people. We never trust a man till we know him, and bad men are better known than trusted. Not so the Lord ; for where his name is ointment poured forth, the virgins love him, fear him, rejoice in him, and repose upon him.— *John Trapp.*

Verse 12.—" *When he maketh inquisition for blood, he remembereth them.*" There is a time when God will make inquisition for innocent blood. The Hebrew word *doresh*, from *darash*, that is here rendered *inquisition,* signifies not barely to seek, to search, but to seek, search, and enquire with all diligence and care imaginable. Oh, there is a time a-coming when the Lord will make a very diligent and careful search and enquiry after all the innocent blood of his afflicted and persecuted people, which persecutors and tyrants have spilt as water upon the ground ; and woe to persecutors when God shall make a more strict, critical, and careful enquiry after the blood of his people than ever was made in the inquisition of Spain, where all things are carried with the greatest diligence, subtlety, secrecy, and severity. O persecutors, there is a time a-coming, when God will make a strict enquiry after the blood of Hooper, Bradford, Latimer, Taylor, Ridley, etc. There is a time a-coming, wherein God will enquire who silenced and suspended such-and-such ministers, and who stopped the mouths of such-and-such, and who imprisoned, confined, and banished such-and-such, who were once burning and shining lights, and who were willing to spend and be spent that sinners might be saved, and that Christ might be glorified. There is a time, when the Lord will make a very narrow enquiry into all the actions and practices of ecclesiastical courts, high commissions, committees, assizes, etc., and deal with persecutors as they have dealt with his people.— *Thomas Brooks.*

Verse 12. —" *When he maketh inquisition for blood, he remembereth them.*" There is *vox sanguinis*, a voice of blood ; and " he that planted the ear, shall he not hear ?" It covered the old world with waters. The earth is filled with cruelty ; it was *vox sanguinis* that cried, and the heavens heard the earth, and the windows of heaven opened to let fall judgment and vengeance upon it. *Edward Marbury*, 1649.

Verse 12.—" *When he maketh inquisition for blood,*" etc. Though God may seem to wink for a time at the cruelty of violent men, yet will call them at last to a strict account for all the innocent blood they have shed, and for their unjust and unmerciful usage of meek and humble persons ; whose cry he never forgets (though he doth not presently answer it), but takes a fit time to be avenged of their oppressors.—*Symon Patrick, D.D.*, 1626—1707.

Verse 12.—" *He maketh inquisition for blood.*" He is so stirred at this sin, that he will up, search out the authors, contrivers, and commissioners of this scarlet sin, he will avenge for blood.— *William Greenhill.*

Verse 12.—" *He forgetteth not the cry of the humble.*" Prayer is a haven to the shipwrecked man, an anchor to them that are sinking in the waves, a staff to the limbs that totter, a mine of jewels to the poor, a healer of diseases, and a guardian of health. Prayer at once secures the continuance of our blessings, and dissipates the clouds of our calamities. O blessed prayer! thou art the unwearied conqueror of human woes, the firm foundation of human happiness, the source of ever-enduring joy, the mother of philosophy. The man who can pray truly, though languishing in extremest indigence, is richer than all beside, whilst the wretch who never bowed the knee, though proudly sitting as monarch of all nations, is of all men most destitute.—*Chrysostom.*

Verse 14.—"*That I may show forth all thy praise,*" etc. To show forth *all* God's praise is to enter largely into the work. An occasional " *God, I thank thee,*" is no fit return for a perpetual stream of rich benefits.—*William S. Plumer.*

Verse 15.—" *The heathen are sunk down in the pit that they made,*" etc. Whilst they are digging pits for others, there is a pit a-digging and a grave a-making for themselves. They have a measure to make up, and a treasure to fill, which at length will be broken open, which, methinks, should take off them which are set upon mischief from pleasing themselves in their plots. Alas! they are but plotting their own ruin, and building a Babel which will fall upon their own heads. If there were any commendation in plotting, then that great plotter of plotters, that great engineer, Satan, would go beyond us all, and take all the credit from us. But let us not envy Satan and his in their glory. They had need of something to comfort them. Let them please themselves with their trade. The day is coming wherein the daughter of Sion shall laugh them to scorn. There will be a time wherein it shall be said, " Arise, Sion, and thresh." Micah iv. 13. And usually the delivery of God's children is joined with the destruction of his enemies ; Saul's death, and David's deliverance ; the Israelites' deliverance, and the Egyptians' drowning. The church and her opposites are like the scales of a balance ; when one goes up, the other goes down.—*Richard Sibbs.*

Verses 15—17. It will much increase the torment of the damned, in that their torments will be as large and strong as their understandings and affections, which will cause those violent passions to be still working. Were their loss never so great, and their sense of it never so passionate, yet if they could but lose the use of their memory, those passions would die, and that loss being forgotten, would little trouble them. But as they cannot lay by their life and being, though then they would account annihilation a singular mercy, so neither can they lay aside any part of their being. Understanding, conscience, affections, memory, must all live to torment them, which should have helped to their happiness. And as by these they should have fed upon the love of God, and drawn forth perpetually the joys of his presence, so by these must they now feed upon the wrath of God, and draw forth continually the dolours of his absence. Therefore, never think, that when I say the hardness of their hearts, and their blindness, dulness, and forgetfulness shall be removed, that therefore they are more holy and happy than before : no, but morally more vile, and hereby far more miserable. Oh, how many times did God by his messengers here call upon them, " Sinners, consider whither you are going. Do but make a stand awhile, and think where your way will end, what is the offered glory that you so carelessly reject : will not this be bitterness in the end ?" And yet, these men would never be brought to consider. But in the latter days, saith the Lord, they shall perfectly consider it, when they are *ensnared in the work of their own hands,* when God hath arrested them, and judgment is passed upon them, and vengeance is poured out upon them to the full, then they cannot choose but consider it, whether they will or no. Now they have no leisure to consider, nor any room in their memories for the things of another life. Ah! but then they shall have leisure enough, they shall be where they shall have nothing else to do but consider it : their memories shall have no other employment to hinder them ; it shall even be engraven upon the tables of their hearts. God would have the doctrine of their eternal state to have been written on the posts of their doors, on their houses, on their hands, and on their hearts : he would have had them mind it and mention it, as they rise and lie down, and as they walk abroad, that so it might have gone well with them at their latter end. And seeing they rejected this counsel of the Lord, therefore shall it be written always before them in the place of their thraldom, that which way soever they look they may still behold it.—*Richard Baxter.*

Verse 16.—" *The Lord is known by the judgment which he executeth.*" Now if the Lord be known by the judgment which he executeth ; then, the judgment which he executeth must be known ; it must be an open judgment ; and such are very many of the judgments of God, they are acted as upon a stage. And I may give you an account in three particulars why the Lord will sometimes do justice in the place of beholders, or in the open sight of others. First, that there may be witnesses enough of what he doth, and so a record of it be kept, at least in the minds and memories of faithful men for the generations to come. Secondly, the Lord doth it not only that he may have witnesses of his justice, but also that his justice and the proceedings of it, may have an effect and a fruit upon those who did not feel it, nor fall under it. This was the reason why the Lord threatened to punish Jerusalem in the sight of the nations. Ezek. v. 6, 7, 8, 14, 15. . . . . God would execute judgment in Jerusalem, a city placed in the midst of the nations, that as the nations had taken notice of the extraordinary favours, benefits, deliverances, and salvations which God wrought for Jerusalem, so they might also take notice of his judgments and sore displeasure against them. Jerusalem was not seated in some nook, corner, or by-place of the world, but in the midst of the nations, that both the goodness and severity of God towards them might be conspicuous. . . . God lets some sinners suffer, or punisheth them openly, both because he would have all others take notice that he dislikes what they have done, as also because he would not have others do the like, lest they be made like them, both in the matter and manner of their sufferings. 'Tis a favour as well as our duty, to be taught by other men's harms, and to be instructed by their strokes to prevent our own. . . . Thirdly, God strikes some wicked men in open view, or in the place of beholders for the comfort of his own people, and for their encouragement. Psalm lviii. 10, 11. " The righteous shall rejoice when he seeth the vengeance ;" not that he shall be glad of the vengeance, purely as it is a hurt or a suffering to the creature ; but the righteous shall be glad when he seeth the vengeance of God as it is a fulfilling of the threatening of God against the sin of man, and an evidence of his own holiness. . . . . It is said (Exod. xiv. 30, 31), that God having overwhelmed the Egyptians in the Red Sea, the Israelites saw the Egyptians dead upon the sea shore : God did not suffer the carcases of the Egyptians to sink to the bottom of the sea, but caused them to lie upon the shore, that the Israelites might see them ; and when Israel saw that dreadful stroke of the Lord upon the Egyptians, it is said, " The people feared the Lord, and believed the Lord, and his servant Moses." Thus they were confirmed in their faith by God's open judgments upon the Egyptians. They were smitten in the place of beholders, or in the open sight of others.—*Condensed from Joseph Caryl.*

Verse 16.—" *The Lord is known by the judgment which he executeth ;*" when he lays his hand upon sinners, saints tremble, consider his power, majesty, greatness, the nature of his judgments, and so judge themselves, and remove out of the way whatever may provoke. . . . . As fire begets a splendour round about where it is, so do the judgments of God set out to the world his glory, justice, holiness.—*William Greenhill.*

Verse 16.—" *Snared in the work of his own hands.*" The wages that sin bargains with the sinner are life, pleasure, and profit ; but the wages it pays him with are death, torment, and destruction. He that would understand the falsehood and deceit of sin, must compare its promises and its payment together. *Robert South, D.D.*, 1633—1716.

Verse 16.—" *Higgaion, Selah,*" that is, as Ainsworth renders it, " Meditation, Selah :" showing this ought to be seriously considered of. The word " *Higgaion*" is again had (Psalm xcii. 3); being mentioned among other musical instruments, whereby we may gather it to be one of them ; for there is psaltery, nable, higgaion, and harp.—*John Mayer.*

Verse 16.—" *The wicked is snared in the work of his own hands.*" Not only do we read it in the word of God, but all history, all experience, records the same righteous justice of God, in snaring the wicked in the work of their own hands. Perhaps the most striking instance on record, next to Haman on his own gallows, is one connected with the horrors of the French Revolution, in which we are told that, " within nine months of the death of the queen Marie Antoinette by the guillotine, every one implicated in her untimely end, her accusers, the judges, the jury, the prosecutors, the witnesses, all, every one at least whose fate is known, perished by the same instrument as their innocent victim." " In the net which they had laid for her was their own foot taken—into the pit which they digged for her did they themselves fall."—*Barton Bouchier,* 1855.

Verse 17.—The ungodly at death must undergo God's fury and indignation. " *The wicked shall be turned into hell.*" I have read of a loadstone in Ethiopia which hath two corners, with one it draws the iron to it, with the other it puts the iron from it : so God hath two hands, of mercy and justice ; with the one he will draw the godly to heaven, with the other he will thrust the sinner to hell ; and oh, how dreadful is that place ! It is called a fiery lake (Rev. xx. 15) ; a lake, to denote the plenty of torments in hell ; a fiery lake, to show the fierceness of them : fire is the most torturing element. Strabo in his geography mentions a lake in Galilee of such a pestiferous nature that it scaldeth off the skin of whatsoever is cast into it ; but, alas ! that lake is cool compared with this fiery lake into which the damned are thrown. To demonstrate this fire terrible, there are two most pernicious qualities in it. 1. It is sulphureous, it is mixed with brimstone (Rev. xxi. 8), which is unsavoury and suffocating. 2. It is inextinguishable ; though the wicked shall be choked in the flames, yet not consumed (Rev. xx. 10); "And the devil was cast into the lake of fire and brimstone, where the beast and the false prophet are, and shall be tormented day and night forever and ever." Behold the deplorable condition of all ungodly ones in the other world, they shall have a life that always dies, and a death that always lives : may not this affright men out of their sins, and make them become godly ? unless they are resolved to try how hot the hell-fire is.—*Thomas Watson.*

Verse 17.—" *The wicked shall be turned into hell,*" etc. By " *the wicked* " here we must understand unregenerate persons, whoever they are that are in a state of unregeneracy. . . . . . . That person is here spoken of as a " *wicked* " man that " *forgets God,*" who does not think of him frequently, and with affection, with fear and delight, and those affections that are suitable to serious thoughts of God. . . . . . . To forget God and to be a wicked person is all one. And these two things will abundantly evince the truth of this assertion : namely, that this forgetfulness of God excludes the prime and main essentials of religion, and also includes in it the highest and most heinous pieces of wickedness, and therefore must needs denominate the subject, a wicked person. . . . . Forgetfulness of God excludes the principal and essential parts of religion. It implies that a man doth neither esteem nor value the all-sufficiency and holiness of God, as his happiness and portion, as his strength and support ; nor doth he fear him, nor live in subjection to his laws and commands, as his rule ; nor doth he aim at the glory of God as his end : therefore every one who thus forgets God, must certainly be a wicked person. . . . . To exclude God out of our thoughts and not to let him have a place there, not to mind, nor think upon God, is the greatest wickedness of the thoughts that can be. And, therefore, though you cannot say of such a one, he will be drunk, or he will swear, cozen, or oppress ; yet if you can say he will forget God, or that he lives all his days never minding nor thinking upon God, you say enough to speak him under wrath, and to turn him into hell without remedy.—*John Howe,* 1630—1705.

Verse 17.—" The wicked shall be turned into hell." לִשְׁאוֹלָה, *Lisholah—head-long into hell, down into hell.* The original is very emphatic.—*Adam Clarke.*

Verse 17.—All wickedness came originally with the wicked one from hell ; thither it will be again remitted, and they who hold on its side must accompany it on its return to that place of torment, there to be shut up for ever. The true state both of·" nations," and the individuals of which they are composed, is to be estimated from one single circumstance ; namely, whether in their doings they remember, or " forget God." Remembrance of him is the well-spring of virtue ; forgetfulness of him, the fountain of vice.—*George Horne, D.D.*

Verse 17.—

> *Hell*, their fit habitation, fraught with fire
> Unquenchable, the house of woe and pain.
>
> *John Milton*, 1608—1674.

Verse 17.—

> Will without power, the element of *hell*,
> Abortive all its acts returning still
> Upon itself; . . . . . . Oh, anguish terrible !
> Meet guerdon of self-love, its proper ill !
> Malice would scowl upon the foe he fears ;
> And he with lip of scorn would seek to kill ;
> But neither sees the other, neither hears—
> For darkness each in his own dungeon bars,
> Lust pines for dearth, and grief drinks its own tears—
> Each in its solitude apart. Hate wars
> Against himself, and feeds upon his chain,
> Whose iron penetrates the soul it scars,
> A dreadful solitude each mind insane,
> Each its own place, its prison all alone,
> And finds no sympathy to soften pain.
>
> *J. A. Heraud.*

Verse 18.—" *For the needy shall not alway be forgotten*," etc. This is a sweet promise for a thousand occasions, and when pleaded before the throne in his name who comprehends in himself every promise, and is indeed himself the great promise of the Bible, it would be found like all others, yea and amen.—*Robert Hawker, D.D.*, 1820.

Verse 18.—" *The expectation of the poor shall not perish.*" A heathen could say, when a bird, scared by a hawk, flew into his bosom, I will not betray thee unto thy enemy, seeing thou comest for sanctuary unto me. How much less will God yield up a soul unto its enemy, when it takes sanctuary in his name, saying, Lord, I am hunted with such a temptation, dogged with such a lust ; either thou must pardon it, or I am damned ; mortify it, or I shall be a slave to it ; take me into the bosom of thy love for Christ's sake ; castle me in the arms of thy everlasting strength ; it is in thy power to save me from, or give me up into the hands of my enemy ; I have no confidence in myself or any other : into thy hands I commit my cause myself, and rely on thee. This dependence of a soul undoubtedly will awaken the almighty power of God for such a one's defence. He hath sworn the greatest oath that can come out of his blessed lips, even by himself, that such as thus fly for refuge to hope in him, shall have strong consolation. Heb. vi. 17. This indeed may give the saint the greater boldness of faith to expect kind entertainment when he repairs to God for refuge, because he cannot come before he is looked for ; God having set up his name and promises as a strong tower, both calls his people into these chambers and expects they should betake themselves thither.—*William Gurnall.*

Verse 18.—As sometimes God is said to hear us in not hearing us, so we may say he should sometimes deny us if he did not delay us. It is (saith Chrysostom) like money, which lying long in the bank, comes home at last with a duck in its mouth, with use upon use ; when money is out a great time, it makes a great return : we can stay thus upon men, and cannot we, shall not we, stay upon the Lord, and for the Lord, for a large return ? God causeth us by delay to make the more prayers ; and the more we pray, the longer we stay, the more comfort we shall have, and the more sure we are that we shall have it in the latter end. Distinguish between denying and delaying. . . . . In God *our Father* are all dimensions of love, and that in an infinite degree ; infinitely infinite : what if he defer us ? so do we our children, albeit we mean no other but to give them their own asking, yet we love to see them wait, that so they may have from us the best things, when they are at the best, in the best time, and in the best manner : if a mother should forget her only boy, yet God hath an infinite memory, he nor can, nor will forget us ; the expectation of the *waiter* shall not fail *for ever*, that is, *never.—Richard Capel.*

Verse 19.—*" Arise, O Lord,"* etc. What does this mean ? Are we to con-sider the psalmist as praying for the destruction of his enemies, as pronouncing a malediction, a curse upon them ? No ; these are not the words of one who is wishing that mischief may happen to his enemies ; they are the words of a prophet, of one who is foretelling, in Scripture language, the evil that must befall them on account of their sins.—*Augustine.*

Verse 20.—*" Put them in fear, O Lord,"* etc. We should otherwise think ourselves gods. We are so inclined to sin that we need strong restraints, and so swelled with a natural pride against God, that we need thorns in the flesh to let out the corrupt matter. The constant hanging the rod over us makes us lick the dust, and acknowledge ourselves to be altogether at the Lord's mercy. Though God hath pardoned us, he will make us wear the halter about our necks to humble us.—*Stephen Charnock.*

Verse 20.—*" That the nations may know themselves to be but men."* The original word is אֱנוֹשׁ, *enosh ;* and therefore it is a prayer that they may know themselves to be but miserable, frail, and dying men. The word is in the singular number, but it is used collectively.—*John Calvin.*

HINTS TO THE VILLAGE PREACHER.

Verse 1.—I. The only object of our praise—" thee, O Lord." II. The abundant themes of praise—" all thy marvellous works." III. The proper nature of praise—" with my whole heart."—*B. Davies.*

Verse 1.—*" I will show forth."* Endless employment and enjoyment.

Verse 1.—*" Thy marvellous works."* Creation, Providence, Redemption, are all marvellous, as exhibiting the attributes of God in such a degree as to excite the wonder of all God's universe. A very suggestive topic.

Verse 2.—Sacred song : its connection with holy gladness.

The duty, excellence, and grounds of holy cheerfulness.

Verse 4.—(1) The rights of the righteous are sure to be assailed, (2) but equally sure to be defended.

Verse 6.—I. The great enemy. II. The destructions he has caused. III. The means of his overthrow. IV. The rest which shall ensue.

Verse 7 (*first clause*).—The eternity of God—the comfort of saints, the terror of sinners.

Verse 8.—The justice of God's moral government, especially in relation to the last great day.

Verse 9.—Needy people, needy times, all-sufficient provision.

Verse 10.—I. All-important knowledge—" know thy name." II. Blessed result—" will put their trust in thee." III. Sufficient reason—" for thou, Lord, hast not forsaken them that seek thee."—*T. W. Medhurst.*

Knowledge, Faith, Experience, the connection of the three.

Verse 10.—The names of God inspire trust. JEHOVAH *Jireh, Tsidkenu, Rophi, Shammah, Shalom, Nissi,* ELOHIM, SHADDAI, ADONAI, etc.

Verse 11.—I. Zion, what is it? II. Her glorious inhabitant, what doth he? III. The twofold occupation of her sons—"sing praises," "declare among the people his doings." IV. Arguments from the first part of the subject to encourage us in the double duty.

Verse 12.—I. God on awful business. II. Remembers his people; to spare, honour, bless, and avenge them. III. Fulfils their cries, in their own salvation, and overthrow of enemies. A consolatory sermon for times of war or pestilence.

Verse 13.—"*Have mercy upon me, O Lord.*" The publican's prayer expounded, commended, presented, and fulfilled.

Verse 13.—"*Thou that liftest me up from the gates of death.*" Deep distresses, Great deliverances. Glorious exaltations.

Verse 14.—"*I will rejoice in thy salvation.*" Especially because it is *thine,* O God, and therefore honours thee. In its freeness, fulness, suitability, certainty, everlastingness. Who can rejoice in this? Reasons why they should always do so.

Verse 15.—*Lex talionis.* Memorable instances.

Verse 16.—Awful knowledge; a tremendous alternative as compared with verse 10.

Verse 17.—A warning to forgetters of God.

Verse 18.—Delays in deliverance. I. Unbelief's estimate of them—"forgotten," "perish." II. God's promise—"not always." III. Faith's duty—wait.

Verse 19. "*Let not man prevail.*" A powerful plea. Cases when employed in Scripture. The reason of its power. Times for its use.

Verse 20.—A needful lesson, and how it is taught.

PSALM X.

*Since this Psalm has no title of its own, it is supposed by some to be a fragment of Psalm
ix. We prefer, however, since it is complete in itself, to consider it as a separate composition. We have had instances already of Psalms which seem meant to form a pair (Ps. i.
and ii., Ps. iii. and iv.,) and this, with the ninth, is another specimen of the double Psalm.*

*The prevailing theme seems to be the oppression and persecution of the wicked, we will,
therefore, for our own guidance, entitle it, THE CRY OF THE OPPRESSED.*

*DIVISION.—The first verse, in an exclamation of surprise, explains the intent of the Psalm,
viz., to invoke the interposition of God for the deliverance of his poor and persecuted people.
From verse 2 to 11, the character of the oppressor is described in powerful language. In
verse 12, the cry of the first verse bursts forth again, but with a clearer utterance. In the
next place (verses 13–15), God's eye is clearly beheld as regarding all the cruel deeds of the
wicked; and as a consequence of divine omniscience, the ultimate judgment of the oppressed
is joyously anticipated (verses 16–18). To the Church of God during times of persecution,
and to individual saints who are smarting under the hand of the proud sinner, this Psalm
furnishes suitable language both for prayer and praise.*

EXPOSITION.

WHY standest thou afar off, O LORD? *why* hidest thou
thyself in times of trouble?

To the tearful eye of the sufferer the Lord seemed to *stand* still, as if he calmly
looked on, and did not sympathize with his afflicted one. Nay, more, the Lord
appeared to be *afar off*, no longer "a very present help in trouble," but an
inaccessible mountain, into which no man would be able to climb. The presence
of God is the joy of his people, but any suspicion of his absence is distracting
beyond measure. Let us, then, ever remember that the Lord is nigh us. The
refiner is never far from the mouth of the furnace when his gold is in the fire,
and the Son of God is always walking in the midst of the flames when his holy
children are cast into them. Yet he that knows the frailty of man will little
wonder that when we are sharply exercised, we find it hard to bear the apparent
neglect of the Lord when he forbears to work our deliverance.

"*Why hidest thou thyself in times of trouble?*" It is not the trouble, but the
hiding of our Father's face, which cuts us to the quick. When trial and desertion
come together, we are in as perilous a plight as Paul, when his ship fell into a
place where two seas met (Acts xxvii. 41). It is but little wonder if we are like
the vessel which ran aground, and the fore-part stuck fast, and remained
unmoveable, while the hinder part was broken by the violence of the waves.
When our sun is eclipsed, it is dark indeed. If we need an answer to the
question, "Why hidest thou thyself?" it is to be found in the fact that there is
a "needs-be," not only for trial, but for heaviness of heart under trial (1 Pet.
i. 6); but how could this be the case, if the Lord should shine upon us while
he is afflicting us? Should the parent comfort his child while he is correcting
him, where would be the use of the chastening? A smiling face and a rod are
not fit companions. God bares the back that the blow may be felt; for it is
only *felt* affliction which can become *blest* affliction. If we were carried in the
arms of God over every stream, where would be the trial, and where the
experience, which trouble is meant to teach us?

2 The wicked in *his* pride doth persecute the poor : let them be
taken in the devices that they have imagined.

3 For the wicked boasteth of his heart's desire, and blesseth the
covetous, *whom* the LORD abhorreth.

4 The wicked, through the pride of his countenance, will not seek *after God :* God *is* not in all his thoughts.

5 His ways are always grievous ; thy judgments *are* far above out of his sight : *as for* all his enemies, he puffeth at them.

6 He hath said in his heart, I shall not be moved : for *I shall* never *be* in adversity.

7 His mouth is full of cursing and deceit and fraud : under his tongue *is* mischief and vanity.

8 He sitteth in the lurking places of the villages : in the secret places doth he murder the innocent : his eyes are privily set against the poor.

9 He lieth in wait secretly as a lion in his den : he lieth in wait to catch the poor : he doth catch the poor, when he draweth him into his net.

10 He croucheth, *and* humbleth himself, that the poor may fall by his strong ones.

11 He hath said in his heart, God hath forgotten : he hideth his face ; he will never see *it*.

2. The second verse contains the formal indictment against the wicked : " *The wicked in his pride doth persecute the poor.*" The accusation divides itself into two distinct charges,—pride and tyranny ; the one the root and cause of the other. The second sentence is the humble petition of the oppressed : " *Let them be taken in the devices that they have imagined.*" The prayer is reasonable, just, and natural. Even our enemies themselves being judges, it is but right that men should be done by as they wished to do to others. We only weigh you in your own scales, and measure your corn with your own bushel. Terrible shall be thy day, O persecuting Babylon ! when thou shalt be made to drink of the wine-cup which thou thyself hast filled to the brim with the blood of saints. There are none who will dispute the justice of God, when he shall hang every Haman on his own gallows, and cast all the enemies of his Daniels into their own den of lions.

3. The indictment being read, and the petition presented, the evidence is now heard upon the first count. The evidence is very full and conclusive upon the matter of *pride*, and no jury could hesitate to give a verdict against the prisoner at the bar. Let us, however, hear the witnesses one by one. The first testifies that he is a boaster. " *For the wicked boasteth of his heart's desire.*" He is a very silly boaster, for he glories in a mere desire : a very brazen-faced boaster, for that desire is villany ; and a most abandoned sinner, to boast of that which is his shame. Bragging sinners are the worst and most contemptible of men, especially when their filthy desires,—too filthy to be carried into act,—become the theme of their boastings. When Mr. Hate-Good and Mr. Heady are joined in partnership, they drive a brisk trade in the devil's wares. This one proof is enough to condemn the prisoner at the bar. Take him away, jailor ! But stay, another witness desires to be sworn and heard. This time, the impudence of the proud rebel is even more apparent ; for he " *blesseth the covetous, whom the Lord abhorreth.*" This is insolence, which is pride unmasked. He is haughty enough to differ from the Judge of all the earth, and bless the men whom God hath cursed. So did the sinful generation in the days of Malachi, who called the proud happy, and set up those that worked wickedness (Mal. iii. 15). These base pretenders would dispute with their Maker ; they would—

" Snatch from his hand the balance and the rod,
   Rejudge his justice, be the god of God."

How often have we heard the wicked man speaking in terms of honour of the covetous, the grinder of the poor, and the sharp dealer! Our old proverb hath it,—

> "I wot well how the world wags;
> He is most loved that hath most bags."

Pride meets covetousness, and compliments it as wise, thrifty, and prudent. We say it with sorrow, there are many professors of religion who esteem a rich man, and flatter him, even though they know that he has fattened himself upon the flesh and blood of the poor. The only sinners who are received as respectable are covetous men. If a man is a fornicator, or a drunkard, we put him out of the church; but who ever read of church discipline against that idolatrous wretch,—the covetous man? Let us tremble, lest we be found to be partakers of this atrocious sin of pride, "blessing the covetous, whom Jehovah abhorreth."

4. The proud boastings and lewd blessings of the wicked have been received in evidence against him, and now his own face confirms the accusation, and his empty closet cries aloud against him. "*The wicked, through the pride of his countenance, will not seek after God.*" Proud hearts breed proud looks and stiff knees. It is an admirable arrangement that the heart is often written on the countenance, just as the motion of the wheels of a clock find their record on its face. A brazen face and a broken heart never go together. We are not quite sure that the Athenians were wise when they ordained that men should be tried in the dark lest their countenances should weigh with the judges; for there is much more to be learned from the motions of the muscles of the face than from the words of the lips. Honesty shines in the face, but villainy peeps out at the eyes.

See the effect of pride; it kept the man from seeking God. It is hard to pray with a stiff neck and an unbending knee. "*God is not in all his thoughts:*" he thought much, but he had no thoughts for God. Amid heaps of chaff there was not a grain of wheat. The only place where God is not is in the thoughts of the wicked. This is a damning accusation; for where the God of heaven is not, the Lord of hell is reigning and raging; and if God be not in our thoughts, our thoughts will bring us to perdition.

5. "*His ways are always grievous.*" To himself they are hard. Men go a rough road when they go to hell. God has hedged-up the way of sin: O what folly to leap these hedges and fall among the thorns! To others, also, his ways cause much sorrow and vexation; but what cares he? He sits like the idol god upon his monstrous car, utterly regardless of the crowds who are crushed as he rolls along. "*Thy judgments are far above out of his sight:*" he looks high, but not high enough. As God is forgotten, so are his judgments. He is not able to comprehend the things of God; a swine may sooner look through a telescope at the stars than this man study the Word of God to understand the righteousness of the Lord. "*As for all his enemies, he puffeth at them.*" He defies and domineers; and when men resist his injurious behaviour, he sneers at them, and threatens to annihilate them with a puff. In most languages there is a word of contempt borrowed from the action of puffing with the lips, and in English we should express the idea by saying, "He cries, 'Pooh! Pooh!' at his enemies." Ah! there is one enemy who will not thus be puffed at. Death will puff at the candle of his life and blow it out, and the wicked boaster will find it grim work to brag in the tomb.

6. The testimony of the sixth verse concludes the evidence against the prisoner upon the first charge of pride, and certainly it is conclusive in the highest degree. The present witness has been prying into the secret chambers of the heart, and has come to tell us what he has heard. "*He hath said in his heart, I shall not be moved: for I shall never be in adversity.*" O impertinence run to seed! The man thinks himself immutable, and omnipotent too, for *he, he* is never to be in adversity. He counts himself a privileged man. He sits alone, and shall see no sorrow. His nest is in the stars, and he dreams not of a hand that shall pluck him thence. But let us remember that this man's house is built upon the sand, upon a foundation no more substantial than the rolling waves of

the sea. He that is too secure is never safe. Boastings are not buttresses, and self-confidence is a sorry bulwark. This is the ruin of fools, that when they succeed they become too big, and swell with self-conceit, as if their summer would last for ever, and their flowers bloom on eternally. Be humble, O man ! for thou art mortal, and thy lot is mutable.

The second crime is now to be proved. The fact that the man is proud and arrogant may go a long way to prove that he is vindictive and cruel. Haman's pride was the father of a cruel design to murder all the Jews. Nebuchadnezzar builds an idol ; in pride he commands all men to bow before it ; and then cruelty stands ready to heat the furnace seven times hotter for those who will not yield to his imperious will. Every proud thought is twin brother to a cruel thought. He who exalts himself will despise others, and one step further will make him a tyrant.

7. Let us now hear the witnesses in court. Let the wretch speak for himself, for out of his own mouth he will be condemned. *"His mouth is full of cursing and deceit and fraud."* There is not only a little evil there, but his mouth is full of it. A three-headed serpent hath stowed away its coils and venom within the den of his black mouth. There is *cursing* which he spits against both God and men, *deceit* with which he entraps the unwary, and *fraud* by which, even in his common dealings, he robs his neighbours. Beware of such a man : have no sort of dealing with him : none but the silliest of geese would go to the fox's sermon, and none but the most foolish will put themselves into the society of knaves. But we must proceed. Let us look under this man's tongue as well as in his mouth ; *"under his tongue is mischief and vanity."* Deep in his throat are the unborn words which shall come forth as mischief and iniquity.

8. Despite the bragging of this base wretch, it seems that he is as cowardly as he is cruel. *"He sitteth in the lurking places of the villages : in the secret places doth he murder the innocent : his eyes are privily set against the poor."* He acts the part of the highwayman, who springs upon the unsuspecting traveller in some desolate part of the road. There are always bad men lying in wait for the saints. This is a land of robbers and thieves ; let us travel well armed, for every bush conceals an enemy. Everywhere there are traps laid for us, and foes thirsting for our blood. There are enemies at our table as well as across the sea. We are never safe, save when the Lord is with us.

9. The picture becomes blacker, for here is the cunning of the lion, and of the huntsman, as well as the stealthiness of the robber. Surely there are some men who come up to the very letter of this description. With watching, perversion, slander, whispering, and false swearing, they ruin the character of the righteous, and murder the innocent ; or, with legal quibbles, mortgages, bonds, writs, and the like, they catch the poor, and draw them into a net. Chrysostom was peculiarly severe upon this last phase of cruelty, but assuredly not more so than was richly merited. Take care, brethren, for there are other traps besides these. Hungry lions are crouching in every den, and fowlers spread their nets in every field.

Quarles well pictures our danger in those memorable lines,—

> " The close pursuers' busy hands do plant
> Snares in thy substance ; snares attend thy wants ;
> Snares in thy credit ; snares in thy disgrace ;
> Snares in thy high estate ; snares in thy base ;
> Snares tuck thy bed ; and snares surround thy board ;
> Snares watch thy thoughts ; and snares attack thy word ;
>
> Snares in thy quiet ; snares in thy commotion ;
> Snares in thy diet ; snares in thy devotion ;
> Snares lurk in thy resolves ; snares in thy doubt ;
> Snares lie within thy heart, and snares without ;
> Snares are above thy head, and snares beneath ;
> Snares in thy sickness ; snares are in thy death."

O Lord ! keep thy servants, and defend us from all our enemies !

10. *" He croucheth and humbleth himself, that the poor may fall by his strong ones."* Seeming humility is often armour-bearer to malice. The lion crouches

that he may leap with the greater force, and bring down his strong limbs upon his prey. When a wolf was old, and had tasted human blood, the old Saxon cried, " Ware, wolf !" and we may cry, " Ware fox !" They who crouch to our feet are longing to make us fall. Be very careful of fawners ; for friendship and flattery are deadly enemies.

11. As upon the former count, so upon this one ; a witness is forthcoming, who has been listening at the keyhole of the heart. Speak up, friend, and let us hear your story. *" He hath said in his heart, God hath forgotten : he hideth his face ; he will never see it."* This cruel man comforts himself with the idea that God is blind, or, at least, forgetful : a fond and foolish fancy, indeed. Men doubt Omniscience when they persecute the saints. If we had a sense of God's presence with us, it would be impossible for us to ill-treat his children. In fact, there can scarcely be a greater preservation from sin than the constant thought of " thou, God, seest me."

Thus has the trial proceeded. The case has been fully stated ; and now it is but little wonder that the oppressed petitioner lifts up the cry for judgment, which we find in the following verse : —

12 Arise, O LORD ; O God, lift up thine hand : forget not the humble.

With what bold language will faith address its God ! and yet what unbelief is mingled with our strongest confidence. Fearlessly the Lord is stirred up to arise and lift up his hand, yet timidly is he begged not to forget the humble ; as if Jehovah could ever be forgetful of his saints. This verse is the incessant cry of the Church, and she will never refrain therefrom until her Lord shall come in his glory to avenge her of all her adversaries.

13 Wherefore doth the wicked contemn God ? he hath said in his heart, Thou wilt not require *it.*

14 Thou hast seen *it ;* for thou beholdest mischief and spite, to requite *it* with thy hand : the poor committeth himself unto thee ; thou art the helper of the fatherless.

15 Break thou the arm of the wicked and the evil *man :* seek out his wickedness *till* thou find none.

In these verses the description of the wicked is condensed, and the evil of his character traced to its source, viz., atheistical ideas with regard to the government of the world. We may at once perceive that this is intended to be another urgent plea with the Lord to show his power, and reveal his justice. When the wicked call God's righteousness in question, we may well beg him to teach them terrible things in righteousness. In verse 13, the hope of the infidel and his heart-wishes are laid bare. He despises the Lord, because he will not believe that sin will meet with punishment : *" he hath said in his heart, Thou wilt not require it."* If there were no hell for other men, there ought to be one for those who question the justice of it. This vile suggestion receives its answer in verse 14. *" Thou hast seen it ; for thou beholdest mischief and spite, to requite it with thy hand."* God is all-eye to see, and all-hand to punish his enemies. From Divine oversight there is no hiding, and from Divine justice there is no fleeing. Wanton mischief shall meet with woeful misery, and those who harbour spite shall inherit sorrow. Verily there is a God which judgeth in the earth. Nor is this the only instance of the presence of God in the world ; for while he chastises the oppressor, he befriends the oppressed. *" The poor committeth himself unto thee."* They give themselves up entirely into the Lord's hands. Resigning their judgment to his enlightenment, and their wills to his supremacy, they rest assured that he will order all things for the best. Nor does he deceive their hope. He preserves them in times of need, and causes them to rejoice in his goodness. *" Thou art the helper of the fatherless."* God is the parent of all orphans. When the earthly father sleeps beneath the sod, a heavenly Father smiles from above.   By some means or other, orphan children are fed, and well they may when they have such a Father.

15. In this verse we hear again the burden of the psalmist's prayer : " *Break thou the arm of the wicked and the evil man.*"   Let the sinner lose his power to sin ; stop the tyrant, arrest the oppressor, weaken the loins of the mighty, and dash in pieces the terrible.   They deny thy justice : let them feel it to the full. Indeed, they shall feel it ; for God shall hunt the sinner for ever : so long as there is a grain of sin in him it shall be sought out and punished.   It is not a little worthy of note, that very few great persecutors have ever died in their beds : the curse has manifestly pursued them, and their fearful sufferings have made them own *that* divine justice at which they could at one time launch defiance.   God permits tyrants to arise as thorn-hedges to protect his church from the intrusion of hypocrites, and that he may teach his backsliding children by them, as Gideon did the men of Succoth with the briers of the wilderness ; but he soon cuts up these Herods, like the thorns, and casts them into the fire. Thales, the Milesian, one of the wise men of Greece, being asked what he thought to be the greatest rarity in the world, replied, " To see a tyrant live to be an old man."   See how the Lord breaks, not only the arm, but the neck of proud oppressors !   To the men who had neither justice nor mercy for the saints, there shall be rendered justice to the full, but not a grain of mercy.

16 The LORD *is* King for ever and ever : the heathen are perished out of his land.

17 LORD, thou hast heard the desire of the humble : thou wilt prepare their heart, thou wilt cause thine ear to hear :

18 To judge the fatherless and the oppressed, that the man of the earth may no more oppress.

The Psalm ends with a song of thanksgiving to the great and everlasting King, because he has granted the desire of his humble and oppressed people, has defended the fatherless, and punished the heathen who trampled upon his poor and afflicted children.   Let us learn that we are sure to speed well, if we carry our complaint to the King of kings.   Rights will be vindicated, and wrongs redressed, at his throne.   His government neglects not the interests of the needy, nor does it tolerate oppression in the mighty.   Great God, we leave ourselves in thine hand ; to thee we commit thy church afresh.   Arise, O God, and let the man of the earth—the creature of a day—be broken before the majesty of thy power.   Come, Lord Jesus, and glorify thy people.   Amen and Amen.

EXPLANATORY NOTES AND QUAINT SAYINGS.

Whole Psalm.—There is not, in my judgment, a Psalm which describes the mind, the manners, the works, the words, the feelings, and the fate of the ungodly with so much propriety, fulness, and light, as this Psalm.   So that, if in any respect there has not been enough said heretofore, or if there shall be anything wanting in the Psalms that shall follow, we may here find a perfect image and representation of iniquity.   This Psalm, therefore, is a type, form, and description of that man, who, though he may be in the sight of himself and of men more excellent than Peter himself, is detestable in the eyes of God ; and this it was that moved Augustine, and those who followed him, to understand the Psalm of ANTICHRIST.   But as the Psalm is without a title, let us embrace the most general and common understanding of it (as I said), and let us look at the picture of ungodliness which it sets before us.   Not that we would deny the propriety of the acceptation in which others receive it, nay, we will, in our general acceptation of the Psalm, include also its reference to ANTICHRIST. And, indeed, it will not be at all absurd if we join this Psalm with the preceding, in its order thus. That David, in the preceding, spoke of the ungodly converted, and prayed for those who were to be converted. But that here he is speaking of the ungodly that are still left so, and in power prevailing over the weak ALMUTH, concerning whom he has no hope, or is in a great uncertainty of mind, whether they ever will be converted or not.—*Martin Luther.*

Verse 1.—" *Why hidest thou thyself in times of trouble ?*" The answer to this is not far to seek, for if the Lord did not hide himself it would not be a time of trouble at all. As well ask why the sun does not shine at night, when for certain there could be no night if he did. It is essential to our thorough chastisement that the Father should withdraw his smile : there is a needs be not only for manifold temptations, but that we be in heaviness through them. The design of the rod is only answered by making us smart. If there be no pain, there will be no profit. If there be no hiding of God, there will be no bitterness, and consequently no purging efficacy in his chastisements.—*C. H. S.*

Verse 1 (*last clause*).—" *Times of trouble*" should be times of confidence ; fixedness of heart on God would prevent fears of heart. Psalm cxii. 7. " He shall not be afraid of evil tidings : his heart is fixed." How ? " Trusting in the Lord. His heart is established, he shall not be afraid." Otherwise without it we shall be as light as a weather-cock, moved with every blast of evil tidings, our hopes will swim or sink according to the news we hear. Providence would seem to sleep unless faith and prayer awaken it. The disciples had but little faith in their Master's accounts, yet that little faith awakened him in a storm, and he relieved them. Unbelief doth only discourage God from showing his power in taking our parts.—*Stephen Charnock.*

Verse 2.—" *The wicked in his pride doth persecute the poor.*" THE OPPRESSOR'S PLEA. I seek but what is my own by law ; it was his own free act and deed— the execution lies for goods and body ; and goods or body I will have, or else my money. What if his beggarly children pine, or his proud wife perish ? they perish at their own charge, not mine ; and what is that to me ? I must be paid, or he lie by it until I have my utmost farthing, or his bones. The law is just and good ; and, being ruled by that, how can my fair proceedings be unjust ? What is thirty in the hundred to a man of trade ? Are we born to thrum caps or pick straws ? and sell our livelihood for a few tears, and a whining face ? I thank God they move me not so much as a howling dog at midnight. I'll give no day if heaven itself would be security. I must have present money, or his bones. . . . Fifteen shillings in the pound composition ! I'll hang first. Come, tell me not of a good conscience : a good conscience is no parcel of my trade ; it hath made more bankrupts than all the loose wives in the universal city. My conscience is no fool : it tells me my own is my own, and that a well crammed bag is no deceitful friend, but will stick close to me when all my friends forsake me. If to gain a good estate out of nothing, and to regain a desperate debt which is as good as nothing, be the fruits and sign of a bad conscience, God help the good. Come, tell me not of griping and oppression. The world is hard, and he that hopes to thrive must gripe as hard. What I give I give, and what I lend I lend. If the way to heaven be to turn beggar upon earth, let them take it that like it. I know not what you call oppression, the law is my direction ; but of the two, it is more profitable to oppress than to be oppressed. If debtors would be honest and discharge, our hands were bound ; but when their failing offends my bags, they touch the apple of my eye, and I must right them.—*Francis Quarles.*

Verse 2.—That famous persecutor, Domitian, like others of the Roman emperors, assumed divine honours, and heated the furnace seven times hotter against Christians because they refused to worship his image. In like manner, when the popes of Rome became decorated with the blasphemous titles of

Masters of the World, and *Universal Fathers*, they let loose their blood-hounds upon the faithful. Pride is the egg of persecution.—*C. H. S.*

Verse 2.—"*Pride*," is a vice which cleaveth so fast unto the hearts of men, that if we were to strip ourselves of all faults one by one, we should undoubtedly find it the very last and hardest to put off.—*Richard Hooker, 1554—1600.*

Verse 3—"*The wicked boasteth*," etc. He braggeth of his evil life, whereof he maketh open profession ; or he boasteth that he will accomplish his wicked designs ; or glorieth that he hath already accomplished them. Or it may be understood that he commendeth others who are according to the desires of his own soul ; that is, he respecteth or honoureth none but such as are like him, and them only he esteemeth. Psalm xxxvi. 4, and xlix. 18 ; Rom. i. 32.—*John Diodati,* 1648.

Verse 3.—"*The wicked. . . . blesseth the covetous.*" Like will to like, as the common proverb is. Such as altogether neglect the Lord's commandments not only commit divers gross sins, but commend those who in sinning are like themselves. For in their affections they allow them, in their speeches they flatter and extol them, and in their deeds they join with them and maintain them.—*Peter Muffet,* 1594.

Verse 3.—"*The covetous.*" Covetousness is the desire of possessing that which we have not, and attaining unto great riches and worldly possessions. And whether this be not the character of trade and merchandise and traffic of every kind, the great source of those evils of over-trading which are everywhere complained of, I refer to the judgment of the men around me, who are engaged in the commerce and business of life. Compared with the regular and quiet diligence of our fathers, and their contentment with small but sure returns, the wild and wide-spread speculation for great gains, the rash and hasty adventures which are daily made, and the desperate gamester-like risks which are run, do reveal full surely that a spirit of covetousness hath been poured out upon men within the last thirty or forty years. And the providence of God corresponding thereto, by wonderful and unexpected revolutions, by numerous inventions for manufacturing the productions of the earth, in order to lead men into temptation, hath impressed upon the whole face of human affairs, a stamp of earnest worldliness not known to our fathers : insomuch that our youth do enter life no longer with the ambition of providing things honest in the sight of men, keeping their credit, bringing up their family, and realising a competency, if the Lord prosper them, but with the ambition of making a fortune, retiring to their ease, and enjoying the luxuries of the present life. Against which crying sin of covetousness, dearly beloved brethren, I do most earnestly call upon you to wage a good warfare. This place is its seat, its stronghold, even this metropolitan city of Christian Britain ; and ye who are called by the grace of God out of the great thoroughfare of Mammon, are so elected for the express purpose of testifying against this and all other the backslidings of the church planted here ; and especially against this, as being in my opinion, one of the most evident and the most common of them all. For who hath not been snared in the snare of covetousness ?—*Edward Irving,* 1828.

Verse 3.—"*The covetous, whom the Lord abhorreth.*" Christ knew what he spake when he said, "No man can serve two masters." Matt. vi. 24. Meaning God and the world, because each would have all. As the angel and the devil strove for the body of Moses (Jude 9), not who should have a part, but who should have the whole, so they strive still for our souls, who shall have all. Therefore, the apostle saith, "The love of this world is enmity to God (James iv. 4), signifying such emulation between these two, that God cannot abide the world should have a part, and the world cannot abide that God should have a part. Therefore, the love of the world must needs be enmity to God, and therefore the lovers of the world must needs be enemies to God, and so no covetous man is God's servant, but God's enemy. For this cause covetousness is called idolatry (Eph. v. 5), which is the most contrary sin to God, because as treason sets up another king in the king's place, so idolatry sets up another god in God's place.—*Henry Smith.*

Verse 4.—" *The wicked, through the pride of his countenance, will not seek after God.*" He is judged a proud man (without a jury sitting on him), who when condemned will not submit, will not stoop so low as to accept of a pardon. I must indeed correct myself, men are willing to be justified, but they would have their duties to purchase their peace and the favour of God. Thousands will die and be damned rather than they will have a pardon upon the sole account of Christ's merits and obedience. Oh, the cursed pride of the heart! When will men cease to be wiser than God? To limit God? When will men be contented with God's way of saving them by the blood of the everlasting covenant? How dare men thus to prescribe to the infinitely wise God? Is it not enough for thee that thy destruction is of thyself? But must thy salvation be of thyself too? Is it not enough that thou hast wounded thyself, but wilt thou die for ever, rather than be beholden to a plaister of free grace? Wilt be damned unless thou mayest be thine own Saviour? God is willing (" God so loved the world that he gave his only Son"), art thou so proud as that thou wilt not be beholden to God? Thou wilt deserve, or have nothing. What shall I say? Poor thou art, and yet proud; thou hast nothing but wretchedness and misery, and yet thou art talking of a purchase. This is a provocation. " God resisteth the proud," especially the spiritually proud. He that is proud of his clothes and parentage, is not so contemptible in God's eyes as he that is proud of his abilities, and so scorns to submit to God's methods for his salvation by Christ, and by his righteousness alone. — *Lewis Stuckley.*

Verse 4.—" *The wicked, through the pride of his countenance, will not seek after God.*" The pride of the wicked is the principal reason why they will not seek after the knowledge of God. This knowledge it prevents them from seeking in various ways. In the first place, it renders God a disagreeable object of contemplation to the wicked, and a knowledge of him as undesirable. Pride consists in an unduly exalted opinion of one's self. It is, therefore, impatient of a rival, hates a superior, and cannot endure a master. In proportion as it prevails in the heart, it makes us wish to see nothing above us, to acknowledge no law but our own wills, to follow no rule but our own inclinations. Thus it led Satan to rebel against his Creator, and our first parents to desire to be as gods. Since such are the effects of pride, it is evident that nothing can be more painful to a proud heart than the thoughts of such a being as God; one who is infinitely powerful, just, and holy; who can neither be resisted, deceived, nor deluded; who disposes, according to his own sovereign pleasure, of all creatures and events; and who, in an especial manner, hates pride, and is determined to abase and punish it. Such a being pride can contemplate only with feelings of dread, aversion, and abhorrence. It must look upon him as its natural enemy, the great enemy, whom it has to fear. But the knowledge of God directly tends to bring this infinite, irresistible, irreconcilable enemy full to the view of the proud man. It teaches him that he has a superior, a master, from whose authority he cannot escape, whose power he cannot resist, and whose will he must obey, or be crushed before him, and be rendered miserable for ever. It shows him what he hates to see, that, in despite of his opposition, God's counsel shall stand, that he will do all his pleasure, and that in all things wherein men deal proudly, God is above them. These truths torture the proud unhumbled hearts of the wicked, and hence they hate that knowledge of God which teaches these truths, and will not seek it. On the contrary, they wish to remain ignorant of such a being, and to banish all thoughts of him from their minds. With this view, they neglect, pervert, or explain away those passages of revelation which describe God's true character, and endeavour to believe that he is altogether such a one as themselves.

How foolish, how absurd, how ruinous, how blindly destructive of its own object, does pride appear! By attempting to soar, it only plunges itself in the mire ; and while endeavouring to erect for itself a throne, it undermines the ground on which it stands, and digs its own grave. It plunged Satan from heaven into hell ; it banished our first parents from paradise ; and it will, in a similar manner, ruin all who indulge in it. It keeps us in ignorance of God, shuts us out from his favour, prevents us from resembling him, deprives us in this world of all the honour and happiness which communion with him would confer ; and in the next, unless previously hated, repented of, and renounced, will bar for ever against us the door of heaven, and close upon us the gates of hell. O then, my friends, beware, above all things, beware of pride ! Beware, lest you indulge it imperceptibly, for it is perhaps, of all sins, the most secret, subtle, and insinuating.—*Edward Payson, D.D.*, 1783—1827.

Verse 4.—David speaks in Psalm x. of great and potent oppressors and politicians, who see none on earth greater than themselves, none higher than they, and think therefore that they may *impunè* prey upon the smaller, as beasts use to do ; and in the fourth verse this is made the root and ground of all, that God is not in all his thoughts. " *The wicked, through the pride of his countenance, will not seek after God : God is not in all his thoughts.*" The words are diversely read, and all make for this sense. Some read it, " No God in all his crafty presumptuous purposes ;" others, " All his thoughts are, there is no God." The meaning whereof is not only that among the swarm and crowd of thoughts that fill his mind, the thought of God is seldom to be found, and comes not in among the rest, which yet is enough for the purpose in hand ; but further, that in all his projects and plots, and consultations of his heart (the first reading of the words intends), whereby he contrives and lays the plot, form, and draught of all his actions, he never takes God or his will into consideration or consultation, to square and frame all accordingly, but proceeds and goes on in all, and carries on all as if there were no God to be consulted with. He takes not him along with him, no more than if he were no God ; the thoughts of him and his will sway him not. As you use to say, when a combination of men leave out some one they should advise with, that such a one is not of their counsel, is not in the plot ; so nor is God in their purposes and advisings, they do all without him. But this is not all the meaning, but farther, all their thought is, that there is no God. This is there made the bottom, the foundation, the groundwork and reason of all their wicked plots and injurious projects, and deceitful carriages and proceedings, that seeing there is no God or power above them to take notice of it, to regard or requite them, therefore they may be bold to go on.—*Thomas Goodwin.*

Verse 4.—" *Of his countenance.*" Which pride he carrieth engraven in his very countenance and forehead, and makes it known in all his carriages and gestures. " *Will not seek,*" namely, he contemneth all divine and human laws, he feareth not, respecteth not God's judgments ; he careth for nothing, so he may fulfil his desires ; enquires after, nor examines nothing ; all things are indifferent to him.—*John Diodati.*

Verse 4.—" *All his thoughts are,* there is *no God ;*" thus some read the passage. Seneca says, there are no atheists, though there would be some ; if any say there is no God, they lie ; though they say it in the day time, yet in the night when they are alone they deny it ; howsoever some desperately harden themselves, yet if God doth but show himself terrible to them, they confess him. Many of the heathens and others, have denied that there is a God, yet when they were in distress, they did fall down and confess him, as Diagoras, that grand atheist, when he was troubled with the strangullion, acknowledged a deity which he had denied. These kind of atheists I leave to the tender mercies of God, of which I doubt it whether there be any for them.—*Richard Stock.*

Verse 4.—" *God is not in all his thoughts.*" It is the black work of an ungodly man or an atheist, that God is not in all his thoughts. What comfort can be had in the being of God without thinking of him with reverence and delight ? A God forgotten is as good as no God to us.—*Stephen Charnock.*

Verse 4.—Trifles possess us, but " *God is not in all our thoughts,*" seldom the sole object of them. We have durable thoughts of transitory things, and flitting thoughts of a durable and eternal good. The covenant of grace engageth the whole heart to God, and bars anything else from engrossing it ; but what strangers are God and the souls of most men ! Though we have the knowledge of him by creation, yet he is for the most part an unknown God in the relations wherein he stands to us, because a God undelighted in. Hence it is, as one observes, that because we observe not the ways of God's wisdom, conceive not of him in his vast perfections, nor are stricken with an admiration of his goodness, that we have fewer good sacred poems than of any other kind. The wits of men hang the wing when they come to exercise their reasons and fancies about God. Parts and strength are given us, as well as corn and wine to the Israelites, for the service of God, but those are consecrated to some cursed Baal, Hosea ii. 8. Like Venus in the poet, we forsake heaven to follow some Adonis. *Stephen Charnock.*

Verses 4, 5.—The world hath a spiritual fascination and witchcraft, by which, where it hath once prevailed, men are enchanted to an utter forgetfulness of themselves and God, and being drunk with pleasures, they are easily engaged to a madness and height of folly. Some, like foolish children, are made to keep a great stir in the world for very trifles, for a vain show ; they think themselves great, honourable, excellent, and for this make a great bustle, when the world hath not added one cubic to their stature of real worth. Others are by this Circe transformed into savage creatures, and act the part of lions and tigers. Others, like swine, wallow in the lusts of uncleanness. Others are unmanned, putting off all natural affections, care not who they ride over, so they may rule over or be made great. Others are taken with ridiculous frenzies, so that a man that stands in the cool shade of a sedate composure would judge them out of their wits. It would make a man admire to read of the frisks of Caius Caligula, Xerxes, Alexander, and many others, who because they were above many men, thought themselves above human nature. They forgot they were born and must die, and did such things as would have made them, but that their greatness overawed it, a laughing-stock and common scorn to children. Neither must we think that these were but some few or rare instances of worldly intoxication, when the Scripture notes it as a general distemper of all that bow down to worship this idol. They live " without God in the world," saith the apostle, that is, they so carry it as if there were no God to take notice of them to check them for their madness. " *God is not in all his thoughts.*" Verse 4. " *The judgments of God are far above out of his sight ;*" he puffs at his enemies (ver. 5), and saith in his heart, he " *shall never be moved.*" Verse 6. The whole Psalm describes the worldling as a man that hath lost all his understanding, and is acting the part of a frantic bedlam. What then can be a more fit engine for the devil to work with than the pleasures of the world ?—*Richard Gilpin.*

Verse 5.—" *Grievous,*" or troublesome ; that is, all his endeavours and actions aim at nothing but at hurting others. " *Are far above,*" for he is altogether carnal, he hath not any disposition nor correspondence with the justice of thy law, which is altogether spiritual ; and therefore cannot lively represent unto himself thy judgments, and the issue of the wicked according to the said law. Rom. vii. 14 ; 1 Cor. ii. 14. " *He puffeth ;*" he doth most arrogantly despise them, and is confident he can overthrow them with a puff.—*John Diodati.*

Verse 5.—" *Thy judgments are far above out of his sight.*" Because God does not immediately visit every sin with punishment, ungodly men do not see that in due time he judges all the earth. Human tribunals must of necessity, by promptness and publicity, commend themselves to the common judgment, but the Lord's modes of dealing with sin are sublimer and apparently more tardy, hence the bat's eyes of godless men cannot see them, and the grovelling wits of men cannot comprehend them. If God sat in the gate of every village and held his court there, even fools might discern his righteousness, but they are not capable of perceiving that for a matter to be settled in the highest court, even in heaven itself, is a far more solemn matter. Let believers take heed lest they fall in a degree into the same error, and begin to criticise the actions of The Great Supreme, when they are too elevated for human reason to comprehend them.— *C. H. S.*

Verse 5.—" *The judgments of God are far above out of his sight.*" Out of his sight, as an eagle at her highest towering so lessens herself to view, that he sees not the talons, nor fears the grip. Thus man presumes till he hath sinned, and then despairs as fast afterwards. At first, " Tush, doth God see it ?" At last, " Alas ! will God forgive it ?" But if a man will not know his sins, his sins will know him ; the eyes which presumption shuts, commonly despair opens. *Thomas Adams.*

Verse 5.—" *As for all his enemies, he puffeth at them.*" David describeth a *proud* man, *puffing at his enemies :* he is puffed up and swelled with high conceits of himself, as if he had some great matter in him, and he puffs at others as if he could do some great matter against them, forgetting that himself is but, as to his being in this world, a puff of wind which passeth away.—*Joseph Caryl.*

Verse 5.—" *As for all his enemies, he puffeth at them ;*" literally, " *He whistles at them.*" He is given over to the dominion of gloomy indifference, and he cares as little for others as for himself. Whosoever may be imagined by him to be an enemy he cares not. Contempt and ridicule are his only weapons ; and he has forgotten how to use others of a more sacred character. His mental habits are marked by scorn ; and he treats with contempt the judgments, opinions, and practices of the wisest of men.—*John Morison.*

Verse 6.—" *He hath said in his heart, I shall not be moved : for I shall never be in adversity.*" Carnal security opens the door for all impiety to enter into the soul. Pompey, when he had in vain assaulted a city, and could not take it by force, devised this stratagem in way of agreement ; he told them he would leave the siege and make peace with them, upon condition that they would let in a few weak, sick, and wounded soldiers among them to be cured. They let in the soldiers, and when the city was secure, the soldiers let in Pompey's army. A carnal settled security will let in a whole army of lusts into the soul.— *Thomas Brooks.*

Verse 6.—" *He hath said in his heart, I shall not be moved : for I shall never be in adversity.*" To consider religion always on the comfortable side ; to congratulate one's self for having obtained the end before we have made use of the means ; to stretch the hands to receive the crown of righteousness before they have been employed to fight the battle ; to be content with a false peace, and to use no efforts to obtain the graces to which true consolation is annexed : this is a dreadful calm, like that which some voyagers describe, and which is a very singular forerunner of a very terrible event. All on a sudden, in the wide ocean, the sea becomes calm, the surface of the water clear as a crystal, smooth as glass—the air serene ; the unskilled passenger becomes tranquil and happy, but the old mariner trembles. In an instant the waves froth, the winds murmur, the heavens kindle, a thousand gulfs open, a frightful light inflames the air, and every wave threatens sudden death. This is an image of many men's assurance of salvation.—*James Saurin,* 1677—1730.

Verse 7.—" *Under his tongue is mischief and vanity.*" The striking allusion of this expression is to certain venomous reptiles, which are said to carry bags of poison under their teeth, and, with great subtlety to inflict the most deadly injuries upon those who come within their reach. How affectingly does this represent the sad havoc which minds tainted with infidelity inflict on the community ! By their perversions of truth, and by their immoral sentiments and practices, they are as injurious to the mind as the deadliest poison can be to the body.—*John Morison.*

Verse 7.—Cursing men are cursed men.—*John Trapp.*

Verses 7, 9.—In Anne Askew's account of her examination by Bishop Bonner, we have an instance of the cruel craft of persecutors : "On the morrow after, my lord of London sent for me at one of the clock, his hour being appointed at three. And as I came before him, he said he was very sorry of my trouble, and desired to know my opinion in such matters as were laid against me. He required me also boldly in any wise to utter the secrets of my heart ; bidding me not to fear in any point, for whatsoever I did say within his house, no man should hurt me for it. I answered, ' For so much as your lordship hath appointed three of the clock, and my friends shall not come till that hour, I desire you to pardon me of giving answer till they come.' " Upon this Bale remarks : "In this preventing of the hour may the diligent perceive the greediness of this Babylon bishop, or bloodthirsty wolf, concerning his prey. ' Swift are their feet,' saith David, ' in the effusion of innocent blood, which have fraud in their tongues, venom in their lips, and most cruel vengeance in their mouths.' David much marvelleth in the spirit that, taking upon them the spiritual governance of the people, they can fall into such frenzy or forgetfulness of themselves, as to believe it lawful thus to oppress the faithful, and to devour them with as little compassion as he that greedily devoureth a piece of bread. If such have read anything of God, they have little minded their true duty therein. ' More swift,' saith Jeremy, ' are our cruel persecutors than the eagles of the air. They follow upon us over the mountains, and lay privy wait for us in the wilderness.' He that will know the crafty hawking of bishops to bring in their prey, let him learn it here. Judas, I think, had never the tenth part of their cunning workmanship.' "—*John Bale, D.D., Bishop of Ossory, 1495—1563, in " Examination of Anne Askew." Parker Society's Publications.*

Verse 8.—" *He sitteth in the lurking places of the villages,*" etc. The Arab robber lurks like a wolf among these sand-heaps, and often springs out suddenly upon the solitary traveller, robs him in a trice, and then plunges again into the wilderness of sand-hills and reedy downs, where pursuit is fruitless. Our friends are careful not to allow us to straggle about, or lag behind, and yet it seems absurd to fear a surprise here—Kaifa before, Acre in the rear, and travellers in sight on both sides. Robberies, however, do often occur, just where we now are. Strange country ! and it has always been so. There are a hundred allusions to just such things in the history, the Psalms, and the prophets of Israel. A whole class of imagery is based upon them. Thus, in Psalm x. 8—10, "He sits in the lurking places of the villages : in the secret places doth he murder the innocent : he lieth in wait secretly as a lion in his den : he lieth in wait to catch' the poor : he doth catch the poor, when he draweth him into his net ; he croucheth and humbleth himself, that the poor may fall by his strong ones." And a thousand rascals, the living originals of this picture, are this day crouching and lying in wait all over the country to catch poor helpless travellers. You observe that all these people we meet or pass are armed ; nor would they venture to go from Acre to Kaifa without their musket, although the cannon of the castles seem to command every foot of the way. Strange, most strange land ! but it tallies wonderfully with its ancient story.—*W. M. Thomson, D.D., in " The Land and the Book," 1859.*

Verse 8.—My companions asked me if I knew the danger I had escaped. "No," I replied ; "What danger?" They then told me that, just after they started, they saw a wild Arab skulking after me, crouching to the ground, with a musket in his hand ; and that, as soon as he had reached within what appeared to them musket-shot of me, he raised his gun ; but, looking wildly around him, as a man will do who is about to perpetrate some desperate act, he caught sight of them and disappeared. Jeremiah knew something of the ways of these Arabs when he wrote, (chap. iii. 2) "In the ways hast thou sat for them, as the Arabian in the wilderness ;" and the simile is used in Psalm x. 9, 10, for the Arabs wait and watch for their prey with the greatest eagerness and perseverance.—*John Gadsby, in " My Wanderings," 1860.*

Verse 8.—" *He sitteth in the lurking places of the villages : in the secret places doth he murder the innocent : his eyes are privily set against the poor.*" All this strength of metaphor and imagery is intended to mark the assiduity, the cunning, the low artifice, to which the enemies of truth and righteousness will often resort in order to accomplish their corrupt and vicious designs. The extirpation of true religion is their great object ; and there is nothing to which they will not stoop in order to effect that object. The great powers which have oppressed the church of Christ, in different ages, have answered to this description. Both heathen and papistical authorities have thus condescended to infamy. They have sat, as it were, in ambush for the poor of Christ's flock ; they have adopted every stratagem that infernal skill could invent ; they have associated themselves with princes in their palaces, and with beggars on their dunghill ; they have resorted to the village, and they have mingled in the gay and populous city ; and all for the vain purpose of attempting to blot out a " name which shall endure for ever, and which shall be continued as long as the sun."—*John Morison.*

Verse 9.—" *He doth catch the poor.*" The poor man is the beast they hunt, who must rise early, rest late, eat the bread of sorrow, sit with many a hungry meal, perhaps his children crying for food, while all the fruit of his pains is served into Nimrod's table. Complain of this while you will, yet, as the orator said of Verres, *pecuniosus nescit damnari.* Indeed, a money-man may not be damnified, but he may be damned. For this is a crying sin, and the wakened ears of the Lord will hear it, neither shall his provoked hands forbear it. *Si tacuerint pauperes loquentur lapides.* If the poor should hold their peace, the very stones would speak. The fines, rackings, enclosures, oppressions, vexations, will cry to God for vengeance. " The stone will cry out of the wall, and the beam out of the timber shall answer it." Hab. ii. 11. You see the beasts they hunt. Not foxes, not wolves, nor boars, bulls, nor tigers. It is a certain observation, no beast hunts its own kind to devour it. Now, if these should prosecute wolves, foxes, &c., they should then hunt their own kind ; for they are these themselves, or rather worse than these, because here *homo homini lupus.* But though they are men they hunt, and by nature of the same kind, they are not so by quality, for they are lambs they persecute. In them there is blood, and flesh, and fleece to be had ; and therefore on these do they gorge themselves. In them there is weak armour of defence against their cruelties ; therefore over these they may domineer. I will speak it boldly : there is not a mighty Nimrod in this land that dares hunt his equal ; but over his inferior lamb he insults like a young Nero. Let him be graced by high ones, and he must not be saluted under twelve score off. ▾ In the country he proves a termagant ; his very scowl is a prodigy, and breeds an earthquake. He would be a Cæsar, and tax all. It is well if he prove not a cannibal ! Only Macro salutes Sejanus so long as he is in Tiberius's favour ; cast him from that pinnacle, and the dog is ready to devour him.—*Thomas Adams.*

Verse 9.—" *He draweth him into his net.*" " They hunt with a net." Micah vii. 2. They have their politic gins to catch men ; gaudy wares and dark shops (and would you have them love the light that live by darkness, as many shopkeepers ?) draw and tole customers in, where the crafty leeches can soon feel their pulses : if they must buy they shall pay for their necessity. And though they plead, We compel none to buy our ware, *caveat emptor ;* yet with fine voluble phrases, damnable protestations, they will cast a mist of error before an eye of simple truth, and with cunning devices hunt them in. So some among us have feathered their nests, not by open violence, but politic circumvention. They have sought the golden fleece, not by Jason's merit, but by Medea's subtlety, by Medea's sorcery. If I should intend to discover these hunters' plots, and to deal punctually with them, I should afford you more matter than you would afford me time. But I limit myself, and answer all their plans with Augustine. Their tricks may hold *in jure fori*, but not *in jure poli*—in the common-pleas of earth, not before the king's bench in heaven.—*Thomas Adams.*

Verse 9.—Oppression turns princes into roaring lions, and judges into ravening wolves. It is an unnatural sin, against the light of nature. No creatures do oppress them of their own kind. Look upon the birds of prey, as upon eagles, vultures, hawks, and you shall never find them preying upon their own kind. Look upon the beasts of the forest, as upon the lion, the tiger, the wolf, the bear, and you shall ever find them favourable to their own kind ; and yet men unnaturally prey upon one another, like the fish in the sea, the great swallowing up the small.—*Thomas Brooks.*

Verse 10.—" *He croucheth, and humbleth himself,*" etc. There is nothing too mean or servile for them, in the attempt to achieve their sinister ends. You shall see his holiness the Pope washing the pilgrims' feet, if such a stratagem be necessary to act on the minds of the deluded multitude ; or you shall see him sitting on a throne of purple, if he wishes to awe and control the kings of the earth.—*John Morison.*

Verse 10.—If you take a wolf in a lambskin, hang him up ; for he is the worst of the generation.—*Thomas Adams.*

Verse 11.—" *He hath said in his heart, God hath forgotten.*" Is it not a senseless thing to be careless of sins committed long ago ? The old sins forgotten by men, stick fast in an infinite understanding. Time cannot raze out that which hath been known from eternity. Why should they be forgotten many years after they were acted, since they were foreknown in an eternity before they were committed, or the criminal capable to practise them ? Amalek must pay their arrears of their ancient unkindness to Israel in the time of Saul, though the generation that committed them were rotten in their graves. 1 Sam. xv. 2. Old sins are written in a book, which lies always before God ; and not only our own sins, but the sins of our fathers, to be requited upon their posterity. " Behold it is written." Isa. lxv. 6. What a vanity is it then to be regardless of the sins of an age that went before us ; because they are in some measure out of our knowledge, are they therefore blotted out of God's remembrance ? Sins are bound up with him, as men do bonds, till they resolve to sue for the debt. " The iniquity of Ephraim is bound up." Hosea xiii. 12. As his foreknowledge extends to all acts that shall be done, so his remembrance extends to all acts that have been done. We may as well say, God foreknows nothing that shall be done to the end of the world, as that he forgets anything that hath been done from the beginning of the world.—*Stephen Charnock.*

Verse 11.—" *He hath said in his heart, God hath forgotten: he hideth his face ; he will never see it.*" Many say in their hearts, " God seeth them not," while with their tongues they confess he is an all-seeing God. The heart hath a tongue in it as well as the head, and these two tongues seldom speak the same language. While the head-tongue saith, " We cannot hide ourselves from the sight of God," the heart-tongue of wicked men will say, " God will hide himself from us, he will not see." But if their heart speak not thus, then as the prophet saith (Isa. xxix. 15), " They dig deep to hide their counsel from the Lord ;" surely they have a hope to hide their counsels, else they would not dig deep to hide them. Their digging is not proper, but tropical ; as men dig deep to hide what they would not have in the earth, so they by their wits, plots, and devices, do their best to hide their counsels from God, and they say, " Who seeth, who knoweth ? We, surely, are not seen either by God or man."—*Joseph Caryl.*

Verse 11.—The Scripture everywhere places sin upon this root. " *God hath forgotten: he hideth his face ; he will never see it.*" He hath turned his back upon the world. This was the ground of the oppression of the poor by the wicked, which he mentions, verses 9, 10. There is no sin but receives both its birth and nourishment from this bitter root. Let the notion of providence be once thrown out, or the belief of it faint, how will ambition, covetousness, neglect of God, distrust, impatience, and all other bitter gourds, grow up in a night !

It is from this topic all iniquity will draw arguments to encourage itself ; for nothing so much discountenances those rising corruptions, and puts them out of heart, as an actuated belief that God takes care of human affairs.—*Stephen Charnock.*

Verse 11.—" *He hath said in his heart,*" etc. " Because sentence against an evil work is not executed speedily, therefore the heart of the sons of men is fully set in them to do evil." Eccl. viii. 11. God forbears punishing, therefore men forbear repenting. He doth not smite upon their back by correction, therefore they do not smite upon their thigh by humiliation. Jer. xxxi. 19. The sinner thinks thus : " God hath spared me all this while, he hath eked out patience into longsuffering ; surely he will not punish." " *He hath said in his heart, God hath forgotten.*" God sometimes in infinite patience adjourns his judgments and puts off the sessions a while longer ; he is not willing to punish. 2 Peter iii. 9. The bee naturally gives honey, but stings only when it is angered. The Lord would have men make their peace with him. Isa. xxvii. 5. God is not like a hasty creditor that requires the debt, and will give no time for the payment ; he is not only gracious, but " waits to be gracious" (Isa. xxx. 18) ; but God by his patience would bribe sinners to repentance ; but alas ! how is this patience abused. God's longsuffering hardens : because God stops the vials of his wrath, sinners stop the conduit of tears.— *Thomas Watson.*

Verse 11.—" *He hath said in his heart, God hath forgotten : he hideth his face ; he will never see it.*" Because the Lord continues to spare them, therefore they go on to provoke him. As he adds to their lives, so they add to their lusts. What is this, but as if a man should break all his bones because there is a surgeon who is able to set them again ? . . . . Because justice seems to *wink*, men suppose her *blind ;* because she delays punishment, they imagine she denies to punish them ; because she does not always reprove them for their sins, they suppose he always approves of their sins. But let such know, that the silent arrow can destroy as well as the roaring cannon. Though the patience of God be *lasting,* yet it is not *everlasting.— William Secker.*

Verses 11, 12, 13.—The atheist denies God's ordering of sublunary matters. " Tush, doth the Lord see, or is there knowledge in the Most High ?" making him a maimed Deity, without an eye of providence, or an arm of power, and at most restraining him only to matters above the clouds. But he that dares to confine the King to heaven, will soon after endeavour to depose him, and fall at last flatly to deny him.— *Thomas Fuller.*

Verse 13.—" *He hath said in his heart, Thou wilt not require it.*" As when the desperate pirate, ransacking and rifling a bottom, was told by the master, that though no law could touch him for the present, he should answer it at the day of judgment, replied, " If I may stay so long ere I come to it, I will take thee and thy vessel too." A conceit wherewith too many land-thieves and oppressors flatter themselves in their hearts, though they dare not utter it with their lips. *Thomas Adams.*

Verses 13, 14.—What, do you think that God doth not remember our sins which we do not regard ? for while we sin the score runs on, and the Judge setteth down all in the table of remembrance, and his scroll reacheth up to heaven. Item, for lending to usury ; item, for racking of rents ; item, for starching thy ruffs ; item, for curling thy hair ; item, for painting thy face ; item, for selling of benefices ; item, for starving of souls ; item, for playing at cards ; item, for sleeping in the church ; item, for profaning the Sabbath-day, with a number more hath God to call to account, for every one must answer for himself. The fornicator, for taking of filthy pleasure ; the careless prelate, for murthering so many thousand souls ; the landlord, for getting money from his poor tenants by racking of his rents ; see the rest, all they shall come like very sheep when the trumpet shall sound, and the heaven and earth shall come to judgment against them ; when the heavens shall vanish like a scroll, and the earth shall consume like fire, and all the creatures standing against them ; the rocks shall cleave asunder, and the mountains shake, and the foundation of the earth shall tremble, and they shall say to the mountains, Cover us, fall upon us, and hide us from the presence of his anger and wrath whom we have not cared to offend. But they shall not be covered and hid ; but then shall they go the back way, to the snakes and serpents, to be tormented of devils for ever.—*Henry Smith.*

Verse 14.—"*Thou hast seen it ; for thou beholdest mischief and spite, to requite it with thy hands,*" etc. This should be a terror to the wicked, to think that whatsoever they do, they do it in the *sight* of him that shall *judge* them, and call them to a strict account for every thought conceived against his majesty ; and therefore, it should make them afraid to sin ; because that when they burn with lust, and toil with hatred, when they scorn the just and wrong the innocent, they do all this, not only *in conspectu Dei*, within the compass of God's sight, but also in *sinu divinitatis*, in the bosom of that Deity, who, though he suffered them for a time to run on, like " a wild ass used to the wilderness," yet he will find them out at the last, and then cut them off and destroy them. And as this is terror unto the wicked, so it may be a comfort unto the godly to think that he who should hear their prayers and send them help, is so near unto them ; and it should move them to rely still upon him, because we are sure of his presence wherever we are.—*G. Williams,* 1636.

Verse 14.—"*The poor committeth himself unto thee.*" The awkwardness of our hearts to suffer comes much from distrust. An unbelieving soul treads upon the promise as a man upon ice ; at first going upon it he is full of fears and tumultuous thoughts lest it should crack. Now, daily resignation of thy heart, as it will give thee an occasion of conversing more with the thoughts of God's power, faithfulness, and other of his attributes (for want of familiarity with which, jealousies arise in our hearts when put to any great plunge), so also it will furnish thee with many experiences of the reality both of his attributes and promises ; which, though they need not any testimony from sense, to gain them credit with us, yet so much are we made of sense, so childish and weak is our faith, that we find our hearts much helped by those experiences we have had, to rely on him for the future. Look, therefore, carefully to this ; every morning leave thyself and ways in God's hand, as the phrase is. Psalm x. 14. And at night look again how well God hath looked to his trust, and sleep not till thou hast affected thy heart with his faithfulness, and laid a stronger charge on thy heart to trust itself again in God's keeping in the night. And when any breach is made, and seeming loss befalls thee in any enjoyment, which thou hast by faith insured of thy God, observe how God fills up that breach, and makes up that loss to thee ; and rest not till thou hast fully vindicated the good name of God to thy own heart. Be sure thou lettest no discontent or dissatisfaction lie upon thy spirit at God's dealings ; but chide thy heart for it, as David did his. Psalm xlii. And thus doing, with God's blessing, thou shalt keep thy faith in breath for a longer race, when called to run it.—*W. Gurnall.*

Verse 14.—"*Thou art the helper of the fatherless.*" God doth exercise a more special providence over men, as clothed with miserable circumstances ; and therefore among his other titles this is one, to be a " *helper of the fatherless.*" It is the argument the church used to express her return to God ; Hosea xiv. 3, " For in thee the fatherless find mercy." Now what greater comfort is there than this, that there is one presides in the world who is so wise he cannot be mistaken, so faithful he cannot deceive, so pitiful he cannot neglect his people, and so powerful that he can make stones even to be turned into bread if he please ! . . . . . . God doth not govern the world only by his will as an absolute monarch, but by his wisdom and goodness as a tender father. It is not his greatest pleasure to show his sovereign power, or his inconceivable wisdom, but his immense goodness, to which he makes the other attributes subservient.—*Stephen Charnock.*

Verse 14.—"*Thou hast seen it,*" etc. If God did not see our ways, we might sin and go unpunished ; but forasmuch as he seeth them with purer eyes than to behold iniquity and approve it, he is engaged both in justice and honour to punish all that iniquity of our ways which he seeth or beholdeth. David makes this the very design of God's superintendency over the ways of men: " *Thou hast seen it; for thou beholdest mischief and spite, to requite it with thy hand: the poor committeth himself unto thee; thou art the helper of the fatherless.*" Thus the psalmist represents the Lord as having taken a view or survey of the ways of men. " *Thou hast seen.*" What hath God seen? Even all that wickedness and oppression of the poor spoken of in the former part of the Psalm, as also the blasphemy of the wicked against himself (verse 13), " *Wherefore doth the wicked contemn God? he hath said in his heart, Thou wilt not require it.*" What saith the psalmist concerning God, to this vain, confident man? " *Thou,*" saith he, " *beholdest mischief and spite;*" but to what purpose? the next words tell us that—" *to requite it with thy hand.*" As thou hast seen what mischief they have done spitefully, so in due time thou wilt requite it righteously. The Lord is not a bare spectator, he is both a rewarder and an avenger. Therefore, from the ground of this truth, that the Lord seeth all our ways, and counteth all our steps, we, as the prophet exhorts (Isaiah iii. 10, 11), may " say to the righteous, that it shall be well with him : for they shall eat the fruit of their doings." We may also say, " Woe unto the wicked ! it shall be ill with him : for the reward of his hands shall be given him." Only idols which have eyes and see not, have hands and strike not.—*Joseph Caryl.*

Verse 14.—" *Thou hast seen it; for thou beholdest mischief and spite, to requite it with thy hand : the poor committeth himself unto thee; thou art the helper of the fatherless.*" Let the poor know that their God doth take care of them, to visit their sins with rods who spoil them, seeing they have forgotten that we are members one of another, and have invaded the goods of their brethren ; God will arm them against themselves, and beat them with their own staves ; either their own compassing and over-reaching wits shall consume their store, or their unthrifty posterity shall put wings upon their riches to make them fly ; or God·shall not give them the blessing to take use of their wealth, but they shall leave to such as shall be merciful to the poor. Therefore let them follow the wise man's counsel (Eccles. x. 20), " Curse not the rich, no, not in thy bedchamber ;" let no railing and unchristian bitterness wrong a good cause ; let it be comfort enough to them that God is both their supporter and avenger. Is it not sufficient to lay all the storms of discontent against their oppressors, that God sees their affliction, and cometh down to deliver and avenge them?— *Edward Marbury.*

Verse 14.—" *Thou hast seen it; for thou beholdest mischief and spite, to requite it with thy hand,*" etc. God considers all your works and ways, and will not you consider the works, the ways of God? Of this be sure, whether you consider the ways of God, his word-ways, or work-ways, of this be sure, God will consider your ways, certainly he will ; those ways of yours which in themselves are not worth the considering or looking upon, your sinful ways, though they are so vile, so abominable, that if yourselves did but look upon them and consider them, you would be utterly ashamed of them ; yea, though they are an abomination to God while he beholds them, yet he will behold and consider them. The Lord who is of purer eyes than to behold any the least iniquity, to approve it, will yet behold the greatest of your iniquities, and your impurest ways to consider them. " *Thou,*" saith David, " *beholdest mischief and spite, to requite it :*" God beholdeth the foulest, dirtiest ways of men, their ways of oppression and unrighteousness, their ways of intemperance and lasciviousness, their ways of wrath and maliciousness, at once to detest, detect, and requite them. If God thus considereth the ways of men, even those filthy and crooked ways of men, should not men consider the holy, just, and righteous ways of God?—*Joseph Caryl.*

Verses 14—18.—" *God delights to help the poor.*" He loves to take part with the best, though the weakest side. Contrary to the course of most, who when a controversy arises use to stand in a kind of indifferency or neutrality, till they see which part is strongest, not which is justest. Now if there be any consideration (besides the cause) that draws or engages God, it is the weakness of the side. He joins with many, because they are weak, not with any, because they are strong ; therefore he is called *the helper of the friendless, and with him the fatherless,* (the orphans) *find mercy.* By fatherless we are not to understand such only whose parents are dead, but any one that is in distress ; as Christ promiseth his disciples ; " *I will not leave you orphans,*" that is, helpless, and (as we translate) *comfortless ;* though ye are as children without a father, yet I will be a father to you. Men are often like those clouds which dissolve into the sea ; they send presents to the rich, and assist the strong ; but God sends his rain upon the dry land, and lends his strength to those who are weak. . . . The prophet makes this report to God of himself (Isaiah xxv. 4) : " *Thou hast been a strength to the poor,* a strength to the needy in his distress, a refuge from the storm,'' etc.—*Joseph Caryl.*

Verse 16.—" *The Lord is King for ever and ever : the heathen are perished out of his land.*" Such confidence and faith must appear to the world strange and unaccountable. It is like what his fellow citizens may be supposed to have felt (if the story be true) toward that man of whom it is recorded, that his powers of vision were so extraordinary, that he could distinctly see the fleet of the Carthaginians entering the harbour of Carthage, while he stood himself at Lilybœum, in Sicily. A man seeing across an ocean, and able to tell of objects so far off ! he could feast his vision on what others saw not. Even thus does faith now stand at its Lilybœum, and see the long tossed fleet entering safely the desired haven, enjoying the bliss of that still distant day, as if it was already come.—*Andrew A. Bonar.*

Verse 17.—There is a humbling act of faith put forth in prayer. Others style it praying in humility ; give me leave to style it praying in faith. In faith which sets the soul in the presence of that mighty God, and by the sight of him, which faith gives us, it is that we see our own vileness, sinfulness, and abhor ourselves, and profess ourselves unworthy of any, much less of those mercies we are to seek for. Thus the sight of God had wrought in the prophet (Isaiah vi. 5), " Then said I, Woe is me ! for I am undone ; because I am a man of unclean lips : for mine eyes have seen the King, the Lord of hosts." And holy Job speaks thus (Job xlii. 5, 6), " Now mine eye seeth thee : wherefore I abhor myself, and repent in dust and ashes." This is as great a requisite to prayer as any other act ; I may say of it alone, as the apostle (James i. 7), that without it we shall receive nothing at the hands of God ! God loves to fill empty vessels, he looks to broken hearts. In the Psalms how often do we read that God hears the prayers of the humble ; which always involves and includes faith in it. Psalm ix. 12, " He forgetteth not the cry of the humble," and Psalm x. 17, " *Lord, thou hast heard the desire of the humble : thou wilt prepare their heart, thou wilt cause thine ear to hear.*" To be deeply humbled is to have the heart prepared and fitted for God to hear the prayer ; and therefore you find the psalmist pleading *sub forma pauperis,* often repeating, " I am poor and needy." And this prevents our thinking much if God do not grant the particular thing we do desire. Thus also Christ himself in his great distress (Psalm xxii.), doth treat God (verse 2), " O my God, I cry in the day-time, but thou hearest not ; and in the night season am not silent. Our fathers trusted in thee. They cried unto thee, and were delivered. But I am a worm, and no man ; reproached of men, and despised of the people ; (verse 6)" and he was " heard " in the end " in what he feared." And these deep humblings of ourselves, being joined with vehement implorations upon the mercy of God to obtain, is reckoned into the account of praying by faith, both by God and Christ. Matt. viii.—*Thomas Goodwin.*

Verse 17.—" *Lord, thou hast heard the desire of the humble.*" A spiritual prayer is a *humble* prayer. Prayer is the asking of an alms, which requires humility. "The publican, standing afar off, would not lift up so much as his eyes unto heaven, but smote upon his breast, saying, God be merciful to me a sinner." *Luke xviii.* 13. God's incomprehensible glory may even amaze us and strike a holy consternation into us when we approach nigh unto him : " O my God, I am ashamed and blush to lift up my face to thee." *Ezra ix.* 6. It is comely to see a poor nothing lie prostrate at the feet of its Maker. "Behold now, I have taken upon me to speak unto the Lord, which am but dust and ashes." *Gen. xviii.* 27. The lower the heart descends, the higher the prayer ascends.—*Thomas Watson.*

Verse 17.—" *Lord, thou hast heard the desire of the humble,*" etc. How pleasant is it, that these benefits, which are of so great a value both on their own account, and that of the divine benignity from whence they come, should be delivered into our hands, marked, as it were, with this grateful inscription, *that they have been obtained by prayer !*—*Robert Leighton.*

Verse 17.—" *The desire of the humble.*" Prayer is the offering up of our desires to God in the name of Christ, for such things as are agreeable to his will. It is an offering of our *desires.* Desires are the soul and life of prayer ; words are but the body ; now as the body without the soul is dead, so are prayers unless they are animated with our desires : " *Lord, thou hast heard the desire of the humble.*" God heareth not words, but *desires.*—*Thomas Watson.*

Verse 17.—God's choice acquaintances are humble men.—*Robert Leighton.*

Verse 17.—He that sits nearest the dust, sits nearest heaven.—*Andrew Gray, of Glasgow,* 1616.

Verse 17.—There is a kind of omnipotency in prayer, as having an interest and prevalency with God's omnipotence. It hath loosed iron chains (Acts xvi. 25, 26) ; it hath opened iron gates (Acts xii. 5—10) ; it hath unlocked the windows of heaven (1 Kings xviii. 41) ; it hath broken the bars of death (John xi. 40, 43). Satan hath three titles given in the Scriptures, setting forth his malignity against the church of God : a dragon, to note his malice ; a serpent, to note his subtlety ; and a lion, to note his strength. But none of all these can stand before prayer. The greatest malice of Haman sinks under the prayer of Esther ; the deepest policy, the counsel of Ahithophel, withers before the prayer of David ; the largest army, a host of a thousand Ethiopians, run away like cowards before the prayer of Asa.—*Edward Reynolds,* 1599—1676.

Verse 18.—" *To judge the fatherless and the oppressed,*" etc. The tears of the poor fall down upon their cheeks, *et ascendunt ad cœlum,* and go up to heaven and cry for vengeance before God, the judge of widows, the father of widows and orphans. Poor people be oppressed even by laws. Woe worth to them that make evil laws against the poor, what shall be to them that hinder and mar good laws ? What will ye do in the day of great vengeance when God shall visit you ? he saith he will hear the tears of the poor women, when he goeth on visitation. For their sake he will hurt the judge, be he never so high, he will for widows' sakes change realms, bring them into temptation, pluck the judges' skins over their heads. Cambyses was a great emperor, such another as our master is, he had many lord deputies, lord presidents, and lieutenants under him. It is a great while ago since I read the history. It chanced he had under him in one of his dominions a briber, a gift-taker, a gratifier of rich men ; he followed gifts as fast as he that followed the pudding ; a handmaker in his office, to make his son a great man, as the old saying is, " Happy is the child whose father goeth to the devil." The cry of the poor widow came to the emperor's ear, and caused him to slay the judge quick, and laid his skin in his chair of judgment, that all judges that should give judgment afterward, should sit in the same skin. Surely it was a goodly sign, a goodly monument, the sign of the judge's skin. I pray God we may once see the sign of the skin in England. Ye will say, peradventure, that this is cruelly and uncharitably spoken. No, no ; I do it charitably, for a love I bear to my country. God saith, " I will visit." God hath two visitations ; the first is when he revealeth his word by preachers ; and where the first is accepted, the second cometh not. The second visitation is vengeance. He went to visitation when he brought the judge's skin over his ears. If this word be despised, he cometh with the second visitation with vengeance.—*Hugh Latimer*, 1480—1555.

Verse 18.—"*Man of the earth*," etc. In the eighth Psalm (which is a circular Psalm, ending as it did begin, "O Lord our God, how excellent is thy name in all the world !" That whithersoever we turn our eyes, upwards or downwards, we may see ourselves beset with his glory round about), how doth the prophet base and discountenance the nature and whole race of man ; as may appear by his disdainful and derogatory interrogation, "What is man that thou art mindful of him ; and the Son of Man, that thou regardest him ?" In the ninth Psalm, "Rise, Lord ; let not man have the upper hand ; let the nations be judged in thy sight. Put them in fear, O Lord, that the heathen may know themselves to be but men." Further, in the tenth Psalm, "Thou judgest the fatherless and the poor, that the man of the earth do no more violence."

The Psalms, as they go in order, so, methinks they grow in strength, and each hath a weightier force to throw down our presumption. 1. We are "men," and the "sons of men," to show our descent and propagation. 2. "Men in our own knowledge," to show that conscience and experience of infirmity doth convict us. 3. "Men of the earth," to show our original matter whereof we are framed. In the twenty-second Psalm, he addeth more disgrace ; for either in his own name, regarding the misery and contempt wherein he was held, or in the person of Christ, whose figure he was, as if it were a robbery for him to take upon him the nature of man, he falleth to a lower style, *at ego sum vermis et non vir ;* but I am a worm, and no man. For as corruption is the father of all flesh, so are the worms his brethren and sisters, according to the old verse—

> "First man, next worms, then stench and loathsomeness,
> Thus man to no man alters by changes."

Abraham, the father of the faithful (Genesis xviii.), sifteth himself into the coarsest man that can be, and resolveth his nature into the elements whereof it first rose : "Behold I have begun to speak to my Lord, being dust and ashes." And if any of the children of Abraham, who succeed him in the faith, or any of the children of Adam, who succeed him in the flesh, thinketh otherwise, let him know that there is a threefold cord twisted by the finger of God, that shall tie him to his first original, though he contend till his heart break. "O earth, earth, earth, hear the word of the Lord " (Jer. xxii.) ; that is, earth by creation, earth by continuance, earth by resolution. Thou camest earth, thou remainest earth, and to earth thou must return.—*John King.*

Verse 18.—"*The man of the earth.*" Man dwelling in the earth, and made of earth.—*Thomas Wilcocks.*

HINTS TO THE VILLAGE PREACHER.

Verse 1.—The answer to these questions furnishes a noble topic for an experimental sermon. Let me suggest that the question is not to be answered in the same manner in all cases. Past sin, trials of graces, strengthening of faith, discovery of depravity, instruction, etc., etc., are varied reasons for the hiding of our Father's face.

Verse 2.—Religious persecution in all its phases based on pride.

Verse 3.—God's hatred of covetousness : show its justice.

Verse 4.—Pride the barrier in the way of conversion.

Verse 4 (last clause).—Thoughts in which God is not, weighed and condemned.

Verse 5.—" *Thy judgments are far above out of his sight.*" Moral inability of men to appreciate the character and acts of God.

Verse 6.—The vain confidence of sinners.

Verse 8.—Dangers of godly men, or the snares in the way of believers.

Verse 9.—The ferocity, craftiness, strength, and activity of Satan.

Verse 9 (*last clause*).—The Satanic fisherman, his art, diligence, success, etc.

Verse 10.—Designing humility unmasked.

Verse 11.—Divine omniscience and the astounding presumption of sinners.

Verse 12.—" *Arise, O Lord.*" A prayer needful, allowable, seasonable, etc.

Verse 13 (*first clause*).—An astounding fact, and a reasonable enquiry.

Verse 13.—Future retribution : doubts concerning it. I. By whom indulged : " *the wicked.*" II. Where fostered : " *in his heart.*" III. For what purpose : *quieting of conscience*, etc. IV. With what practical tendency : " *contemn God.*" He who disbelieves hell distrusts heaven.

Verses 13, 14.—Divine government in the world. I. Who doubt it ? and why ? II. Who believe it ? and what does this faith cause them to do ?

Verse 14 (*last clause*).—A plea for orphans.

Verse 16.—The Eternal Kingship of Jehovah.

Verse 17 (*first clause*).—I. The Christian's character—" *humble.*" II. An attribute of the Christian's whole life—" *desire :*" he desires more holiness, communion, knowledge, grace, and usefulness ; and then he desires glory. III. The Christian's great blessedness—" *Lord, thou hast heard the desire of the humble.*"

Verse 17 (*whole verse*).—I. Consider the *nature* of gracious desires. II. Their *origin*. III. Their *result*. The three sentences readily suggest these divisions, and the subject may be very profitable.

PSALM XI.

SUBJECT.—*Charles Simeon gives an excellent summary of this Psalm in the following sentences :—" The Psalms are a rich repository of experimental knowledge. David, at the different periods of his life, was placed in almost every situation in which a believer, whether rich or poor, can be placed ; in these heavenly compositions he delineates all the workings of the heart. He introduces, too, the sentiments and conduct of the various persons who were accessory either to his troubles or his joys ; and thus sets before us a compendium of all that is passing in the hearts of men throughout the world. When he penned this Psalm he was under persecution from Saul, who sought his life, and hunted him ' as a partridge upon the mountains.' His timid friends were alarmed for his safety, and recommended him to flee to some mountain where he had a hiding-place, and thus to conceal himself from the rage of Saul. But David, being strong in faith, spurned the idea of resorting to any such pusillanimous expedients, and determined confidently to repose his trust in God."*

To assist us to remember this short, but sweet Psalm, we will give it the name of " THE SONG OF THE STEDFAST."

DIVISION.—*From 1 to 3, David describes the temptation with which he was assailed, and from 4 to 7, the arguments by which his courage was sustained.*

EXPOSITION.

I N the LORD put I my trust : how say ye to my soul, Flee *as* a bird to your mountain ?

2 For, lo, the wicked bend *their* bow, they make ready their arrow upon the string, that they may privily shoot at the upright in heart.

3 If the foundations be destroyed, what can the righteous do ?

These verses contain an account of a temptation to distrust God, with which David was, upon some unmentioned occasion, greatly exercised. It may be, that in the days when he was in Saul's court, he was advised to flee at a time when this flight would have been charged against him as a breach of duty to the king, or a proof of personal cowardice. His case was like that of Nehemiah, when his enemies, under the garb of friendship, hoped to entrap him by advising him to escape for his life. Had he done so, they could then have found a ground of accusation. Nehemiah bravely replied, " Shall such a man as I flee ?" and David, in a like spirit, refuses to retreat, exclaiming, " *In the Lord put I my trust : how say ye to my soul, Flee as a bird to your mountain ?*" When Satan cannot overthrow us by presumption, how craftily will he seek to ruin us by distrust ! He will employ our dearest friends to argue us out of our confidence, and he will use such plausible logic, that unless we once for all assert our immovable trust in Jehovah, he will make us like the timid bird which flies to the mountain whenever danger presents itself. How forcibly the case is put ! The bow is bent, the arrow is fitted to the string : " Flee, flee, thou defenceless bird, thy safety lies in flight ; begone, for thine enemies will send their shafts into thy heart ; haste, haste, for soon wilt thou be destroyed !" David seems to have felt the force of the advice, for it came home *to his soul ;* but yet he would not yield, but would rather dare the danger than exhibit a distrust in the Lord his God. Doubtless, the perils which encompassed David were great and imminent ; it was quite true that his enemies were *ready* to *shoot privily* at him ; it was equally correct that the very *foundations* of law and justice were *destroyed* under Saul's unrighteous government : but what were all these things to the man whose trust was in God alone ? He could brave the dangers, could escape the enemies, and defy the injustice which surrounded him. His answer to the question, " What can the righteous do ?" would be

10

the counter-question, "What cannot they do?" When prayer engages God on our side, and when faith secures the fulfilment of the promise, what cause can there be for flight, however cruel and mighty our enemies? With a sling and a stone, David had smitten a giant before whom the whole hosts of Israel were trembling, and the Lord, who delivered him from the uncircumcised Philistine, could surely deliver him from King Saul and his myrmidons. There is no such word as "impossibility" in the language of faith; that martial grace knows how to fight and conquer, but she knows not how to flee.

4 The LORD *is* in his holy temple, the LORD's throne *is* in heaven : his eyes behold, his eyelids try, the children of men.

5 The LORD trieth the righteous : but the wicked and him that loveth violence his soul hateth.

6 Upon the wicked he shall rain snares, fire and brimstone, and an horrible tempest : *this shall be* the portion of their cup.

7 For the righteous LORD loveth righteousness ; his countenance doth behold the upright.

David here declares the great source of his unflinching courage. He borrows his light from heaven—from the great central orb of deity. The God of the believer is never far from him ; he is not merely the God of the mountain fastnesses, but of the dangerous valleys and battle plains.

"*Jehovah is in his holy temple.*" The heavens are above our heads in all regions of the earth, and so is the Lord ever near to us in every state and condition. This is a very strong reason why we should not adopt the vile suggestions of distrust. There is one who pleads his precious blood in our behalf in the temple above, and there is one upon the throne who is never deaf to the intercession of his Son. Why, then, should we fear? What plots can men devise which Jesus will not discover? Satan has doubtless desired to have us, that he may sift us as wheat, but Jesus is in the temple praying for us, and how can our faith fail? What attempts can the wicked make which Jehovah shall not behold? And since he is in his holy temple, delighting in the sacrifice of his Son, will he not defeat every device, and send us a sure deliverance?

"*Jehovah's throne is in the heavens ;*" he reigns supreme. Nothing can be done in heaven, or earth, or hell, which he doth not ordain and over-rule. He is the world's great Emperor. Wherefore, then, should we flee? If we trust this King of kings, is not this enough? Cannot he deliver us without our cowardly retreat? Yes, blessed be the Lord our God, we can salute him as Jehovah-nissi ; in his name we set up our banners, and, instead of flight, we once more raise the shout of war.

"*His eyes behold.*" The eternal Watcher never slumbers ; his eyes never know a sleep. "*His eyelids try the children of men :*" he narrowly inspects their actions, words, and thoughts. As men, when intently and narrowly inspecting some very minute object, almost close their eyelids to exclude every other object, so will the Lord look all men through and through. God sees each man as much and as perfectly as if there were no other creature in the universe. He sees us always ; he never removes his eye from us ; he sees us entirely, reading the recesses of the soul as readily as the glancings of the eye. Is not this a sufficient ground of confidence, and an abundant answer to the solicitations of despondency? My danger is not hid from him ; he knows my extremity, and I may rest assured that he will not suffer me to perish while I rely alone on him. Wherefore, then, should I take wings of the timid bird, and flee from the dangers which beset me?

"*The Lord trieth the righteous :*" he doth not hate them, but only tries them. They are precious to him, and therefore he refines them with afflictions. None of the Lord's children may hope to escape from trial, nor, indeed, in our right minds, would any of us desire to do so, for trial is the channel of many blessings.

" 'Tis my happiness below
Not to live without the cross;
But the Saviour's power to know,
Sanctifying every loss.

*   *   *   *.   *

Trials make the promise sweet;
Trials give new life to prayer;
Trials bring me to his feet—
Lay me low, and keep me there.

Did I meet no trials here—
No chastisement by the way—
Might I not, with reason, fear
I should prove a cast-away?

Bastards may escape the rod,
Sunk in earthly vain delight;
But the true-born child of God
Must not—would not, if he might."—*William Cowper.*

Is not this a very cogent reason why we should not distrustfully endeavour to shun a trial?—for in so doing we are seeking to avoid a blessing.

" *But the wicked and him that loveth violence his soul hateth:*" why, then, shall I flee from these wicked men? If God hateth them, I will not fear them. Haman was very great in the palace until he lost favour, but when the king abhorred him, how bold were the meanest attendants to suggest the gallows for the man at whom they had often trembled! Look at the black mark upon the faces of our persecutors, and we shall not run away from them. If God is in the quarrel as well as ourselves, it would be foolish to question the result, or avoid the conflict. Sodom and Gomorrah perished by a fiery hail, and by a brimstone shower from heaven; so shall all the ungodly. They may gather together like Gog and Magog to battle, but the Lord will rain upon them " an overflowing rain, and great hailstones, fire, and brimstone:" Ezek. xxxviii. 22. Some expositors think that in the term " horrible tempest," there is in the Hebrew an allusion to that burning, suffocating wind, which blows across the Arabian deserts, and is known by the name of Simoom. " A burning storm," Lowth calls it, while another great commentator reads it " wrathwind;" in either version the language is full of terrors. What a tempest will that be which shall overwhelm the despisers of God! Oh! what a shower will that be which shall pour out itself for ever upon the defenceless heads of impenitent sinners in hell! Repent, ye rebels, or this fiery deluge shall soon surround you. Hell's horrors shall be your inheritance, your entailed estate, " the portion of your cup." The dregs of that cup you shall wring out, and drink for ever. A drop of hell is terrible, but what must a full cup of torment be? Think of it—a cup of misery, but not a drop of mercy. O people of God, how foolish is it to fear the faces of men who shall soon be faggots in the fire of hell! Think of their end, their fearful end, and all fear of them must be changed into contempt of their threatenings, and pity for their miserable estate.

The delightful contrast of the last verse is well worthy of our observation, and it affords another overwhelming reason why we should be stedfast, unmovable, not carried away with fear, or led to adopt carnal expedients in order to avoid trial. " *For the righteous Lord loveth righteousness.*" It is not only his office to defend it, but his nature to love it. He would deny himself if he did not defend the just. It is essential to the very being of God that he should be just; fear not, then, the end of all your trials, but " be just, and fear not." God approves, and, if men oppose, what matters it? " *His countenance doth behold the upright.*" We need never be out of countenance, for God countenances us. He observes, he approves, he delights in the upright. He sees his own image in them, an image of his own fashioning, and therefore with complacency he regards them. Shall we dare to put forth our hand unto iniquity in order to escape affliction? Let us have done with by-ways and short turnings, and let us keep to that fair path of right along which Jehovah's smile shall light us. Are we tempted to put our light under a bushel, to conceal our religion from our neighbours? Is it suggested to us that there are ways of avoiding the cross, and shunning the reproach of Christ? Let us not hearken to the voice of the charmer, but seek an increase of faith, that we may wrestle with principalities and powers, and follow the Lord, fully going without the camp, bearing his reproach. Mammon, the flesh, the devil, will all whisper in our ear, "Flee as a bird to your mountain;" but let us come forth and defy them all. "Resist the devil, and he will flee from you." There is no room or reason for retreat. Advance! Let the vanguard push on! To the front! all ye powers and passions of our soul. On! on! in God's name, on! for "the Lord of hosts is with us; the God of Jacob is our refuge."

EXPLANATORY NOTES AND QUAINT SAYINGS.

Whole Psalm.—The most probable account of the occasion of this Psalm is that given by Amyraldus. He thinks it was composed by David while he was in the court of Saul, at a time when the hostility of the king was beginning to show itself, and before it had broken out into open persecution. David's friends, or those professing to be so, advised him to flee to his native mountains for a time, and remain in retirement, till the king should show himself more favourable. David does not at that time accept the counsel, though afterwards he seems to have followed it. This Psalm applies itself to the establishment of the church against the calumnies of the world and the compromising counsel of man, in that confidence which is to be placed in God the Judge of all.—*W. Wilson, D.D., in loc.,* 1860.

Whole Psalm.—If one may offer to make a modest conjecture, it is not improbable this Psalm might be composed on the sad murder of the priests by Saul (1 Sam. xxii. 19), when after the slaughter of Abimelech, the high priest, Doeg, the Edomite, by command from Saul, "slew in one day fourscore and five persons which wore a linen ephod." I am not so carnal as to build the spiritual church of the Jews on the material walls of the priests' city at Nob (which then by Doeg was smitten with the edge of the sword), but this is most true, that "knowledge must preserve the people;" and (Mal. ii. 7), "The priests' lips shall preserve knowledge;" and then it is easy to conclude, what an earthquake this massacre might make in the *foundations of religion.*—*Thomas Fuller.*

Whole Psalm.—Notice how remarkably the whole Psalm corresponds with the deliverance of Lot from Sodom. This verse, with the angel's exhortation, "Escape to the mountains, lest thou be consumed," and Lot's reply, "I cannot escape to the mountains, lest some evil take me and I die." Genesis xix. 17—19. And again, "*The Lord's seat is in heaven,* and *upon the ungodly he shall rain snares, fire, brimstone, storm and tempest,*" with "Then the Lord rained upon Sodom and Gomorrah brimstone and fire out of heaven:" and again, "*His countenance will behold the thing that is just,*" with "Delivered just Lot . . . . . for that righteous man vexed his righteous soul with their ungodly deeds." 2 Peter ii. 7, 8.—*Cassiodorus* (A.D., 560) *in John Mason Neale's "Commentary on the Psalms, from Primitive and Mediæval Writers,"* 1860.

Whole Psalm.—The combatants at the Lake Thrasymene are said to have been so engrossed with the conflict, that neither party perceived the convulsions of nature that shook the ground—

> "An earthquake reeled unheedingly away,
> None felt stern nature rocking at his feet."

From a nobler cause, it is thus with the soldiers of the Lamb. They believe, and, therefore, make no haste ; nay, they can scarcely be said to feel earth's convulsions as other men, because their eager hope presses forward to the issue at the advent of the Lord.—*Andrew A. Bonar.*

Verse 1.—" *I trust in the Lord : how do ye say to my soul, Swerve on to your mountain like a bird ?*" (others, " *O thou bird.*") Saul and his adherents mocked and jeered David with such taunting speeches, as conceiving that he knew no other shift or refuge, but so betaking himself unto wandering and lurking on the mountains ; hopping, as it were, from one place to another like a silly bird ; but they thought to ensnare and take him well enough for all that, not considering God who was David's comfort, rest and refuge.—*Theodore Haak's* " *Translation of the Dutch Annotations, as ordered by the Synod of Dort, in* 1618." London, 1657.

Verse 1.—" *With Jehovah I have taken shelter ; how say ye to my soul, Flee, sparrows, to your hill ?*" " *Your hill,*" that hill from which you say your help cometh : a sneer. Repair to that boasted hill, which may indeed give you the help which it gives the sparrow : a shelter against the inclemencies of a stormy sky, no defence against our power.—*Samuel Horsley, in loc.*

Verse 1.—" *In the Lord put I my trust : how say ye to my soul, Flee as a bird to your mountain ?*" The holy confidence of the saints in the hour of great trial is beautifully illustrated by the following ballad which Anne Askew, who was burned at Smithfield in 1546, made and sang when she was in Newgate :—

Like as the armèd knight,
Appointed to the field,
With this world will I fight,
And Christ shall be my shield.

Faith is that weapon strong,
Which will not fail at need :
My foes, therefore, among,
Therewith will I proceed.

As it is had in strength
And force of Christe's way,
It will prevail at length,
Though all the devils say nay.

Faith in the fathers old
Obtained righteousness ;
Which make me very bold
To fear no world's distress.

I now rejoice in heart,
And hope bids me do so ;
For Christ will take my part,
And ease me of my woe.

Thou say'st Lord, whoso knock,
To them wilt thou attend :
Undo therefore the lock,
And thy strong power send.

More enemies now I have
Than hairs upon my head :
Let them not me deprave,
But fight thou in my stead.

On thee my care I cast,
For all their cruel spite :
I set not by their haste ;
For thou art my delight.

I am not she that list
My anchor to let fall
For every drizzling mist,
My ship substantial.

Not oft use I to write,
In prose, nor yet in rhyme ;
Yet will I shew one sight
That I saw in my time.

I saw a royal throne,
Where justice should have sit,
But in her stead was one
Of moody, cruel wit.

Absorbed was righteousness,
As of the raging flood :
Satan, in his excess,
Sucked up the guiltless blood.

Then thought I, Jesus Lord,
When thou shall judge us all,
Hard it is to record
On these men what will fall.

Yet, Lord, I thee desire,
For that they do to me,
Let them not taste the hire
Of their iniquity.

Verse 1.—" *How say ye to my soul, Flee as a bird to your mountain ?*" We may observe, that David is much pleased with the metaphor in frequently comparing himself to a bird, and that of several sorts : first, to an eagle (Psalm ciii. 5), " My youth is renewed like the eagle's ;" sometimes to an owl (Psalm cii. 6), " I am like an owl in the desert ;" sometimes to a pelican, in the same verse, " Like a pelican in the wilderness ;" sometimes to a sparrow (Psalm cii. 7), " I watch, and am as a sparrow ;" sometimes to a partridge, " As when one doth hunt a partridge." I cannot say that he doth compare himself to a dove, but he would compare himself (Psalm lv. 6), " O that I had the wings of a dove, for then I would flee away, and be at rest." Some will say, How is it possible that birds of so different a feather should all so fly together as to meet in the character of David? To whom we answer, That no two men can more differ one from another, that the same servant of God at several times differeth from himself. David in prosperity, when commanding, was like an *eagle;* in adversity, when contemned, like an *owl;* in devotion, when retired, like a *pelican;* in solitariness, when having no company, like a *sparrow;* in persecution, when fearing too much company (of *Saul*), like a *partridge.* This general metaphor of a *bird,* which David so often used on himself, his enemies in the first verse of this Psalm used on him, though not particularising the kind thereof : " *Flee as a bird to your mountain;*" that is, speedily betake thyself to thy God, in whom thou hopest for succour and security.

Seeing this counsel was both good in itself, and good at this time, why doth David seem so angry and displeased thereat? Those his words, " *Why say you to my soul, Flee as a bird to your mountain?*" import some passion, at leastwise, a disgust of the advice. It is answered, David was not offended with the counsel, but with the manner of the propounding thereof. His enemies did it ironically in a gibing, jeering way, as if his flying thither were to no purpose, and he unlikely to find there the safety he sought for. However, David was not hereby put out of conceit with the counsel, beginning this Psalm with this his firm resolution, " *In the Lord put I my trust : how say ye then to my soul,*" etc. Learn we from hence, when men give us good counsel in a jeering way, let us take the counsel, and practise it ; and leave them the jeer to be punished for it. Indeed, corporal cordials may be envenomed by being wrapped up in poisoned papers ; not so good spiritual advice where the good matter receives no infection from the ill manner of the delivery thereof. Thus, when the chief priests mocked our Saviour (Matt. xxvii. 43), " He trusted in God, let him deliver him now if he will have him." Christ trusted in God never a whit the less for the fleere and flout which their profaneness was pleased to bestow upon him. Otherwise, if men's mocks should make us to undervalue good counsel, we might in this age be mocked out of our God, and Christ, and Scripture, and heaven ; the apostle Jude, verse 18, having foretold that in the last times there should be mockers, walking after their own lusts.—*Thomas Fuller.*

Verse 1.—It is as great an offence to make a new, as to deny the true God. " *In the Lord put I my trust;*" how then " *say ye unto my soul* " (ye seducers of souls), " *that she should fly unto the mountains as a bird;*" to seek unnecessary and foreign helps, as if the Lord alone were not sufficient? " The Lord is my rock, and my fortress, and he that delivereth me, my God, and my strength ; in him will I trust : my shield, the horn of my salvation, and my refuge. I will call upon the Lord, who is worthy to be praised, so shall I be safe from mine enemies." " Whom have I in heaven but thee," amongst those thousands of angels and saints, what Michael or Gabriel, what Moses or Samuel, what Peter, what Paul? " and there is none in earth that I desire in comparison of thee." *John King,* 1608.

Verse 1.—In temptations of inward trouble and terror, it is not convenient to dispute the matter with Satan. David in Psalm xlii. 11, seems to correct himself for his mistake ; his soul was cast down within him, and for the cure of that temptation, he had prepared himself by arguments for a dispute ; but perceiving himself in a wrong course, he calls off his soul from disquiet to an immediate application to God and the promises, " Trust still in God, for I shall yet praise him ;" but here he is more aforehand with his work ; for while his enemies were acted by Satan to discourage him, he rejects the temptation at first, before it settled upon his thoughts, and chaseth it away as a thing that he would not give ear to. " *In the Lord put I my trust : how say ye to my soul, Flee as a bird to your mountain?*" And there are weighty reasons that should dissuade us from entering the lists with Satan in temptation of inward trouble.—*Richard Gilpin.*

Verse 1.—The shadow will not cool except in it. What good to have the shadow though of a mighty rock, when we sit in the open sun? To have almighty power engaged for us, and we to throw ourselves out of it, by bold sallies in the mouth of temptation! The saints' falls have been when they have run out of their trench and stronghold; for, like the conies, they are a weak people in themselves, and their strength lies in the rock of God's almightiness, which is their habitation.—*William Gurnall.*

Verse 1.—The saints of old would not accept deliverances on base terms. They scorned to fly away for the enjoyment of rest except it were with the wings of a dove, covered with silver innocence. As willing were many of the martyrs to die as to dine. The tormentors were tired in torturing Blandina. "We are ashamed, O Emperor! The Christians laugh at your cruelty, and grow the more resolute," said one of Julian's nobles. This the heathen counted obstinacy; but they knew not the power of the Spirit, nor the secret armour of proof which saints wear about their hearts.—*John Trapp.*

Verse 2.—"*For, lo, the wicked bend their bow,*" etc. This verse presents an unequal combat betwixt *armed power, advantaged with policy,* on the one side; and *naked innocence* on the other. First, *armed power:* "*They bend their bows, and make ready their arrows,*" being all the artillery of that age; secondly, *advantaged with policy:* "*that they may privily shoot,*" to surprise them with an ambush unawares, probably pretending amity and friendship unto them; thirdly, *naked innocence:* if innocence may be termed naked, which is its own armour; "*at the upright in heart.*"—*Thomas Fuller.*

Verse 2.—"*For, lo, the ungodly bend their bow, and make ready their arrows within the quiver: that they may privily shoot at them which are true of heart.*" The plottings of the chief priests and Pharisees that they might take Jesus by subtlety and kill him. They bent their bow, when they hired Judas Iscariot for the betrayal of his Master; they made ready their arrows within the quiver when they sought "false witnesses against Jesus to put him to death." Matt. xxvi. 59. "*Them which are true of heart.*" Not alone the Lord himself, the only true and righteous, but his apostles, and the long line of those who should faithfully cleave to him from that time to this. And as with the Master, so with the servants: witness the calumnies and the revilings that from the time of Joseph's accusation by his mistress till the present day, have been the lot of God's people. —*Michael Ayguan,* 1416, in *J. M. Neale's Commentary.*

Verse 2.—"*That they may secretly shoot at them which are upright in heart.*" They bear not their bows and arrows as scarecrows in a garden of cucumbers, to fray, but *to shoot,* not at stakes, but men; their arrows are *jacula mortifera* (Psalm vii.), deadly arrows, and lest they should fail to hit, they take advantage of the dark, of privacy and secrecy; they shoot *privily.* Now this is the covenant of hell itself. For what created power in the earth is able to dissolve that work which *cruelty* and *subtlety,* like Simeon and Levi, brothers in evil, are combined and confederate to bring to pass? Where subtlety is ingenious, insidious to invent, cruelty barbarous to execute, subtlety giveth counsel, cruelty giveth the stroke. Subtlety ordereth the time, the place, the means, accommodateth, concinnateth circumstances; cruelty undertaketh the act: subtlety hideth the knife, cruelty cutteth the throat: subtlety with a cunning head layeth the ambush, plotteth the train, the stratagem; and cruelty with as savage a heart, sticketh not at the dreadfullest, direfullest objects, ready to wade up to the ankles, the neck, in a whole red sea of human, yea, country blood: how fearful is their plight that are thus assaulted!—*John King.*

Verse 3.—"*If the foundations be destroyed, what can the righteous do?*" But now we are met with a giant objection, which with Goliath must be removed, or else it will obstruct our present proceedings. Is it possible that the *foundations of religion* should be destroyed? Can God be in so long a sleep, yea, so long a lethargy, as patiently to permit the ruins thereof? If he looks on, and yet doth not see these *foundations* when destroyed, where then is his *omnisciency?*

If he seeth it, and cannot help it, where then is his *omnipotency?* If he seeth it, can help it, and will not, where then is his *goodness* and *mercy?* Martha said to Jesus (John xi. 21), "Lord, if thou hadst been here, my brother had not died." But many will say, Were God effectually present in the world with his aforesaid attributes, surely the *foundations* had not *died*, had not been *destroyed.* We answer negatively, that it is impossible that the *foundations* of religion should ever be *totally* and *finally destroyed*, either in relation to the church in general, or in reference to every true and lively member thereof. For the first, we have an express promise of Christ. Matt. xvi. 18. "The gates of hell shall not prevail against it." *Fundamenta tamen stant inconcussa Sionis.* And as for every particular Christian (2 Tim. ii. 19), "Nevertheless, the foundation of God standeth sure, having this seal, the Lord knoweth them that are his." However, though for the reasons aforementioned in the objections (the inconsistency thereof with the attributes of God's omnipotency, omnisciency, and goodness), the *foundations* can never totally and finally, yet may they partially be destroyed, *quoad gradum*, in a fourfold degree, as followeth. First, *in the desires and utmost endeavours of wicked men*,

They bring their $\begin{cases} 1. \textit{ Hoc velle,} \\ 2. \textit{ Hoc agere,} \\ 3. \textit{ Totum posse.} \end{cases}$

If they *destroy* not the foundations, it is no thanks to them, seeing all the world will bear them witness they have done *their best* (that is, *their worst*), what their might and malice could perform. Secondly, *in their own vainglorious imaginations:* they may not only vainly boast, but also verily believe that they have *destroyed the foundations.* Applicable to this purpose, is that high rant of the Roman emperor (Luke ii. 1) : "And it came to pass in those days, that there went out a decree from Cæsar Augustus, that all the world should be taxed." All the world ! whereas he had, though much, not all in Europe, little in Asia, less in Africa, none in America, which was so far from being conquered, it was not so much as known to the Romans. But *hyperbole* is not a figure, but the ordinary language of pride ; because indeed Augustus had very much he proclaimeth himself to have all the world. . . . . Thirdly, *the foundations may be destroyed* as to all outward visible illustrious apparition. The church in persecution is like unto a ship in a tempest ; down go all their masts, yea, sometimes for the more speed they are forced to cut them down : not a piece of canvas to play with the winds, no sails to be seen ; they lie close knotted to the very keel, that the tempest may have the less power upon them, though when the storm is over, they can hoist up their sails as high, and spread their canvas as broad as ever before. So the church in time of persecution *feared*, but especially *felt*, loseth all gayness and gallantry which may attract and allure the eyes of beholders, and contenteth itself with its own secrecy. In a word, on the work-days of affliction she weareth her worst clothes, whilst her best are laid up in her wardrobe, in sure and certain hope that God will give her a *holy* and *happy day*, when with joy she shall wear her best garments. Lastly, they may be *destroyed* in the *jealous apprehensions* of the best saints and servants of God, especially in their melancholy fits. I will instance in no puny, but in a star of the first magnitude and greatest eminency, even Elijah himself complaining (1 Kings xix. 10) : "And I, even I only, am left ; and they seek my life, to take it away."—*Thomas Fuller.*

Verse 3.—" *If.*" It is the only word of comfort in the text, that what is said is not *positive, but suppositive ;* not thetical, but hypothetical. And yet this comfort which is but a spark (at which we would willingly kindle our hopes), is quickly sadded with a double consideration. First, impossible suppositions produce impossible consequences, "As is the mother, so is the daughter." Therefore, surely God's Holy Spirit would not suppose such a thing but what was feasible and possible, but what either had, did, or might come to pass. Secondly, the Hebrew word is not the conditional *im, si, si forte*, but *chi, quia, quoniam*, because, and (although here it be favourably rendered *if*), seemeth to import, more therein, that the sad case had already happened in David's days. I see, therefore, that this *if*, our only hope in the text, is likely to prove with Job's friends, but a miserable comforter. Well, it is good to know the worst of things, that we may provide ourselves accordingly ; and therefore let us behold this doleful case, not as doubtful, but as done ; not as feared, but felt ; not as suspected, but at this time really come to pass.—*Thomas Fuller.*

Verse 3.—" *If the foundations*," etc. My text is an answer to a tacit objection which some may raise ; namely, that the righteous are wanting to themselves, and by their own easiness and inactivity (not daring and doing so much as they might and ought), betray themselves to that bad condition. In whose defence David shows, that if God in his wise will and pleasure seeth it fitting, for reasons best known to himself, to suffer religion to be reduced to terms of extremity, it is not placed in the power of the best man alive to remedy and redress the same. " *If the foundations be destroyed, what can the righteous do ?*" My text is hung about with *mourning*, as for a funeral sermon, and contains : First, a sad case supposed, " *If the foundations be destroyed.*" Secondly, a sad question propounded, " *What can the righteous do ?*" Thirdly, a sad answer implied, namely, that they can do just nothing, as to the point of re-establishing the destroyed foundation.—*Thomas Fuller.*

Verse 3.—" *If the foundations be destroyed,*" etc. The civil foundation of a nation or people, is their laws and constitutions. The order and power that's among them, that's the foundation of a people ; and when once this foundation is destroyed, " *What can the righteous do ?*" What can the best, the wisest in the world, do in such a case ? What can any man do, if there be not a foundation of government left among men ? There is no help nor answer in such a case but that which follows in the fourth verse of the Psalm, " *The Lord is in his holy temple, the Lord's throne is in heaven : his eyes behold, his eyelids try, the children of men ;*" as if he had said, in the midst of these confusions, when as it is said (Psalm lxxxii. 5), " All the foundations of the earth are out of course ;" yet God keeps his course still, he is where he was and as he was, without variableness or shadow of turning.—*Joseph Caryl.*

Verse 3.—" *The righteous.*" The righteous indefinitely, equivalent to the righteous universally ; not only the righteous as a single arrow, but in the whole sheaf ; not only the righteous in their personal, but in their diffusive capacity. Were they all collected into one body, were all the righteous living in the same age wherein the *foundations are destroyed*, summoned up and modelled into one corporation, all their joint endeavours would prove ineffectual to the re-establishing of the fallen *foundations*, as not being man's work, but only God's work to perform.—*Thomas Fuller.*

Verse 3.—" *The foundations.*" *Positions*, the things formerly fixed, placed, and settled. It is not said, if the roof be ruinous, or if the side walls be shattered, but if the *foundations*.

Verse 3.—" *Foundations be destroyed.*" In the plural. Here I will not warrant my skill in architecture, but conceive this may pass for an undoubted truth : it is possible that a building settled on several entire *foundations* (suppose them *pillars*) close one to another, if one of them fall, yet the structure may still stand, or rather hang (at the least for a short time) by virtue of the *complicative*, which it receiveth from such foundations which still stand secure. But in case there be a total rout, and an utter ruin of all the *foundations*, none can fancy to themselves a possibility of that building's subsistence.—*Thomas Fuller.*

Verse 3.—" *What* CAN *the righteous ?*" The *can* of the righteous is a limited *can*, confined to the rule of God's word ; they *can* do nothing but what they *can* lawfully do. 2 Cor. xiii. 8. " For we *can* do nothing against the truth, but for the truth :" *Illud possumus, quod jure possumus.* Wicked men can do anything ; their conscience, which is so wide that it is none at all, will bear them out to act anything how unlawful soever, to stab, poison, massacre, by any means, at any time, in any place, whosoever standeth betwixt them and the effecting their desires.   Not so the righteous ; they have a rule whereby to walk, which they will not, they must not, they dare not, cross.   If therefore a righteous man were assured, that by the breach of one of God's commandments he might restore decayed religion, and re-settle it *statu quo prius*, his hands, head, and heart are tied up, he *can* do nothing, because *their damnation is just who say* (Rom. iii. 8), " *Let us do evil that good may come thereof.*"

Verse 3.—" *Do.*"   It is not said, *What can they think ?*   It is a great blessing which God hath allowed injured people, that though otherwise oppressed and straitened, they may freely enlarge themselves in their thoughts.—*Thomas Fuller.*

Verse 3.—Sinning times have ever been the saints' praying times : this sent Ezra with a heavy heart to confess the sin of his people, and to bewail their abominations before the Lord.   Ezra ix.   And Jeremiah tells the wicked of his degenerate age, that " his soul should weep in secret places for their pride." Jer. xiii. 17.   Indeed, sometimes sin comes to such a height, that this is almost all the godly can do, to get into a corner, and bewail the general pollutions of the age.   " *If the foundations be destroyed, what can the righteous do ?*"   Such dismal days of national confusion our eyes have seen, when foundations of government were destroyed, and all hurled into military confusion.   When it is thus with a people, " *What can the righteous do ?*"   Yes, this they may, and should do, " fast and pray."   There is yet a God in heaven to be sought to, when a people's deliverance is thrown beyond the help of human policy or power.   Now is the fit time to make their appeal to God, as the words following hint : " *The Lord is in his holy temple, the Lord's throne is in heaven ;*" in which words God is presented sitting in heaven as a temple, for their encouragement, I conceive, in such a desperate state of affairs, to direct their prayers thither for deliverance.   And certainly this hath been the engine that hath been instrumental, above any, to restore this poor nation again, and set it upon the foundation of that lawful government from which it had so dangerously departed.— *William Gurnall.*

Verse 4.—The infinite understanding of God doth exactly know the sins of men ; he knows so as to consider.   He doth not only know them, but intently behold them : " *His eyelids try the children of men,*" a metaphor taken from men, that contract the eyelids when they would wistly and accurately behold a thing : it is not a transient and careless look.—*Stephen Charnock.*

Verse 4.—" *His eyes behold,*" etc.   God searcheth not as man searcheth, by enquiring into that which before was hid from him ; his searching is no more but his beholding ; he seeth the heart, he beholdeth the reins ; God's very sight is searching.   Heb. iv. 13.   " All things are naked, and opened unto his eyes," τετραχηλισμένα, *dissected or anatomised.*   He hath at once as exact a view of the most hidden things, the very entrails of the soul, as if they had been with never so great curiosity anatomised before him.—*Richard Alleine*, 1611—1681.

Verse 4.—" *His eyes behold,*" etc.   Consider that God not only sees into all you do, but he sees it to that very end that he may examine and search into it. He doth not only behold you with a common and indifferent look, but with a searching, watchful, and inquisitive eye : he pries into the reasons, the motives, the ends of all your actions.   " *The Lord's throne is in heaven : his eyes behold, his eyelids try, the children of men.*"   Rev. i. 14, where Christ is described, it is said, *his eyes are as a flame of fire :* you know the property of fire is to search and make trial of those things which are exposed unto it, and to separate the dross from the pure metal : so, God's eye is like fire, to try and examine the actions of men : he knows and discerns how much your very purest duties have in them of mixture, and base ends of formality, hypocrisy, distractedness, and deadness : he sees through all your specious pretences, that which you cast as a mist before the eyes of men when yet thou art but a juggler in religion : all your tricks and sleights of outward profession, all those things that you use to cozen and delude men withal, cannot possibly impose upon him : he is a God that can look through all those fig-leaves of outward profession, and discern the nakedness of your duties through them.— *Ezekiel Hopkins, D.D.*

Verse 4.—" *His eyes behold,*" etc. Take God into thy counsel. Heaven overlooks hell. God at any time can tell thee what plots are hatching there against thee.— *William Gurnall.*

Verse 4.—" *His eyes behold, his eyelids try, the children of men.*" When an offender, or one accused for any offence, is brought before a judge, and stands at the bar to be arraigned, the judge looks upon him, eyes him, sets his eye upon him, and he bids the offender look up in his face : " Look upon me," saith the judge, " and speak up :" guiltiness usually clouds the forehead and clothes the brow ; the weight of guilt holds down the head ! *the evil doer hath an ill look,* or dares not look up ; how glad is he if the judge looks off him. We have such an expression here, speaking of the Lord, the great Judge of heaven and earth : " *His eyelids try the children of men,*" as a judge tries a guilty person with his eye, and reads the characters of his wickedness printed in his face. Hence we have a common speech in our language, such a one *looks suspiciously,* or, *he hath a guilty look.* At that great gaol-delivery described in Rev. vi. 16, All the prisoners cry out *to be hid from the face of him that sat upon the throne.* They could not look upon Christ, and they could not endure Christ should look on them ; the eyelids of Christ try the children of men. . . . . Wickedness cannot endure to be under the observation of any eye, much less of the eye of justice. Hence the actors of it say, " *Who seeth us ?*" It is very hard not to show the guilt of the heart in the face, and it is as hard to have it seen there.— *Joseph Caryl.*

Verse 5.—" *The Lord trieth the righteous.*" Except our sins, there is not such plenty of anything in all the world as there is of troubles which come from sin, as one heavy messenger came to Job after another. Since we are not in paradise, but in the wilderness, we must look for one trouble after another. As a bear came to David after a lion, and a giant after a bear, and a king after a giant, and Philistines after a king, so, when believers have fought with poverty, they shall fight with envy ; when they have fought with envy, they shall fight with infamy ; when they have fought with infamy, they shall fight with sickness ; they shall be like a labourer who is never out of work.— *Henry Smith.*

Verse 5.—" *The Lord trieth the righteous.*"—Times of affliction and persecution will distinguish the precious from the vile, it will difference the counterfeit professor from the true. Persecution is a Christian's touchstone, it is a *lapis lydius* that will try what metal men are made of, whether they be silver or tin, gold or dross, wheat or chaff, shadow or substance, carnal or spiritual, sincere or hypocritical. Nothing speaks out more soundness and uprightness than a pursuing after holiness, even then when holiness is most afflicted, pursued, and persecuted in the world : to stand fast in fiery trials argues much integrity within.— *Thomas Brooks.*

Verse 5.—Note the singular opposition of the two sentences. God hates the wicked, and therefore in contrast he loves the righteous ; but it is here said that he tries them : therefore it follows that to try and to love are with God the same thing.— *C. H. S.*

Verse 6.—" *Upon the wicked he shall rain snares.*" Snares to hold them ; then if they be not delivered, follow fire and brimstone, and they cannot escape. This is the case of a sinner if he repent not ; if God pardon not, he is in the snare of Satan's temptation, he is in the snare of divine vengeance ; let him therefore cry aloud for his deliverance, that he may have his feet in a large room. The wicked lay snares for the righteous, but God either preventeth them that their souls ever escape them, or else he subventeth them : " The snares are broken, and we are delivered." No snares hold us so fast as those of our own sins ; they keep down our heads, and stoop us that we cannot look up : a very little ease they are to him that hath not a seared conscience.—*Samuel Page*, 1646.

Verse 6.—"*He shall rain snares.*" As in hunting with the lasso, the huntsman casts a snare from above upon his prey to entangle its head or feet, so shall the Lord from above with many twistings of the line of terror, surround, bind, and take captive the haters of his law.—*C. H. S.*

Verse 6.—"*He shall rain snares,*" etc. He shall rain upon them when they least think of it, even in the midst of their jollity, as rain falls on a fair day. Or, he shall rain down the vengeance when he sees good, for it rains not always. Though he defers it, yet it will rain.—*William Nicholson, Bishop of Gloucester, in "David's Harp Strung and Tuned,"* 1662.

Verse 6.—"*Upon the wicked he shall rain snares, fire and brimstone, and an horrible tempest.*" The strange dispensation of affairs in this world is an argument which doth convincingly prove that there shall be such a day wherein all the *involucra* and entanglements of providence shall be clearly unfolded. Then shall the riddle be dissolved, why God hath given this and that profane wretch so much wealth, and so much power to do mischief : is it not *that they might be destroyed for ever ?* Then shall they be called to a strict account for all that plenty and prosperity for which they are now envied ; and the more they have abused, the more dreadful will their condemnation be. Then it will be seen that God gave them not as mercies, but as "*snares.*" It is said that God "*will rain on the wicked snares, fire and brimstone, and an horrible tempest :*" when he scatters abroad the desirable things of this world, riches, honours, pleasures, etc., then he rains "*snares*" upon them ; and when he shall call them to an account for these things, then he will rain upon them "*fire and brimstone, and an horrible tempest* " of his wrath and fury. Dives, who caroused on earth, yet, in hell could not obtain so much as one poor drop of water to cool his scorched and flaming tongue : had not his excess and intemperance been so great in his life, his fiery thirst had not been so tormenting after death ; and therefore, in that sad item that Abraham gives him (Luke xvi. 25), he bids him "*remember, that thou, in thy lifetime, receivedst thy good things, and likewise Lazarus evil things ; but now he is comforted, and thou art tormented.*" I look upon this as a most bitter and a most deserved sarcasm ; upbraiding him for his gross folly, in making the trifles of this life his good things. Thou hast received thy good things, but now thou art tormented. Oh, never call Dives's purple and delicious fare *good things*, if they thus end in torments ! Was it good for him to be wrapped in purple who is now wrapped in flames ? Was it good for him to fare deliciously who was only thereby fatted up against the day of slaughter ?—*Ezekiel Hopkins.*

Verse 6.—"*Snares, fire and brimstone, storm and tempest : this shall be the portion of their cup.*" After the judgment follows the condemnation : prefigured as we have seen, by the overthrow of Sodom and Gomorrah. "*Snares :*" because the allurements of Satan in this life will be their worst punishments in the next ; the fire of anger, the brimstone of impurity, the tempest of pride, the lust of the flesh, the lust of the eyes, and the pride of life. "*This shall be their portion ;*" compare it with the psalmist's own saying, "The Lord himself is the portion of my inheritance and my cup." Psalm xvi. 5.—*Cassiodorus, in J. M. Neale's Commentary.*

Verse 6.—"*The portion of their cup.*" Heb., the allotment of their cup. The expression has reference to the custom of distributing to each guest his mess of meat.—*William French and George Skinner*, 1842.

Verse 7.—That God may give grace without glory is intelligible ; but to admit a man to communion with him in glory without grace, is not intelligible. It is not agreeable to God's holiness to make any inhabitant of heaven, and converse freely with him in a way of intimate love, without such a qualification of grace : "*The righteous Lord loveth righteousness ; his countenance doth behold the upright ;*" he looks upon him with a smiling eye, and therefore he cannot favourably look upon an unrighteous person ; so that this necessity is not founded only in the command of God that we should be renewed, but in the very nature of the thing, because God, in regard of his holiness, cannot converse with an impure creature. God must change his nature, or the sinner's nature must be changed. There can be no friendly communion between two of different natures without the change of one of them into the likeness of the other. Wolves and sheep, darkness and light, can never agree. God cannot love a sinner as a sinner, because he hates impurity by a necessity of nature as well as a choice of will. It is as impossible for him to love it as to cease to be holy.— *Stephen Charnock.*

HINTS TO THE VILLAGE PREACHER.

Verse 1.—Faith's bold avowal, and brave refusal.

Verse 1.—Teacheth us to trust in God, how great soever our dangers be ; also that we shall be many times assaulted to make us put far from us this trust, but yet that we must cleave unto it, as the anchor of our souls, sure and steadfast.—*Thomas Wilcocks.*

Verse 1.—The advice of cowardice, and the jeer of insolence, both answered by faith. Lesson—Attempt no other answer.

Verse 2.—The craftiness of our spiritual enemies.

Verse 3.—This may furnish a double discourse. I. *If God's oath and promise could remove,* what could we do ? Here the answer is easy. II. *If all earthly things fail,* and the very State fall to pieces, what can we do ? We can suffer joyfully, hope cheerfully, wait patiently, pray earnestly, believe confidently, and triumph finally.

Verse 3.—Necessity of holding and preaching foundation truths.

Verse 4.—The elevation, mystery, supremacy, purity, everlastingness, invisibility, etc., of the throne of God.

Verses 4, 5.—In these verses mark the fact that the children of men, as well as the righteous, are tried ; work out the contrast between the two trials in their design and result, etc.

Verse 5.—" *The Lord trieth the righteous.*" I. Who are tried ? II. What in them is tried ?—Faith, love, etc. III. In what manner ?—Trials of every sort. IV. How long ? V. For what purposes ?

Verse 5.—" *His soul hateth.*" The thoroughness of God's hatred of sin. Illustrate by providential judgments, threatenings, sufferings of the Surety, and the terrors of hell.

Verse 5.—The trying of the gold, and the sweeping out of the refuse.

Verse 6.—" *He shall rain.*" Gracious rain and destroying rain.

Verse 6.—The portion of the impenitent.

Verse 7.—The Lord possesses righteousness as a personal attribute, loves it in the abstract, and blesses those who practise it.

PSALM XII.

TITLE.—*This Psalm is headed* "To the Chief Musician upon Sheminith, a Psalm of David," *which title is identical with that of the sixth Psalm, except that Neginoth is here omitted. We have nothing new to add, and therefore refer the reader to our remarks on the dedication of Psalm VI. As Sheminith signifies the eighth, the Arabic version says it is concerning the end of the world, which shall be the eighth day, and refers it to the coming of the Messiah: without accepting so fanciful an interpretation, we may read this song of complaining faith in the light of His coming who shall break in pieces the oppressor. The subject will be the better before the mind's eye if we entitle this Psalm:* "GOOD THOUGHTS IN BAD TIMES." *It is supposed to have been written while Saul was persecuting David, and those who favoured his cause.*

DIVISION.—*In the first and second verses David spreads his plaint before the Lord concerning the treachery of his age; verses 3 and 4 denounce judgments upon proud traitors; in verse 5, Jehovah himself thunders out his wrath against oppressors; hearing this, the Chief Musician sings sweetly of the faithfulness of God and his care of his people, in verses 6 and 7; but closes on the old key of lament in verse 8, as he observes the abounding wickedness of his times. Those holy souls who dwell in Mesech, and sojourn in the tents of Kedar, may read and sing these sacred stanzas with hearts in full accord with their mingled melody of lowly mourning and lofty confidence.*

EXPOSITION.

H ELP, LORD; for the godly man ceaseth; for the faithful fail from among the children of men.

2 They speak vanity every one with his neighbour : *with* flattering lips *and* with a double heart do they speak.

"*Help, Lord.*" A short, but sweet, suggestive, seasonable, and serviceable prayer; a kind of angel's sword, to be turned every way, and to be used on all occasions. Ainsworth says the word rendered "help," is largely used for all manner of saving, helping, delivering, preserving, etc. Thus it seems that the prayer is very full and instructive. The Psalmist sees the extreme danger of his position, for a man had better be among lions than among liars; he feels his own inability to deal with such sons of Belial, for "he who shall touch them must be fenced with iron;" he therefore turns himself to his all-sufficient Helper, the Lord, whose help is never denied to his servants, and whose aid is enough for all their needs. "*Help, Lord,*" is a very useful ejaculation which we may dart up to heaven on occasions of emergency, whether in labour, learning, suffering, fighting, living, or dying. As small ships can sail into harbours which larger vessels, drawing more water, cannot enter, so our brief cries and short petitions may trade with heaven when our soul is wind-bound, and business-bound, as to longer exercises of devotion, and when the stream of grace seems at too low an ebb to float a more laborious supplication. "*For the godly man ceaseth;*" the death, departure, or decline of godly men should be a trumpet-call for more prayer. They say that fish smell first at the head, and when godly men decay, the whole commonwealth will soon go rotten. We must not, however, be rash in our judgment on this point, for Elijah erred in counting himself the only servant of God alive, when there were thousands whom the Lord held in reserve. The present times always appear to be peculiarly dangerous, because they are nearest to our anxious gaze, and whatever evils are rife are sure to be observed, while the faults of past ages are further off, and are more easily overlooked. Yet we expect that in the latter days, "because iniquity shall abound, the love of many shall wax cold," and then we must the more thoroughly turn from man, and address ourselves to the Churches'

Lord, by whose help the gates of hell shall be kept from prevailing against us. "*The faithful fail from among the children of men;*" when godliness goes, faithfulness inevitably follows ; without fear of God, men have no love of truth. Common honesty is no longer common, when common irreligion leads to universal godlessness. David had his eye on Doeg, and the men of Ziph and Keilah, and perhaps remembered the murdered priests of Nob, and the many banished ones who consorted with him in the cave of Adullam, and wondered where the state would drift without the anchors of its godly and faithful men. David, amid the general misrule, did not betake himself to seditious plottings, but to solemn petitionings ; nor did he join with the multitude to do evil, but took up the arms of prayer to withstand their attacks upon virtue.

"*They speak vanity every one with his neighbour.*" They utter that which is vain *to hear*, because of its frivolous, foolish, want of worth ; vain *to believe*, because it was false and lying ; vain to *trust to*, since it was deceitful and flattering ; vain to *regard*, for it lifted up the hearer, filling him with proud conceit of himself. It is a sad thing when it is the fashion to talk vanity. " Ca'me, and I'll ca'thee," is the old Scotch proverb ; give me a high-sounding character, and I will give you one. Compliments and fawning congratulations are hateful to honest men ; they know that if they take they must give them, and they scorn to do either. These accommodation-bills are most admired by those who are bankrupt in character. Bad are the times when every man thus cajoles and cozens his neighbour. "*With flattering lips and with a double heart do they speak.*" He who puffs up another's heart, has nothing better than wind in his own. If a man extols me to my face, he only shows me one side of his heart, and the other is black with contempt for me, or foul with intent to cheat me. Flattery is the sign of the tavern where duplicity is the host. The Chinese consider a man of two hearts to be a very base man, and we shall be safe in reckoning all flatterers to be such.

3 The LORD shall cut off all flattering lips, *and* the tongue that speaketh proud things :

4 Who have said, With our tongue will we prevail ; our lips *are* our own : who *is* lord over us ?

Total destruction shall overwhelm the lovers of flattery and pride, but meanwhile how they hector and fume ! Well did the apostle call them " raging waves of the sea, foaming out their own shame." Free-thinkers are generally very free-talkers, and they are never more at ease than when railing at God's dominion, and arrogating to themselves unbounded license. Strange is it that the easy yoke of the Lord should so gall the shoulders of the proud, while the iron bands of Satan they bind about themselves as chains of honour : they boastfully cry unto God, " Who is lord over us ?" and hear not the hollow voice of the evil one, who cries from the infernal lake, " I am your lord, and right faithfully do ye serve me." Alas, poor fools, their pride and glory shall be cut off like a fading flower ! May God grant that our soul may not be gathered with them. It is worthy of observation that flattering lips, and tongues speaking proud things, are classed together : the fitness of this is clear, for they are guilty of the same vice, the first flatters another, and the second flatters himself, in both cases a lie is in their right hands. One generally imagines that flatterers are such mean parasites, so cringing and fawning, that they cannot be proud ; but the wise man will tell you that while all pride is truly meanness, there is in the very lowest meanness no small degree of pride. Cæsar's horse is even more proud of carrying Cæsar, than Cæsar is of riding him. The mat on which the emperor wiped his shoes, boasts vaingloriously, crying out, " I cleaned the imperial boots." None are so detestably domineering as the little creatures who creep into office by cringing to the great ; those are bad times, indeed, in which these obnoxious beings are numerous and powerful. No wonder that the justice of God in cutting off such injurious persons is matter for a psalm, for both

earth and heaven are weary of such provoking offenders, whose presence is a
very plague to the people afflicted thereby. Men cannot tame the tongues of
such boastful flatterers ; but the Lord's remedy if sharp is sure, and is an unanswerable answer to their swelling words of vanity.

5 For the oppression of the poor, for the sighing of the needy,
now will I arise, saith the LORD ; I will set *him* in safety *from him
that* puffeth at him.

In due season the Lord will hear his elect ones, who cry day and night unto
him, and though he bear long with their oppressors, yet will he avenge them
speedily. Observe that the mere oppression of saints, however silently they bear
it, is in itself a cry to God : Moses was heard at the Red Sea, though he said
nothing ; and Hagar's affliction was heard despite her silence. Jesus feels with
his people, and their smarts are mighty orators with him. By-and-by, however,
they begin to sigh and express their misery, and then relief comes post-haste.
Nothing moves a father like the cries of his children ; he bestirs himself, wakes
up his manhood, overthrows the enemy, and sets his beloved in safety. A *puff*
is too much for the child to bear, and the foe is so haughty, that he laughs the
little one to scorn ; but the Father comes, and then it is the child's turn to
laugh, when he is set above the rage of his tormentor. What virtue is there
in a poor man's sighs, that they should move the Almighty God to arise from
his throne. The needy did not dare to speak, and could only sigh in secret,
but the Lord heard, and could rest no longer, but girded on his sword for the
battle. It is a fair day when our soul brings God into her quarrel, for when
his bare arm is seen, Philistia shall rue the day. The darkest hours of the
Church's night are those which precede the break of day. Man's extremity is
God's opportunity. Jesus will come to deliver just when his needy ones shall
sigh, as if all hope had gone for ever. O Lord, set thy *now* near at hand, and
rise up speedily to our help. Should the afflicted reader be able to lay hold
upon the promise of this verse, let him gratefully fetch a fulness of comfort
from it. Gurnal says, " As one may draw out the wine of a whole hogshead
at one tap, so may a poor soul derive the comfort of the whole covenant to
himself through one promise, if he be able to apply it." He who promises to
set us in safety, means thereby preservation on earth, and eternal salvation in
heaven.

6 The words of the LORD *are* pure words : *as* silver tried in a
furnace of earth, purified seven times.

7 Thou shalt keep them, O LORD, thou shalt preserve them
from this generation for ever.

Verse 6. What a contrast between the vain words of man, and the pure
words of Jehovah. Man's words are yea and nay, but the Lord's promises are
yea and amen. For truth, certainty, holiness, faithfulness, the words of the
Lord are pure as well-refined silver. In the original there is an allusion to the
most severely-purifying process known to the ancients, through which silver was
passed when the greatest possible purity was desired ; the dross was all consumed, and only the bright and precious metal remained ; so clear and free
from all alloy of error or unfaithfulness is the book of the words of the Lord.
The Bible has passed through the furnace of persecution, literary criticism,
philosophic doubt, and scientific discovery, and has lost nothing but those human
interpretations which clung to it as alloy to precious ore. The experience of
saints has tried it in every conceivable manner, but not a single doctrine or
promise has been consumed in the most excessive heat. What God's words
are, the words of his children should be. If we would be Godlike in conversation, we must watch our language, and maintain the strictest purity of integrity
and holiness in all our communications.

7. To fall into the hands of an evil generation, so as to be baited by their cruelty, or polluted by their influence, is an evil to be dreaded beyond measure ; but it is an evil foreseen and provided for in the text. In life many a saint has lived a hundred years before his age, as though he had darted his soul into the brighter future, and escaped the mists of the beclouded present : he has gone to his grave unreverenced and misunderstood, and lo ! as generations come and go, upon a sudden the hero is unearthed, and lives in the admiration and love of the excellent of the earth ; preserved for ever from the generation which stigmatised him as a sower of sedition, or burned him as a heretic. It should be our daily prayer that we may rise above our age as the mountain-tops above the clouds, and may stand out as heaven-pointing pinnacle high above the mists of ignorance and sin which roll around us. O Eternal Spirit, fulfil in us the faithful saying of this verse ! Our faith believes those two assuring words, and cries, " *Thou shalt*," " *thou shalt*."

8 The wicked walk on every side, when the vilest men are exalted.

8. Here we return to the fount of bitterness, which first made the psalmist run to the wells of salvation, namely, the prevalence of wickedness. When those in power are vile, their underlings will be no better. As a warm sun brings out noxious flies, so does a sinner in honour foster vice every-where. Our turf would not so swarm with abominables if those who are styled honourables did not give their countenance to the craft. Would to God that the glory and triumph of our Lord Jesus would encourage us to walk and work on every side ; as like acts upon like, since an exalted sinner encourages sinners, our exalted Redeemer must surely excite, cheer, and stimulate his saints. Nerved by a sight of his reigning power we shall meet the evils of the times in the spirit of holy resolution, and shall the more hopefully pray, " Help, Lord."

EXPLANATORY NOTES AND QUAINT SAYINGS.

Verse 1.—" *Help, Lord*." 'Twas high time to call to heaven for help, when Saul cried, " Go, kill me up the priests of Jehovah" (the occasion as it is thought of making this Psalm), and therein committed the sin against the Holy Ghost, as some grave divines are of opinion. 1 Sam. xxii. 17. David, after many sad thoughts about that slaughter, and the occasion of it, Doeg's malicious information, together with the paucity of his fast friends, and the multitude of his sworn enemies at court, breaks forth abruptly into these words, " *Help, Lord*," help at a dead lift. The Arabic version hath it, *Deliver me by main force*, as with weapons of war, for " the Lord is a man of war." Ex. xv. 3. *John Trapp*.

Verse 1.—" *The faithful*." " *A faithful man*," as a parent, a reprover, an adviser, one " without guile," " *who can find ?*" Prov. xx. 6. Look close. View thyself in the glass of the word. Does thy neighbour or thy friend, find thee *faithful* to him ? What does our daily intercourse witness ? Is not the attempt to speak what is agreeable oft made at the expense of truth ? Are not professions of regard sometimes utterly inconsistent with our real feelings ? In common life, where gross violations are restrained, a thousand petty offences are allowed, that break down the wall between sin and duty, and, judged by the divine standard, are indeed guilty steps upon forbidden ground.—*Charles Bridges*, 1850.

Verse 1. —A *"faithful"* man must be, first of all, faithful to himself ; then, he must be faithful to God ; and then, he must be faithful to others, particularly the church of God. And this, as it regards ministers, is of peculiar importance. *Joseph Irons,* 1840.

Verse 1.—Even as a careful mother, seeing her child in the way when a company of unruly horses run through the streets in full career, presently whips up her child in her arms and taketh him home ; or as the hen, seeing the ravenous kite over her head, clucks and gathers her chickens under her wings ; even so when God hath a purpose to bring a heavy calamity upon a land, it hath been usual with him to call and cull out to himself such as are his dearly beloved. He takes his choice servants from the evil to come. Thus was Augustine removed a little before Hippo (wherein he dwelt) was taken ; Parœus died before Heidelburg was sacked ; and Luther was taken off before Germany was overrun with war and bloodshed.—*Ed. Dunsterville in a Sermon at the Funeral of Sir Sim. Harcourt,* 1642.

Verse 1.—" *Help, Lord ; for the godly man ceaseth,*" etc. :—

> Back, then, complainer, loathe thy life no more,
> Nor deem thyself upon a desert shore,
>   Because the rocks the nearer prospect close.
> Yet in fallen Israel are there hearts and eyes,
> That day by day in prayer like thine arise ;
>   Thou knowest them not, but their Creator known.
> Go, to the world return, nor fear to cast
> Thy bread upon the waters, sure at last
>   In joy to find it after many days.
>   *John Keble,* 1792—1866.

Verses 1, 2, 4.—Consider our markets, our fairs, our private contracts and bargains, our shops, our cellars, our weights, our measures, our promises, our protestations, our politic tricks and villanous Machiavelism, our enhancing of the prices of all commodities, and tell, whether the twelfth Psalm may not as fitly be applied to our times as to the days of the man of God ; in which the feigning, and lying, and facing, and guile, and subtlety of men provoked the psalmist to cry out, " *Help, Lord ; for there is not a godly man left : for the faithful are failed from among the children of men : they speak deceitfully every one with his neighbour, flattering with their lips, and speak with a double heart, which have said, With our tongue we will prevail ; our lips are our own : who is Lord over us ?*"—*R. Wolcombe,* 1612.

Verse 2.—" *They speak vanity every one with his neighbour : with flattering lips and with a double heart do they speak.*" The feigned zeal is just like a waterman, that looks one way and rows another way ; for this man *pretends* one thing and *intends* another thing ; as Jehu pretended the zeal of God's glory, but his aim was at his master's kingdom ; and his zeal to God's service was but to bring him to the sceptre of the kingdom. So Demetrius professed great love unto Diana, but his drift was to maintain the honour of his profession ; and so we have too many that make great show of holiness, and yet their hearts aim at other ends ; but they may be sure, though they can deceive the world and destroy themselves, yet not God, who knoweth the secrets of all hearts.— *Gr. Williams,* 1636.

Verse 2.—" *They speak vanity.*"—

> Faithless is earth, and faithless are the skies !
> Justice is fled, and truth is now no more !
>   *Virgil's Æneid,* IV. 373.

Verse 2.—" *With a double heart.*" Man is nothing but insincerity, falsehood, and hypocrisy, both in regard to himself and in regard to others. He does not wish that he should be told the truth, he shuns saying it to others ; and all these moods, so inconsistent with justice and reason, have their roots in his heart.—*Blaise Pascal.*

Verse 2.—" *With flattering lips and with a double heart do they speak.*" There is no such stuff to make a cloak of as religion ; nothing so fashionable, nothing so profitable : it is a livery wherein a wise man may serve two masters, God and the world, and make a gainful service by either. I serve both, and in both myself, by prevaricating with both. Before man none serves his God with more severe devotion ; for which, among the best of men, I work my own ends, and serve myself. In private, I serve the world ; not with so strict devotion, but with more delight ; where fulfilling of her servants' lusts, I work my end and serve myself. The house of prayer who more frequents than I ? In all Christian duties who more forward than I ? I fast with those who fast, that I may eat with those that eat. I mourn with those that mourn. No hand more open to the cause than mine, and in their families none prays longer and with louder zeal. Thus when the opinion of a holy life hath cried the goodness of my conscience up, my trade can lack no custom, my wares can want no price, my words can need no credit, my actions can lack no praise. If I am covetous, it is interpreted providence ; if miserable, it is counted temperance ; if melancholy, it is construed godly sorrow ; if merry, it is voted spiritual joy ; if I be rich, it is thought the blessing of a godly life ; if poor, supposed the fruit of conscionable dealing ; if I be well spoken of, it is the merit of holy conversation ; if ill, it is the malice of malignants. Thus I sail with every wind, and have my end in all conditions. This cloak in summer keeps me cool, in winter warm, and hides the nasty bag of all my secret lusts. Under this cloak I walk in public fairly with applause, and in private sin securely without offence, and officiate wisely without discovery. I compass sea and land to make a proselyte ; and no sooner made, but he makes me. At a fast I cry Geneva, and at a feast I cry Rome. If I be poor, I counterfeit abundance to save my credit ; if rich, I dissemble poverty to save charges. I most frequent schismatical lectures, which I find most profitable ; from thence learning to divulge and maintain new doctrines ; they maintain me in suppers thrice a week. I use the help of a lie sometimes, as a new stratagem to uphold the gospel ; and I colour oppression with God's judgments executed upon the wicked. Charity I hold an extraordinary duty, therefore not ordinarily to be performed. What I openly reprove abroad, for my own profit, that I secretly act at home, for my own pleasure. But stay, I see a handwriting in my heart which damps my soul. It is charactered in these sad words, " Woe be to you, hypocrites." Matt. xxiii. 13. *Francis Quarles*' " *Hypocrite's Soliloquy.*"

Verse 2.—" *With flattering lips,*" etc. The world indeed says that society could not exist if there were perfect truthfulness and candour between man and man ; and that the world's propriety would be as much disturbed if every man said what he pleased, as it was in those days of Israelitish history, when every man did that which was right in his own eyes. The world is assuredly the best judge of its own condition and mode of government, and therefore I will not say what a libel does such a remark contain, but oh, what a picture does it present of the social edifice, that its walls can be cemented and kept together only by flattery and falsehood !—*Barton Bouchier.*

Verse 2.—" *Flattering lips.*" The philosopher Bion being asked what animal he thought the most hurtful, replied, " That of wild creatures a tyrant, and of tame ones a flatterer." The flatterer is the most dangerous enemy we can have. Raleigh, himself a courtier, and therefore initiated into the whole art of flattery, who discovered in his own career and fate its dangerous and deceptive power, its deep artifice and deeper falsehood, says, " A flatterer is said to be a beast that biteth smiling. But it is hard to know them from friends—they are so obsequious and full of protestations ; for as a wolf resembles a dog, so doth a flatterer a friend."—*The Book of Symbols,* 1844.

Verse 2.—" *They speak with a double heart.*" The original is, " A heart and a heart :" one for the church, another for the change ; one for Sundays, another for working-days ; one for the king, another for the pope. A man without a heart is a wonder, but a man with two hearts is a monster. It is said of Judas

"There were many hearts in one man;" and we read of the saints, "There was one heart in many men." Acts iv. 32. *Dabo illis cor unum;* a special blessing.—*Thomas Adams.*

Verse 2.—When men cease to be faithful to their God, he who expects to find them so to each other, will be much disappointed. The primitive sincerity will accompany the primitive piety in her flight from the earth; and then interest will succeed conscience in the regulation of human conduct, till one man cannot trust another farther than he holds him by that tie. Hence, by the way, it is, that though many are infidels themselves, yet few choose to have their families and dependants such; as judging, and rightly judging, that true Christians are the only persons to be depended on for the exact discharge of social duties.—*George Horne.*

Verse 3.—"*The Lord shall cut off all flattering lips,*" etc. They who take pleasure in deceiving others, will at the last find themselves most of all deceived, when the Sun of truth, by the brightness of his rising, shall at once detect and consume hypocrisy.—*George Horne.*

Verse 3.—"*Cut off lips and tongues.*" May there not be here an allusion to those terrible but suggestive punishments which Oriental monarchs were wont to execute on criminals? Lips were cut off and tongues torn out when offenders were convicted of lying or treason. So terrible and infinitely more so are the punishments of sin.—*C. H. S.*

Verses 3, 4.—It need not now seem strange to tell you that the Lord is the owner of our bodies, that he has so much propriety therein that they are more his than ours. The apostle tells us as much. 1 Cor. vi. 20. "Glorify God in your bodies which are his." Our bodies, and every member thereof, are his; for if the whole be so, no part is exempted. And therefore they spake proud things, and presumptuously usurped the propriety of God, who said, "*Our lips are our own;*" as though their lips had not been his who is Lord and Owner of all, but they had been lords thereof, and might have used them as they list. This provoked God to show what right he had to dispose of such lips and tongues, by *cutting them off.*—*David Clarkson.*

Verse 4.—"*Who have said, With our tongues will we prevail; who is Lord over us?*" So it was: twelve poor and unlearned men on the one side, all the eloquence of Greece and Rome arrayed on the other. From the time of Tertullus to that of Julian the apostate, every species of oratory, learning, wit, was lavished against the church of God; and the result, like the well-known story of that dispute between the Christian peasant and the heathen philosopher, when the latter, having challenged the assembled fathers of a synod to silence him, was put to shame by the simple faith of the former "In the name of our Lord Jesus Christ, I command thee to be dumb." *Who is Lord over us?* "Who is the Lord, that I should obey his voice to let Israel go?" Ex. v. 2. "What is the Almighty, that we should serve him?" Job xxi. 15. "Who is that God that shall deliver you?" Dan. iii. 15.—*Michael Ayguan, in J. M. Neale's Commentary.*

Verse 4.—"*Our lips are our own.*" If we have to do with God, we must quit claim to ourselves and look on God as our owner; but this is fixed in the hearts of men, We will be our own; we will not consent to the claim which God makes to us: "*Our lips are our own.*" Wicked men might as well say the same thing of their whole selves; our bodies, strength, time, parts, etc., are our own, and who is Lord over us?—*John Howe.*

Verse 4.—From the faults of the wicked we must learn three contrary lessons; to wit: 1. That nothing which we have is our own. But, 2. Whatsoever is given to us of God is for service to be done to him. 3. That whatsoever we do or say, we have a Lord over us to whom we must be answerable when he calleth us to account.—*David Dickson.*

Verse 5.—"*For the oppression of the poor,*" etc. When oppressors and persecutors do snuff and puff at the people of God, when they defy them, and scorn them, and think that they can with a blast of their breath blow them away, then God will arise to judgment, as the Chaldee has it ; at that very nick of time when all seems to be lost, and when the poor, oppressed, and afflicted people of God can do nothing but sigh and weep, and weep and sigh, then the Lord will arise and ease them of their oppressions, and make their day of extremity a glorious opportunity to work for his own glory and his people's good. Matt. xxii. 6, 7. " And the remnant took his servants, and entreated them spitefully, and slew them. But when the king heard thereof, he was wroth : and he sent forth his armies and destroyed those murderers, and burned up their city."—*Thomas Brooks.*

Verse 5.—Fear ye, whosoever ye be, that do wrong the poor ; you have power and wealth, and the favour of the judges, but they have the strongest weapons of all, sighings and groanings, which fetch help from heaven for them. These weapons dig down houses, throw up foundations, overthrow whole nations.— *Chrysostom.*

Verse 5.—"*For the sighing of the needy, now will I arise, saith the Lord.*" God is pleased to take notice of *every grace,* even the least and lowest, and every gracious inclination in any of his servants. *To fear his name* is no great matter, yet these have a promise. *To think on his name* less, yet set down in a " book of remembrance." God sets down how many good *thoughts* a poor soul hath had. As evil thoughts in wicked men are taken notice of—they are the first fruits of the evil heart (Matt. xv. 19)—so good thoughts are they which lie uppermost, and best discover a good heart. A *desire* is a small matter, especially of the poor man, yet God regards the desire of the poor, and calls a good desire the greatest kindness ; " The desire of a man is his kindness." A *tear* makes no great noise, yet hath a voice, " God hath heard the voice of my weeping." It is no pleasant water, yet God bottles it up. A *groan* is a poor thing, yet is the best part of a prayer sometimes (Rom. viii. 26) ; a *sigh* is less, yet *God is awakened and raised up by it.* Psalm xii. 5. A *look* is less than all these, yet this is regarded (Jonah ii. 4) ; *breathing* is less, yet (Lam. iii 56), the church could speak of no more ; *panting* is less than breathing, when one is spent for lack of breath, yet this is all the godly can sometimes boast of. Psalm xlii. 1. The description of a godly man is ofttimes made from his least *quod sic.* Blessed are the *poor,* the *meek,* they that *mourn,* and they who *hunger* and *thirst.* Never did Hannah pray better than when she could get out never a word, but cried, " Hard, hard heart." Nor did the publican, than when he smote his breast and cried, "Lord, be merciful to me a sinner." Nor Mary Magdalene, than when she came behind Christ, sat down, wept, but kept silence. How sweet is music upon the *waters!* How fruitful are the lowest valleys ! Mourning hearts are most musical, lowest most fruitful. The good shepherd ever takes most care of his weak lambs and feeble sheep. The father makes most of the least, and the mother looks most after the sick child. How comfortable is that of our Saviour, " It is not the will of your Father which is in heaven that one of these little ones should perish !" And that heaven is not to be entered but by such as are like the little child.—*John Sheffield,* 1654.

Verse 5.—" *The oppression of the poor.*" Insolent and cruel oppressing of the poor is a sin that brings desolating and destroying judgments upon a people. God sent ten wasting judgments one after another upon Pharaoh, his people, and land, to revenge the cruel oppression of his poor people. " Rob not the poor, because he is poor : neither oppress the afflicted in the gate : for the Lord will plead their cause." Prov. xxii. 22, 23. To rob and oppress the rich is a great sin ; but to rob and oppress the poor is a greater ; but to rob and oppress the poor because he is poor, and wants money to buy justice, is the top of all inhumanity and impiety. To oppress any one is sin ; but to oppress the oppressed is the height of sin. Poverty, and want, and misery, should be motives to pity ; but oppressors make them the whetstones of their cruelty and severity, and therefore the Lord will plead the cause of his poor oppressed people against their oppressors without fee or fear ; yea, he will plead their cause with pestilence, blood, and fire. God was a great oppressor of the poor (Ezekiel xxxviii. 8—14), and God pleads against him with pestilence, blood, and fire (verse 22); "and I will plead against him, with pestilence and with blood; and I will rain upon him, and upon his bands, and upon the many people that are with him, an overflowing rain, and great hailstones, fire, and brimstone."—*Thomas Brooks.*

Verse 6.—"*The words of the Lord are pure words,*" etc. How beautifully is this verse introduced, by way of contrast to what was said before concerning! Do sinners talk of vanity? let saints then speak of Jesus and his gospel. Do they talk impure words? then let the faithful use the pure words of God, which like silver, the more used the more melted in the fire, the more precious will they be. It is true, indeed, despisers will esteem both God and his word as trifling; but oh, what an unknown treasure doth the word, the promises, the covenant relation of the divine things of Jesus contain! They are more to be desired than gold, yea, than pure gold; sweeter also than honey and the honey-comb.—*Robert Hawker.*

Verse 6.—"*The words of the Lord are pure words,*" etc. They that purify silver to the purpose, use to put it in the fire again and again, that it may be thoroughly tried. So is the truth of God; there is scarce any truth but hath been tried over and over again, and still if any dross happen to mingle with it, then God calls it in question again. If in former times there have been Scriptures alleged that have not been pertinent to prove it, that truth shall into the fire again, that what is dross may be burnt up; the Holy Ghost is so curious, so delicate, so exact, he cannot bear that falsehood should be mingled with the truths of the gospel. That is the reason, therefore, why that God doth still, age after age, call former things in question, because that there is still some dross one way or other mingled with them; either in the stating the opinions themselves, or else in the Scriptures that are brought and alleged for them, that have passed for current, for he will never leave till he have purified them. The doctrine of God's free grace hath been tried over, and over, and over again. Pelagius begins, and he mingles his dross with it: he saith, grace is nothing but nature in man. Well, his doctrine was purified, and a great deal of dross purged out. Then come the semi-Pelagians, and they part stakes; they say, nature can do nothing without grace, but they make nature to concur with grace, and to have an influence as well as grace; and the dross of that was burnt up. The Papists, they take up the same quarrel, but will neither be Pelagians nor semi-Pelagians, yet still mingle dross. The Arminians, they come, and they refine popery in that point anew; still they mingle dross. God will have this truth tried seven times in the fire, till he hath brought it forth as pure as pure may be. And I say it is because that truth is thus precious. *Thomas Goodwin.*

Verse 6.—The Scripture is the sun; the church is the clock. The sun we know to be sure, and regularly constant in his motions; the clock, as it may fall out, may go too fast or too slow. As then, we should condemn him of folly that should profess to trust the clock rather than the sun, so we cannot but justly tax the credulity of those who would rather trust to the church than to the Scripture.—*Bishop Hall.*

Verse 6.—"*The words of the Lord are pure words.*" Men may inspect detached portions of the Book, and please themselves with some things, which, at first view, have the semblance of conniving at what is wrong. But let them read it, let them read the whole of it; let them carry along in their minds the character of the persons to which the different portions of it were addressed; the age of the world, and the circumstances under which the different parts of it were written, and the particular objects which even those portions of it have in view, which to an infidel mind appear the most exceptionable; and they may be rationally convinced that, instead of originating in the bosom of an impostor, it owes its origin to men who wrote "as they were moved by the Holy Ghost."

Let them scrutinise it with as much severity as they please ; only let their scrutiny be well informed, wisely directed, and with a fair and ingenuous mind, and we have no fears for the issue. There are portions of it on which ignorance and folly have put constructions that are forced and unnatural, and which impure minds have viewed in shadows reflected from their own impurity. Montesquieu said of Voltaire, *Lorsque Voltaire lit un livre, il le fait, puis il écrit contre ce qu'il a fait :* "When Voltaire reads a book, he makes it what he pleases, and then writes against what he has made." It is no difficult matter to besmear and blot its pages, and then impute the foul stains that men of corrupt minds have cast upon it, to its stainless Author. But if we honestly look at it as it is, we shall find that like its Author, it is without blemish and without spot.—*Gardiner Spring, D.D.*

Verse 6.—"*The words of the Lord are pure words: as silver tried in a furnace of earth, purified seven times.*" The expression may import two things : first, the infallible certainty of the word ; and, secondly, the exact purity. First, the infallible certainty of the word, as gold endureth in the fire when the dross is consumed. Vain conceits comfort us not in a time of trouble ; but the word of God, the more it is tried, the more you will find the excellency of it—the promise is tried, as well as we are tried, in deep afflictions ; but, when it is so, it will be found to be most pure. "The word of the Lord is tried ; he is a buckler to all those that trust in him" (Prov. xxx. 5) ; as pure gold suffers no loss by the fire, so the promises suffer no loss when they are tried, but stand to us in our greatest troubles. Secondly, it notes the exact perfection of the word : there is no dross in silver and gold that hath been often refined ; so there is no defect in the word of God.—*Thomas Manton.*

Verse 6.—Fry thus translates this verse :—

> The words of Jehovah are pure words—
> Silver refined in the crucible—
> Gold, seven times washed from the earth.

מְזֻקָּק though sometimes applied to express the purity of silver, is more strictly an epithet of gold, from the peculiar method made use of in separating it from the soil by repeated washings and decantations.—*John Fry, in loc.*

Verse 6.—"*Seven times.*" I cannot but admit that there may be a mystic meaning in the expression "seven times," in allusion to the seven periods of the church, or to that perfection, implied in the figure seven, to which it is to be brought at the revelation of Jesus Christ. This will be more readily allowed by those who admit of the prophetic interpretation of the seven epistles of the Book of Revelation.—*W. Wilson, D.D., in loc.*

Verse 8.—"*When the vilest men are exalted :*" Heb., *vilities*, οὐτίδανοι, the abstract for the concrete, *quisquiliæ*, οὐτίδανοι. Oft, empty vessels swim aloft, rotten posts are gilt with adulterate gold, the worst weeds spring up bravest. Chaff will get to the top of the fan, when good corn, as it lieth at the bottom of the heap, so it falls low at the feet of the fanner. The reason why wicked men "*walk*" on every side, are so brisk, so busy (and who but they ?) is given to be this, because losels and rioters were exalted. See Prov. xxviii. 12, 18, and xxix. 2. As rheums and catarrhs fall from the head to the lungs, and cause a consumption of the whole body, so it is in the body politic. As a fish putrefies first in the head and then in all the parts, so here. Some render the text thus, "*When they* (that is, the wicked) *are exalted,*" it is a "*shame* for the sons of men," that other men who better deserve preferment, are not only slighted, but vilely handled by such worthless ambitionists, who yet the higher they climb, as apes, the more they discover their deformities."—*John Trapp.*

Verse 8.—Good thus translates this verse :—

> Should the wicked advance on every side ;
> Should the dregs of the earth be uppermost ?

The original is given literally. זֻלּוּת means "fœces, fœculences, dregs." כְּרֻם is here an adverb, and imports *uppermost*, rather than *exalted*.—*J. Mason Good, in loc.*

HINTS TO THE VILLAGE PREACHER.

Verse 1.—" *Help, Lord.*"   I. The Prayer itself, short, suggestive, seasonable, rightly directed, vehement.   II. Occasions for its use.   III. Modes of its answer.   IV. Reasons for expecting gracious reply.

First two clauses.—Text for funeral of an eminent believer.

Whole verse.—I. *The fact bewailed*—describe godly and faithful, and show how they fail.   II. *The feeling excited.*   Mourning the loss, fears for church, personal need of such companions, appeal to God.   III. *The forebodings aroused.*   Failure of the cause, judgments impending, etc.   IV. *The faith remaining :* " Help, Lord."

Verse 1.—Intimate connection between yielding honour to God and honesty to man, since they decline together.

Verse 2 (first clause).—A discourse upon the prevalence and perniciousness of vain talk.

The whole verse.—Connection between flattery and treachery.

" *A double heart.*"   Right and wrong kinds of hearts, and the disease of duplicity.

Verse 3.—God's hatred of those twin sins of the lips—Flattery and Pride (which is self flattery).   Why he hates them.   How he shows his hatred.   In whom he hates them most.   How to be cleansed from them.

Verses 3, 4.—I. *The revolt of the tongue.*   Its claim of power, self-possession, and liberty.   Contrast between this and the believer's confession, " we are not our own."   II. *The method of its rebellion*—" flattery, and speaking proud things."   III. *The end of its treason*—" cut off."

Verse 5.—The Lord aroused—How ! Why ! What to do ! When !

Last clause.—Peculiar danger of believers from those who despise them and their special safety.   Good practical topic.

Verse 6.—The purity, trial, and permanency of the words of the Lord.

Seven crucibles in which believers try the word.   A little thought will suggest these.

Verse 7.—Preservation from one's generation in this life and for ever.   A very suggestive theme.

Verse 8.—*Sin in high places specially infectious.*   Call to the rich and prominent to remember their responsibility.   Thankfulness for honourable rulers.   Discrimination to be used in choice of our representatives, or civic magistrates.

WORK UPON THE TWELFTH PSALM.

In " *A Godly Meditacion upon* xx *select Psalms.* . . . . By Sir ANTHONY COPE, Knight, 1547," a thin, black letter 4to., is an Exposition, or rather Meditation, on this Psalm.   Reprinted 1848.

PSALM XIII.

OCCASION.—*The Psalm cannot be referred to any especial event or period in David's history. All attempts to find it a birthplace are but guesses. It was, doubtless, more than once the language of that much tried man of God, and is intended to express the feelings of the people of God in those ever-returning trials which beset them. If the reader has never yet found occasion to use the language of this brief ode, he will do so ere long, if he be a man after the Lord's own heart. We have been wont to call this the "How Long Psalm." We had almost said the Howling Psalm, from the incessant repetition of the cry "how long?"*

DIVISION.—*This Psalm is very readily to be divided into three parts ;—the question of anxiety, 1, 2 ; the cry of prayer, 3, 4 ; the song of faith, 5, 6.*

EXPOSITION.

HOW long wilt thou forget me, O Lord? for ever? how long wilt thou hide thy face from me?

2 How long shall I take counsel in my soul, *having* sorrow in my heart daily? how long shall mine enemy be exalted over me?

"*How long?*"—This question is repeated no less than four times. It betokens very intense desire for deliverance, and great anguish of heart. And what if there be some impatience mingled therewith ; is not this the more true a portrait of our own experience? It is not easy to prevent desire from degenerating into impatience. O for grace that, while we wait on God, we may be kept from indulging a murmuring spirit! "*How long?*" Does not the oft-repeated cry become a very HOWLING? And what if grief should find no other means of utterance? Even then, God is not far from the voice of our roaring ; for he does not regard the music of our prayers, but his own Spirit's work in them in exciting desire and inflaming the affections.

"*How long?*" Ah! how long do our days appear when our soul is cast down within us!

> "How wearily the moments seem to glide
> O'er sadness! How the time
> Delights to linger in its flight!"

Time flies with full-fledged wing in our summer days, but in our winters he flutters painfully. A week within prison-walls is longer than a month at liberty. Long sorrow seems to argue abounding corruption ; for the gold which is long in the fire must have had much dross to be consumed, hence the question "how long?" may suggest deep searching of heart. "*How long wilt thou forget me?*" Ah, David! how like a fool thou talkest! Can God *forget?* Can Omniscience fail in memory? Above all, can Jehovah's heart forget his own beloved child? Ah! brethren, let us drive away the thought, and hear the voice of our covenant God by the mouth of the prophet, "But Zion said, The Lord hath forsaken me, and my Lord hath forgotten me. Can a woman forget her sucking child, that she should not have compassion on the son of her womb? yea, they may forget, yet will I not forget thee. Behold, I have graven thee upon the palms of my hands ; thy walls are continually before me." "*For ever?*" Oh, dark thought! It was surely bad enough to suspect a temporary forgetfulness, but shall we ask the ungracious question, and imagine that the Lord will for ever cast away his people? No, his anger may endure for a night, but his love shall abide eternally. "*How long wilt thou hide thy face from me?*" This is a far more rational question, for God may hide his face, and yet he may remember still. A hidden face is no sign of a forgetful heart. It is in love that his face is turned away ; yet to a real child of God, this hiding of his Father's face is terrible, and he will never be at ease until, once more he hath his Father's smile. "*How long shall I take counsel, in my soul, having sorrow in my heart daily?*" There is in the original the idea of "laying up" counsels in his heart, as if his devices had become innumerable but unavailing. Herein we have often been like David, for we have considered and reconsidered day after day, but have not discovered the happy device by which to escape from our trouble. Such store is a sad sore. Ruminating upon trouble is bitter work. Children fill their mouths with bitterness when they rebelliously chew the pill which they ought obediently to have taken at once. "*How long shall mine enemy be exalted over me?*" This is like wormwood in the gall, to see the wicked enemy exulting while our soul is bowed down within us. The laughter of a foe grates horribly upon the ears of grief. For the devil to make mirth of our misery is the last ounce of our complaint, and quite breaks down our patience; therefore let us make it one chief argument in our plea with mercy.

Thus the careful reader will remark that the question "how long?" is put in four shapes. The writer's grief is viewed, as it seems to be, as it is, as it affects himself within, and his foes without. We are all prone to play most on the worst string. We set up monumental stones over the graves of our joys, but who thinks of erecting monuments of praise for mercies received? We write four books of Lamentations and only one of Canticles, and are far more at home in wailing out a *Miserere* than in chanting a *Te Deum*.

3 Consider *and* hear me, O Lord my God : lighten mine eyes, lest I sleep the *sleep* of death ;

4 Lest mine enemy say, I have prevailed against him ; *and* those that trouble me rejoice when I am moved.

But now prayer lifteth up her voice, like the watchman who proclaims the daybreak. Now will the tide turn, and the weeper shall dry his eyes. The mercy-seat is the life of hope and the death of despair. The gloomy thought of God's having forsaken him is still upon the psalmist's soul, and he therefore cries, "*Consider and hear me.*" He remembers at once the root of his woe, and cries aloud that it may be removed. The final absence of God is Tophet's fire, and his temporary absence brings his people into the very suburbs of hell. God is here entreated to *see* and *hear*, that so he may be doubly moved to pity. What should we do if we had no God to turn to in the hour of wretchedness?

Note the cry of faith, "*O Lord* MY *God!*" Is it not a very glorious fact that our interest in our God is not destroyed by all our trials and sorrows? We may lose our gourds, but not our God. The title-deed of heaven is not written in the sand, but in eternal brass.

"*Lighten mine eyes:*" that is, let the eye of my faith be clear, that I may see my God in the dark ; let my eye of watchfulness be wide open, lest I be entrapped, and let the eye of my understanding be illuminated to see the right way. Perhaps, too, here is an allusion to that cheering of the spirits so frequently called the enlightening of the eyes because it causes the face to brighten, and the eyes to sparkle. Well may we use the prayer, "Lighten our darkness, we beseech thee, O Lord!" for in many respects we need the Holy Spirit's illuminating rays. "*Lest I sleep the sleep of death.*" Darkness engenders sleep, and despondency is not slow in making the eyes heavy. From this faintness and dimness of vision, caused by despair, there is but a step to the iron sleep of death. David feared that his trials would end his life, and he rightly uses his fear as an argument with God in prayer ; for deep distress has in it a kind of claim upon compassion, not a claim of right, but a plea which has power with grace. Under the pressure of heart sorrow, the psalmist does not look forward to the sleep of death with hope and joy, as assured believers do, but he shrinks from it with dread, from which we gather that bondage from fear of death is no new thing.

Another plea is urged in the fourth verse, and it is one which the tried believer may handle well when on his knees. We make use of our arch-enemy for once, and compel him, like Samson, to grind in our mill while we use his cruel arrogance as an argument in prayer. It is not the Lord's will that the great enemy of our souls should overcome his children. This would dishonour God, and cause the evil one to boast. It is well for us that our salvation and God's honour are so intimately connected, that they stand or fall together.

Our covenant God will complete the confusion of all our enemies, and if for awhile we become their scoff and jest, the day is coming when the shame will change sides, and the contempt shall be poured on those to whom it is due.

5 But I have trusted in thy mercy ; my heart shall rejoice in thy salvation.

6 I will sing unto the Lord, because he hath dealt bountifully with me.

What a change is here ! Lo, the rain is over and gone, and the time of the singing of birds is come. The mercy-seat has so refreshed the poor weeper, that he clears his throat for a song. If we have mourned with him, let us now dance with him. David's heart was more often out of tune than his harp. He begins many of his psalms sighing, and ends them singing ; and others he begins in joy and ends in sorrow ; " so that one would think," says Peter Moulin, " that those Psalms had been composed by two men of a contrary humour." It is worthy to be observed that the joy is all the greater because of the previous sorrow, as calm is all the more delightful in recollection of the preceding tempest.

" Sorrows remembered sweeten present joy."

Here is his avowal of his confidence : " *But I have trusted in thy mercy.*" For many a year it had been his wont to make the Lord his castle and tower of defence, and he smiles from behind the same bulwark still. He is sure of his faith, and his faith makes him sure ; had he doubted the reality of his trust in God, he would have blocked up one of the windows through which the sun of heaven delights to shine. Faith is now in exercise, and consequently is readily discovered ; there is never a doubt in our heart about the existence of faith while it is in action : when the hare or partridge is quiet we see it not, but let the same be in motion and we soon perceive it. All the powers of his enemies had not driven the psalmist from his stronghold. As the shipwrecked mariner clings to the mast, so did David cling to his faith ; he neither could nor would give up his confidence in the Lord his God. O that we may profit by his example and hold by our faith as by our very life !

Now hearken to the music which faith makes in the soul. The bells of the mind are all ringing, " *My heart shall rejoice in thy salvation.*" There is joy and feasting within doors, for a glorious guest has come, and the fatted calf is killed. Sweet is the music which sounds from the strings of the heart. But this is not all ; *the voice* joins itself in the blessed work, and the tongue keeps tune with the soul, while the writer declares, " *I will sing unto the Lord.*"

" I will praise thee every day,
    Now thine anger's past away ;
Comfortable thoughts arise
    From the bleeding sacrifice."

The Psalm closes with a sentence which is a refutation of the charge of forgetfulness which David had uttered in the first verse, " *He hath dealt bountifully with me.*" So shall it be with us if we wait awhile. The complaint which in our haste we utter shall be joyfully retracted, and we shall witness that the Lord hath dealt bountifully with us.

EXPLANATORY NOTES AND QUAINT SAYINGS.

Verse 1.—" *How long wilt thou forget me, O Lord ?*" etc. The departures of God from true believers are never final ; they may be tedious, but they are temporary.   As the evil spirit is said to depart from Christ for a season (Luke iv. 13 ; though he quitted that temptation, he did not quit his design, so as to tempt no more), so the good Spirit withdraws from those that are Christ's, for a season only, 'tis with a purpose of coming again.   When he hath most evidently forsaken, 'tis as unquestionable that sooner or later he will return ; and the happiness of his return will richly recompense for the sadness of his desertion ; Isa. liv. 7, " For a small moment have I forsaken thee ; but with great mercies will I gather thee ;" here is not only a gathering after a forsaking, but " *great mercies*" to make amends for " *a small moment.*" He who hath engaged to be our God for ever, cannot depart for ever.—*Timothy Cruso,* 1696.

Verse 1.—" *How long wilt thou forget me, O Lord ?*" Whatever be the pressing need of Christ's followers in troubles, and their constant cleaving to duty for all that ; and whatever be Christ's purpose of love towards them, yet he seeth it fit ofttimes not to come to them at first, but will let the trial go on till it come to a height, and be a trial indeed, and put them seriously to it ; for before he came he lets them row " about five and twenty or thirty furlongs" (the last of which make near four miles, eight furlongs going to a mile) ; and (Mark vi. 48) he came not till the fourth watch of the night, which is the morning watch.   We are indeed very sparing of ourselves in trouble, and do soon begin to think that we are low and tried enough, and therefore would be delivered ; but our wise Lord seeth that we need more.— *George Hutcheson,* 1657.

Verse 1.—" *How long,*" etc. Enquire into the causes of God's anger. He is never angry but when there is very great reason, when we force him to be so. What is that accursed thing in our hearts, or in our lives, for which God hides his face, and frowns upon us ? What particular disobedience to his commands is it for which he has taken up the rod ? Job x. 2 ; " I will say unto God, Do not condemn me ; shew me wherefore thou contendest with me ;" as if he should say, Lord, my troubles and my sorrows are very well known. . . . . We must not cease to be solicitous to know what are the particular sins that have made him to tear us up by the roots, to throw us down as with a whirlwind ; what is it that has made him so long angry with us, and so long to delay his help, that if any evil be undiscovered in our souls, we may lament it with a seasonable grief, and get a pardon for it. It is not the common course of God's providence to cover his servants with so thick a darkness as this is, which our troubled souls labour under in the day, or rather in the night of his displeasure ; and, therefore, we may with humility desire to know why he proceeds with us in a way that is so singular ; for it is some way delightful to the understanding to pierce into the reasons and causes of things.—*Timothy Rogers.*

Verse 1.—" *How long wilt thou forget me,*" etc. For God *to forget* David, not to mind him, or look after him, is much ! If his eye be never so little once off us, the spiritual adversary is ready presently to seize on us, as the kite on the chick if the hen look not carefully after it. . . . . As a father will sometimes cross his son to try the child's disposition, to see how he will take it, whether he will mutter and grumble at it, and grow humorous and wayward, neglect his duty to his father because his father seemeth to neglect him, or make offer to run away and withdraw himself from his father's obedience because he seemeth to carry himself harshly and roughly towards him, and to provoke him thereunto ; so doth God likewise ofttimes cross his children and seemeth to neglect them, so to try their disposition, what metal they are made of, how they stand affected towards him : whether they will neglect God because God seemeth to neglect them, forbear to serve him because he seemeth to forget them, cease to depend upon him because he seemeth not to look after them, to provide for them, or to protect them. Like Joram's prophane pursuivant, "This evil," saith he, "is of the Lord ; what should I wait for the Lord any longer ?" Or whether they will still constantly cleave to him, though he seem not to regard them, nor to have any care of them ; and say with Isaiah, "Yet will I wait upon God, though he have hid his face from us, and I will look for him though he look not on us ;" for, "They are blessed that wait on him ; and he will not fail in due time to show mercy unto all them that do so constantly wait on him." Isa. viii. 17 ; xxx. 18. As Samuel dealt with Saul ; he kept away till the last hour, to see what Saul would do when Samuel seemed not to keep touch with him. So doth God with his saints, and with those that be in league with him ; he withdraweth himself oft, and keeps aloof off for a long time together to try what they will do, and what courses they will take when God seemeth to break with them and to leave them in the suds, as we say ; amidst many difficulties much perplexed, as it was with David at this time.—*Thomas Gataker*, 1637.

Verse 1.—1. For desertions. I think them like lying fallow of lean and weak land for some years, while it gathers sap for a better crop. It is possible to gather gold, where it may be had, with moonlight. Oh, if I could but creep one foot, or half a foot, nearer in to Jesus, in such a dismal night as that when he is away, I should think it a happy absence ! 2. If I knew that the Beloved were only gone away for trial, and further humiliation, and not smoked out of the house with new provocations, I would forgive desertions and hold my peace at his absence. But Christ's bought absence (that I bought with my sin), is two running boils at once, one upon each side ; and what side then can I lie on ? 3. I know that, as night and shadows are good for flowers, and moonlight and dews are better than a continual sun, so is Christ's absence of special use, and that it hath some nourishing virtue in it, and giveth sap to humility, and putteth an edge on hunger, and furnisheth a fair field to faith to put forth itself, and to exercise its fingers in gripping it seeth not what.—*Samuel Rutherford*, 1600-1661.

Verses 1, 2.—That which the French proverb hath of sickness is true of all evils, that they come on horseback and go away on foot ; we have often seen that a sudden fall, or one meal's surfeit, has stuck by many to their graves ; whereas pleasures come like oxen, slow and heavily, and go away like post-horses, upon the spur. Sorrows, because they are lingering guests, I will entertain but moderately, knowing that the more they are are made of the longer they will continue : and for pleasures, because they stay not, and do but call to drink at my door, I will use them as passengers with slight respect. He is his own best friend that makes the least of both of them.—*Joseph Hall.*

Verses 1, 2.—"How LONG *wilt thou forget me ?* How LONG *wilt thou hide thy face from me ?* How LONG *shall I take counsel in my soul ?*" The intenseness of the affliction renders it trying to our fortitude ; but it is by the continuance of it that patience is put to the test. It is not under the sharpest, but the longest trials, that we are most in danger of fainting. In the first case, the soul collects all its strength, and feels in earnest to call in help from above ; but, in the last, the mind relaxes, and sinks into despondency. When Job was accosted with evil tidings, in quick sucession, he bore it with becoming fortitude ; but when he could see no end to his troubles, he sunk under them.—*Andrew Fuller.*

Verses 1—4.—Everything is strangely changed ; all its comeliness, and beauty, and glory, vanishes when the *life* is gone : life is the pleasant thing ; 'tis sweet and comfortable ; but death with its pale attendants, raises a horror and aversion to it everywhere. The saints of God dread the removal of his favour, and the hiding of his face ; and when it is hid, a faintness and a cold amazement and fear seizes upon every part, and they feel strange bitterness, and anguish, and tribulation, which makes their joints to tremble, and is to them as the very pangs of death.—*Timothy Rogers.*

Verses 1, 5, 6.—Prayer helps towards the increase and growth of grace, by drawing the habits of grace into exercise. Now, as exercise brings benefit to the body, so does prayer to the soul. Exercise doth help to digest or breathe forth those humours that clog the spirits. One that stirs little we see grow pursy, and is soon choked up with phlegm, which exercise clears the body of. Prayer is the saint's exercise-field, where his graces are breathed ; it is as the wind to the air, it brightens the soul ; as bellows to the fire, which clears the coal of those ashes that smother them. The Christian, while in this world, lives in an unwholesome climate ; one while, the delights of it deaden and dull his love to Christ ; another while, the trouble he meets in it damps his faith on the promise. How now should the Christian get out of these distempers, had he not a throne of grace to resort to, where, if once his soul be in a melting frame, he (like one laid in a kindly sweat), soon breathes out the malignity of his disease, and comes into his right temper again ? How often do we find the holy prophet, when he first kneels down to pray, full of fears and doubts, who, before he and the duty part, grows into a sweet familiarity with God, and repose in his own spirit ! (Psalm xiii. 1), he begins his prayer as if he thought God would never give him a kind look more : "*How long wilt thou forget me, O Lord? for ever?*" But by that time he had exercised himself a little in duty, his distemper wears off, the mists scatter, and his faith breaks out as the sun in its strength, verses 5, 6 : "*I have trusted in thy mercy; my heart shall rejoice in thy salvation. I will sing unto the Lord.*" Thus his faith lays the cloth, expecting a feast ere long to be set on : he that now questioned whether he should ever hear good news from heaven, is so strong in faith as to make himself merry with the hopes of that mercy which he is assured will come at last. Abraham began with fifty, but his faith got ground on God every step, till he brought down the price of their lives to ten.—*William Gurnall.*

Verses 1, 6.—Whatever discouragements thou meetest with in thine attendance on God in ordinances, be like the English jet, fired by water, and not like our ordinary fires, quenched by it ; let them add to, not diminish, thy resolution and courage ; let not one repulse beat thee off ; be violent, give a second storm to the kingdom of heaven. Parents sometimes hide themselves to make their children continue seeking. He that would not at first open his mouth, nor vouchsafe the woman of Canaan a word, doth, upon her continued and fervent petitions, at last open his hand and give her whatsoever she asks : "O woman, be it unto thee as thou wilt." Continued importunity is undeniable oratory. And truly, if after all thy pains thou findest Jesus Christ, will it not make amends for thy long patience ? Men that venture often at a lottery, though they take blanks twenty times, if afterwards they get a golden bason and ewer, it will make them abundant satisfaction. Suppose thou shouldst continue knocking twenty, nay, forty years, yet if at last, though but one hour before thou diest thy heart be opened to Christ, and he be received into thy soul, and when thou diest heaven be opened to thee, and thy soul received into it, will it not infinitely requite thee for all thy labour ? Oh, think of it, and resolve never to be dumb while God is deaf, never to leave off prayer till God return a gracious answer. And for thy comfort, know that he who began his Psalm with, "*How long wilt thou forget me, O Lord? for ever? how long wilt thou hide thy face from me?*" comes to conclude it with, "*I will sing unto the Lord, because he hath dealt bountifully with me.*"—*George Swinnock.*

Verse 2.—"*How long?*" There are many situations of the believer in this life in which the words of this Psalm may be a consolation, and help to revive sinking faith. A certain man lay at the pool of Bethesda, who had an infirmity thirty and eight years. John v. 5. A woman had a spirit of infirmity eighteen years, before she was "loosed." Luke xiii. 11. Lazarus all his life long laboured under disease and poverty, till he was released by death and transferred to Abraham's bosom. Luke xvi. 20—22. Let every one, then, who may be tempted to use the complaints of this Psalm, assure his heart that God does not forget his people, help will come at last, and, in the meantime, all things shall work together for good to them that love him.—*W. Wilson, D.D.*

Verse 2.—"*How long shall I take counsel in my soul, having sorrow in my heart daily?*" There is such a thing as to pore on our guilt and wretchedness, to the overlooking of our highest mercies. Though it be proper to know our own hearts, for the purposes of conviction, yet, if we expect consolation from this quarter, we shall find ourselves sadly disappointed. Such, for a time, appears to have been the case of David. He seems to have been in great distress; and, as is common in such cases, his thoughts turned inward, casting in his mind what he should do, and what would be the end of things. While thus exercised, he had *sorrow in his heart daily:* but, betaking himself to God for relief, he succeeded, *trusting in his mercy, his heart rejoiced in his salvation.* There are many persons, who, when in trouble, imitate David in the former part of this experience : I wish we may imitate him in the latter.—*Andrew Fuller.*

Verses 2, 4.—"*How long shall mine enemy be exalted over me?*" 'Tis a great relief to the miserable and afflicted, to be pitied by others. It is some relief when others, though they cannot help us, yet seem to be truly concerned for the sadness of our case ; when by the kindness of their words and of their actions they do a little smooth the wounds they cannot heal ; but 'tis an unspeakable addition to the cross, when a man is brought low under the sense of God's displeasure, to have men to mock at his calamity, or to revile him, or to speak roughly ; this does inflame and exasperate the wound that was big enough before ; and it is a hard thing when one has a dreadful sound in his ears to have every friend to become a son of thunder. It is a small matter for people that are at ease, to deal severely with such as are afflicted, but they little know how their severe speeches and their angry words pierce them to the very soul. 'Tis easy to blame others for complaining, but if such had felt but for a little while what it is to be under the fear of God's anger, they would find that they could not but complain. It cannot but make any person restless and uneasy when he apprehends that God is his enemy. It is no wonder if he makes every one that he sees, and every place that he is in, a witness of his grief ; but now it is a comfort in our temptations and in our fears, that we have so compassionate a friend as Christ is to whom we may repair, "For we have not an high priest which cannot be touched with the feeling of our infirmities ; but was in all points tempted like as we are, yet without sin." Heb. iv. 15.—*Timothy Rogers.*

Verse 3.—"*Lighten mine eyes, lest I sleep the sleep of death.*" In time of sickness and grief, the "eyes" are dull and heavy ; and they grow more and more so as death approaches, which closes them in darkness. On the other hand, health and joy render the organs of vision bright and sparkling, seeming, as it were, to impart "light" to them from within. The words, therefore, may be fitly applied to a recovery of the body natural, and thence, of the body politic, from their respective maladies. Nor do they less significantly describe the restoration of the soul to a state of spiritual health and holy joy, which will manifest themselves in like manner, by "the eyes of the understanding being enlightened ;" and in this case, the soul is saved from the sleep of sin, as the body is in the other, from the sleep of death.—*George Horne.*

Verse 3.—Why dost *thou hide thy face?* happily thou wilt say, None can see thy face and live. Ah, Lord, let me die, that I may see thee ; let me see thee, that I may die : I would not live, but die ; that I may see Christ, I desire death ; that I may live with Christ, I despise life.—*Augustine.*

Verse 3.—"*How long wilt thou hide thy face from me?*" Oh, excellent hiding, which is become my perfection ! My God, thou hidest thy treasure, to kindle my desire ! Thou hidest thy pearl, to inflame the seeker ; thou delayest to give, that thou mayest teach me to importune ; seemest not to hear, to make me persevere.—*John Anselm*, 1034—1109.

Verse 4.—

> Ah ! can you bear contempt; the venom'd tongue
> Of those whom ruin pleases, the keen sneer,
> The lewd reproaches of the rascal herd ;
> Who for the selfsame actions, if successful,
> Would be as grossly lavish in your praise ?
> To sum up all in one—can you support
> The scornful glances, the malignant joy,
> Or more detested pity of a rival—
> Of a triumphant rival ?

James Thomson, 1700—1748.

Verse 4.—"And those that trouble me rejoice when I am moved"—compose comedies out of my tragedies.—*John Trapp.*

Verse 5.—" I have trusted in thy mercy ; my heart shall rejoice in thy salvation." Faith rejoiceth in tribulations, and triumpheth before the victory. The patient is glad when he feels his physic to work, though it make him sick for the time ; because he hopes it will procure health. We rejoice in afflictions, not that they are joyous for the present, but because they shall work for our good. As faith rejoiceth, so it triumpheth in assurance of good success ; for it seeth not according to outward appearance, but when all means fail, it keepeth God in sight, and beholdeth him present for our succour.—*John Ball.*

Verse 5.—" I have trusted in thy mercy; my heart shall rejoice in thy salvation." Though passion possess our bodies, let " patience possess our souls." The law of our profession binds us to a warfare ; *patiendo vincimus*, our troubles shall end, our victory is eternal. Here David's triumph (Psalm xviii. 38—40), " I have wounded them, that they were not able to rise ; they are fallen under my feet. Thou hast subdued under me those that rose up against me. Thou hast also given me the neck of mine enemies," etc. They have wounds for their wounds ; and the treaders down of the poor are trodden down by the poor. The Lord will subdue those to us that would have subdued us to themselves ; and though for a short time they rode over our heads, yet now at last we shall everlastingly tread upon their necks. Lo, then, the reward of humble patience and confident hope. *Speramus et superamus.* Deut. xxxii. 31. " Our God is not as their God, even our enemies being judges." Psalm xx. 7. " Some put their trust in chariots, and some in horses." But no chariot hath strength to oppose, nor horse swiftness to escape, when God pursues. Verse 8. " They are brought down and fallen ; we are risen and stand upright." Their trust hath deceived them ; down they fall, and never to rise. Our God hath helped us ; we are risen, not for a breathing space, but to stand upright for ever.—*Thomas Adams.*

Verse 5.—None live so easily, so pleasantly, as those that live by faith.—*Matthew Henry.*

Verse 5.—Wherefore I say again, " Live by faith ;" again I say, always live by it, rejoice through faith in the Lord. I dare boldly say it is thy fault and neglect of its exercise if thou suffer either thy own melancholy humour or Satan to interrupt thy mirth and spiritual alacrity, and to detain thee in dumps and pensiveness at any time. What if thou beest of a sad constitution ? of a dark complexion ? Is not faith able to rectify nature ? Is it not stronger than any hellebore ? Doth not an experienced divine and physician worthily prefer one dram of it before all the drugs in the apothecary's shop for this effect ? Hath it not sovereign virtue in it, to excerebrate all cares, expectorate all fears and griefs, evacuate the mind of all ill thoughts and passions, to exhilarate the whole man ? But what good doth it to any to have a cordial by him if he use it not ? To wear a sword, soldier-like, by his side, and not to draw it forth in an assault ? When a dump overtakes thee, if thou wouldst say to thy soul in a word or two, " Soul, why art thou disquieted ? know and consider in whom thou believest," would it not presently return to its rest again ? Would not the Master rebuke the winds and storms, and calm thy troubled mind presently ? Hath not every man something or other he useth to put away dumps, to drive away the evil spirit, as David with his harp ? Some with merry company, some with a cup of sack, most with a pipe of tobacco, without which they cannot ride or go. If they miss it a day together they are troubled with rheums, dulness of spirits. They that live in fens and ill airs dare not stir out without a morning draught of some strong liquor. Poor, silly, smoky helps, in comparison with the least taste (but for dishonouring faith I would say whiff) or draught of faith.—*Samuel Ward,* 1577--1653.

Verse 6.—" *I will sing unto the Lord, because he hath dealt bountifully with me.*" Faith keeps the soul from sinking under heavy trials, by bringing in former experiences of the power, mercy, and faithfulness of God to the afflicted soul. Hereby was the psalmist supported in distress. Oh, saith faith, remember what God hath done both for thy outward and inward man : he hath not only delivered thy body when in trouble, but he hath done great things for thy soul ; he hath brought thee out of a state of black nature, entered into a covenant relation with thee, made his goodness pass before thee ; he hath helped thee to pray, and many times hath heard thy prayers and thy tears. Hath he not formerly brought thee out of the horrible pit, and out of the miry clay, and put a new song in thy mouth, and made thee to resolve never to give way to such unbelieving thoughts and fears again ? and how unbecoming is it for thee now to sink in trouble ?—*John Willison,* 1680—1750.

Verse 6.—" *I will sing unto the Lord.*" Mr. John Philpot having lain for some time in the bishop of London's coal-house, the bishop sent for him, and amongst other questions, asked him why they were so merry in prison ? singing (as the prophet speaks) *Exultantes in rebus pessimis,* rejoicing in your naughtiness, whereas you should rather lament and be sorry. Mr. Philpot answered, " My lord, the mirth which we make is but in singing certain Psalms, as we are commanded by Paul, to rejoice in the Lord, singing together hymns and Psalms, for we are in a dark, comfortless place, and therefore, we thus solace ourselves. I trust, therefore, your lordship will not be angry, seeing the apostle saith, ' If any be of an upright heart, let him sing Psalms ;' and we, to declare that we are of an upright mind to God, though we are in misery, yet refresh ourselves with such singing." After some other discourse, saith he, " I was carried back to my lord's coal-house, where I, with my six fellow prisoners, do rouze together in the straw, as cheerfully (I thank God) as others do in their beds of down." And in a letter to a friend, he thus writes : " Commend me to Mr. Elsing and his wife, and thank them for providing me some ease in my prison ; and tell them that though my lord's coal-house be very black, yet it is more to be desired of the faithful than the Queen's palace. The world wonders how we can be so merry under such extreme miseries ; but our God is omnipotent, who turns misery into felicity. Believe me, there is no such joy in the world, as the people of God have under the cross of Christ : I speak by experience, and therefore believe me, and fear nothing that the world can do unto you, for when they imprison our bodies, they set our souls at liberty to converse with God ; when they cast us down, they lift us up ; when they kill us, then do they send us to everlasting life. What greater glory can there be than to be made conformable to our Head, Christ ? And this is done by affliction. O good God, what am I, upon whom thou shouldst bestow so great a mercy ? This is the day which the Lord hath made ; let us rejoice and be glad in it. This is the way, though it be narrow, which is full of the peace of God, and leadeth to eternal bliss. Oh, how my heart leapeth for joy that I am so near the apprehension thereof ! God forgive me my unthankfulness, and unworthiness of so great glory. I have so much joy, that though I be in a place of darkness and mourning, yet I cannot lament ; but both night and day

12

am so full of joy as I never was so merry before ; the Lord's name be praised
for ever. Our enemies do fret, fume, and gnash their teeth at it. O pray
instantly that this joy may never be taken from us ; for it passeth all the
delights in this world. This is the peace of God that passeth all understanding.
This peace, the more his chosen be afflicted, the more they feel it, and therefore cannot faint neither for fire nor water."—*Samuel Clarke's* "*Mirrour*," 1671.

   Verse 6.—"*I will sing unto the Lord.*" How far different is the end of this
Psalm from the beginning !—*John Trapp.*

   Verse 6.—"*I will sing unto the Lord,*" etc. I never knew what it was for
God to stand by me at all turns, and at every offer of Satan to afflict me, etc.,
as I have found him since I came in hither ; for look how fears have presented
themselves, so have supports and encouragements ; yea, when I have started,
even as it were at nothing else but my shadow, yet God, as being very tender
of me, hath not suffered me to be molested, but would with one Scripture or
another, strengthen me against all ; insomuch that I have often said, *Were it
lawful, I could pray for greater trouble, for the greater comfort's sake.* Eccles.
vii. 14 ; 2 Cor. i. 5.—*John Bunyan,* 1628—1688.

HINTS TO THE VILLAGE PREACHER.

   Verse 1.—The apparent length of sorrow, only apparent. Contrast with days
of joy, with eternal misery and eternal joy. Impatience, and other evil passions,
cause the seeming length. Means of shortening, by refusing to forestall, or to
repine afterwards.

   Verse 1 (*second clause*).—Hiding of the divine face. Why at all ? Why from
me ? Why so long ?

   Verse 2.—Advice to the dejected, or the soul directed to look out of itself
for consolation.—*A. Fuller.*

   Verse 2 (*first clause*).—*Self-torture,* its cause, curse, crime, and cure.

   Verse 2.—"*Having sorrow in my heart daily.*" I. The cause of daily sorrow.
Great enemy, unbelief, sin, trial, loss of Jesus' presence, sympathy with others,
mourning for human ruin. II. The necessity of daily sorrow. Purge corruptions, excite graces, raise desires heavenward. III. The cure of daily sorrow.
Good food from God's table, old wine of promises, walks with Jesus, exercise in
good works, avoidance of everything unhealthy.—*B. Davies.*

   Verse 2 (*second clause*).—Time anticipated when defeat shall be turned into
victory.

   Verse 3.—By accommodating the text to the believer. I. True character of
Satan, "enemy." II. Remarkable fact that this enemy is exalted over us.
III. Pressing enquiry, "How long ?"—*B. Davies.*

   Verse 3.—"*Lighten mine eyes.*" A prayer fit for (1) Every benighted sinner.
(2) Every seeker of salvation. (3) Every learner in Christ's school. (4) Every
tried believer. (5) Every dying saint.—*B. Davies.*

   Verse 4.—Noteth the nature of the wicked two ways ; namely, the more they
prevail the more insolent they are ; they wonderfully exult over those that are
afflicted.—*T. Wilcocks.*

   Verse 5.—Experience and perseverance. "I have," "my heart shall."

   Verse 6.—The bountiful giver and the hearty singer.

   The whole Psalm would make a good subject, showing the stages from mourning to rejoicing, dwelling especially upon the turning point, prayer. There are
two verses for each, mourning, praying, rejoicing.—*A. G. Brown.*

PSALM XIV.

TITLE.—*This admirable ode is simply headed, "*To the Chief Musician, by David.*" The dedication to the Chief Musician stands at the head of fifty-three of the Psalms, and clearly indicates that such psalms were intended, not merely for the private use of believers, but to be sung in the great assemblies by the appointed choir at whose head was the overseer, or superintendent, called in our version, "the Chief Musician," and by Ainsworth, "the Master of the Music." Several of these psalms have little or no praise in them, and were not addressed directly to the Most High, and yet were to be sung in public worship; which is a clear indication that the theory of Augustine lately revived by certain hymn-book makers, that nothing but praise should be ·sung, is far more plausible than scriptural. Not only did the ancient Church chant hallowed doctrine and offer prayer amid her spiritual songs, but even the wailing notes of complaint were put into her mouth by the sweet singer of Israel who was inspired of God. Some persons grasp at any nicety which has a gloss of apparent correct- ness upon it, and are pleased with being more fancifully precise than others; nevertheless it will ever be the way of plain men, not only to magnify the Lord in sacred canticles, but also, according to Paul's precept, to teach and admonish one another in psalms and hymns and spiritual songs, singing with grace in their hearts unto the Lord.*

As no distinguishing title is given to this Psalm, we would suggest as an assistance to the memory, the heading—CONCERNING PRACTICAL ATHEISM. *The many conjectures as to the occasion upon which it was written are so completely without foundation, that it would be a waste of time to mention them at length. The apostle Paul, in Romans iii., has shown in- cidentally that the drift of the inspired writer is to show that both Jews and Gentiles are all under sin; there was, therefore, no reason for fixing upon any particular historical occasion, when all history reeks with terrible evidence of human corruption. With instructive alterations, David has given us in Psalm liii. a second edition of this humiliating psalm, being moved of the Holy Ghost thus doubly to declare a truth which is ever distasteful to carnal minds.*

DIVISION.—*The world's foolish creed (verse* 1); *its practical influence in corrupting morals,* 1, 2, 3. *The persecuting tendencies of sinners,* 4; *their alarms,* 5; *their ridicule of the godly,* 6; *and a prayer for the manifestation of the Lord to his people's joy.*

EXPOSITION.

THE fool hath said in his heart, *There is* no God. They are corrupt, they have done abominable works, *there is* none that doeth good.

"*The fool.*" The Atheist is *the* fool pre-eminently, and *a* fool universally. He would not deny God if he were not a fool by nature, and having denied God it is no marvel that he becomes a fool in practice. Sin is always folly, and as it is the height of sin to attack the very existence of the Most High, so is it also the greatest imaginable folly. To say there is no God is to belie the plainest evidence, which is obstinacy; to oppose the common consent of mankind, which is stupidity; to stifle consciousness, which is madness. If the sinner could by his atheism destroy the God whom he hates there were some sense, although much wickedness, in his infidelity; but as denying the existence of fire does not prevent its burning a man who is in it, so doubting the existence of God will not stop the Judge of all the earth from destroying the rebel who breaks his laws; nay, this atheism is a crime which much provokes heaven, and will bring down terrible vengeance on the fool who indulges it. The proverb says, "A fool's tongue cuts his own throat," and in this instance it kills both soul and body for ever: would to God the mischief stopped even there, but alas! one fool makes hundreds, and a noisy blasphemer spreads his horrible doctrines as lepers spread the plague. Ainsworth, in his "Annotations," tells us that the word here used is *Nabal*, which has the signification of fading, dying, or falling away, as a withered leaf or flower; it is a title given to the foolish man as having lost the juice and sap of wisdom, reason, honesty, and godliness. Trapp hits the mark when he calls him " that sapless fellow, that carcase of a man, that walking sepulchre of himself, in whom all religion and right reason is withered and wasted, dried up and decayed." Some translate it *the apostate*, and others *the wretch*. With what earnestness should we shun the appearance of doubt as to the presence, activity, power and love of God, for all such mistrust is of the nature of folly, and who among us would wish to be ranked with the fool in the text ? Yet let us never forget that all unregenerate men are more or less such fools.

The fool " *hath said in his heart.*" May a man with his mouth profess to believe, and yet in heart say the reverse ? Had he hardly become audacious enough to utter his folly with his tongue ? Did the Lord look upon his thoughts as being in the nature of words to Him though not to man ? Is this where man first becomes an unbeliever ?—in his heart, not in his head ? And when he talks atheistically, is it a foolish heart speaking, and endeavouring to clamour down the voice of conscience ? We think so. If the affections were set upon truth and righteousness, the understanding would have no difficulty in settling the question of a present personal Deity, but as the heart dislikes the good and the right, it is no wonder that it desires to be rid of that Elohim, who is the great moral Governor, the Patron of rectitude and the Punisher of iniquity. While men's hearts remain what they are, we must not be surprised at the prevalence of scepticism ; a corrupt tree will bring forth corrupt fruit. " Every man," says Dickson, " so long as he lieth unrenewed and unreconciled to God is nothing in effect but a madman." What wonder then if he raves ? Such fools as those we are now dealing with are common to all time, and all countries ; they grow without watering, and are found all the world over. The spread of mere intellectual enlightenment will not diminish their number, for since it is an affair of the heart, this folly and great learning will often dwell together. To answer sceptical cavillings will be labour lost until grace enters to make the mind willing to believe ; fools can raise more objections in an hour than wise men can answer in seven years, indeed it is their mirth to set stools for wise men to stumble over. Let the preacher aim at the heart, and preach the all-conquering love of Jesus, and he will by God's grace win more doubters to the faith of the gospel than any hundred of the best reasoners who only direct their arguments to the head.

" *The fool hath said in his heart, There is no God,*" or " *no God.*" So monstrous is the assertion, that the man hardly dared to put it as a positive statement, but went very near to doing so. Calvin seems to regard this saying " no God," as hardly amounting to a syllogism, scarcely reaching to a positive, dogmatical declaration ; but Dr. Alexander clearly shows that it does. It is not merely the wish of the sinner's corrupt nature, and the hope of his rebellious heart, but he manages after a fashion to bring himself to assert it, and at certain seasons he thinks that he believes it. It is a solemn reflection that some who worship God with their lips may in their hearts be saying, " no God." It is worthy of observation that he does not say there is no Jehovah, but there is no Elohim ; Deity in the abstract is not so much the object of attack, as the covenant, personal, ruling and governing presence of God in the world. God as ruler, lawgiver, worker, Saviour, is the butt at which the arrows of human wrath are shot. How impotent the malice ! How mad the rage which raves and foams against Him in whom we live and move and have our being ! How horrible the insanity which leads a man who owes his all to God to cry out," *No God*" ! How terrible the depravity which makes the whole race adopt this as their hearts' desire, " no God !"

" *They are corrupt.*" This refers to all men, and we have the warrant of the Holy Ghost for so saying ; see the third chapter of the Epistle to the Romans. Where there is enmity to God, there is deep, inward depravity of mind. The words are rendered by eminent critics in an active sense, " they have done corruptly :" this may serve to remind us that sin is not only in our nature passively as the source of evil, but we ourselves actively fan the flame and corrupt ourselves, making that blacker still which was black as darkness itself already. We rivet our own chains by habit and continuance.

" *They have done abominable works.*" When men begin with renouncing the Most High God, who shall tell where they will end ? When the Master's eyes are put out, what will not the servants do ? Observe the state of the world before the flood, as pourtrayed in Genesis vi. 12, and remember that human nature is unchanged. He who would see a terrible photograph of the world without God must read that most painful of all inspired Scriptures, the first chapter of the epistle to the Romans. Learned Hindoos have confessed that the description is literally correct in Hindostan at the present moment ; and were it not for the restraining grace of God, it would be so in England. Alas ! it is even here but too correct a picture of things which are done of men in secret. Things loathsome to God and man are sweet to some palates.

" *There is none that doeth good.*" Sins of omission must abound where transgressions are rife. Those who do the things which they ought not to have done, are sure to leave undone those things which they ought to have done. What a picture of our race is this ! Save only where grace reigns, there is none that doeth good ; humanity, fallen and debased, is a desert without an oasis, a night without a star, a dunghill without a jewel, a hell without a bottom.

2 The LORD looked down from heaven upon the children of men, to see if there were any that did understand, *and* seek God.

3 They are all gone aside, they are *all* together become filthy : *there is* none that doeth good, no, not one.

" *The Lord looked down from heaven upon the children of men.*" As from a watchtower, or other elevated place of observation, the Lord is represented as gazing intently upon men. He will not punish blindly, nor like a tyrant command an indiscriminate massacre because a rumour of rebellion has come up to his ears. What condescending interest and impartial justice are here imaged ! The case of Sodom, visited before it was overthrown, illustrates the careful manner in which Divine Justice beholds the sin before it avenges it, and searches out the righteous that they perish not with the guilty. Behold then the eyes of Omniscience ransacking the globe, and prying among every people and nation, " *to see if there were any that did understand and seek God.*" He who is looking down knows the good, is quick to discern it, would be delighted to find it ; but as he views all the unregenerate children of men his search is fruitless, for of all the race of Adam, no unrenewed soul is other than an enemy to God and goodness. The objects of the Lord's search are not wealthy men, great men, or learned men ; these, with all they can offer, cannot meet the demands of the great Governor : at the same time, he is not looking for superlative eminence in virtue, he seeks for *any that understand* themselves, their state, their duty, their destiny, their happiness ; he looks for any that *seek God*, who, if there be a God, are willing and anxious to find him out. Surely this is not too great a matter to expect ; for if men have not yet known God, if they have any right understanding, they will seek him. Alas ! even this low degree of good is not to be found even by him who sees all things ; but men love the hideous negation of " No God," and with their backs to their Creator, who is the sun of their life, they journey into the dreary region of unbelief and alienation, which is a land of darkness as darkness itself, and of the shadow of death without any order and where the light is as darkness.

" *They are all gone aside.*" Without exception, all men have apostatized from the Lord their Maker, from his laws, and from the eternal principles of right. Like stubborn heifers they have sturdily refused to receive the yoke, like errant sheep they have found a gap and left the right field. The original speaks of the race as a whole, as a totality ; and humanity as a whole has become depraved in heart and defiled in life. " *They have altogether become filthy ;*" as a whole they are spoiled and soured like corrupt leaven, or, as some put it, they have become putrid and even stinking. The only reason why we do not more clearly see this foulness is because we are accustomed to it, just as those who work daily among offensive odours at last cease to smell them. The miller does not observe the noise of his own mill, and we are slow to discover our own ruin and depravity. But are there no special cases, are all men sinful ? " Yes," says the Psalmist, in a manner not to be mistaken, " they are." He has put it positively, he repeats it negatively, " *There is none that doeth good, no, not one.*" The Hebrew phrase is an utter denial concerning any mere man that he of himself doeth good. What cáñ be more sweeping ? This is the verdict of the all-seeing Jehovah, who cannot exaggerate or mistake. As if no hope of finding a solitary specimen of a good man among the unrenewed human family might be harboured for an instant. The Holy Spirit *is not* content with saying all and altogether, but adds the crushing threefold negative, " *none, no, not one.*" What say the opponents to the doctrine of natural depravity to this ? Rather what do we *feel* concerning it ? Do we not confess that we by nature are corrupt, and do we not bless the sovereign grace which has renewed us in the spirit of our minds, that sin may no more have dominion over us, but that grace may rule and reign ?

4 Have all the workers of iniquity no knowledge ? who eat up my people *as* they eat bread, and call not upon the LORD.

Hatred of God and corruptness of life are the motive forces which produce persecution. Men who having no saving knowledge of divine things, enslave themselves to become workers of iniquity, have no heart to cry to the Lord for deliverance, but seek to amuse themselves with devouring the poor and despised people of God. It is hard bondage to be a " *worker of iniquity ;*" a worker at the galleys, or in the mines of Siberia, is not more truly degraded and wretched ; the toil is hard and the reward dreadful ; those who have no knowledge choose such slavery, but those who are taught of God cry to be rescued from it. The same ignorance which keeps men bondsmen to evil, makes them hate the free-born sons of God ; hence they seek to eat them up " *as they eat bread,*"—daily, ravenously, as though it were an ordinary, usual, every-day matter to oppress the saints of God. As pikes in a pond eat up little fish, as eagles prey on smaller birds, as wolves rend the sheep of the pasture, so sinners naturally and as a matter of course, persecute, malign, and mock the followers of the Lord Jesus. While thus preying, they forswear all praying, and in this act consistently, for how could they hope to be heard while their hands are full of blood ?

5 There were they in great fear : for God *is* in the generation of the righteous.

Oppressors have it not all their own way, they have their fits of trembling and their appointed seasons of overthrow. *There*—where they denied God and hectored against his people ; *there*—where they thought of peace and safety, they were made to quail. " *There were they*"—these very loud-mouthed, iron-handed, proud-hearted Nimrods and Herods, these heady, high-minded sinners—" *there were they in great fear.*" A panic terror seized them : " they feared a fear," as the Hebrew puts it ; an undefinable, horrible, mysterious dread crept over them. The most hardened of men have their periods when conscience casts them into a cold sweat of alarm. As cowards are cruel, so all cruel men are at heart cowards. The ghost of past sin is a terrible spectre to haunt any man, and though unbelievers may boast as loudly as they will, a sound is in their ears which makes them ill at ease.

" *For God is in the generation of the righteous.*" This makes the company of godly men so irksome to the wicked because they perceive that God is with them. Shut their eyes as they may, they cannot but perceive the image of God in the character of his truly gracious people, nor can they fail to see that he works for their deliverance. Like Haman, they instinctively feel a trembling when they see God's Mordecais. Even though the saint may be in a mean position, mourning at the gate where the persecutor rejoices in state, the sinner feels the influence of the believer's true nobility and quails before it, for God is there. Let scoffers beware, for they persecute the Lord Jesus when they molest his people ; the union is very close between God and his people, it amounts to a mysterious indwelling, for God is in the generation of the righteous.

6 Ye have shamed the counsel of the poor, because the LORD *is* his refuge.

Notwithstanding their real cowardice, the wicked put on the lion's skin and lord it over the Lord's poor ones. Though fools themselves, they mock at the truly wise as if the folly were on their side ; but this is what might be expected, for how should brutish minds appreciate excellence, and how can those who have owl's eyes admire the sun ? The special point and butt of their jest seems to be the confidence of the godly in their Lord. What can your God do for you now ? Who is that God who can deliver out of our hand ? Where is the reward of all your praying and beseeching ? Taunting questions of this sort they thrust into the faces of weak but gracious souls, and tempt them to feel ashamed of their refuge. Let us not be laughed out of our confidence by them, let us scorn their scorning and defy their jeers ; we shall need to wait but a little, and then the Lord our refuge will avenge his own elect, and ease himself of his adversaries, who once made so light of him and of his people.

7 Oh that the salvation of Israel *were come* out of Zion ! when the LORD bringeth back the captivity of his people, Jacob shall rejoice, *and* Israel shall be glad.

Natural enough is this closing prayer, for what would so effectually convince atheists, overthrow persecutors, stay sin, and secure the godly, as the manifest appearance of Israel's great Salvation ? The coming of Messiah was the desire of the godly in all ages, and though he has already come with a sin-offering to purge away iniquity, we look for him to come a second time, to come without a sin-offering unto salvation. O that these weary years would have an end ! Why tarries he so long ? He knows that sin abounds and that his people are down-trodden ; why comes he not to the rescue ? His glorious advent will restore his ancient people from literal captivity, and his spiritual seed from spiritual sorrow. Wrestling Jacob and prevailing Israel shall alike rejoice before him when he is revealed as their salvation. O that he were come ! What happy, holy, halcyon, heavenly days should we then see ! But let us not count him slack, for behold, he comes, he comes quickly ! Blessed are all they that wait for him.

EXPLANATORY NOTES AND QUAINT SAYINGS.

Whole Psalm.—There is a peculiar mark put upon this Psalm, in that it is twice in the Book of Psalms. The fourteenth Psalm and the fifty-third Psalm are the same, with the alteration of one or two expressions at most. And there is another mark put upon it, that the apostle transcribes a great part of it.—Rom. iii. 10—12.

It contains a description of a most deplorable state of things in the world—ay, in Israel ; a most deplorable state, by reason of the general corruption that was befallen all sorts of men, in their principles, and in their practices, and in their opinions.

First, it was a time when there was a mighty prevalent *principle* of atheism got into the world, got among the great men of the world. Saith he, " That is their principle, they say in their hearts, ' There is no God.' " It is true, they did not absolutely profess it ; but it was the principle whereby all their actings were regulated, and which they conformed unto. " *The fool,*" saith he, " *hath said in his heart, There is no God.*" Not this or that particular man, but the fool—that is, those foolish men ; for in the next word he tells you, " *They are corrupt ;*" and verse 3, " *They are all gone aside.*" " The fool " is taken indefinitely for the great company and society of foolish men, to intimate that whatsoever they were divided about else, they were all agreed in this. " They are all a company of atheists," saith he, " practical atheists."

Secondly, their *affections* were suitable to this principle, as all men's affections and actions are suitable to their principles. What are you to expect from men whose principle is, that there is no God? Why, saith he, for their affections, "They are corrupt;" which he expresseth again (verse 3), "They are all gone aside, they are all together become filthy." "All gone aside." The word in the original is, "They are all grown sour;" as drink, that hath been formerly of some use, but when grown vapid—lost all its spirits and life—it is an insipid thing, good for nothing. And, saith he, "*They are altogether become filthy*"—"become stinking," as the margin hath it. They have corrupt affections, that have left them no life, no savour; but stinking, corrupt lusts prevail in them universally. They say, "There is no God;" and they are filled with stinking, corrupt lusts.

Thirdly, if this be their principle and these their affections, let us look after their *actions*, to see if they be any better. But consider their actions. They be of two sorts;—1. How they act in the world, 2. How they act towards the people of God.

1. How do they act in the world? Why, consider that, as to their duties which they omit, and as to the wickednesses which they perform. What good do they do? Nay, saith he, "*None of them doeth good.*" Yea, some of them. "*No, not one.*" Saith he, verses 1, 3, "There is none that doeth good, no, not one." If there was any one among them that did attend to what was really good and useful in the world, there was some hope. "No," saith he, "their principle is atheism, their affections are corrupt; and for good, there is not one of them doeth any good—they omit all duties."

What do they do for evil? Why, saith he, "*They have done abominable works*"—"works," saith he, "not to be named, not to be spoken of—works which God abhors, which all good men abhor." "Abominable works," saith he, "such as the very light of nature would abhor;" and give me leave to use the expression of the psalmist—"stinking, filthy works." So he doth describe the state and condition of things under the reign of Saul, when he wrote this Psalm.

2. "If thus it be with them, and if thus it be with their own ways, yet they let the people of God alone; they will not add that to the rest of their sins." Nay, it is quite otherwise, saith he, "*They eat up my people as they eat bread.*" "Those workers of iniquity have no knowledge, who eat up my people as they eat bread, and call not upon the LORD." What is the reason why he brings it in in that manner? Why could he not say, "They have no knowledge that do such abominable things;" but brings it in thus, "They have no knowledge who eat up my people as they eat bread?" "It is strange, that after all my dealings with them and declaration of my will, they should be so brutish as not to know this would be their ruin. Don't they know this will devour them, destroy them, and be called over again in a particular manner?" In the midst of all the sins, and greatest and highest provocations that are in the world, God lays a special weight upon the eating of his people. They may feed upon their own lusts what they will; but, "Have they no knowledge, that they eat up my people as they eat bread?"

There are very many things that might be observed from all this; but I aim to give but a few hints from the Psalm.

Well, what is the state of things now? You see what it was with them. How was it with the providence of God in reference unto them? Which is strange, and a man would scarce believe it in such a course as this is, he tells you (verse 5), notwithstanding all this, they were in great fear. "*There were they in great fear,*" saith he. May be so, for they saw some evil coming upon them. No, there was nothing but the hand of God in it; for in Psalm liii. 5, where these words are repeated, it is, "There were they in great fear, where no fear was"—no visible cause of fear; yet they were in great fear.

God by his providence seldom gives an absolute, universal security unto men in their height of sin, and oppression, and sensuality, and lusts; but he will secretly put them in fear where no fear is : and though there be nothing seen that should cause them to have any fear, they shall act like men at their wits' end with fear.

But whence should this fear arise ? Saith he, it ariseth from hence, " *For God is in the generation of the righteous.*" Plainly they see their work doth not go on ; their meat doth not digest with them ; their bread doth not go well down. " They were eating and devouring my people, and when they came to devour them, they found God was among them (they could not digest their bread) ; and this put them in fear ; quite surprised them." They came, and thought to have found them a sweet morsel : when engaged, God was there filling their mouth and teeth with gravel ; and he began to break out the jaw-bone of the terrible ones when they came to feed upon them. Saith he, " God was there." (Verse 5.)

The Holy Ghost gives an account of the state of things that was between those two sorts of people he had described—between the fool and the people of God—them that were devouring, and them that had been utterly devoured, had not God been among them. Both were in fear—they that were to be devoured, and those that did devour. And they took several ways for their relief ; and he showeth what those ways were, and what judgment they made upon the ways of one another. Saith he, " *Ye have shamed the counsel of the poor, because the Lord is his refuge.*"

There are the persons spoken of—they are " the poor ;" and that is those who are described in the verses foregoing, the people that were ready to be eaten up and devoured.

And there is the hope and refuge that these poor had in such a time as this, when all things were in fear ; and that was " the LORD." The poor maketh the Lord his refuge.

And you may observe here, that as he did describe all the wicked as one man, " the fool," so he describes all his own people as one man, " the poor"—that is, the poor man : " Because the LORD is his refuge." He keeps it in the singular number. Whatsoever the people of God may differ in, they are all as one man in this business.

And there is the way whereby these poor make God their refuge. They do it by " counsel," saith he. It is not a thing they do by chance, but they look upon it as their wisdom. They do it upon consideration, upon advice. It is a thing of great wisdom.

Well, what thoughts have the others concerning this acting of theirs ? The poor make God their refuge ; and they do it by counsel. What judgment, now, doth the world make of this counsel of theirs ? Why, they " shame it ;" that is, they cast shame upon it, contemn it as a very foolish thing, to make the Lord their refuge. " Truly, if they could make this or that great man their refuge, it were something ; but to make the Lord their refuge, this is the foolishest thing in the world," say they. To shame men's counsel, to despise their counsel as foolish, is as great contempt as they can lay upon them.

Here you see the state of things as they are represented in this Psalm, and spread before the Lord : which being laid down, the psalmist showeth what our duty is upon such a state of things—what is the duty of the people of God, things thus being stated. Saith he, " Their way is to go to prayer :" verse 7, " *O that the salvation of Israel were come out of Zion ! when the Lord bringeth back the captivity of his people, Jacob shall rejoice, and Israel shall be glad.*" If things are thus stated. then cry, then pray, " O that the salvation of Israel were come out of Zion," etc. There shall a revenue of praise come to God out of Zion, to the rejoicing of his people.—*John Owen.*

Verse 1.—" *The fool.*" That sapless fellow, that carcase of a man, that walking sepulchre of himself, in whom all religion and right reason is withered and wasted, dried up and decayed. That apostate in whom natural principles are extinct, and from whom God is departed, as when the prince is departed, hangings are taken down. That mere animal that hath no more than a reasonable soul, and for little other purpose than as salt, to keep his body from putrefying. That wicked man hereafter described, that studieth atheism.—*John Trapp.*

Verse 1.—" *The fool,*" etc. The world we live in is a world of fools. The far greater part of mankind act a part entirely irrational. So great is their infatuation, that they prefer time to eternity, momentary enjoyments to those that shall never have an end, and listen to the testimony of Satan in preference to that of God. Of all folly, that is the greatest, which relates to eternal objects, because it is the most fatal, and when persisted in through life, entirely remediless. A mistake in the management of temporal concerns may be afterwards rectified. At any rate, it is comparatively of little importance. But an error in spiritual and eternal matters, as it is in itself of the greatest moment, if carried through life, can never be remedied ; because after death there is no redemption. The greatest folly that any creature is capable of, is that of denying or entertaining unjust apprehensions of the being and perfections of the great Creator. Therefore, in a way of eminence, the appellation of *fool* is given by the Spirit of God, to him who is chargeable with this guilt. " *The fool hath said in his heart, There is no God.*"—*John Jamieson,* M.A., 1789.

Verse 1.—" *The fool,*" a term in Scripture signifying a wicked man, used also by the heathen philosophers to signify a vicious person, נָבֵל as coming from נָבֵל signifies the extinction of life in men, animals, and plants ; so the word נָבֵל is taken, Isaiah, xl. 7, צִיץ נָבֵל " the flower fadeth" (Isaiah xxviii. 1), a plant that hath lost all that juice that made it lovely and useful. So, a fool is one that hath lost his wisdom and right notion of God and divine things, which were communicated to man by creation ; one dead in sin, yet one not so much void of rational faculties, as of grace in those faculties ; not one that wants reason, but abuses his reason.—*Stephen Charnock.*

Verse 1.—" *The fool hath said,*" etc. This folly is bound up in every heart. It is bound, but it is not tongue-tied ; it speaks blasphemous things against God, *it says* there is " *no God.*" There is a difference indeed in the language : gross sins speak this louder, there are crying sins ; but though less sins speak it not so loud, they whisper it. But the Lord can hear the language of the heart, the whisperings of its motions, as plainly as we hear one another in our ordinary discourse. Oh, how heinous is the least sin, which is so injurious to the very being of the great God !—*David Clarkson.*

Verse 1.—" *The fool hath said in his heart, There is no God.*" If you will turn over some few leaves, as far as the fifty-third Psalm, you shall not only find my text, but this whole Psalm, without any alteration, save only in the fifth verse, and that not at all in the sense neither. What shall we say ? Took the Holy Spirit of God such especial particular notice of the sayings and deeds of a *fool,* that one expression of them would not serve the turn ? Or, does the babbling and madness of a fool so much concern us, as that we need to have them urged upon us once and again, and a third time in the third of the Romans ? Surely not any one of us present here, is this fool ! Nay, if any one of us could but tell where to find such a fool as this, that would offer to say, though in his heart, " *There is no God,*" he should not rest in quiet, he should soon perceive we were not of his faction. We that are able to tell David an article or two of faith more than ever he was acquainted with ! Nay, more ; can we with any imaginable ground of reason be supposed liable to any suspicion of atheism, that are able to read to David a lecture out of his own Psalms, and explain the meaning of his own prophecies much clearer than himself which held the pen to the Holy Spirit of God ? Though we cannot deny but that in other things there may be found some spice of folly and imperfection in us, but it cannot be imagined that we, who are almost cloyed with the heavenly manna of God's word, that can instruct our teachers, and are able to maintain opinions and tenets, the scruples whereof not both the universities in this land, nor the whole clergy are able to resolve, that it should be possible for us ever to come to that perfection and excellency of folly and madness, as to entertain thought that *there is no God:* nay, we are not so uncharitable as to charge a Turk or an infidel with such a horrible imputation as this.

Beloved Christians, be not wise in your own conceits : if you will seriously examine the third of Romans (which I mentioned before), you shall find that Paul, out of this Psalm, and the like words of Isaiah, doth conclude the whole posterity of Adam (Christ only excepted), under sin and the curse of God ; which inference of his were weak and inconcluding, unless every man of his own nature were such a one as the prophet here describes ; and the same apostle in another place expresses, " *Even altogether without God in the world,*" *i.e.,* not maintaining it as an opinion which they would undertake by force of argument to confirm, That there is no God : for we read not of above three or four among the heathens, that were of any fashion, which went thus far ; but such as though in their discourse and serious thoughts they do not question a deity, but would abhor any man that would not liberally allow unto God all his glorious attributes, yet in their hearts and affections they deny him ; they live as if there was no God, having no respect at all to him in all their projects, and therefore, indeed and in God's esteem, become formally, and in strict propriety of speech, very atheists.—*William Chillingworth,* 1602—1643.

Verse 1.—" *The fool hath said in his heart, There is no God.*" Why do men resist God's authority, against which they cannot dispute ? and disobey his commands, unto which they cannot devise to frame an exception ? What but the spirit of enmity, can make them regret " so easy a yoke," reject so " light a burden," shun and fly off from so peaceful and pleasant paths ? yea, and take ways that so manifestly " take hold of hell, and lead down to the chambers of death," rather choosing to perish than obey ? Is not this the very height of enmity ? What further proof would we seek of a disaffected and implacable heart ? Yet to all this we may cast in that fearful addition, their saying in their heart, " *No God ;*" as much as to say, " O that there were none !" This is enmity not only to the highest pitch of *wickedness,* to wish their common parent extinct, the author of their being, but even unto *madness* itself. For in the forgetful heat of this transport, it is not thought on that they wish the most absolute impossibility ; and that, if it were possible, they wish, with his, the extinction of their own and of all being ; and that the sense of their hearts, put into words, would amount to no less than a direful and most horrid execration and curse upon God and the whole creation of God at once ! As if, by the blasphemy of their poisonous breath, they would wither all nature, blast the whole universe of being, and make it fade, languish, and drop into nothing. This is to set their mouth against heaven and earth, themselves, and all things at once, as if they thought their feeble breath should overpower the omnipotent Word, shake and shiver the adamantine pillars of heaven and earth, and the Almighty *fiat* be defeated by their *nay,* striking at the root of all ! So fitly is it said, " The *fool* hath in his heart " muttered thus. Nor are there few such fools ; but this is plainly given us as the common character of apostate man, the whole revolted race, of whom it is said in very general terms, " They are all gone back, there is none that doeth good." This is their sense, one and all, that is, comparatively ; and the true state of the case being laid before them, it is more their temper and sense to say, " No God," than to repent, " and turn to him." What mad enmity is this ! Nor can we devise into what else to resolve it.— *John Howe.*

Verse 1.—" *The fool hath said in his heart, there is no God.*" He that shall deny there is a God, sins with a very high hand against the light of nature ; for every creature, yea, the least gnat and fly, and the meanest worm that crawls upon the ground will confute and confound that man that disputes whether there be a God or no. The name of God is written in such full, fair, and shining characters upon the whole creation, that all men may run and read that there is a God. The notion of a deity is so strongly and deeply impressed upon the tables of all men's hearts, that to deny a God is to quench the very principles of common nature ; yea, it is formally *deicidium,* a killing of God, as much a sin

the creature lies.   There are none of these atheists in hell, for the devils believe
and tremble.   James ii. 19.   The Greek word φρίσσουσι, that is here used,
signifies properly the roaring of the sea ; it implies such an extreme fear, as
causeth not only trembling, but also a roaring and screeching out.   Mark vi. 49 ;
Acts xvi. 29.   The devils believe and acknowledge four articles of our faith.
Matt. viii. 29.   (1.) They acknowledge God ; (2.) Christ ; (3.) The day of
judgment ; (4.) That they shall be tormented then ; so that he that doth not
believe that there is a God, is more vile than a devil.   To deny there is a God.
is a sort of atheism that is not to be found in hell.

> " On earth are atheists many,
>   In hell there is not any."

Augustine, speaking of atheists, saith, " That albeit there be some who think, or
would persuade themselves, that there is no God, yet the most vile and
desperate wretch that ever lived would not say, there was no God."   Seneca
hath a remarkable speech, *Mentiuntur qui dicunt se non sentire Deum esse: nam
etsi tibi affirmant interdiù noctu tamen dubitant.*   They lie, saith he, who say they
perceive not there is a God ; for although they affirm it to thee in the day-
time, yet by night they doubt of it.   Further, saith the same author, I have
heard of some that deny that there was a God ; yet never knew the man, but
when he was sick he would seek unto God for help ; therefore they do but lie
that say there is no God ; they sin against the light of their own consciences ;
they who most studiously go about to deny God, yet cannot do it but some check
of conscience will fly in their faces.   Tully would say that there was never any
nation under heaven so barbarous as to deny that there was a God.—*T. Brooks.*

Verse 1.—" *The fool hath said in his heart, There is no God.*"   Popery has
not won to itself so great wits as atheism ; it is the superfluity of wit that makes
atheists.   These will not be beaten down with impertinent arguments ; disordered hail-shot of Scriptures will never scare them ; they must be convinced
and beaten by their own weapons.   " Hast thou appealed to Cæsar ?   To Cæsar
thou shalt go."   Have they appealed to reason ?   Let us bring reason to them,
that we may bring them to reason.   We need not fear the want of weapons in
that armoury, but our own ignorance and want of skill to use them.   There is
enough even in philosophy to convince atheism, and make them confess, " We
are foiled with our own weapons ;" for with all their wit atheists are fools.—
Thomas Adams.

Verse 1.—As there is no wound more mortal than that which plucketh forth
man's heart or soul ; so, likewise, is there no person or pestilence of greater
force suddenly in men to kill all faith, hope, and charity, with the fear of God,
and consequently to cast them headlong into the pit of hell, than to deny the
principle and foundation of all religion—namely, that there is a God.—*Robert
Cawdray's " Treasury or Storehouse of Similes,"* 1609.

Verse 1.—" *The fool hath said in his heart, There is no God.*"—Who in the
world is a verier fool, a more ignorant, wretched person, than he that is an
atheist ?   A man may better believe there is no such man as himself, and that
he is not in being, than that there is no God ; for himself can cease to be, and
once was not, and shall be changed from what he is, and in very many periods
of his life knows not that he is ; and so it is every night with him when he
sleeps ; but none of these can happen to God ; and if he knows it not, he is a
fool.   Can anything in this world be more foolish than to think that all this rare
fabric of heaven and earth can come by chance, when all the skill of art is not
able to make an oyster ?   To see rare effects, and no cause ; an excellent
government and no prince ; a motion without an immovable ; a circle without
a centre ; a time without eternity ; a second without a first ; a thing that begins
not from itself, and therefore, not to perceive there is something from whence
it does begin, which must be without beginning ; these things are so against
philosophy and natural reason, that he must needs be a beast in his understanding that does not assent to them ; this is the atheist : " *The fool hath said in*

his heart, There is no God." That is his character ; the thing framed, says that nothing framed it ; the tongue never made itself to speak, and yet talks against him that did ; saying, that which is made, is, and that which made it, is not. But this folly is as infinite as hell, as much without light or bound, as the chaos or the primitive nothing.—*Jeremy Taylor*, 1613—1667.

Verse 1.—" *The fool hath said in his heart, There is no God.*" A wise man, that lives up to the principles of reason and virtue, if one considers him in his solitude as taking in the system of the universe, observing the mutual dependence and harmony by which the whole frame of it hangs together, beating down his passions, or swelling his thoughts with magnificent ideas of providence, makes a nobler figure in the eye of an intelligent being, than the greatest conqueror amidst the pomps and solemnities of a triumph. On the contrary, there is not a more ridiculous animal than an atheist in his retirement. His mind is incapable of rapture or elevation : he can only consider himself as an insignificant figure in a landscape, and wandering up and down in a field or a meadow, under the same terms as the meanest animals about him, and as subject to as total a mortality as they, with this aggravation, that he is the only one amongst them who lies under the apprehension of it. In distresses he must be of all creatures the most helpless and forlorn ; he feels the whole pressure of a present calamity, without being relieved by the memory of anything that is past, or the prospect of anything that is to come. Annihilation is the greatest blessing that he proposes to himself, and a halter or a pistol the only refuge he can fly to. But if you would behold one of these gloomy miscreants in his poorest figure, you must consider him under the terrors or at the approach of death. About thirty years ago, I was a shipboard with one of these vermin, when there arose a brisk gale, which could frighten nobody but himself. Upon the rolling of the ship he fell upon his knees, and confessed to the chaplain, that he had been a vile atheist, and had denied a Supreme Being ever since he came to his estate. The good man was astonished, and a report immediately ran through the ship, that there was an atheist upon the upper deck. Several of the common seamen, who had never heard the word before, thought it had been some strange fish ; but they were more surprised when they saw it was a man, and heard out of his own mouth, " That he never believed till that day that there was a God." As he lay in the agonies of confession, one of the honest tars whispered to the boatswain, " That it would be a good deed to heave him overboard." But we were now within sight of port, when of a sudden the wind fell, and the penitent relapsed, begging all of us that were present, as we were gentlemen, not to say anything of what had passed. He had not been ashore above two days, when one of the company began to rally him upon his devotion on shipboard, which the other denied in so high terms, that it produced the lie on both sides, and ended in a duel. The atheist was run through the body, and after some loss of blood, became as good a Christian as he was at sea, till he found that his wound was not mortal. He is at present one of the free-thinkers of the age, and now writing a pamphlet against several received opinions concerning the existence of fairies. *Joseph Addison* (1671—1719), *in " The Tattler."*

Verse 1 :—

" ' There is no God,' the fool in secret said :
There is no God that rules or earth or sky.'
Tear off the band that binds the wretch's head,
That God may burst upon his faithless eye !
Is there no God ?—The stars in myriads spread,
If he look up, the blasphemy deny ;
While his own features, in the mirror read,
Reflect the image of Divinity.
Is there no God ?—The stream that silver flows,
The air he breathes, the ground he treads, the trees,
The flowers, the grass, the sands, each wind that blows,
All speak of God ; throughout, one voice agrees,
And, eloquent, his dread existence shows :
Blind to thyself, ah, see him, fool, in these ! "

Giovanni Cotta.

Verse 1 :—

> "The owlet, *Atheism*,
> Sailing on obscene wings across the noon,
> Drops his blue-fringed lids, and shuts them close,
> And, hooting at the glorious sun in heaven,
> Cries out, ' Where is it ? ' "

Samuel Taylor Coleridge, 1772—1834.

Verse 1.—" *They are corrupt, they have done abominable works.*" Sin pleaseth the flesh. *Omne simile nutrit simile.* Corruption inherent is nourished by the accession of corrupt actions. Judas's covetousness is sweetened with unjust gain. Joab is heartened and hardened with blood. 1 Kings ii. 5. Theft is fitted to and fatted in the thievish heart with obvious booties. Pride is fed with the officious compliments of observant grooms. Extortion battens in the usurer's affections by the trolling in of his moneys. Sacrilege thrives in the church-robber by the pleasing distinctions of those sycophant priests, and helped with their not laborious profit. Nature is led, is fed with sense. And when the citadel of the heart is once won, the turret of the understanding will not long hold out. As the suffumigations of the oppressed stomach surge up and cause the headache, or as the thick spumy mists, which vapour up from the dark and foggy earth, do often suffocate the brighter air, and to us more than eclipse the sun, the black and corrupt affections, which ascend out of the nether part of the soul, do no less darken and choke the understanding. Neither can the fire of grace be kept alive at God's altar (man's heart), when the clouds of lust shall rain down such showers of impiety on it. *Perit omne judicium, cum res transit ad affectum.* Farewell the perspicuity of judgment, when the matter is put to the partiality of affection.—*Thomas Adams.*

Verse 1.—" *They are corrupt, they have done abominable things : there is none that doeth good.*" " Men," says Bernard, " because they are *corrupt* in their minds, become *abominable* in their doings : *corrupt* before God, *abominable* before men. There are three sorts of men of which none doeth good. There are those who neither understand nor seek God, and they are the dead : there are others who understand him, but seek him not, and they are the wicked. There are others that seek him but understand him not, and they are the fools." " O God," cries a writer of the middle ages, " how many are here at this day who, under the name of Christianity, worship idols, and are abominable both to thee and to men ! For every man worships that which he most loves. The proud man bows down before the idol of worldly power ; the covetous man before the idol of money ; the adulterer before the idol of beauty ; and so of the rest." And of such, saith the apostle, " They profess that they know God, but in works deny him, being *abominable* and disobedient, and unto every good work reprobate." Titus i. 16. " *There is none that doeth good.*" Notice how Paul avails himself of this testimony of the psalmist, among those which he heaps together in the third chapter of the epistle to the Romans, where he is proving concerning " both Jews and Gentiles, that they are all under sin." Rom. iii. 9.—*John Mason Neale, in loc.*

Verse 1.—The argument of my text is the atheist's divinity, the brief of his belief couched all in one article, and that negative too, clean contrary to the fashion of all creeds, " *There is no God.*" The article but one ; but so many absurdities tied to the train of it, and itself so irreligious, so prodigiously profane, that he dares not speak it out, but saith it softly to himself, in secret, " *in his heart.*" So the text yields these three points ; Who is he ? A " *fool.*" What he saith, " *no God.*" How he speaks it, " *in his heart.*" A fool, his bolt, and his draught. I will speak of them severally. . . . . . There is a child in years, and there is a child in manners, *ætate et moribus,* saith Aristotle. So there is a fool ; for fools and children both are called νηπιοι. There is a fool in wit, and there is a fool in life ; *stultus in scientia, et stultus in conscientia,* a witless and a graceless fool. The latter is worthy of the title as the first ; both void of reason ; not of the faculty but of the use. Yea, the latter fool is indeed the more kindly of the twain ; for the sot would use his reason if he could ; the sinner will not though he may. It is not the natural, but the moral fool that David means, the wicked and ungracious person, for so is the sense of the original term. . . . . . It is time we leave the person, and come unto the act. What hath this fool done ? Surely nothing ; he hath only *said*. What hath he *said ?* Nay, nothing either ; he hath only *thought :* for to *say in heart*, is but to *think*. There are two sorts of saying in the Scripture, one meant indeed so properly, the other but in hope ; one by word of mouth, the other by thought of heart. You see the psalmist means here the second sort. The bolt the fool here shoots is atheism : he makes no noise at the loss of it, as bowmen use ; he draws and delivers closely, and stilly, out of sight, and without sound : he saith " *God is not*," but " *in heart.*" The heart hath a mouth ; *intus est os cordis*, saith Augustine. God, saith Cyprian, is *cordis auditor*, he hears the heart ; then be-like it hath some speech. When God said to Moses, *quare clamas ?* why criest thou ? we find no words he uttered : *silens auditur*, saith Gregory, he is heard through saying nothing. There is a silent speech (Psalm iv. 4), " Commune with your own heart," saith David, " and be still." Speech is not the heart's action, no more than meditation is the mouth's. But sometimes the heart and mouth exchange offices ; *lingua mea meditabitur*, saith David. Psalm xxxv. 28. There is *lingua meditans*, a musing tongue ; here is *cor loquens*, a speaking heart. And to say the truth, the philosopher saith well, it is the heart doth all things, *mens videt, mens audit, mens loquitur*. It is the heart that speaks, the tongue is but the instrument to give the sound. It is but the heart's echo to repeat the words after it. Except when the tongue doth run before the wit, the heart doth dictate to the mouth ; it suggests what it shall say. The heart is the soul's herald : look what she will have proclaimed, the heart reads it, and the mouth cries it. The tongue saith nought but what the heart saith first. Nay, in very deed, the truest and kindest speech is the heart's. The tongue and lips are Jesuits, they lease, and lie, and use equivocations : flattery, or fear, or other by-respect, other wry respect adulterate their words. But the heart speaks as it means, worth twenty mouths, if it could speak audibly.—*Richard Clerke, D.D.*, ——1634 *(one of the translators of our English Bible)*.

Verses 1, 4.—The Scripture gives this as a cause of the notorious courses of wicked men, that " God is not in all their thoughts." Psalm x. 4. They forget there is a God of vengeance and a day of reckoning. " *The fool* " would needs enforce upon his heart, that " *there is no God*," and what follows : " *Corrupt they are, there is none doth good : they eat up my people as bread*," etc. They make no more bones of devouring men and their estates, than they make con-science of eating a piece of bread. What a wretched condition hath sin brought man unto, that the great God who " filleth heaven and earth" (Jer. xxiii. 24) should yet have no place in the heart which he hath especially made for him-self ! The sun is not so clear as this truth, that God is, for all things in the world are because God is. If he were not, nothing could be. It is from him that wicked men have that strength they have to commit sin, therefore sin proceeds from atheism, especially these plotting sins ; for if God were more thought on, he would take off the soul from sinful contrivings, and fix it upon himself.—*Richard Sibbes*.

Verse 2.—" *To see if there were any that did understand . . seek God.*" None seek him aright, and as he ought to be sought, nor can do while they live in sin : for men in seeking God fail in many things : as, First, men seek him not for himself. Secondly, they seek him not alone, but other things with him. Thirdly, they seek other things before him, as worldlings do. Fourthly, they seek him coldly or carelessly. Fifthly, they seek him inconstantly ; example of Judas and Demas. Sixthly, they seek him not in his word, as heretics do. Seventhly, they seek him not in all his word, as hypocrites do. Lastly, they seek him not seasonably and timely, as profane, impenitent sinners do ; have no care to depend upon God's word, but follow their own lusts and fashions of this world.—*Thomas Wilson*, 1653.

Verses 2, 3.—What was the issue of God's so looking upon men ? " *They are all gone aside,*" that is, from him and his ways ; " *They are altogether become filthy ;*" their practices are such as make them stink ; " *There is none that doeth good, no not one ;*" of so many millions of men as are upon the earth, there is not one doeth good.   There were men of excellent parts then in the world, men of soul, but not one of them did know God, or seek after God : Paul therefore hath laid it down for a universal maxim, that the animal, natural, or intellectual man, receives not the things of the Spirit of God, for they are foolishness unto him, and so are rejected by him.—*William Greenhill.*

Verse 3.—The ungodly are " vile" persons (Nah. i. 14).   " I will make thy grave ; for thou art vile."   Sin makes men base, it blots their name, it taints their blood : " *They are altogether become filthy ;*" in the Hebrew it is, they are become stinking.   Call wicked men ever so bad, you cannot call them out of their name ; they are " swine" (Matt. vii. 6) ; " vipers" (Matt. iii. 7) ; " devils" (John vi. 70).   The wicked are the dross and refuse (Psa. cxix. 119) ; and heaven is too pure to have any dross mingle with it.—*Thomas Watson.*

Verse 3.—"*Altogether become filthy.*"   Thus the Roman satirist describes his own age :

> " Nothing is left, nothing, for future times
> To add to the full catalogue of crimes ;
> The baffled sons must feel the same desires,
> And act the same mad follies as their sires,
> Vice has attained its zenith."
>
> *Juvenal, Sat.* 1.

Verse 3.—" *There is none that doeth good, no, not one.*"   Origen maketh a question, how it could be said that there was none, neither among the Jews nor Gentiles, that did any good ; seeing there were many among them which did clothe the naked, feed the hungry, and did other good things : he hereunto maketh this answer :—That like as one that layeth a foundation, and buildeth upon it a wall or two, yet cannot be said to have built a house till he have finished it ; so although those might do some good things, yet they attained not unto perfect goodness, which was only to be found in Christ.   But this is not the apostle's meaning only to exclude men from the perfection of justice ; for even the faithful and believers were short of that perfection which is required ; he therefore showeth what men are by nature, all under sin and in the same state of damnation, without grace and faith in Christ : if any perform any good work, either it is of grace, and so not of themselves, or if they did it by the light of nature, they did it not as they ought, and so it was far from a good work indeed.—*Andrew Willet* (1562—1621), *on Romans* iii. 10.

Verse 4.—" *Have the workers of iniquity no knowledge ?*"   Men's ignorance is the reason why they fear not what they should fear.   Why is it that the ungodly fear not sin ?   Oh, it's because they know it not.   " *Have the workers of iniquity no knowledge ?*"   Sure enough they have none, for " *they eat up my people as they eat bread ;*" such morsels would scald their mouths, they would not dare to be such persecutors and destroyers of the people of God ; they would be afraid to touch them if they did but know what they did.—*Richard Alleine.*

Verse 4.—" *Who eat up my people as they eat bread.*"   That is, *quotidiè*, daily, saith Austin ; as duly as they eat bread ; or, with the same eagerness and voracity.   These man-eaters, these Λαοβόροι, cruel cannibals, make no more conscience to undo a poor man, than to eat a good meal when they are hungry.   Like pickerels in a pond, or sharks in the sea, they devour the poorer, as those do the lesser fishes ; and that many times with a plausible, invisible consumption ; as the usurer, who, like the ostrich, can digest any metal ; but especially money.—*John Trapp.*

Verse 4.—" *Who eat up my people as they eat bread.*"   Oh, how few consult and believe the Scriptures setting forth the enmity of wicked men against God's people !   The Scripture tells us " *they eat up God's people as bread,*" which implies a strange inclination in them to devour the saints, and that they take as great delight therein as a hungry man in eating, and that it is natural to them to molest them. The Scripture compares them, for their hateful qualities, to the lions and bears, to foxes for subtlety, to wild bulls, to greedy swine, to scorpions, to briers and thorns (grievous and vexing things). The Scripture represents them as industrious and unwearied in their bloody enterprises, they cannot sleep without doing mischief. Herodias had rather have the blood of a saint than half a kingdom. Haman would pay a great fine to the king that the scattered Jews (who keep not the king's laws) may be cut off. Wicked men will run the hazard of damning their own souls, rather than not fling a dagger at the apple of God's eye. Though they know what one word—aha!—cost, yet they will break through all natural, civil, and moral obligations, to ruin God's people. The Holy Ghost calls them "implacable" men, fierce and headstrong; they are like the hot oven for fury, like the sea for boundless rage; yet "who hath believed" this Scripture "report?" Did we believe what enemies all wicked men are unto all saints, we should not lean to our own prudence and discretion to secure us from any danger by these men; we would get an ark to secure us from the deluge of their wrath; if at any time we be cast among them and delivered, we would bless God with the three children, that the hot fiery oven did not consume us; we would not wonder when we hear of any of their barbarous cruelty, but rather wonder at God's restraining them every day; we would be suspicious of receiving hurt when cast among light and frothy companions; we would shun their company as we do lions and scorpions; we would never commit any trust or secret into their hands; we would not be light-hearted whilst in their society; we would not rely on their promises any more than we would on the promise of the devil, their father; we would long for heaven, to be delivered from "the tents of Kedar;" we would not count any of the saints secured from danger, though related to any great wicked man; we would not twist ourselves with them by matching ourselves or children to these sons and daughters of Belial; neither would we make choice of devils to be our servants.—*Lewis Stuckley.*

Verse 4.—This is an evil world. It hates the people of God. "Because ye are not of the world, therefore the world hateth you." John xv. 19. Haman's hatred was against the whole seed of the Jews. When you can find a serpent without a sting, or a leopard without spots, then may you expect to find a wicked world without hatred to the saints. Piety is the target which is aimed at. "They are mine adversaries because I follow the thing that good is." Psalm xxxviii. 20. The world pretends to hate the godly for something else, but the ground of the quarrel is holiness. The world's hatred is implacable: anger may be reconciled, hatred cannot. You may as soon reconcile heaven and hell as the two seeds. If the world hated Christ, no wonder that it hates us. "The world hated me before it hated you." John xv. 18. Why should any hate Christ? This blessed Dove had no gall, this rose of Sharon did send forth a most sweet perfume; but this shows the world's baseness, it is a Christ-hating and a *saint-eating* world.—*Thomas Watson.*

Verse 5.—"*There were they in great fear.*" That we may not mistake the meaning of the point, we must understand that this faintheartedness and cowardliness doth not always come upon presumptuous sinners when they behold imminent dangers, for though none of them have true courage and fortitude, yet many of them have a kind of desperate stoutness and resolution when they do, as it were, see death present before their faces; which proceedeth from a kind of deadness, that is upon their hearts, and a brawniness that hath overgrown their consciences to their greater condemnation. But when it pleaseth the Lord to waken them out of the dead slumber, and to set the worm of conscience awork within them, then this doctrine holdeth true without any exception, that the boldest sinners prove at length the basest cowards: and they that have been most audacious in adventuring upon the most mischievous evils, do become of

13

all others most timorous when God's revenging hand seizeth upon them for the same.—*John Dod*, 1547—1645.

Verse 5.—" *God is in the generation of the righteous ;*" that is, he favours that generation or sort of men ; God is in all generations, but such he delights in most : the wicked have cause enough to fear those in whom God delights.—*Joseph Caryl.*

Verse 5.—The King of Glory cannot come into the heart (as he is said to come into the hearts of his people as such ; Psalm xxiv. 9, 10), but some glory of himself will appear ; and as God doth accompany the word with majesty because it is his word, so he doth accompany his own children, and their ways, with majesty, yea, even in their greatest debasements. As when Stephen was brought before the council, as a prisoner at the bar for his life, then God manifested his presence to him, for it is said, " his face shone as the face of an angel of God " (Acts vi. 15) ; in a proportionable manner it is ordinarily true what Solomon says of all righteous men, " A man's wisdom makes his face to shine." Eccles. viii. 1. Thus Peter also speaks (1 Peter iv. 14) : " If you be reproached for the name of Christ, happy are you, for the Spirit," not only of God, or of grace, but " of glory, resteth upon you." And so in the martyrs ; their innocency, and carriage, and godly behaviour, what majesty had it with it ! What an amiableness in the sight of the people, which daunted, dashed, and confounded their most wretched oppressors ; so that although the wicked persecutors " *did eat up God's people as bread* " (verse 4), yet it is added that they were in great fear upon this very account, that " *God is in the generation of the just.*" Verse 5. God stands, as it were, astonished at their dealings : " *Have the workers of iniquity no knowledge,*" (so in the words afore) " *that eat up my people as bread,*" and make no more ado of it than a man doth that heartily eats of his meat ? They seem to do thus, they would carry it and bear it out ; but for all that they are in great fear whilst they do thus, and God strikes their hearts with terror then when they most insult. Why ? For, " *God is in the generation of, or dwelleth in the just,*" and God gives often some glimmerings, hints, and warnings to the wicked (such as Pilate had concerning Christ), that his people are righteous. And this you may see in Phil. i. 28 : " And in nothing terrified by your adversaries, which is to them an evident token of perdition, but to you of salvation, and that of God." In that latter passage, I observe that an assurance of salvation, and a spirit of terror, and that of God, is given to either. In the Old Testament it is recorded of David (1 Sam. xviii. 12), that although Saul hated him (verse 9), and sought to destroy him (verses 10, 11), " yet Saul was afraid of David, because the Lord was with him, and was departed from Saul ;" which is the reason in hand. God manifested his presence in David, and struck Saul's conscience with his godly and wise carriage, and that made him afraid.—*Thomas Goodwin.*

Verse 6.—" *Ye have shamed the counsel of the poor, because the Lord is his refuge.*" In the fifty-third Psalm it is, " Thou hast put them to shame, because God hath despised them." Of course, the allusion is totally different in each ; in this Psalm it is the indignant remonstrance of the Psalmist with " the workers of iniquity" for undervaluing and putting God's poor to shame ; the other affirms the final shame and confusion of the ungodly, and the contempt in which the Lord holds them. In either case it sweetly illustrates God's care of his poor, not merely the poor in spirit, but literally the poor and lowly ones, the oppressed and the injured. It is this character of God which is so conspicuously delineated in his word. We may look through all the Shasters and Vedas of the Hindoo, the Koran of the Mahometan, the legislation of the Greek, and the code of the Roman, aye, and the Talmud of the Jew, the bitterest of all ; and not in one single line or page shall we find a vestige or trace of that tenderness, compassion, or sympathy for the wrongs, and oppressions, and trials, and sorrows of God's poor, which the Christian's Bible evidences in almost every page. *Barton Bouchier.*

Verse 6.—" *Ye have shamed.*" Every fool that saith in his heart there is no God, hath out of the same quiver a bolt to shoot at goodness. Barren Michal hath too many sons, who, like their mother, jeer at holy David.—*John Trapp.*

Verse 6.—" *Ye have shamed,*" saith he, "*the counsel of the poor.*" There is nothing that wicked men do so despise as the making God a refuge—nothing which they scorn in their hearts like it. " They shame it," saith he, " It is a thing to be cast out of all consideration. The wise man trusts in his wisdom, the strong man in his strength, the rich man in his riches ; but this trusting in God is the foolishest thing in the world." The reasons of it are—1. They know not God ; and it is a foolish thing to trust one knows not whom. 2. They are enemies to God, and God is their enemy ; and they account it a foolish thing to trust their enemy. 3. They know not the way of God's assistance and help. And—4. They seek for such help, such assistance, such supplies, as God will not give ; to be delivered, to serve their lusts ; to be preserved, to execute their rage, filthiness, and folly. They have no other design or end of these things ; and God will give none of them. And it is a foolish thing in any man to trust God to be preserved in sin. It is true, their folly is their wisdom, considering their state and condition. It is a folly to trust in God to live in sin, and despise the counsel of the poor.—*John Owen.*

Verse 6.—" *Ye have made a mock of the counsel of the poor :*" and why ? " *because the Lord is his trust.*" This is the very true cause, whatsoever other pretences there be. Whence observe this doctrine ; that true godliness is that which breeds the quarrel between God's children and the wicked. Ungodly men may say what they list, as, namely, that they hate and dislike them for that they are proud and saucy in meddling with their betters ; for that they are so scornful and disdainful towards their neighbours ; for that they are malcontent, and turbulent, and I know not what ; but the true reason is yielded by the Lord in this place, to wit, because they make him their stay and their confidence, and will not depend upon lying vanities as the men of the world do.—*John Dod.*

Verse 6.—" *The Lord is his refuge.*"—Be persuaded actually to hide yourselves with Jesus Christ. To have a hiding-place and not to use it, is as bad as to want one ; fly to Christ ; run into the holes of this Rock.—*Ralph Robinson,* 1656.

Verse 7.—" *O that the salvation,*" etc. Like as when we be in quiet, we do pray either nothing at all, or very coldly unto God ; so in adversity and trouble, our spirit is stirred up and enkindled to prayer, whereof we do find examples everywhere in the Psalms of David ; so that affliction is as it were the sauce of prayer, as hunger is unto meat. Truly their prayer is usually unsavoury who are without afflictions, and many of them do not pray truly, but do rather counterfeit a prayer, or pray for custom.—*Wolfgang Musculus,* 1497—1563.

Verse 7.—" *Out of Zion.*" Zion, the church is no Saviour, neither dare we trust in her ministers or ordinances, and yet salvation comes to men through her. The hungry multitudes are fed by the hands of the disciples, who delight to act as the servitors of the gospel feast. Zion becomes the site of the fountain of healing waters which shall flow east and west till all nations drink thereat. What a reason for maintaining in the utmost purity and energy all the works of the church of the living God !—*C. H. S.*

Verse 7.—" *When the Lord turneth the captivity of his people : then shall Jacob rejoice, and Israel shall be glad.*"—Notice that by Israel we are to understand those other sheep which the Lord has that are not of this fold, but which he must also bring, that they may hear his voice. For it is Israel, not Judah ; Sion, not Jerusalem. " When the Lord turneth the captivity of his people." " Then," as it is in the parallel passage, " *were we like unto them that dream.*" A glorious dream indeed, in which, fancy what we may, the half of the beauty, the half of the splendour, will not be reached by our imagination. " *The captivity*" of our souls to the law of concupiscence, of our bodies to the law of death ; the captivity of our senses to fear ; the captivity, the conclusion of which is so

beautifully expressed by one of our greatest poets :—namely, *Giles Fletcher*
(1588—1623), *in his " Christ's Triumph over Death."*

> " No sorrow now hangs clouding on their brow;
> No bloodless malady impales their face ;
> No age drops on their hairs his silver snow ;
> No nakedness their bodies doth embase ;
> No poverty themselves and theirs disgrace;
> No fear of death the joy of life devours ;
> No unchaste sleep their precious time deflowers ;
> No loss, no grief, no change, wait on their winged hours."

John Mason Neale, in loc.

HINTS TO THE VILLAGE PREACHER.

Verse 1 (*first clause*).—The folly of atheism.

Verse 1.—Atheism of the heart.—*Jamieson's Sermons on the Heart.*

Verse 1 (*whole verse*).—Describe : I. The creed of the fool. II. The fool who holds the creed : or thus, Atheism. I. Its source : *" the heart."* II. Its creed : *" no God."* III. Its fruits : *" corrupt,"* etc.

Verse 1.—I. The great source of sin—alienation from God. II. Its place of dominion—the heart. III. Its effect upon the intellect—makes man a fool. IV. Its manifestations in the life—acts of commission and omission.

Verse 1 (*last clause*).—The lantern of Diogenes. Hold it up upon all classes, and denounce their sins.

Verse 2.—I. Condescending search. II. Favoured subjects. III. Generous intentions.

Verse 2.—What God looks for, and what we should look for. Men usually are quick to see things congruous to their own character.

Verses 2, 3.—God's search for a naturally good man ; the result ; lessons to be learned therefrom.

Verse 3.—Total depravity of the race.

Verse 4.—*" Have all the workers of iniquity no knowledge?"* If men rightly knew God, his law, the evil of sin, the torment of hell, and other great truths, would they sin as they do ? Or if they know these and yet continue in their iniquities, how guilty and foolish they are ! Answer the question both positively and negatively, and it supplies material for a searching discourse.

Verse 4 (*first clause*).—The crying sin of transgressing against light and knowledge.

Verse 4 (*last clause*).—Absence of prayer, a sure mark of a graceless state.

Verse 5.—The foolish fears of those who have no fear of God.

Verse 5.—The Lord's nearness to the righteous, its consequences to the persecutor, and its encouragement to saints.

Verse 6.—The wisdom of making the Lord our refuge.—*John Owen.*

Verse 6.—Describe, I. The poor man here intended. II. His counsel. III. His reproach. IV. His refuge.

Verse 6.—Trust in God, a theme for mockery to fools only. Show its wisdom.

Verse 7.—Longings for the Advent.

Verse 7.—*" Out of Zion."* The church, the channel of blessings to men.

Verse 7.—Discourse to promote revival. I. Frequent condition of the church, " captivity." II. Means of revival—the Lord's coming in grace. III. Consequences, " rejoice," " be glad."

Verse 7.—Captivity of soul. What it is. How provided for. How accomplished. With what results.

PSALM XV.

SUBJECT, &c.—*This Psalm of David bears no dedicatory title at all indicative of the occasion upon which it was written, but it is exceedingly probable that, together with the twenty-fourth Psalm, to which it bears a striking resemblance, its composition was in some way connected with the removal of the ark to the holy hill of Zion. Who should attend upon the ark was a matter of no small consequence, for because unauthorized persons had intruded into the office, David was unable on the first occasion to complete his purpose of bringing the ark to Zion. On the second attempt he is more careful, not only to allot the work of carrying the ark to the divinely appointed Levites* (1 Chron. xv. 2), *but also to leave it in charge of the man whose house the Lord had blessed, even Obed-edom, who, with his many sons, ministered in the house of the Lord.* (1 Chron. xxvi. 8, 12.) *Spiritually we have here a description of the man who is a child at home in the Church of God on earth, and who will dwell in the house of the Lord for ever above. He is primarily Jesus, the perfect man, and in him all who through grace are conformed to his image.*

DIVISION.—*The first verse asks the question; the rest of the verses answer it. We will call the Psalm* THE QUESTION AND ANSWER.

EXPOSITION.

L ORD, who shall abide in thy tabernacle? who shall dwell in thy holy hill?

1.—THE QUESTION. *Jehovah.* Thou high and holy One, who shall be permitted to have fellowship with thee? The heavens are not pure in thy sight, and thou chargedst thine angels with folly, who then of mortal mould shall dwell with thee, thou dread consuming fire? A sense of the glory of the Lord and of the holiness which becomes his house, his service, and his attendants, excites the humble mind to ask the solemn question before us. Where angels bow with veiled faces, how shall man be able to worship at all? The unthinking many imagine it to be a very easy matter to approach the Most High, and when professedly engaged in his worship they have no questionings of heart as to their fitness for it; but truly humbled souls often shrink under a sense of utter unworthiness, and would not dare to approach the throne of the God of holiness if it were not for him, our Lord, our Advocate, who can abide in the heavenly temple, because his righteousness endureth for ever. " *Who shall abide in thy tabernacle?*" Who shall be admitted to be one of the household of God, to sojourn under his roof and enjoy communion with himself? " *Who shall dwell in thy holy hill?*" Who shall be a citizen of Zion, and an inhabitant of the heavenly Jerusalem? The question is raised, because it is a question. All men have not this privilege, nay, even among professors there are aliens from the commonwealth, who have no secret intercourse with God. On the grounds of law no mere man can dwell with God, for there is not one upon earth who answers to the just requirements mentioned in the succeeding verses. The questions in the text are asked of the *Lord*, as if none but the Infinite Mind could answer them so as to satisfy the unquiet conscience. We must know from the Lord of the tabernacle what are the qualifications for his service, and when we have been taught of him, we shall clearly see that only our spotless Lord Jesus, and those who are conformed unto his image, can ever stand with acceptance before the Majesty on high.

Impertinent curiosity frequently desires to know who and how many shall be saved; if those who thus ask the question, " Who shall dwell in thy holy hill?" would make it a soul-searching enquiry in reference to themselves they would act much more wisely. Members of the visible church, which is God's tabernacle of worship, and hill of eminence, should diligently see to it, that they have the preparation of heart which fits them to be inmates of the house of God. Without the wedding-dress of righteousness in Christ Jesus, we have no right to sit at the banquet of communion. Without uprightness of walk we are not fit for the imperfect church on earth, and certainly we must not hope to enter the perfect church above.

2 He that walketh uprightly, and worketh righteousness, and speaketh the truth in his heart.

3 *He that* backbiteth not with his tongue, nor doeth evil to his neighbour, nor taketh up a reproach against his neighbour.

4 In whose eyes a vile person is contemned ; but he honoureth them that fear the LORD. *He that* sweareth to *his own* hurt, and changeth not.

5 *He that* putteth not out his money to usury, nor taketh reward against the innocent. He that doeth these *things* shall never be moved.

2.—THE ANSWER. The Lord in answer to the question informs us by his Holy Spirit of the character of the man who alone can dwell in his holy hill. In perfection this holiness is found only in the Man of Sorrows, but in a measure it is wrought in all his people by the Holy Ghost. Faith and the graces of the Spirit are not mentioned, because this is a description of outward character, and where fruits are found the root may not be seen, but it is surely there. Observe the accepted man's *walk, work, and word.* " *He that walketh uprightly,*" he keeps himself erect as those do who traverse high ropes ; if they lean on one side over they must go, or as those who carry precious but fragile ware in baskets on their heads, who lose all if they lose their perpendicular. True believers do not cringe as flatterers, wriggle as serpents, bend double as earth-grubbers, or crook on one side as those who have sinister aims ; they have the strong backbone of the vital principle of grace within, and being themselves upright, they are able to walk uprightly. Walking is of far more importance than talking. He only is right who is *up*right in walk and *down*right in honesty. " *And worketh righteousness.*" His faith shows itself by good works, and therefore is no dead faith. God's house is a hive for workers, not a nest for drones. Those who rejoice that everything is done for them by another, even the Lord Jesus, and therefore hate legality, are the best doers in the world upon gospel principles. If we are not positively serving the Lord, and doing his holy will to the best of our power, we may seriously debate our interest in divine things, for trees which bear no fruit must be hewn down and cast into the fire. " *And speaketh the truth in his heart.*" The fool in the last psalm spoke falsely in his heart ; observe both here and elsewhere in the two psalms, the striking contrast. Saints not only desire to love and speak truth with their lips, but they seek to be true within ; they will not lie even in the closet of their hearts, for God is there to listen ; they scorn double meanings, evasions, equivocations, white lies, flatteries, and deceptions. Though truths, like roses, have thorns about them, good men wear them in their bosoms. Our heart must be the sanctuary and refuge of truth, should it be banished from all the world beside, and hunted from among men ; at all risk we must entertain the angel of truth, for truth is God's daughter. We must be careful that the heart is really fixed and settled in principle, for tenderness of conscience towards truthfulness, like the bloom on a peach, needs gentle handling, and once lost it were hard to regain it. Jesus was the mirror of sincerity and holiness. Oh, to be more and more fashioned after his similitude !

3. After the positive comes the negative. " *He that backbiteth not with his tongue.*" There is a sinful way of backbiting with the heart when we think too hardly of a neighbour, but it is the tongue which does the mischief. Some men's tongues bite more than their teeth. The tongue is not steel, but it cuts, and its

wounds are very hard to heal; its worst wounds are not with its edge to our face, but with its back when our head is turned. Under the law, a night hawk was an unclean bird, and its human image is abominable everywhere. All slanderers are the devil's bellows to blow up contention, but those are the worst which blow at the back of the fire. " *Nor doeth evil to his neighbour.*" He who bridles his tongue will not give a licence to his hand. Loving our neighbour as ourselves will make us jealous of his good name, careful not to injure his estate, or by ill example to corrupt his character. " *Nor taketh up a reproach against his neighbour.*" He is a fool if not a knave who picks up stolen goods and harbours them ; in slander as well as robbery, the receiver is as bad as the thief. If there were no gratified hearers of ill reports, there would be an end of the trade of spreading them. Trapp says, that " the tale-bearer carrieth the devil in his tongue, and the tale-hearer carries the devil in his ear." The original may be translated, " endureth ;" implying that it is a sin to endure or tolerate tale-bearers. " Show that man out !" we should say of a drunkard, yet it is very questionable if his unmannerly behaviour will do us so much mischief as the tale-bearer's insinuating story. " Call for a policeman !" we say if we see a thief at his business ; ought we to feel no indignation when we hear a gossip at her work ? Mad dog ! Mad dog ! ! is a terrible hue and cry, but there are few curs whose bite is so dangerous as a busybody's tongue. Fire ! fire ! ! is an alarming note, but the tale bearer's tongue is set on fire of hell, and those who indulge it had better mend their manners, or they may find that there is fire in hell for unbridled tongues. Our Lord spake evil of no man, but breathed a prayer for his foes ; we must be like him, or we shall never be with him.

4. " *In whose eyes a vile person is contemned ; but he honoureth them that fear the Lord.*" We must be as honest in paying respect as in paying our bills. Honour to whom honour is due. To all good men we owe a debt of honour, and we have no right to hand over what is their due to vile persons who happen to be in high places. When bad men are in office, it is our duty to respect the office, but we cannot so violate our consciences as to do otherwise than contemn the men ; and on the other hand, when true saints are in poverty and distress, we must sympathize with their afflictions and honour the men none the less. We may honour the roughest cabinet for the sake of the jewels, but we must not prize false gems because of their setting. A sinner in a gold chain and silken robes is no more to be compared with a saint in rags than a rushlight in a silver candlestick with the sun behind a cloud. The proverb says, that " ugly women, finely dressed, are the uglier for it," and so mean men in high estate are the more mean because of it. " *He that sweareth to his own hurt, and changeth not.*" Scriptural saints under the New Testament rule " swear not at all," but their word is as good as an oath : those men of God who think it right to swear, are careful and prayerful lest they should even seem to overshoot the mark. When engagements have been entered into which turn out to be unprofitable, " the saints are men of honour still." Our blessed Surety swore to his own hurt, but how gloriously he stood to his suretyship ! what a comfort to us that he changeth not, and what an example to us to be scrupulously and precisely exact in fulfilling our covenants with others ! The most far-seeing trader may enter into engagements which turn out to be serious losses, but whatever else he loses, if he keeps his honour, his losses will be bearable ; if that be lost all is lost.

5. " *He that putteth not out his money to usury.*" Usury was and is hateful both to God and man. That a lender should share with the borrower in gains made by his money is most fitting and proper ; but that the man of property should eat up the poor wretch who unfortunately obtained a loan of him is abominable. Those who grind poor tradesmen, needy widows, and such like, by charging them interest at intolerable rates, will find that their gold and their silver are cankered. The man who shall ascend into the hill of the Lord must shake off this sin as Paul shook the viper into the fire. " *Nor taketh reward against the innocent.*" Bribery is a sin both in the giver and the receiver. It was frequently practised in Eastern courts of justice ; that form of it is now

under our excellent judges almost an unheard-of thing ; yet the sin survives in various forms, which the reader needs not that we should mention ; and under every shape it is loathsome to the true man of God. He remembers that Jesus instead of taking reward against the innocent died for the guilty.

5. *" He that doeth these things shall never be moved."* No storm shall tear him from his foundations, drag him from his anchorage, or uproot him from his place. Like the Lord Jesus, whose dominion is everlasting, the true Christian shall never lose his crown. He shall not only be *on* Zion, but *like* Zion, fixed and firm. He shall dwell in the tabernacle of the Most High, and neither death nor judgment shall remove him from his place of privilege and blessedness.

Let us betake ourselves to prayer and self-examination, for this Psalm is as fire for the gold, and as a furnace for silver. Can we endure its testing power ?

EXPLANATORY NOTES AND QUAINT SAYINGS.

Verse 1.—*" Lord, who shall abide in thy tabernacle ?"*—In that the church of Christ upon earth is a *" tabernacle,"* we may note, that neither the church itself, nor the members of it, have any fixed or firm seat of habitation in this world : " Arise, depart, for this is not your rest." Micah ii. 10. " Here have we no continuing city, but we seek one to come." Heb. xiii. 14. God's tabernacle, being a movable temple, wandered up and down, sometimes in the desert, sometimes in Shiloh, sometimes among the Philistines, sometimes in Kirjath-jearim, and never found any settled place till it was translated into the mountain of God : even so the church of God wandereth as a straggler and a stranger in the wilderness of this world, being destitute, tormented, and afflicted on every side, persecuted from this city to that, and never enjoying any constant habitation of sound and sure rest until it be translated unto *" God's holy hill."* The verb נור *gur* (as the learned in Hebrew note) signifying to dwell as a stranger, or a sojourner, imports that a citizen of heaven is a pilgrim on earth. . . . . In that the church is a *tabernacle,* we may see that it is not a fort, compassed about with any strong walls, armed with any human forces ; and yet such as keep within her are defended from heat of sun, and hurt of storms. Her strength is not here, but from above, for Christ her Head is in all her troubles a present help, a refuge against the tempest, a shadow against the heat. Isa. xxv. 4. The church on earth is indeed a *tabernacle,* but it is *God's* tabernacle, wherein he dwelleth as in his house ; " Lord, who shall abide in *thy* tabernacle ?" for to this end the Lord commanded the tabernacle to be made, that he might dwell among them ; and again, whereas he promised by Moses to set his tabernacle among them, the blessed apostle construeth it of his dwelling among them. 2 Cor. vi. 16. " You are," saith he, " the temple of the living God, as God hath said, I will dwell in them, and walk in them." To the same purpose, God is said elsewhere to dwell in Sion, and to walk in the midst of the seven golden candlesticks, that is, in the midst of the seven churches, in the midst of his city (Psa. xlvi. 5), in the midst of his people. Isa. xii. 6.—*John Boys, D.D., Dean of Canterbury,* 1571—1625.

Verse 1.—*" Lord, who shall abide,"* etc. If David, a man endued with an excellent and divine spirit, one in whom singular wisdom, rare knowledge, and deep understanding of hidden secrets appeared, who being taught of God in heavenly things, far surpassed and exceeded in wisdom all his teachers and counsellors, did notwithstanding desire to know the sheep from the goats, the good from the bad, the saints from the hypocrites, the true worshippers of God from dissemblers, the true inhabitants of the holy tabernacle from the intruders of the wicked, lest therein he should be deceived ; how great cause have we, in whom neither the like spirit, neither such wisdom, nor equal knowledge, nor comparable understanding, by many degrees appeareth, to fear our own weakness, to doubt of our own judgments, to confess our own infirmity, and to suspect the subtle sleights and coloured pretences of men : and for further knowledge in hidden, deep, and secret things, with David to demand and ask this question, "Lord, who shall abide in thy tabernacle? who shall dwell in thy holy hill?" . . . . Where David saith, "Who shall abide in thy holy hill?" he giveth us to understand that there is no true and sound rest but in the *holy hill of the Lord*, which is the church. Then the wicked and ungodly which are not of God's house, of his *holy hill*, of the church, have no quiet, rest, nor sound peace ; but they are in continual perplexity, continual torment, continual disquietness of their minds.—*Richard Turnbull*, 1606.

Verse 1.—"*Abide in thy tabernacle*," etc. The worshippers in the outer court only will get their eternal abode without among the dogs, sorcerers, etc.; but they that shall be inhabitants of heaven, come further in, even unto the tabernacle itself : their souls are fed at his table, they find the smell of his garments as of myrrh, aloes, and cassia ; and if they miss it at any time, it is the grief of their souls, and they are never at rest till they recover it again.—*Thomas Boston*.

Verse 1.—"*Who shall dwell*," etc.

> " Now, who is he? Say, if ye can,
> Who *so* shall gain the firm abode?
> Pilate shall say, ' Behold the Man ! '
> And John, ' Behold the Lamb of God ! ' "
>
> *John Barclay, quoted by A. A. Bonar, in loc.*

Verse 1.—"*Holy hill*." Heaven is aptly compared to a hill, hell to a hole. Now who shall ascend unto this holy mount? None but those whom this mount comes down unto, that have sweet communion with God in this life present, whose conversation is in heaven, though their commoration be for awhile upon earth, who do here eat, and drink, and sleep, eternal life.—*John Trapp*.

Verses 1, 2.—The disguising and counterfeiting of hypocrites in all ages, occasioned haply this query : for, as Paul speaks, "all are not Israel that are of Israel," a great many living in the church are not of the church, according to that of the doctors upon this place, *multi sunt corpore qui non sunt fide, multi nomine qui non sunt nomine*. Wherefore, David, here perceiving that sundry people were shuffled into God's tabernacle like goats among the sheep, and tares among the corn, being Jews outwardly, but not inwardly, deceiving others often, and, sometimes, themselves also, with a bare profession of religion, and false opinion of true piety, cometh unto God (as to the searcher and trier of the hearts of men, acquainted with all secrets, and best understanding who are his own), saying unto him, O Lord, forsomuch as there is so much unsoundness and hypocrisy reigning among those that dwell in thy tabernacle, professing thy word, and frequenting the places of thy worship ; I beseech thee most humbly, to declare to thy people some tokens and cognizances by which a true subject of thy knigdom may be discerned from the children of this world. Here then, observe, that an external profession of faith, and outward communion with the church of God, is not sufficient unto salvation, unless we lead an incorrupt life correspondent to the same, doing the thing which is right, and speaking the truth in our heart. And, therefore, the silly Papist is exceedingly deceived in relying so much upon the church's outside, to wit, upon the succession of Roman bishops, upon the multitudes of Roman Catholics, upon the power and pomp of the Roman synagogue, crying as the Jews in old time, " The temple of the Lord, the temple of the Lord," our church is the temple of the Lord. The carnal and careless gospeller is deceived also, placing all his religion in the formal observation of outward service, for a mere verbal Christian is a real atheist, according to that of Paul (Titus i. 16), " In word they profess that they know God, but in their works they deny him ;" and so many who seem to sojourn in God's tabernacle for a time, shall never rest upon his " *holy hill ;*" and this assertion is expressly confirmed by Christ himself : " Not every one (saith he) that saith unto me, Lord, Lord, shall enter into the kingdom of heaven ; but he that doeth the will of my Father which is in heaven. Many will say to me in that day, Lord, Lord, have we not prophesied in thy name? and in thy name have cast out devils? and in thy name done many wonderful works? And then will I profess unto them, I never knew you : depart from me, ye that work iniquity." Matt. vii. 21—23. Consider this, all ye which are Christians in lip only but not in life, making a mask of religion, or rather a very vizard, with eyes, and mouth, and nose, fairly painted and proportioned to all pretences and purposes. O think on this, all ye that forget God, he that dwelleth on high, and beholds the things here below, suffers none *to rest upon the mountain of his holiness* but such as *walk uprightly, doing that which is just, and speaking that which is true.—John Boys.*

Verse 2.—" He that walketh uprightly," etc. If neither the golden reason of excellency can move us, nor the silver reason of profit allure us, then must the iron reason of necessity enforce us to *integrity* and *uprightness of heart.* For first, such is the necessity thereof, that without integrity the best graces we seem to have are counterfeit, and, therefore, but glorious sins ; the best worship we can perform is but hypocrisy, and therefore abominable in God's sight. For uprightness is the soundness of all grace and virtues, as also of all religion and worship of God, without which they are unsound and nothing worth. And first, as touching graces, if they be not joined with uprightness of heart, they are sins under the masks or vizards of virtue, yea, as it may seem, double sins : for as Augustine saith, *Simulata æquitas est duplex iniquitas, quia et iniquitas est, et simulatio :* Feigned equity is double iniquity, both because it is iniquity, and because it is feigning.—*George Downame, D.D.,* 1604.

Verse 2.—" He that walketh uprightly." Here two questions are moved ; First. Why David describes a sound member of the church, and inheritor of heaven, by works rather than by faith, seeing the kingdom of heaven is promised unto faith, and the profession thereof also maketh one a member of the visible church? Secondly. Why, among all the fruits of faith, almost innumerable, he makes choice of those duties especially which concern our neighbours? To the first, answer may be, that in this, and in all other places of Holy Scripture, where good works are commanded or commended in any, faith is ever presupposed, according to that apostolical maxim, " Whatsoever is not of faith is sin ;" " Without me," saith our blessed Saviour, " ye can do nothing" (John xv. 5); and without faith in him it is impossible to please God (Heb. xi. 6) ; *fides est operum fomes,* as Paulinus wittily : " *Faith* (as our church speaks), *is the nest of good works ;* albeit our birds be never so fair, though haply we *do that which is right, and speak that which is true,* yet all these will be lost, except it be brought forth in a true belief." Aristides was so just in his government that he would not tread awry for any respect to friend or despite of foe. Pomponius is said to have been so true, that he never made lie himself, nor suffered a lie in other. Curtius at Rome, Menæceus at Thebes, Codrus at Athens, exposed themselves unto voluntary death, for the good of their neighbours and country : yet, because they wanted the rest of true faith in the world's Saviour, where to lay their young, we cannot (if we speak with our prophet here from God's oracle), say that they shall ever rest upon his holy hill. Another answer may be, that faith is an inward and hidden grace, and many deceive themselves and others with a feigned profession thereof, and therefore the Holy Spirit will have every man's faith to be tried and known by their fruits, and howsoever, eternal life be promised to faith, and eternal damnation be threatened against infidelity, yet the sentence of salvation and condemnation shall be pronounced according to works, as the clearest evidence of both. It is truly said, out of Bernard, that although our good works are not *causa regnandi,* yet they be *via regni,* the causeway wherein, albeit not the cause wherefore, we must ascend God's holy hill. To the second demand, why the duties immediately belonging to God, are not mentioned here, but only such as concern our brother? Answer is made, that this question is propounded of such as, living in the visible church, openly profess the faith, and would seem to be devout, hearing the word of God, and calling upon his name ; for of such as are profane atheists, and do not so much as make a semblance of holiness, there is no question to be made, for, without all doubt, there can be no resting place for such in the kingdom of heaven. Now that we may discern aright which of those that profess religion are sound, and which unsound ; the marks are not to be taken from an outward hearing of the word, or receiving of the sacraments, and much less from a formal observation of human traditions in God's tabernacle (for all these things hypocrites usually perform), but from the duties of righteousness, giving every man his due, because the touchstone of piety towards God is charity towards our brother. "Herein," saith John, "are the children of God known, and the children of the devil : whosoever doth not righteousness is not of God, neither he that loveth not his brother."—*John Boys.*

Verse 2.—There is no ascertaining the quality of a tree but by its fruits. When the wheels of a clock move within, the hands on the dial will move without. When the heart of a man is sound in conversion, then the life will be fair in profession. When the conduit is walled in, how shall we judge of the spring but by the waters which run through the pipes ?— *William Secker.*

Verse 2.—" *And worketh righteousness.*" A man must first be righteous before he can work righteousness of life. " He that doeth righteousness is righteous, even as he is righteous." 1 John iii. 7. The tree makes the fruit, not the fruit the tree ; and therefore the tree must be good before the fruit can be good. Matt. vii. 18. A righteous man may make a righteous work, but no work of an unrighteous man can make him righteous. Now we become righteous only by faith, through the righteousness of Christ imputed to us. Rom. v. 1. . . . . . Wherefore let men work as they will, if they be not true believers in Christ, they are not workers of righteousness ; and, consequently, they will not be dwellers in heaven. Ye must then close with Christ in the first place, and by faith receive the gift of imputed righteousness, or ye will never truly bear this character of a citizen of Zion. A man shall as soon force fruit out of a branch broken off from the tree and withered, as work righteousness without believing in, and uniting with Christ. These are two things by which those that hear the gospel are ruined.— *Thomas Boston.*

Verse 2.—" *Worketh righteousness.*" Jacob's ladder had stairs, upon which he saw none standing still, but all either ascending, or else descending by it. Ascend you likewise to the top of the ladder, to heaven, and there you shall hear one say, " My Father doth now work, and I work also." Whereupon Basil noteth that King David having first said, " *Lord, who shall dwell in thy tabernacle?*" adds then, not he that hath wrought righteousness heretofore, but *he that doth now work righteousness,* even as Christ saith, " My Father doth now work, and I work also."—*Thomas Playfere.*

Verse 2.—But here observe, David saith, " that *worketh* righteousness ;" not that talks about, thinks about, or hears of, righteousness ; because, " not the hearers of the law, but the doers of the law, shall be justified." What then do we owe unto others ? That which Christ saith (Matt. vii.), " Whatsoever ye would that men should do unto you, do ye also unto them," even unto your enemies : that is, to injure no one, to succour those that suffer injury, and to do good unto all men. But these things, I say, are spoken especially unto those who have respect of persons ; as if he had said, It is not because thou art a priest, nor because thou art of a religious order, nor because thou prayest much, nor because thou doest miracles, nor because thou teachest excellently, nor because thou art dignified with the title of father, nor because thou art the doer of any work (except righteousness), that thou shalt rest in the holy hill of the Lord ; for if thou be destitute of the work of righteousness, neither all thy good works, nor thy indulgences, nor thy votes and suffrages, nor thy intercessions, shall avail thee anything. Therefore, the truth is firm ; that it is the walker without spot, and the doer of righteousness, that shall rest in the tabernacle of the Lord. Yet how many are there, who build, increase and adorn churches, monasteries, altars, vessels, garments, etc., who, all the while, never so much as think of the works of righteousness ; nay, who tread righteousness under foot that they may work these their own works, and because of them hope to gain the pardon of their unrighteousness, while thousands are deceived by these means ! Hence, in the last day, Christ will say, "I was an hungered, I was thirsty, I was naked, I was in prison, I was a stranger." He will not say one word about those works which are done and admired at this day. And, on the other hand, it is of no account against thee that thou art a layman, or poor, or sick, or contemptible, or how vile soever thou art, if thou workest righteousness, thou shalt be saved. The only work that we must hope will be considered and accounted of, is the work of righteousness : all other works that either urge or allure us on under a show of godliness, are a thing of nought.—*Martin Luther.*

Verse 2.—"*And speaketh the truth in his heart.*" Anatomists have observed that the tongue in man is tied with a double string to the heart. And so in *truth spoken* there is necessary a double agreement of our words. 1. With our heart. That is, to the speaking of truth, it is necessary our words agree with our mind and thoughts about the thing. We must speak as we think, and our tongues must be faithful interpreters of our mind : otherwise we lie, not speaking as we think. So what is truth in itself may be spoken by a man, and yet he be a liar ; namely, if he does not think as he speaks. 2. With the thing as it is in itself. Though we think a thing to be so, which is not so, we lie, when we affirm it ; because it is not as we say, though we really think it is so. For our mistaken notions of things can never stamp lies to pass current for truths. 2 Thess. ii. 11.—*Thomas Boston.*

Verse 2.—I this day heard a sermon from Psalm xv. 2, "*And speaketh the truth in his heart.*" . . . . . . O my soul, receive the admonition that has been given thee ! Study truth in the inward parts ; let integrity and truth always accompany thee, and preserve thee : speak the truth in thy heart. I am thankful for any conviction and sense I have of the evil of lying ; Lord, increase my abhorrence of it : as a further assistance and help against this mean, sordid, pernicious vice, I would endeavour, and resolve, in pursuit of the directions laid before us in the sermon, to mortify those passions and corruptions from whence this sin of lying more ordinarily flows, and which are the chief occasion of it, as "out of the heart proceed evil thoughts" (Matt. xv. 19) ; so, from the same fountain proceed evil words. And I would, with the greatest zeal, set myself against such corruptions as upon observation I find more commonly betray me into this iniquity : pride often indites our speech, and coins many a lie ; so envy, covetousness, malice, etc. I would endeavour to cleanse myself from all this filthiness : there never will be a mortified tongue while there is an unmortified heart. If I love the world inordinately, it is a thousand to one I shall be often stretching a point to promote a worldly interest ; and if I hate my brother, it is the same odds I shall reproach him. Lord, help me to purge the fountain, and then the streams will be pure. When the spring of a clock, and all the movements are right, the hand will go right ; and so it is here. The tongue follows the inward inclination. I would resolve to do nothing that may need a lie. If Gehazi's covetousness had not shamed him, he had not wanted a lie to excuse him, "He that walks uprightly, walks surely" and safely in this, as well as other respects. Prov. x. 9. May I do nothing that is dishonourable and mean, nothing that cannot bear the light, and then I shall have little temptation to lying. I would endeavour for a lively sense of the eye of God upon me, acting and speaking in his presence. Lord, I desire to set thee always before me ; thou understandest my thoughts as perfectly as others do my words. I would consider before I speak, and not speak much or rashly. Prov. xxix. 20. I would often think of the severity of a future judgment, when every secret shall be made manifest, and the hypocrite and liar exposed before angels and men. Lastly, I would frequently beg divine assistance herein. Psalm cxix. 29 ; Prov. xxx. 8. O my God, help me in my future conduct,

remove from me the way of lying ; may the law of kindness and truth be in my
tongue ; may I take heed to my ways, that I sin not with my tongue. I bewail
my past miscarriages in this respect, and flee to thy mercy through the blood of
Christ ; bless to me the instructions that have been this day given me ; let no
iniquity prevail against me ; " Keep back thy servant from presumptuous sins,
and cleanse me from secret faults." I commit my thoughts, desires, and tongue,
to thy conduct and government ; may I think and act in thy fear, and always
speak the truth in my heart.—*Benjamin Bennet's " Christian Oratory,"* 1728.

Verses 2, 5.—As the eagle casteth off her beak, and so reneweth her youth,
and the snake strippeth off her old skin, and so maketh herself smooth : even
so he that will enter into the joys of God, and rest upon his holy mountain,
must, as the Scripture speaks, put off the old man and put on the new, which,
after God, is created in righteousness and true holiness, repenting truly
speedily, steadily.—*Robert Cawdray.*

Verse 3.—*" He that backbiteth not with his tongue, nor doeth evil to his
neighbour."* Lamentation for the gross neglect of this duty, or the frequent
commission of this sin. What tears are sufficient to bewail it ? How thick do
censures and reproaches fly in all places, at all tables, in all conventions ! And
this were the more tolerable, if it were only the fault of ungodly men, of
strangers and enemies to religion ; for so saith the proverb, " Wickedness
proceedeth from the wicked." When a man's heart is full of hell, it is not
unreasonable to expect that his tongue should be set on fire of hell ; and it is
no wonder to hear such persons reproach good men, yea, even for their goodness. But alas ! the disease doth not rest here, this plague is not only among
the Egyptians but Israelites too. It is very doleful to consider how professors
sharpen their tongues like swords against professors ; and one good man
censures and reproaches another, and one minister traduceth another ; and who
can say, " I am clean from this sin ?" O that I could move your pity in this
case ! For the Lord's sake pity yourselves, and do not pollute and wound
your consciences with this crime. Pity your brethren ; let it suffice that godly
ministers and Christians are loaded with reproaches by wicked men—there is no
need that you should combine with them in this diabolical work. You should
support and strengthen their hands against the reproaches of the ungodly
world, and not add affliction to the afflicted. O pity the world, and pity the
church which Christ hath purchased with his own blood, which methinks bespeaks you in these words, " Have pity upon me, have pity upon me, O ye
my friends ; for the hand of God hath touched me." Job xix. 21. Pity the
mad and miserable world, and help it against this sin ; stop the bloody issue ;
restrain this wicked practice amongst men as much as possibly you can, and
lament it before God, and for what you cannot do yourselves, give God no rest
until he shall please to work a cure.—*Matthew Poole,* 1624—1679.

Verse 3.—*" He that backbiteth not,"* etc. Detraction or slander is not lightly
to be passed over, because we do so easily fail in this point. For the good
name of a man, as saith Solomon, is a precious thing to every one, and to be
preferred before much treasure, insomuch that it is no less grievous to hurt a
man with the tongue than with a sword : nay, ofttimes the stroke of a tongue
is grievouser than the wound of a spear, as it is in the French proverb. And
therefore the tongue must be bridled, that we hurt not in any wise the good
name of our neighbour ; but preserve it unto him safe and sound, as much as
in us shall lie. That which he addeth touching evil or injury not to be done
to our neighbour, is like unto that which we have seen already concerning the
working or exercising of righteousness. He would have us therefore so to
exercise all upright dealing, that we might be far from doing any damage or
wrong to our neighbours. And by the name of neighbour, is meant every man
and woman, as it is plain and evident. For we are all created of God, and
placed in this world that we might live uprightly and sincerely together.
And therefore he breaketh the law of human society (for we are all tied and

bound by this law of nature) that doth hurt or injury to another. The third member of this verse is, *nor that reproacheth another*, or, that maintaineth not a false report give one against another ; which latter particle seemeth to be the better, since he had spoken before expressly, touching the good name of another, not to be hurt or wronged with our tongue. To the which fault this is next in degree, wherewith we are too much encumbered, and which we scarce acknowledge to be a fault, when we further and maintain the slanders devised and given out by another against a man, either by hearing them or by telling them forth to others, as we heard them. For why ? It seemeth for the most part to be enough for us if we can say, that we feign not this or that, nor make it of our own heads, but only tell it forth as we heard it of others, without adding anything of our own brain. But as oft as we do this we fail in our duty doing, in not providing for our neighbour's credit, as were requisite for the things, which being uttered by others ought to be passed over in silence and to lie dead, we gather up, and by telling them forth, disperse them abroad, which whether it be a sin or no, when as we ought by all means possible to wish and do well unto our neighbour, all men do see. And therefore thou that travellest towards eternal life, must not only not devise false reports and slanders against other men, but also not so much as have them in thy mouth being devised by others, neither by any means assist or maintain them in slandering ; but by all honest and lawful means, provide for the credit and estimation of thy neighbour, so much as in thee lieth.—*Peter Baro, D.D.*, 1560.

Verse 3.—" *He that backbiteth not with his tongue.*" The Hebrew word רָגַל signifieth to play the spy, and by a metaphor, to *backbite* or *slander*, for *back-biters* and whisperers, after the manner of spies, go up and down dissembling their malice, that they may espy the faults and defects of others, whereof they may make a malicious relation to such as will give ear to their slanders. So that *backbiting* is a malicious defamation of a man behind his back. . . . . . . And that the citizen of heaven doth and ought to abhor from *backbiting*, the horrible wickedness of this sin doth evince. For first, Lev. xix. 16, where it is straightly forbidden, the "*tale-bearer*" is compared to a pedlar : " Thou shalt not walk about with tales and slanders, as it were a pedlar among thy people." So much רָכִיל signifieth. For as the pedlar having bought his wares of some one or more, goeth about from house to house that he may sell the same to others ; so *backbiters* and *tale-bearers*, gathering together tales and rumours, as it were wares, go from one to another, that such wares as either themselves have invented, or have gathered by report, they may utter in the absence of their neighbour to his infamy and disgrace. Likewise Psalm l. 20, it is con-demned as a notable crime, which God will not suffer to go unpunished ; Ezek. xxii. 9, it is reckoned among the abominations of Jerusalem, for which destruction is denounced against it ; and Rom. i. 29, 30, among the crimes of the heathen, given over unto a reprobate sense, this is placed : they were " *whisperers and backbiters.*"—*George Downame.*

Verse 3.—" *He that backbiteth not.*" He that is guilty of backbiting, that speaks evil of another behind his back, if that which he speaks be false, is guilty of lying, which is prejudicial to salvation. If that which he speaks be true, yet he is void of charity in seeking to defame another. For as Solomon observes, " Love covereth all sins." Prov. x. 12. Where there is love and charity, there will be a covering and concealing of men's sins as much as may be. Now, where charity is wanting, their salvation is not to be expected. 1 Cor. xiii. 1, etc. ; 1 John iii. 14, 15.—*Christopher Cartwright*, 1602—1658.

Verse 3.—" *Backbiteth not.*" This crime is a conjugation of evils, and is productive of infinite mischiefs ; it undermines peace, and saps the foundation of friendship ; it destroys families, and rends in pieces the very heart and vitals of charity ; it makes an evil man party, and witness, and judge, and executioner of the innocent.—*Bishop Taylor.*

Verse 3.—" *Backbiteth.*" The scorpion hurteth none but such as he toucheth with the tip of his tail ; and the crocodile and basilisk slay none but such as either the force of their sight, or strength of their breath reacheth. The viper woundeth none but such as it biteth ; the venomous herbs or roots kill none but such as taste, or handle, or smell them, and so come near unto them ; but the poison of slanderous tongues is much more rank and deadly ; for that hurteth and slayeth, woundeth and killeth, not only near, but afar off ; not only at hand, but by distance of place removed ; not only at home, but abroad ; not only in our own nation, but in foreign countries ; and spareth neither quick nor dead.—*Richard Turnbull.*

Verse 3.—" *Backbiteth.*" The word here used comes from a root signifying *foot,* and denotes a person who goes about from house to house, speaking things he should not (1 Tim. v. 13) ; and a word from this root signifies *spies ;* and the phrase here may point at persons who creep into houses, pry into the secrets of families, divulge them, and oftentimes represent them in a false light. Such are ranked among the worst of men, and are very unfit to be in the society of saints, or in a church of Christ. See Rom. i. 30.—*John Gill.*

Verse 3.—" *Nor taketh up a reproach against his neighbour.*" The saints of God must not be too light of hearing, much less of believing all tales, rumours, and reports of their brethren ; and charity requireth that we do not only stop and stay them, but that we examine them before we believe them. Saul, the king, too light of belief in this point, believed the slanderous and false reports of David's enemies, who put into Saul's head that David imagined evil against him. Yea, David himself showed his great infirmity in that, that without due examination and proof of the matter, he believed the false report of Ziba against Mephibosheth, the son of Jonathan ; of whom to David the king, persecuted by Absalom his son, Ziba reported falsely, that he should say, " This day shall the house of Israel restore unto me the kingdom of my father." The example of whose infirmity in Scripture reproved, must not we follow ; but let us rather embrace the truth of that heavenly doctrine which, through God's Spirit, here he preacheth, that we believe not false reports against our neighbours.—*Richard Turnbull.*

Verse 3.—Despise not thy neighbour, but think thyself as bad a sinner, and that the like defects may befall thee. If thou canst not excuse his doing, excuse his intent which may be good ; or if the deed be evil, think it was done of ignorance ; if thou canst no way excuse him, think some great temptation befell him, and that thou shouldst be worse if the like temptation befell thee ; and give God thanks that the like as yet hath not befallen thee. Despise not a man being a sinner, for though he be evil to-day, he may turn to-morrow.—*William Perkins,* 1558—1602.

Verses 3, 4, 5.—They that cry down moral honesty, cry down that which is a great part of religion, my duty towards God, and my duty towards man. What care I to see a man run after a sermon, if he cozens and cheats as soon as he comes home ? On the other side, morality must not be without religion, for if so, it may change as I see convenience. Religion must govern it. He that has not religion to govern his morality, is not a dram better than my mastiff-dog ; so long as you stroke him, and please him, and do not pinch him, he will play with you as finely as may be, he is a very good moral mastiff ; but if you hurt him, he will fly in your face, and tear out your throat.—*John Seldon,* 1584—1654.

Verse 4.—" *In whose eyes a vile person is contemned,*" etc. When wicked Jehoram, king of Israel, came to Eliseus, the prophet, to ask counsel of the Lord, and to entreat for waters, having in company Jehoshaphat, the king of Judah, being virtuous ; the prophet showeth his contempt to the one, being wicked, and his reverence to the other, being godly, faithful and virtuous, said, " As the Lord of hosts liveth, before whom I stand, were it not that I regard the presence of Jehoshaphat, the king of Judah, I would not look toward thee, nor see thee." 2 Kings iii. 14. Thus was the wicked *vile* in his sight ; thus did he not flatter the ungodly. In like manner godly Mordecai, the Jew, having Haman the ambitious and proud Agagite in contempt, would in no wise bow the knee unto him in sign of honour, as the rest of the people did ; for which cause he was extremely hated, menaced, and molested of proud and wicked Haman. To wink at their wickedness, to uphold them in their iniquity, to fawn upon them and flatter them, to praise them when they deserve just reproof, is, as it were, an honouring of them ; to which, as to a most grievous sin, the prophet denounceth a most bitter curse : " Woe unto them that call evil good, and good evil ; that put darkness for light, and light for darkness ; that put bitter for sweet, and sweet for bitter !" Isaiah v. 20.— *Richard Turnbull.*

Verse 4.—" *In whose eyes a vile person is contemned.*" To *contemn* the wicked and honour the godly, are opposite the one to the other. But the former may seem not to be sufficiently beseeming to a godly man. For why should he contemn or despise others, who is commanded by all means to care for the credit of others, as we heard even now ? Nay, a godly man, letting others go, ought to search into himself, and to accuse himself, but not to judge of others. But this saying of the prophet is to be understood rather of the faults than of the person. As every man therefore is to be loved, so are the faults of every man to be hated of the godly. For so is God himself, whom we desire to be like unto, that we might dwell with him, affected and disposed. For why ? he hateth no man, nay, he hateth nothing at all in this whole universal world, but only sin. For he is the author and preserver of all things that be ; and therefore doth good and wisheth well to all ; only of sin he is not the author, but the free and unconstrained will of man and Satan. Notwithstanding God doth so greatly hate sin, that by reason thereof he doth sometimes neglect and forsake men, yea, and have them in contempt. So then a godly man hateth no man, nor contemneth any ; but yet notwithstanding he disliketh sin in sinful men, and that he sticketh not to let them perceive either by reproving them, or shunning their company, or by doing of some other thing, whereby they may know they are misliked of good men for their enormities, and see themselves to be contemned of others for their wicked and ungodly life. A good man therefore must not flatter the ungodly in their ungracious attempts, but must freely declare that he disalloweth their course and conversation.— *Peter Baro.*

Verse 4.—" *In whose eyes a vile person is contemned.*" Augustine, as Posidonius writeth, showing what hatred he had to tale-bearers and false reporters of others, had two verses written over his table ; by translation these : —

> " He that doth love with bitter speech the absent to defame,
> Must surely know that at this board no place is for the same."

> —*Richard Turnbull.*

Verse 4.—" *In whose eyes a vile person is contemned.*" The burgess of the New Jerusalem, *reprobos reprobat, et probos probat ;* he cannot flatter any man, nor fancy such as in whom he findeth not *aliquid Christi,* something of the image of God. A golden Colosse, stuffed with rubbish, he cannot stoop to, " But he honoureth them that fear the Lord," as the only earthly angels, though never so mean and despicable in the world's eye. Mr. Fox, being asked whether he remembered not such a poor servant of God who had received succour from him in time of trouble ? answered, " I remember him well ; I tell you, I forget the lords and ladies, to remember such."—*John Trapp.*

Verse 4.—" *He honoureth them that fear the Lord.*" Though the godly some way or other be injurious unto us, we ought nevertheless to honour and not to despise them. So Joseph did Mary, though he supposed her to have dealt injuriously with him ; and she had done so, indeed, if it had been with her as he imagined. Calvin's resolution concerning Luther was very admirable in this respect. They differed much about the presence of Christ in the sacrament ; and Luther being of a vehement spirit, wrote bitterly against those that did hold otherwise in that point than himself did. This enforced some, who were more nearly concerned in the business, to prepare to answer Luther ; which Calvin understanding, and fearing lest they being provoked by Luther's tartness, should deal with him in the like kind, he wrote unto Bullinger, a prime man among them, persuading and exhorting him to carry the business so as to show all due respect unto Luther, considering what worth and excellency there was in him, however he had demeaned himself in that particular. And he adds, that he often used to say, that although Luther should call him devil, yet he would do him that honour, to acknowledge him a choice servant of God.— *Christopher Cartwright.*

Verse 4.—" *He honoureth them that fear the Lord.*" I have read of one that said, If he should meet a preacher and an angel together, he would first salute the preacher and then the angel.—*Charles Bradbury's "Cabinet of Jewels,"* 1785.

Verse 4.—" *He that sweareth to his own hurt, and changeth not.*"

> " His words are bonds, his oaths are oracles ;
> His love sincere, his thoughts immaculate ;
> His tears pure messengers, sent from his heart ;
> His heart as far from fraud as heaven from earth."
>
> *William Shakspere.*

Verse 5.—The Puritanic divines are almost all of them against the taking of any interest upon money, and go the length of saying that one penny per cent. per annum will shut a man out of heaven if persisted in. It appeared to me to be useless to quote opinions in which I cannot agree, especially as this would occupy space better employed. The demanding of excessive and grinding interest is a sin to be detested ; the taking of the usual and current interest in a commercial country is not contrary to the law of love. The Jews were not engaged in commerce, and to lend money even at the lowest interest to their fellow farmers in times of poverty would have been usurious ; but they might lend to strangers, who would usually be occupied in commerce, because in the commercial world, money is a fruitful thing, and the lender has a right to a part of its products ; a loan to enable a non-trader to live over a season of want is quite another matter.— *C. H. S.*

Verse 5.—" *He that putteth not out his money to usury.*" By usury is generally understood the gain of anything above the principal, or that which was lent, exacted only in consideration of the loan, whether it be in money, corn, wares, or the like. It is most commonly taken for an unlawful profit which a person makes of his money or goods. The Hebrew word for usury signifies biting. The law of God prohibits rigorous imposing conditions of gain for the loan of money or goods, and exacting them without respect to the condition of the borrower, whether he gain or lose ; whether poverty occasioned his borrowing, or a visible prospect of gain by employing the borrowed goods. It is said in Exod. xxii. 25, 26, " If thou lend money to any of my people that is poor by thee, thou shalt not be to him as an *usurer*, neither shalt thou lay upon him *usury*," etc. And in Lev. xxv. 35, 36, 37, " If thy brother be waxen poor, and fallen into decay with thee, then thou shalt relieve him ; yea, though he be a stranger, or a sojourner, that he may live with thee : take thou no *usury* of him," etc. This law forbids the taking *usury* from a brother that was poor, an Israelite reduced to poverty, or from a proselyte ; but in Deut. xxiii. 20, God seems to tolerate *usury* towards strangers ; " Unto a stranger thou mayest lend upon *usury*." By *strangers*, in this passage, some understand the Gentiles in general, or all such as were not Jews, excepting proselytes. Others think that by *strangers* are meant the Canaanites, and the other people that were devoted to slavery and subjection ; of these the Hebrews were permitted to exact *usury*, but not of such *strangers* with whom they had no quarrel, and against whom the Lord had not denounced his judgments. The Hebrews were plainly commanded in Exod. xxii. 25, etc., not to receive *usury* for money from any that borrowed from necessity, as in that case in Neh. v. 5, 7. And such

14

provision the law made for the preserving of estates to their families by the year of jubilee ; for a people that had little concern in trade, could not be supposed to borrow money but out of necessity : but they were allowed to lend upon *usury* to strangers, whom yet they must not oppress. This law, therefore, in the strictness of it, seems to have been peculiar to the Jewish state ; but in the equity of it, it obligeth us to show mercy to those we have advantage against, and to be content to share with those we lend to in loss, as well as profit, if Providence cross them. And upon this condition, a valuable commentator says, " It seems as lawful for me to receive interest for money, which another takes pains with, improves, but runs the hazard of in trade, as it is to receive rent for my land, which another takes pains with, improves, but runs the hazard of in husbandry."—*Alexander Cruden*, 1701—1770.

Verse 5.—" *He that putteth not out his money to usury.*" " *If thou lend money to any of my people that is poor by thee.*" Exod. xxii. 25. Rather, according to the letter of the original, " If thou lend money to my people, even to a poor man with thee." The Israelites were a people but little engaged in commerce, and therefore could not in general be supposed to borrow money but from sheer necessity ; and of that necessity the lender was not to take advantage by usurious exactions. The law is not to be understood as a prohibition of interest at any rate whatever, but of excessive interest or usury. The clause, " Thou shalt not be to him as an usurer," is equivalent to saying, ' Thou shalt not domineer and lord it over him rigorously and cruelly.' That this class of men were peculiarly prone to be extortionate and oppressive in their dealings with debtors would seem to be implied by the etymology of the original term for *usury* (נֶשֶׁךְ *neshek*), which comes from a root signifying *to bite ;* and in Neh. v. 2—5, we have a remarkable case of the bitter and grinding effects resulting from the exercise of the creditor's rights over the debtor. A large portion of the people had not only mortgaged their lands, vineyards, and houses, but had actually sold their sons and daughters into bondage, to satisfy the claims of their grasping creditors. In this emergency Nehemiah espoused the cause of the poor, and compelled the rich, against whom he called the people together, to remit the whole of their dues ; and, moreover, exacted from them an oath that they would never afterwards oppress their poor brethren for the payment of those debts. This was not because every part of those proceedings had been contrary to the letter of the Mosaic law, but because it was a flagrant breach of equity under the circumstances. It was taking a cruel and barbarous advantage of the necessities of their brethren, at which God was highly indignant, and which his servants properly rebuked. From this law the Hebrew canonists have gathered a general rule, that " Whoso exacteth of a poor man, and knoweth that he hath not aught to pay him with, he transgresseth against this prohibition, Thou shalt not be to him as an exacting creditor." (*Maimonides, in Ainsworth.*) We nowhere learn from the institutes delivered by Moses that the simple taking of interest, especially from the neighbouring nations (Deut. xxiii. 19, 20), was forbidden to the Israelites ; but the divine law would give no countenance to the griping and extortionate practices to which miserly money-lenders are always prone. The deserving and industrious poor might sometimes be reduced to such straits, that pecuniary accommodations might be very desirable to them ; and towards such God would inculcate a mild, kind, and forbearing spirit, and the precept is enforced by the relation which they sustained to him : *q.d.*, " Remember that you are lending to *my* people, *my* poor ; and therefore take no advantage of their necessities. Trust me against the fear of loss, and treat them kindly and generously."—*George Bush, in " Notes on the Book of Exodus,"* 1856.

Verse 5.—" *He that putteth not out his money to usury.*" With respect to the first clause, as David seems to condemn all kinds of usury in general, and without exception, the very name has been everywhere held in detestation. But crafty men have invented specious names under which to conceal the vice ; and thinking by this artifice to escape, they have plundered with greater excess than if they had lent on usury avowedly and openly. God, however, will not be dealt with and imposed upon by sophistry and false pretences. He looks upon the thing as it really is. There is no worse species of usury than an unjust way of making bargains, where equity is disregarded on both sides. Let us, then, remember that all bargains, in which the one party unrighteously strives to make gain by the loss of the other party, whatever name may be given to them, are here condemned. It may be asked, whether all kinds of usury are to be put into this denunciation, and regarded as alike unlawful? If we condemn all without distinction, there is a danger lest many, seeing themselves brought into such a strait as to find that sin must be incurred, in whatever way they can turn themselves, may be rendered bolder by despair, and may rush headlong into all kinds of usury without choice or discrimination. On the other hand, whenever we concede that something may be lawfully done in this way, many will give themselves loose reins, thinking that a liberty to exercise usury, without control or moderation, has been granted them. In the first place, therefore, I would, above all things, counsel my readers to beware of ingeniously contriving deceitful pretexts by which to take advantage of their fellow men, and let them not imagine that anything can be lawful to them which is grievous and hurtful to others. . . . . It is not without cause that God has in Lev. xxv. 35, 36, forbidden usury, adding this reason : " And if thy brother be waxen poor, and fallen in decay with thee ; then thou shalt relieve him : yea, though he be a stranger, or a sojourner ; that he may live with thee. Take thou no usury of him, or increase." We see that the end for which the law was framed was that man should not cruelly oppress the poor, who ought rather to receive sympathy and compassion. This was, indeed, a part of the judicial law which God appointed for the Jews in particular ; but it is a common principle of justice, which extends to all nations, and to all ages, that we should keep ourselves from plundering and devouring the poor who are in distress and want. Whence it follows, that the gain which he who lends his money upon interest acquires, without doing injury to any one, is not to be included under the head of unlawful usury. The Hebrew word נֶשֶׁךְ neshek, which David employs, being derived from another word which signifies to bite, sufficiently shows that usuries are condemned in so far as they involve in them, or lead to, a license of robbing or plundering our fellow men. Ezekiel, indeed (chapters xviii. 17, and xxii. 12), seems to condemn the taking of any interest whatever upon money lent ; but he, doubtless, has an eye to the unjust and crafty arts of gaining by which the rich devoured the poor people. In short, provided we had engraven on our hearts the rule of equity which Christ prescribes in Matt. vii. 12, " Therefore, all things whatsoever ye would that men should do to you, do ye even so to them," it would not be necessary to enter into lengthened disputes concerning usury.—*John Calvin, in loc.*

Verse 5 (*first clause*).—The Mosaic law forbids the lending of money for interest to an Israelite. Exod. xxii. 25 ; Lev. xxv. 37 ; Deut. xxiii. 19 ; Prov. xxviii. 8 ; Ezek. xviii. 8. In several of the passages referred to, it is expressly supposed that money is lent only to the poor, a supposition which has its ground in the simple relations of the Mosaic times, in which lending, for the purpose of speculation and gain, had no existence. Such lending ought only to be a work of brotherly love ; and it is a great violation of that if any one, instead of helping his neighbour, takes advantage of his need to bring him into still greater straits. The Mosaic regulation in question has, accordingly, its import also for New Testament times. With the interest-lending of capitalists, who borrow for speculation, it has nothing to do. This belongs to a quite different matter, as is implied even by the name נֶשֶׁךְ, a mordendo, according to which only such usury can be meant as plagues and impoverishes a neighbour. By unseasonable comparison with our modes of speech, many would expound, "His money he puts not to interest."—*E. W. Hengstenberg.*

Verse 5 (*first clause*).—The worm called in Latin *teredo*, whereof Pliny hath reported something in his story, breeding in wood, to the touch is soft, yet it hath such teeth as endeavoureth and consumeth the hard timber. So the usurer is a soft beast at first to handle, but in continuance of time the hardness of his teeth will eat thee up, both flesh and bone, if thou beware not. He pleadeth love, but not for thy sake, but for his own ; for as the ivy colleth and claspeth the oak as a lover, but thereby it groweth up and overtoppeth the oak, and sucketh out the juice and sap thereof, that it cannot thrive nor prosper ; so the usurer colleth, embraceth, and claspeth in arms the borrower, that thereby himself may grow richer, and suck all wealth, goods, and riches from him, that he never thriveth or prospereth after. The pleasure the usurer showeth is like the playing of the cat with the silly mouse : the cat playeth with the mouse, but the play of the cat is the death of the mouse. The usurer pleasureth the borrower ; but the pleasure of the usurer is the undoing of the borrower. The fox through craft slideth and tumbleth, and maketh much pastime till he come to the prey, then he devoureth : the usurer maketh many fair speeches, giveth out many fair promises, pretendeth very great kindness, until he have got thee within his compass, then he crusheth and cruciateth thee. The usurer preyeth upon the poor, he waxeth rich of the penury of his brother, he clotheth himself with the coat of the naked, he gathereth riches of the indigency and want of his neighbour ; he feedeth himself of the bread of the hungry, and devoureth his poor brother, as the great beasts do the smaller ; than which, saith Ambrose, there is no greater inhumanity and cruelty, no greater wretchedness and iniquity, as Chrysostom in many places, and Basil upon this Psalm, have well observed.—*Richard Turnbull.*

Verse 5.—The rich make the poor to fill them ; for *usurers* feed upon the poor, even as great fishes devour the small. Therefore, he which said, Let there not be a beggar in Israel (Deut. xv. 4), 'said too, Let there not be an usurer in Israel. For if there be usurers in Israel there will be beggars in Israel ; for usurers make beggars, even as lawyers make quarrellers. . . . It is a miserable occupation to live by sin, and a great comfort to a man when he looketh upon his gold and silver, and his heart telleth him, All this is well gotten ; and when he lieth upon his death-bed, and must leave all to his children, he can say unto them, I leave you mine own ; but the usurer cannot say, I leave you mine own, but I leave you other men's ; therefore the usurer can never die in peace, because if he die before he maketh restitution, he dieth in his sin.—*Henry Smith.*

Verse 5.—Biting *usurers* were so abhorred in the primitive church, that as they condemned the usurer himself, so they made the scribes, who wrote the bonds, and also the witnesses, incapable of any benefit ; and that no testament or latter will, written by such should be valid. The house of the usurer was called *domus Satanæ,* the house of the devil ; and they ordained that no man should eat or drink with such usurers, nor fetch fire from them ; and after they were dead that they should not be buried in Christian burial. The conclusion of this is (Ezek. xviii. 13), this sin is matched with theft ; and verse 11, with adultery ; and verse 12, with violence ; it is the daughter of oppression and sister to idolatry, and he that doth these things shall not *dwell in God's holy hill.* Albeit, these worldlings think themselves more honest than thieves and adulterers, yet the Lord maketh their case all alike.—*John Weemse,* 1636.

Verse 5.—"*Taketh reward against the innocent.*" I am sure this is *scala inferni,* the right way to hell, to be covetous, to take bribes, and pervert justice. If a judge should ask me the way to hell, I should show him this way : First, let him be a covetous man ; let his heart be poisoned with covetousness. Then let him go a little further and take bribes ; and, lastly, pervert judgments. Lo, here is the mother, and the daughter, and the daughter's daughter. Avarice is the mother ; she brings forth bribe-taking, and bribe-taking perverting of judgment. There lacks a fourth thing to make up the mess, which, so help me God, if I were judge, should be *hangum tuum,* a Tyburn tippet to take with him ; an it were the judge of the King's Bench, my Lord Chief Judge of England, yea, an it were my Lord Chancellor himself, to Tyburn with him.—*Hugh Latimer.*

Verse 5.—" *Taketh reward against the innocent.*" I come to corrupt lawyers and advocates, who so often *take rewards against the innocent*, as they do take upon them the defence of such causes as they in their own conscience are persuaded to be evil and unjust. Which being so common a fault among lawyers, as that very few which plead causes, either in civil or ecclesiastical courts, do seem to make any conscience thereof, to whom all is fish that cometh to their nets ; therefore all lawyers are to be exhorted to apply this note unto themselves.—*George Downame.*

Verse 5.—" *He that doeth.*" 'Tis not said he that *professes* this or that, or he that *believes* thus and thus, or he that is of such or such an *opinion* or *way of worship*, or he that sets up *new lights*, and pretends the *Spirit* for his immediate guide *;* 'tis not he that *hears* much or *talks* much of religion ; no, nor he that *preaches* and *prays* much, nor he that *thinks* much of these things, and *means well* ; but 'tis he that " *doeth these things*"—that is actually employed about them—that is the religious and truly godly man. 'Tis not, I say, a formal *professor*, a confidant *solifidian*, a wild *opinionist*, a high-flown *perfectist ;* it is not a constant *hearer*, or a mighty *talker*, or a laborious *teacher*, or a *gifted brother*, or a simple *well-wisher* must pass ; but 'tis the honest and sincere *doer* of these things, that will abide the test and stand the trial ; when all other flashy pretences shall, in those searching flames, be burnt and consumed like " hay and stubble," as the apostle expresses it. To wear Christ's livery and to do him no service is but to mock a gracious Master ; to own him in our *profession* and deny him in our *practice*, is, with Judas, to betray him with a kiss of homage ; with the rude soldiers to bow the knee before him, and, in the meantime to beat his sacred head with his reeden sceptre, and with Pilate to crown him with thorns, to crucify the Lord and write over his head, " King of the Jews :" in a word, to grieve him with our honours, and wound him with our acknowledgments. A Christian profession without a life answerable, will be so far from saving any one, that 'twill highly aggravate his condemnation ; when a dissembled friendship at the great day of discoveries shall be looked upon as the worst of enmities. A mere outside formality of worship, is at best but Prometheus' sacrifice, a skeleton of bones and a religious cheat. . . . The harmless humour of *meaning well* is not enough to approve a man's spiritual state, to acquit obligations, or to ascertain his expectations. For he that bids us " eschew evil" does immediately subjoin, that we must " follow" and " hold fast that which is good." It will be no good account not to have done evil, unless we make it appear that we have been doing good too ; since the non-commission of great sins will not excuse our omission of great duties. In the busy commonwealth of bees, the drone without a sting, as she has no weapon for mischief, so, wanting a tool for employ, is deservedly cashiered the hive.—*Condensed from Adam Littleton, D.D.*, 1627—1694.

Verse 5.—" *He that doeth these things, shall never be moved.*" Mark how the prophet saith not, he that readeth these things, or he that heareth these things, but he that *doth* them, shall never be removed. For were it enough to read or hear these precepts, then should an infinite number of vain and wicked persons enter into, and continue in the church, which notwithstanding have no place therein ; for there are very few, or none at all, which have not read, or at least have not heard these things, yet they will not do them. Neither doth he say, he that talketh of these things, but he that *doth* them ; for many now in these days can talk gloriously of uprightness, justice, truth, in whom notwithstanding, there is neither upright dealings, nor sound righteousness, nor unfeigned truth to be found. Many can say that slander is sin, injury is iniquity, to receive false reports is uncharitable, that it becometh not the saints to flatter the wicked, that to break promise and falsify their oaths is unseemly, to give upon usury is oppression, to receive bribes against the innocent is extreme cruelty ; yet themselves backbite and hurt their neighbour, they themselves believe every tale that is brought them, they flatter and fawn upon the wicked for advantage, they swear and forswear for commodity, they oppress through usury, and receive gifts of bribery against the innocent ; and so in word they speak of these things, but *do them not* indeed. . . . . Neither doth David say he that preacheth these, "*shall never be removed,*" for then not only many other wicked persons, which can speak of, yea, many ungodly men which can also preach of virtue, should have the place in the Lord's tabernacle, and rest upon his holy hill ; but also among others, even Balaam the covetous prophet, should have a sure place in God's tabernacle ; for he could say, "If Balak would give me his house full of silver and gold, I cannot go beyond the word of the Lord my God, to do less or more" (Num. xxii. 18) ; yet he took rewards ; yet he was carried away with covetousness, as much as in him lay, to work the destruction of Israel, the innocent people of the Lord.—*Richard Turnbull.*

Verse 5.—"*Shall never be moved.*" Moved he may be for a time, but not removed for ever. His soul is bound up in the bundle of life, near unto the throne of glory ; when the souls of the wicked are restless as a stone in the midst of a sling, saith the Targum in 1 Sam. xxv.—*John Trapp.*

Verse 5 (last clause).—The holy soul is the love of God, the joy of angels ; her eyes dare look upon the glorious Judge whom she knows to be her Saviour. Her heart is courageous ; she dares stand the thunder ; and when guilty minds creep into corners, she is confident in him that he will defend her. She challengeth the whole world to accuse her of injustice, and fears not the subornation of false witnesses, because she knows the testimony of her own conscience. Her language is free and bold, without the guiltiness of broken stops. Her forehead is clear and smooth, as the brow of heaven. Her knees are ever bent to the throne of grace ; her feet travelling towards Jerusalem ; her hands weaving the web of righteousness. Good men bless her ; good angels guard her ; the Son of God doth kiss her ; and when all the world shall be turned to a burning pile, she shall be brought safe to the mountain of joy, and set in a throne of blessedness for ever.—*Thomas Adams.*

HINTS TO THE VILLAGE PREACHER.

Verse 1.—Qualifications for church membership on earth and in heaven. A subject for self-examination.

Verse 1.—I. *Comparison of the church to the tabernacle.* God's presence manifested, sacrifice offered, and vessels of grace preserved in it ; mean externally, glorious within. II. *Comparison of its double position to that of the tabernacle.* Moving in the wilderness, and fixed on the hill. III. Enquire into qualifications for admittance into church and tabernacle. Parallel with the priests, etc.

Verse 1.—The great question. Asked by idle curiosity, despair, godly fear, earnest enquirer, soul troubled by falls of others, holy faith. Give answer to each.

Verse 1.—The citizen of Zion described.—*Thomas Boston's Sermons.*

Verse 1.—Anxiety to know the true saints, how far lawful and profitable.

Verse 1.—God the only infallible discerner of true saints.

Verse 2.—"*He that walketh uprightly.*" I. What he must be. He must be upright in heart. A man himself bent double cannot walk uprightly. II. How he must act. Neither from impulse, ambition, gain, fear, or flattery. He must not be warped in any direction, but stand perpendicularly. III. What he must expect. Snares, etc., to trip him. IV. Where he must walk. Path of duty, the only one in which he can walk uprightly. V. Where he must look. Up, right-up, and then he will be upright.

Verse 2.—"*Speaketh the truth in his heart.*" Subject :—Heart falsehood and heart truth.

Verse 2 (first clause).—The citizen of Zion, an upright walker.

Verse 2 (middle clause).—The citizen of Zion, a worker of righteousness.

Verse 2 (*last clause*).—The citizen of Zion, a speaker of truth.—*Four Sermons in Thomas Boston's Works.*

Verse 3.—The evils of detraction. It affects three persons here mentioned : the backbiter, the suffering neighbour, and the taker-up of the reproach.

Verse 3.—" *Nor taketh up a reproach.*" The sin of being too ready to believe ill reports. Common, cruel, foolish, injurious, wicked.

Verse 4.—The duty of practically honouring those who fear the Lord. Commendation, deference, assistance, imitation, etc.

Verse 4.—The sin of estimating persons other than by their practical characters.

Verse 4 (*last clause*).—The Lord Jesus as our unchanging Surety, his oath and his hurt.

Verse 5.—The evidences and privileges of godly men.

Verse 5 (*last clause*).—The fixedness and safety of the godly.

WORKS UPON THE FIFTEENTH PSALM.

Fower Sermons and Two Questions, as they were uttered and disputed by that learned Frenchman, P[ETER] B[ARO]. 1560.

Lectures on the XV. Psalme read in the Cathedral Church of St. Paul, in London. By GEORGE DOWNAME, Doctor of Divinitie, London. 1604. 4to.

Four Sermons, by way of Exposition of Psalm XV., by RICHARD TURNBULL, are found at the end of the old 4to containing his Exposition of the Epistles of James and Jude. There is no separate title page to the Exposition of the Psalm ; the date of the book is 1606.

The Works of John Boys, D.D., Deane of Canterburie, 1629, folio, contains Expositions of Psalms II., IX., and XV. (The folio edition of Boys' Works consists of Expositions of the Scriptures used in the Liturgy.)

A Practical and Polemical Commentary, or Exposition on the whole Fifteenth Psalm, wherein the text is learnedly and fruitfully explained, some *controversies* discussed, sundry *cases of conscience* are cleared ; more especially that of USURIE. By CHRISTOPHER CARTWRIGHT, late minister of Saint-Martin's, in the city of York. 1658. 4to.

PSALM XVI.

TITLE.—MICHTAM OF DAVID. *This is usually understood to mean* THE GOLDEN PSALM, *and such a title is most appropriate, for the matter is as the most fine gold. Ainsworth calls it " David's jewel, or notable song." Dr. Hawker, who is always alive to passages full of savour, devoutly cries, " Some have rendered it* precious, *others* golden, *and others*, precious jewel; *and as the Holy Ghost, by the apostles* Peter *and* Paul, *hath shown us that it is all about the Lord Jesus Christ, what is here said of him is* precious, *is* golden, *is a jewel indeed!" We have not met with the term* Michtam *before, but if spared to write upon Psalms* lvi., lvii., lviii., lix. *and* lx., *we shall see it again, and shall observe that like the present these psalms although they begin with prayer, and imply trouble, abound in holy confidence and close with songs of assurance as to ultimate safety and joy. Dr. Alexander, whose notes are peculiarly valuable, thinks that the word is most probably a simple derivative of a word signifying to hide, and signifies a secret or mystery, and indicates the depth of doctrinal and spiritual import in these sacred compositions. If this be the true interpretation it well accords with the other, and when the two are put together, they make up a name which every reader will remember, and which will bring the precious subject at once to mind.* THE PSALM OF THE PRECIOUS SECRET.

SUBJECT. *We are not left to human interpreters for the key to this golden mystery, for, speaking by the Holy Ghost, Peter tells us, " David speaketh concerning* HIM." (Acts ii. 25.) *Further on in his memorable sermon he said, " Men and brethren, let me freely speak unto you of the patriarch David, that he is both dead and buried, and his sepulchre is with us unto this day. Therefore being a prophet, and knowing that God had sworn with an oath to him, that of the fruit of his loins, according to the flesh, he would raise up Christ to sit on his throne; he seeing this before* spake of the resurrection of Christ, *that his soul was not left in hell, neither his flesh did see corruption."* (Acts ii. 29—31.) *Nor is this our only guide, for the apostle Paul, led by the same infallible inspiration, quotes from this psalm, and testifies that David wrote of the man through whom is preached unto us the forgiveness of sins.* (Acts xiii. 35—38.) *It has been the usual plan of commentators to apply the psalm both to David, to the saints, and to the Lord Jesus, but we will venture to believe that in it " Christ is all;" since in the ninth and tenth verses, like the apostles on the mount, we can see " no man but Jesus only."*

DIVISION.—*The whole is so compact that it is difficult to draw sharp lines of division. It may suffice to note our Lord's prayer of faith, verse 1, avowal of faith in Jehovah alone, 2, 3, 4, 5, the contentment of his faith in the present, 6, 7, and the joyous confidence of his faith for the future* (8, 11).

EXPOSITION.

PRESERVE me, O God : for in thee do I put my trust.

" *Preserve me,*" *keep, or save me,* or as Horsley thinks, " *guard me,*" even as body-guards surround their monarch, or as shepherds protect their flocks. Tempted in all points like as we are, the manhood of Jesus needed to be preserved from the power of evil ; and though in itself pure, the Lord Jesus did not confide in that purity of nature, but as an example to his followers, looked to the Lord, his God, for preservation. One of the great names of God is " the Preserver of men," (Job vii. 20,) and this gracious office the Father exercised towards our Mediator and Representative. It had been promised to the Lord Jesus in express words, that he should be preserved, Isa. xlix. 7, 8. " Thus saith the Lord, the Redeemer of Israel and his Holy One, to him whom man despiseth, to him whom the nation abhorreth, I will preserve thee, and give thee for a covenant of the people." This promise was to the letter fulfilled, both by providential deliverance and sustaining power, in the case of our Lord. Being preserved himself, he is able to restore the preserved of Israel, for we are " preserved in Christ Jesus and called." As one with him, the elect were preserved in his preservation, and we may view this mediatorial supplication as the petition of the Great High Priest for all those who are in him. The intercession recorded in John xvii. is but an amplification of this cry, " Holy Father, keep through thine own name those whom thou hast given me, that they may be one, as we *are.*" When he says " preserve me," he means his members, his mystical body, himself, and all in him. But while we rejoice in the fact that the Lord Jesus used this prayer for his members, we must not forget that he employed it most surely for himself ; he had so emptied himself, and so truly taken upon him the form of a servant, that as man he needed divine keeping even as we do, and often cried unto the strong for strength. Frequently on the mountain-top he breathed forth this desire, and on one occasion in almost the same words, he publicly prayed, " Father, save me from this hour." (John xii. 27.) If Jesus looked out of himself for protection, how much more must we, his erring followers, do so !

" *O God.*" The word for God here used is EL 7ֆ, by which name the Lord Jesus, when under a sense of great weakness, as for instance when upon the cross, was wont to address the Mighty God, the Omnipotent Helper of his people. We, too, may turn to *El,* the Omnipotent One, in all hours of peril, with the confidence that he who heard the strong cryings and tears of our faithful High Priest, is both able and willing to bless us in him. It is well to study the name and character of God, so that in our straits we may know how and by what title to address our Father who is in heaven.

" *For in thee do I put my trust,*" or, *I have taken shelter in thee.* As chickens run beneath the hen, so do I betake myself to thee. Thou art my great overshadowing Protector, and I have taken refuge beneath thy strength. This is a potent argument in pleading, and our Lord knew not only how to *use* it with God, but how to yield to its power when wielded by others upon himself. " According to thy faith be it done unto thee," is a great rule of heaven in dispensing favour, and when we can sincerely declare that we exercise faith in the Mighty God with regard to the mercy which we seek, we may rest assured that our plea will prevail. Faith, like the sword of Saul, never returns empty ; it overcomes heaven when held in the hand of prayer. As the Saviour prayed, so let us pray, and as he became more than a conqueror, so shall we also through him ; let us when buffeted by storms right bravely cry to the Lord as he did, " in thee do I put my trust."

2 *O my soul,* thou hast said unto the LORD, Thou *art* my Lord : my goodness *extendeth* not to thee :

3 *But* to the saints that *are* in the earth, and *to* the excellent, in whom *is* all my delight.

4 Their sorrows shall be multiplied *that* hasten *after* another *god :* their drink offerings of blood will I not offer, nor take up their names into my lips.

5 The LORD *is* the portion of mine inheritance and of my cup : thou maintainest my lot.

" *O my soul, thou hast said unto the Lord, Thou art my Lord.*" In his inmost heart the Lord Jesus bowed himself to do service to his Heavenly Father, and before the throne of Jehovah his soul vowed allegiance to the Lord for our sakes. We are like him when our soul, truly and constantly in the presence of the heart-searching God, declares her full consent to the rule and government of the Infinite Jehovah, saying, " Thou art my Lord." To avow this with the lip is little, but for *the soul* to say it, especially in times of trial, is a gracious evidence of spiritual health ; to profess it before men is a small matter, but to declare it before Jehovah himself is of far more consequence. This sentence may also be viewed as the utterance of appropriating faith, laying hold upon the Lord by personal covenant and enjoyment ; in this sense may it be our daily song in the house of our pilgrimage.

" *My goodness extendeth not to thee.*" The work of our Lord Jesus was not needful on account of any necessity in the Divine Being. Jehovah would have been inconceivably glorious had the human race perished, and had no atonement been offered. Although the life-work and death-agony of the Son did reflect unparalleled lustre upon every attribute of God, yet the Most Blessed and Infinitely Happy God stood in no need of the obedience and death of his Son ; it was for our sakes that the work of redemption was undertaken, and not because of any lack or want on the part of the Most High. How modestly does the Saviour here estimate his own goodness ! What overwhelming reasons have we for imitating his humility ! " If thou be righteous, what givest thou him ? or what receiveth he of thine hand ?" (Job xxxv. 7.)

" *But to the saints that are in the earth.*" These sanctified ones, although still upon the earth, partake of the results of Jesus' mediatorial work, and by his goodness are made what they are. The peculiar people, zealous for good works, and hallowed to sacred service, are arrayed in the Saviour's righteousness and washed in his blood, and so receive of the goodness treasured up in him ; these are the persons who are profited by the work of the man Christ Jesus ; but that work added nothing to the nature, virtue, or happiness of God, who is blessed for evermore. How much more forcibly is this true of us, poor unworthy servants not fit to be mentioned in comparison with the faithful Son of God ! Our hope must ever be that haply some poor child of God may be served by us, for the Great Father can never need our aid. Well may we sing the verses of Dr. Watts :

> " Oft have my heart and tongue confess'd
> How empty and how poor I am ;
> My praise can never make thee blest,
> Nor add new glories to thy name.
> Yet, Lord, thy saints on earth may reap
> Some profit by the good we do ;
> These are the company I keep,
> These are the choicest friends I know."

Poor believers are God's receivers, and have a warrant from the Crown to receive the revenue of our offerings in the King's name. Saints departed we cannot bless ; even prayer for them is of no service ; but while they are here we should practically prove our love to them, even as our Master did, for they are *the excellent of the earth*. Despite their infirmities, their Lord thinks highly of them, and reckons them to be as nobles among men. The title of " His Excellency" more properly belongs to the meanest saint than to the greatest governor. The true aristocracy are believers in Jesus. They are the only Right Honourables. Stars and garters are poor distinctions compared with the graces of the Spirit. He who knows them best says of them, " *in whom is all my delight.*" They are his Hephzibah and his land Beulah, and before all worlds his delights were with these chosen sons of men. Their own opinion of themselves is far other than their Beloved's opinion of them ; they count themselves to be less than nothing, yet he makes much of them, and sets his heart towards them. What wonders the eyes of Divine Love can see where the hands of Infinite Power have been graciously at work. It was this quicksighted affection which led Jesus to see in us a recompense for all his agony, and sustained him under all his sufferings by the joy of redeeming us from going down into the pit.

The same loving heart which opens towards the chosen people is fast closed against those who continue in their rebellion against God. Jesus hates all wickedness, and especially the high crime of idolatry. The text while it shows our Lord's abhorrence of sin, shows also the sinner's greediness after it. Professed believers are often slow towards the true Lord, but sinners " *hasten after another god.*" They run like madmen where we creep like snails. Let their zeal rebuke our tardiness. Yet theirs is a case in which the more they haste the worse they speed, for *their sorrows are multiplied* by their diligence in multiplying their sins. Matthew Henry pithily says, " They that multiply gods multiply griefs to themselves ; for whosoever thinks one god too little, will find two too many, and yet hundreds not enough." The cruelties and hardships which men endure for their false gods is wonderful to contemplate ; our missionary reports are a noteworthy comment on this passage ; but perhaps our own experience is an equally vivid exposition ; for when we have given our heart to idols, sooner or later we have had to smart for it. Near the roots of our self-love all our sorrows lie, and when that idol is overthrown, the sting is gone from grief. Moses broke the golden calf and ground it to powder, and cast it into the water of which he made Israel to drink, and so shall our cherished idols become bitter portions for us, unless we at once forsake them. Our Lord had no selfishness ; he served but one Lord, and served him only. As for those who turn aside from Jehovah, he was separate from them, bearing their reproach without the camp. Sin and the Saviour had no communion. He came to destroy, not to patronize or be allied with the works of the devil. Hence he refused the testimony of unclean spirits as to his divinity, for in nothing would he have fellowship with darkness. We should be careful above measure not to connect ourselves in the remotest degree with falsehood in religion ; even the most solemn of Popish rites we must abhor. " *Their drink offerings of blood will I not offer.*" The old proverb says, " It is not safe to eat at the devil's mess, though the spoon be never so long." The mere mentioning of ill names it were well to avoid,—" *nor take up their names into my lips.*" If we allow poison upon the lip, it may ere long penetrate to the inwards, and it is well to keep out of the mouth that which we would shut out from the heart. If the Church would enjoy union with Christ, she must break all the bonds of impiety, and keep herself pure from all the pollutions of carnal will-worship, which now pollute the service of God. Some professors are guilty of great sin in remaining in the communion of Popish churches, where God is as much dishonoured as in Rome herself, only in a more crafty manner.

" *The Lord is the portion of mine inheritance and of my cup.*" With what confidence and bounding joy does Jesus turn to Jehovah, whom his soul possessed and delighted in ! Content beyond measure with his portion in the Lord his God, he had not a single desire with which to hunt after other gods ; his cup was full, and his heart was full too ; even in his sorest sorrows he still laid hold with both his hands upon his Father, crying, " My God, my God ;" he had not so much as a thought of falling down to worship the prince of this world, although tempted with an " all these will I give thee." We, too, can make our boast in the Lord ; he is the meat and the drink of our souls. He is our portion, supplying all our necessities, and our cup yielding royal luxuries ; our cup in this life, and our inheritance in the life to come. As children of the Father who is in heaven, we inherit, by virtue of our joint heirship with Jesus, all the riches of the covenant of grace ; and the portion which falls to us sets upon our table the bread of heaven and the new wine of the kingdom. Who would not be satisfied with such dainty diet ? Our shallow cup of sorrow we may well drain with resignation, since the deep cup of love stands side by side with it, and will never be empty. " *Thou maintainest my lot.*" Some tenants have a covenant in their leases that they themselves shall maintain and uphold, but in our case Jehovah himself maintains our lot. Our Lord Jesus delighted in this truth, that the Father was on his side, and would maintain his right against all the wrongs of men. He knew that his elect would be reserved for him, and that almighty power would preserve them as his lot and reward for ever. Let us also be glad, because the Judge of all the earth will vindicate our righteous cause.

6 The lines are fallen unto me in pleasant *places ;* yea, I have a goodly heritage.

7 I will bless the LORD, who hath given me counsel : my reins also instruct me in the night seasons.

Jesus found the way of obedience to lead into " *pleasant places.*" Notwithstanding all the sorrows which marred his countenance, he exclaimed, " Lo, I come ; in the volume of the book it is written of me, I delight to do thy will, O my God : yea, thy law is within my heart." It may seem strange, but while no other man was ever so thoroughly acquainted with grief, it is our belief that no other man ever experienced so much joy and delight in service, for no other served so faithfully and with such great results in view as his recompense of reward. The joy which was set before him must have sent some of its beams of splendour a-down the rugged places where he endured the cross, despising the shame, and must have made them in some respects pleasant places to the generous heart of the Redeemer. At any rate, we know that Jesus was well content with the blood-bought portion which the lines of electing love marked off as his spoil with the strong and his portion with the great. Therein he solaced himself on earth, and delights himself in heaven ; and he asks no more "GOODLY HERITAGE" than that his own beloved may be with him where he is and behold his glory. All the saints can use the language of this verse, and the more thoroughly they can enter into its contented, grateful, joyful spirit the better for themselves, and the more glorious to their God. Our Lord was poorer than we are, for he had not where to lay his head, and yet when he mentioned his poverty he never used a word of murmuring ; discontented spirits are as unlike Jesus as the croaking raven is unlike the cooing dove. Martyrs have been happy in dungeons. "From the delectable orchard of the Leonine prison the Italian martyr dated his letter, and the presence of God made the gridiron of Laurence pleasant to him." Mr. Greenham was bold enough to say, "They never felt God's love, or tasted forgiveness of sins, who are discontented." Some divines think that discontent was the first sin, the rock which wrecked our race in paradise ; certainly there can be no paradise where this evil spirit has power, its slime will poison all the flowers of the garden.

"*I will bless the Lord, who hath given me counsel.*" Praise as well as prayer was presented to the Father by our Lord Jesus, and we are not truly his followers unless our resolve be, "I will bless the Lord." Jesus is called Wonderful, Counsellor, but as man he spake not of himself, but as his Father had taught him. Read in confirmation of this, John vii. 16 ; viii. 28 ; and xii. 49, 50 ; and the prophecy concerning him in Isaiah xi. 2, 3. It was our Redeemer's wont to repair to his Father for direction, and having received it, he blessed him for giving him counsel. It would be well for us if we would follow his example of lowliness, cease from trusting in our own understanding, and seek to be guided by the Spirit of God. "*My reins also instruct me in the night seasons.*" By the reins understand the inner man, the affections and feelings. The communion of the soul with God brings to it an inner spiritual wisdom which in still seasons is revealed to itself. Our Redeemer spent many nights alone upon the mountain, and we may readily conceive that together with his fellowship with heaven, he carried on a profitable commerce with himself ; reviewing his experience, forecasting his work, and considering his position. Great generals fight their battles in their own mind long before the trumpet sounds, and so did our Lord win our battle on his knees before he gained it on the cross. It is a gracious habit after taking counsel from above to take counsel within. Wise men see more with their eyes shut by night than fools can see by day with their eyes open. He who learns from God and so gets the seed, will soon find wisdom within himself growing in the garden of his soul ; "Thine ears shall hear a voice behind thee, saying, This is the way, walk ye in it, when ye turn to the right hand and when ye turn to the left." The night season which the sinner chooses for his sins is the hallowed hour of quiet when believers hear the soft still voices of heaven, and of the heavenly life within themselves.

8 I have set the LORD always before me : because *he is* at my right hand, I shall not be moved.

9 Therefore my heart is glad, and my glory rejoiceth : my flesh also shall rest in hope.

10 For thou wilt not leave my soul in hell ; neither wilt thou suffer thine Holy One to see corruption.

11 Thou wilt shew me the path of life : in thy presence *is* fulness of joy ; at thy right hand *there are* pleasures for evermore.

The fear of death at one time cast its dark shadow over the soul of the Redeemer, and we read that " he was heard in that he feared." There appeared unto him an angel, strengthening him ; perhaps the heavenly messenger reassured him of his glorious resurrection as his people's surety, and of the eternal joy into which he should admit the flock redeemed by blood. Then hope shone full upon our Lord's soul, and, as recorded in these verses, he surveyed the future with holy confidence because he had a continued eye to Jehovah, and enjoyed his perpetual presence. He felt that, thus sustained, he could never be driven from his life's grand design ; nor was he, for he stayed not his hand till he could say, " It is finished." What an infinite mercy was this for us ! In this immoveableness, caused by simple faith in the divine help, Jesus is to be viewed as our exemplar ; to recognize the presence of the Lord is the duty of every believer ; *" I have set the Lord always before me ;"* and to *trust* the Lord as our champion and guard is the privilege of every saint ; *" because he is at my right hand, I shall not be moved."* The apostle translates this passage, " I foresaw the Lord always before my face ;" Acts ii. 25 ; the eye of Jesus' faith could discern beforehand the continuance of divine support to his suffering Son, in such a degree that he should never be moved from the accomplishment of his purpose of redeeming his people. By the power of God at his right hand he foresaw that he should smite through all who rose up against him, and on that power he placed the firmest reliance. He clearly foresaw that he must die, for he speaks of his flesh resting, and of his soul in the abode of separate spirits ; death was full before his face, or he would not have mentioned corruption ; but such was his devout reliance upon his God, that he sang over the tomb, and rejoiced in vision of the sepulchre. He knew that the visit of his soul to Sheol, or the invisible world of disembodied spirits, would be a very short one, and that his body in a very brief space would leave the grave, uninjured by its sojourn there ; all this made him say, *" my heart is glad,"* and moved his tongue, the *glory* of his frame, to *rejoice* in God, the strength of his salvation. Oh, for such holy faith in the prospect of trial and of death ! It is the work of faith, not merely to create a peace which passeth all understanding, but to fill the heart full of gladness until the tongue, which, as the organ of an intelligent creature, is our glory, bursts forth in notes of harmonious praise. Faith gives us living joy, and bestows dying rest. *" My flesh also shall rest in hope."*

Our Lord Jesus was not disappointed in his hope. He declared his Father's faithfulness in the words, *" thou wilt not leave my soul in hell,"* and that faithfulness was proven on the resurrection morning. Among the departed and disembodied Jesus was not left ; he had believed in the resurrection, and he received it on the third day, when his body rose in glorious life, according as he had said in joyous confidence, *" neither wilt thou suffer thine Holy One to see corruption."* Into the outer prison of the grave his body might go, but into the inner prison of corruption he could not enter. He who in soul and body was pre-eminently God's " Holy One," was loosed from the pains of death, because it was not possible that he should be holden of it. This is noble encouragement to all the saints ; die they must, but rise they shall, and though in their case they shall see corruption, yet they shall rise to everlasting life. Christ's resurrection is the cause, the earnest, the guarantee, and the emblem of the rising of all his people. Let them, therefore, go to their graves as to their beds, resting their flesh among the clods as they now do upon their couches.

"Since Jesus is mine, I'll not fear undressing,
But gladly put off these garments of clay ;
To die in the Lord is a covenant blessing,
Since Jesus to glory through death led the way."

Wretched will that man be who, when the Philistines of death invade his soul, shall find that, like Saul, he is forsaken of God ; but blessed is he who has

the Lord at his right hand, for he shall fear no ill, but shall look forward to
an eternity of bliss.

11. "*Thou wilt shew me the path of life.*" To Jesus first this way was shown,
for he is the first-begotten from the dead, the first-born of every creature. He
himself opened up the way through his own flesh, and then trod it as the forerunner of his own redeemed. The thought of being made the path of life to
his people, gladdened the soul of Jesus. "*In thy presence is fulness of joy.*" Christ
being raised from the dead ascended into glory, to dwell in constant nearness
to God, where joy is at its full for ever : the foresight of this urged him
onward in his glorious but grievous toil. To bring his chosen to eternal happiness was the high ambition which inspired him, and made him wade through a
sea of blood. O God, when the worldling's mirth has all expired, for ever with
Jesus may we dwell "*at thy right hand,*" where "*there are pleasures for evermore ;*"
and meanwhile, may we have an earnest by tasting thy love below. Trapp's
note on the heavenly verse which closes the Psalm is a sweet morsel, which
may serve for a contemplation, and yield a foretaste of our inheritance. He
writes, "Here is as much said as can be, but words are too weak to utter it.
For *quality* there is in heaven joy and pleasures ; for *quantity*, a fulness, a torrent
whereat they drink without let or loathing ; for *constancy*, it is at God's right
hand, who is stronger than all, neither can any take us out of his hand ; it
is a constant happiness without intermission : and for *perpetuity* it is for evermore.
Heaven's joys are without measure, mixture, or end."

EXPLANATORY NOTES AND QUAINT SAYINGS.

Title.—There is a diversity of opinion as to the meaning of the title of this
Psalm. It is called "*Michtam of David,*" but *Michtam* is the Hebrew word
untranslated—the Hebrew word in English letters—and its signification is involved in obscurity. According to some, it is derived from a verb which means
to hide, and denotes a mystery or secret. Those who adopt this view, regard
the title as indicating a depth of doctrinal and spiritual import in the Psalm,
which neither the writer nor any of his contemporaries had fathomed. According to others, it is derived from a verb which means *to cut, to grave, to write,*
and denotes simply a writing of David. With this view agree the Chaldee and
Septuagint versions, the former translating it, "a straight sculpture of David :"
and the latter, "an inscription upon a pillar to David." Others again, look
upon "*Michtam,*" as being derived from a noun which means gold, and they
understand it as denoting a golden Psalm—a Psalm of surpassing excellence, and
worthy of being written in letters of gold. This was the opinion of our translators, and hence they have rendered it on the margin—"*A golden Psalm of
David.*" The works of the most excellent Arabian poets were called golden,
because they were written in letters of gold ; and this golden song may have
been written and hung up in some conspicuous part of the Temple. Many other
interpretations have been given of this term, but at this distance of time, we
can only regard it as representing some unassignable peculiarity of the composition.—*James Frame*, 1858.

Title.—Such are the riches of this Psalm, that some have been led to think
the obscure title, "*Michtam,*" has been prefixed to it on account of its *golden
stores.* For כֶּתֶם is used of the "gold of Ophir" (*e.g.*, Psalm xlv. 9), and
מכתם might be a derivative from that root. But as there is a group of five
other Psalms (namely, lvi., lvii., lviii., lix., lx.), that bear this title, whose subject-
matter is various, but which all end in a *tone of triumph*, it has been suggested
that the Septuagint may be nearly right in their Στηλογραφία, as if "A Psalm to
be hung up or inscribed on a pillar to commemorate victory." It is, however,

more likely still that the term " *Michtam*" (like " *Maschil* "), is a musical term, whose real meaning and use we have lost, and may recover only when the ransomed house of Israel return home with songs. Meanwhile, the subject-matter of this Psalm itself is very clearly this—*the righteous one's satisfaction with his lot.—Andrew A. Bonar.*

Whole Psalm.—Allow that in verse ten it is clear that our Lord is in this Psalm, yet the application of every verse to Jesus in *Gethsemane* appears to be far-fetched, and inaccurate. How verse nine could suit the agony and bloody sweat, it is hard to conceive, and equally so is it with regard to verse six. The " cup" of verse five is so direct a contrast to that cup concerning which Jesus prayed in anguish of spirit, that it cannot be a reference to it. Yet we think it right to add, that Mr. James Frame has written a very valuable work on this Psalm, entitled, " Christ in Gethsemane," and he has supported his theory by the opinion of many of the ancients. He says, " All the distinguished interpreters of ancient days, such as Eusebius, Jerome, and Augustine, explain the Psalm as referring to the Messiah, in his passion and his victory over death and the grave, including his subsequent exaltation to the right hand of God ;" and, in a foot note he gives the following quotations : *Jerome.*—" The Psalm pertains to Christ, who speaks in it. . . . . It is the voice of our King, which he utters in the human nature that he had assumed, but without detracting from his divine nature. . . . . . The Psalm pertains to his passion." *Augustine.*—" Our King speaks in this Psalm in the person of the human nature that he assumed, at the time of his passion, the royal title inscribed will show itself conspicuous."—*C. H. S.*

Whole Psalm.—The present Psalm is connected in thought and language with the foregoing, and linked on to the following Psalm by catchwords. It is entitled in the Syriac and Arabic versions, a Psalm on the Election of the Church, and on the Resurrection of Christ."—*Christopher Wordsworth, D.D.*, 1868.

Verse 1.—" Preserve me, O God." Here David desireth not deliverance from any special trouble, but generally prayeth to be fenced and defended continually by the providence of God, wishing that the Lord would continue his mercy towards him unto the end, and in the end ; whereby he foresaw it was as needful for him to be safe guarded by God, his protection in the end, as at the time present ; as also how he made no less account of it in his prosperity than in adversity. So that the man of God still feared his infirmity, and therefore acknowledgeth himself ever to stand in need of God his help. And here is a sure and undoubted mark of the child of God, when a man shall have as great a care to continue and grow in well-doing, as to begin ; and this praying for the gift of final perseverance is a special note of the child of God. This holy jealousy of the man of God made him so to desire to be preserved at all times, in all estates, both in soul and body.—*Richard Greenham, 1531—1591.*

Verse 1.—" For in thee do I put my trust." Here the prophet setteth down the cause why he prayeth to God ; whereby he declareth, that none can truly call upon God unless they believe. Rom. x. 14. " How shall they call on him in whom they have not believed ?" In regard whereof, as he prayeth to God to be his Saviour, so he is fully assured that God will be his Saviour. If, then, without faith we cannot truly call upon God, the men of this world rather prate like parrots than pray like Christians, at what time they utter these words ; for that they trust not in God they declare both by neglecting the lawful means, and also in using unlawful means. Some we see trust in friends ; some shoulder out, as they think, the cross with their goods ; some fence themselves with authority ; others bathe and baste themselves in pleasure to put the evil day far from them ; others make flesh their arm ; and others make the wedge of gold their confidence ; and these men when they seek for help at the Lord, mean in their hearts to find it in their friends, good authority and pleasure, howsoever for fear, they dare not say this outwardly. Again, here we are to observe under

what shelter we may harbour ourselves in the showers of adversity, even under
the protection of the Almighty.   And why ?   " Whoso dwelleth in the secret of
the Most High, shall abide in the shadow of the Almighty."   And here in effect
is showed, that whosoever putteth his trust in God shall be preserved ; otherwise the prophet's reason here had not been good.   Besides, we see he pleadeth
not by merit, but sueth by faith, teaching us that if we come with like faith, we
may obtain the like deliverance.—*Richard Greenham.*

Verse 2.—" *O my soul, thou hast said unto the Lord, Thou art my Lord.*"   I
wish I could have heard what you said to yourself when these words were first
mentioned.   I believe I could guess the language of some of you.   When you
heard me repeat these words, " *O my soul, thou hast said unto the Lord, Thou
art my Lord,*" you thought, " I have never said anything to the Lord, unless
when I cried out, Depart from me, for I desire not the knowledge of thy ways."
Has not something like this passed in your minds ?   I will try again.   When I
first mentioned the text, " Let me consider," you secretly said, " I believe that I
did once say to the Lord, Thou art my Lord ; but it was so long ago, that I had
almost forgotten it ; but I suppose that it must have been at such a time when
I was in trouble.   I had met with disappointments in the world ; and then,
perhaps, I cried, Thou art my portion, O Lord.   Or, perhaps, when I was under
serious impressions, in the hurry of my spirits, I might look up to God and say,
Thou art my Lord.   But, whatever I could or did formerly say, I am certain
that I cannot say it at present."   Have none of you thought in this manner ?
I will hazard one conjecture more ; and I doubt not but in this case I shall
guess rightly.   When I repeated these words, " O my soul, thou hast said unto
the Lord, Thou art my Lord ;" " So have I," thought one ; " So have I," thought
another ; I have said it often, but I said it with peculiar solemnity and pleasure,
when, in an act of humble devotion, I lately threw my ransomed, rescued,
grateful soul at his feet, and cried, " O Lord, truly I am thy servant ; I am thy
servant ; thou hast loosed my bonds."   The very recollection of it is pleasant ;
and I shall now have an opportunity of renewing my vows, and hope to recover
something of the divine serenity and joy which I at that time experienced."—
Samuel Lavington's Sermons, 1810.
Verse 2.—" *Thou art my Lord.*"   He acknowledgeth the Lord Jehovah ; but
he seeth him not as it were then afar off, but drawing near unto him, he sweetly
embraceth him ; which thing is proper unto faith, and to that particular applying
which we say to be in faith.—*Robert Rollock,* 1600.
Verse 2.—" *My goodness extendeth not to thee.*"   I think the words should be
understood of what the Messiah was doing for men.   My goodness, טוֹבָתִי
tobhathi, " my bounty" is not to thee.   What I am doing can add nothing to
thy divinity ; thou art not providing this astonishing sacrifice because thou
canst derive any excellence from it ; but this bounty extends *to the saints*—
to all the spirits of just men made perfect, whose bodies are still in the earth ;
and to the excellent, אַדִּירֵי *addirey,* " the noble or super-eminent ones," those
who through faith and patience inherit the promises.   The saints and illustrious
ones not only taste of my goodness, but enjoy my salvation.   Perhaps *angels*
themselves may be intended ; they are not uninterested in the incarnation,
passion, death, and resurrection of our Lord.   They *desire to look into these*
things ; and the victories of the cross in the conversion of sinners cause joy
among the angels of God.—*Adam Clarke.*
Verse 2.—" *My goodness extendeth not to thee ;*" " My well-doing extendeth
not to thee."   Oh, what shall I render unto thee, my God, for all thy benefits
towards me ?   what shall I repay ?   Alas ! I can do thee no good, for mine
imperfect goodness cannot pleasure thee who art most perfect and goodness
itself ; my well-doing can do thee no good, my wickedness can do thee no harm.
I receive all good from thee, but no good can I return to thee ; wherefore I acknowledge thee to be most rich, and myself to be most beggarly ; so far off is
it that thou standest in any need of me.   Wherefore I will join myself to thy

people, that whatsoever I have they may profit by it ; and whatsoever they have I may profit by it, seeing the things that I have received must be put out to loan, to gain some comfort to others. Whatsoever others have, they have not for their own private use, but that by them, as by pipes and conduits, they liberally should be conveyed unto me also. Wherefore in this strain we are taught, that if we be the children of God, we must join ourselves in a holy league to his people, and by mutual participation of the gifts of God, we must testify each to other, that we be of the number and communion of saints ; and this is an undoubted badge and cognizance of him that loveth God, if he also loveth them that are begotten of God. Wherefore, if we so profess ourselves to be of God and to worship him, then we must join ourselves to the church of God which with us doth worship God. And this must we do of necessity, for it is a branch of our belief that there is a communion of saints in the church ; and if we believe that there is a God, we must also believe that there is a remnant of people, unto whom God revealeth himself, and communicateth his mercies, in whom we must have all our delight, to whom we must communicate according to the measure of grace given unto every one of us.—*Richard Greenham.*

Verse 2.—" *My goodness extendeth not to thee.* " Oh, how great is God's goodness to you ! He calls upon others for the same things, and conscience stands as Pharaoh's taskmasters, requiring the tale of bricks but not allowing straw ; it impels and presseth, but gives no enlargement of heart, and buffets and wounds them for neglect : as the hard creditor that, taking the poor debtor by the throat, saith, " Pay me that thou owest me," but yields him no power to do it ; thus God might deal with you also, for *he oweth not assistance to us ;* but *we owe obedience* to him. Remember, we had power, and it is just to demand what we cannot do, because the weakness that is in us is of ourselves : we have impoverished ourselves. Therefore, when in much mercy he puts forth his hand into the work with thee, be very thankful. If the work be not done, he is no loser ; if done, and well done, he is no gainer. Job xxii. 2 ; xxxv. 6—8. But the gain is all to thee ; all the good that comes by it is to thyself. *Joseph Symonds,* 1639.

Verse 2 (last clause).—It is a greater glory to us that we are allowed to serve God, than it is to him that we offer him that service. He is not rendered happy by us ; but we are made happy by him. He can do without such earthly servants ; but we cannot do without such a heavenly Master.— *William Secker.*

Verse 2 (last clause).—There is nothing added to God : he is so perfect, that no sin can hurt him ; and so righteous, that no righteousness can benefit him. *O Lord, my righteousness extendeth not to thee ! thou hast no need of my righteousness.* Acts xvii. 24, 25. God hath no need of anything.—*Richard Stock,* 1641.

Verse 2.—As Christ is the head of man, so is God the head of Christ (1 Cor. xi. 3) ; and as man is subject unto Christ, so is Christ subject to God ; not in regard of the divine nature, wherein there is an equality, and consequently no dominion or jurisdiction ; nor only in his human nature, but in the economy of a Redeemer, considered as one designed, and consenting to be incarnate, and take our flesh ; so that after this agreement, God had a sovereign right to dispose of him according to the articles consented to. In regard of his undertaking and the advantage he was to bring to the elect of God upon earth, he calls God by the solemn title of " his Lord." " O my soul, thou hast said unto the Lord, Thou art my Lord : my goodness extendeth not to thee ; but to the saints that are in the earth." It seems to be the speech of Christ in heaven, mentioning the saints on earth as at a distance from him. I can add nothing to the glory of thy majesty, but the whole fruit of my mediation and suffering will redound to the saints on earth.—*Stephen Charnock.*

Verses 2, 3.—" *My goodness extendeth not to thee ; but to the saints.* " God's goodness to us should make us merciful to others. It were strange indeed a soul should come out of his tender bosom with a hard uncharitable heart. Some children do not indeed take after their earthly parents, as Cicero's son, who had nothing of his father but his name ; but God's children all partake of their heavenly Father's nature. Philosophy tells us, that there is no reaction from the earth to the heavens ; they indeed shed their influences upon the lower world, which quicken and fructify it, but the earth returns none back to make the sun shine the better. David knew that *his goodness extended not unto God*, but this made him reach it forth to his brethren. Indeed, God hath left his poor saints to receive the rents we owe unto him for his mercies. An ingenuous guest, though his friend will take nothing for his entertainment, yet, to show his thankfulness, will give something to his servants.—*William Gurnall*.

Verse 3.—" But to the saints that are in the earth, and to the excellent, in whom is all my delight." My brethren, look upon saintship as the greatest excellency to love it. So did Christ. His eye was " upon the excellent ones in the earth ;" that is, upon the saints, who were excellent to him ; yea, also even when not saints, because God loved them. Isaiah xliii. 4. It is strange to hear how men by their speeches will undervalue a saint as such, if without some other outward excellency. For whilst they acknowledge a man a saint, yet in other respects, they will contemn him ; " He is a holy man," they will say, " but he is weak," etc. But is he a saint ? And can there be any such other imperfection or weakness found as shall lay him low in thy thoughts in comparison of other carnal men more excellent ? Hath not Christ loved him, bought him, redeemed him ?— *Thomas Goodwin*.

Verse 3.—" But to the saints." I understand that a man then evinces affection towards God, and towards those who love God, when his soul yearns after them —when he obliges himself to love them by practically serving and benefiting them—acting towards them as he would act towards God himself were he to see him in need of his service, as David says he did.—*Juan de Valdes*, 1550.

Verse 3.—" The saints." The Papists could abide no saints but those which are in heaven ; which argueth that they live in a kingdom of darkness, and err, not knowing the Scriptures, nor the power of God ; for if they were but meanly conversant in the Scriptures, in the holy epistles, they should find almost in every epistle mention made of the saints who are thereunto called in Jesus Christ, through whom they are sanctified by the Holy Ghost. And mark, he calleth them *" excellent."* Some think rich men to be excellent, some think learned men to be excellent, some count men in authority so to be, but here we are taught that those men are *excellent* who are sanctified by God's graces. *Richard Greenham*.

Verse 3.—By David's language, there were many singular saints in his day : " *To the saints that are in the earth, and to the excellent, in whom is all my delight.*" Was it so then, and should it not be so now ? We know the New Testament outshines the Old as much as the sun outshines the moon. If we then live in a more glorious dispensation, should we not maintain a more glorious conversation ? . . . . " *The excellent.*" Were the sun to give no more delight than a star, you could not believe he was the regent of the day ; were he to transmit no more heat than a glow-worm, you would question his being the source of elementary heat. Were God to do no more than a creature, where would his Godhead be ? Were a man to do no more than a brute, where would his manhood be ? Were not a saint to *excel* a sinner, where would his sanctity be ?— *William Secker*.

Verse 3.—Ingo, an ancient king of the Draves, who making a stately feast, appointed his nobles, at that time Pagans, to sit in the hall below, and commanded certain poor Christians to be brought up into his presence-chamber, to sit with him at his table, to eat and drink of his kingly cheer, at which many wondering, he said, he accounted Christians, though never so poor, a greater ornament to his table, and more worthy of his company than the greatest peers unconverted to the Christian faith ; for when these might be thrust down to hell, those might be his comforts and fellow princes in heaven. Although you see the stars sometimes by their reflections in a puddle, in the bottom of a well, or in a stinking ditch, yet the stars have their situation in heaven. So, although you see a godly man in a poor, miserable, low, despised condition, for the things of this world, yet he is fixed in heaven, in the region of heaven : "Who hath raised us up," saith the apostle, "and made us sit together in heavenly places in Christ Jesus."—*Charles Bradbury's " Cabinet of Jewels,"* 1785.

Verse 3.—To sum up all, we must know that we neither do nor can love the godly so well as we should do ; but all is well if we would love them better, and do like ourselves the less because we do love them no more, and that this is common or usual with me, then I am right : so that we are to love the godly first because God commands it, because they are good ; and in these cases our faith doth work by our love to good men. Next, when I am at the worst, like a sick sheep, I care not for the company of other sheep, but do mope in a corner by myself ; but yet I do not delight in the society of goats or dogs, it proves that I have some good blood left in me ; it is because for the present I take little or no delight in myself or in my God, that I delight no better in the godly : yet as I love myself for all that, so I may be said to love them for all this. Man indeed is a sociable creature, a company-keeper by nature when he is himself ; and if we do not associate ourselves with the ungodly, though for the present, and care not much to show ourselves amongst the godly, the matter is not much, it is a sin of infirmity, not a fruit of iniquity. The disciples went from Christ, but they turned not to the other side as Judas did, who did forsake his Master and joined himself to his Master's enemies, but they got together. Some say Demas did repent (which I think to be the truth), and then he did "embrace this present world," but for the present fit : put case he did forsake Paul ; so did better men than he. Indeed as long as a man hath his delights about him, he will embrace the delights of this present world, or the delights which belong to the world to come ; join with Paul, or cleave to the world. In this temptation our stay is, first, that we care not for the company of goats ; next, that as we should, so we would, and desire that we may take delight in the company of sheep, to count them the only *excellent* men in the world, *in whom is all our delight.* The conclusion is, that to love the saints as saints, is a sound proof of faith ; the reason is, for that we cannot master our affections by love, but first we must master our understandings by faith.—*Richard Capel,* 1586—1656.

Verse 4.—"*Drink offerings of blood.*" The Gentiles used to offer, and sometimes to drink part of the blood of their sacrifices, whether of beasts or of men, as either of them were sacrificed.—*Matthew Poole.*

Verse 4.—"*Drink offerings of blood.*" It is uncertain whether this expression is to be understood literally to be blood, which the heathen actually mixed in their libations when they bound themselves to the commission of some dreadful deed, or whether their libations are figuratively called offerings of blood to denote the horror with which the writer regarded them.—*George R. Noyes, in loc.* 1846.

Verse 4 (*last clause*).—A sin rolled under the tongue becomes soft and supple, and the throat is so short and slippery a passage, that insensibly it may slide down from the mouth into the stomach ; and contemplative wantonness quickly turns into practical uncleanness.—*Thomas Fuller.*

Verse 5.—"*The Lord is the portion of mine inheritance.*" If the Lord be thy portion, then thou mayest conclude, omnipotency is my portion, immensity, all-sufficiency, etc. Say not, If so, then I should be omnipotent, etc. There is a vast difference betwixt identity and interest, betwixt conveying of a title, and transmutation of nature. A friend gives thee an invaluable treasure, and all the securities of it that thou canst desire ; wilt thou deny it is thine because thou art not changed into its nature ? The attributes are thine, as thy inheritance, as thy lands are thine ; not because thou art changed into their nature, but because the title is conveyed to thee, it is given thee, and improved for thy benefit. If another manage it, who can do it with greater advantage to thee than thou to thyself, it is no infringement of thy title. . . . . . . The Lord is our *portion*, and this is incomparably more than if we had heaven and earth ; for all the earth is but as a point compared with the vastness of the heavens, and the heavens themselves are but a point compared with God. What a large possession have we then ! There is no confiscation of it, no banishment from it. Our portion fills heaven and earth, and is infinitely above heaven and below earth, and beyond both. Poor men boast and pride themselves of a kingdom, but we have more than all the kingdoms of the world and the glory thereof. Christ has given us more than the devil could offer him.— *David Clarkson.*

Verse 5.—"*Portion of mine inheritance and of my cup,*" may contain an allusion to the daily supply of food, and also to the inheritance of Levi. Deut. xviii. 1, 2.—"*Critical and Explanatory Pocket Bible.*" *By A. R. Fausset and B. M. Smith,* 1867.

Verses 5, 6.—" *The Lord is the portion of mine inheritance: the lines are fallen unto me in pleasant places ; yea, I have a goodly heritage.*" " Blessed are the people that are in such a case ; yea, blessed are the people whose God is the Lord." No greater mercy can be bestowed upon any people, family, or person, than this, for God to dwell among them. If we value this mercy according to the excellence and worth of that which is bestowed, it is the greatest ; if we value it according to the good will of him that gives it, it will appear likewise to be the greatest favour. The greatness of the good will of God in giving himself to be our acquaintance, is evident in the nature of the gift. A man may give his estate to them to whom his love is not very large, but he never gives himself but upon strong affection. God gives abundantly to all the works of his hands ; he causeth the sun to shine upon the evil and upon the good, and the rain to descend upon the just and the unjust ; but it cannot be conceived that he should give himself to be a portion, a friend, father, husband, but in abundance of love. Whosoever therefore shall refuse acquaintance with God, slighteth the greatest favour that ever God did bestow upon man. Now, consider what a high charge this is ; to abuse such a kindness from God is an act of the greatest vileness. David was never so provoked as when the king of Ammon abused his kindness, in his ambassadors, after his father's death. And God is highly provoked when his greatest mercies, bestowed in the greatest love, are rejected and cast away. What could God give more and better than himself ? . . . . . Ask David what he thinks of God ; he was well acquainted with him, he dwelt in his house, and by his good will would never be out of his more immediate presence and company ; enquire, I pray, what he found amiss in him. That you may know his mind the better, he hath left it upon record in more than one or two places, what a friend he hath had of God. " *The lines are fallen unto me in pleasant places ; yea, I have a goodly heritage.*" Why, what is that you boast of so much, O David ? Have not others had kingdoms as well as you ? No, that's not the thing ; a crown is one of the least jewels in my cabinet : " *The Lord is the portion of mine inheritance and of my cup.*"— *James Janeway.*

Verses 5, 6.—Take notice not only of the mercies of God, but of God in the mercies. Mercies are never so savoury as when they savour of a Saviour.— *Ralph Venning,* 1620—1673.

Verse 6.—" *The lines are fallen unto me in pleasant places ; yea, I have a goodly heritage.*" Bitter herbs will go down very well, when a man has such delicious " meats which the world knows not of." The sense of our Father's love is like honey at the end of every rod ; it turns stones into bread, and water into wine, and the valley of trouble into a door of hope ; it makes the biggest evils seem as if they were none, or better than none ; for it makes our deserts like the garden of the Lord, and when we are upon the cross for Christ, as if we were in paradise with Christ. Who would quit his duty for the sake of suffering, that hath such relief under it? Who would not rather walk in truth, when he hath such a cordial to support him, than by the conduct of fleshly wisdom, to take any indirect or irregular method for his own deliverance?—*Timothy Cruso.*

Verse 6.—" The lines." Probably alluding to the division of the land by lot, and the measuring of it off by ropes and lines. David believed in an overruling destiny which fixed the bounds of his abode, and his possessions; he did more, he was satisfied with all the appointment of the predestinating God.—*C. H. S.*

Verse 7.—" I will bless the Lord, who hath given me counsel." The Holy Ghost is a spirit of counsel, powerfully instructing and convincingly teaching how to act and walk, for he directs us to set right steps, and to walk with a right foot, and thereby prevents us of many a sin, by seasonable instruction set on upon our hearts with a strong hand; as Isaiah viii. 11. For, as the same prophet says (Isaiah xi. 2), he is the spirit of counsel and of might. Of counsel to direct; of might, to strengthen the inner man. Such he was to Christ the Head, of whom it is there spoken. For instance, in that agony (on the determination of which our salvation depended), and conflict in the garden, when he prayed, "Let this cup pass," it was this good Spirit that counselled him to die; and he blesseth God for it: "I bless the Lord that hath given me counsel." It was that counsel that in that case caused his heart to say, "Not my will, but thine."—*Thomas Goodwin.*

Verse 7.—" My reins." Common experience shows that the workings of the mind, particularly the passions of joy, grief, and fear, have a very remarkable effect on the reins or kidneys, and from their retired situation in the body, and their being hid in fat, they are often used in Scripture to denote the most secret working of the soul and affections.—*John Parkhurst.*

Verse 7.—" My reins also instruct me in the night seasons." This shows that God, who, he says, was always present to him, had given him some admonition in his dreams, or at least his waking thoughts by night, from whence he gathered a certain assurance of his recovery; possibly he might be directed to some remedy. Antonine thanks the gods for directing him in his sleep to remedies.—*Z. Mudge, in loc,* 1744.

Verse 7.—" My reins also instruct me in the night seasons." We have a saying among ourselves, that "the pillow is the best counsellor;" and there is much truth in the saying, especially if we have first committed ourselves in prayer to God, and taken a prayerful spirit with us to our bed. In the quiet of its silent hours, undisturbed by the passions, and unharassed by the conflicts of the world, we can commune with our own heart, and be instructed and guarded as to our future course even " *in the night season.*" David especially seems to have made these seasons sources of great profit as well as delight. Sometimes he loved to meditate upon God as he lay upon his bed; and it was no doubt as he meditated on the Lord's goodness, and on the way by which he had led him, that he was, as it were, constrained, even at midnight, to arise and pray. While, therefore, we acknowledge the pillow to be a good counsellor, let us with David here acknowledge also that it is the Lord who gives the counsel, and sends the instruction in the night season.—*Barton Bouchier.*

Verse 8.—" I have set the Lord always before me." David did not by fits and starts set the Lord before him; but he "*always*" set the Lord before him in his course; he had his eye upon the Lord, and so much the Hebrew word imports: I have equally set the Lord before me; that is the force of the original word, that is, I have set the Lord before me, at one time as well as another, without any irregular affections or passions, etc. In every place, in every condition, in every company, in every employment, and in every enjoyment, I have set the Lord equally before me; and this raised him, and this will raise any Christian, by degrees, to a very great height of holiness.—*Thomas Brooks.*

Verse 8.—" I have set the Lord always before me." Hebrew, I have *equally* set, or proposed. The apostle translateth it, "I foresaw the Lord always before my face." Acts ii. 25. I set the eye of my faith full upon him, and suffer it not to take to other things ; I look him in the face, *oculo irretorto*, as the eagle looketh upon the sun ; and *oculo adamantino*, with an eye of adamant, which turns only to one point : so here, *I have equally set the Lord before me*, without irregular affections and passions. And this was one of those lessons that his *reins had taught* him, that the Holy Spirit had dictated unto him.—*John Trapp*.

Verse 8.—"*I have set the Lord* ALWAYS *before me.*" Like as the gnomon doth ever behold the north star, whether it be closed and shut up in a coffer of gold, silver, or wood, never losing its nature ; so a faithful Christian man, whether he abound in wealth or be pinched with poverty, whether he be of high or low degree in this world, ought continually to have his faith and hope surely built and grounded upon Christ, and to have his heart and mind fast fixed and settled in him, and to follow him through thick and thin, through fire and water, through wars and peace, through hunger and cold, through friends and foes, through a thousand perils and dangers, through the surges and waves of envy, malice, hatred, evil speeches, railing sentences, contempt of the world, flesh, and devil, and even in death itself, be it never so bitter, cruel, and tyrannical, yet never to lose sight and view of Christ, never to give over faith, hope, and trust in him.—*Robert Cawdray*.

Verse 8.—"*I have set the Lord always before me.*" By often thinking of God, the heart will be enticed into desires after him. Isaiah xxvi. 8. "The desire of our soul is to thy name, and to the remembrance of thee ;" and see what follows, verse 9 : "With my soul have I desired thee in the night ; yea, with my spirit within me will I seek thee early." Love sets the soul on musing, and from musing to praying. Meditation is prayer in bullion, prayer in the ore—soon melted and run into holy desires. The laden cloud soon drops into rain ; the piece charged soon goes off when fire is put to it. A meditating soul is in *proxima potentia* to prayer.—*William Gurnall*.

Verse 8.—"*I have set the Lord always before me,*" etc. He that by faith eyes God continually as his protector in trouble "*shall not be moved*" with any evil that he suffers, and he that eyes God by faith as his pattern in holiness, shall not be moved from doing that which is good. This thought—*the Lord is at our right hand*—keeps us from turning either to the right hand or to the left. It is said of Enoch, that "he walked with God" (Genesis v. 22), and though the history of his life be very short, yet 'tis said of him a second time (verse 24), that "he walked with God." He walked so much with God that he walked as God : he did not "*walk*" (which kind of walking the apostle reproves, 1 Cor. iii. 3), "*as men.*" He walked so little like the world, that his stay was little in the world. "He was not," saith the text, "for God took him." He took him from the world to himself, or, as the author to the Hebrews reports it, "he was translated that he should not see death, for he had this testimony, that he pleased God."—*Joseph Caryl*.

Verse 8.—"*Because he is at my right hand,*" etc. Of ourselves we stand not at any time, by his power we may overcome at all times. And when we are sorest assaulted he is ever ready *at our right hand* to support and stay us that we shall not fall. He hath well begun, and shall happily go forward in his work, who hath in truth begun. For true grace well planted in the heart, how weak soever, shall hold out for ever. All total decays come from this—that the heart was never truly mollified, nor grace deeply and kindly rooted therein.—*John Ball*.

Verse 8.—"*He is at my right hand.*" This phrase of speech is borrowed from those who, when they take upon them the patronage, defence, or tuition of any, will set them on their right hand, as in place of most safeguard. Experience confirmeth this in children, who in any imminent danger shroud and shelter themselves under their father's arms or hands, as under a sufficient buckler. Such was the estate of the man of God, as here appeareth, who was hemmed and hedged in with the power of God, both against present evils, and dangers to come.—*Richard Greenham*.

Verse 8.—Even as a column or pillar is sometimes on thy right hand, and sometimes on thy left hand, because thou dost change thy standing, sitting, or walking, for it is unmovable and keepeth one place ; so God is sometimes favourable and bountiful unto thee, and sometimes seemeth to be wroth and angry with thee, because thou dost fall from virtue to vice, from obedience and humility to pride and presumption ; for in the Lord there is no change, no, not so much as any shadow of change. He is immutable, always one and everlasting. If thou wilt bend thyself to obedience, and to a virtuous and godly life, thou shalt ever have him a strong rock, whereupon thou mayst boldly build a castle and tower of defence. He will be unto thee a mighty pillar, bearing up heaven and earth, whereto thou mayst lean and not be deceived, wherein thou mayst trust and not be disappointed. He will ever be at thy right hand, that thou shalt not fall. He will take thy part, and will mightily defend thee against all enemies of thy body and of thy soul ; but if thou wilt shake hands with virtue, and bid it adieu and farewell, and, forsaking the ways of God, wilt live as thou list, and follow thy own corruption, and make no conscience of aught thou doest, defiling and blemishing thyself with all manner of sin and iniquity, then be sure the Lord will appear unto thee in his fury and indignation. From his justice and judgments none shall ever be able to deliver thee.—*Robert Cawdray.*

Verse 9.—*" My heart is glad."* Men may for a time be hearers of the gospel, men may for order's sake pray, sing, receive the sacraments ; but if it be without joy, will not that hypocrisy in time break out ? Will they not begin to be weary ? Nay, will they not be as ready to hear any other doctrine ? Good things cannot long find entertainment in our corruptions, unless the Holy Ghost hath changed us from our old delights to conceive pleasure in these things.—*Richard Greenham.*

Verse 9.—*" My heart is glad, and my glory rejoiceth."* His inward joy was not able to contain itself. We testify our pleasure on lower occasions, even at the gratification of our senses ; when our ear is filled with harmonious melody, when our eye is fixed upon admirable and beauteous objects, when our smell is recreated with agreeable odours, and our taste also by the delicacy and rareness of provisions ; and much more will our soul show its delight, when its faculties, that are of a more exquisite constitution, meet with things that are in all respects agreeable and pleasant to them ; and in God they meet with all those : with his light our understanding is refreshed, and so is our will with his goodness and his love.—*Timothy Rogers.*

Verse 9.—*" Therefore my heart is glad,"* etc. That is, I am all over in very good plight, as well as heart can wish, or require ; I do over-abound exceedingly with joy ; " God forgive me mine unthankfulness and unworthiness of so great glory" (as that martyr said) : " In all the days of my life I was never so merry as now I am in this dark dungeon," etc. Wicked men rejoice in appearance, and not in heart (2 Cor. v. 12) ; their joy is but skin deep, their mirth frothy and flashy, such as wetteth the mouth, but warmeth not the heart. But David is *totus totus, quantus quantus exultabundus ;* his *heart, glory, flesh,* (answerable, as some think to that of the apostle, 1 Thess. v. 23 ; *spirit, soul, and body*) were all overjoyed.—*John Trapp.*

Verse 9.—*" My flesh shall rest in hope."* If a Jew pawned his bed-clothes, God provided mercifully that it should be restored before night : " For," saith he, " that is his covering : wherein shall he sleep ?" Exodus xxii. 27. Truly, hope is the saint's covering, wherein he wraps himself, when he lays his body down to sleep in the grave : " My flesh," saith David, " *shall rest in hope."* O Christian, bestir thyself to redeem thy hope before this sun of thy temporal life goes down upon thee, or else thou art sure to lie down in sorrow. A sad going to the bed of the grave he hath who hath no hope of a resurrection to life.—*William Gurnall.*

Verse 9.—*" My flesh shall rest in hope."* That hope which is grounded on the word, gives rest to the soul ; 'tis an anchor to keep it steady. Heb. vi. 13. Which shows the unmovableness of that which our anchor is fastened to. The promise sustains our faith, and our faith is that which supports us. He that hopes in the Word as David did (Psalm cxix. 81), lays a mighty stress upon it ; as Samson did when he leaned upon the pillars of the house, so as to pull it down upon the Philistines. A believer throws the whole weight of all his affairs and concernments, temporal, spiritual, and eternal, upon the promises of God, like a man resolved to stand or fall with them. He ventures himself, and all that belongs to him, entirely upon this bottom, which is in effect to say, if they will not bear me up, I am content to sink ; I know that there shall be a performance of those things which have been told me from the Lord, and therefore I will incessantly look for it.—*Timothy Cruso.*

Verse 10.—" *For thou wilt not leave my soul in hell,*" etc. The title of this golden text may be—*The embalming of the dead saints :* the force whereof is to free the souls from dereliction in the state of death, and to secure the bodies of God's saints from corruption in the grave. It is the art which I desire to learn, and at this time, teach upon this sad occasion,* even the preparing of this confection against our burials.—*George Hughes,* 1642.

Verse 10.—Many of the elder Reformers held that our Lord in soul actually descended into hell, according to some of them to suffer there as our surety, and according to others to make a public triumph over death and hell. This idea was almost universally, and, as we believe, most properly repudiated by the Puritans. To prove this fact, it may be well to quote from Corbet's witty itinerary of,

> " Foure clerkes of Oxford, doctors two, and two
> That would be doctors."

He laments the secularisation of church appurtenances at Banbury, by the Puritans, whom he describes as,

> ———————" They which tell
> That Christ hath nere descended into hell,
> But to the grave."

C. H. S.   The quotation is from Richard Corbet's Poems, 1632.

Verse 10.—" *My soul in hell.*"   Christ in soul descended into hell, when as our surety he submitted himself to bear those hellish sorrows (or equivalent to them), which we were bound by our sins to suffer for ever. His descension is his projection of himself into the sea of God's wrath conceived for our sins, and his ingression into most unspeakable straits and torments in his soul, which we should else have suffered for ever in hell. This way of Christ's descending into hell is expressly uttered in the person of David, as the type of Christ. Psalm lxxxvi. 13 ; cxvi. 3 ; lxix. 1--3. Thus the prophet Isaiah saith, " His soul was made an offering." Isaiah liii. 10. And this I take it David means, when he said of Christ, " *Thou wilt not leave my soul in hell.*" Psalm xvi. ; Acts ii. And thus Christ descended into hell when he was alive, not when he was dead. Thus his soul was in hell when in the garden he did sweat blood, and on the cross when he cried so lamentably, " My God, my God, why hast thou forsaken me ?" Matt. xxvi. 38.—*Nicholas Byfield's " Exposition of the Creed,"* 1676.

Verse 10.—" *In hell.*"   *Sheol* here, as *hades* in the New Testament, signifies the state of the dead, the separate state of souls after death, the invisible world of souls, where Christ's soul was, though it did not remain there, but on the third day returned to its body again. It seems best of all to interpret this word of the grave as it is rendered ; Gen. xlii. 38 ; Isaiah xxxviii. 18.—*John Gill.*

Verse 10.—" *Thine Holy One.*"   *Holiness* preserves the soul from dereliction, in the state of death, and the body of the saint from corruption in the grave. If it be desired by any that doubt of it, to see the clear issue of this from the

---

* A Funeral Sermon.

text, I shall guide them to read this text with a great accent upon that term, " *Thine Holy One*," that they may take special notice of it, even the quality of that man exempted from these evils. In this the Spirit of God puts an emphasis upon *holiness*, as counter-working and prevailing over death and the grave. It is this and nothing but this, that thus keeps the man, dead and buried, from desertion in death, and corruption in the grave.—*George Hughes*.

Verse 10.—The great promise to Christ is, that though he took a corruptible body upon him, yet he should " *not see corruption*," that is, *partake of corruption :* corruption should have no communion with, much less power over him.—*Joseph Caryl*.

Verse 10.—Quoted by the apostle Peter (Acts ii. 27); on which Hackett (*Com. in loc.*) observes :—" The sense then may be expressed thus : Thou wilt not give me up as a prey to death ; he shall not have power over me, to dissolve the body and cause it to return to dust."

Verse 11.—In this verse are four things observable :—1. *A Guide*, THOU. 2. *A Traveller*, ME. 3. *A Way*, THE PATH. 4. *The End*, LIFE, described after. For that which follows is but the description of this life.

This verse is a proper subject for a *meditation*. For, all three are solitary. *The guide* is but one, the *traveller*, one ; the *way* one ; and the *life*, the only one. To meditate well on this is to bring all together ; and at last make them all but *one*. Which that we may do, let us first seek our *Guide*.

The Guide. Him we find named in the first verse—Jehovah. Here we may begin, as we ought in all holy exercises, with *adoration*. For " unto him all knees shall bow ;" nay, unto his *name*. For holy is his name. Glory be to thee, O God ! He is *Deus*, therefore *holy ;* he is *Deus fortis*, therefore *able*. " For the strength of the hills is his ;" and if there be a *way* on earth, he can " *show*" it ; for in his hands are all the corners of the earth. But is he *willing* to " *show* "? Yes, though he be *Deus, holy* (which is a word terrible to poor flesh and blood), yet he is *Deus meus*, my holiness. That takes away servile fear. He is *meus,* we have a property in him ; and he is willing : " *Thou wilt show*," etc. And that you may know *he will guide*, David shows a little above, how diligently he will guide. First, he will *go before*, he will lead the way himself : if I can but follow, I shall be sure to go right. And he that hath a *guide* before him, and will not follow, is worthy to be left behind. But say, I am willing, I do desire to go, and I do follow : what if, through faintness in the long way, I fall often ? or, for want of care step out of the way, shall I not then be left behind ? Fear not ; for " He is at my right hand, so that I shall not slip." *Verse* 8. This is some comfort indeed. But we are so soon weary in this way, and do fall and err so often, that it would weary the patience of a good *guide* to lead us but one day. Will he bear with us, and continue to the end ? Yes, always ; or this text deceives us ; for all this is found in the eighth verse. We must have *him* or none ; for he is one, and the only one. So confessed Asaph : " Whom have I on earth but thee ?" Seek this *good Guide*, he is easy to be found : " Seek, and ye shall find." You shall find that he is first *holy ;* secondly, *able ;* thirdly, *willing ;* fourthly, *diligent ;* and fifthly, *constant*. O my soul ! to follow him, and he will make thee both *able* to follow to the end ; and *holy* in the end.

The traveller. Having found the *Guide*, we shall not long seek for one that wants him ; for, see, here is *a man out of his way*. And that will soon appear if we consider his condition. For, he is a *stranger* (" *Thou wilt show me*") ; and what am I ? " I am a stranger, and a sojourner, as all my fathers were," says he, in another place. But this was in the old time under the law ; what, are we, their sons, in the gospel, any other ? Peter tells us no : that we are strangers and pilgrims too ; that is, travellers. We travel, as being *out of our country ;* and we are strangers to those we converse with. For neither the natives be our friends, nor anything we possess truly our own. It is time we had *animum revertendi ;* and surely so we have if we could but pray on the *way,*

Converte nos Domine. But it is so long since we came hither, we have forgot
the way home : *obliti sunt montis mei.* Yet still we are travelling ; and, we
think, homewards. For all hope well : *oculi omnium sperant in te.* But *right*,
like pilgrims, or rather, wanderers. For we scarce know if we go right ; and,
which is worse, have little care to enquire.

" *Me.*" David still keeps the singular number. As there is but *one* guide,
so he speaks in the person but of *one traveller.* There is somewhat, peradventure, in that. It is to show his *confidence.* The Lord's prayer is in
the plural, but the creed in the singular. We may pray that God would guide
all ; but we can be confident for none but ourselves. " *Thou wilt show*," or
thou dost, or hast, as some translate : all is but to show particular confidence.
" *Thou wilt show me ;*" me, not *us*, a number indefinite wherein I *may be* one ;
but *me* in particular that am out of the way ; that am myself *alone ;* that must
walk in " *the path*" *alone.* Either I must follow, or go before others ; I must
work for myself alone ; believe for myself alone ; and be saved by one alone.
The way in this text that I must walk is but one ; nay, it is but a " *path*" where
but one can go : this is no highway, but a *way* of sufferance by favour : it is
none of ours. It is no *road ;* you cannot hurry here, or gallop by troops : it is
but *semita*, a small *footpath* for one to go alone in. Nay, as it is a *way* for *one
alone*, so it is *a lonely way : preparate vias ejus in solitudine*, saith John, and he
knew which way God went, who is our *Guide in solitudine :* there is the sweetness of solitariness, the comforts of meditation. For God is never more familiar
with man than when man is *in solitudine, alone,* in his *path* by himself. Christ
himself came thus, all *lonely ;* without troop, or noise, and ever avoided the
tumultuous multitude, though they would have made him a king. And he
never spake to them but in parables ; but to *his* that sought him, *in solitudine,*
in private, he spake plain ; and so doth he still love to do to the soul, in private
and particular. Therefore well said David, " *Thou wilt show me*," in particular,
and in the singular number. But how shall I know that I, in particular, shall
be taught and *showed* this *way ?* This prophet, that had experience, will tell
us : *mites docebit*, the *humble he will teach.* Psalm xxv. 9. If thou canst
humble thyself, thou mayst be sure to see thy *guide ;* Christ hath crowned this
virtue with a blessing : " Blessed are the meek ;" for then he will call to him
and teach. But thou must be humble then. For heaven is built like' our
churches, high-roofed within, but with a strait low gate ; they then that enter
there must stoop, ere they can see God. Humility is the mark at every cross,
whereby thou shalt know if thou be in the way : if any be otherwise minded,
God also shall reveal it unto you, for, " *Thou wilt show.*"

" *The path.*" But let us now see *what* he will *show* us : " *the path.*" We
must know, that as men have *many paths* out of their highway—the world—but
they all end in destruction ; so God hath *many paths* out of his highway, the word,
but they all end in salvation. Let us oppose ours to his (as indeed they are opposite), and see how they agree. *Ours* are not worth *marking*, *his* marked with
an *attendite*, to begin withal ; *ours* bloody, *his* unpolluted ; *ours* crooked, *his*
straight ; *ours* lead to hell, *his* to heaven. Have not we strayed then ? We had
need to turn and take another path, and that quickly : we may well say, *semitas
nostras, à viâ tuâ.* Well, here is *the Book*, and here are the *ways* before you ;
and he will *show* you. Here is *semita mandatorum*, in the one hundred-and-
nineteenth Psalm, verse thirty-five : here is *semita pacifica* (Prov. iii. 17) ; here
is *semita æquitatis* (Prov. iv. 11) ; here is *semita justitiæ* (Psalm xxiii. 3) ; here
is *semita judicii* (Prov. xvii. 23) ; and many others. These are, every one of
them, *God's ways ;* but these are somewhat too many and too far off : we must
seek the *way* where all these meet, and that will bring us into " *the path ;*" these
are many, but I will show you yet " a more excellent way," saith Paul. 1 Cor.
xii. 31.

We must begin to enter at *via mandatorum ;* for till then we are in the dark
and can distinguish no *ways*, whether they be good or bad. But there we shall
meet with a *lantern* and a *light* in it. Thy commandment is a lantern, and thy

law a light. Prov. vi. 23. Carry this with thee (as a good man should, *lex Dei in corde ejus*) ; and it will bring thee into the *way*. And see how careful our *Guide* is ; for lest the wind should blow out this light, he hath put it into a lantern to preserve it. For the fear, or sanction, of the " commandments," preserves the memory of the law in our hearts, as a lantern doth a light burning within it. The law is the light, and the commandment the lantern. So that neither flattering Zephyrus, nor blustering Boreas shall be able to blow it out, so long as the fear of the sanction keeps it in. This is *lucerna pedibus* (Psalm cxix. 105) ; and will not only *show* thee where thou shalt tread, but what pace thou shalt keep. When thou hast this light, take Jeremy's counsel ; enquire for *semita antiqua*, before thou goest any further. " Stand (saith he) in the ways, and behold and ask for the old way ; which is the good way, and walk therein, and ye shall find rest for your souls." This will bring you some whither where you may *rest* awhile. And whither is that ? Trace this *path*, and you shall find this " old way" to run quite through all the Old Testament till it end in the New, the gospel of peace, and there is *rest*. And that this is so Paul affirms. For the law, which is the " old way," is but the pedagogue to the gospel. This then is " a more excellent way" than the law, the ceremonies whereof in respect of this were called " beggarly rudiments." When we come there, we shall find the way pleasant and very *light*, so that we shall plainly see before us that *very path*, that *only path*, " the path of life" (*semita vitæ*), in which the gospel ends, as the law ends in the gospel. Now what is *semita vitæ* that we seek for ? " All the ways of God are *truth*," saith David. Psalm cxix. 151. He doth not say they are *veræ*, or *veritates*, but *veritas ;* all one truth. So, all the *ways* of God end in one truth. *Semita vitæ*, then, is *truth*. And so sure a *way* to life is *truth*, that John says, he had " no greater joy" than to hear that his sons " walked in truth." 3 John i. 3. " No greater joy :" for it brings them certainly to a joy, than which there is none greater. *Via veritatis* is " the gospel of truth," but *semita vitæ* is the truth itself. Of these, Esay prophesied, " *et erit ibi semita et via*," etc. " There shall be a path, and a way ;" and the way shall be called *holy*, the proper epithet of the gospel : " *the holy gospel*," that is *the way*. But the *path* is the epitome of this *way* (called in our text, by way of excellence, " *the path*," in the singular) ; than which there is no other. " The gospel of your salvation," saith Paul, is " the word of truth ;" and " thy word is truth," saith our Saviour to his Father. *Truth*, then, is " *the path of life*," for it is the epitome of the gospel, which is the *way*. This is that truth which Pilate (unhappy man) asked after, but never stayed to be resolved of. He himself is the word ; the word is the truth ; and the truth is " *the path of life*," trodden by all the patriarchs, prophets, apostles, martyrs and confessors, that ever went to heaven before us. The abstract of the gospel, the gate of heaven, *semita vitæ*, " *the path of life*," even Jesus Christ the righteous, who hath beaten the way for us, gone himself before us, and left us the prints of his footsteps for us to follow, where he himself sits ready to receive us. So, the law is the light, the gospel is the way, and Christ is " *the path of life*."— *William Austin*, 1637.

Verse 11.—It is Christ's triumphing in the consideration of his exaltation, and taking pleasure in the fruits of his sufferings : " *Thou wilt show me the paths of life*." God hath now opened the way to paradise, which was stopped up by a flaming sword, and made the path plain by admitting into heaven the head of the believing world. This is a part of the joy of the soul of Christ ; he hath now a fulness of joy, a satisfying delight instead of an overwhelming sorrow ; a " fulness of joy," not only some sparks and drops as he had now and then in his debased condition ; and that in the presence of his Father. His soul is fed and nourished with a perpetual vision of God, in whose face he beholds no more frowns, no more designs of treating him as a servant, but such smiles that shall give a perpetual succession of joy to him, and fill his soul with fresh and pure flames. Pleasures they are, pleasantness in comparison whereof the greatest joys in this life are anguish and horrors. His soul hath joys without mixture, pleasures without number, a fulness without want, a constancy without interruption, and a perpetuity without end.—*Stephen Charnock.*

Verse 11.—"*In thy presence,*" etc. To the blessed soul resting in Abraham's bosom, there shall be given an immortal, impassible, resplendent, perfect, and glorious body. Oh, what a happy meeting will this be, what a sweet greeting between the soul and the body, the nearest and dearest acquaintance that ever were! What a welcome will that soul give to her beloved body! Blessed be thou (will she say), for thou hast aided me to the glory I have enjoyed since I parted with thee ; blessed art thou that sufferedst thyself to be mortified, giving "thy members as weapons of righteousness unto God." Rom. vi. 13. Cheer up thyself, for now the time of labour is past, and the time of rest is come. Thou wast sown and buried in the dust of earth with ignominy, but now raised in glory ; sown in weakness, but raised in power ; sown a natural body, but raised a spiritual body ; sown in corruption, but raised in incorruption. 1 Cor. xv. 43. O my dear companion and familiar, we took sweet counsel together, we two have walked together as friends in God's house (Psalm lv. 14), for when I prayed inwardly, thou didst attend my devotions with bowed knees and lifted-up hands outwardly. We two have been fellow labourers in the works of the Lord, we two have suffered together, and now we two shall ever reign together ; I will enter again into thee, and so both of us together will enter into our Master's joy, where we shall have *pleasures at his right hand for evermore.*

The saints, entered as it were into the chamber of God's presence, shall have joy to their ears in hearing their own commending and praise, "Well done, good and faithful servant" (Matt. xxv. 21) ; and in hearing the divine language of heavenly Canaan ; for our bodies shall be *vera et viva,* perfect like Christ's glorious body, who did both hear other and speak himself after his resurrection, as it is apparent in the gospels' history. Now, then, if the words of the wise spoken in due places be like "apples of gold with pictures of silver" (Prov. xxv. 11), if the mellifluous speech of Origen, the silver trumpet of Hillary, the golden mouth of Chrysostom, bewitched as it were their auditory with exceeding great delight ; if the gracious eloquence of heathen orators, whose tongues were never touched with a coal from God's altar, could steal away the hearts of their hearers, and carry them up and down whither they would, what a "*fulness of joy*" will it be to hear not only the sanctified, but also the glorified tongues of saints and angels in the kingdom of glory ? . . . . . . Bonaventure fondly reports at all adventure, that St. Francis hearing an angel a little while playing on a harp, was so moved with extraordinary delight, that he thought himself in another world. Oh ! what a "*fulness of joy*" will it be to hear more than twelve legions of angels, accompanied with a number of happy saints which no man is able to number, all at once sing together, "Hallelujah, holy, holy, holy, Lord God Almighty, which was, and is, and is to come." "And every creature which is in heaven, and on the earth, and under the earth, and such as are in the sea, and all that are in them, heard I saying, Blessing, and honour, and glory, and power, be unto him that sitteth upon the throne, and unto the Lamb for ever and ever." Rev. iv. 8 ; v. 13. If the voices of mortal men, and the sound of cornet, trumpet, harp, sackbut, psaltery, dulcimer, and other well-tuned instruments of music, passing through our dull ears in this world be so powerful, that all our affections are diversly transported according to the divers kinds of harmony, then how shall we be ravished in God's presence when we shall hear heavenly airs with heavenly ears !

Concerning "*fulness of joy*" to the rest of the senses, I find a very little or nothing in holy Scriptures, and therefore seeing God's Spirit will not have a pen to write, I may not have a tongue to speak. Divines in general affirm, that the smelling, and taste, and feeling, shall have joy proportionable to their blessed estate, for this corruptible must put on incorruption, and this mortal immortality ; the body which is sown in weakness is to be raised in power ; it is sown a natural body, but it is raised a spiritual body ; buried in dishonour, raised in glory ; that is, capable of good, and, as being impassible, no way subject to suffer evil, insomuch that it cannot be hurt if it should be cast into hell fire, no more than Shadrach, Meshech, and Abednego, were hurt in the burning oven. In one word, God is not only to the souls, but also to the bodies of the saints, *all in all things ;* a glass to their sight, honey to their taste, music to their hearing, balm to their smelling.—*John Boys.*

Verse 11.—*" In thy presence is fulness of joy."* The saints on earth are all but *viatores,* wayfaring men, wandering pilgrims far from home ; but the saints in heaven are *comprehensores,* safely arrived at the end of their journey. All we here present for the present, are but mere strangers in the midst of danger, we are losing ourselves and losing our lives in the land of the dying. But ere long, we may find our lives and ourselves again in heaven with the Lord of life, being found of him in the land of the living. If when we die, we be in the Lord of life, our souls are sure to be bound up in the bundle of life, that so when we live again we may be sure to find them in the life of the Lord. Now we have but a dram, but a scruple, but a grain of happiness, to an ounce, to a pound, to a thousand weight of heaviness ; now we have but a drop of joy to an ocean of sorrow ; but a moment of ease to an age of pain ; but then (as St. Austin very sweetly in his *Soliloquies),* we shall have endless ease without any pain, true happiness without any heaviness, the greatest measure of felicity without the least of misery, the fullest measure of joy that may be, without any mixture of grief. Here therefore (as St. Gregory the divine adviseth us), let us ease our heaviest loads of sufferings, and sweeten our bitterest cups of sorrows with the continual meditation and constant expectation of *the fulness of joy in the presence of God, and of the pleasure at his right hand for evermore.*

" In thy presence, IS*,"* etc., *there it is,* not there it was, nor there it may be, nor there it will be, but *there it is,* there it *is* without cessation or intercision, there it always hath been, and is, and must be. It is an assertion *æternæ veritatis,* that is always true, it may at any time be said that there it *is.* " In thy presence *is* the fulness of joy ;" and herein consists the consummation of felicity ; for what does any man here present wish for more than joy ? And what measure of joy can any man wish for more than fulness of joy ? And what kind of fulness would any man wish for rather than this fulness, the fulness κατ᾽ ἐξοχὴν ? And where would any man wish to enjoy this fulness of joy rather than in the presence of God, which is the ever-flowing and the over-flowing fountain of joy ? And when would any man wish for this enjoyment of the fulness of joy in the very fountain of joy rather than presently, constantly, and incessantly ? Now all these desirables are encircled within the compass of the first remarkable, to make up the consummation of true felicity. *" In thy presence is fulness of joy."*—*" The Consummation of Felicity,"* by *Edward Willan,* 1645.

Verse 11.—The human nature of Christ in heaven hath a double capacity of glory, happiness and delight ; one on that mere fellowship and communion with his Father and the other persons, through his personal union with the Godhead. Which joy of his in this fellowship, Christ himself speaks of as to be enjoyed by him : *" In thy presence is fulness of joy, and at thy right hand are pleasures for evermore."* And this is a constant and settled fulness of pleasure, such as admits not any addition or diminution, but is always one and the same, and absolute and entire in itself ; and of itself alone sufficient for the Son of God, and heir of all things to live upon, though he should have had no other comings in of joy and delight from any creature. And this is his natural inheritance.—*Thomas Goodwin.*

Verse 11.—*" In thy presence is* FULNESS *of joy."* In heaven they are free from want ; they can want nothing there unless it be want itself. They may find the want of evil, but never feel the evil of want. Evil is but the want of good, and the want of evil is but the absence of want. God is good, and no want of good can be in God. What want then can be endured in the presence of God, where no evil is, but all good, that the fulness of joy may be enjoyed ? Here some men eat their meat without any hunger, whilst others hunger without any meat to eat, and some men drink extremely without any thirst, whilst others thirst extremely without any drink. But in the glorious presence of God, not any one can be pampered with too much, nor any one be pined with too little. They that gather much of the heavenly manna, "have nothing over ;" and "they that gather little have no lack." They that are once possessed of that presence of God, are so possessed with it that they can never feel the misery of thirst or hunger.—*Edward Willan.*

Verse 11.—"*Fulness.*" Every soul shall there enjoy an infinite happiness, because it shall enjoy an infinite goodness. And it shall be for ever enjoyed, without disliking of it, or losing of it, or lacking any of it. Every soul shall enjoy as much good in that presence, by the presence of that good, as it shall be able to receive, or to desire to receive. As much as shall make it fully happy. Every one shall be filled so proportionably full ; and every desire in any soul shall be fulfilled so perfectly in that presence of glory, with the glory of that presence, that no one shall ever wish for any more, or ever be weary of that it has, or be willing to change it for any other.—*Edward Willan.*

Verse 11.—"*Fulness of joy.*" When a man comes to the sea, he doth not complain that he wants his cistern of water : though thou didst suck comfort from thy relations ; yet when thou comest to the ocean, and art with Christ, thou shalt never complain that thou hast left thy cistern behind. There will be nothing to breed sorrow in heaven ; there shall be *joy, and nothing but joy :* heaven is set out by that phrase, " Enter thou into the joy of thy Lord." Here joy enters into us, there we enter into joy ; the joys we have here are from heaven ; the joys that we shall have with Christ are without measure and with-out mixture. " *In thy presence is fulness of joy.*"—*Thomas Watson.*

Verse 11.—" *In thy presence is fulness of joy.*" In this life our joy is mixed with sorrow like a prick under the rose. Jacob had joy when his sons returned home from Egypt with the sacks full of corn, but much sorrow when he per-ceived the silver in the sack's mouth. David had much joy in bringing up the ark of God, but at the same time great sorrow for the breach made upon Uzza. This is the Lord's great wisdom to temper and moderate our joy. As men of a weak constitution must have their wine qualified with water for fear of distemper, so must we in this life (such is our weakness), have our joy mixed with sorrow, lest we turn giddy and insolent. Here our joy is mixed with fear (Psalm ii.), " Rejoice with trembling ;" the women departed from the sepulchre of our Lord " with fear and great joy." Matthew xxviii. 8. In our regenerate estate, though we have joy from Christ that is " formed in us," yet the impression of the terrors of God before the time of our new birth remains in us ; as in a commotion of the sea by a great tempest after a stormy wind hath ceased, yet the impression of the storm remains and makes an agitation. The tender mother recovering her young child from danger of a fall hath joy from the recovery ; but with much fear with the impression of the danger : so after we are recovered here from our dangerous falls by the rich and tender mercies of our God, sometime prevening us, sometime restoring us ; though we rejoice in his mercy, and in our own recovery out of the snares of Satan, yet in the midst of our joy the remembrance of former guiltiness and danger do humble our hearts with much sorrow, and some trepidation of heart. As our joy here is mixed with fears, so with sorrow also. Sound believers do look up to Christ crucified, and do rejoice in his incomparable love, that such a person should have died such a death for such as were enemies to God by sinful inclinations and wicked works ; they look down also upon their own sins that have wounded and crucified the Lord of glory, and this breaketh the heart, as a widow should mourn, who by her froward and lewd behaviour hath burst the heart of a kind and loving husband.

The sound believers look to their small beginnings of grace, and they rejoice in the work of God's hands ; but when they compare it with that original and primitive righteousness, they mourn bitterly, as the elders of Israel did at the rebuilding of the temple (Ezra iii. 12) ; " They who had seen the first house wept.'' But in heaven our joy will be full, without mixture of sorrow (John xvi. 20) ; "Your sorrow," saith our Lord, "shall be turned into joy." Then will there be no sorrow for a present trouble, nor present fear of future troubles. Then their eye will deeply affect their heart ; the sight and knowledge of God the supreme and infinite good will ravish, and take up all their heart with joy and delight. Peter in the Mount (Matthew xvii.), was so affected with that glorious sight, that he forgot both the delights and troubles that were below ; "It is good to be here," said he. How much more will all worldly troubles and delights be forgot at that soul-satisfying sight in heaven, which is as far above that of Peter in the Mount, as the third heaven is above that Mount, and as the uncreated is above the created glory !—*William Colvill's "Refreshing Streams,"* 1655.

Verse 11.—"*In thy presence is fulness of joy ; at thy right hand there are pleasures for evermore.*" Mark, for quality, there are *pleasures ;* for quantity, *fulness ;* for dignity, *at God's right hand ;* for eternity, *for evermore.* And millions of years multiplied by millions, make not up one minute to this eternity of joy that the saints shall have in heaven. In heaven there shall be no sin to take away your joy, nor no devil to take away your joy ; nor no man to take away your joy. "Your joy no man taketh from you." John xvi. 22. The joy of the saints in heaven is never ebbing, but always flowing to all content-ment. The joys of heaven never fade, never wither, never die, nor never are lessened nor interrupted. The joy of the saints in heaven is a constant joy, an everlasting joy, in the root and in the cause, and in the matter of it and in the objects of it. "Their joy lasts for ever whose objects remain for ever."—*Thomas Brooks.*

Verse 11.—"*Pleasures for evermore.*" The soul that is once landed at the heavenly shore is past all storms. The glorified soul shall be for ever bathing itself in the *rivers of pleasure.* This is that which makes heaven to be heaven, "We shall be ever with the Lord." 1 Thess. iv. 17. Austin saith, "Lord, I am content to suffer any pains and torments in this world, if I might see thy face one day ; but alas ! were it only a day, then to be ejected heaven, it would rather be an aggravation of misery ;" but this word, "*ever with the Lord,*" is very accumulative, and makes up the garland of glory : a state of eternity is a state of security.—*Thomas Watson.*

Verse 11.—This then may serve for a ground of comfort to every soul dis-tressed with the tedious bitterness of this life ; for short sorrow here, we shall have eternal joy ; for a little hunger, an eternal banquet ; for light sickness and affliction, everlasting health and salvation ; for a little imprisonment, endless liberty ; for disgrace, glory. Instead of the wicked who oppress and afflict them, they shall have the angels and saints to comfort and solace them, in-stead of Satan to torment and tempt them, they shall have Jesus to ravish and affect them. Joseph's prison shall be turned into a palace ; Daniel's lions' den into the presence of the Lion of the Tribe of Judah ; the three children's hot fiery furnace, into the New Jerusalem of pure gold ; David's Gath, into the tabernacle of the living God.—*John Cragge's "Cabinet of Spirituall Jewells,"* 1657.

Verse 11.—This heavenly feast will not have an end, as Ahasuerus's feast had, though it lasted many days ; but "*At thy right hand are pleasures for ever-more.*"—*William Colvill.*

HINTS TO THE VILLAGE PREACHER.

Michtam of David.—Under the title of "The Golden Psalm," Mr. Canon Dale has published a small volume, which is valuable as a series of good simple discourses, but ought hardly to have been styled "an exposition." We have thought it right to give the headings of the chapters into which his volume is divided, for there is much showiness, and may be some solidity in the suggestions.

Verse 1.—The seeking of the gold. The believer conscious of danger, trusting in God only for deliverance.

Verses 2, 3.—The possessing of the gold. The believer looking for justification to the righteousness of God alone, while maintaining personal holiness by companionship with the saints.

Verses 4, 5.—The testing of the gold. The believer finding his present portion, and expecting his eternal inheritance in the Lord.

Verse 6.—The prizing or valuing of the gold. The believer congratulating himself on the pleasantness of his dwelling and the goodness of his heritage.

Verses 7, 8.—The occupying of the gold. The believer seeking instruction from the counsels of the Lord by night, and realising his promise by day.

Verses 9, 10.—The summing or reckoning of the gold. The believer rejoicing and praising God for the promise of a rest in hope and resurrection into glory.

Verse 11.—The perfecting of the gold. The believer realising at God's right hand the fulness of joy and the pleasures for evermore.

Upon this suggestive Psalm we offer the following few hints out of many—

Verse 1.—The prayer and the plea. The preserver and the truster. The dangers of the saints and the place of their confidence.

Verse 2.—"Thou art my Lord." The soul's appropriation, allegiance, assurance, and avowal.

Verses 2, 3.—The influence and sphere of goodness. No profit to God, or departed saints or sinners, but to *living men.* Need of promptness, etc.

Verses 2, 3.—Evidences of true faith. I. Allegiance to divine authority. II. Rejection of self-righteousness. III. Doing good to the saints. IV. Appreciation of saintly excellence. V. Delight in their society.

Verse 3.—Excellent of the earth. May be translated noble, wonderful, magnificent. They are so in their new birth, nature, clothing, attendance, heritage, etc., etc.

Verse 3.—"In whom is all my delight." Why Christians should be objects of our delight. Why we do not delight in them more. Why they do not delight in us. How to make our fellowship more delightful.

Verse 3.—Collection sermon for poor believers. I. Saints. II. Saints on the earth. III. These are excellent. IV. We must delight in them. V. We must extend our goodness to them.—*Matthew Henry.*

Verse 4.—Sorrows of idolatry illustrated in heathens and ourselves.

Second clause.—The duty of complete separation from sinners in life and lip.

Verse 5.—Future inheritance and present cup found in God. (See Exposition.)

Last clause.—What our "lot" is. What danger it is in. Who defends it.

Verse 6.—"Pleasant places." Bethlehem, Calvary, Olivet, Tabor, Zion, Paradise, etc. II. *Pleasant purposes,* which made these lines fall to me. III. *Pleasant praises.* By service, sacrifice, and song.

Verse 6 (second clause).—I. A heritage. II. A goodly heritage. III. I have it. IV. Yea, or the Spirit's witness.

Verse 6.—"*A goodly heritage.*" That which makes our portion good is—I. The favour of God with it. II. That it is from a Father's hand. III. That it comes through the covenant of grace. IV. That it is the purchase of Christ's blood. V. That it is an answer to prayer, and a blessing from above upon honest endeavours.

Verse 6.—We may put this acknowledgment into the mouth of—I. *An indulged child of providence.* II. *An inhabitant of this favoured country.* III. *A Christian with regard to his spiritual condition.*—*William Jay.*

Verse 7.—*Taking counsel's opinion.* Of whom? Upon what? Why? When? How? What then?

Verse 7.—Upward and inward, or two schools of instruction.

Verse 8.—Set the Lord always before you as—I. Your *protector.* II. Your *leader.* III. Your *example.* IV. Your *observer.*—*William Jay.*

Verses 8, 9.—A sense of the divine presence our best support. It yields, I. Good confidence concerning things without. "*I shall not be moved.*" II. Good cheer within. "*My heart is glad.*" III. Good music for the living tongue. "*My glory rejoiceth.*" IV." Good hope for the dying body. "*My flesh also,*" etc.

Verse 9 (*last clause*).—I. The saint's Sabbath (*rest*). II. His sarcophagus (*in hope*). III. His salvation (for which he *hopes*).

Verses 9, 10.—Jesus cheered in prospect of death by the safety of his soul and body; our consolation in him as to the same.

Verse 10.—Jesus dead, the place of his soul and his body. A difficult but interesting topic.

Verses 10, 11.—Because he lives we shall live also. The believer, therefore, can also say, "Thou wilt show *me* the path of life." This life means the blessedness reserved in heaven for the people of God after the resurrection. It has three characters. The first regards its *source*—it flows from "*his presence.*" The second regards its plenitude—it is "*fulness*" of joy. The third regards its *permanency*—the pleasures are "*for evermore.*"—*William Jay.*

Verse 11.—A sweet picture of heaven. (See Exposition.)

WORKS UPON THE SIXTEENTH PSALM.

An Exposition upon some select Psalms of David. . . . . . By ROBERT ROLLOCK. 1600. 16mo.

A Godly Exposition of the Sixteenth Psalm: in R. Greenham's "Works:" pp. 316—331. Folio: 1612.

In the "Works" of John Boys, 1626, folio, pp. 898—908, there is an Exposition of Psalm Sixteen.

"*Devotions Augustinianæ Flamma; or, Certayne Devout, Godly, and Learned Meditations.* Written by the excellently accomplisht gentleman, WILLIAM AUSTIN, of Lincolnes Inne, Esquire. . . . . 1637," contains "Notes on the Sixteenth Psalme; more particularly on the last verse." Small folio.

The Golden Psalm. Being an Exposition practical, experimental, and prophetical of Psalm Sixteenth. By the Rev. THOMAS DALE, M.A. Canon Residentiary of St. Paul's, London, and Vicar of St. Pancras, Middlesex. London: 1847.

Christ in Gethsemane. An Exposition of Psalm Sixteen. By JAMES FRAME, Minister of Queen Street Chapel, Ratcliff, London: 1858.

PSALM XVII.

TITLE and SUBJECT.—A Prayer of David. *David would not have been a man after God's own heart, if he had not been a man of prayer. He was a master in the sacred art of supplication. He flies to prayer in all times of need, as a pilot speeds to the harbour in the stress of tempest. So frequent were David's prayers that they could not all be dated and entitled ; and hence this simply bears the author's name, and nothing more. The smell of the furnace is upon the present psalm, but there is evidence in the last verse that he who wrote it came unharmed out of the flame. We have in the present plaintive song,* AN APPEAL TO HEAVEN *from the persecutions of earth. A spiritual eye may see Jesus here.*

DIVISIONS.—*There are no very clear lines of demarcation between the parts ; but we prefer the division adopted by that precious old commentator, David Dickson. In verses 1—4, David craves justice in the controversy between him and his oppressors. In verses 5 and 6, he requests of the Lord grace to act rightly while under the trial. From verse 7—12, he seeks protection from his foes, whom he graphically describes ; and in verses 13 and 14, pleads that they may be disappointed ; closing the whole in the most comfortable confidence that all would certainly be well with himself at the last.*

EXPOSITION.

HEAR the right, O LORD, attend unto my cry, give ear unto my prayer, *that goeth* not out of feigned lips.

2 Let my sentence come forth from thy presence ; let thine eyes behold the things that are equal.

3 Thou hast proved mine heart ; thou hast visited *me* in the night ; thou hast tried me, *and* shalt find nothing ; I am purposed *that* my mouth shall not transgress.

4 Concerning the works of men, by the word of thy lips I have kept *me from* the paths of the destroyer.

1. "*Hear the right, O Lord.*" He that has the worst cause makes the most noise ; hence the oppressed soul is apprehensive that its voice may be drowned, and therefore pleads in this one verse for a hearing no less than three times. The troubled heart craves for the ear of the great Judge, persuaded that with him to hear is to redress. If our God could not or would not hear us, our state would be deplorable indeed ; and yet some professors set such small store by the mercy-seat, that God does not hear them for the simple reason that they neglect to plead. As well have no house if we persist like gipsies in living in the lanes and commons ; as well have no mercy-seat as be always defending our own cause and never going to God. There is more fear that *we* will not hear the Lord than that the Lord will not hear us. "*Hear the right ;*" it is well if our case is good in itself and can be urged as a right one, for right shall never be wronged by our righteous Judge ; but if our suit be marred by our infirmities, it is a great privilege that we may make mention of the righteousness of our Lord Jesus, which is ever prevalent on high. *Right* has a voice which Jehovah always hears ; and if my wrongs clamour against me with great force and fury, I will pray the Lord to hear that still louder and mightier voice of the right, and the rights of his dear Son. "Hear, O God, the just One ;" *i.e.*, "hear the Messiah," is a rendering adopted by Jerome, and admired by Bishop Horsley, whether correct or not as a translation, it is proper enough as a plea. Let the reader plead it at the throne of the righteous God, even when all other arguments are unavailing.

"*Attend unto my cry.*" This shows the vehemence and earnestness of the petitioner ; he is no mere talker, he weeps and laments. Who can resist a cry ? A real hearty, bitter, piteous cry, might almost melt a rock, there can be no fear of its prevalence with our heavenly Father. A cry is our earliest utterance, and

in many ways the most natural of human sounds ; if our prayer should like the
infant's cry be more natural than intelligent, and more earnest than elegant, it
will be none the less eloquent with God. There is a mighty power in a child's
cry to prevail with a parent's heart. " *Give ear unto my prayer.*" Some repetitions are not vain. The reduplication here used is neither superstition nor
tautology, but is like the repeated blow of a hammer hitting the same nail on
the head to fix it the more effectually, or the continued knocking of a beggar
at the gate who cannot be denied an alms. " *That goeth not out of feigned lips.*"
Sincerity is a *sine quâ non* in prayer. Lips of deceit are detestable to man and
much more to God. In intercourse so hallowed as that of prayer, hypocrisy even
in the remotest degree is as fatal as it is foolish. Hypocritical piety is double
iniquity. He who would feign and flatter had better try his craft with a fool
like himself, for to deceive the all-seeing One is as impossible as to take the
moon in a net, or to lead the sun into a snare. He who would deceive God is
himself already most grossly deceived. Our sincerity in prayer has no merit in
it, any more than the earnestness of a mendicant in the street ; but at the same
time the Lord has regard to it, through Jesus, and will not long refuse his ear
to an honest and fervent petitioner.

2. " *Let my sentence come forth from thy presence.*" The psalmist has now
grown bold by the strengthening influence of prayer, and he now entreats the
Judge of all the earth to give sentence upon his case. He had been libelled,
basely and maliciously libelled ; and having brought his action before the highest
court, he, like an innocent man, has no desire to escape the enquiry, but even
invites and sues for judgment. He does not ask for secresy, but would have the
result come forth to the world. He would have sentence pronounced and executed forthwith. In some matters we may venture to be as bold as this ; but except
we can plead something better than our own supposed innocence, it were terrible
presumption thus to challenge the judgment of a sin-hating God. With Jesus
as our complete and all-glorious righteousness we need not fear, though the day
of judgment should commence at once, and hell open her mouth at our feet, but
might joyfully prove the truth of our hymn writer's holy boast—

> " Bold shall I stand in that great day ;
> For who aught to my charge shall lay ?
> While, through thy blood, absolved I am
> From sin's tremendous curse and shame."

" *Let thine eyes behold the things that are equal.*" Believers do not desire
any other judge than God, or to be excused from judgment, or even to be judged
on principles of partiality. No ; our hope does not lie in the prospect of favouritism
from God, and the consequent suspension of his law ; we expect to be judged
on the same principles as other men, and through the blood and righteousness
of our Redeemer we shall pass the ordeal unscathed. The Lord will weigh us
in the scales of justice fairly and justly ; he will not use false weights to
permit us to escape, but with the sternest equity those balances will be used
upon us as well as upon others ; and with our blessed Lord Jesus as our all in
all we tremble not, for we shall not be found wanting. In David's case, he
felt his cause to be so right that he simply desired the Divine eyes to rest upon
the matter, and he was confident that equity would give him all that he needed.

3. " *Thou hast proved mine heart.*" Like Peter, David uses the argument,
" Thou knowest all things, thou knowest that I love thee." It is a most assuring thing to be able to appeal at once to the Lord, and call upon our Judge to be
a witness for our defence. " Beloved, if our heart condemn us not, then have
we confidence towards God." " *Thou hast visited me in the night.*" As if he had
said, " Lord, thou hast entered my house at all hours ; and thou hast seen me
when no one else was nigh ; thou hast come upon me unawares and marked my
unrestrained actions, and thou knowest whether or no I am guilty of the crimes
laid at my door." Happy man who can thus remember the omniscient eye, and
the omnipresent visitor, and find comfort in the remembrance. We hope we
have had our midnight visits from our Lord, and truly they are sweet ; so sweet

that the recollection of them sets us longing for more of such condescending communings. Lord, if, indeed, we had been hypocrites, should we have had such fellowship, or feel such hungerings after a renewal of it ? " *Thou hast tried me, and shalt find nothing.*" Surely the Psalmist means nothing hypocritical or wicked in the sense in which his slanderers accused him ; for if the Lord should put the best of his people into the crucible, the dross would be a fearful sight, and would make penitence open her sluices wide. Assayers very soon detect the presence of alloy, and when the chief of all assayers shall, at the last, say of us that he has found nothing, it will be a glorious hour indeed—"They are without fault before the throne of God." Even here, as viewed in our cove- nant Head, the Lord sees no sin in Jacob, nor perverseness in Israel ; even the all-detecting glance of Omniscience can see no flaw where the great Substitute covers all with beauty and perfection. " *I am purposed that my mouth shall not transgress.*" Oh those sad lips of ours ! we had need purpose to purpose if we would keep them from exceeding their bounds. The number of diseases of the tongue is as many as the diseases of all the rest of the man put together, and they are more inveterate. Hands and feet one may bind, but who can fetter the lips ? iron bands may hold a madman, but what chains can restrain the tongue ? It needs more than a purpose to keep this nimble offender within its proper range. Lion-taming and serpent-charming are not to be mentioned in the same day as tongue-taming, for the tongue can no man tame. Those who have to smart from the falsehoods of others should be the more jealous over themselves ; perhaps this led the Psalmist to register this holy resolution ; and, moreover, he intended thereby to aver that if he had said too much in his own defence, it was not intentional, for he desired in all respects to tune his lips to the sweet and simple music of truth. Notwithstanding all this David was slandered, as if to show us that the purest innocence will be bemired by malice. There is no sunshine without a shadow, no ripe fruit unpecked by the birds.

4. " *Concerning the works of men.*" While we are in the midst of men we shall have their works thrust under our notice, and we shall be compelled to keep a corner in our diary headed " concerning the works of men." To be quite clear from the dead works of carnal humanity is the devout desire of souls who are quickened by the Holy Spirit. " *By the word of thy lips I have kept me from the paths of the destroyer.*" He had kept the highway of Scripture, and not chosen the bye-paths of malice. We should soon imitate the example of the worst of men if the grace of God did not use the Word of God as the great preservative from evil. The paths of the destroyer have often tempted us ; we have been prompted to become destroyers too, when we have been sorely provoked, and resentment has grown warm ; but we have remembered the example of our Lord, who would not call fire from heaven upon his enemies, but meekly prayed, "Father, forgive them." All the ways of sin are the paths of Satan,—the Apollyon or Abaddon, both of which words signify the destroyer. Foolish indeed are those who give their hearts to the old murderer, because for the time he panders to their evil desires. That heavenly Book which lies neglected on many a shelf is the only guide for those who would avoid the enticing and entangling mazes of sin ; and it is the best means of preserving the youthful pilgrim from ever treading those dangerous ways. We must follow the one or the other ; the Book of Life, or the way of death ; the word of the Holy Spirit, or the suggestion of the Evil Spirit. David could urge as the proof of his sincerity that he had no part or lot with the ungodly in their ruinous ways. How can we venture to plead our cause with God, unless we also can wash our hands clean of all connection with the enemies of the Great King ?

5 Hold up my goings in thy paths, *that* my footsteps slip not.

6 I have called upon thee, for thou wilt hear me, O God : incline thine ear unto me, *and hear* my speech.

5. Under trial it is not easy to behave ourselves aright ; a candle is not easily kept alight when many envious mouths are puffing at it. In evil times prayer is

peculiarly needful, and wise men resort to it at once. Plato said to one of his disciples, " When men speak ill of thee, live so that no one will believe them ;" good enough advice, but he did not tell us how to carry it out. We have a precept here incorporated in an example ; if we would be preserved, we must cry to the Preserver, and enlist divine support upon our side. *" Hold up my goings"*—as a careful driver holds up his horse when going down hill. We have all sorts of paces, both fast and slow, and the road is never long of one sort, but with God to hold up our goings, nothing in the pace or in the road can cast down. He who has been down once and cut his knees sadly, even to the bone, had need redouble his zeal when using this prayer ; and all of us, since we are so weak on our legs through Adam's fall, had need use it every hour of the day. If a perfect father fell, how shall an imperfect son dare to boast ? *" In thy paths."* Forsaking Satan's paths, he prayed to be upheld in God's paths. We cannot keep *from* evil without keeping *to* good. If the bushel be not full of wheat, it may soon be once more full of chaff. In all the appointed ordinances and duties of our most holy faith, may the Lord enable us to run through his upholding grace ! *" That my footsteps slip not."* What ! slip in God's ways ? Yes, the road is good, but our feet are evil, and therefore slip, even on the King's highway. Who wonders if carnal men slide and fall in ways of their own choosing, which, like the vale of Siddim, are full of deadly slime-pits ? One may trip over an ordinance as well as over a temptation. Jesus Christ himself is a stumbling-block to some, and the doctrines of grace have been the occasion of offence to many. Grace alone can hold up our goings in the paths of truth.

6. *" I have called upon thee, for thou wilt hear me, O God."* Thou hast always heard me, O my Lord, and therefore I have the utmost confidence in again approaching thine altar. Experience is a blessed teacher. He who has tried the faithfulness of God in hours of need, has great boldness in laying his case before the throne. The well of Bethlehem, from which we drew such cooling draughts in years gone by, our souls long for still ; nor will we leave it for the broken cisterns of earth. *" Incline thine ear unto me, and hear my speech."* Stoop out of heaven and put thine ear to my mouth ; give me thine ear all to myself, as men do when they lean over to catch every word from their friend. The Psalmist here comes back to his first prayer, and thus sets us an example of pressing our suit again and again, until we have a full assurance that we have succeeded.

7 Shew thy marvellous lovingkindness, O thou that savest by thy right hand them which put their trust *in thee* from those that rise up *against them*.

8 Keep me as the apple of the eye, hide me under the shadow of thy wings,

9 From the wicked that oppress me, *from* my deadly enemies, *who* compass me about.

10 They are inclosed in their own fat : with their mouth they speak proudly.

11 They have now compassed us in our steps : they have set their eyes bowing down to the earth ;

12 Like as a lion *that* is greedy of his prey, and as it were a young lion lurking in secret places.

7. *" Shew thy marvellous lovingkindness."* Marvellous in its antiquity, its distinguishing character, its faithfulness, its immutability, and above all, marvellous in the wonders which it works. That marvellous grace which has redeemed us with the precious blood of God's only begotten, is here invoked to come to the rescue. That grace is sometimes hidden ; the text says, " Shew it." Present enjoyments of divine love are matchless cordials to support fainting hearts.

Believer, what a prayer is this ! Consider it well. O Lord, shew thy marvellous lovingkindness ; shew it to my intellect, and remove my ignorance ; shew it to my heart, and revive my gratitude ; shew it to my faith, and renew my confidence ; shew it to my experience, and deliver me from all my fears. The original word here used is the same which in Psalm iv. 3 is rendered *set apart*, and it has the force of, Distinguish thy mercies, set them out, and set apart the choicest to be bestowed upon me in this hour of my severest affliction. " *O thou that savest by thy right hand them which put their trust in thee from those that rise up against them.*" The title here given to our gracious God is eminently consolatory. He is the God of salvation ; it is his present and perpetual habit to save believers ; he puts forth his best and most glorious strength, using his right hand of wisdom and might, to save all those, of whatsoever rank or class, who trust themselves with him. Happy faith thus to secure the omnipotent protection of heaven ! Blessed God, to be thus gracious to unworthy mortals, when they have but grace to rely upon thee ! The right hand of God is interposed between the saints and all harm ; God is never at a loss for means ; his own bare hand is enough. He works without tools as well as with them.

8. " *Keep me as the apple of the eye.*" No part of the body more precious, more tender, and more carefully guarded than the eye ; and of the eye, no portion more peculiarly to be protected than the central apple, the pupil, or, as the Hebrew calls it, " the daughter of the eye." The all-wise Creator has placed the eye in a well-protected position ; it stands surrounded by projecting bones like Jerusalem encircled by mountains. Moreover, its great Author has surrounded it with many tunics of inward covering, besides the hedge of the eyebrows, the curtain of the eyelids, and the fence of the eyelashes ; and, in addition to this, he has given to every man so high a value for his eyes, and so quick an apprehension of danger, that no member of the body is more faithfully cared for than the organ of sight. Thus, Lord, keep thou me, for I trust I am one with Jesus, and so a member of his mystical body. " *Hide me under the shadow of thy wings.*" Even as the parent bird completely shields her brood from evil, and meanwhile cherishes them with the warmth of her own heart, by covering them with her wings, so do thou with me, most condescending God, for I am thine offspring, and thou hast a parent's love in perfection. This last clause is in the Hebrew in the future tense, as if to show that what the writer had asked for but a moment before he was now sure would be granted to him. Confident expectation should keep pace with earnest supplication.

9. " *From the wicked that oppress me, from my deadly enemies, who compass me about.*" The foes from whom David sought to be rescued were *wicked* men. It is hopeful for us when our enemies are God's enemies. They were *deadly enemies*, whom nothing but his death would satisfy. The foes of a believer's soul are mortal foes most emphatically, for they who war against our faith aim at the very life of our life. Deadly sins are deadly enemies, and what sin is there which hath not death in its bowels ? These foes *oppressed* David, they laid his spirit waste, as invading armies ravage a country, or as wild beasts desolate a land. He likens himself to a besieged city, and complains that his foes *compass him about*. It may well quicken our business upward, when all around us, every road, is blockaded by deadly foes. This is our daily position, for all around us dangers and sins are lurking. O God, do thou protect us from them all.

10. " *They are inclosed in their own fat.*" Luxury and gluttony beget vainglorious fatness of heart, which shuts up its gates against all compassionate emotions and reasonable judgments. The old proverb says that full bellies make empty skulls, and it is yet more true that they frequently make empty hearts. The rankest weeds grow out of the fattest soil. Riches and self-indulgence are the fuel upon which some sins feed their flames. Pride and fulness of bread were Sodom's twin sins. (Ezek. xvi. 49.) Fed hawks forget their masters ; and the moon at its fullest is furthest from the sun. Eglon was a notable instance that a well-fed corporation is no security to life, when a sharp message comes from God, addressed to the inward vitals of the body. " *With*

their mouth they speak proudly." He who adores himself, will have no heart to adore the Lord. Full of selfish pleasure within his heart, the wicked man fills his mouth with boastful and arrogant expressions. Prosperity and vanity often lodge together. Woe to the fed ox when it bellows at its owner, the poleaxe is not far off.

11. " *They have now compassed us in our steps.*" The fury of the ungodly is aimed not at one believer alone, but at all the band ; they have compassed *us.* All the race of the Jews were but a morsel for Haman's hungry revenge, and all because of one Mordecai. The prince of darkness hates all the saints for their Master's sake. The Lord Jesus is one of the *us,* and herein is our hope. He is the Breaker, and will clear a way for us through the hosts which environ us. The hatred of the powers of evil is continuous and energetic, for they watch every *step,* hoping that the time may come when they shall catch us by surprise. If our spiritual adversaries thus compass every step, how anxiously should we guard all our movements, lest by any means we should be betrayed into evil ! " *They have set their eyes bowing down to the earth.*" Trapp wittily explains this metaphor by an allusion to a bull when about to run at his victim ; he lowers his head, looks downward, and then concentrates all his force in the dash which he makes. It most probably denotes the malicious jealousy with which the enemy watches the steps of the righteous ; as if they studied the ground on which they trod, and searched after some wrong foot-mark to accuse them for the past, or some stumbling-stone to cast in their future path to trip them in days to come.

12. Lions are not more greedy, nor their ways more cunning than are Satan and his helpers when engaged against the children of God. The blood of souls the adversary thirsts after, and all his strength and craft are exercised to the utmost to satisfy his detestable appetite. We are weak and foolish like sheep ; but we have a shepherd wise and strong, who knows the old lion's wiles, and is more than a match for his force ; therefore will we not fear, but rest in safety in the fold. Let us beware, however, of our lurking foe ; and in those parts of the road where we feel most secure, let us look about us lest, peradventure, our foe should leap upon us.

13 Arise, O LORD, disappoint him, cast him down : deliver my soul from the wicked, *which is* thy sword :

14 From men *which are* thy hand, O LORD, from men of the world, *which have* their portion in *this* life, and whose belly thou fillest with thy hid *treasure :* they are full of children, and leave the rest of their *substance* to their babes.

13. " *Arise, O Lord.*" The more furious the attack, the more fervent the Psalmist's prayer. His eye rests singly upon the Almighty, and he feels that God has but to rise from the seat of his patience, and the work will be performed at once. Let the lion spring upon us, if Jehovah steps between we need no better defence. When God meets our foe face to face in battle, the conflict will soon be over. " *Disappoint him.*" Be beforehand with him, outwit and outrun him. Appoint it otherwise than he has appointed, and so disappoint him. " *Cast him down.*" Prostrate him. Make him sink upon his knees. Make him bow as the conquered bows before the conqueror. What a glorious sight will it be to behold Satan prostrate beneath the foot of our glorious Lord ! Haste, glorious day ! " *Deliver my soul from the wicked, which is thy sword.*" He recognizes the most profane and oppressive as being under the providential rule of the King of kings, and used as a sword in the divine hand. What can a sword do unless it be wielded by a hand ? No more could the wicked annoy us, unless the Lord permitted them so to do. Most translators are, however, agreed that this is not the correct reading, but that it should be as Calvin puts it, " Deliver my soul from the ungodly man by thy sword." Thus David contrasts the sword of the Lord with human aids and reliefs, and rests assured that he is safe enough under the patronage of heaven.

14. Almost every word of this verse has furnished matter for discussion to

scholars, for it is very obscure. We will, therefore, rest content with the common version, rather than distract the reader with divers translations. "*From men which are thy hand.*" Having styled the ungodly a sword in his Father's hand, he now likens them to that hand itself, to set forth his conviction that God could as easily remove their violence as a man moves his own hand. He will never slay his child with his own hand. "*From men of the world,*" mere earthworms ; not men of the world to come, but mere dwellers in this narrow sphere of mortality ; having no hopes or wishes beyond the ground on which they tread. "*Which have their portion in this life.*" Like the prodigal, they have their portion, and are not content to wait their Father's time. Like Passion in the "Pilgrim's Progress," they have their best things first, and revel during their little hour. Luther was always afraid lest he should have his portion here, and therefore frequently gave away sums of money which had been presented to him. We cannot have earth and heaven too for our choice and portion ; wise men choose that which will last the longest. "*Whose belly thou fillest with thy hid treasure.*" Their sensual appetite gets the gain which it craved for. God gives to these swine the husks which they hunger for. A generous man does not deny dogs their bones ; and our generous God gives even his enemies enough to fill them, if they were not so unreasonable as never to be content. Gold and silver which are locked up in the dark treasuries of the earth are given to the wicked liberally, and they therefore roll in all manner of carnal delights. Every dog has his day, and they have theirs, and a bright summer's day it seems ; but ah ! how soon it ends in night ! "*They are full of children.*" This was their fondest hope, that a race from their loins would prolong their names far down the page of history, and God has granted them this also ; so that they have all that heart can wish. What enviable creatures they seem, but it is only seeming ! "*They are full of children, and leave the rest of their substance to their babes.*" They were fat housekeepers, and yet leave no lean wills. Living and dying they lacked for nothing but grace, and alas ! that lack spoils everything. They had a fair portion within the little circle of time, but eternity entered not into their calculations. They were penny wise, but pound foolish ; they remembered the present, and forgot the future ; they fought for the shell, and lost the kernel. How fine a description have we here of many a successful merchant, or popular statesman ; and it is, at first sight, very showy and tempting, but in contrast with the glories of the world to come, what are these paltry molehill joys. Self, self, self, all these joys begin and end in basest selfishness ; but oh, our God, how rich are those who begin and end in thee ! From all the contamination and injury which association with worldly men is sure to bring us, deliver thou us, O God !

15 As for me, I will behold thy face in righteousness : I shall be satisfied, when I awake, with thy likeness.

15. "*As for me.*" "I neither envy nor covet these men's happiness, but partly have and partly hope for a far better." To behold God's face and to be changed by that vision into his image, so as to partake in his righteousness, this is my noble ambition ; and in the prospect of this I cheerfully waive all my present enjoyments. My satisfaction is to come ; I do not look for it as yet. I shall sleep awhile, but I shall wake at the sound of the trumpet ; wake to everlasting joy, because I arise in thy likeness, O my God and King ! Glimpses of glory good men have here below to stay their sacred hunger, but the full feast awaits them in the upper skies. Compared with this deep, ineffable, eternal fulness of delight, the joys of the worldling are as a glowworm to the sun, or the drop of a bucket to the ocean.

EXPLANATORY NOTES AND QUAINT SAYINGS.

Title.—"*A prayer of David.*" Since many of the Psalms consist of *prayers*, the question may be asked why such an inscription more especially belongs to this. But though the others contain divers prayers mixed with other matters, this is a supplication through its whole course.—*The Venerable Bede, 672—735.*

Verse 1.—"*Hear . . . attend . . . give ear.*" This petition repeated thrice, indicates a great power of feeling and many tears ; because the craft of the ungodly, in truth, grieves and afflicts the spiritual man more than their power and violence, for we can get a knowledge of open force and violence, and, when we see the danger, can in some way guard against it.—*Martin Luther.*

Verse 1.—"*That goeth not out of feigned lips.*"—There are such things as "*feigned lips ;* " a contradiction between the heart and the tongue, a clamour in the voice and scoffing in the soul, a crying to God, " Thou art my father, the guide of my youth ;" and yet speaking and doing evil to the utmost of our power (Jer. iii. 4, 5), as if God could be imposed upon by fawning pretences, and, like old Isaac, take Jacob for Esau, and be cozened by the smell of his garments ; as if he could not discern the negro heart under an angel's garb. . . . . This is an unworthy conceit of God, to fancy that we can satisfy for inward sins, and avert approaching judgments by external offerings, by a loud voice, with a false heart, as if God (like children), would be pleased with the glittering of an empty shell, or the rattling of stones, the chinking of money, a mere voice, and crying without inward frames and intentions of service.—*Stephen Charnock.*

Verse 1.—"*Not out of feigned lips.*" It is observable that the eagle soareth on high, little intending to fly to heaven, but to gain her prey ; and so it is that many do carry a great deal of seeming devotion in lifting up their eyes towards heaven ; but they do it only to accomplish with more ease, safety, and applause their wicked and damnable designs here on earth ; such as without are Catos, within Neros ; hear them, no man better ; search and try them, no man worse ; they have Jacob's voice, but Esau's hands ; they profess like saints, but practise like Satans ; they have their long prayers, but short prayings ; they are like apothecaries' gallipots—having without the title of some excellent preservative, but within they are full of deadly poison ; counterfeit holiness is their cloak for all manner of villanies, and the midwife to bring forth all their devilish designs. *Peter Bales, in Spencer's " Things New and Old.*"

Verse 1.—"*Not out of feigned lips.*" Not only a righteous cause, but a righteous prayer are urged as motives why God should hear. Calvin remarks on the importance of joining prayer to the testimony of a good conscience, lest we defraud God of his honour by not committing all judgment to him. *J. J. Stewart Perowne.*

Verse 1.—Though thy prayers be never so well framed in regard of words, and reverently performed as to thy external gestures ; yet all is nothing, *if thy heart be not in the duty.* For prayer is not a work of the head, or hand, or eyes only, but chiefly a work of the heart, and therefore called in Scripture, the " pouring out of the soul " (1 Sam. i. 15) ; and the " pouring out of the heart." Psalm lxii. 8. And, indeed, the very soul of prayer lieth in the pouring out of the soul before the Lord. Whensoever, therefore, thou drawest near unto God in prayer, let it be with thine heart and soul, otherwise thou canst have no assurance of audience, and acceptance ; for as Cyprian speaketh, *Quomodo te audiri a Deo postulas,* etc. How canst thou expect the Lord should hear thee, when thou hearest not thyself ? or that he should regard thy prayers, when thou regardest not what thou prayest ? Certainly that prayer reacheth not the heart of God, which reacheth not our own.—*Thomas Gouge, 1605—1681.*

Verse 2.—David appeals unto God to judge the righteousness of his heart towards Saul—" *Let my sentence come forth from thy presence.*" From Saul and his courtiers there comes a hard sentence ; they call me traitor, they call me rebel ; but, Lord, leave me not unto their sentence, " *Let my sentence come from thy presence ;*" that I know will be another sentence than what cometh from them, for thou hast proved me, and tried me, and findest nothing in me.—*Jeremiah Burroughs.*

Verse 3.—" *Thou hast proved mine heart :*"—

What ! take it at adventure, and not try
What metal it is made of? No, not I.
   Should I now lightly let it pass,
Take sullen lead for silver, sounding brass,
     Instead of solid gold, alas !
What would become of it in the great day
Of making jewels, 'twould be cast away.

The heart thou giv'st me must be such a one,
As is the same throughout. I will have none
   But that which will abide the fire.
'Tis not a glitt'ring outside I desire,
     Whose seeming shows do soon expire :
But real worth within, which neither dross,
Nor base alloys, make subject unto loss.

If, in the composition of thine heart,
A stubborn, steely wilfulness have part,
   That will not bow and bend to me,
Save only in a mere formality
     Of tinsel-trimm'd hypocrisy,
I care not for it, though it show as fair
As the first blush of the sun-gilded air.

The heart that in my furnace will not melt,
When it the glowing heat thereof hath felt,
   Turn liquid, and dissolve in tears
Of true repentance for its faults, that hears
     My threat'ning voice, and never fears,
Is not an heart worth having. If it be
An heart of stone, 'tis not an heart for me.

The heart, that, cast into my furnace, spits,
And sparkles in my face, fall into fits
   Of discontented grudging, whines
When it is broken of its will, repines
     At the least suffering, declines
My fatherly correction, is an heart
On which I care not to bestow mine art.

   *   *   *   *   *

The heart that vapours out itself in smoke,
And with these cloudy shadows thinks to cloke
   Its empty nakedness, how much
Soever thou esteemest, it is such
     As never will endure my touch.

I'll bring it to my furnace, and there see
What it will prove, what it is like to be.
   If it be gold, it will be sure
The hottest fire that can be to endure,
     And I shall draw it out more pure.
Affliction may refine, but cannot waste
That heart wherein my love is fixed fast.

                         Francis Quarles.

Verse 3.—" *Thou hast visited me in the night,*" etc. In the night the soul is free from business with the world, and therefore freest for business with God ; and then did God prove and visit David, that is, examine and sift him, by calling to his mind all his ways and works in former passages ; and the issue of this trial was, *he found nothing ;* not that his soul was empty of good things, or that there was nothing evil in him ; but God, upon examination, found nothing of that evil in him which some men suspected him of ; namely either any ill will or evil design against Saul, in reference to whom he called his cause a righteous cause, or "*the right*" (verse 1) ; "Hear the right, O Lord."—*Joseph Caryl.*

Verse 3 (third clause, New Translation).—"*Thou hast smelted me, and found in me no dross.*" A metaphor taken from the smelting of metals to purify them from extraneous matter.—*Geddes.*

Verse 3.—"*Proved . . . visited in the night . . . tried.*" Tribulation whereby, when examined, I was found righteous, is called not only night, in that it is wont to disturb with fear, but fire in that it actually burns.—*Augustine.*

Verse 3.—"*I am purposed that my mouth shall not transgress:*"—Wherefore, if thou be upon a mountain, look not backward again unto Sodom as Lot's wife did ; if thou be within the ark, fly not out again into the world as Noah's crow did ; if thou be well washed, return not again to the mire as the hog doth ; if thou be clean, run not again to thy filth, as the dog doth ; if thou be going towards the land of Canaan, think not on the flesh-pots of Egypt ; if thou be marching against the host of Midian, drink not of the waters of Harod ; if thou be upon the housetop, come not down ; if thou have set thy hand to the plough, look not behind thee ; remember not those vices which are behind thee.—*Thomas Playfere.*

Verses 3, 4. 5.—Where there is true grace, there is hatred of all sin, for hatred is πρὸς τὸ γένος. Can a man be resolved to commit what he hates ? No, for his inward aversion would secure him more against it than all outward obstacles. As this inward purpose of a good man is against all sin, so more particularly against that which doth so easily beset him. David seems in several places to be naturally inclined to lying, but he takes up a particular resolution against it : (verse 3), "*I am purposed that my mouth shall not transgress ;*" זַמֹּתִי—I have contrived to waylay and intercept the sin of lying when it hath an occasion to approach me. A good man hath not only purposes, but he endeavours to fasten and strengthen those purposes by prayer ; so David (verse 5), "*Hold up my goings in thy paths, that my footsteps slip not.*" He strengthens himself by stirring up a liveliness in duty, and by avoiding occasions of sin ; (verse 4), "*I have kept me from the paths of the destroyer ;*" whereas, a wicked man neither steps out of the way of temptation, nor steps up to God for strength against it.—*Stephen Charnock.*

Verse 4.—"*Concerning the works of men, by the word of thy lips I have kept me from the paths of the destroyer :*" as if he had said, Would you know how it comes to pass that I escape those ungodly works and practices which men ordinarily take liberty to do ? I must ascribe it to the good word of God ; it is this I consult with, and by it I am kept from those foul ways whereinto others, that make no use of the word for their defence, are carried by Satan the destroyer. Can we go against sin and Satan with a better weapon than Christ used to vanquish the tempter with ? And, certainly, Christ did it to set us an example how we should come armed into the field against them ; for Christ could with one beam shot from his Deity (if he had pleased to exert it), have as easily laid the bold fiend at his foot, as afterward he did them that came to attack him ; but he chose rather to conceal the majesty of his Divinity, and let Satan come up closer to him, that so he might confound him with the word, and thereby give him a proof of that sword of his saints, which he was to leave them for their defence against the same enemy. The devil is set out by the leviathan (Isaiah xxvii. 1), him God threatens to punish with his strong sword ; alluding to that great fish, the whale, which fears no fish like the sword-fish, by whom this great devourer of all other fish is so often killed ; for, receiving one prick from his sword, he hasteneth to the shore, and beats himself against it till he dies. Thus the devil, the great devourer of souls, who sports himself in the sea of this world, as the leviathan in the waters, and swallows the greatest part of mankind without any power to make resistance against him, is himself vanquished by the word. When he has to do with a saint armed with this sword, and instructed how to use this weapon, he then, and not till then, meets his match. —*William Gurnall.*

Verse 4.—"*By the word of thy lips,*" etc. It is a great relief against temptations to have the word ready. The word is called, "The sword of the Spirit." Eph. vi. 17. In spiritual conflicts there is none like to that. Those that ride abroad in time of danger, will not be without a sword. We are in danger, and had need handle the sword of the Spirit. The more ready the Scripture is with us, the greater advantage in our conflicts and temptations. When the devil came to assault Christ, he had Scripture ready for him, whereby he overcame the tempter. The door is barred upon Satan, and he cannot find such easy entrance when the word is hid in our hearts, and made use of pertinently. "I write unto you, young men, because ye are strong." Where lies their strength? "And the word of God abideth in you, and ye have overcome the wicked one." 1 John ii. 14. Oh, it is a great advantage when we have the word not only by us, but in us, engrafted in the heart; when it is present with us, we are more able to resist the assaults of Satan. Either a man forgets the word, or hath lost his affection to it, before he can be drawn to sin.—*Thomas Manton.*

Verse 5.—"*Hold up my goings in thy paths, that my footsteps slip not.*" Lord, whatsoever the wrath of Saul be against me, yet let neither that, nor any other thing put me out of thy way, but keep my heart close unto thee, and keep my paths in thy way; let not my footsteps so much as slide from thee, for, Lord, they watch for my halting; if they can find but the least slip from me, they take advantage of it to the utmost; and I am a poor and a weak creature, therefore Lord help me, that my footsteps may not slide.—*Jeremiah Burroughs.*

Verse 5.—"*Hold up my goings in thy paths, that my footsteps slip not.*" As a stone cast up into the air cannot go any higher, neither yet there abide when the power of the hurler ceaseth to drive it; even so, seeing our corrupt nature can go downward only, and the devil, the world, and the flesh, driveth to the same way; how can we proceed further in virtue, or stand therein, when we are tempted, if our merciful and good God do not by his Holy Spirit, from time to time, guide and govern us?—*Robert Cawdray.*

Verse 5.—"*Hold up my goings in thy paths, that my footsteps slip not.*" Lord, hold me up, that I may hold out. Thou hast set the crown at the end of the race; let me run the race, that I may wear the crown. It was Beza's prayer, and let it be ours, "Lord, perfect what thou hast begun in me, that I may not suffer shipwreck when I am almost at the haven."—*Thomas Watson.*

Verse 5.—In fierce assaults and strong temptations, when Satan layeth siege to the soul, shooting his fiery darts, and using stratagems of policy, joining his endeavours with our corruptions, as wind with tide, then we have cause to pray as David, "*Hold up my goings in thy paths, that my footsteps slip not.*" The apostle also found he had need of help from heaven when he was assaulted, and therefore he prayed "*thrice,*" that the thing that he feared might depart from him. 2 Cor. xii. Christ hath taught us to pray daily, "Lead us not into temptation," for it is dangerous; and then temptations are most dangerous, when, 1. *Most suitable*—when Satan joins with our disposition or constitution; 2. *Continual;* 3. When *opportunity* and power is greatest.—*Joseph Symonds.*

Verse 6.—"*I have called upon thee, for thou wilt hear me.*" I have cried, says the Psalmist, because thou hast heard me. One would think he should have said contrariwise: thou hast heard me because I have cried; yet, he says, I have cried because thou hast heard me; to show that crying doth not always go before hearing with God, as it doth with us; but that God will not only hear our cry, but also hear us before we cry, and will help us.—*T. Playfere.*

Verse 6.—"*I have called upon thee,*" etc. Prayer is the best remedy in a calamity. This is indeed a true *catholicon,* a general remedy for every malady. Not like the empiric's *catholicon,* which sometimes may work, but for the most part fails, but that which upon assured evidence and constant experience hath its *probatum est ;* being that which the most wise, learned, honest, and skilful Physician that ever was, or can be, hath prescribed, even he that teacheth us how to bear what is to be borne, or how to heal and help what hath been borne. *William Gouge,* 1575—1653.

Verse 6.—I have called upon thee formerly, therefore, Lord, hear me now. It will be a great comfort to us if trouble, when it comes, finds the wheels of prayer a-going, for then may we come with the more boldness to the throne of grace. Tradesmen are willing to oblige those that have been long their customers. *Matthew Henry.*

Verse 8.—*" Keep me as the apple of the eye."* He prays for deliverance (verse 7), *" Show thy marvellous lovingkindness"* to me ; Lord, my straits they are marvellous, I know not what to do, whither to turn me, but my eyes are towards thee ; as straits are marvellous, so let the lovingkindness of God be marvellous towards me, and *" Keep me as the apple of thy eye."* O Lord, unto them I am but a dog, a vile creature in the eyes of Saul and those about him ; but blessed be thy name, I can look up to thee, and know that I am dear unto thee *as the apple of thy eye.* All the saints of God are dear to God at all times, but the persecuted saints, they are the apple of God's eye ; if at any time they are dear to God, then especially when they are most persecuted ; now they are *the apple of his eye,* and *the apple of an eye* is weak, and little able to resist any hurt, but so much the more is the man tender of the apple of his eye. The saints are weak and shiftless for themselves, but the Lord is so much the more tender over them.—*Jeremiah Burroughs.*

Verse 8.—Does it not appear to thee to be a work of providence, that considering the weakness of the eye, he has protected it with eyelids, as with doors, which whenever there is occasion to use it are opened, and are again closed in sleep ? And that it may not receive injury from the winds, he has planted on it eyelashes like a strainer ; and over the eyes has disposed the eyebrows like a penthouse, so that the sweat from the head may do no mischief.—*Socrates, in Xenophon.*

Verse 9.—*" From the wicked:"* as though he had said, "They are equally enemies to thee and me ; not more opposite to me by their cruelty, than by their wickedness they are to thee. Vindicate then, at once, thyself, and deliver me." *John Howe.*

Verse 10.—*" They are inclosed in their own fat,"* or *their fat has inclosed them ;* either their eyes, that they can hardly see out of them, or their hearts, so that they are stupid and senseless, and devoid of the fear of God ; the phrase is expressive of the multitude of their wealth, and increase of power, by which they were swelled with pride and vanity, and neither feared God nor regarded man ; so the Targum paraphrases it, " their riches are multiplied, their fat covers them." *John Gill.*

Verse 10.—*" They are inclosed in their own fat."* Their worldly prosperity puffeth them up, and makes them insensible and obdurate against all reason and just fear ; and the Scripture doth use this term of a fattened heart in this sense, because that the fat of man hath no feeling in it, and those that are very fat are less subject to the passion of fear.—*John Diodati.*

Verse 10.—*" They are inclosed in their own fat."* To say a man is fat, often means he is very proud. Of one who speaks pompously it is said, " What can we do ? *tassi kullap inâl,"* that is, " from the fat of his flesh he declares himself." " Oh, the fat of his mouth ! how largely he talks ! " " Take care, fellow ! or I will restrain the fat of thy mouth."—*J. Roberts, in " Oriental Illustrations,"* 1844.

Verse 11.—*" They have now compassed us in our steps : they have set their eyes bowing down to the earth."* A man who has people watching him to find out a cause for accusation against him to the king, or to great men, says, " Yes, they are around my legs and my feet ; their eyes are always open ; they are ever watching my ' *suvadu*,' ' steps ; ' " that is, they are looking for the impress or footsteps in the earth. For this purpose the eyes of the enemies of David were " *bowing down to the earth.*"—*Joseph Roberts.*

Verse 11.—" *They have now compassed us in our steps.*" Like those who destroy game by battue, and so make a ring around their prey from which their victims cannot escape.—*C. H. S.*

Verse 11.—" *They have set their eyes bowing down to the earth.*" The allusion probably is to the huntsman tracing the footmarks of the animal he pursues.--*Religious Tract Society's Commentary.*

Verse 11.—" *They have set their eyes bowing to the earth.*" It is an allusion, as I conceive, to hunters, who go poring upon the ground to prick the hare, or to find the print of the hare's claw, when the hounds are at a loss, and can make nothing of it by the scent.—*Joseph Caryl.*

Verse 12.—" *Like a lion,*" etc. In " *Paradise Lost,*" we have a fine poetical conception of the arch enemy prowling around our first parents when he first beheld their happiness, and resolved to ruin them.

> — About them round
> A lion now, he stalks with fiery glare ;
> Then, as a tiger, who by chance hath spied
> In some purlieu, two gentle fawns at play,
> Straight crouches close, then rising, changes oft
> His couchant watch, as one who chose his ground,
> Whence rushing he might surest seize them both,
> Grip'd in each paw.
>
> *John Milton.*

Verse 12.—We were consulting as to the best means of getting at a rhinoceros cow which we saw standing at some distance under a tree, when a troop of impalas came charging down, with a fine old lioness after them. We went and saw her lying down, but so flat to the ground, head and all, that no man could shoot with any certainty ; and she never for a moment took her eyes from us. When we got up to her, she was lying down flat as a plate to the ground ; but her head might have been on a pivot, as her watchful eye glared on us all round, without appearing to move her body, as we decreased the circle, in the hopes she would stand up and give us a fair chance of a shot behind the shoulder. . . . . I looked for a tree to climb up, near enough to make tolerably sure of my shot, and was just getting up one, when the lioness made off.—*William Charles Baldwin, F.R.G.S., in " African Hunting,"* 1863.

Verse 13.—" *The wicked, which is thy sword.*" The devil and his instruments both are God's instruments, therefore " *the wicked* " are called his " *sword,*" his " axe" (Psalm xvii. 13 ; Isaiah x. 15) ; now let God alone to wield the one, and handle the other. He is but a bungler that hurts and hackles his own legs with his own axe ; which God should do if his children should be the worse for Satan's temptations. Let the devil choose his way, God is a match for him at every weapon. If he will try it by force of arms, and assaults the saints by persecution, as the " Lord of hosts" he will oppose him. If by policy and subtlety, he is ready there also. The devil and his whole council are but fools to God ; nay, their wisdom foolishness.—*William Gurnall.*

Verses 13, 14.—" *Thy sword. . . . thy hand.*" Thou canst as easily command and manage them, as a man may wield his sword, or move his hand. Wilt thou suffer thine own sword, thine own hand, to destroy thine own servant ?—*J. Howe.*

Verse 14 (*first clause*).—How wonderful are the dispensations of the providence of God, who can use even the wicked to promote the present happiness and the final salvation of his saints !—*J. Edwards, M.A.,* 1856.

Verse 14.—" *Men of the world, which have their portion in this life.*" Time and this lower world, bound all their hopes and fears. They have no serious believing apprehensions of anything beyond this present life ; therefore, have nothing to withhold them from the most injurious violence, if thou withhold them not ; men that believe not another world, are the ready actors of any imaginable mischiefs and tragedies in this.—*John Howe.*

Verse 14.—" *Men which are thy hand,*" etc. What shall we say then ? Because God maketh use of thy sins, art thou excused ? Is not thine evil evil, because he picketh good out of it ? Deceive not thyself therein. When thou hast done such service to thy Master and Maker, though seven and seven years, as Jacob did service to Laban, thou shalt lose thy wages and thy thanks too. Oh, well were thou if thou didst but lose, for thou shalt also gain a sorrowful advantage. It is unprofitable, nay, miserable service which thou hast thus bestowed. Babylon shall be the hammer of the Lord a long time to bruise the nations, himself afterwards bruised : Asshur his rod to scourge his people, but Asshur shall be more scourged. These hammers, rods, axes, saws, other instruments, when they have done their offices, which they never meant, shall be thrown themselves into the fire, and burnt to ashes. Satan did service to God, it cannot be denied, in the afflicting of Job, winnowing of Peter, buffeting of Paul, executing of Judas, and God did a work in all these either to prove patience, or to confirm faith, or to try strength, or to commend justice ; yet is Satan " reserved in chains, under darkness, to the retribution of the great day." Judas did service to God, in getting honour to his blessed name for the redemption of mankind, whilst the world endureth, yet was his wages an alder-tree to hang himself upon, and, which is worse, he hangeth in hell for eternal generations. He had his wages, and lost his wages. That which the priest gave him, he lost, and lost his apostleship, but gained the recompense of everlasting unhappiness, and lies in the lowest lake, for the worm and death to gnaw upon without ceasing.—*John King.*

Verse 14.—" *Thy hand.*" The hand of God, his correcting or cherishing hand, sometimes is an immediate, and sometimes a mediate hand. Sometimes it is immediate, when God by himself doth chasten, or punish, or afflict, when no second cause doth appear or intervene. So it may seem Satan means, when he saith (Job i. 11), " *Put forth thy hand,*" that is, do it thine own self, let no other have the handling of Job but thyself. God doth send such immediate afflictions ; a man is afflicted in his body, in his estate, and many other ways, and he cannot find anything in the creature whence it should come ; it is an immediate stroke of God, he cannot see how, or which way, or at what door this evil came in upon him ; therefore it is called a creating of evil. Isaiah xlv. 7. " I make peace, and create evil." Now creation is out of nothing, there is nothing out of which it is wrought. So many times God bringeth evil upon a people or person when there is no appearance of second causes, no matter out of which it is made, but it comes as a creature, formed by the only hand of God. Sometimes likewise it is called God's hand, when it is the hand of a creature ; it is God's hand in a creature's hand ; God's hand when it is the hand of wicked men, God's hand when it is Satan's hand. So that place is translated (Psalm xvii. 13, 14), " *Deliver my soul from the wicked, which is thy sword : from men which are thy hand :*" so that " *thy hand* " may be understood of an instrument ; Satan himself is God's hand to punish in that sense, as wicked men here are said to be God's hand : " *from men which are thy hand,*" though there be other readings of that place ; some read it, *deliver me from men by thy hand ;* and others, *deliver me from men of thy hand ;* but our translation may very well carry the sense of the original in it, " *from men which are thy hand ;*" as Nebuchadrezzar, that wicked king, is called *God's servant* (Jer. xliii. 10), " I will send and take Nebuchadrezzar my servant :" God speaks of him as his servant, or as his *hand* in the thing.—*Joseph Caryl.*

Verse 14.—" *Men of the world, which have their portion in this life.*" The large portion of the wicked in the things of this world, may tell the righteous of how little value this is, in the account of God ; in that these things are often given to his enemies plentifully, when denied in such a measure to his children. Now this cannot be because he loves or favours his enemies most ; but because these lower things, given them in what degree soever, are so mean in his account, as that his chosen may learn by his distribution of them, to regard them as he does ; namely, as no part of their felicity, but as common favours to all his creatures, good or bad, enemies or friends.—*Daniel Wilcox.*

Verse 14.—"*Men which have their portion in this life.*" God gives wicked men a portion here to show unto them what little good there is in all these things, and to show the world what little good there is in all the things that are here below in the world. Certainly if they were much good they should never have them ; it is an argument there is no great excellency in the strength of body, for an ox hath it more than you ; an argument there is no great excellency in agility of body, for a dog hath it more than you ; an argument no great excellency in gay clothes, for a peacock hath them more than you ; an argument there is not any great excellency in gold and silver, for the Indians that know not God have them more than you ; and if these things had any great worth in them, certainly God would never give them to wicked men—a certain argument. As it is an argument there is no great evil in affliction in this world, because that the saints are so much afflicted ; so no great argument there is any great good in this world, for the wicked they enjoy so much of it. Luther hath such an expression as this in his comment upon Genesis, saith he, " The Turkish empire, as great as it is, is but a crumb, that the Master of the family, that God, casts to dogs :" the whole Turkish empire, such an esteem had Luther of it ; and indeed, it is no more. All the things of the world, God in giving of them to Turks and wicked ones, his enemies, shows there is not much excellency and good in them : God therefore will cast them promiscuously up and down in the world, because he looks upon them as worthless things ; God doth not so much regard whether men be prepared to give him the glory of them, yea or no, they shall have them ; however he is content to venture them. Indeed, when God comes unto his choice mercies in Christ, there he looks to have glory from them, and he doth never give them to any, but first he prepares them, that they may give him the glory of those mercies. But it is otherwise with others ; as, suppose you see a man gathering of crabs, although swine be under the tree, he cares not much to drive them away ; they are but crabs, let them have them ; but if he were gathering any choice and precious fruit, if any swine should come under, he drives them away. As for outward things, crabs, the Lord suffers the swine of the world to come grunting and take them up ; but when he comes to his choice mercies in his Christ, there he makes a distinction. Oh, this is precious fruit ! A blacksmith that is working upon iron, though a great many cinders and little bits of iron fly up and down, he regards them not ; but a goldsmith that is working upon gold, he preserves every rag, and every dust of gold ; and a lapidary that is working upon precious stones, every little bit he will be sure to preserve ; a carpenter that is only hewing of timber, he regards it not much if chips fly up and down ; but it is not so with a lapidary. So these outward things are but as the chips and cinders, and such kind of things as those are, and therefore God ever gives a portion to wicked men out of them.—*Jeremiah Burroughs.*

Verse 14.—"*Men which have their portion in this life.*" I have read of Gregory, that being advanced to preferment, professed that there was no Scripture that went so to his heart, that struck such a trembling into his spirit, that daunted him so much, as this Scripture did :—" Here you have your reward, son ; in your lifetime you have had your pleasure." Oh, this was a dreadful Scripture that sounded in his ears continually, as Hierom speaks of that Scripture, " Arise, ye dead, and come to judgment ;" night and day he thought that Scripture sounded in his ears : so Gregory :—" Here you have your reward ; in this life you have had your pleasure." This was the Scripture that night and day sounded in his ears. O that it might please God to assist so far, to speak out of this Scripture to you, that I might make this Scripture ring in your ears even when you lie upon our beds, after the sermon is done ; that yet you may think this Scripture rings in your ears : " *Men of this world, who have their portion in this life.*"—*Jeremiah Burroughs.*

Verse 14.—" *Which have their portion in this life.*" The earth and the commodities thereof God distributeth without respect of persons, even to them that are his children by creation only, and not by adoption. But yet there is a difference between the prosperity of the one and the other ; for the one is but with anxiety of heart (even in laughter their heart is heavy) ; the others' is with cheerfulness and joy in the Spirit ; the one's is a pledge of the greater preferment in the world to come, the others' is their *whole* portion, and as if God should say, " Let them take *that* and look for no more." The one's is with the blessing of the people, who wish they had more ; the others' with their curse and hatred, who are grieved that they have so much."—*Miles Smith.*

Verse 14.—" *Their portion in this life.*" The good man's *best*, and the bad man's worst, lie in *shall be's* (Isaiah iii. 10, 11), in reversion. Here Dives had nothing but his " good things," but hereafter he had no good thing. Here Lazarus had his " evil things," but afterwards no evil thing. The good man when he dies, takes his leave of, and departs from, all evil ; and the evil man when he dies, takes his leave of, and departs from, all his goods, which was all the good he had. " Now he is comforted, but thou art tormented." Luke xvi. 25. Oh ! 'tis a sad thing to have one's *portion of good* only in this life.—*Ralph Venning's* " *Helps to Piety,*" 1620—1673.

Verse 14.—" *This life.*" There is yet another thing to be seen far more monstrous in this creature ; that whereas he is endued with reason and counsel, and knoweth that this life is like unto a shadow, to a dream, to a tale that is told, to a watch in the night, to smoke, to chaff which the wind scattereth, to a water-bubble, and such-like fading things ; and that life to come shall never have end ; he yet nevertheless setteth his whole mind most carefully upon this present life, which is to-day, and to-morrow is not ; but of the life which is everlasting he doth not so much as think. If this be not a monster, I know not what may be called monstrous.—*Thomas Tymme.*

Verse 14.—What wicked men possess of this world is all that ever they can hope for : why should we grudge them filled bags, or swelling titles ! it is their whole portion ; they now receive their good things. Hast thou food and clothing? that is children's fare ; envy not ungodly men, who flaunt it in the gallantry of the world : they have more than you ; but it is all they are like to have : the psalmist gives us an account of their estate. They are *the men of* this *world, which have their portion in this life, and whose bellies God filleth with his hid treasure.* Whereas thou, O Christian, who possessest nothing, art heir-apparent of heaven, co-heir with Jesus Christ, who is the heir of all things, and hast an infinite mass of riches laid up for thee ; so great and infinite, that all the stars of heaven are too few to account it by : you have no reason to complain of being kept short ; for all that God hath is yours, whether prosperity or adversity, life or death, all is yours. What God gives is for your comfort ; what he denies or takes away is for your trial : it is for the increase of those graces which are far more gracious than any temporal enjoyment. If, by seeing wicked and ungodly men flow in wealth and ease, when thou art forced to struggle against the inconveniences and difficulties of a poor estate, thou hast learnt a holy contempt and disdain of the world, believe it, God hath herein given thee more than if he had given thee the world itself.—*Ezekiel Hopkins.*

Verse 14.—To show that wicked men have often the greatest *portion in this world,* I need not speak much : the experience of all ages since the beginning of the world confirms it, your own observation, I believe, can seal to it ; however, Scripture abundantly evinces it. The first *murderer* that ever was, carries possession in his very name : *Cain* signifies so much. Gen. iv. 8. Go on in the whole series of Scripture, and you shall find Joseph persecuted by his brethren ; Esau (as Rivet observes on Gen. xxxii.), advanced in the world for a time far above Jacob ; go on, and you find the Israelites, God's peculiar, in captivity,

and Pharaoh upon the throne ; Saul ruling, and David in a cave, or in a wilderness ; Job upon the dunghill ; Jeremy in the dungeon ; Daniel in the den, and
the children in the furnace, and Nebuchadnezzar on the throne.   In the New
Testament you have Felix on the bench, Paul at the bar ; Dives in the palace,
Lazarus at his gate (Luke xvi. 19) ; he clothed in purple, Lazarus in rags and
overspread with sores ; he banqueted and fared deliciously every day, the other
desired but the crumbs from the table, and could not have them ; Dives beset
with his rich and stately attendance, Lazarus hath no other society but the
dogs which came to lick his sores ; all which Austin and Tertullian against
Marcion (lib. 4), conceive to be a true history of what was really acted, though
others think it parabolical.   Job tells us that " the tabernacles of robbers"
sometimes "prosper" (Job xii. 6), which prosperity he at large describes
(chap. xxi. from verses 7 to 14) ; exalted in " *power*," verse 7 ; multiplied in their
posterity, verses 8, 11 ; *safe at home*, verse 9 ; *increased abroad*, verse 10 ; have
their fill of *pleasure*, verse 12, and *wealth* at will, verse 13.   David speaks his
own experience of this.   Psalm xxxvii. 35 ; lxxiii. 7.   So in the text, they enjoy
not only common favours, as air to breathe in, earth to walk on ; their bellies
are filled with his " *hid treasure*," and that not for themselves only, but for their
posterity too ; they " *leave the rest of their substance to their babes ;*" in a word,
" *they have their portion in this life.*"—*John Frost*, 1657.

Verse 14.—A master or lord pays his *servant* his present wages, while he cuts
his *son* short in his allowance during his nonage, that he may learn to depend
upon his father for the inheritance.   Thus doth God, the great Lord of all, deal
with his *slaves*, who serve him for the hire of some temporal advantage ; he
gives them their present reward and wages ; but though his goodness hath
determined a better *portion* to be a reward to the piety and obedience of his
children, yet he gives it them in reversion, little in hand, that they may learn to
live upon the promise, and by faith to depend upon the goodness and faithfulness of their Father for their heavenly inheritance ; that they, walking not by
sight but faith (which is a Christian's work and condition here), may "not
look at the things which are seen," etc.   2 Cor. iv. 18. . . . . . This discovers
that rotten foundation upon which many men build their hopes of heaven.
Surely (are many ready to argue) if God did not love me he would not give
me such a portion in the world.   Deceive not thyself in a matter of so great
concernment.   Thou mayest as well say God loved Judas, because he had the
bags, or Dives, because he fared deliciously, who are now roaring in hell.—*John
Frost*.

Verse 14.—The word which denotes the " *belly*" may have been fixed, by the
divine Spirit, to indicate the fact, that a very great proportion of the sin of
worldly and depraved characters is connected with the indulgence of base and
degrading lusts ; and that they abuse the very bounty of heaven, in riveting
the chain of sense upon their unhappy souls.   But let them remember, that
their sensual idolatries will, at last, be followed up by the most fearful visitations of divine wrath.—*John Morison*.

Verse 14.—" *Whose belly thou fillest with thy hid treasure.*"   Wicked men
may abound in earthly things.   They may have the earth and the fulness of it,
the earth, and all that is earthly ; their bellies are filled by God himself with
hidden treasure.   Precious things are usually hidden, and all that's named
treasure, though it be but earthly, hath a preciousness in it.   Hidden treasures
of earth fill their bellies who slight the treasures of heaven, and whose souls
shall never have so much as a taste of heavenly treasures : riches and honour
are the lots of their inheritance who have no inheritance among those whose lot
is glory.   They have the earth in their hands (Job ix. 24), who have nothing of
heaven in their hearts ; they bear sway in the world who are slaves to the
world ; they govern and order others at their will who are led captive by Satan
at his will.   Be not offended and troubled to see the reins of government in
their hands who know not how to govern themselves, or to see them rule the
world who are unworthy to live in the world.—*Joseph Caryl*.

Verse 14.—" *Whose belly thou fillest with thy hid treasure.*" The hearts of saints only are filled with the " *hidden manna,*" but the bellies of the wicked are often filled with *hidden treasure;* that is, with those dainties and good things which are virtually hidden in, and formally spring out of, the belly and bowels of the earth. The Lord easily grants them their wish in such things, and gives them " *their portion,*" which is all their portion, " *in this life.*" For as they are but common professors, so these are but common mercies, such as many of his enemies receive, who are but fatted as oxen for the slaughter, and fitted for destruction. True happiness is not to be judged by lands or houses, by gold or silver. The world is a narrow bound : unless we get beyond the creature, and set our hopes above this world, we cannot be happy. As hypocrites desire, so they attain much of the world, but they shall attain no more, how much soever they seem to desire it.—*Joseph Caryl.*

Verse 14.—" *Whose belly thou fillest.*" That is, their sensual appetite, as oftentimes that term is used (Rom. xvi. 18 ; Phil. iii. 19), " *with thy hid treasures ;*" namely, the riches which either God is wont to hide in the bowels of the earth, or lock up in the repository of providence, dispensing them at his own pleasure.—*John Howe.*

Verse 14.—" *Whose belly thou fillest,*" etc . :—

> Thou from thy hidden store,
> Their bellies, Lord, hast fill'd ;
> Their sons are gorg'd, and what is o'er,
> To their sons' sons they yield.
>
> *Richard Mant.*

Verse 14.—" *They are full of children.*" So it appears by that which follows, it ought to be read, and not according to that gross, but easy (νῶν for νἱῶν), mistake of some transcribers of the seventy. As if in all this he pleaded thus : " Lord, thou hast abundantly indulged those men already, what need they more ? They have themselves, from thy unregarded bounty, their own vast swollen desires sufficiently filled, enough for their own time ; and when they can live no longer in their persons, they may in their posterity, and leave not strangers, but their numerous offspring, their heirs. Is it not enough that their avarice be gratified, except their malice be also ? that they have whatsoever they can conceive desirable for themselves, unless they may also infer whatever they can think mischievous on me ?" To this description of his enemies, he *ex opposito,* subjoins some account of himself in this his closure of the Psalm. " *As for me,*" here he is at his statique point ; and, after some appearing discomposure, his spirit returns to a consistency, in consideration of his own more happy state, which he opposes and prefers to theirs, in the following respects. That *they* were wicked, *he* righteous. " I will behold thy face in righteousness." That *their* happiness was worldly, terrene, such only as did spring from the earth ; *his* heavenly and divine, such as should result from the face and image of God. *Theirs* present, temporary, compassed within this life ; *his* future, everlasting, to be enjoyed when he should awake. *Theirs* partial, defective, such as would but gratify their bestial part, fill their bellies ; *his* adequate, complete (the εὐδαιμονία τοῦ συνετοῦ, *a happiness of proportion*), such as should satisfy the man. " I shall be *satisfied,*" etc.—*John Howe.*

Verse 14.—" *They are full of children.*" Margin, *their children are full.* The margin probably expresses the sense of the Hebrew better than the text. The literal rendering would be, " satisfied are their sons ;" that is, they have enough to satisfy the wants of their children. The expression, " they are full of children," is harsh and unnatural, and is not demanded by the original, or by the main thought in the passage. The obvious signification is, that they have enough for themselves and for their children.—*Albert Barnes.*

Verse 15.—" *I will behold thy face.*" I look upon the face of a stranger and it moves me not ; but upon a friend and his face presently transforms mine into a lively, cheerful aspect. " As iron sharpeneth iron, so doth the face of a man his friend" (Prov. xxvii. 17), puts a sharpness and a quickness into his looks. The soul that loves God, opens itself to him, admits his influences and impressions, is easily moulded and wrought to his will, yields to the transforming power of his appearing glory. There is no resistant principle remaining when the love of God is perfected in it ; and so overcoming is the first sight of his glory upon the awaking soul, that it perfects it, and so his likeness, both at once.—*John Howe.*

Verse 15.—"*I will behold*," etc.—In the words we have, 1. The time of his complete and consummate happiness—"*When I awake.*" 2. The matter of his happiness, and the manner of enjoying it ; the matter and object— "*God's face, or likeness ;*" the manner of enjoying—"*I will behold thy face.*" 3. His perfect disposition and condition in the state of happiness—"*I shall behold in righteousness,*" having my heart perfectly conformed to the will of God, the perfect and adequate rule of righteousness. 4. The measure of his happiness—"*I shall be satisfied ;*" my happiness will be full in the measure, without want of anything that can make me happy ; all my desires shall be satisfied, and my happiness in respect of duration shall be eternal, without a shadow or fear of a change.— *William Colvill.*

Verse 15.—He doth profess his resolution, yet notwithstanding all the danger he was in, to go on in the ways of God, and expects a gracious issue ; *but I,* saith he, "*will behold thy face in righteousness ;*" indeed, I cannot behold the face of the king without danger to me ; there are a great many that run to kill me, and they desire his face ; but though I cannot see his face, yet, Lord, I shall behold *thy* face ; "*I will behold thy face,*" and it shall be "*in righteousness ;*" I will still keep on in the ways of righteousness, and "*when I awake*"—for I believe that these troubles will not hold long—I shall not sleep in perpetual sleep, but *I shall awake* and be delivered, and then "*I shall be satisfied with thy likeness :*" there shall be the manifestation of thy glory to me, that shall satisfy me for all the trouble that I have endured for thy name's sake, that my soul shall say, I have enough.—*Jeremiah Burroughs.*

Verse 15.—"*I shall be satisfied,*" etc. The fulness of the felicity of heaven may appear if we *compare it with the joys and comforts of the Holy Spirit.* Such they are, as that the Scripture styles them *strong consolations* (Heb. vi. 17) ; *full joys* (John xv. 11) ; *joy unspeakable and full of glory* (1 Pet. i. 8) ; *abounding consolations.* 2 Cor. i. 5. And yet all the joy and peace that believers are partakers of in this life is but as a drop to the ocean, as a single cluster to the whole vintage, as the thyme or honey upon the thigh of a bee to the whole hive fully fraught with it, or as the break and peep of day to the bright noontide. But yet these tastes of the water, wine, and honey of this celestial Canaan, with which the Holy Spirit makes glad the hearts of believers, are both far more desirable and satisfactory than the overflowing streams of all earthly felicities. And there are none who have once tasted of them, but say as the Samaritan woman did, "Lord, give me that water, that I thirst not, neither come hither to draw." John iv. 15. So also the first and early dawnings of the heavenly light fill the soul with more serenity, and ravish it with more pure joy, than the brightest sunshine of all worldly splendour can ever do. I have read of a devout person who but dreaming of heaven, the signatures and impressions it made upon his fancy were so strong, as that when he awaked he knew not his cell, could not distinguish the night from the day, nor difference by his taste, oil from wine ; still he was calling for his vision and saying, *Redde mihi campos floridos, columnam auream, comitem Hieronymum, assistentes angelos :* give me my fresh and fragrant fields again, my golden pillar of light, Jerome my companion, angels my assistants. If heaven in a dream produce such ecstasies as drown and overwhelm the exercises of the senses to inferior objects, what trances and complacencies must the fruition of it work in those who have their whole rational appetite filled, and their body beautified with its endless glory ?—*William Spurstow,* 1656.

Verse 15.—"*I shall be satisfied.*" Have you never seen how when they were finishing the interior of buildings they kept the scaffolding up? The old Pope, when he had Michael Angelo employed in decorating the interior of that magnificent structure, the Sistine Chapel, demanded that the scaffolding should be taken down so that he could see the glowing colours that with matchless skill were being laid on. Patiently and assiduously did that noble artist labour, toiling by day, and almost by night, bringing out his prophets and sibyls and pictures wondrous for their beauty and significance, until the work was done. The day before it was done, if you had gone into that chapel and looked up, what would you have seen? Posts, planks, ropes, lime, mortar, slop, dirt. But when all was finished, the workmen came, and the scaffolding was removed. And then, although the floor was yet covered with rubbish and litter, when you looked up, it was as if heaven itself had been opened, and you looked into the courts of God and angels. Now, the scaffolding is kept around men long after the fresco is commenced to be painted; and wondrous disclosures will be made when God shall take down this scaffolding body, and reveal what you have been doing. By sorrow and by joy; by joys which are but bright colours, and by sorrows which are but shadows of bright colours; by prayer; by the influences of the sanctuary; by your pleasures; by your business; by reverses; by successes and by failures; by what strengthened your confidence, and by what broke it down; by the things that you rejoiced in, and by the things that you mourned over—by all that God is working in you. And you are to be perfected, not according to the things that you plan, but according to the divine pattern. Your portrait and mine are being painted, and God by wondrous strokes and influences is working us up to his own ideal. Over and above what you are doing for yourself, God is working to make you like him. And the wondrous declaration is, that when you stand before God, and see what has been done for you, you shall be "*satisfied.*" Oh, word that has been wandering solitary and without a habitation ever since the world began, and the morning stars sang together for joy! Has there ever been a human creature that could stand on earth while clothed in the flesh, and say, "I am satisfied?" What is the meaning of the word? Sufficiently filled; filled full; filled up in every part. And when God's work is complete, we shall stand before him, and, with the bright ideal and glorified conception of heavenly aspiration upon us, looking up to God, and back on ourselves, we shall say, "I am satisfied;" for we shall be like him. Amen. Why should we not be satisfied?—*Henry Ward Beecher, in "Royal Truths,"* 1862.

Verse 15.—"*When I awake, I shall be satisfied with thy likeness.*" He speaks here of the resurrection; he calls it an awaking, for you know death is called a sleep. "Those that are asleep in the Lord shall rise first." He had spoken before of those that had put their happiness in the comforts of this life, suitable to their bodies, to the animal state of their bodies; that is clear by the fourteenth verse, "Deliver me from the men that are thine hand, O Lord, who have their portion in this life, whose belly thou fillest with thy treasure: they are full of children, and leave to them outward things," bodily things. "But as for me," saith he, "I will behold thy face in thy righteousness" (there is the vision of God which is his happiness in his soul): "and I shall be satisfied when I awake" (when I rise again), "with thine image." It is not the image of God only upon himself that he means here. Why? Because that doth not satisfy a holy heart, but it is that image of the invisible God which the human nature of Jesus Christ is, who, in opposition to all these outward pleasures, will be all in all to us; he is a spiritual creature, his human nature is spiritualised, made glorious, and our bodies shall be made spiritual likewise. "The body is made for the Lord, and the Lord for the body," and this when they are both raised up; Christ is raised up already, and because he hath ordained the one to be serviceable to the other, he will also raise up our bodies; and when he doth raise me up, saith David, though other men have their bellies full here, and have animal pleasures they delight in; yet when I shall awake at latter day, and shall see this image of thine, shall see thy Son, I shall be satisfied: "When I awake, I shall be satisfied with thine image."—*Thomas Goodwin.*

Verse 15.—*" I shall be satisfied, when I awake, with thy likeness."* In this Psalm holy David's afflictions are neither few nor small : his *innocency* that is wounded by malicious slanderers, his *life* that is in jeopardy by deadly enemies that compass him about ; his *present condition* that is embittered unto him by the pressing wants of a barren wilderness, while his foes live deliciously in Saul's court. And yet under the weight and combination of so many sore evils, David carries himself as one that is neither hopeless nor forsaken, yea, lays his estate in the balance against theirs, and in this low ebb of his, vies with them for happiness ; and at last shutting up the Psalm with a triumphant *epiphonema*, concludes himself to be by far the better man. *" As for me, I will behold thy face in righteousness ; I shall be satisfied, when I awake with thy likeness."* They, 'tis true, enjoy the face of their king, whose favour is as a cloud of latter rain promising a fruitful harvest of many blessings, *" but I,"* saith he, *" shall behold the face of God* in righteousness," whose lovingkindness is better than life, clothed with all its royalties. They have their bellies filled with hidden treasure, having more than a common hand of bounty opened unto them ; but I have more gladness put into my heart, more than in the time that their corn and wine increased. They have their portion in hand, and as being men of this world ; but I have mine laid up in the other : *" I shall be satisfied, when I awake, with thy likeness."* In these words we have his and every believer's eternal happiness in the other life, set forth in three particulars as a most effectual antidote against present troubles and temptations that arise from the malice of wicked men against them.—*William Spurstow.*

Verse 15.—*" I shall be satisfied when I awake with thy likeness."* The saints in heaven have not yet awaked in God's likeness. The bodies of the righteous still sleep, but they are to be satisfied on the resurrection morn, when they awake. When a Roman conqueror had been at war, and won great victories, he would return to Rome with his soldiers, enter privately into his house, and enjoy himself till the next day, when he would go out of the city to re-enter it publicly in triumph. Now, the saints, as it were, enter privately into heaven without their bodies ; but on the last day, when their bodies wake up, they will enter into their triumphal chariots. Methinks I see that grand procession, when Jesus Christ first of all, with many crowns on his head, with his bright, glorious, immortal body, shall lead the way. Behind him come the saints, each of them clapping their hands, or pouring sweet melody from their golden harps ; all entering in triumph. And when they come to heaven's gates, and the doors are opened wide to let the King of glory in, how will the angels crowd at the windows and on the housetops, like the inhabitants in the Roman triumphs, to watch the pompous procession, and scatter heaven's roses and lilies upon them, crying, *" Hallelujah ! hallelujah ! hallelujah ! the Lord God Omnipotent reigneth."* *" I shall be satisfied "* in that glorious day when all the angels of God shall come to see the triumphs of Jesus, and when his people shall be victorious with him.—*Spurgeon's Sermons.*

Verse 15.—*" I shall be satisfied . . . with thy likeness."* Let a man who is thirsty be brought to an ocean of pure water, and he has enough. If there be enough in God to satisfy the angels, then sure there is enough to satisfy us. The soul is but finite, but God is infinite. Though God be a good that satisfies, yet he does not surfeit. Fresh joys spring continually from his face ; and he is as much to be desired after millions of years by glorified souls as at the first moment. There is a fulness in God that satisfies, and yet so much sweetness that the soul still desires. God is a *delicious* good. That which is the chief good must ravish the soul with pleasure ; there must be in it rapturous delight and quintessence of joy. *In Deo quadam dulcedine delectatur anima immo rapitur :* the love of God drops such infinite suavity into the soul as is unspeakable and full of glory. If there be so much delight in God, when we see him only by faith (1 Peter i. 8), what will the joy of vision be, when we shall see him face to face ! If the saints have found so much delight in God while they were suffering, oh, what joy and delight will they have when they are being crowned ! If flames are beds of roses, what will it be to lean on the bosom of Jesus ! What a bed of roses that will be ! God is a *superlative* good. He is better than anything you can put in competition with him ; he is better than health, riches, honour. Other things maintain life, he gives life. Who would put anything in balance with the Deity ? Who would weigh a feather against a mountain of gold ? God excels all other things more infinitely than the sun the light of a taper. God is an *eternal* good. He is the Ancient of days, yet never decays, nor waxes old. Daniel vii. 9. The joy he gives is eternal, the crown fadeth not away. 1 Peter v. 4. The glorified soul shall be ever solacing itself in God, feasting on his love, and sunning itself in the light of his countenance. We read of the river of pleasure at God's right hand ; but will not this in time be dried up ? No. There is a fountain at the bottom which feeds it. Psalm xxxvi. 9. "With the Lord is a fountain of life." Thus God is the chief good, and the enjoyment of God for ever is the highest felicity of which the soul is capable.—*Thomas Watson.*

Verse 15.—" *When I awake,*" etc. The sincere Christian is progressive, never at his journey's end till he gets to heaven ; this keeps him always in motion, advancing in his desires and endeavours forward : he is thankful for little grace, but not content with great measures of grace. " *When I awake,*" saith David, " *I shall be satisfied with thy likeness.*" He had many a sweet entertainment at the house of God in his ordinances. The Spirit of God was the messenger that brought him many a covered dish from God's table, inward consolations which the world knew not of. Yet David has not enough, it is heaven alone that can give him his full draught. They say the Gauls, when they first tasted of the wines of Italy, were so taken with their lusciousness and sweetness, that they could not be content to trade thither for this wine, but resolved they would conquer the land where they grew. Thus the sincere soul thinks it not enough to receive a little now and then of grace and comfort from heaven, by trading and holding commerce at a distance with God in his ordinances here below, but projects and meditates a conquest of that holy land and blessed place from which such rich commodities come, that he may drink the wine of that kingdom in that kingdom.—*William Gurnall.*

Verse 15.—" *When I awake.*" How apt and obvious is the analogy between our awaking out of natural sleep, and the holy soul's rising up out of the darkness and torpor of its present state into the enlivening light of God's presence ? It is truly said so to *awake* at its first quitting these darksome regions, when it lays aside its cumbersome night-veil. It doth so more perfectly in the joyful morning of the resurrection-day when mortality is swallowed up in life, and all the yet hovering shadows of it are vanished and fled away. And how known and usual an application this is of the metaphorical terms of sleeping and awaking in Holy Writ, I need not tell them who have read the Bible. Nor doth this interpretation less fitly accord to the other contents of this verse ; for to what state do the sight of God's face, and satisfaction with his likeness, so fully agree, as to that of future blessedness in the other world ? But then the contexture of discourse in this and the foregoing verse together, seems plainly to determine us to this sense : for what can be more conspicuous in them, than a purposed comparison, an opposition of two states of felicity mutually to each other ? That of the wicked whom he calls *men of time* (as the words מְמְתִים מֵחֶלֶד are rendered by Pagninus—*Homines de tempore*—and do literally signify) and whose portion, he tells us, is in this life : and the righteous man's, his own ; which he expected not to be till he should awake, that is, not till after this life.—*John Howe.*

Verse 15.—There is a sleep of deadness of spirit, out of which the shining of God's loving countenance doth awake a believer and revive the spirit of the contrite ones ; and there is a sleep of death bodily, out of which the loving-kindness of the Lord shall awake all his own in the day of the resurrection, when he shall so change them into the similitude of his own holiness and glorious felicity that they shall be fully contented for ever : and this first and second delivery out of all trouble may every believer expect and promise to himself. " I shall be satisfied when I awake with thy likeness."—*David Dickson.*

Verse 15.—There is a threefold meaning in this verse, inasmuch as it is in Christ alone, the firstborn from the dead, the express image of Jehovah's glory, that the saints will rise immortal, incorruptible, and be like the angels in heaven. 1. They will greatly delight in the glorious state in which they will rise. 2. They will greatly delight in Jesus, in whom, and by whom, resurrection and immortality are brought to light; and 3. They will delight greatly in beholding the blessed and reconciled countenance of Jehovah, the Father, whom no eye of flesh can see. This is the difference between the appearance of God to Israel on Mount Sinai, and the happy state in which the saints will behold him in the resurrection. Glorious as the scene on Sinai was, yet the Lord said to Israel, " You have seen no תְּמוּנָה (*Temunah*), no manner of similitude," or likeness, or countenance; but David speaks of the spiritual glory of the triumphant saints in the resurrection, when they shall see Jehovah as he is, and rejoice in his beatific presence for ever and ever.—*Benjamin Weiss, in loc,* 1858.

Verse 15.—Everlasting life and salvation in heaven, is not a truth revealed only by the gospel, but was well known, clearly revealed, and firmly believed, by the saints of old. They had assurance of this, that they should live with God for ever in glory. " *When I awake, with thy likeness.*" Psalm xvii. 15. " Thou wilt receive me to glory." Psalm lxxiii. 24. " *In thy presence is fulness of joy; at thy right hand there are pleasures for evermore.*" Psalm xvi. 11. They looked for another country, whereof Canaan was but a type and shadow, as the apostle shows in the epistle to the Hebrews, chap. xi. 16. They knew there was an eternal state of happiness for the saints, as well as an eternal state of misery for the wicked; they did believe this in those days.—*Samuel Mather on the " Types,"* 1705.

HINTS TO THE VILLAGE PREACHER.

Verse 1.—The voice of Jesus—our Righteousness, and our own voice. Work out the thought of both coming up to the ear of heaven, noting the qualities of our prayer as indicated by the psalmist's language, such as earnestness, perseverance, sincerity, etc.

Verse 2.—" *Let my sentence come forth from thy presence.*" I. When it will come. II. Who dare meet it *now.* III. How to be among them.

Verse 3.—" *Thou hast proved mine heart.*" The metal, the furnace, the refiner, etc.

Verse 3.—" *Thou hast visited me in the night.*" I. Glorious visitor. II. Favoured individual. III. Peculiar season. IV. Refreshing remembrance. V. Practical result.

Verse 3 (last sentence).—Transgressions of the lip, and how to avoid them.

Verse 4.—The highway and the by-paths. *The world and sin.* " *The paths of the destroyer*"—a significant name for transgression.

Verse 5.—" *Hold up.*" I. Who? God. II. What? " *My goings.*" III. When? Present tense. IV. Where? " *In thy paths.*" V. Why? " *That my footsteps slip not.*"

Verse 5.—Let me observe David and learn to pray as he prayed, " Hold up my goings in thy paths, that my footsteps slip not." I. See his *course.* He speaks of his " goings." Religion does not allow a man to sit still. He speaks of his goings " in God's paths." These are threefold. (1). The path of his *commands.* (2). The path of his *ordinances.* (3). The path of his *dispensations.* II. His *concern* respecting this course. It is the language of—(1) *conviction;* (2) of *apprehension;* (3) of *weakness;* (4) of *confidence.* —*William Jay.*

Verse 6.—*Two words*, both great, though little, "call" and "hear." *Two persons*, one little and the other great, "I," "Thee, O God." *Two tenses:* past, "I have;" future, "Thou wilt." *Two wonders*, that we do not call more, and that God hears such unworthy prayers.

Verse 7 (first sentence).—See Exposition. A view of divine lovingkindness desired.

Verse 7.—"O thou," etc. God, the Saviour of believers.

Verse 8.—Two most suggestive emblems of tenderness and care. Involving in the one case *living unity*, as the eye with the body, and in the other, *loving relationship*, as the bird and its young.

Verse 14.—"Men of the world, which have their portion in this life." Who they are? What they have? Where they have it? What next?

Verse 14.—"Men which are thy hand." Providential control and use of wicked men.

Verse 15.—This is the language (1) of a man whose mind is made up; who has decided for himself; who does not suspend his conduct upon the resolution of others. (2). Of a man rising in life, and with great prospects before him. (3). It is the language of a Jew.

Verse 15.—*The beholding of God's face* signifies two things. I. The enjoyment of his favour. II. Intimate communion with him.—*William Jay.*

Verse 15.—See "Spurgeon's Sermons," No. 25. Title, "The Hope of Future Bliss." Divisions. I. The Spirit of this utterance. II. The matter of it. III. The contrast implied in it.

Verse 15.—To see God and to be like him, the believer's desire.—*J. Fawcett.*

PSALM XVIII.

TITLE.—"To the Chief Musician *a Psalm* of David, the servant of the Lord, who spake unto the Lord the words of this song in the day *that* the Lord delivered him from the hand of all his enemies, and from the hand of Saul." *We have another form of this Psalm with significant variations* (2 Sam. xxii.), *and this suggests the idea that it was sung by David at different times when he reviewed his own remarkable history, and observed the gracious hand of God in it all. Like Addison's hymn beginning, " When all thy mercies, O my God," this Psalm is the song of a grateful heart overwhelmed with a retrospect of the manifold and marvellous mercies of God. We will call it* THE GRATEFUL RETROSPECT. *The title deserves attention. David, although at this time a king, calls himself " the servant of Jehovah," but makes no mention of his royalty ; hence we gather that he counted it a higher honour to be the Lord's servant than to be Judah's king. Right wisely did he judge. Being possessed of poetic genius, he served the Lord by composing this Psalm for the use of the Lord's house ; and it is no mean work to conduct or to improve that delightful part of divine worship, the singing of the Lord's praises. Would that more musical and poetical ability were consecrated, and that our chief musicians were fit to be trusted with devout and spiritual psalmody. It should be observed that the words of this song were not composed with the view of gratifying the taste of men, but were spoken unto Jehovah. It were well if we had a more single eye to the honour of the Lord in our singing, and in all other hallowed exercises. That praise is little worth which is not directed solely and heartily to the Lord. David might well be thus direct in his gratitude, for he owed all to his God, and in the day of his deliverance he had none to thank but the Lord, whose right hand had preserved him. We too should feel that to God and God alone we owe the greatest debt of honour and thanksgiving.*

If it be remembered that the second and the forty-ninth verses are both quoted in the New Testament (Heb. ii. 13 ; Rom. xv. 9) *as the words of the Lord Jesus, it will be clear that a greater than David is here. Reader, you will not need our aid in this respect ; if you know Jesus you will readily find him in his sorrows, deliverance, and triumphs all through this wonderful psalm.*

DIVISION.—*The first three verses are the proem or preface in which the resolve to bless God is declared. Delivering mercy is most poetically extolled from verse 4 to verse 19 ; and then the happy songster from verse 20 to 28, protests that God had acted righteously in thus favouring him. Filled with grateful joy he again pictures his deliverance, and anticipates future victories from verse 29—45 ; and in closing speaks with evident prophetic foresight of the glorious triumphs of the Messiah, David's seed and the Lord's anointed.*

EXPOSITION.

I WILL love thee, O LORD, my strength.

2 The LORD *is* my rock, and my fortress, and my deliverer ; my God, my strength, in whom I will trust ; my buckler, and the horn of my salvation, *and* my high tower.

3 I will call upon the LORD, *who is worthy* to be praised : so shall I be saved from mine enemies.

1. *" I will love thee, O Lord."* With strong, hearty affection will I cling to thee ; as a child to its parent, or a spouse to her husband. The word is intensely forcible, the love is of the deepest kind. " I will love heartily, with my inmost bowels." Here is a fixed resolution to abide in the nearest and most intimate union with the Most High. Our triune God deserves the warmest love of all our hearts. Father, Son and Spirit have each a claim upon our love. The solemn purpose never to cease loving naturally springs from present fervour of affection. It is wrong to make rash resolutions, but this when made in the strength of God is most wise and fitting. *" My strength."* Our God is the strength of our life,

our graces, our works, our hopes, our conflicts, our victories. This verse is not found in 1 Sam. xxii., and is a most precious addition, placed above all and after all to form the pinnacle of the temple, the apex of the pyramid. Love is still the crowning grace.

2. "*The Lord is my rock and my fortress.*" Dwelling among the crags and mountain fastnesses of Judea David had escaped the malice of Saul, and here he compares his God to such a place of concealment and security. Believers are often hidden in their God from the strife of tongues and the fury of the storm of trouble. The clefts of the Rock of Ages are safe abodes. "*My deliverer,*" interposing in my hour of peril. When almost captured the Lord's people are rescued from the hand of the mighty by him who is mightier still. This title of "*deliverer*" has many sermons in it, and is well worthy of the study of all experienced saints. "*My God;*" this is all good things in one. There is a boundless wealth in this expression ; it means, my perpetual, unchanging, infinite, eternal good. He who can say truly "my God," may well add, "my heaven, my all." "*My strength;*" this word is really "*my rock,*" in the sense of strength and immobility. My sure, unchanging, eternal confidence and support. Thus the word rock occurs twice, but it is no tautology, for the first time it is a rock for concealment, but here a rock for firmness and immutability. "*In whom I will trust.*" Faith must be exercised, or the preciousness of God is not truly known ; and God must be the object of faith, or faith is mere presumption. "*My buckler,*" warding off the blows of my enemy, shielding me from arrow or sword. The Lord furnishes his warriors with weapons both offensive and defensive. Our armoury is completely stored so that none need go to battle unarmed. "*The horn of my salvation,*" enabling me to push down my foes, and to triumph over them with holy exultation. "*My high tower,*" a citadel high planted on a rocky eminence beyond the reach of my enemies, from the heights of which I look down upon their fury without alarm, and survey a wide landscape of mercy reaching even unto the goodly land beyond Jordan. Here are many words, but none too many ; we might profitably examine each one of them had we leisure, but summing up the whole, we may conclude with Calvin, that David here equips the faithful from head to foot.

3. In this verse the happy poet resolves to invoke the Lord in joyful song, believing that in all future conflicts his God would deal as well with him as in the past. It is well to pray to God as to one who deserves to be praised, for then we plead in a happy and confident manner. If I feel that I can and do bless the Lord for all his past goodness, I am bold to ask great things of him. That word *So* has much in it. To be saved singing is to be saved indeed. Many are saved mourning and doubting ; but David had such faith that he could fight singing, and win the battle with a song still upon his lips. How happy a thing to receive fresh mercy with a heart already sensible of mercy enjoyed, and to anticipate new trials with a confidence based upon past experiences of divine love !

> "No fearing or doubting with Christ on our side,
> We hope to die shouting, 'The Lord will provide.'"

4 The sorrows of death compassed me, and the floods of ungodly men made me afraid.

5 The sorrows of hell compassed me about : the snares of death prevented me.

6 In my distress I called upon the LORD, and cried unto my God : he heard my voice out of his temple, and my cry came before him, *even* into his ears.

7 Then the earth shook and trembled ; the foundations also of the hills moved and were shaken, because he was wroth.

8 There went up a smoke out of his nostrils, and fire out of his mouth devoured : coals were kindled by it.

9 He bowed the heavens also, and came down : and darkness *was* under his feet.

10 And he rode upon a cherub, and did fly : yea, he did fly upon the wings of the wind.

11 He made darkness his secret place ; his pavilion round about him *were* dark waters *and* thick clouds of the skies.

12 At the brightness *that was* before him his thick clouds passed, hail *stones* and coals of fire.

13 The LORD also thundered in the heavens, and the Highest gave his voice ; hail *stones* and coals of fire.

14 Yea, he sent out his arrows, and scattered them ; and he shot out lightnings, and discomfited them.

15 Then the channels of waters were seen, and the foundations of the world were discovered at thy rebuke, O LORD, at the blast of the breath of thy nostrils.

16 He sent from above, he took me, he drew me out of many waters.

17 He delivered me from my strong enemy, and from them which hated me : for they were too strong for me.

18 They prevented me in the day of my calamity : but the LORD was my stay.

19 He brought me forth also into a large place ; he delivered me, because he delighted in me.

In most poetical language the Psalmist now describes his experience of Jehovah's delivering power. Poesy has in all her treasures no gem more lustrous than the sonnet of the following verses ; the sorrow, the cry, the descent of the Divine One, and the rescue of the afflicted, are here set to a music worthy of the golden harps. The Messiah our Saviour is evidently, over and beyond David or any other believer, the main and chief subject of this song ; and while studying it we have grown more and more sure that every line here has its deepest and profoundest fulfilment in Him ; but as we are desirous not to extend our comment beyond moderate bounds, we must leave it with the devout reader to make the very easy application of the passage to our once distressed but now triumphant Lord.

4. " *The sorrows of death compassed me.*" Death like a cruel conqueror seemed to twist round about him the cords of pain. He was environed and hemmed in with threatening deaths of the most appalling sort. He was like a mariner broken by the storm and driven upon the rocks by dreadful breakers, white as the teeth of death. Sad plight for the man after God's own heart, but thus it is that Jehovah dealeth with his sons. " *The floods of ungodly men made me afraid.*" Torrents of ungodliness threatened to swamp all religion, and to hurry away the godly man's hope as a thing to be scorned and despised ; so far was this threat fulfilled, that even the hero who slew Goliath began to be afraid. The most seaworthy bark is sometimes hard put to it when the storm fiend is abroad. The most courageous man, who as a rule hopes for the best, may sometimes fear the worst. Beloved reader, he who pens these lines has known better than most men what this verse means, and feels inclined to weep, and yet to sing, while he writes upon a text so descriptive of his own experience. On the night of the lamentable accident at the Surrey Music Hall, the floods of Belial were let loose, and the subsequent remarks of a large portion of the press were exceedingly malicious and wicked ; our soul was afraid as we stood encompassed with the sorrows of death and the blasphemies of the cruel. But oh, what mercy was there in it all, and what honey of goodness was extracted

by our Lord out of this lion of affliction ! Surely God hath heard me ! Art thou in an ill plight? Dear friend, learn thou from our experience to trust in the Lord Jehovah, who forsaketh not his chosen.

5. " *The sorrows of hell compassed me about.*" From all sides the hell-hounds barked furiously. A cordon of devils hemmed in the hunted man of God ; every way of escape was closed up. Satan knows how to blockade our coasts with the iron war-ships of sorrow, but, blessed be God, the port of all prayer is still open, and grace can run the blockade bearing messages from earth to heaven, and blessings in return from heaven to earth. " *The snares of death prevented me.*" The old enemy hunts for his prey, not only with the dogs of the infernal kennel, but also with the snares of deadly craft. The nets were drawn closer and closer until the contracted circle completely prevented the escape of the captive :

" About me cords of hell were wound,
And snares of death my footsteps bound."

Thus hopeless was the case of this good man, as hopeless as a case could be, so utterly desperate that none but an almighty arm could be of any service. According to the four metaphors which he employs, he was bound like a malefactor for execution ; overwhelmed like a shipwrecked mariner ; surrounded and standing at bay like a hunted stag ; and captured in a net like a trembling bird. What more of terror and distress could meet upon one poor defenceless head ?

6. " *In my distress I called upon the Lord, and cried unto my God.*" Prayer is that postern gate which is left open even when the city is straitly besieged by the enemy ; it is that way upward from the pit of despair to which the spiritual miner flies at once when the floods from beneath break forth upon him. Observe that he *calls,* and then *cries ;* prayer grows in vehemence as it proceeds. Note also that he first invokes his God under the name of Jehovah, and then advances to a more familiar name, " *my God ;*" thus faith increases by exercise, and he whom we at first viewed as Lord is soon seen to be our God in covenant. It is never an ill time to pray ; no distress should prevent us from using the divine remedy of supplication. Above the noise of the raging billows of death, or the barking dogs of hell, the feeblest cry of a true believer will be heard in heaven. " *He heard my voice out of his temple, and my cry came before him, even into his ears.*" Far up within the bejewelled walls, and through the gates of pearl, the cry of the suffering suppliant was heard. Music of angels and harmony of seraphs availed not to drown or even to impair the voice of that humble call. The king heard it in his palace of light unsufferable, and lent a willing ear to the cry of his own beloved child. O honoured prayer, to be able thus through Jesus' blood to penetrate the very ears and heart of Deity. The voice and the cry are themselves heard directly by the Lord, and not made to pass through the medium of saints and intercessors ; " My cry came before *Him ;*" the operation of prayer with God is immediate and personal. We may cry with confident and familiar importunity, while our Father himself listens.

7. There was no great space between the cry and its answer. The Lord is not slack concerning his promise, but is swift to rescue his afflicted. David has in his mind's eye the glorious manifestations of God in Egypt, at Sinai, and on different occasions to Joshua and the judges ; and he considers that his own case exhibits the same glory of power and goodness, and that, therefore, he may accommodate the descriptions of former displays of the divine majesty into his hymn of praise. " *Then the earth shook and trembled.*" Observe how the most solid and immovable things feel the force of supplication. Prayer has shaken houses, opened prison doors, and made stout hearts to quail. Prayer rings the alarm bell, and the Master of the house arises to the rescue, shaking all things beneath his tread. " *The foundations also of the hills moved and were shaken, because of his wrath.*" He who fixed the world's pillars can make them rock in their sockets, and can upheave the corner-stones of creation. The huge roots of the towering mountains are torn up when the Lord bestirs himself in anger to smite the enemies of his people. How shall puny man be

able to face it out with God when the very mountains quake with fear? Let not the boaster dream that his present false confidence will support him in the dread day of wrath.

8. " *There went up a smoke out of his nostrils.* " A violent oriental method of expressing fierce wrath. Since the breath from the nostrils is heated by strong emotion, the figure portrays the Almighty Deliverer as pouring forth smoke in the heat of his wrath and the impetuousness of his zeal. Nothing makes God so angry as an injury done to his children. He that toucheth you toucheth the apple of mine eye. God is not subject to the passions which govern his creatures, but acting as he does with all the energy and speed of one who is angry, he is here aptly set forth in poetic imagery suitable to human understandings. The opening of his lips is sufficient to destroy his enemies ; " *and fire out of his mouth devoured.* " This fire was no temporary one but steady and lasting ; " *Coals were kindled by it.* " The whole passage is intended to depict God's descent to the help of his child, attended by earthquake and tempest : at the majesty of his appearing the earth rocks, the clouds gather like smoke, and the lightning as flaming fire devours, setting the world on a blaze. What grandeur of description is here ! Bishop Mant very admirably rhymes the verse thus :—

> " Smoke from his heated nostrils came,
> And from his mouth devouring flame ;
> Hot burning coals announced his ire,
> And flashes of careering fire."

9. Amid the terror of the storm Jehovah the Avenger descended, bending beneath his foot the arch of heaven. " *He bowed the heavens also, and came down.* " He came in haste, and spurned everything which impeded his rapidity. The thickest gloom concealed his splendour, " *and darkness was under his feet ;* " he fought within the dense vapours, as a warrior in clouds of smoke and dust, and found out the hearts of his enemies with the sharp falchion of his vengeance. Darkness is no impediment to God ; its densest gloom he makes his tent and secret pavilion. See how prayer moves earth and heaven, and raises storms to overthrow in a moment the foes of God's Israel. Things were bad for David before he prayed, but they were much worse for his foes so soon as the petition had gone up to heaven. A trustful heart, by enlisting the divine aid, turns the tables on its enemies. If I must have an enemy let him not be a man of prayer, or he will soon get the better of me by calling in his God into the quarrel.

10. There is inimitable grandeur in this verse. Under the Mosaic system the cherubim are frequently represented as the chariot of God ; hence Milton, in " Paradise Lost," writes of the Great Father,—

> " He on the wings of cherubim
> Uplifted, in paternal glory rode
> Far into chaos."

Without speculating upon the mysterious and much-disputed subject of the cherubim, it may be enough to remark that angels are doubtless our guards and ministering friends, and all their powers are enlisted to expedite the rescue of the afflicted. " *He rode upon a cherub, and did fly.* " Nature also yields all her agents to be our helpers, and even the powers of the air are subservient : " *yea, he did fly upon the wings of the wind.* " The Lord comes flying when mercy is his errand, but he lingers long when sinners are being wooed to repent. The flight here pictured is as majestic as it is swift : " flying all abroad " is Sternhold's word, and he is not far from correct. As the eagle soars in easy grandeur with wings outspread, without violent flapping and exertion, so comes the Lord with majesty of omnipotence to aid his own.

11. The storm thickened, and the clouds pouring forth torrents of rain combined to form the secret chamber of the invisible but wonder-working God. " Pavilioned in impervious shade" faith saw him, but no other eye could gaze through the " *thick clouds of the skies.* " Blessed is the darkness which encurtains

my God ; if I may not see him, it is sweet to know that he is working in secret for my eternal good. Even fools can believe that God is abroad in the sunshine and the calm, but faith is wise, and discerns him in the terrible darkness and threatening storm.

12. Suddenly the terrible artillery of heaven was discharged ; the *brightness* of lightning lit up the clouds as with a glory proceeding from him who was concealed within the cloudy pavilion ; and volleys of hailstones and coals of fire were hurled forth upon the enemy. The lightnings seemed to cleave the clouds and kindle them into a blaze, and then hailstones and flakes of fire with flashes of terrific grandeur terrified the sons of men.

13. Over all this splendour of tempest pealed the dread thunder. " *The Lord also thundered in the heavens, and the Highest gave his voice.*" Fit accompaniment for the flames of vengeance. How will men bear to hear it at the last when addressed to them in proclamation of their doom, for even now their hearts are in their mouths if they do but hear it muttering from afar ? In all this terror David found a theme for song, and thus every believer finds even in the terrors of God a subject for holy praise. " *Hailstones and coals of fire*" are twice mentioned to show how certainly they are in the divine hand, and are the weapons of Heaven's vengeance. Horne remarks that " every thunderstorm should remind us of that exhibition of power and vengeance, which is hereafter to accompany the general resurrection ;" may it not also assure us of the real power of him who is our Father and our friend, and tend to assure us of our safety while he fights our battles for us. The prince of the power of the air is soon dislodged when the cherubic chariot is driven through his dominions ; therefore let not the legions of hell cause us dismay. He who is with us is greater than all they that be against us.

14. The lightnings were darted forth as forked arrows upon the hosts of the foe, and speedily " *scattered them.*" Boastful sinners prove to be great cowards when Jehovah enters the lists with them. They despise his words, and are very tongue-valiant, but when it comes to blows they fly apace. The glittering flames, and the fierce bolts of fire " *discomfited them.*" God is never at a loss for weapons. Woe be unto him that contendeth with his Maker ! God's arrows never miss their aim ; they are feathered with lightning, and barbed with everlasting death. Fly, O sinner, to the rock of refuge before these arrows stick fast in thy soul.

15. So tremendous was the shock of God's assault in arms that the order of nature was changed, and the bottoms of rivers and seas were laid bare. " *The channels of waters were seen ;*" and the deep cavernous bowels of the earth were upheaved till " *the foundations of the world were discovered.*" What will not Jehovah's " *rebuke*" do ? If " *the blast of the breath of thy nostrils,*" O Lord, be so terrible, what must thine arm be ? Vain are the attempts of men to conceal anything from him whose word unbars the deep, and lifts the doors of earth from their hinges ! Vain are all hopes of resistance, for a whisper of his voice makes the whole earth quail in abject terror.

16. Now comes the rescue. The Author is divine, " *He sent ;*" the work is heavenly, " *from above ;*" the deliverance is marvellous, " *He drew me out of many waters.*" Here David was like another Moses, drawn from the water ; and thus are all believers like their Lord, whose baptism in many waters of agony and in his own blood has redeemed us from the wrath to come. Torrents of evil shall not drown the man whose God sitteth upon the floods to restrain their fury.

17. When we have been rescued, we must take care to ascribe all the glory to God by confessing our own weakness, and remembering the power of the conquered enemy. God's power derives honour from all the incidents of the conflict. Our great spiritual adversary is a " *strong enemy*" indeed, much too strong for poor, weak creatures like ourselves, but we have been delivered hitherto and shall be even to the end. Our weakness is a reason for divine help ; mark the force of the " *for*" in the text.

18. It was an ill day, a day of *calamity*, of which evil foes took cruel advantage,

while they used crafty means utterly to ruin him, yet David could say, "*but the Lord is my stay.*" What a blessed *but* which cuts the Gordian knot, and slays the hundred-headed hydra ! There is no fear of deliverance when our stay is in Jehovah.

19. "*He brought me forth also into a large place.*" After pining awhile in the prison-house Joseph reached the palace, and from the cave of Adullam David mounted to the throne. Sweet is pleasure after pain. Enlargement is the more delightful after a season of pinching poverty and sorrowful confinement. Besieged souls delight in the broad fields of the promise when God drives off the enemy and sets open the gates of the environed city. The Lord does not leave his work half done, for having routed the foe he leads out the captive into liberty. Large indeed is the possession and place of the believer in Jesus, there need be no limit to his peace, for there is no bound to his privilege. "*He delivered me, because he delighted in me.*" Free grace lies at the foundation. Rest assured, if we go deep enough, sovereign grace is the truth which lies at the bottom of every well of mercy. Deep sea fisheries in the ocean of divine bounty always bring the pearls of electing, discriminating love to light. Why Jehovah should delight in us is an answerless question, and a mystery which angels cannot solve ; but that he does delight in his beloved is certain, and is the fruitful root of favours as numerous as they are precious. Believer, sit down, and inwardly digest the instructive sentence now before us, and learn to view the uncaused love of God as the cause of all the lovingkindness of which we are the partakers.

20 The LORD rewarded me according to my righteousness ; according to the cleanness of my hands hath he recompensed me.

21 For I have kept the ways of the LORD, and have not wickedly departed from my God.

22 For all his judgments *were* before me, and I did not put away his statutes from me.

23 I was also upright before him, and I kept myself from mine iniquity.

24 Therefore hath the LORD recompensed me according to my righteousness, according to the cleanness of my hands in his eyesight.

25 With the merciful thou wilt shew thyself merciful ; with an upright man thou wilt shew thyself upright ;

26 With the pure thou wilt shew thyself pure ; and with the froward thou wilt shew thyself froward.

27 For thou wilt save the afflicted people ; but wilt bring down high looks.

28 For thou wilt light my candle : the LORD my God will enlighten my darkness.

20. "*The Lord rewarded me according to my righteousness.*" Viewing this psalm as prophetical of the Messiah, these strongly-expressed claims to righteousness are readily understood, for his garments were white as snow ; but considered as the language of David they have perplexed many. Yet the case is clear, and if the words be not strained beyond their original intention, no difficulty need occur. Albeit that the dispensations of divine grace are to the fullest degree sovereign and irrespective of human merit, yet in the dealings of Providence there is often discernible a rule of justice by which the injured are at length avenged, and the righteous ultimately delivered. David's early troubles arose from the wicked malice of envious Saul, who no doubt prosecuted his persecutions under cover of charges brought against the character of "the man after God's own heart." These charges David declares to have been

utterly false, and asserts that he possessed a grace-given righteousness which the Lord had graciously rewarded in defiance of all his calumniators. Before God the man after God's own heart was a humble sinner, but before his slanderers he could with unblushing face speak of the " *cleanness of his hands*" and the righteousness of his life. He knows little of the sanctifying power of divine grace who is not at the bar of human equity able to plead innocence. There is no self-righteousness in an honest man knowing that he is honest, nor even in his believing that God rewards him in providence because of his honesty, for such is often a most evident matter of fact ; but it would be self-righteousness indeed if we transferred such thoughts from the region of providential government into the spiritual kingdom, for there grace reigns not only supreme but sole in the distribution of divine favours. It is not at all an opposition to the doctrine of salvation by grace, and no sort of evidence of a Pharisaic spirit, when a gracious man, having been slandered, stoutly maintains his integrity, and vigorously defends his character. A godly man has a clear conscience, and knows himself to be upright ; is he to deny his own consciousness, and to despise the work of the Holy Ghost, by hypocritically making himself out to be worse than he is ? A godly man prizes his integrity very highly, or else he would not be a godly man at all ; is he to be called proud because he will not readily lose the jewel of a reputable character ? A godly man can see that in divine providence uprightness and truth are in the long run sure to bring their own reward ; may be not, when he sees that reward bestowed in his own case, praise the Lord for it ? Yea rather, must he not show forth the faithfulness and goodness of his God ? Read the cluster of expressions in this and the following verses as the song of a good conscience, after having safely outridden a storm of obloquy, persecution, and abuse, and there will be no fear of our upbraiding the writer as one who set too high a price upon his own moral character.

21. Here the assertion of purity is repeated, both in a positive and a negative form. There is " *I have*" and " *I have not,*" both of which must be blended in a truly sanctified life ; constraining and restraining grace must each take its share. The words of this verse refer to the saint as a traveller carefully keeping to " *the ways of the Lord,*" and " *not wickedly,*" that is, designedly, wilfully, persistently, defiantly forsaking the ordained pathway in which God favours the pilgrim with his presence. Observe how it is implied in the expression, " *and have not wickedly departed from my God,*" that David lived habitually in communion with God, and knew him to be his own God, whom he might speak of as " *my God.*" God never departs from his people, let them take heed of departing from him.

22. " *For all his judgments were before me.*" The word, the character, and the actions of God should be evermore before our eyes ; we should learn, consider, and reverence them. Men forget what they do not wish to remember, but the excellent attributes of the Most High are objects of the believer's affectionate and delighted admiration. We should keep the image of God so constantly before us that we become in our measure conformed unto it. This inner love to the right must be the main spring of Christian integrity in our public walk. The fountain must be filled with love to holiness, and then the streams which issue from it will be pure and gracious. " *I did not put away his statutes from me.* ' To put away the Scriptures from the mind's study is the certain way to prevent their influencing the outward conversation. Backsliders begin with dusty Bibles, and go on to filthy garments.

23. " *I was also upright before him.*" Sincerity is here claimed ; sincerity, such as would be accounted genuine before the bar of God. Whatever evil men might think of him, David felt that he had the good opinion of his God. Moreover, freedom from his one great besetting sin he ventures also to plead, " *I kept myself from mine iniquity.*" It is a very gracious sign when the most violent parts of our nature have been well guarded. If the weakest link in the chain is not broken, the stronger links will be safe enough. David's impetuous

18

temper might have led him to slay Saul when he had him in his power, but grace enabled him to keep his hands clean of the blood of his enemy ; but what a wonder it was, and how well worthy of such a grateful record as these verses afford ! It will be a sweet cordial to us one of these days to remember our self-denials, and to bless God that we were able to exhibit them.

24. God first gives us holiness, and then rewards us for it. We are his work-manship ; vessels made unto honour ; and when made, the honour is not withheld from the vessel ; though, in fact, it all belongs to the Potter upon whose wheel the vessel was fashioned. The prize is awarded to the flower at the show, but the gardener reared it ; the child wins the prize from the schoolmaster, but the real honour of his schooling lies with the master, although instead of receiving he gives the reward.

25. The dealings of the Lord in his own case, cause the grateful singer to remember the usual rule of God's moral government ; he is just in his dealings with the sons of men, and metes out to each man according to his measure. " *With the merciful thou wilt shew thyself merciful ; with an upright man thou wilt shew thyself upright.*" Every man shall have his meat weighed in his own scales, his corn meted in his own bushel, and his land measured with his own rod. No rule can be more fair, to ungodly men more terrible, or to the generous more honourable. How would men throw away their light weights, and break their short yards, if they could but believe that they themselves are sure to be in the end the losers by their knavish tricks ! Note that even the merciful need mercy ; no amount of generosity to the poor, or forgiveness to enemies, can set us beyond the need of mercy. Lord, have mercy upon me, a sinner.

26. " *With the pure thou wilt shew thyself pure ; and with the froward thou wilt shew thyself froward.*" The sinner's frowardness is sinful and rebellious, and the only sense in which the term can be applied to the Most Holy God is that of judicial opposition and sternness, in which the Judge of all the earth will act at cross-purposes with the offender, and let him see that all things are not to be made subservient to wicked whims and wilful fancies. Calvin very forcibly says, " This brutish and monstrous stupidity in men compels God to invent new modes of expression, and as it were to clothe himself with a different character. There is a similar sentence in Leviticus xxvi. 21—24, where God says, " and if ye walk contrary unto (or perversely with) me, then will I also walk contrary unto (or perversely, or roughly, or at random with) you." As if he had said that their obstinacy and stubbornness would make him on his part forget his accustomed forbearance and gentleness, and cast himself recklessly or at random against them. We see then what the stubborn at length gain by their obduracy ; it is this, that God hardens himself still more to break them in pieces, and if they are of stone, he causes them to' feel that he has the hardness of iron." The Jewish tradition was that the manna tasted according to each man's mouth ; certainly God shows himself to each individual according to his character.

27. " *For thou wilt save the afflicted people.*" This is a comforting assurance for the poor in spirit whose spiritual griefs admit of no sufficient solace from any other than a divine hand. They cannot save themselves nor can others do it, but God will save them. " *But wilt bring down high looks.*" Those who look down on others with scorn shall be looked down upon with contempt ere long. The Lord abhors a proud look. What a reason for repentance and humiliation ! How much better to be humble than to provoke God to humble us in his wrath ! A considerable number of clauses occur in this passage in the future tense ; how forcibly are we thus brought to remember that our present joy or sorrow is not to have so much weight with us as the great and eternal future !

28. " *For thou wilt light my candle.*" Even the children of the day sometimes need candle-light. In the darkest hour light will arise ; a candle shall be lit, it will be comfort such as we may fittingly use without dishonesty—it will be our own candle ; yet God himself will find the holy fire with which the candle

shall burn ; our evidences are our own, but their comfortable light is from above. Candles which are lit by God the devil cannot blow out. All candles are not shining, and so there are some graces which yield no present comfort ; but it is well to have candles which may by and by be lit, and it is well to possess graces which may yet afford us cheering evidences. The metaphor of the whole verse is founded upon the dolorous nature of darkness and the delightfulness of light ; " truly the light is sweet, and a pleasant thing it is for the eyes to behold the sun ;" and even so the presence of the Lord removes all the gloom of sorrow, and enables the believer to rejoice with exceeding great joy. The lighting of the lamp is a cheerful moment in the winter's evening, but the lifting up of the light of God's countenance is happier far. It is said that the poor in Egypt will stint themselves of bread to buy oil for the lamp, so that they may not sit in darkness ; we could well afford to part with all earthly comforts if the light of God's love could but constantly gladden our souls.

29 For by thee I have run through a troop ; and by my God have I leaped over a wall.

30 *As for* God, his way *is* perfect : the word of the LORD is tried: he *is* a buckler to all those that trust in him.

31 For who *is* God save the LORD ? or who *is* a rock save our God ?

32 *It is* God that girdeth me with strength, and maketh my way perfect.

33 He maketh my feet like hinds' *feet*, and setteth me upon my high places.

34 He teacheth my hands to war, so that a bow of steel is broken by mine arms.

35 Thou hast also given me the shield of thy salvation : and thy right hand hath holden me up, and thy gentleness hath made me great.

36 Thou hast enlarged my steps under me, that my feet did not slip.

37 I have pursued mine enemies, and overtaken them : neither did I turn again till they were consumed.

38 I have wounded them that they were not able to rise : they are fallen under my feet.

39 For thou hast girded me with strength unto the battle : thou hast subdued under me those that rose up against me.

40 Thou hast also given me the necks of mine enemies ; that I might destroy them that hate me.

41 They cried, but *there was* none to save *them : even* unto the LORD, but he answered them not.

42 Then did I beat them small as the dust before the wind : I did cast them out as the dirt in the streets.

43 Thou hast delivered me from the strivings of the people ; *and* thou hast made me the head of the heathen : a people *whom* I have not known shall serve me.

44 As soon as they hear of me, they shall obey me : the strangers shall submit themselves unto me.

45 The strangers shall fade away, and be afraid out of their close places.

Some repetitions are not vain repetitions. Second thoughts upon God's mercy should be and often are the best. Like wines on the lees our gratitude grows stronger and sweeter as we meditate upon divine goodness. The verses which we have now to consider are the ripe fruit of a thankful spirit ; they are apples of gold as to matter, and they are placed in baskets of silver as to their language. They describe the believer's victorious career and his enemies' confusion.

29. "*For by thee I have run through a troop; and by my God have I leaped over a wall.*" Whether we meet the foe in the open field or leap upon them while they lurk behind the battlements of a city, we shall by God's grace defeat them in either case ; if they hem us in with living legions, or environ us with stone walls, we shall with equal certainty obtain our liberty. Such feats we have already performed, hewing our way at a run through hosts of difficulties, and scaling impossibilities at a leap. God's warriors may expect to have a taste of every form of fighting, and must by the power of faith determine to quit themselves like men ; but it behoves them to be very careful to lay all their laurels at Jehovah's feet, each one of them saying, "*by my God*" have I wrought this valiant deed. Our *spolia optima*, the trophies of our conflicts, we hereby dedicate to the God of Battles, and ascribe to him all glory and strength.

30. "*As for God, his way is perfect.*" Far past all fault and error are God's dealings with his people ; all his actions are resplendent with justice, truth, tenderness, mercy, and holiness. Every way of God is complete in itself, and all his ways put together are matchless in harmony and goodness. Is it not very consolatory to believe that he who has begun to bless us will perfect his work, for all his ways are "*perfect.*" Nor must the divine "*word*" be without its song of praise. "*The word of the Lord is tried,*" like silver refined in the furnace. The doctrines are glorious, the precepts are pure, the promises are faithful, and the whole revelation is superlatively full of grace and truth. David had tried it, thousands have tried it, we have tried it, and it has never failed. It was meet that when way and word had been extolled, the Lord himself should be magnified ; hence it is added, "*He is a buckler to all those that trust in him.*" No armour of proof or shield of brass so well secures the warrior as the covenant God of Israel protects his warring people. He himself is the buckler of trustful ones ; what a thought is this ! What peace may every trusting soul enjoy !

31. Having mentioned his God, the psalmist's heart burns, and his words sparkle ; he challenges heaven and earth to find another being worthy of adoration or trust in comparison with Jehovah. His God, as Matthew Henry says, is a None-such. The idols of the heathen he scorns to mention, snuffing them all out as mere nothings when Deity is spoken of. "*Who is God save the Lord?*" Who else creates, sustains, foresees, and overrules ? Who but he is perfect in every attribute, and glorious in every act ? To whom but Jehovah should creatures bow ? Who else can claim their service and their love ? "*Who is a rock save our God?*" Where can lasting hopes be fixed ? Where can the soul find rest ? Where is stability to be found ? Where is strength to be discovered ? Surely in the Lord Jehovah alone can we find rest and refuge.

32. Surveying all the armour in which he fought and conquered, the joyful victor praises the Lord for every part of the panoply. The girdle of his loins earns the first stanza : "*It is God that girdeth me with strength, and maketh my way perfect.*" Girt about the loins with power from heaven, the warrior was filled with vigour, far above all created might ; and, whereas, without this wondrous belt he would have been feeble and effeminate, with relaxed energies and scattered forces, he felt himself, when braced with the girdle of truth, to be compact in purpose, courageous in daring, and concentrated in power ; so that his course was a complete success, so undisturbed by disastrous defeat as to be called "perfect." Have we been made more than conquerors over sin, and has our life hitherto been such as becometh the gospel ? Then let us

ascribe all the glory to him who girt us with his own inexhaustible strength, that we might be unconquered in battle and unwearied in pilgrimage.

33. The conqueror's feet had been shod by a divine hand, and the next note must, therefore, refer to them. *"He maketh my feet like hinds' feet, and setteth me upon my high places."* Pursuing his foes the warrior had been swift of foot as a young roe, but, instead of taking pleasure in the legs of a man, he ascribes the boon of swiftness to the Lord alone. When our thoughts are nimble, and our spirits rapid, like the chariots of Amminadib, let us not forget that our best Beloved's hand has given us the choice favour. Climbing into impregnable fortresses, David had been preserved from slipping, and made to stand where scarce the wild goat can find a footing ; herein was preserving mercy manifested. We, too, have had our *high places* of honour, service, temptation, and danger, but hitherto we have been kept from falling. Bring hither the harp, and let us emulate the psalmist's joyful thanksgiving ; had we fallen, our wailings must have been terrible ; since we have stood, let our gratitude be fervent.

34. *"He teacheth my hands to war."* Martial prowess and skill in the use of weapons are gratefully acknowledged to be the result of divine teaching ; no sacrifice is offered at the shrine of self in praise of natural dexterity, or acquired skilfulness ; but, regarding all warlike prowess as a gift of heavenly favour, thankfulness is presented to the Giver. The Holy Spirit is the great Drill-master of heavenly soldiers. *"So that a bow of steel is broken by mine arms."* A bow of brass is probably meant, and these bows could scarcely be bent by the arms alone, the archer had to gain the assistance of his foot ; it was, therefore, a great feat of strength to bend the bow, so far as even to snap it in halves. This was meant of the enemies' bow, which he not only snatched from his grasp, but rendered useless by breaking it in pieces. Jesus not only destroyed the fiery suggestions of Satan, but he broke his arguments with which he shot them, by using Holy Scripture against him ; by the same means we may win a like triumph, breaking the bow and cutting the spear in sunder by the sharp edge of revealed truth. Probably David had by nature a vigorous bodily frame ; but it is even more likely that, like Samson, he was at times clothed with more than common strength ; at any rate, he ascribes the honour of his feats entirely to his God. Let us never wickedly rob the Lord of his due, but faithfully give unto him the glory which is due unto his name.

35. *"Thou hast also given me the shield of thy salvation."* Above all we must take the shield of faith, for nothing else can quench Satan's fiery darts ; this shield is of celestial workmanship, and is in all cases a direct gift from God himself ; it is the channel, the sign, the guarantee, and the earnest of perfect salvation. *"Thy right hand hath holden me up."* Secret support is administered to us by the preserving grace of God, and at the same time Providence kindly yields us manifest aid. We are such babes that we cannot stand alone ; but when the Lord's right hand upholds us, we are like brazen pillars which cannot be moved. *"Thy gentleness hath made me great."* There are several readings of this sentence. The word is capable of being translated, "thy *goodness* hath made me great." David saw much of benevolence in God's action towards him, and he gratefully ascribed all his greatness not to his own goodness, but to the goodness of God. "Thy *providence*" is another reading, which is indeed nothing more than goodness in action. Goodness is the bud of which providence is the flower ; or goodness is the seed of which providence is the harvest. Some render it, "thy *help*," which is but another word for providence ; providence being the firm ally of the saints, aiding them in the service of their Lord. Certain learned annotators tell us that the text means, "thy *humility* hath made me great." "Thy *condescension*" may, perhaps, serve as a comprehensive reading, combining the ideas which we have already mentioned, as well as that of humility. It is God's making himself little which is the cause of our being made great. We are so little that if God should manifest his greatness without condescension, we should be trampled under his feet ; but God, who must stoop to view the skies and bow to see what angels do, looks to the lowly and contrite,

and makes them great.   While these are the translations which have been given to the adopted text of the original, we find that there are other readings altogether ; as for instance, the Septuagint, which reads, " thy discipline"—thy fatherly correction—" hath made me great ;" while the Chaldee paraphrase reads, " thy word hath increased me."   Still the idea is the same.   David ascribes all his own greatness to the condescending goodness and graciousness of his Father in heaven.   Let us all feel this sentiment in our own hearts, and confess that whatever of goodness or greatness God may have put upon us, we must cast our crowns at his feet, and cry, " *thy gentleness hath made me great.*"

36. " *Thou hast enlarged my steps.*" A smooth pathway leading to spacious possessions and camping-grounds had been opened up for him. Instead of threading the narrow mountain paths, and hiding in the cracks and corners of caverns, he was able to traverse the plains and dwell under his own vine and fig tree. It is no small mercy to be brought into full Christian liberty and enlargement, but it is a greater favour still to be enabled to walk worthily in such liberty, not being permitted to slip with our feet. To stand upon the rocks of affliction is the result of gracious upholding, but that aid is quite as much needed in the luxurious plains of prosperity.

37. The preservation of the saints bodes ill for their adversaries. The Amelekites thought themselves clear away with their booty, but when David's God guided him in the pursuit, they were soon overtaken and cut in pieces. When God is with us sins and sorrows flee, and all forms of evil are " *consumed* " before the power of grace. What a noble picture this and the following verses present to us of the victories of our glorious Lord Jesus !

38. The destruction of our spiritual enemies is complete. We may exult over sin, death and hell, as disarmed and disabled *for* us by our conquering Lord ; may he graciously give them a like defeat *within* us.

39 and 40. It is impossible to be too frequent in the duty of ascribing all our victories to the God of our salvation. It is true that we have to wrestle with our spiritual antagonists, but the triumph is far more the Lord's than ours. We must not boast like the ambitious votaries of vainglory, but we may exult as the willing and believing instruments in the Lord's hands of accomplishing his great designs.

41. " *They cried, but there was none to save them ; even unto the Lord, but he answered them not.*" Prayer is so notable a weapon that even the wicked will take to it in their fits of desperation. Bad men have appealed to God against God's own servants, but all in vain ; the kingdom of heaven is not divided, and God never succours his foes at the expense of his friends. There are prayers to God which are no better than blasphemy, which bring no comfortable reply, but rather provoke the Lord to greater wrath. Shall I ask a man to wound or slay his own child to gratify my malice ? Would he not resent the insult against his humanity ? How much less will Jehovah regard the cruel desires of the enemies of the church, who dare to offer their prayers for its destruction, calling its existence schism, and its doctrine heresy !

42. The defeat of the nations who fought with King David was so utter and complete that they were like powders pounded in a mortar ; their power was broken into fragments and they became as weak as dust before the wind, and as mean as the mire of the roads. Thus powerless and base are the enemies of God now become through the victory of the Son of David upon the cross. Arise, O my soul, and meet thine enemies, for they have sustained a deadly blow, and will fall before thy bold advance.

> " Hell and my sins resist my course,
> But hell and sin are vanquish'd foes
> My Jesus nail'd them to his cross,
> And sung the triumph when he rose."

43. " *Thou hast delivered me from the strivings of the people.*" Internal strife is very hard to deal with. A civil war is war in its most miserable form ; it is a subject for warmest gratitude when concord rules within. Our poet

praises Jehovah for the union and peace which smiled in his dominions, and if we have peace in the three kingdoms of our spirit, soul, and body, we are in duty bound to give Jehovah a song. Unity in a church should assuredly excite like gratitude. " *Thou hast made me the head of the heathen ; a people whom I have not known shall serve me.*" The neighbouring nations yielded to the sway of Judah's prince. Oh when shall all lands adore King Jesus, and serve him with holy joy ? Surely there is far more of Jesus than of David here. Missionaries may derive rich encouragement from the positive declaration that heathen lands shall own the Headship of the Crucified.

44. " *As soon as they hear of me, they shall obey me.*" Thus readily did the once struggling captain become a far-renowned victor, and thus easy shall be our triumphs. We prefer, however, to speak of Jesus. In many cases the gospel is speedily received by hearts apparently unprepared for it. Those who have never heard the gospel before, have been charmed by its first message, and yielded obedience to it ; while others, alas ! who are accustomed to its joyful sound, are rather hardened than softened by its teachings. The grace of God sometimes runs like fire among the stubble, and a nation is born in a day. " Love at first sight" is no uncommon thing when Jesus is the wooer. He can write Cæsar's message without boasting, *Veni, vidi, vici ;* his gospel is in some cases no sooner heard than believed. What inducements to spread abroad the doctrine of the cross !

45. " *The strangers shall fade away.*" Like sear leaves or blasted trees our foes and Christ's foes shall find no sap and stamina remaining in them. Those who are strangers to Jesus are strangers to all lasting happiness ; those must soon fade who refuse to be watered from the river of life. " *And be afraid out of their close places.*" Out of their mountain fastnesses the heathen crept in fear to own allegiance to Israel's king, and even so, from the castles of self-confidence and the dens of carnal security, poor sinners come bending before the Saviour, Christ the Lord. Our sins which have entrenched themselves in our flesh and blood as in impregnable forts, shall yet be driven forth by the sanctifying energy of the Holy Spirit, and we shall serve the Lord in singleness of heart.

Thus with remembrances of conquests in the past, and with glad anticipations of victories yet to come, the sweet singer closes the description, and returns to exercise of more direct adoration of his gracious God.

46 The LORD liveth ; and blessed *be* my rock ; and let the God of my salvation be exalted.

47 *It is* God that avengeth me, and subdueth the people under me.

48 He delivereth me from mine enemies : yea, thou liftest me up above those that rise up against me : thou hast delivered me from the violent man.

49 Therefore will I give thanks unto thee, O LORD, among the heathen, and sing praises unto thy name.

50 Great deliverance giveth he to his king ; and sheweth mercy to his anointed, to David, and to his seed for evermore.

46. " *The Lord liveth.*" Possessing underived, essential, independent and eternal life. We serve no inanimate, imaginary, or dying God. He only hath immortality. Like loyal subjects let us cry, Live on, O God. Long live the King of kings. By thine immortality do we dedicate ourselves afresh to thee. As the Lord our God liveth so would we live to him. " *And blessed be my rock.*" He is the ground of our hope, and let him be the subject of our praise. Our hearts bless the Lord, with holy love extolling him.

> Jehovah lives, my rock be blessed !
> Praised be the God who gives me rest !

" *Let the God of my salvation be exalted.*" As our Saviour, the Lord should more than ever be glorified. We should publish abroad the story of the covenant and the cross, the Father's election, the Son's redemption, and the Spirit's regeneration. He who rescues us from deserved ruin should be very dear to us. In heaven they sing, "Unto him that loved us and washed us in his blood;" the like music should be common in the assemblies of the saints below.

47. "*It is God that avengeth me, and subdueth the people under me.*" To rejoice in personal revenge is unhallowed and evil, but David viewed himself as the instrument of vengeance upon the enemies of God and his people, and had he not rejoiced in the success accorded to him he would have been worthy of censure. That sinners perish is in itself a painful consideration, but that the Lord's law is avenged upon those who break it is to the devout mind a theme for thankfulness. We must, however, always remember that vengeance is never ours, vengeance belongeth unto the Lord, and he is so just and withal so long-suffering in the exercise of it, that we may safely leave its administration in his hands.

48. From all enemies, and especially from one who was pre-eminent in violence, the Lord's anointed was preserved, and at the last over the head of Saul and all other adversaries he reigned in honour. The like end awaits every saint, because Jesus who stooped to be lightly esteemed among men is now made to sit far above all principalities and powers.

49. Paul cites this verse (Rom. xv. 9): "And that the Gentiles might glorify God for his mercy; as it is written, For this cause I will confess to thee among the Gentiles, and sing unto thy name." This is clear evidence that David's Lord is here, but David is here too, and is to be viewed as an example of a holy soul making its boast in God even in the presence of ungodly men. Who are the despisers of God that we should stop our mouths for them? We will sing to our God whether they like it or no, and force upon them the knowledge of his goodness. Too much politeness to traitors may be treason to our King.

50. This is the winding up verse into which the writer throws a fulness of expression, indicating the most rapturous delight of gratitude. "*Great deliverance.*" The word "*deliverance*" is plural, to show the variety and completeness of the salvation; the adjective "*great*" is well placed if we consider from what, to what, and how we are saved. All this mercy is given to us in our King, the Lord's Anointed, and those are blessed indeed who as his seed may expect mercy to be built up for evermore. The Lord was faithful to the literal David, and he will not break his covenant with the spiritual David, for that would far more involve the honour of his crown and character.

The Psalm concludes in the same loving spirit which shone upon its commencement; happy are they who can sing on from love to love, even as the pilgrims marched from strength to strength.

EXPLANATORY NOTES AND QUAINT SAYINGS.

Whole Psalm.—The general argument of the Psalm may be thus stated: it is a magnificent eucharistic ode. It begins with a celebration of the glorious perfections of the Divinity, whose assistance the speaker had so often experienced. He describes, or rather, he delineates, his perils, the power of his enemies, his sudden deliverance from them, and the indignation and power of his divine deliverer manifested in their overthrow. He paints these in so lively colours, that while we read we seem to see the lightning, to hear the thunders, to feel the earthquake. He afterwards describes his victories, so that we seem to be eye-witnesses of them, and take part in them. He predicts a wide-extended empire, and concludes with a lofty expression of grateful adoration of Jehovah, the Author of all his deliverances and triumphs. The style is highly oratorical and poetical, sublime, and full of uncommon figures of speech. It is the natural language of a person of the highest mental endowments, under a divine inspiration, deeply affected by remarkable divine benefits, and filled with the most lofty conceptions of the divine character and dispensations.—*John Brown, D.D.*, 1853.

Whole Psalm.—Kitto, in "The Pictorial Bible," has the following note upon 2 Samuel xxii. :—"This is the same as the eighteenth Psalm. . . . The Rabbins reckon up seventy-four differences between the two copies, most of them very minute. They probably arose from the fact that the poem was, as they conjecture, composed by David in his youth, and revised in his later days, when he sent it to the chief musician. The present is, of course, supposed to be the earlier copy."

Whole Psalm.—The eighteenth Psalm is called by Michaelis more artificial, and less truly terrible, than the Mosaic odes. In structure it may be so, but surely not in spirit. It appears to many besides us, one of the most magnificent lyrical raptures in the Scriptures. As if the poet had dipped his pen in "the brightness of that light which was before his eye," so he describes the descending God. Perhaps it may be objected that the *nodus* is hardly worthy of the *vindex*— to deliver David from his enemies, could Deity ever be imagined to come down? But the objector knows not the character of the ancient Hebrew mind. God in its view had not to descend from heaven; he was nigh—a cloud like a man's hand might conceal—a cry, a look might bring him down. And why should not David's fancy clothe him, as he came, in a panoply befitting his dignity, in clouds spangled with coals of fire? If he was to descend, why not in state? The proof of the grandeur of this Psalm is in the fact, that it has borne the test of almost every translation, and made doggerel erect itself, and become divine. Even Sternhold and Hopkins its fiery whirlwind lifts up, purifies, touches into true power, and then throws down, helpless and panting, upon their ancient common. Perhaps the great charm of the eighteenth, apart from the poetry of the descent, is the exquisite and subtle alternation of the *I* and the *Thou*. We have spoken of parallelism, as the key to the mechanism of Hebrew song. We find this as existing between David and God—the delivered and the deliverer— beautifully pursued throughout the whole of this Psalm. "I will love thee, O Lord, my strength." "I will call upon the Lord, who is worthy to be praised." "He sent from above; he took me; he drew me out of many waters." "Thou wilt light my candle." "Thou hast given me the shield of thy salvation." "Thou hast girded me with strength unto battle." "Thou hast given me the necks of mine enemies." "Thou hast made me the head of the heathen." It has been ingeniously argued, that the existence of the *I* suggests, inevitably as a polar opposite, the thought of the *Thou*, that the personality of man proves thus the personality of God; but, be this as it may, David's perception of that personality is nowhere so intense as here. He seems not only to see, but to feel and touch, the object of his gratitude and worship.—*George Gilfillan, in "The Bards of the Bible,"* 1852.

Whole Psalm.—He that would be wise, let him read the Proverbs; he that would be holy, let him read the Psalms. Every line in this book breathes peculiar sanctity. This Psalm, though placed among the first, was penned among the last, as the preface assures us, and is left as the epitome of the general history of David's life. It is twice recorded in the Scripture (2 Sam. xxii., and in this book of Psalms), for the excellency and sweetness thereof; surely that we should take double notice of it. Holy David, being near the shore, here looks on his former dangers and deliverances with a thankful heart, and writes this Psalm to bless the Lord: as if each of you that are grown into years should review your lives and observe the wonderful goodness and providence of God towards you; and then sit down and write a modest memorial of his most remarkable mercies, for the comfort of yourselves and posterity; an excellent practice. What a comfort would it be for you to read how good your God was to your father or grandfather, that are dead and gone! So would your children rejoice in the Lord upon the reading of his goodness to you; and you cannot have a better pattern for this than holy David, who wrote this Psalm when he was threescore and seven years old; when he had outlived most of his troubles, and almost ready for his journey to his Father in heaven, he resolves to leave this good report of him upon earth. And I pray mark how he begins: he sets not up trophies to himself, but triumphs in his God—"*I will love thee, O Lord, my strength.*" As the *love of God* is the beginning of all our mercies, so *love to God* should be the end and effect of them all. As the stream leads us to the spring, so all the gifts of God must lead us to the giver of them. Lord, thou hast saved me from sickness, "*I will love thee;*" from death and hell, "*I will love thee;*" on me thou hast bestowed grace and comfort, "*I will love thee, O Lord, my strength.*" And after he had heaped on God all the sweet names he could devise (verse 2), as the true saint thinks he can never speak too well of God, or too ill of himself, then he begins his narrative. 1. Of his *dangers* (verse 4); "*Snares of death,*" "*Floods of ungodly men,*" "*Sorrows of hell.*" Hell and earth are combined against each holy man, and will trouble sufficiently in this world, if they cannot keep him out of a better. 2. Of his *retreat*, and that was, earnest prayer to God (verse 6), "*I called upon the Lord, and cried unto my God.*" When our prayers are cries ardent and importunate, then they speed: "*My cry came before him, even into his ears.*" The mother trifles while the child whimpers, but when he raises his note—strains every nerve and cries every vein—then she throws all aside, and gives him his desire. While our prayers are only whispers, our God can take his rest; but when we fall to crying, "Now will I arise, saith the Lord." 3. Of his *rescue* (verses 7 to 20), by the powerful and terrible arm of the Lord, who is in a lofty strain brought in to his servant's help, as if he would mingle heaven and earth together, rather than leave his child in the lion's paws. 4. Of the *reason* of this gracious dealing of God with him (verse 20, etc.). He was a righteous person, and he had a righteous cause. And thereupon he turns to God, saying, Thou hast dealt with me just as thou art wont to do, for "*with the merciful thou wilt show thyself merciful; with an upright man thou wilt show thyself upright.*"—*Richard Steele's* "*Plain Discourse upon Uprightness,*" 1670.

Whole Psalm.—Sometimes the Lord cheers and comforts the hearts of his people with smiling and reviving providences, both public and personal. There are times of lifting up, as well as casting down by the hand of providence. The scene changes, the aspects of providence are very cheerful and encouraging; their winter seems to be over; they put off their garments of mourning; and then, ah, what sweet returns are made to heavenly gracious souls! Doth God lift them up by prosperity? they also will lift up their God by praises. See title, and verses 1—3 of Psalm xviii. So Moses, and the people with him (Exodus xv.), when God had delivered them from Pharaoh, how do they exalt him in a song of thanksgiving, which for the elegancy and spirituality of it, is made an emblem of the doxologies given to God in glory by the saints. Rev. xv. 1. *John Flavel.*

Title.—"*The servant of the Lord;*"—the name given to Moses (Josh. i. 1, 13, 15, and in nine other places of that book) and to Joshua (Josh. xxiv. 29; Judg. ii. 8); but to none other except David (here, and in the title to Ps. xxxvi). Cp. Acts xiii. 36, ὑπηρετήσας. This is significant; reminding us of the place occupied by David in the history of Israel. He was the appointed successor of Moses and Joshua, who extended the power of Israel over the whole region allotted to them by Divine promise.—*W. Kay*, 1871.

Title.—This Psalm, which is entitled a *shirah* (or song), is David's hymn of praise to God for his deliverance from all his enemies (see the title, and above, 2 Sam. xxii), and has an appropriate place in the present group of Psalms, which speak of resurrection after suffering. It is entitled a Psalm of David, "*the servant of the Lord,*" and thus is coupled with another psalm of deliverance, Ps. xxxvi.—*Christopher Wordsworth.*

Verse 1.—"*I will love thee, O Lord.*"—The word whereby the psalmist expresseth his entire affection, in the noun signifieth a womb, and importeth such an affection as cometh from the innermost part of man (רחם matrix), from his bowels, from the bottom of his heart, as we speak. It is, therefore, oft put for such pity and compassion as moveth the bowels. Some, therefore, thus translate that phrase, "From my innermost bowels will I love thee, O Lord." To give evidence of his entire and ardent love of God, he oft professeth his wonderful great love to God's commandments, whereof he saith with admiration, "Oh, how I love thy law! I love thy commandments above gold; yea, above fine gold. I love them exceedingly" (Psalm cxix. 97, 127, 167); therefore, he saith to God, "Consider how I love thy precepts" (verse 159).—*William Gouge*, 1575–1653.

Verse 1.—"*I will love thee.*" Intimately as a mother loves the child that comes out of her womb.—*Westminster Assembly's Annotations*, 1651.

Verses 1, 2.—God hath, as it were, made himself over to believers. David doth not say, God will give or bestow salvation upon me; but he saith, "He is the horn of my salvation." It is God himself who is the salvation and the portion of his people. They would not care much for salvation if God were not their salvation. It more pleaseth the saints that they enjoy God, than that they enjoy salvation. False and carnal spirits will express a great deal of desire after salvation, for they like salvation, heaven, and glory well; but they never express any longing desire after God and Jesus Christ. They love salvation, but they care not for a Saviour. Now that which faith pitcheth most upon is God himself; he shall be my salvation, let me have him, and that is salvation enough; he is my life, he is my comfort, he is my riches, he is my honour, and he is my all. Thus David's heart acted immediately upon God, "*I will love thee, O Lord, my strength. The Lord is my rock, and my fortress, and my deliverer; my God, my strength, in whom I will trust; my buckler, and the horn of my salvation, and my high tower.*" It pleased holy David more that God was his strength, than that God gave him strength; that God was his deliverer, than that he was delivered; that God was his fortress, his buckler, his horn, his high tower, than that he gave him the effect of all these. It pleased David, and it pleases all the saints more that God is their salvation, whether temporal or eternal, than that he saves them: the saints look more at God than at all that is God's.—*Joseph Caryl.*

Verses 1, 2.—David speaks like one in love with God, for he doth adorn him with confession of praise, and his mouth is filled with the praise of the Lord, which he expresseth in this exuberancy and redundancy of holy oratory.—*Edward Marbury.*

Verse 2.—"*The Lord is my rock.*" As the rocks that are hard to be clambered unto are good refuges to fly unto from the face of pursuers, so God is the safety of all such as in distress do fly to him for succour.—*Robert Cawdray.*

Verse 2.—"*My deliverer.*" He who betook himself to one of these inaccessible retreats, was sometimes obliged by famine to surrender to his enemy, who lay in wait for him beneath; but Jehovah gives him not only security but liberty; not only preserves him, as it were, in an inaccessible retreat, but at the same time enables him to go forth in safety.—*Jarchi.*

Verse 2.—"*The horn of my salvation.*" The allusion here is doubtful. Some have supposed the reference to be to the horns of animals, by which they defend themselves and attack their enemies. "God is to me, does for me, what their horns do for them." Others consider it as referring to the well-established fact, that warriors were accustomed to place horns, or ornaments like horns, on their helmets. The horn stands for the helmet; and "the helmet of salvation" is an expression equivalent to "a saving, a protecting helmet." Others consider the reference as to the corners or handles of the altar in the court of the tabernacle or temple, which are called its horns. Others suppose the reference to be to the highest point of a lofty and precipitous mountain, which we are accustomed to call its peak. No doubt, in the Hebrew language, horn is used for mountain as in Isaiah v. 1. A very fertile mountain is called a horn of oil. The sense is substantially the same, whichever of these views we take ; though, from the connection with "shield" or "buckler," I am induced to consider the second of these views as the most probable. It seems the same idea as that expressed, Psalm cxl. 7, "Thou hast covered," and thou wilt cover "my head in the day of battle."—*John Brown*.

Verse 2.—"*The horn of my salvation*" Horns are the well-known emblems of strength and power, both in the sacred and profane writers ; by a metaphor taken from horned animals, which are frequently made subjects of comparison by poetical writers, and the strength of which, whether for offence or defence, consists principally in their horns. Bruce speaks of a remarkable head-dress worn by the governors of provinces in Abyssinia, consisting of a large broad fillet, bound upon their foreheads and tied behind their heads, and having in the middle of it a horn, or a conical piece of silver, gilt, about four inches long, much in the shape of our common candle extinguishers. It is called *kirn* or horn, and is only worn on reviews or parades after victory. He supposes this, like other Abyssinian usages, to be taken from the Hebrews, and is of opinion that there are many allusions to the practice in Scripture, in the expressions, "lifting up the horn," "exalting the horn," and the like.—*Richard Mant*.

Verse 2.—"*The Lord is my high tower*." If a man do run to a tower, yet if that be a weak and an insufficient tower, without men and munition, and a ruinous shaken tower ; or if a man do make choice of a tower, a strong sufficient tower, yet if in his danger he betake not himself to that tower, but he sit still ; or if he sit not still, yet he but only go and walk on easily towards it, he may well be met withal, and a danger may arrest him, surprise him, and cut him off before he get the tower over his head. But the man that will be safe, as he must choose a strong tower, so he must go to, nay, *run* into that tower. Running will not secure a man unless the tower be strong. . . . . David was got unto his *tower*, and in that *tower* there was thundering ordnance, and David put fire to them by prayer, verse 6, "In my distress I called upon the Lord, and cried unto my God : he heard my voice out of his temple, and my cry came before him, even into his ears." Here David prays and gives fire to the cannon, and what followed ? See verses 7, 8, 13, 14. "Then the earth shook and trembled," etc. "There went up a smoke out of his nostrils," etc. "The Lord also thundered in the heavens, and the Highest gave his voice ; hail stones and coals of fire. Yea, he sent out his arrows, and scattered them ; and he shot out lightnings, and discomfited them." There were no guns nor ordnance invented and in use in David's time, and yet David's prayers being in this tower, did him as good service against his enemies as all the ordnance and cannons in the world have done. David had thundering ordnance, and with them discomfited his enemies long before powder and guns were invented. It is a memorable and well known story of that Christian legion that was in Marcus Aurelius's army : the enemy being in great straits, those Christian soldiers did by their prayers not only procure rain, by which his languishing army was refreshed, but also obtained hail mixed with thunderbolts against his enemies, upon which he honoured them with the name of *Legio fulminatrix*, the Thundering Legion. They used David's cannon against the enemy, and discharged that thundering ordnance by their prayers, and that to the confusion of their enemies.—*Jeremiah Dyke's* "*Righteous Man's Tower*," 1639.

Verse 2.—"*My high tower*." Even as the fowls of the air, that they may escape the nets and snares of the fowlers, are wont to fly up on high ; so we, to avoid the infinite snares of innumerable temptations, must fly to God ; and lift up ourselves from the corruptions, lying vanities, and deceitful sleights of the world.—*Robert Cawdray*.

Verse 3.—"*I will call upon the Lord, who is worthy to be praised*." Prayer and invocation of God should always be joined with praises and thanksgivings, and used as a means whereby faith shall extract the good which it knoweth is in God, and of which he hath made promise.—*David Dickson.*

Verse 3.—"*So shall I be saved from mine enemies.*" Whoso comes to God as he should will not call in vain. The right kind of prayer is the most potent instrumentality known on earth.—*William S. Plumer.*

Verse 4.—"*Sorrows of death.*" It is heaven's peculiar to be the land of the living ; all this life is at most but the *shadow* of death, the *gate* of death, the *sorrows* of death, the *snares* of death, the *terrors* of death, the *chambers* of death, the *sentence* of death, the *savour* of death, the *ministration* of death, the *way* of death.—*Matthew Griffith,* 1634.

Verse 4.—"*The bands or cords of death encompassed me.*" It is not very easy to fix the precise meaning of the phrase, "bands" or "cords" of death. It may either be considered as equivalent to "the bands by which the dead are bound," in which case, to be encircled with the bands of death is just a figurative expression for being dead ; or it may be considered as equivalent to the bands in which a person is bound in the prospect of a violent death, and by which his violent death is secured, he being prevented from escaping. It has been supposed by some, that the allusion is to the ancient mode of hunting wild animals. A considerable tract of country was surrounded with strong ropes. The circle was gradually contracted, till the object of pursuit was so confined as to become an easy prey to the hunter. These cords were the cords of death, securing the death of the animal. The phrase is applicable to our Lord in both senses ; but as "the floods" of wickedness, or the wicked, are represented as making him afraid subsequently to his being encircled with the cords of death, I am disposed to understand it in the latter of these two senses.—*John Brown.*

Verse 4.—"*The floods.*" There is no metaphor of more frequent occurrence with the sacred poets, than that which represents dreadful and unexpected calamities under the image of overwhelming waters. This image seems to have been especially familiar with the Hebrews, inasmuch as it was derived from the peculiar habit and nature of their own country. They had continually before their eyes the river Jordan, annually overflowing its banks, when at the approach of summer the snows of Libanus and the neighbouring mountains melted, and, suddenly pouring down in torrents, swelled the current of the river. Besides, the whole country of Palestine, although it was not watered by many perennial streams, was, from the mountainous character of the greater part of it, liable to numerous torrents, which precipitated themselves through the narrow valleys after the periodical rainy seasons. This image, therefore, however known and adopted by other poets, may be considered as particularly familiar, and, as it were, domestic with the Hebrews ; who accordingly introduce it with greater frequency and freedom.—*Robert Lowth (Bishop),* 1710—1787.

Verse 5.—"*The snares of death prevented me.*" The word "*snares,*" signifies such traps or gins as are laid for birds and wild beasts. The English word "prevent" has changed its meaning in some measure since our authorised translation of the Bible was made. Its original meaning is to "come before."—*John Brown.*

Verse 6.—"*In my distress.*" If you listen even to David's harp, you shall hear as many hearse-like airs as carols ; and the pencil of the Holy Spirit hath laboured more in describing the afflictions of Job than the felicities of Solomon. Prosperity is not without many fears and distastes ; and adversity is not without comforts and hopes. We see, in needleworks and embroideries, it is more pleasing to have a lively work upon a sad and solemn ground, than to have a dark and melancholy work upon a lightsome ground ; judge, therefore, of the pleasures of the heart by the pleasures of the eye. Certainly virtue is like precious odours — most fragrant when they are crushed ; for prosperity doth best discover vice. but adversity doth best discover virtue.—*Francis Bacon, Baron of Verulam, etc.,* 1561—1626.

Verse 6.—"*I called upon the Lord and cried.*" Prayer is not eloquence but earnestness; not the definition of helplessness, but the feeling of it; it is the cry of faith to the ear of mercy.—*Hannah Moore,* 1745—1833.

Verse 6.—"*He heard my voice out of his temple,*" etc. The Ædiles or chamberlains among the Romans, had ever their doors standing open for all who had occasion of request or complaint to have free access to them. "God's mercy-doors are wide open to the prayers of his faithful people." The Persian kings held it a piece of their silly glory to deny an easy access to their greatest subjects. It was death to solicit them uncalled. Esther herself was afraid. But the king of heaven manifesteth himself to his people, he calls to his spouse, with, "Let me see thy face, let me hear thy voice," etc., and assigneth her negligence herein as the cause of her soul-sickness. The door of the tabernacle was not of any hard or debarring matter, but a veil, which is easily penetrable. And whereas in the temple none came near to worship, but only the high priest, others stood without in the outer court. God's people are now a kingdom of priests, and are said to worship in the temple, and at the altar. Rev. xi. 1. "Let us therefore draw near with a true heart in full assurance of faith:" "let us come boldly to the throne of grace, that we may obtain mercy, and find grace to help in time of need." Heb. x. 22; iv. 16.—*Charles Bradbury's* "*Cabinet of Jewels,*" 1785.

Verse 6.—Oh! how true is that saying, that "Faith is safe when in danger, and in danger when secure; and prayer is fervent in straits, but in joyful and prosperous circumstances, if not quite cold and dead, at least lukewarm." Oh, happy straits, if they hinder the mind from flowing forth upon earthly objects, and mingling itself with the mire; if they favour our correspondence with heaven, and quicken our love to celestial objects, without which, what we call life, may more properly deserve the name of death!—*Robert Leighton, D.D.*

Verses 6, 7.—The prayer of a single saint is sometimes followed with wonderful effects; "*In my distress I called upon the Lord, and cried unto my God: he heard my voice out of his temple, and my cry came before him, even into his ears. Then the earth shook and trembled; the foundations also of the hills moved and were shaken, because he was wroth:*" what then can a thundering legion of such praying souls do? It was said of Luther, *iste vir potuit cum Deo quicquid voluit,* That man could have of God what he would; his enemies felt the weight of his prayers; and the church of God reaped the benefits thereof. The Queen of Scots professed she was more afraid of the prayers of Mr. Knox, than of an army of ten thousand men. These were mighty wrestlers with God, howsoever contemned and vilified among their enemies. There will a time come when God will hear the prayers of his people who are continually crying in his ears, "How long, Lord, how long?"—*John Flavel.*

Verse 7.—"*Then the earth shook and trembled.*" The word גָּעַשׁ signifies, to move or shake violently: it is employed, also, to denote the reeling and staggering of a drunken man. Jer. xxv. 16.—*John Morison, in loc.*

Verse 7.—Let no appearing impossibilities make you question God's accomplishment of any of his gracious words. Though you cannot see how the thing can be done, 'tis enough if God hath said that he will do it. There can be no obstructions to promised salvation which we need to fear. He who is the God of this salvation and the Author of the promise will prepare his own way for the doing of his own work, so that "every valley shall be filled, and every mountain and hill shall be brought low." Luke iii. 5. Though the valleys be so deep that we cannot see the bottom, and the mountains so high that we cannot see the tops of them, yet God knows how to raise the one and level the other. Isaiah lxiii. 1. "I that speak in righteousness (or faithfulness) am mighty to save." If anything would keep back the kingdom of Christ, it would be our infidelity; but he will come though he should find no faith on the earth. See Rom. iii. 3. Cast not away your confidence because he defers his performances. Though providences run cross, though they move backwards and forwards, you have a sure and faithful word to rely upon. Promises, though they be for a time seemingly delayed, cannot be finally frustrated. Dare not to harbour such a thought within yourselves as Psalm lxxvii. 8; "Doth his promise fail for evermore?" The being of God may as well fail as the promise of God. That which does not come in your time, will be hastened in his time, which is always the more convenient season. Accuse him not of slowness who hath said, "I come quickly," that is, he comes as soon as all things are ready and ripe for his appearance. 'Tis as true that "the Lord is not slack concerning his promise" (2 Peter iii. 9), as that he is never guilty of breaking his promise. Wait, therefore, how long soever he tarry; do not give over expecting : the heart of God is not turned though his face be hid ; and prayers are not flung back, though they be not instantly answered.—*Timothy Cruso.*

Verses 7, 8.—The volcanic phenomena of Palestine open a question of which the data are, in a scientific point of view, too imperfect to be discussed ; but there is enough in the history and literature of the people to show that there was an agency of this kind at work. The valley of the Jordan, both in its desolation and vegetation, was one continued portent ; and from its crevices ramified even into the interior of Judæa the startling appearances, if not of the volcano, at least of the earthquake. Their historical effect in the special theatres of their operation will appear as we proceed ; but their traces on the permanent feeling of the nation must be noticed here. The writings of the psalmists and prophets abound with indications which escape the eye of a superficial reader. Like the soil of their country, they actually heave and labour with the fiery convulsions which glow beneath their surface.—*Arthur Penrhyn Stanley.*

Verses 7—9. While Jesus hung on the cross, a preternatural "darkness covered all the land ;" and no sooner had he yielded up his spirit, than "the vail of the temple was rent in twain from the top even to the bottom, and the earth did quake, and the rocks rent, and the graves were opened ; and many bodies of the saints that slept arose, and came out of the graves, after his resurrection, and went into the holy city, and appeared unto many."—*John Brown.*

Verses 7—9. In the night in which the Idumæans lay before Jerusalem, there arose a prodigious tempest and fierce winds, with most vehement rains, frequent lightnings, and terrible thunderings, and great roarings of the shaken earth ; and it was manifest that the state of the universe was disordered at the slaughter of men ; so that one might guess that these were signs of no small calamity. . . . . At the day of Pentecost, when the priests, by night, went into the inner temple, according to their custom, to execute their office, they said they perceived, first of all, a shake and a noise, and after that a sudden voice, "Let us go hence." . . . . A few days after the feast of unleavened bread, a strange and almost incredible sight was seen, which would, I suppose, be taken for a mere fable, were it not related by such as saw it, and did not the miseries which followed appear answerable to the signs ; for, before the sun set, were seen on high, in the air, all over the country, chariots and armed regiments moving swiftly in the clouds, and encompassing the city.—*Flavius Josephus,* 37—103.

Verse 8. —"*There went up a smoke out of his nostrils,*" עָלָה עָשָׁן בְּאַפּוֹ. Or there *ascended into his nose,* as the words, literally rendered, signify. The ancients placed the seat of anger in the nose, or nostrils ; because when it grows warm and violent, it discovers itself, as it were, by a heated vehement breath, that proceeds from them.—*Samuel Chandler, D.D., F.R. and A.S.S.,* 1766.

Verses 8—19.—David calls the full force of poetical imagery to aid, to describe in a becoming manner the marvels of his deliverances. He means to say that they were as manifest as the signs of heaven and earth, as sudden and powerful as the phenomena in the kingdom of nature surprise terrified mortals.

Deliverance being his theme, he might have taken the figure from the *peaceable* phenomena of the heavens. But since man heeds heaven more in *anger* than in *blessing*, and regards God more when he descends on earth in the *storm* than in the *rainbow*, David describes the blessed condescension of God by the figure of a tempest. In order to thoroughly appreciate the beauty and truthfulness of this figure, we should endeavour to realise the full power of an Oriental storm, as it is described in Psalm xxix. Solitary lightning precedes the discharge— this is meant by the *coals* in verse 8 : the clouds approach the mountain summits—*the heavens bow*, as verse 9 has it ; the storm shakes its pinions ; en- wrapped in thick clouds as in a tent, God descends to the earth ; hail (not unfrequently attending Eastern storms) and lightning issue from the black clouds, through the dissolving layers of which is seen the fiery splendour which hides the Lord of nature. He speaks, and thunder is his voice ; he shoots, and flashes of lightning are his arrows. At his rebuke, and at the blast of his breath the earth recedes—the sea foams up, and its beds are seen—the land bursts, and the foundations of the world are discovered. And lo ! an arm of deliverance issues forth from the black clouds, and the destructive fire grasps the wretched one who had cried out from the depths, pulls him forth, and delivers him from all his enemies ! Yes, the hand of the Lord has done marvellous things in the life of David. But the *eye of faith* alone could perceive in them all the hand of God. Thousands whose experiences of the delivering hand of God are not less signal than those of David, stop short at the powers of nature, and instead of bending the knee before the All-merciful God, content themselves to express with cold hearts their admiration of the changes of the destiny of man.—*Augustus F. Tholuck, D.D., Ph.D.*—1856.

Verse 9.—"*He bowed the heavens also, and came down.*" As in a tempest the clouds come nearer to the earth, and from the mountains to the valleys, so the psalmist adopts this figure peculiar to such occasions as described God's near approach to judgment (Psalm cxliv. 5, etc. ; Heb. iii. 6) ; "*and darkness* was *under his feet.*" We have here the increase of the horrors of the tempest, and its still nearer approach, but God is not yet revealed, it is darkness under his feet. Thick darkness was the accompaniment of God's descent on Mount Sinai (Exod. xx. 21 ; Deut. iv. 11) : and it invests his throne, to veil from us the overwhelming majesty of deity. Psalm xcvii. 2. But this darkness, while it hides his coming judgment, bespeaks sorrow and anguish to the objects of his wrath. Luke xxi. 25, 26.—*W. Wilson, in loc.*

Verses 9—11 :—

> " He also bowed the heavens,
> And thence he did descend ;
> And thickest clouds of darkness did
> Under his feet attend.
>
> And he upon a cherub rode,
> And thereon he did fly ;
> Yea, on the swift wings of the wind,
> His flight was from on high.
>
> He darkness made his secret place ;
> About him for his tent
> Dark waters were, and thickest clouds
> Of the airy firmament."

Verses 9—12 : —   *Scotch Version, 1649.*

> " In his descent, bow'd heaven with earth did meet,
> And gloomy darkness roll'd beneath his feet ;
> A golden winged cherub he bestrid,
> And on the swiftly flying tempest rid.
>
> He darkness made his secret cabinet ;
> Thick fogs and dropping clouds about him set ;
> The beams of his bright presence these expel,
> Whence showers of burning coals and hailstones fell."

George Sandys, 1577—1643.

Verse 10.—" *Cherub.*" The Hebrew name hath affinity with *Rechub*, a chariot, used in Psalm civ. 3, almost in like sense as " *cherub*" is here ; and the *cherubims* are called a chariot, 1 Chron. xxviii. 18 ; and God's angels are his chariots, Psalm lxviii. 18, and they seem to be meant in this place ; for as the angels are said to fly, Dan. ix. 21 ; so the *cherubims* had wings, Exod. xxv. 20, and are by the apostle called " cherubims of glory," Heb. ix. 5. In Psalm lxxx. 2, God is said " to sit on the cherubims," as here, to ride ; and " *a cherub*" may be put for many, or all the *cherubims*, as chariot for chariots, Psalm lxviii. 18. *Henry Ainsworth.*

Verse 10.—" *Cherubs.*" The " *cherub*" with the countenances of man, the lion, the bull, and the eagle (combining in itself, as it were, the intelligence, majesty, strength, and life of nature), was a symbol of the powers of nature. When powerful elements, as in a storm, are serving God, he is said to " *ride on a cherub.*"—*Augustus F. Tholuck.*

Verse 10.—" *Cherub.*"—

> " He on the wings of *cherub* rode sublime
> On the crystalline sky."
>
> *John Milton.*

Verse 10.—When God comes to punish his foes and rescue his people, nothing has ever surprised his friends or foes more than the admirable swiftness with which he moves and acts : He flies " *upon the wings of the wind.*"—*William S. Plumer.*

Verse 10.—Every circumstance that can add to the splendour of Jehovah's descent upon his enemies is thrown into the narrative by the inspired poet. It is not enough that the heavens should bend beneath him, and that clouds of darkness should be seen rolling, in terrible majesty, under his feet ; cherubic legions also are the willing supporters of his throne, and, swift as air, he flies " *upon the wings of the wind.*" Into this amazing scene the awful appendages of the mercy-seat are introduced ; on the bending heavens, the cloudy chariot rides sublime, and the winds of heaven bear it majestically along.—*J. Morison.*

Verse 12.—" *Coals of fire.*" The word signifies, living *burning coals.* Where the lightning fell, it devoured all before it, and burned whatever it touched into burning embers.—*Samuel Chandler.*

Verse 14.—" *Yea, he sent out his arrows, and scattered them,*" etc. O that you who are now strangers to God would but consider these things ! O that you would but think what this battle may be, where the combatants are so unequal ! Stand still, O sun, in the valley of Ajalon, till the Lord have avenged him of his enemies ! Muster yourselves, O ye stars, and fight in your courses against those miserable sinners that have waged war against their Maker ; plant your mighty cannons, shoot down huge hailstones, arrows of fire, and hot thunderbolts ! Oh, how do the wounded fall ! How many are the slain of the Lord, multitudes in the Valley of Decision, for the day of the Lord is terrible. Behold God's enemies falling by thousands, behold the garments rolling in blood, hear the prancing of his terrible ones, the mountains are covered with horses and chariots of fire. God's soldiers run from one place to another with their flaming swords in their hands, armed with the justice of God, jealousy, power, and indignation ! Oh, the dreadful slaughter that is made ! Millions, millions fall ; they are not able to stand ; not one of them can lift up his hand ; their hearts fail them ; paleness and trembling hath seized upon the stoutest of them all. The bow of the Lord is strong ; from the blood of the slain, from the fat of the mighty, the bow of the Lord turneth not back, the sword of the Almighty returns not empty. How do the mighty ones fall in this battle ! A hot battle indeed, in which none escape ! Who is he that cometh from Edom, with dyed garments from Bozrah ? He that is glorious in his apparel, and thy garments like him that treadeth the wine fat ? I have trodden the wine-press alone, and of the people there was none with me. For I will tread them in mine anger,

and trample them in my fury ; and I will bring down their strength to the earth :
the hand of the Lord shall be known, the power of the mighty Jehovah shall be
felt, and his indignation towards his enemies. For behold he will come with
fire and with chariots like a whirlwind, to render his anger with fury, and his
rebuke with flames of fire ; for by fire and by his sword will he plead with all
flesh ; and the slain of the Lord shall be many, and the saints shall go forth and
look upon the carcases of the men that have transgressed against me.   For their
worm shall not die, neither shall their fire be quenched, and they shall be an
abhorring unto all flesh.   Upon the wicked he shall rain snares, fire, and brimstone, and a horrible tempest.   This shall be the portion of their cup !   This it
is to fight against God !   This it is to defy the Lord of Hosts !—*James Janeway.*

Verse 14.—" *He shot out his lightnings.*" בְּרָקִים רָב. LXX ἀστραπὰς ἐπλήθυνε.
Falgura multiplicavit : Vulg. and so all the versions. He multiplied his
thunderbolts ; or, shot them out thick one after another ; as the word properly
signifies.

וַיְהֻמֵּם. And discomfited them, as we render the word ; or rather, as I think it
should be translated, *and melted them ;* namely, the heavens.—*Samuel Chandler.*

Verse 14 (last clause).—It is written, " *destroyed them,*" because the Holy
Ghost would not so much as name, by the mouth of his prophet, the evil
spirits to whom he refers.—*Euthymius Zigabenus* (1125) *quoted by J. M. Neale.*

Verse 15.—" *The foundations of the world were discovered ;* i.e.*, such large
and deep chasms, or apertures, were made by the violence of the earthquake,
as one might almost see the very foundations, or as Jonah calls them, *the bottoms,*
or rather, *the extremities of the mountains,* in the bottom of the sea.   Jonah ii. 6.
Samuel Chandler.

Verse 15.—The Lord interposed with the same notoriety of his presence, as
when the waters of the sea were driven back by a strong east wind, and the deep
turned into dry ground (Ex. xiv. 21, 22), to give the Israelites a safe passage
out of their thraldom, and to drown the Egyptians.—*Henry Hammond.*

Verse 16.—" *He sent from above,*" etc.   He " *sent* " angels, or assistance otherwise.—*Matthew Poole.*

Verse 16.—" *He took.*"   God's grasp cannot be broken.   None can pluck his
chosen out of his hand.—*William S. Plumer.*

Verse 16.—" *Drew me out of many waters.*"   This hath reference to Moses'
case, who was " drawn out of the water," and thereupon called *Mosheh* (Ex. ii.
10) ; that word *Mashah* is used here by David, and nowhere else in Scripture.
" *Waters,*" signify *troubles,* and sometimes multitudes of *people.*—*H. Ainsworth.*

Verse 18.—" *They prevented me in the day of my calamity ;*" i.e.*, came on me
suddenly, unawares, when I was unprovided and helpless, and must have
destroyed me had not God upheld and supported me when I was in danger of
perishing.   God was to the psalmist לְמִשְׁעָן, *for a staff* to support him.   What
the staff is to one that is ready to fall, the means of recovering and preserving
him ; that was God to David in the time of his extremity.   For he several times
preserved him from Saul, when he, David, thought his destruction by him almost
unavoidable.   See 1 Sam. xxiii. 26, 27.—*Samuel Chandler.*

Verse 18.—" *They prevented me in the day of my calamity : but the Lord was
my stay.*"   When Henry the Eighth had spoken and written bitterly against
Luther ; saith Luther, Tell the Henries, the bishops, the Turks, and the devil
himself, do what they can, we are the children of the kingdom, worshipping of
the true God, whom they, and such as they, spit upon and crucified.   And of
the same spirit were many martyrs.   Basil affirms of the primitive saints, that
they had so much courage and confidence in their sufferings, that many of the
heathens seeing their heroic zeal and constancy, turned Christians.—*Charles
Bradbury.*

Verse 20.—" *The Lord rewarded me according to my righteousness ; according to the clearness of my hands hath he recompensed me.*" We must stand our ground, and be stiff for ourselves against all misjudgings. It is good to be zealously affected always in a good matter, whether it respects the glory of God immediately and alone, or whether it respects the credit of our brethren or our own. To desire to be famous in the world, and as those giants in the old world (Gen. vi. 4), men of renown, or, as the original text hath it, men of name, is a very great vanity ; but to protect and preserve our good name is a great and necessary duty.—*Joseph Caryl.*

Verse 21.—" *I have not wickedly departed from my God ;*" that is, with a purpose and resolution of heart to continue in a way of sinning ; and that is the property of sincerity. A man indeed may be overtaken and surprised by a temptation, but it is not with a resolution to forsake God and to cleave unto the sin, or rest in it. He will not sleep in it, spare it, or favour it ; that is, to do wickedly against God, to have a double heart and a double eye ; to look upon two objects, partly at God and partly at sin ; so to keep God, as to keep some sin also, as it is with all false-hearted men in the world. They look not upon God alone, let them pretend to religion never so much, yet they look not unto God alone, but upon something else together with God ; as Herod regarded John, but regarded his Herodias more ; and the young man in the gospel, comes to Christ, yet he looks after his estate ; and Judas followed Christ, yet looks after the bag ; this is *to depart wickedly from God.*—*William Strong,* 1650.

Verse 21 (*last clause*).—Although a godly man may break a particular commandment again and again against knowledge, yet his knowledge never suffers him to go so far as to venture knowingly to break the covenant of grace with God, and to depart from him ; when he hath gone on so far in a sin as he comes to apprehend he must break with God, and lose him if he goes on any further, this apprehension stays him, stops and brings him back again ; he may presumptuously venture (though seldom ; and always to his cost) to commit an act of sin against knowledge, because he may withal think, that by one act the covenant is not broken, nor all friendship and love hazarded between God and him, nor his interest in the state of grace, nor God, quite lost by it, though he may well think he would be displeased with him ; but if he should begin to allow himself in it, and to continue to go on again and again in it, then he knows the covenant would be broken, it cannot stand with grace ; and when this apprehension comes, and comes in strongly, he cannot sin against it, for this were to cast away the Lord, and to depart wickedly from him, now so he doth not. So David, though he sinned highly and presumptuously, yet says he, " *I have not departed wickedly from my God ;*" that is, I have not so far departed from him as though I apprehended I should utterly lose my interest in him, yet I would go on. No ; for he is my God, there lies the consideration that kept him from departing from him. So Psalm xliv. 17, " We have not dealt falsely in thy covenant," says the church there. Many acts of displeasing him may pass and be ventured, but if the holy soul thinks that the covenant lay at stake, that he and God must utterly part and break off, thus far he will never go.—*Thomas Goodwin.*

Verses 22, 23.—An unsound soul will not take notice of such a precept as opposeth his special sin ; such a precept must go for a blank, which the soul throws by, and will not think of, but as conscience now and then puts him in mind of it, whether he will or no. But it is not so with a man in whom sincerity is : that precept which doth most oppose that sin to which he is most inclined, he labours to obey as well as any other. An unsound soul sets so many of God's statutes before him, as rules to walk by, as suits with himself and the times, and no more. Such precepts as oppose his special corruptions, or displease the times, and so expose him to suffering, these he baulks and puts away, as David

292 EXPOSITIONS OF THE PSALMS.

here saith, and calls them as the rotten Scribes and Pharisees were wont to do,
"least commandments," small things not to be regarded ; which rottenness
Christ took up roundly in those ironical words, "Whosoever shall break one of
these least commandments, shall be called the least in the kingdom of God."
Godly sincerity makes no difference of greatest and least between the precepts of God, but sets all before a man as a rule to walk by, and makes the soul
laborious to observe all. "Then shall I not be ashamed, when I have respect
unto all thy commandments." Psalm cxix. 6.—*Nicholas Lockyer*, 1649.

Verse 23.—"*I was also upright before him, and I kept myself from mine
iniquity.*" He who says, "Lo, I come : in the volume of the book it is written
of me, I delight to do thy will, O my God ; yea, thy law is within my heart ;"
and who by the apostle in the tenth chapter of the epistle to the Hebrews, is
identified with Jesus Christ, says also (verse 12), "innumerable evils have
compassed me about ; mine iniquities have taken hold upon me, so that I am
not able to look up : they are more than the hairs of mine head ; therefore
mine heart faileth me ;" and in the forty-first psalm, "He whose familiar friend,
to whom he had committed a trust, who ate of his bread, lifted up his heel
against him," whom our Lord in the thirteenth chapter of the gospel of John
identifies with himself, says (verse 4), "Lord, be merciful to me : heal my soul,
for I have sinned ;" I am guilty "before thee." The difficulty is removed by
the undoubtedly true principle—the principle which, above all others, gives
Christianity its peculiar character—"He who knew no sin, was made sin ;" "On
his righteous servant, Jehovah made to fall the iniquities of us all." In this
sense, "innumerable iniquities compassed him," the iniquities made to fall
on him—made "his" as to their liabilities—by divine appointment laid hold of
him. In the sense of *culpa*—blame-worthiness—he had no sin. In the sense of
reatus—liability to the penal effects of sin—never had any one so much sin to
bear as he—"He bore the sins of many."—*John Brown.*
Verse 23.—"*I was upright before him.*" Hence observe :—first, that a godly
man may have his heart upright and perfect even in the imperfection of his
ways. Secondly, a man that is sincere is in God's account a perfect man :
sincerity is the truth of all grace, the highest pitch that is to be attained here.
Thirdly, sincerity of heart gives a man boldness even in the presence of God,
notwithstanding many failings. The Lord doth "charge his angels with folly,"
how much more man that "dwells in a house of clay" ? Job iv. David, whose
faith failed, and who had said, "I shall one day perish by the hand of Saul," and
whose tongue had faltered also to Abimelech, the priest ; three or four several
lies he had told ; yet David can say to God, that he was *perfect* with him for all
that. It is a strange boldness that the saints have in the presence of God by
virtue of the new covenant. All their sins shall be laid open at the last day as
a cancelled bond, that they wonder how they shall look upon them and not
blush ; but the same spirit of sonship that shall give them perfect boldness then,
doth give them boldness in a great measure even now in this life ; that they
shall be able to say, "Neither height nor depth," etc., nothing "shall separate
us from the love of Christ."—*William Strong.*
Verse 23.—"*I was upright,*" etc. An upright Christian will not allow himself in any known sin ; he dares not touch the forbidden fruit. Gen. xxxix. 9.
"How then can I do this great wickedness, and sin against God ?" Though it
be a complexion-sin, he disinherits it. There is no man but doth propend and
incline more to one sin than another ; as in the body there is one humour
predominant, or as in the hive there is one master-bee ; so in the heart there is
one master-sin ; there is one sin which is not only near to a man as the garment,
but dear to him as the right eye. This sin is Satan's fort-royal, all his strength
lies here ; and though we beat down his out-works, gross sin, yet if we let him
hold this fort of complexion-sin, it is as much as he desires. The devil can
hold a man as fast by this one link, as by a whole chain of vices. The fowler
hath the bird fast enough by one wing. Now, an upright Christian will not

Indulge himself in this complexion-sin : "*I was upright before him, and kept myself from mine iniquity.*" An upright Christian takes the sacrificing knife of mortification, and runs it through his dearest sin. Herod did many things, but there was one sin so dear to him, that he would sooner behead the prophet, than behead that sin. Herod would have a gap for his incest. An upright heart is not only angry with sin (which may admit of reconciliation), but hates sin ; and if he sees this serpent creeping into his bosom, the nearer it is the more he hates it.—*Thomas Watson.*

Verse 23.—"*I kept myself.*" Keep himself ! Who made man his own keeper ? It's the Lord that is his keeper : he is the keeper of Israel, and the preserver of man. If a man cannot keep himself from sorrow, how is he able to keep himself from sin ? God indeed in our first conversion works upon us as he did upon the earth, or Adam's body in paradise, before he breathed a soul into it, and made it a living creature ; such a power as Christ put forth on Lazarus in his grave, for we are " dead in trespasses and sins ;" but yet being living he must walk and act of himself, the Lord will have us to co-operate together with him, for we are built upon Christ, not as dead, but as " living stones." 1 Pet. ii. 5. The grace whereby we are made alive is his, and the power is his ; he it is that works in us both to will and to do, when we perform anything ; and yet by his grace we do it also ; *ille facit ut nos faciamus, quæ præcepit (Augustine).—William Strong.*

Verse 23.—"*I kept myself from mine iniquity.*" It is possible to keep ourselves from such sins as David did ; who professes here of himself great sincerity, that he had *kept* himself from that *iniquity* to which he was strongly tempted, and which he was prone to fall into. The method which holy David made use of gives us the first and the best direction ; and that is, by constant and fervent prayer to implore the divine aid and the continual assistance of his Holy Spirit, that God would not only keep us from falling into them, but even turn our hearts from inclining to them, and help us to see our folly and our danger. For alas! we are not able of ourselves to help ourselves, not so much as to think a good thought, much less to resist an evil inclination, or a strong temptation; but " our sufficiency is of God :" " It is God (says the psalmist here), that girdeth me with strength, and maketh my way perfect :" verse 32. . . . . . Next, that we take care to avoid such things and decline such occasions as are most likely to snare us and gain upon us, lest one thing hook in another, and we be caught in the gin before we suspect the danger.—*Henry Dove,* 1690.

Verse 23.—"*Mine iniquity.*" A man's darling sin may change with the change of a man's condition, and some occasion that may present itself. What was Saul's and Jehu's sin before they came unto the crown we know not : but surely it was that wherein their lust did afterwards run out—the establishing a kingdom upon their posterity. Wantonness may be the darling of a man's youth, and worldliness the darling of his age ; and a man's being raised unto honour, and having the opportunities that he had not in times past, the lust may run in another channel, he having now such an opportunity as before he never expected.—*William Strong.*

Verse 23.—"*Mine iniquity.*" There is some particular sin to which one is more prone than to another, of which he may say by way of emphasis, 'tis " *mine iniquity,*" at which he may point with his finger, and say, " That's it." . . There are more temptations to some sins than others, from the different professions or courses of life men take upon themselves. If they follow the court I need not tell you what temptations and snares there are to divers sins, and what danger there is of falling into them, unless your vows for virtue, and a tender regard to the honour which cometh of God only, keep you upright. If they be listed in the camp, that tempts them to rapine and violence, neglect of God's worship, and profaneness. If they exercise trading and merchandise, they meet with greater enticements to lying and cozening, over-reaching, and unjust dealing ; and the mystery of some trades, as bad men manage them, is a downright "mystery of iniquity." If husbandry, to anxiety about the things of the world, a distrust of God's providence, or murmuring against it. Nay, I could wish in the most sacred profession of all there might be an exception made in this particular ; but Paul tells us that even in his days " some preached Christ even of envy and strife," some for filthy lucre only, as well as " some of good will." Phil. i. 15.—*Henry Dove.*

Verse 23.—" *Mine iniquity.*" The actual reign of sin is commonly of some particular master-lust, which is as the viceroy over all the rest of the sins in the soul, and commands them all as lord paramount, and makes them all subservient and subordiante unto it ; and this is according to custom, calling, constitution, abilities, relations, and according to the different administrations of the Spirit of God ; for though God be not the author of sin, yet he is the orderer of sin. So that it is that way of sin and death that a man chooseth to himself, he having looked abroad upon all the contentments of the world, his own corrupt inclination doth choose unto himself to follow with greatest sweetness and contentment and delight, as that wherein the happiness of his life consists ; that as in the body there is in every one some predominant humour, so there is in the body of sin also ; that as in the natural man, though there be all the faculties, yet some faculties are in some more lively and vigorous than in others, some are more witty, some are more strong, some quick of sight, some have a ready ear, and others a nimble tongue, etc. So it is in the old man also ; there is all the power of sin in an unregenerate man, but in some more dexterous one way than another ; as men in the choice of calling, some have a greater inclination to one thing than to another, so it is in the choice of contentments also : as in the appetite for food, so it is in lust, being nothing else but the appetite of the creature corrupted to some sinful object.— *William Strong.*

Verse 23.—*Growth in mortification. . . . . .* Men may deceive themselves when they estimate their progress herein by having overcome such lusts as their natures are not so prone unto. The surest way is to take a judgment of it from the decay of a man's bosom-sin, even as David did estimate his uprightness by his " *keeping himself from his iniquity ;*" so a man of his growth in uprightness. When physicians would judge of a consumption of the whole, they do it not by the falling away of any part whatever, as of the flesh in the face alone, or any the like ; such a particular abatement of flesh in some one part may come from some other cause ; but they use to judge by the falling away of the brawn of the hands, or arms and thighs, etc., for these are the more solid parts. The like judgments do physicians make upon other diseases, and of the abatement of them from the decrease in such symptoms as are pathognomical, and proper, and peculiar to them. In like manner also the estimate of the progress of the victories of a conqueror in an enemy's kingdom is not taken from the taking or burning of a few villages or dorps, but by taking the forts and strongest holds, and by what ground he hath won upon the chief strength, and by what forces he hath cut off of the main army. Do the like in the decrease of, and victory over, your lusts.— *Thomas Goodwin.*

Verse 23.—We must remember always that though the grace of God prevents us, that we may have a good will, and works in us when we have it, that so we may find success ; yet in vain do we expect the continuance of his help without diligent endeavours. Whilst he assists our weakness, he does not intend to encourage our laziness, and therefore we are also " to labour, and strive according to his working, which worketh in us mightily," as the apostle expresses it, Col. i. 29.—*Henry Dove.*

Verses 24—26.—As you may see a proportion between sins and punishments which are the rewards of them, that you can say, Such a sin brought forth this affliction, it is so like the father ; so you might see the like proportion between your prayers and your walking with God, and God's answers to you, and his dealings with you. So did David ; " *According to the cleanness of my hands hath he recompensed me,*" etc. His speech notes some similitude or likeness ; as, for example, the more by-ends or carnal desires you had in praying, and the more you mingled of these with your holy desires, and the more want of zeal, fervency, etc., were found in your prayers, the more you shall, it may be, find of bitterness mingled with the mercy, when it is granted, and so much imperfection, and want of comfort in it. So says David in this same Psalm (verses 25, 26), "*With the pure thou wilt show thyself pure.*" Pure prayers have pure blessings ; *et è contra*, "*With the froward thou wilt show thyself froward.*" And again, as you in praying sometimes slackened and grew cold, so you might see the business in like manner to cool, and cast backward ; as, When Moses's hands were down, Amalek prevailed ; but when they were lifted up, Israel had the better. Exod. xvii. 12. God let him see a proportion, which argued his prayer was the means of prevailing. A man finds in praying that his suit sometimes sticks, and goes not on as he expected ; this is because he gives not so good a fee as he was wont, and doth not ply God and solicit him ; but on the contrary, when he was stirred up to pray, then still he found things to go well. By this a man may clearly see that it was the prayer which God did hear and regarded. Thus, likewise, when a man sees hills and dales in a business, fair hopes often, and then all dashed again, and the thing in the end brought to pass, let him look back upon his prayers. Didst not thou in like manner just thus deal with God ? when thou hadst prayed earnestly, and thought thou hadst even carried it, then dash all again by interposing some sin, and thus again and again ? Herein God would have you observe a proportion, and it may help you to discern how and when they are answered and obtained by prayer, because God deals thus with you therein in such a proportion to your prayers. — *Thomas Goodwin.*

Verses 24—27.—Even as the sun, which, unto eyes being sound and without disease, is very pleasant and wholesome, but unto the same eyes, when they are feeble, sore, and weak, is very troublesome and hurtful, yet the sun is ever all one and the selfsame that was before ; so God, who hath ever shown himself benign and bountiful to those who are kind and tender-hearted towards his saints, and are merciful to those who show mercy. But unto the same men, when they fall into wickedness and grow to be full of beastly cruelty, the Lord showeth himself to be very wrathful and angry, and yet is one and the same immutable God from everlasting to everlasting.—*Robert Cawdray.*

Verse 25.—"*With the merciful thou wilt shew thyself merciful ; with an upright man thou wilt shew thyself upright.*" "*An upright*"—the same word is oft translated "perfect," he is good throughout, though not thoroughly ; not one that personates religion, but that is a religious person. He is perfect, because he would be so. So Noah is termed (Gen. vi. 9) ; "Noah was a just man and perfect (*i.e.*, upright) in his generation :" he was a good man in a bad age. He was like a glowing spark of fire in a sea of water, which is pefect goodness ; and therefore the Holy Ghost doth so hang upon his name, as if he could not give over—it is an excellent preacher's observation—verse 8, "But Noah was a just man and perfect in his generations, and Noah walked with God. And Noah found grace in the eyes of the Lord. These are the generations of Noah : Noah begat three sons." Noah, Noah, Noah, I love the sound of thy name ; and so are all your names precious to God, though hated by men, if the name of God be dear and sweet to you. 'Tis also sometimes translated "plain." Gen. xxv. 27. Jacob was אִישׁ תָּם, "a plain," that is, an upright man, "dwelling in tents." Esau was "a *cunning* hunter," but Jacob was a plain man without welt or gard ; you might well know his heart by his tongue, save once when Rebekah put a cunning trick into his head, otherwise he was a most "*upright*," downright man. And the plain meaning of it is, a simple, cordial, unfeigned, and exact man : this is the man we are looking for.

"*Man.*" This substantive the Hebrews use to drown in the adjective, but here the Holy Ghost exhibits a word, and a choice one too, signifying *a strong, valiant man ;* the same word (Psalm xlv. 3), "O mighty man !" that's meant of our Lord Christ, who was a most strong and valiant man, that could meet the wrath of God, the malice of the devil, and the sin of man, in the face, and come off with triumph. And so the Dutch translate this clause in 2 Sam. xxii. : " With the right valiant person, thou behavest thyself upright." In short, if the words were literally translated, they run thus :—*a man of uprightness :* that is, every way you behold him, an upright man : like an even die, cast him which way you will he will be found square and right ; a stiff and strong man to tread down both lusts within and temptations without ; an *Athanasius contra mundum*, a *Luther contra Roman ;* this is a man of an excellent spirit, and such is our upright man. " *Thou wilt shew thyself upright,*" or, " wilt be upright with him ;" for one word in the Hebrew makes all these six, " Thou wilt *upright* it with him." If men will deal plainly with God, he will deal plainly with them. He that is upright in performing his duty shall find God upright in performing his promises. It is God's way to carry to men as they carry to him. If thou hast a design to please him, he will have a design to please thee ; if thou wilt echo to him when he calls, he'll echo to thee when thou callest. On the other side ; if a man will wrestle with God, he will wrestle with him ; if thou wilt be fast and loose with him, and walk *frowardly* towards him, thou shalt have as good as thou bringest ; if thou wilt provoke him with never-ending sins, he will pursue thee with never-ending torments ; if thou wilt sin in *tuo eterno*, thou must suffer in *suo eterno*, and every man shall find like for like. . . . . An *upright* heart is *single without division.* Unto an hypocrite there be "gods many and lords many," and he must have an heart for each ; but to the *upright* there is but one God the Father, and one Lord Jesus Christ, and one heart will serve them both. He that fixes his heart upon the creatures, for every creature he must have an heart, and the dividing of his heart destroys him. Hos. ₄ 2. Worldly profits knock at the door, he must have an heart for them ; carnal pleasures present themselves, he must have an heart for them also ; sinful preferments appear, they must have an heart too—*Necessariorum numerus parvus, opinionum nullus ;* of necessary objects the number is few, of needless vanities the number is endless. The *upright* man hath made choice of God and hath enough.—*Richard Steele.*

Verse 25.—" *With the merciful,*" etc. In Jupiter's hall-floor there are set two barrels of gifts, the one of good gifts or blessings, the other of evil gifts or plagues. Thus spake Homer falsely of Jupiter ; it may truly be spoken of the true God, Jehovah ; that he hath in his hand two cups, the one of comforts, the other of crosses, which he poureth out indifferently for the good and for the bad ; " *with the kind (or merciful) he will shew himself kind, and with the froward, froward.*" Now this is not to make God the author of evil, but of justice, which is good ; *qrorum deus non est author eorum est justus ultor*, saith Augustine ; " God is not the author of sin, but he punisheth the sinner justly." *Miles Smith (Bishop),* 1632.

Verse 26.—" *With the pure thou wilt shew thyself pure,*" etc. But doth the Lord take colour from every one he meets, or change his temper as the company changes ? That's the weakness of sinful man : he cannot do so with whom there is no variableness nor shadow of changing. God is pure and upright with the unclean and hypocritical, as well as with the pure and upright, and his actions show him to be so. God shows himself froward with the froward when he deals with him as he hath said he will deal with the froward—deny them and reject them. God shows himself pure with the pure, when he deals with them as he hath said he will—hear them and accept them. Though there be nothing in purity and sincerity which deserveth mercy, yet we cannot expect mercy without them. Our comforts are not grounded upon our graces, but our comforts are the fruits or consequences of our graces.—*Joseph Caryl.*

Verse 26.—" *The froward one.*" Here, as in the first promise, the two combatants stand contrasted—the seed of the woman and the serpent—the benignantly bountiful, perfect, pure One, and the froward one, whose works he came to destroy, and who made it his great business to circumvent him whom he feared.

The literal meaning of the word is "tortuous," or "crooked," and both the ideas of perversity and cunning which the figure naturally suggests, are very applicable to "that old serpent the devil." From the concluding part of the sentence, I think there is no doubt that it is the latter idea that is intended to be conveyed. God cannot deal perversely with any one ; but he outwits the wise, and takes the cunning in their own craftiness.—*John Brown.*

Verse 26.—" *With the froward thou wilt shew thyself froward.*" The Hebrew word in the root signifieth to wrest or writhe a thing, or to wrest or turn a thing, as wrestlers do their bodies. Hence by a trope, it is translated often to wrestle, because a cunning man in wrestling, turneth and windeth his body, and works himself in and out every way, to get an advantage of his adversary any way ; therefore your cunning-headed men, your crafty men, are fitly presented under this word ; they are like wrestlers who turn and wind themselves in and out, and lie for all advantages ; or as we speak, they " lie at catch." A man knows not where to have them, or what they mean when they speak plainest, or swear solemnest ; when we think we see their faces, we see but their vizards ; all their promises and performances too are under a disguise. . . . . And this word is applied to the Lord himself, " *With the froward thou wilt shew thyself froward;*" that is, if men will be winding and turning, and thinking to catch others, or over-reach the Lord himself with tricks and turnings of wit, the Lord will meet and answer them in their own kind ; he can turn as fast as they, he can put himself into such intricate labyrinths of infinite wisdom and sacred craft, as shall entangle and ensnare the most cunning wrestler or tumbler of them all. He will Cretize the Cretians, supplant the supplanters of his people.—*Joseph Caryl.*

Verse 26.—" *Wilt shew thyself froward.*" It is a similitude taken from wrestlers, and noteth a writhing of one's self against an adversary. Compare herewith Deut. xxxii. 5. " They are a perverse and crooked generation," the same two words that are here in this text ; the latter importeth that they wriggled and writhed after the manner of wrestlers that wave up and down, and wind the other way, when one thinks to have him here or there. But all will not serve their turn to save them from punishment. God will be sure to meet with them, his Word will lay hold on them, and their sin shall find them out.—*John Trapp.*

Verse 27.—" *The afflicted people.*" The word rendered " *afflicted,*" properly signifies " poor," or " needy." The persons spoken of are obviously afflicted ones, for they need to be saved or delivered ; but it is not their affliction, so much as their poverty, that is indicated by the epithet here given them ; and, from the poor being contrasted, not with the wealthy, but with the proud—for that is the meaning of the figurative expression, " the man of high looks"—it seems plain that, though the great body of the class referred to have always been found among the comparatively " poor in this world," the reference is to those poor ones whom our Lord represents as " poor in spirit."—*John Brown.*

Verse 27.—" *High looks :*" namely, *the proud ;* the raising up of the eyebrows being a natural sign of that vice. Psalm ci. 5 ; Prov. vi. 17.—*John Diodati.*

Verse 28.—" *For thou wilt light my candle,*" etc. The psalmist speaks in this place of artificial light ; " *a candle,*" or " lamp ;" which has been supposed to be illustrated by the custom prevailing in Egypt of never suffering their houses to be without lights, but burning lamps even through the night, so that the poorest people would rather retrench part of their food than neglect it. Supposing this to have been the ancient custom, not only in Egypt, but in the neighbouring countries of Arabia and Judæa, " the lighting of the lamp" in this passage may have had a special allusion. In the parallel passage, 2 Sam. xxii. 29, Jehovah is figuratively styled the " lamp" of the psalmist, as above.—*Richard Mant.*

Verse 28 (*first clause*).—" *Thou also shalt*"—when none else can. And notice, too, how here, and often elsewhere, the psalmist begins with speaking *of* God, and ends with speaking *to* him.   So the bride in the Canticles, "Let him kiss me with the kisses of *his* mouth, for *thy* love is better than wine."—*Dionysius the Carthusian* (1471), *quoted by J. M. Neale.*

Verse 29.—"*By thee I have run through a troop,*" etc.   David ascribes his victories to God, declaring that, under his conduct, he *had broken through the wedges or phalanxes* of his enemies, and had taken by storm their fortified cities. Thus we see that, although he was a valiant warrior, and skilled in arms, he arrogates nothing to himself.—*John Calvin.*

Verse 29.—"*By my God have I leaped over a wall;*" or, "taken a fort."— *Henry Hammond.*

Verse 29.—"*Leaped over a wall.*"   This probably refers to his having taken some remarkable town by scaling the ramparts.—*John Kitto, in* "*The Pictorial Bible.*"

Verse 31.—"*For who is God save the Lord?*"   Here first in the Psalms, occurs the name *Eloah*, rendered *God.*   It occurs more than *fifty* times in the Scriptures, but only *four* times in the Psalms.   It is the singular of Elohim. Many have supposed that this name specially refers to God as an object of religious worship.   That idea may well be prominent in this place.—*William S. Plumer.*

Verse 32.—"*It is God that girdeth me with strength.*"   One of the few articles of Eastern dress which I wore in the East, was the *girdle*, which was of great use as a support to the body in the long and weary camel-rides through the Desert.   The support and *strengthening* I received in this way, gave me a clearer idea than I had before of the meaning of the psalmist.—*John Anderson, in* "*Bible Light from Bible Lands,*" 1856.

Verse 33.—"*He maketh my feet like hinds' feet, and setteth me upon my high places:*" that is, he doth give swiftness and speed to his church ; as Augustine interpreteth it, *transcendendo spinosa, et umbrosa implicamenta hujus sæculi,* passing lightly through the thorny and shady incumbrances of this world.   "He will make me walk upon my high places."   David saith, "He setteth me upon high places."   For, consider David, as he then was, when he composed this Psalm, it was at the time when God had delivered him from the hand of all his enemies, and from the hand of Saul.   For then God set his feet on high places, settling his kingdom, and establishing him in the place of Saul. *Edward Marbury.*

Verse 33.—"*He maketh my feet like hinds' feet:*" מְשַׁוֶּה רַגְלַי כָּאַיָּלוֹת.   Celerity of motion was considered as one of the qualities of an ancient hero.   Achilles is celebrated for being πόδας ὠκύς.   Virgil's Nisus is hyperbolically described, "*Et ventis et fulminis ocior alis;*" and the men of God, who came to David, "Men of might, and men of war fit for the battle, that could handle shield and buckler," are said to have had "faces like the faces of lions," and to have been "as swift as the roes upon the mountains."   1 Chron. xii. 8.   Asahel is described as "light of foot as a wild roe" (2 Sam. ii. 18) ; and Saul seems called the *roe* (in the English translation, "the beauty") of Israel."   2 Sam. i. 19.   It has been said that the legs of the hind are straighter than those of the buck, and that *she* is swifter than *he* is ; but there is no sufficient proof of this.   Gataker gives the true account of it when he says, "The female formula is often used for the species."   This is not uncommon in Hebrew.   The female ass obviously stands for the ass species.   Gen. xii. 16 ; Job i. 3 ; xlii. 12.   Some (at the head of whom is Bochart, *Hierozoicon*, P. i. L. ii. c. 17), have supposed the reference to be to the peculiar hardness of the hoof of the roe, which enables it to walk firmly, without danger of falling, on the roughest and rockiest places.   Virgil calls the hind "*æri-pedem,*" brass-footed.   Others suppose the reference to be to its agility and celerity. There is nothing to prevent our supposing that there is a reference to both these distinguishing qualities of the hind's feet.—*John Brown.*

Verse 33.—*" He maketh my feet like hinds' feet,"* etc. *He maketh me able to stand on the sides of mountains and rocks,* which were anciently used as fastnesses in time of war. The feet of the sheep, the goat, and the hart are particularly adapted to standing in such places. Mr. Merrick has here very appositely cited the following passage from Xenophon ; *Lib. de Venatione :* Ἐπισκοπεῖν δεῖ ἔχοντα τὰς κύνας τὰς μὲν ἐν ὄρεσι ἑστώσας ᾽λαφους. See also Psalm civ. 18, where the same property of standing on the rocks and steep cliffs is attributed to the wild goat.—*Stephen Street, M.A., in loc.,* 1790.

Verse 34.—*" He teacheth my hands to war,"* etc. To him I owe all that military skill, or strength, or courage, which I have. My strength is sufficient, not only to bend *" a bow of steel,"* but to *break* it.—*Matthew Poole.*

Verse 34.—*" Steel."* The word so rendered in the authorised version, properly means "copper" (נְחוּשָׁה). It is doubtful if the Hebrews were acquainted with the process of hardening iron into steel, for though the " northern iron" of Jer. xv. 12, has been supposed by some to be steel, this is by no means certain ; it may have only been a superior sort of iron.—*William Lindsay Alexander, in " Kitto's Cyclopædia."*

Verse 34.—The drawing of a mighty bow was a mark of great slaughter and skill.

> " So the great master drew the mighty bow,
> And drew with ease. One hand aloft display'd
> The bending horns, and one the string essay'd."
>
> *Alexander Pope,* 1688—1744. [*Translation of Homer.*

Verses 37, 38 :—

> Oh, I have seen the day,
> When with a single word,
> God helping me to say,
> " My trust is in the Lord ;"
> My soul has quelled a thousand foes,
> Fearless of all that could oppose.
>
> *William Cowper,* 1731—1800.

Verse 38.—*" I have wounded them,"* etc. Greater is he that is in us than he that is against us, and God shall bruise Satan under our feet shortly. Rom. xv. 20. *W. Wilson.*

Verses 38—40.—Though passion possess our bodies, let " patience possess our souls." The law of our profession binds us to a warfare ; *patiendo vincimus,* our troubles shall end, our victory is eternal. Hear David's triumph, " *I have wounded them that they were not able to rise : they are fallen under my feet. Thou hast subdued under me those that rose up against me. Thou hast given me the necks of mine enemies,"* etc. They have wounds for their wounds ; and the treaders down of the poor are trodden down by the poor. The Lord will subdue those to us that would have subdued us to themselves ; and though for a short time they rode over our heads, yet now at last we shall everlastingly tread upon their necks. Lo, then, the reward of humble patience and confident hope !— *Thomas Adams.*

Verse 39.—To be well girt was to be well armed in the Greek and Latin idioms, as well as in the Hebrew.—*Alexander Geddes, LL.D.,* 1737—1802.

Verse 41.—*" They shall cry, but there shall be none to help them,"* etc. Sad examples enough there are of the truth of this prophecy. Of Esau it is written that he " found no place of repentance, though he sought it carefully with tears." Heb. xii. 17. Of Antiochus, though he vowed in his last illness, " that also he would become a Jew himself, and go through all the world that was inhabited, and declare the power of God, yet," continues the historian, " for all this his pains would not cease, for the just judgment of God was come upon him." 2 Macc. ix. 17, 18. But most appropriately to this passage, it is written of Saul, " When he enquired of the Lord, the Lord answered him not, neither by dreams, nor by Urim, nor by prophets." 1 Sam. xxviii. 6. And therefore, the prophet warns us : " Give glory to the Lord your God, before he cause darkness, and before your feet stumble upon the dark mountains (Jer. xiii. 16) : as Saul's feet, indeed, stumbled on the dark mountains of Gilboa. *" Even unto the Lord shall they cry:*" but not, as it has been well remarked, by a Mediator : and so, crying to him in their own name, and by their own merits, they cry in vain.—*John Lorinus* (1569—1634), *and Remigius* (900), *quoted by J. M. Neale.*

Verse 41.—" Even unto the Lord." As, nature prompteth men in an extremity to look up for help ; but because it is but the prayer of the flesh for ease, and not of the Spirit for grace, and a good use of calamities, and not but in extreme despair of help elsewhere, therefore God hears them not. In Samuel it is, " They looked, but there was none to save them," *q.d.*, If they could have made any other shift, God should never have heard of them.—*John Trapp.*

Verse 42.—" I did cast them out as the dirt in the streets," or rather " of the streets." In the East, all household refuse and filth is cast forth into the streets, where all of it that is at all edible is soon cleared away by birds and dogs, and all that is not is speedily dried up by the sun. To cast forth any one, therefore, as the dirt of the streets, is a strong image of contempt and rejection. *John Kitto.*

Verses 43, 44.—If these words can be explained literally of David, they apply much more naturally to Jesus Christ, who has been delivered from the strivings of the Jewish people ; when, after the terrible opposition he met with on their part, to the establishment of the gospel, he was made the head of the Gentiles who were a strange people, and whom he had not formerly acknowledged as his, but who nevertheless obeyed him with astonishing readiness as soon as they heard his voice.—*Louis Isaac le Maistre de Sacy*, 1613—1684.

Verse 45.—The first clause is comparatively easy. *" The strangers shall fade away"*—" shall gradually wither and disappear ;" but the second clause is very difficult, *" They shall be afraid out of their close places."* One Jewish scholar interprets it, " They shall fear for the prisons in which I will throw them and keep them confined." * Another, " They shall tremble in their castles to which they have betaken themselves for fear of me." Another,† " They shall surrender themselves from their fortresses." The general meaning is plain enough. The class referred to are represented as reduced to a state of complete helpless subjugation. As to the event referred to, if we keep to the rendering of our translators the meaning may be, " The Pagans, retired now generally to villages and remote places, shall gradually dwindle away, and fearfully anticipate the complete extinction of their religion." This exactly accords with history. If with some interpreters we read, " The strangers shall fade away, and be afraid because of their prisons," then the meaning may be, " that they who only feigned submission, when persecution for the word should arise should openly apostatise." This, too, would be found consonant with fact. The first of these interpretations seems the more probable.—*John Brown.*

Verse 46.—" The Lord liveth ; and blessed be my rock ; and let the God of my salvation be exalted."—Let us unite our hearts in this song for a close of our praises. Honours *die*, pleasures *die*, the world *dies ;* but *" The Lord liveth."* My flesh is as *sand ;* my fleshly life, strength, glory, is as *a word written on sand ;* but *" blessed be my* Rock." Those are for a moment ; this stands for ever. The curse shall devour those ; everlasting blessings on the head of this. Let

---

* Jarchi.   † Abenezra.

outward salvations vanish ; let the saved be crucified ; let the " *God* " of our salvations " *be exalted.*" This Lord is *my rock;* this God is *my salvation.*—
Peter Sterry, 1649.

Verse 46.—" *The Lord liveth.*" Why do you not oppose one God to all the armies of evils that beset you round? why do you not take the more content in God when you have the less of the creature to take content in? why do you not boast in your God? and bear up yourselves big with your hopes in God and expectations from him? Do you not see young heirs to great estates act and spend accordingly? And, why shall you, being the King of heaven's son, be lean and ragged from day to day, as though you were not worth a groat? O sirs, live upon your portion, chide yourselves for living besides what you have. There are great and precious promises, rich, enriching mercies ; you may make use of God's all-sufficiency ; you can blame none but yourselves if you be defective or discouraged. A woman, truly godly for the main, having buried a child, and sitting alone in sadness, did yet bear up her heart with the expression, " God lives ;" and having parted with another, still she redoubled, " Comforts die, but God lives." At last her dear husband dies, and she sat oppressed and most overwhelmed with sorrow. A little child she had yet surviving, having observed what before she spoke to comfort herself, comes to her and saith, " Is God dead, mother? is God dead?" This reached her heart, and by God's blessing recovered her former confidence in her God, who is a *living* God. Thus do you chide yourselves ; ask your fainting spirits under pressing outward sorrows, is not God alive? and why then doth not thy soul revive? why doth thy heart die within thee when comforts die! Cannot a living God support thy dying hopes? Thus, Christians, argue down your discouraged and disquieted spirits as David did.—*Oliver Heywood's " Sure Mercies of David,"* 1672.

Verse 47.—" *It is God.*" Sir, this is none other than the hand of God ; and to him alone belongs the glory, wherein none are to share with him. The General served you with all faithfulness and honour ; and the best commendation I can give him is that I dare say he attributes all to God, and would rather perish than assume to himself.—*Written to the Speaker of the House of Commons, after the battle of Naseby, June* 14, 1645, *by* OLIVER CROMWELL.

Verse 49.—I admire King David a great deal more when I see him in the quire than when I see him in the camp ; when I see him singing as the sweet singer of Israel, than when I see him fighting as the worthy warrior of Israel. For fighting with others he did overcome all others ; but singing, and delighting himself, he did overcome himself.—*Thomas Playfere.*

HINTS TO THE VILLAGE PREACHER.

Verse 1.—Love's resolve, love's logic, love's trials, love's victories.
James Hervey has two sermons upon " Love to God " from this text.
Verse 2.—The many excellences of Jehovah to his people.
Verse 2.—God the all-sufficient portion of his people.—*C. Simeon's Works*, Vol. v. p. 85.
Verse 3.—Prayer resolved upon ; praise rendered ; result anticipated.
Verses 4—6.—Graphic picture of a distressed soul, and its resorts in the hour of extremity.
Verse 5 (*first clause*).—The condition of a soul convinced of sin.
Verse 5 (*second clause*).—The way in which snares and temptations are, by Satanic craft, arranged so as to forestall or prevent us.
Verse 6.—The time, the manner, the hearing, and the answering of prayer.
Verse 7.—The quaking of all things in the presence of an angry God.
Verse 10.—Celestial and terrestrial agencies subservient to the divine purposes.
Verse 11.—The darkness in which Jehovah hides. Why ? When ? What then ? etc.
Verse 13.—" *Hailstones and coals of fire.*" The terrific in its relation to Jehovah.
Verse 16.—The Christian, like Moses, " one taken out of the water." The whole verse a noble subject ; may be illustrated by life of Moses.
Verse 17.—The saint's pæan of victory over Satan, and all other foes.
Verse 17 (*last clause*).—Singular but sound reason for expecting divine help.
Verse 18.—The enemy's " craft," " *They prevented me in the day of my calamity.*" The enemy chained. " *But the Lord was my stay.*"
Verse 19.—The reason of grace, and the position in which it places its chosen ones.
Verse 21.—Integrity of life, its measure, source, benefit, and dangers.
Verse 22.—The need of considering sacred things, and the wickedness of carelessly neglecting them.
Verse 23.—The upright heart and its darling sin.—*W. Strong's Sermons.*
Verse 23.—*Peccata in deliciis ;* a discourse of bosom sins.—*P. Newcome.*
Verse 23.—The sure trial of uprightness.—*Dr. Bates.*
Verse 25.—Equity of the divine procedure.—*C. Simeon.*
Verse 26.—Echoes, in providence, grace, and judgment.
Verse 27.—Consolation for the humble, and desolation for the proud.
Verse 27 (*second clause*).—The bringing down of high looks. In a way of grace and justice. Among saints and sinners, etc. A wide theme.
Verse 28.—A comfortable hope for an uncomfortable state.
Verse 29.—Believing exploits recounted. Variety, difficulty in themselves, ease in performance, completeness, impunity, and dependence upon divine working.
Verse 30.—God's way, word, and warfare.
Verse 31.—A challenge. I. To the *gods*. World, pleasure, etc. Which among these deserve the name ? II. To the *rocks*, self-confidence, superstition, etc. On which can we trust ?
Verses 32—34.—Trying positions, gracious adaptations, graceful accomplishments, secure abidings, grateful acknowledgment.
Verse 35.—" *The shield of thy salvation.*" What it is ? Faith. Whence it comes ? " Thou hast given." What it secures ? " Salvation." Who have received it ?
Verse 35.—See " Spurgeon's Sermons," No. 683. " Divine Gentleness Acknowledged."
Verse 36.—Divine benevolence in the arranging of our lot.
Verse 39.—The Red Cross Knight armed for the fray.
Verse 41.—Unavailing prayers—on earth and in hell.

Verse 42.—The sure overthrow, final shame, and ruin of evil.

Verse 43 (*last clause*).—Our natural and sinful distance from Christ, no bar to grace.

Verse 44.—Rapid advances of the gospel in some places, slow progress in others. Solemn considerations.

Verse 46.—The living God, and how to bless and exalt him.

Verse 50.—The greatness of salvation, "*great deliverance;*" its channel, "*the King;*" and its perpetuity, "*for evermore.*"

WORKS UPON THE EIGHTEENTH PSALM.

There is "An Exposition" of this Psalm in "*A Critical History of the Life of David*. By SAMUEL CHANDLER, D.D., F.R., and A.S.S.," 1766. 2 vols., 8vo.

The Sufferings and Glories of the Messiah: an Exposition of Psalm XVIII., and *Isaiah* lii. 13 ; liii. 12. By JOHN BROWN, D.D., 1853.

PSALM XIX.

SUBJECT.—*It would be idle to enquire into the particular period when this delightful poem was composed, for there is nothing in its title or subject to assist us in the enquiry. The heading, " To the chief Musician, a Psalm of David," informs us that David wrote it, and that it was committed to the Master of the service of song in the sanctuary for the use of the assembled worshippers. In his earliest days the psalmist, while keeping his father's flock, had devoted himself to the study of God's two great books—nature and Scripture; and he had so thoroughly entered into the spirit of these two only volumes in his library that he was able with a devout criticism to compare and contrast them, magnifying the excellency of the Author as seen in both. How foolish and wicked are those who instead of accepting the two sacred tomes, and delighting to behold the same divine hand in each, spend all their wits in endeavouring to find discrepancies and contradictions. We may rest assured that the true " Vestiges of Creation" will never contradict Genesis, nor will a correct " Cosmos" be found at variance with the narrative of Moses. He is wisest who reads both the world-book and the Word-book as two volumes of the same work, and feels concerning them, " My Father wrote them both."*

DIVISION.—*This song very distinctly divides itself into three parts, very well described by the translators in the ordinary heading of our version. The creatures show God's glory, 1—6: The word showeth his grace, 7—11. David prayeth for grace, 12—14. Thus praise and prayer are mingled, and he who here sings the work of God in the world without, pleads for a work of grace in himself within.*

EXPOSITION.

THE heavens declare the glory of God ; and the firmament sheweth his handywork.

2 Day unto day uttereth speech, and night unto night sheweth knowledge.

3 *There is* no speech nor language, *where* their voice is not heard.

4 Their line is gone out through all the earth, and their words to the end of the world. In them hath he set a tabernacle for the sun,

5 Which *is* as a bridegroom coming out of his chamber, *and* rejoiceth as a strong man to run a race.

6 His going forth *is* from the end of the heaven, and his circuit into the ends of it : and there is nothing hid from the heat thereof.

1. " *The heavens declare the glory of God.*" The book of nature has three leaves, heaven, earth, and sea, of which heaven is the first and the most glorious, and by its aid we are able to see the beauties of the other two. Any book without its first page would be sadly imperfect, and especially the great Natural Bible, since its first pages, the sun, moon, and stars, supply light to the rest of the volume, and are thus the keys, without which the writing which follows would be dark and undiscerned. Man walking erect was evidently made to scan the skies, and he who begins to read creation by studying the stars begins the book at the right place.

The *heavens* are plural for their variety, comprising the watery heavens with their clouds of countless forms, the aerial heavens with their calms and tempests, the solar heavens with all the glories of the day, and the starry heavens with all the marvels of the night ; what the Heaven of heavens must be hath not entered into the heart of man, but there in chief all things are telling the glory of God. Any part of creation has more instruction in it than human mind will ever exhaust, but the celestial realm is peculiarly rich in spiritual lore. The heavens *declare*, or are *declaring*, for the continuance of their testimony is intended by the participles employed ; every moment God's existence, power, wisdom, and goodness, are being sounded abroad by the heavenly heralds which shine upon us from above. He who would guess at divine sublimity should gaze upward into the starry vault ; he who would imagine infinity must peer into the boundless expanse ; he who desires to see divine wisdom should consider the balancing of the orbs ; he who would know divine fidelity must mark the regularity of the planetary motions ; and he who would attain some conceptions of divine power, greatness, and majesty, must estimate the forces of attraction, the magnitude of the fixed stars, and the brightness of the whole celestial train. It is not merely glory that the heavens declare, but the *"glory of God,"* for they deliver to us such unanswerable arguments for a conscious, intelligent, planning, controlling, and presiding Creator, that no unprejudiced person can remain unconvinced by them. The testimony given by the heavens is no mere hint, but a plain, unmistakeable declaration ; and it is a declaration of the most constant and abiding kind. Yet for all this, to what avail is the loudest declaration to a deaf man, or the clearest showing to one spiritually blind ? God the Holy Ghost must illuminate us, or all the suns in the milky way never will.

" *The firmament sheweth his handy-work ;*" not *handy,* in the vulgar use of that term, but hand-work. The expanse is full of the works of the Lord's skilful, creating hands ; hands being attributed to the great creating Spirit to set forth his care and workmanlike action, and to meet the poor comprehension of mortals. It is humbling to find that even when the most devout and elevated minds are desirous to express their loftiest thoughts of God, they must use words and metaphors drawn from the earth. We are children, and must each confess, " I think as a child, I speak as a child." In the expanse above us God flies, as it were, his starry flag to show that the King is at home, and hangs out his escutcheon that atheists may see how he despises their denunciations of him. He who looks up to the firmament and then writes himself down an atheist, brands himself at the same moment as an idiot or a liar. Strange is it that some who love God are yet afraid to study the God-declaring book of nature ; the mock-spirituality of some believers, who are too heavenly to consider the heavens, has given colour to the vaunts of infidels that nature contradicts revelation. The wisest of men are those who with pious eagerness trace the goings forth of Jehovah as well in creation as in grace ; only the foolish have any fears lest the honest study of the one should injure our faith in the other. Dr. M'Cosh has well said, " We have often mourned over the attempts made to set the works of God against the Word of God, and thereby excite, propagate, and perpetuate jealousies fitted to separate parties that ought to live in closest union. In particular, we have always regretted that endeavours should have been made to depreciate nature with a view of exalting revelation ; it has always appeared to us to be nothing else than the degrading of one part of God's works in the hope thereby of exalting and recommending another. Let not science and religion be reckoned as opposing citadels, frowning defiance upon each other, and their troops brandishing their armour in hostile attitude. They have too many common foes, if they would but think of it, in ignorance and prejudice, in passion and vice, under all their forms, to admit of their lawfully wasting their strength in a useless warfare with each other. Science has a foundation, and so has religion ; let them unite their foundations, and the basis will be broader, and they will be two compartments of one great fabric reared to the glory of God. Let the one be the outer and the other the inner court. In the one, let all look, and admire and adore ; and in the other, let those who have faith kneel, and pray, and praise. Let the one be the sanctuary where human learning may present its richest incense as an offering to God, and the other the holiest of all, separated from it by a veil now rent in twain, and in which, on a blood-sprinkled mercy-seat, we pour out the love of a reconciled heart, and hear the oracles of the living God."

2. " *Day unto day uttereth speech, and night unto night sheweth knowledge.*" As if one day took up the story where the other left it, and each night passed over the wondrous tale to the next. The original has in it the thought of

pouring out, or welling over, with speech ; as though days and nights were but as a fountain flowing evermore with Jehovah's praise.   Oh to drink often at the celestial well, and learn to utter the glory of God !   The witnesses above cannot be slain or silenced ; from their elevated seats they constantly preach the knowledge of God, unawed and unbiassed by the judgments of men.   Even the changes of alternating night and day are mutely eloquent, and light and shade equally reveal the Invisible One ; let the vicissitudes of our circumstances do the same, and while we bless the God of our days of joy, let us also extol him who giveth " songs in the night."

The lesson of day and night is one which it were well if all men learned.   It should be among our day-thoughts and night-thoughts to remember the flight of time, the changeful character of earthly things, the brevity both of joy and sorrow, the preciousness of life, our utter powerlessness to recall the hours once flown, and the irresistible approach of eternity.   Day bids us labour, night reminds us to prepare for our last home ; day bids us work for God, and night invites us to rest in him ; day bids us look for endless day, and night warns us to escape from everlasting night.

3. " *There is no speech nor language, where their voice is not heard.*"   Every man may hear the voices of the stars.   Many are the languages of terrestrials, to celestials there is but one, and that one may be understood by every willing mind.   The lowest heathen are without excuse, if they do not discover the invisible things of God in the works which he has made.   Sun, moon, and stars are God's travelling preachers ; they are apostles upon their journey confirming those who regard the Lord, and judges on circuit condemning those who worship idols.

The margin gives us another rendering, which is more literal, and involves less repetition ; " *no speech, no words, their voice is not heard ;*" that is to say, their teaching is not addressed to the ear, and is not uttered in articulate sounds ; it is pictorial, and directed to the eye and heart ; it touches not the sense by which faith comes, for faith cometh by hearing.   Jesus Christ is called the Word, for he is a far more distinct display of Godhead than all the heavens can afford ; they are, after all, but dumb instructors ; neither star nor sun can arrive at a word, but Jesus is the express image of Jehovah's person, and his name is the Word of God.

4. " *Their line is gone out through all the earth, and their words to the end of the world.*"   Although the heavenly bodies move in solemn silence, yet in reason's ear they utter precious teachings.   They give forth no literal *words*, but yet their instruction is clear enough to be so described.   Horne says that the phrase employed indicates a language of signs, and thus we are told that the heavens speak by their significant actions and operations.   Nature's words are like those of the deaf and dumb, but grace tells us plainly of the Father.   By their line is probably meant the *measure* of their domain which, together with their testimony, has gone out to the utmost end of the habitable earth.   No man living beneath the copes of heaven dwells beyond the bounds of the diocese of God's Court-preachers ; it is easy to escape from the light of ministers, who are as stars in the right hand of the Son of Man ; but even then men, with a conscience yet unseared, will find a Nathan to accuse them, a Jonah to warn them, and an Elijah to threaten them in the silent stars of night.   To gracious souls the voices of the heavens are more influential far, they feel the sweet influences of the Pleiades, and are drawn towards their Father God by the bright bands of Orion.

" *In them hath he set a tabernacle for the sun.*"   In the midst of the heavens the sun encamps, and marches like a mighty monarch on his glorious way.   He has no fixed abode, but as a traveller pitches and removes his tent, a tent which will soon be taken down and rolled together as a scroll.   As the royal pavilion stood in the centre of the host, so the sun in his place appears like a king in the midst of attendant stars.

5. " *Which is as a bridegroom coming out of his chamber.*"   A bridegroom comes forth sumptuously apparelled, his face beaming with a joy which he imparts

to all around ; such, but with a mighty emphasis, is the rising Sun. "*And rejoiceth as a strong man to run a race.*" As a champion girt for running cheerfully addresses himself to the race, so does the sun speed onward with matchless regularity and unwearying swiftness in his appointed orbit. It is but mere play to him ; there are no signs of effort, flagging, or exhaustion. No other creature yields such joy to the earth as her bridegroom the sun ; and none, whether they be horse or eagle, can for an instant compare in swiftness with that heavenly champion. But all his glory is but the glory of God ; even the sun shines in light borrowed from the Great Father of Lights.

> "Thou sun, of this great world both eye and soul,
> Acknowledge Him thy greater ; sound His praise
> Both when thou climb'st, and when high noon hast gained,
> And when thou fall'st."

6. "*His going forth is from the end of the heaven, and his circuit unto the ends of it.*" He bears his light to the boundaries of the solar heavens traversing the zodiac with steady motion, denying his light to none who dwell with his range. "*And there is nothing hid from the heat thereof.*" Above, beneath, around, the heat of the sun exercises an influence. The bowels of the earth are stored with the ancient produce of the solar rays, and even yet earth's inmost caverns feel their power. Where light is shut out, yet heat and other more subtle influences find their way.

There is no doubt a parallel intended to be drawn between the heaven of grace and the heaven of nature. God's way of grace is sublime and broad, and full of his glory ; in all its displays it is to be admired and studied with diligence ; both its lights and its shades are instructive ; it has been proclaimed, in a measure, to every people, and in due time shall be yet more completely published to the ends of the earth. Jesus, like a sun, dwells in the midst of revelation, tabernacling among men in all his brightness ; rejoicing, as the Bridegroom of his church, to reveal himself to men ; and, like a champion, to win unto himself renown. *He* makes a circuit of mercy, blessing the remotest corners of the earth ; and there are no seeking souls, however degraded and depraved, who shall be denied the comfortable warmth and benediction of his love—even death shall feel the power of his presence, and resign the bodies of the saints, and this fallen earth shall be restored to its pristine glory.

7 The law of the Lord *is* perfect, converting the soul : the testimony of the Lord *is* sure, making wise the simple.

8 The statutes of the LORD *are* right, rejoicing the heart : the commandment of the LORD *is* pure, enlightening the eyes.

9 The fear of the LORD *is* clean, enduring for ever : the judgments of the LORD *are* true *and* righteous altogether.

10 More to be desired *are they* than gold, yea, than much fine gold : sweeter also than honey and the honeycomb.

11 Moreover by them is thy servant warned : *and* in keeping of them *there is* great reward.

In the three following verses we have a brief but instructive hexapla containing six descriptive titles of the word, six characteristic qualities mentioned and six divine effects declared. Names, nature, and effect are well set forth.

7. "*The law of the Lord is perfect ;*" by which he means not merely the law of Moses but the doctrine of God, the whole run and rule of sacred Writ. The doctrine revealed by God he declares to be perfect, and yet David had but a very small part of the Scriptures, and if a fragment, and that the darkest and most historical portion, be perfect, what must the entire volume be ? How more than perfect is the book which contains the clearest possible display of divine love, and gives us an open vision of redeeming grace. The gospel is a complete scheme or law of gracious salvation, presenting to the needy sinner everything

that his terrible necessities can possibly demand. There are no redundancies and no omissions in the Word of God, and in the plan of grace ; why then do men try to paint this lily and gild this refined gold ? The gospel is perfect in all its parts, and perfect as a whole : it is a crime to add to it, treason to alter it, and felony to take from it.

"*Converting the soul.*"—Making the man to be returned or restored to the place from which sin had cast him. The practical effect of the Word of God is to turn the man to himself, to his God, and to holiness ; and the turn or conversion is not outward alone, " *the soul* " is moved and renewed. The great means of the conversion of sinners is the Word of God, and the more closely we keep to it in our ministry the more likely are we to be successful. It is God's Word rather than man's comment on God's Word which is made mighty with souls. When the law drives and the gospel draws, the action is different but the end is one, for by God's Spirit the soul is made to yield, and cries, " Turn me, and I shall be turned." Try men's depraved nature with philosophy and reasoning, and it laughs your efforts to scorn, but the Word of God soon works a transformation.

" *The testimony of the Lord is sure.*" God bears his testimony against sin, and on behalf of righteousness ; he testifies of our fall and of our restoration ; this testimony is plain, decided, and infallible, and is to be accepted as sure. God's witness in his Word is so sure that we may draw solid comfort from it both for time and eternity, and so sure that no attacks made upon it however fierce or subtle can ever weaken its force. What a blessing that in a world of uncertainties we have something sure to rest upon ! We hasten from the quicksands of human speculations to the *terra firma* of Divine Revelation.

" *Making wise the simple.*" Humble, candid, teachable minds receive the word, and are made wise unto salvation. Things hidden from the wise and prudent are revealed unto babes. The persuadable grow wise, but the cavillers continue fools. As a law or plan the Word of God converts, and then as a testimony it instructs ; it is not enough for us to be converts, we must continue to be disciples ; and if we have felt the power of truth, we must go on to prove its certainty by experience. The perfection of the gospel converts, but its sureness edifies ; if we would be edified it becomes us not to stagger at the promise through unbelief, for a doubted gospel cannot make us wise, but truth of which we are assured will be our establishment.

8. " *The statutes of the Lord are right.*" His precepts and decrees are founded in righteousness, and are such as are right or fitted to the right reason of man. As a physician gives the right medicine, and a counsellor the right advice, so does the Book of God. " *Rejoicing the heart.*" Mark the progress ; he who was converted was next made wise and is now made happy ; that truth which makes the heart right then gives joy to the right heart. Free grace brings heart-joy. Earthborn mirth dwells on the lip, and flushes the bodily powers ; but heavenly delights satisfy the inner nature, and fill the mental faculties to the brim. There is no cordial of comfort like that which is poured from the bottle of Scripture.

> " Retire and read thy Bible to be gay."

" *The commandment of the Lord is pure.*" No mixture of error defiles it, no stain of sin pollutes it ; it is the unadulterated milk, the undiluted wine. " *Enlightening the eyes,*" purging away by its own purity the earthly grossness which mars the intellectual discernment : whether the eye be dim with sorrow or with sin, the Scripture is a skilful oculist, and makes the eye clear and bright. Look at the sun and it puts out your eyes, look at the more than sunlight of Revelation and it enlightens them ; the purity of snow causes snow-blindness to the Alpine traveller, but the purity of God's truth has the contrary effect, and cures the natural blindness of the soul. It is well again to observe the gradation ; the convert became a disciple and next a rejoicing soul, he now obtains a discerning eye, and as a spiritual man discerneth all things, though he himself is discerned of no man.

9. " *The fear of the Lord is clean.*" The doctrine of truth is here described

by its spiritual effect, viz., inward piety, or the fear of the Lord ; this is clean in itself, and cleanses out the love of sin, sanctifying the heart in which it reigns. Mr. Godly-fear is never satisfied till every street, lane, and alley, yea, and every house and every corner of the town of Mansoul is clean rid of the Diabolonians who lurk therein. *" Enduring for ever."* Filth brings decay, but cleanness is the great foe of corruption. The grace of God in the heart being a pure principle, is also an abiding and incorruptible principle, which may be crushed for a time, but cannot be utterly destroyed. Both in the Word and in the heart, when the Lord writes, he says with Pilate, " What I have written, I have written ;" he will make no erasures himself, much less suffer others to do so. The revealed will of God is never changed ; even Jesus came not to destroy but to fulfil, and even the ceremonial law was only changed as to its shadow, the substance intended by it is eternal. When the governments of nations are shaken with revolution, and ancient constitutions are being repealed, it is comforting to know that the throne of God is unshaken, and his law unaltered.

" The judgments of the Lord are true and righteous altogether ;"—jointly and severally the words of the Lord are true ; that which is good in detail is excellent in the mass ; no exception may be taken to a single clause separately, or to the book as a whole. God's judgments, all of them together, or each of them apart, are manifestly just, and need no laborious excuses to justify them. The judicial decisions of Jehovah, as revealed in the law, or illustrated in the history of his providence, are truth itself, and commend themselves to every truthful mind ; not only is their power invincible, but their justice is unimpeachable.

10. *" More to be desired are they than gold, yea, than much fine gold."* Bible truth is enriching to the soul in the highest degree ; the metaphor is one which gathers force as it is brought out ;—gold—fine gold—much fine gold ; it is good, better, best, and therefore it is not only to be desired with a miser's avidity, but with more than that. As spiritual treasure is more noble than mere material wealth, so should it be desired and sought after with greater eagerness. Men speak of solid gold, but what is so solid as solid truth ? For love of gold pleasure is forsworn, ease renounced, and life endangered ; shall we not be ready to do as much for love of truth ? *" Sweeter also than honey and the honeycomb."* Trapp says, " Old people are all for profit, the young for pleasure ; here's gold for the one, yea, the finest gold in great quantity ; here's honey for the other, yea, live honey dropping from the comb." The pleasures arising from a right understanding of the divine testimonies are of the most delightful order ; earthly enjoyments are utterly contemptible, if compared with them. The sweetest joys, yea, the sweetest of the sweetest falls to his portion who has God's truth to be his heritage.

11. *" Moreover by them is thy servant warned."* We are warned by the Word both of our duty, our danger, and our remedy. On the sea of life there would be many more wrecks, if it were not for the divine storm-signals, which give to the watchful a timely warning. The Bible should be our Mentor, our Monitor, our Memento Mori, our Remembrancer, and the Keeper of our Conscience. Alas, that so few men will take the warning so graciously given ; none but servants of God will do so, for they alone regard their Master's will. Servants of God not only find his service delightful in itself, but they receive good recompense ; *" In keeping of them there is great reward."* There is a wage, and a great one ; though we earn no wages of debt, we win great wages of grace. Saints may be losers for a time, but they shall be glorious gainers in the long run, and even now a quiet conscience is in itself no slender reward for obedience. He who wears the herb called heart's-ease in his bosom is truly blessed. However, the main reward is yet to come, and the word here used hints as much, for it signifies *the heel,* as if the reward would come to us at the end of life when the work was done ;—not while the labour was in the hand, but when it was gone and we could see the heel of it. Oh the glory yet to be revealed ! It is enough to make a man faint for joy at the prospect of it. Our light affliction, which is but for a moment, is not worthy to be compared with the glory which shall be

revealed in us. Then shall we know the value of the Scriptures when we swim in that sea of unutterable delight to which their streams will bear us, if we commit ourselves to them.

12 Who can understand *his* errors? cleanse thou me from secret *faults*.

13 Keep back thy servant also from presumptuous *sins* ; let them not have dominion over me : then shall I be upright, and I shall be innocent from the great transgression.

14 Let the words of my mouth, and the meditation of my heart, be acceptable in thy sight, O LORD, my strength, and my redeemer.

12. " *Who can understand his errors ?*" A question which is its own answer. It rather requires a note of exclamation than of interrogation. By the law is the knowledge of sin, and in the presence of divine truth, the psalmist marvels at the number and heinousness of his sins. He best knows himself who best knows the Word, but even such an one will be in a maze of wonder as to what he does not know, rather than on the mount of congratulation as to what he does know. We have heard of a comedy of errors, but to a good man this is more like a tragedy. Many books have a few lines of errata at the end, but our errata might well be as large as the volume if we could but have sense enough to see them. Augustine wrote in his older days a series of Retractations ; ours might make a library if we had enough grace to be convinced of our mistakes and to confess them. " *Cleanse thou me from secret faults.*" Thou canst mark in me faults entirely hidden from myself. It were hopeless to expect to see all my spots ; therefore, O Lord, wash away in the atoning blood even those sins which my conscience has been unable to detect. Secret sins, like private conspirators, must be hunted out, or they may do deadly mischief ; it is well to be much in prayer concerning them. In the Lateran Council of the Church of Rome, a decree was passed that every true believer must confess his sins, all of them, once in a year to the priest, and they affixed to it this declaration, that there is no hope of pardon but in complying with that decree. What can equal the absurdity of such a decree as that ? Do they suppose that they can tell their sins as easily as they can count their fingers ? Why, if we could receive pardon for all our sins by telling every sin we have committed in one hour, there is not one of us who would be able to enter heaven, since, besides the sins that are known to us and that we may be able to confess, there are a vast mass of sins, which are as truly sins 'as those which we lament, but which are secret, and come not beneath our eye. If we had eyes like those of God, we should think very differently of ourselves. The transgressions which we see and confess are but like the farmer's small samples which he brings to market, when he has left his granary full at home. We have but a very few sins which we can observe and detect, compared with those which are hidden from ourselves and unseen by our fellow-creatures.

13. " *Keep back thy servant also from presumptuous sins ; let them not have dominion over me.*"—This earnest and humble prayer teaches us that saints may fall into the worst of sins unless restrained by grace, and that therefore they must watch and pray lest they enter into temptation. There is a natural proneness to sin in the best of men, and they must be held back as a horse is held back by the bit or they will run into it. Presumptuous sins are peculiarly dangerous. All sins are great sins, but yet some sins are greater than others. Every sin has in it the very venom of rebellion, and is full of the essential marrow of traitorous rejection of God ; but there be some sins which have in them a greater development of the essential mischief of rebellion, and which wear upon their faces more of the brazen pride which defies the Most High. It is wrong to suppose that because all sins will condemn us, that therefore one sin is not greater than another. The fact is, that while all transgression is a greatly grievous and sinful thing, yet there are some transgressions which have a deeper

shade of blackness, and a more double scarlet-dyed hue of criminality than others. The presumptuous sins of our text are the chief and worst of all sins ; they rank head and foremost in the list of iniquities. It is remarkable that though an atonement was provided under the Jewish law for every kind of sin, there was this one exception : " But the soul that sinneth presumptuously shall have no atonement ; it shall be cut off from the midst of my people." And now under the Christian dispensation, although in the sacrifice of our blessed Lord there is a great and precious atonement for presumptuous sins, whereby sinners who have erred in this manner are made clean, yet without doubt, presumptuous sinners, dying without pardon, must expect to receive a double portion of the wrath of God, and a more terrible portion of eternal punishment in the pit that is digged for the wicked. For this reason is David so anxious that he may never come under the reigning power of these giant evils. " *Then shall I be upright, and I shall be innocent from the great transgression.*" He shudders at the thought of the unpardonable sin. Secret sin is a stepping-stone to presumptuous sin, and that is the vestibule of " the sin which is unto death." He who is not wilful in his sin, will be in a fair way to be innocent so far as poor sinful man can be ; but he who tempts the devil to tempt him is in a path which will lead him from bad to worse, and from the worse to the worst.

14. " *Let the words of my mouth, and the meditation of my heart, be acceptable in thy sight, O Lord, my strength, and my Redeemer.*" A sweet prayer, and so spiritual that it is almost as commonly used in Christian worship as the apostolic benediction. *Words of the mouth* are mockery if the heart does not *meditate;* the shell is nothing without the kernel ; but both together are useless unless *accepted;* and even if accepted by man, it is all vanity if not acceptable in *the sight of God.* We must in prayer view Jehovah as our *strength* enabling, and our *Redeemer* saving, or we shall not pray aright, and it is well to feel our personal interest so as to use the word *my,* or our prayers will be hindered. Our near Kinsman's name, our Goel or Redeemer, makes a blessed ending to the Psalm ; it began with the heavens, but it ends with him whose glory fills heaven and earth. Blessed Kinsman, give us now to meditate acceptably upon thy most sweet love and tenderness.

EXPLANATORY NOTES AND QUAINT SAYINGS.

Whole Psalm.—The magnificent scenery to which the poem alludes is derived entirely from a contemplation of nature, in a state of pastoral seclusion ; and a contemplation indulged in, at noontide or in the morning, when the sun was travelling over the horizon, and eclipsing all the other heavenly bodies by his glory. On which account it forms a perfect contrast with the eighth Psalm, evidently composed in the evening, and should be read in connection with it, as it was probably written nearly at the same time ; and as both are songs of praise derived from natural phenomena, and therefore peculiarly appropriate to rural or pastoral life.—*John Mason Good.*

Whole Psalm.—The world resembleth a divinity-school, saith Plutarch, and Christ, as the Scripture telleth, is our doctor, instructing us by his works, and by his words. For as Aristotle had two sorts of writings, one called *exoterical,* for his common auditors, another acromatical, for his private scholars and familiar acquaintance : so God hath two sorts of books, as David intimates in this Psalm ; namely, the book of his creatures, as a common-place book for all men in the world : " *The heavens declare the glory of God,*" verses 1—6 ; the book of his Scriptures as a statute-book for his domestical auditory, the church : " *The law of the Lord is an undefiled law,*" verses 7, 8. The great book of the creatures in folio, may be termed aptly *the shepherd's kalendar,* and the *ploughman's alphabet,* in which even the most ignorant may run (as the prophet speaks) and read. It is a letter patent, or open epistle for all, as David, in our text, *Their sound is gone out into all lands, and their words unto the ends of the world ; there is neither speech nor language but have heard of their preaching.* For albeit, heaven, and the sun in heaven, and the light in the sun are mute, yet *their voices* are well understood, catechising plainly the first elements of religion, as, namely, that there is a God, and that this God is but one God, and that this one God excelleth all other things infinitely both in might and majesty. *Universus mundus* (as one pithily) *nihil aliud est quàm Deus explicatus :* the whole world is nothing else but God expressed. So St. Paul, Rom. i. 20 : God's *invisible things*, as his eternal power and Godhead, " are clearly seen" by the creation of the world, " being understood by the things that are made." The heavens declare this, and the firmament showeth this, and the day telleth this, and the night certifieth this, the sound of the thunder proclaimeth, as it were, this in all lands, and the words of the whistling wind unto the ends of the world. More principally *the sun, which as a bridegroom cometh out of his chamber, and rejoiceth as a giant to run his course.* The body thereof (as mathematicians have confidently delivered) is one hundred and sixty-six times bigger than the whole earth, and yet it is every day carried by the finger of God so great a journey, so long a course, that if it were to be taken on the land, it should run every several hour of the day two hundred and twenty-five German miles. It is true that God is incapable to sense, yet he makes himself, as it were, visible in his works ; as the divine poet (Du Bartas) sweetly :—

> " Therein our fingers feel, our nostrils smell,
> Our palates taste his virtues that excel,
> He shows him to our eyes, talks to our ears,
> In the ordered motions of the spangled spheres."

So " *the heavens declare,*" that is, they make men declare the glory of God, by their admirable structure, motions, and influence. Now, the preaching of *the heavens* is wonderful in three respects. 1. As preaching all the night and all the day without intermission : verse 2. *One day telleth another, and one night certifieth another.* 2. As preaching in every kind of language : verse 3. *There is neither speech, nor language, but their voices are heard among them.* 3. As preaching in every part of the world, and in every parish of every part, and in every place of every parish : verse 4, *Their sound is gone into all lands, and their words unto the ends of the world.* They be diligent pastors, as preaching at all times ; and learned pastors, as preaching in all tongues ; and catholic pastors, as preaching in all towns. Let us not then in this University (where the voices of so many great doctors are heard), be like to truants in other schools, who gaze so much upon the babies,* and gilded cover, and painted margent of their book, that they neglect the text and lesson itself. This is *God's primer*, as it were, for all sorts of people ; but he hath another book proper only for his domestical auditory the church : " He sheweth his word unto Jacob, his statutes and his judgments unto Israel. He hath not dealt so with any nation, neither have the heathen knowledge of his laws." Psa. cxlvii. 19, 20. Heathen men read in his primer, but Christian men are well acquainted with his Bible. The primer is a good book, but it is imperfect ; for after a man hath learned it he must learn more ; but " *the law of the Lord,*" that is, the body of the Holy Scriptures, is a most absolute canon of all doctrines appertaining either to faith or good manners ; it is a *perfect law, converting the soul, giving wisdom to the simple, sure, pure, righteous, and rejoicing the heart,*" etc.—*John Boys.*

Whole Psalm.—Saint Chrysostom conjectures that the main intention of the greatest part of this Psalm consists in the discovery of divine providence, which manifests itself in the motions and courses of the heavenly bodies, concerning which the psalmist speaketh much, from verse 1 to verse 7. Saint Austin upon the place, is of a quite different opinion, who conjectures that Christ is the whole subject of this Psalm ; whose person is compared to the sun for excellency

---

* The pictures or illustrations of a book.

and beauty, and the course of whose doctrine was dispersed round about the world by his apostles, to which Saint Paul alludes (Rom. x. 18) ; "Have they not heard ? Yes, verily, their sound went into all the earth," etc., and the efficacy of whose gospel is like the heat of the sun, which pierceth into the very heart of the earth, so that into the secrets of the soul. I confess this allegorical exposition is not altogether impertinent, neither is that literal exposition of Saint Chrysostom to be blamed, for it hath its weight. But to omit all variety of conjectures, this Psalm contains in it :

1. A double kind of *the knowledge of God*, of which one is *by the book of the creature ;* and this divines call a natural knowledge : there is not any one creature but it is a leaf written all over with the description of God ; his eternal power and Godhead may be understood by the things that are seen, saith the apostle. Rom. i. 20. And, as every creature, so especially "*the heavens*" do lead us to the knowledge of a God ; so verse 1 of this Psalm : "*The heavens declare the glory of God, and the firmament sheweth his handywork ;*" they are the theatres, as it were, of his wisdom, and power, and glory. Another is *by the book of Scripture ;* and this knowledge is far more distinct and explicit : with the other even the heathens do grope after a deity, but with this Christians do behold God, as it were, with open face. The characters here are now fresh, spiritual, complete, and lively. The word of God is the singular means to know God aright. Look, as the light which comes from the sun, so that word of God, which is light, is the clearest way to know God who is light itself. Hence it is that the psalmist stands much upon this from verse 7 to verse 12, where he sets open the word in its several encomiums and operations ; namely, in its perfection, its certainties, and firmness ; its righteousness, and purity, and truth ; and then in its efficacy—that it is a converting word, an enlightening word, an instructing word, a rejoicing word, a desirable word, a warning word, and a rewarding word.

2. *A singular and experimental knowledge of himself.*—So it seemeth, that that word which David did so much commend, he did commend it from an experimental efficacy ; he had found it to be a righteous, and holy, and pure, and discovering word, laying open, not only visible and gross transgressions, but also, like the light of the sun, those otherwise unobserved and secret atoms of senses flying within the house ; I mean in the secret chambers of the soul.—*Obadiah Sedgwick.* 1660.

Verse 1.—"*The heavens declare the glory of God,*" etc.—The eminent saints of ancient times were watchful observers of the objects and operations of nature. In every event they saw the agency of God ; and, therefore, they took delight in its examination. For they could not but receive pleasure from witnessing the manifestations of his wisdom and beneficence, whom they adored and loved. They had not learned, as we have in modern times, to interpose unbending laws between the Creator and his works ; and then, by giving inherent power to these laws, virtually to remove God away from his creation into an ethereal extramundane sphere of repose and happiness. I do not say that this is the universal feeling of the present day. But it prevails extensively in the church, and still more in the world. The ablest philosophers of modern times do, indeed, maintain that a natural law is nothing more than the uniform mode in which God acts ; and that, after all, it is not the efficiency of the law, but God's own energy, that keeps all nature in motion ; that he operates immediately and directly, not remotely and indirectly, in bringing about every event, and that every natural change is as really the work of God as if the eye of sense could see his hand turning round the wheels of nature. But, although the ablest philosophy of modern times has reached this conclusion, the great mass of the community, and even of Christians, are still groping in the darkness of that mechanical system which ascribes the operations of the natural world to nature's laws instead of nature's God. By a sort of figure, indeed, it is proper, as the advocates of this system admit, to speak of God as the author of natural events, because he originally ordained the laws of nature. But they have no idea that he exerts any direct and immediate agency in bringing them about ; and, therefore, when they look upon these events they feel no impression of the presence and active agency of Jehovah.

But how different, as already remarked, were the feelings of ancient saints. The psalmist could not look up to heaven without exclaiming, " *The heavens declare the glory of God ; and the firmament sheweth his handywork. Day unto day uttereth speech, and night unto night sheweth knowledge. There is no speech nor language where their voice is not heard.*" When he cast his eyes abroad upon the earth, his full heart cried out, " O Lord, how manifold are thy works ! In wisdom hast thou made them all ; the earth is full of thy riches." In his eye everything was full of God. It was God who " sent springs into the valleys, which run among the hills." When the thunder-storm passed before him, it was " God's voice in the heavens, and his lightnings that lighted the world." When he heard the bellowings, and saw the smoke of the volcano, it was " God who looketh on the earth, and it trembleth ; he toucheth the hills, and they smoke."— *Edward Hitchcock, D.D., LL.D.,* 1867.

Verse 1.—" *The heavens declare,*" etc. Man has been endued by his Creator with mental powers capable of cultivation. He has employed them in the study of the wonderful works of God which the universe displays. His own habitation has provided a base which has served him to measure the heavens. He compares his own stature with the magnitude of the earth on which he dwells ; the earth, with the system in which it is placed ; the extent of the system, with the distance of the nearest fixed stars ; and that distance again serves as a unit of measurement for other distances which observation points out. Still no approach is made to any limit. How extended these wonderful works of the Almighty may be no man can presume to say. The sphere of creation appears to extend around us indefinitely on all sides ; " to have its centre everywhere, its circumference nowhere." These are considerations which from their extent almost bewilder our minds. But how should they raise our ideas toward their great Creator, when we consider that all these were created from nothing, by a word, by a mere volition of the Deity. " Let them be," said God, and they were. " By the word of the Lord were the heavens made, and all the host of them by the breath of his mouth." " For he spake, and it was done. He commanded, and it stood fast." Psalm xxxiii. 6, 9. What must be that power which so formed worlds on worlds ; worlds in comparison of which this earth which we inhabit sinks into utter nothingness ! Surely when we thus lift up our thoughts to the heavens, the moon and the stars which he hath ordained, we must feel, if we can ever feel, how stupendous and incomprehensible is that Being who formed them all ; that " *the heavens*" do indeed " *declare the glory of God ; and the firmament sheweth his handywork.*"—*Temple Chevallier, in " The Hulsean Lectures for* 1827."

Verse 1.—I have often been charmed and awed at the sight of the nocturnal heavens, even before I knew how to consider them in their proper circumstances of majesty and beauty. Something like magic has struck my mind, on transient and unthinking survey of the æthereal vault, tinged throughout with the purest azure, and decorated with innumerable starry lamps. I have felt, I know not what, powerful and aggrandising impulse, which seemed to snatch me from the low entanglements of vanity, and prompted an ardent sigh for sublimer objects. Methought I heard, even from the silent spheres, a commanding call to spurn the abject earth, and pant after unseen delights. Henceforth I hope to imbibe more copiously this moral emanation of the skies, when, in some such manner as the preceding, they are rationally seen, and the sight is duly improved. The stars, I trust, will teach as well as shine, and help to dispel both nature's gloom and my intellectual darkness. To some people they discharge no better a service than that of holding a flambeau to their feet, and softening the horrors of their night. To me and my friends may they act as ministers of a superior order, as counsellors of wisdom, and guides to happiness ! Nor will they fail to execute this nobler office, if they gently light our way into the knowledge of their adored Maker—if they point out with their silver rays our path to his beatific presence.—*James Hervey, A.M.*, 1713—1758.

Verse 1.—Should a man live underground, and there converse with the works of art and mechanism, and should afterwards be brought up into the open day, and see the several glories of the heaven and earth, he would immediately pronounce them the works of such a Being as we define God to be.—*Aristotle.*

Verse 1.—When we behold "*the heavens,*" when we contemplate the celestial bodies, can we fail of conviction? Must we not acknowledge that there is a Divinity, a perfect Being, a ruling intelligence, which governs; a God who is everywhere and directs all by his power? Anybody who doubts this may as well deny there is a sun that lights us. Time destroys all false opinions, but it confirms those which are formed by nature. For this reason, with us as well as with other nations, the worship of the gods and the holy exercises of religion, increase in purity and extent every day.—*Cicero.*

Verse 1.—"*The heavens declare the glory of God,*" etc.—They discover his *wisdom*, his *power*, his *goodness;* and so there is not any one creature, though never so little, but we are to admire the Creator in it. As a chamber hung round about with looking-glasses represents the face upon every turn, thus all the world doth the mercy and the bounty of God; though that be visible, yet it discovers an invisible God and his invisible properties.—*Anthony Burgess,* 1656.

Verse 1.—None of the elect are in that respect so unwise as to refuse to hear and consider the works and words of God as not appertaining unto him. God forbid. No man in the world doth with more fervency consider the works of God, none more readily lift up their ears to hear God speak than even they who have the inward revelation of the Holy Spirit.—*Wolfgang Musculus.*

Verse 1.—During the French revolution Jean Bon St. André, the Vendean revolutionist, said to a peasant, "I will have all your steeples pulled down, that you may no longer have any object by which you may be reminded of your old superstitions." "But," replied the peasant, "*you cannot help leaving us the stars.*"—*John Bate's* "*Cyclopædia of Moral and Religious Truths,*" 1865.

Verse 1.—" *The heavens declare the glory of God* "—

How beautiful this dome of sky,
And the vast hills in fluctuation fixed
At thy command, how awful! Shall the soul,
Human and rational, report of Thee
Even less than these? Be mute who will, who can,
Yet I will praise thee with impassioned voice.
My lips, that may forget thee in the crowd,
Cannot forget thee here, where thou hast built
For thine own glory, in the wilderness!

William Wordsworth, 1770—1850.

Verse 1.—" *The firmament sheweth his handiwork* "—

The giltt'ring stars
By the deep ear of meditation heard,
Still in their midnight watches sing of him.
He nods a calm. The tempest blows his wrath:
The thunder is his voice; and the red flash
His speedy sword of justice. At his touch
The mountains flame. He shakes the solid earth,
And rocks the nations. Nor in these alone—
In ev'ry common instance God is seen.

Verse 1.   *James Thomson.*

These are thy glorious works, Parent of good,
Almighty! Thine this universal frame,
Thus wondrous fair; Thyself how wondrous, then!
Unspeakable, who sitt'st above these heavens
To us invisible, or dimly seen
In these thy lowest works; yet these declare
Thy goodness beyond thought, and power divine.

John Milton.

Verses 1, 2.—In order more fully to illustrate the expressive richness of the
Hebrew, I would direct the attention of my reader to the beautiful phraseology
of the XIX. Psalm. The literal reading of the first and second verses may be
thus given :—

> " The heavens are *telling* the glory of God,
> The firmament *displaying* the work of his hands ;
> Day unto day *welleth forth* speech,
> Night unto night *breatheth out* knowledge."

Thus the four distinct terms in the original are preserved in the translation ;
and the overflowing fulness with which day unto day pours forth divine instruction, and the gentle whisperings of the silent night, are contrasted as in the
Hebrew.—*Henry Craik*, 1860.

Verses 1—4.—Though all preachers on earth should grow silent, and every
human mouth cease from publishing the glory of God, the heavens above will
never cease to declare and proclaim his majesty and glory. They are for ever
preaching ; for, like an unbroken chain, their message is delivered from day to
day and from night to night. At the silence of one herald another takes up his
speech. One day, like the other, discloses the same spectacles of his glory, and
one night, like the other, the same wonders of his majesty. Though nature be
hushed and *quiet* when the sun in his glory has reached the zenith on the azure
sky—though the world keep her *silent* festival, when the stars shine brightest at
night—yet, says the psalmist, *they speak ;* ay, holy silence itself is a speech,
provided there be the ear to hear it.—*Augustus T. Tholuck.*

Verses 1—4.—" *The heavens declare the glory of God, and the firmament showeth
his handiwork.*" If the heavens declare the glory of God, we should observe
what that glory is which they declare. The heavens preach to us every day.
. . . . . . " *Their line is gone out through all the earth, and their words to the
end of the world.*" Sun, moon, and stars are preachers ; they are universal,
they are natural apostles. The world is their charge ; " *their words,*" saith the
Psalm, " *go to the end of the world.*" We may have good doctrine from them,
especially this doctrine in the text, of the wisdom and power of God. And it is
very observable that the apostle alludes to this text in the Psalm for a proof of
gospel preaching to the whole world. Rom. x. 18. The gospel, like the sun,
casts his beams over, and sheds his light into all the world. David in the Psalm
saith, " *Their line is gone out,*" etc. By which word he shows that the
heavens, being so curious a fabric, made, as it were, by a line and level, do
clearly, though silently, preach the skill and perfections of God. Or, that we
may read divine truths in them as a line formed by a pen into words and
sentences (the original signifies both a measuring line and a written line),
letters and words in writing being nothing but lines drawn into several forms or
figures. But the Septuagint, whose translation the apostle citeth, for *Kavam,
their line*, read *Kolam, their sound ;* either misreading the word or studiously
mollifying the sense into a nearer compliance with the latter clause of the
verse, " *And their words to the end of the world.*"—*Joseph Caryl.*

Verses 1—4.—Like as the sun with his light beneficially comforteth all the
world, so Christ, the Son of God, reacheth his benefits unto all men, so that they
will receive them thankfully, and not refuse them disobediently.—*Robert
Cawdray.*

Verse 2.—" *Day unto day,*" etc. But what is the meaning of the next word—
One day telleth another, and one night certifieth another ? Literally, *dies diem
dicit*, is nothing else but *dies diem docet*. One day telleth another, is one day
teacheth another. The day past is instructed by the day present : every new
day doth afford new doctrine. The day is a most apt time to learn by reading
and conference ; the night a most fit time for invention and meditation. Now
that which thou canst not understand this day thou mayest haply learn the
next, and that which is not found out in one night may be gotten in another.
Mystically (saith Hierom), Christ is this " *day*," who saith of himself, " I am

the light of the world," and his twelve apostles are the twelve hours of the day ; for Christ's Spirit revealed by the mouths of his apostles the mysteries of our salvation, in other ages not so fully known unto the sons of men. *One day telleth another*, that is, the spiritual utter this unto the spiritual ; and *one night certifieth another*, that is, Judas insinuates as much unto the Jews in the night of ignorance, saying, " Whomsoever I shall kiss, that is he, lay hold on him." Matt. xxvi. 28. Or, the Old Testament only shadowing Christ is *the night*, and the New Testament plainly showing Christ, is *the day.—John Boys.*

Verse 2.—" Day unto day," or day after day ; the vicissitude or continual succession of day and night speaketh much divine knowledge. The assiduity and constancy without any intermission by the heavens preaching is hereby expressed.—*John Richardson.*

Verse 2.—" Uttereth," poureth forth abundantly ; *" sheweth,"* demonstrates clearly and effectively, without ambiguity. Job xxxvi. 2. Many in the full light of gospel day, hear not that speech, who yet in the night of affliction and trouble, or in the conviction of their natural darkness, have that knowledge communicated to them which enables them to realise the joy that cometh in the morning.—*W. Wilson.*

Verse 2.—" Sheweth knowledge." We may illustrate the differing measures in which natural objects convey knowledge to men of differing mental and spiritual capacity by the story of our great English artist. He is said to have been engaged upon one of his immortal works, and a lady of rank looking on remarked, " But, Mr. Turner, I do not see in nature all that you describe there." " Ah, Madam," answered the painter, " do you not wish you could ?"—*C. H. S.*

Verse 3.—" There is no speech," etc. The sunset was one of the most glorious I ever beheld, and the whole earth seemed so still that *the voice of neither God nor man was heard.* There was not a ripple upon the waters, not the leaf of a tree nor even of a blade of grass moving, and the rocks upon the opposite shore reflected the sun's " after-glow," and were again themselves reflected from or in the river during the brief twilight, in a way I do not remember ever to have beheld before. No ! I will not say *the voice of God* was not heard ; it spoke in the very stillness as loud as in roaring thunder, in the placid scene as in rocks and cliffs impassable, and louder still in *the heavens and in the firmament,* and in the magnificent prospect around me. His wondrous works declared him to be near, and I felt as if the very ground upon which I was treading was holy.—*John Gadsby.*

Verse 4.—" Their line is gone out," etc. " Their *sound* went," etc. Rom. x. 18. The relations which the gospel of Christ Jesus hath to the Psalms of David I find to be more than to all the Bible besides, that seldom anything is written in the New Testament, but we are sent to fetch our proofs from these. The margin here sends me to the Psalm, and the Psalm sends me back to this again ; showing that they both speak one thing. How comes it then that it is not one, for " *line*" and " *sound* " are not one thing ? Is there not some mistake here ? Answer—To fetch a proof from a place is one thing, an allusion is another. Sometimes the evangelists are enforced to bring their proofs for what they write out of the Old Testament, else we should never believe them, and then they must be very sure of the terms, when they say, " This was done that it might be fulfilled which was spoken," etc. But the apostle was not now upon that account ; only showing to the Romans the marvellous spreading of the gospel, alluding to this passage of David discoursing of " *the heavens,*" to which the prophet compared the publication of the word ; the sun and moon and stars not only shining through, but round all the earth. The same subject Paul was now upon, and for his purpose makes use of a term fitter to express the preaching of the gospel, by the word " *sound,*" than that other word expressing the limitations of the law, by the word " *line :*" both of these agreeing that there is no fitter comparison to be fetched from anything in nature than from "*the heavens,*" their motions, revolutions, influences upon sublunary bodies ; also in their eclipses, when one text seems to darken another, as if it were put out altogether by crossing and opposing, which is but seemingly so to the ignorant, they agree sweetly enough in themselves ; no bridegroom can agree better with his bride, nor rejoice more to run his course.   So they both conclude in this, that the sun never saw that nation yet where the word of truth, in one degree or other (all the world, you must think, cannot be right under the meridian) hath not shined.—*William Streat, in " The Dividing of the Hoof,*" 1654.

Verse 4.—"*Unto the end of the world.*"   Venantius Fortunatus eleven hundred years ago witnesses to the peregrinations of Paul the apostle.

> He passed the ocean's curled wave,
> As far as islands harbours have;
> As far as Brittain yields a bay,
> Or Iceland's frozen shore a stay.   *John Cragge,* 1557.

Verse 4.—" *Their line is gone out through all the earth,*" etc.   The molten sea did stand upon twelve oxen, that is, as Paul doth interpret it, upon twelve apostles (1 Cor. ix. 10) ; which in that they looked four ways, east, west, north, and south, they did teach all nations.   And in that they looked three and three together, they did represent the blessed Trinity.   Not only teaching all nations, but also in that sea of water, baptising them in the name of the Father, and of the Son, and of the Holy Ghost.   Wherefore, though the two kine which carried the ark wherein were the tables of the law, went straight and kept one path, turning neither to the right hand nor to the left ; yet these twelve oxen which carried the molten sea, signifying the doctrine of the gospel, went not straight, neither kept one path, but turned into the way of the Gentiles ; yea, they looked all manner of ways, east, west, north, and south.   And those two kine stood still and lowed no more when they came to the field of Joshua, dwelling in Bethshemesh, that is, the house of the sun.   To note, that all the kine, and calves, and sacrifices, and ceremonies of the old law were to cease and stand still when they came to Jesus, who is the true Joshua, dwelling in heaven, which is the true Bethshemesh.   But these twelve oxen were so far from leaving off, either to go, or to low, when they came to Christ, that even then they went much faster and lowed much louder ; so that now " *their sound is gone out into all lands, and their words to the end of the world ;*" and " *in them hath God set* " Bethshemesh, that is, a house or " *tabernacle for the sun.*"   Therefore, as the material sun, through the twelve signs of the Zodiac, goeth forth from the uttermost parts of the heaven, and runneth about to the end of it again : in like sort, the spiritual *Sun of Righteousness,* by the twelve apostles, as by twelve signs, hath been borne round about the world, that he might be not only " the glory of his people Israel," but also " a light to lighten the Gentiles ;" and that all, " *all* the ends of the earth might see the salvation of our God."—*Thomas Playfere.*

Verses 4—6.—It appears to me very likely that the Holy Ghost in these expressions, which he most immediately uses about the rising of the sun, has an eye to the rising of the Sun of Righteousness from the grave, and that the expressions that the Holy Ghost here uses are conformed to such a view.   The times of the Old Testament are times of night in comparison of the gospel day, and are so represented in Scripture, and therefore the approach of the day of the New Testament dispensation in the birth of Christ, is called the day-spring from on high visiting the earth (Luke i. 78), " Through the tender mercy of our God ; whereby the dayspring from on high hath visited us ;" and the commencing of the gospel dispensation as it was introduced by Christ, is called the Sun of Righteousness rising.   Mal. iv. 2.   But this gospel dispensation commences with the resurrection of Christ.   Therein the Sun of Righteousness rises from under the earth, as the sun appears to do in the morning, and comes forth as a bridegroom.   He rose as the joyful, glorious bridegroom of his church ; for Christ, especially as risen again, is the proper bridegroom, or husband, of his church, as the apostle teaches (Rom. vii. 4), "Wherefore, my brethren, ye also are become dead to the law by the body of Christ; that ye should be married to another, even to him who is raised from the dead, that we should bring forth fruit unto God." He that was covered with contempt, and overwhelmed in a deluge of sorrow, has purchased and won his spouse, for he loved the church, and gave himself for it, that he might present it to himself; now he comes forth as a bridegroom to bring home his purchased spouse to him in spiritual marriage, as he soon after did in the conversion of such multitudes, making his people willing in the day of his power, and hath also done many times since, and will do in a yet more glorious degree. And as the sun when it rises comes forth like a bridegroom gloriously adorned, so Christ in his resurrection entered on his state of glory. After his state of sufferings, he rose to shine forth in ineffable glory as the King of heaven and earth, that he might be a glorious bridegroom, in whom his church might be unspeakably happy. Here the psalmist says that God *has placed a tabernacle for the sun in the heavens:* so God the Father had prepared an abode in heaven for Jesus Christ; he had set a throne for him there, to which he ascended after he rose. The sun after it is risen ascends up to the midst of heaven, and then at that end of its race descends again to the earth; so Christ when he rose from the grave ascended up to the height of heaven, and far above all heavens, but at the end of the gospel day will descend again to the earth. It is here said that the risen sun " rejoiceth as a strong man to run a race." So Christ, when he rose, rose as a man of war, as the Lord strong and mighty, the Lord mighty in battle; he rose to conquer his enemies, and to show forth his glorious power in subduing all things to himself, during that race which he had to run, which is from his resurrection to the end of the world, when he will return to the earth again. . . . . That the Holy Ghost here has a mystical meaning, and has respect to the light of the Sun of Righteousness, and not merely the light of the natural sun, is confirmed by the verses that follow, in which the psalmist himself seems to apply them to the word of God, which is the light of that Sun, even of Jesus Christ, who himself revealed the word of God : see the very next words, " The law of the Lord is perfect," etc.—*Jonathan Edwards,* 1703—1758.

Verse 5.—" *Which is as a bridegroom,*" etc. The sun is described like a bridegroom coming out of his chamber, dressed and prepared, and as a giant rejoicing to run his race ; but though the sun be thus prepared, and dressed, and ready, yet if the Lord send a writ and a prohibition to the sun to keep within his chamber, he cannot come forth, his journey is stopped. Thus also he stops man in his nearest preparations for any action. If the Lord will work, who shall let it? Isaiah xliii. 13. That is, there is no power in heaven or earth which can hinder him. But if the Lord will let, who shall work? Neither sun, nor stars, nor men, nor devils, can work, if he forbids them. The point is full of comfort. —*Joseph Caryl.*

Verse 5.—" *Which is as a bridegroom,*" etc. The Sun of Righteousness appeared in three signs especially ; *Leo, Virgo, Libra.* 1. In *Leo,* roaring as a lion, in the law ; so that the people could not endure his voice. 2. In *Virgo,* born of a pure virgin in the gospel. 3. In *Libra,* weighing our works in his balance at the day of judgment. Or as Bernard distinguisheth his threefold coming aptly—*venit ad homines, venit in homines, venit contra homines:* in the time past he came *unto* men as upon this day ;* in the time present, he comes by his spirit *into* men every day ; in the time future, he shall come *against* men at the last day. The coming here mentioned is his coming in the flesh—for so the fathers usually gloss the text—he came forth of the virgin's womb, " *as a bridegroom out of his chamber.*" As a *bridegroom,* for the King of heaven at this holy time made a great wedding for his Son. Matt. xxii. 1. Christ is the *bridegroom,* man's nature the bride, the conjunction and blessed union of both in one person is his marriage. The best way to reconcile two disagreeing

---

* The Nineteenth Psalm is one " appointed to be read" on *Christmas Day.*

families is to make some marriage between them : even so, the Word became flesh, and dwelt among us in the world that he might hereby make our peace, reconciling God to man and man to God. By this happy match the Son of God is become the Son of Man, even flesh of our flesh, and bone of our bones ; and the sons of men are made the sons of God, " of his flesh and of his bones," as Paul saith, Eph. v. 30. So that now the church being Christ's own spouse, saith, " I am my Beloved's, and my Beloved is mine." Cant. vi. 3. My sin is his sin, and his righteousness is my righteousness. He who knew no sin, for my sake was made sin ; and I, contrariwise, having no good thing, am made the righteousness of God in him : I which am *brown* by persecution, and *black* by nature (Cant. i. 5), so foul as the sow that walloweth in the mire, through his favour am comely, without spot or wrinkle, so white as the snow, like a lily among thorns, even the fairest among women. Cant. ii. 2. This happy *marriage* is not a *mar age*, but it makes a *merry age*, being " the consolation of Israel," and comfort of Jerusalem's heart. Indeed, Christ our husband doth absent himself from us in his body for a time ; but when he did ascend into heaven he took with him our pawn, namely, his flesh ; and he gave us his pawn, namely, his Spirit, assuring us that we shall one day, when the world is ended, enter with him into the wedding chamber, and there feast with him, and enjoy his blessed company for evermore.—*John Boys.*

Verse 6.—" *There is nothing hid from the heat thereof.*"—This is literally the case. The earth receives its heat from the sun, and by conduction, a part of it enters the crust of our globe. By convection, another portion is carried to the atmosphere, which it warms. Another portion is radiated into space, according to laws yet imperfectly understood, but which are evidently connected with the colour, chemical composition, and mechanical structure of parts of the earth's surface. At the same time the ordinary state of the air, consisting of gases and vapour, modifies the heat rays and prevents scorching. Thus, the solar heat is equalised by the air. Nothing on earth or in air is hid from the heat of the sun. . . . . Even the colour of some bodies is changed by heat. . . . Heat also is in bodies in a state which is not sensible, and is therefore called latent heat, or heat of fluidity, because it is regarded as the cause of fluidity in ponderable substances. It can fuse every substance it does not decompose below the melting point, as in the case of wood. Every gas may be regarded as consisting of heat, and some basis of ponderable matter, whose cohesion it overcomes, imparting a tendency to great expansion, when no external obstacle prevents, and this expansive tendency is their elasticity or tension. Certain gases have been liquified under great pressure, and extreme cold. Heat, also, at certain temperatures, causes the elasticity of vapours to overcome the atmospheric pressure which can no longer restrain them. An example of this is the boiling point of water ; and, indeed, in every case the true instance is the boiling point. Philosophers are agreed that the affinity of heat for any ponderable substance is superior to all other forces acting upon it. No ponderable matters can combine without disengagement of heat. . . . And the same occurs from every mechanical pressure and condensation of a body. In all these cases, and many more, there are like evidences of the presence and influences of heat ; but the facts now advanced are sufficient to show us the force of the expression, that in terrestrial things nothing is hid from, or can by any possibility escape the agency of heat.—*Edwin Sidney, A.M., in* " *Conversations on the Bible and Science,*" 1866.

Verse 6 (last clause). " *There is nothing hid from the heat,*" nothing from the light of Christ. It is not solely on the mountain top that he shines, as in the day before he was fully risen, when his rays, although unseen by the rest of the world, formed a glory round the heads of his prophets, who saw him while to the chief part of mankind he was still lying below the horizon. Now, however, that he is risen, he pours his light through the valley, as well as over the mountain ; nor is there any one, at least in these countries, who does not catch some gleams of that light, except those who burrow and hide themselves in the dark caverns of sin. But it is not light alone that Christ sheds from his heavenly tabernacle. As nothing is hid from his light, neither is anything hid from his heat. He not only enlightens the understanding, so that it shall see and know the truth ; he also softens, and melts, and warms the heart, so that it shall love the truth, and calls forth fruit from it, and ripens the fruit he has called forth ; and that too on the lowliest plant which creeps along the ground, as well as the loftiest tree. . . . .

Though while he was on earth, he had fullest power of bestowing every earthly gift, yet, in order that he should be able to bestow heavenly gifts with the same all-healing power, it was necessary that he should go up into heaven. When he had done so, when he had ascended into *his tabernacle in the heavens*, then, he promises his disciples, he would send down the Holy Spirit of God, who should bring them heavenly gifts, yea, who should enter into their hearts, and make them bring forth all the fruits of the Spirit in abundance ; should make them abound in love, in peace, in longsuffering, in gentleness, in goodness, in faith, in meekness, in temperance. These are the bright heavenly rays, which, as it were, make up the pure light of Christ ; *and from this heat nothing is hid.* Even the hardest heart may be melted by it ; even the foulest may be purified.— *Julius Charles Hare, M.A.*, 1841.

Verse 7.—" *The law of the Lord is perfect, converting the soul.*" To man fallen, the law only convinceth of sin, and bindeth over to death, it is nothing but a killing letter ; but the gospel, accompanied by the power of the Spirit, bringeth life. Again, it is said, " *The law of the Lord is perfect, converting the soul;*" therefore it seems the law may also be a word of salvation to the creature. I answer ; by the law there, is not meant only that part of the word which we call the covenant of works, but there it is put for the whole word, for the whole doctrine of the covenant of life and salvation; as Psalm i. 2 : "His delight is in the law of the Lord ; and in his law doth he meditate day and night." And if you take it in that stricter sense, then it converteth the soul but by accident, as it is joined with the gospel, which is the misery of life and righteousness, but in itself it is the law of sin and death. Look, as a thing taken simply, would be poison and deadly in itself, yet mixed with other whole-some medicines, it is of great use, is an excellent physical ingredient ; so the law is of great use as joined with the gospel, to awaken and startle the sinner, to show him his duty, to convince him of sin and judgment ; but it is the gospel properly that pulls in the heart.— *Thomas Manton.*

Verse 7.— *The law,* or doctrine, an orderly manner of instruction, an institu-tion or disposition, called in Hebrew *torah,* which implies both doctrine and an orderly disposition of the same. Therefore where one prophet, relating David's words, saith *the law* of man (2 Sam. vii. 19), another saith, *the orderly estate,* or, *course* of man. 1 Cor. xvii. 17. The Holy Ghost, in Greek, calls it *Nomos,* a law (Heb. viii. 10), from Jer. xxxi. 33. This name is most commonly ascribed to the precepts given by Moses at Mount Sinai (Deut. xxxii. 4 ; Mal. iv. 4 ; John i. 17, and vii. 19) ; it is also largely used for all his writings. For the history of Genesis is called *law* (Gal. iv. 21), from Gen. xvi. And though some-times the law be distinguished from the Psalms and Prophets (Luke xvi. 16, and xxiv. 24), yet the other prophets' books are called *law* (1 Cor. xiv. 21), from Isa. xxviii. 11 ; the Psalms are also thus named (John x. 24 and xv. 25), from Psalm lxxxii. 6 and xxxv. 19. Yea, one Psalm is called a *law* (Psalm lxxviii. 1) ; and the many branches of Moses' doctrine as the *law* of the sin-offering, etc. Lev. vi. 25. And generally it is used for any *doctrine,* as the *law* of works, the *law* of faith, etc. Rom. iii. 27.—*Henry Ainsworth.*

Verse 7.—" *Converting the soul.*" This version conveys a sense good and true in itself, but is not in accordance with the design of the psalmist, which is, to express the divine law on the feelings and affections of good men.. The Hebrew terms properly mean, "bringing back the spirit," when it is depressed.

by adversity, by refreshing and consoling it ; like food, it restores the faint, and communicates vigour to the disconsolate."—*William Walford*, 1837.

Verse 7.—" Converting the soul." The heart of man is the most free and hard of anything to work upon, and to make an impression and stamp upon this hard heart, this heart that is so stony, adamantine, " harder than the nether millstones," as the Scripture teacheth. To compel this free-will, this *Domina sui actus*, the queen in the soul, the empress, it cannot be without a divine power, without a hand that is omnipotent ; but the ministers do this by the Word—they mollify, and wound, and break this heart, they incline, and bow, and draw this free-will whither the spirit listeth. And Clemens Alexandrinus is not afraid to say, that if the fables of Orpheus and Amphion were true— that they drew birds, beasts, and stones, with their ravishing melody—yet the harmony of the Word is greater, which translates men from Helicon to Zion, which softens the hard heart of man obdurate against the truth, that " raises up children to Abraham of stones," that is (as he interprets), of unbelievers, which he calls stocks and stones, that put their trust in stones and stocks ; which metamorphoses men that are beastlike, wild birds for their lightness and vanity, serpents for their craft and subtlety, lions for their wrath and cruelty, swine for voluptuousness and luxury, etc. ; and charms them so that of wild beasts they become tame men ; that makes living *stones* (as he did others) come of their own accord to the building of the walls of Jerusalem (as he of Thebes), to the building of a living temple to the everliving God. This must needs be a truly persuasive charm, as he speaks.—*John Stoughton's " Choice Sermons,"* 1640.

Verse 7.—" Making wise the simple." The apostle Paul in Eph. i. 8, ex-presseth conversion, and the whole work inherently wrought in us, by the making of a man wise. It is usual in the Scriptures, and you may ofttimes meet with it ; *" converting the soul," "making wise the simple."* The beginning of conversion, and so all along, the increase of all grace to the end, is expressed by wisdom entering into a man's heart, " If wisdom enter into thy heart," and so goes on to do more and more ; not unto thy head only—a man may have all that, and be a fool in the end, but when it entereth into the heart, and draws all the affections after it, and along with it, " when knowledge is pleasant to thy soul," then a man is converted ; when God breaks open a man's heart, and makes wisdom fall in, enter in, and make a man wise.—*Thomas Goodwin.*

Verse 7.—This verse, and the two next following, which treat of God's law, are in Hebrew, written each of them with ten words, according to the number of the ten commandments, which are called the ten words. Exodus xxxiv. 28.— *Henry Ainsworth.*

Verses 7, 8.—" The testimony of the Lord is sure, enlightening the eyes," revealing the object, ennobling the organ.—*Richard Stock.*

Verses 7—11.—All of us are by nature the children of wrath ; our souls are like the *porches* of Bethesda (John v.), in which are lodged a great many " sick folk, blind, halt, withered ;" and the Scriptures are like the *pool* of Bethesda, into which whosoever entereth, after God's Holy Spirit hath a little stirred the water, is " made whole of whatsoever disease he hath." He that hath anger's frenzy, being as furious as a lion, by stepping into this pool shall in good time become as gentle as a lamb ; he that hath the blindness of intemperance, by washing in this pool shall easily see his folly ; he that hath envy's rust, avarice's leprosy, luxury's palsy, shall have means and medicines here for the curing of his mala-dies. *The word of God* is like the drug *catholicon*, that is instead of all purges ; and like the herb *panaces*, that is good for all diseases. Is any man heavy ? *the statutes of the Lord rejoice the heart :* is any man in want ? *the judgments of the Lord are more to be desired than gold, yea, than much fine gold, and by keep-ing of them there is great reward :* is any man ignorant ? *the testimonies of the Lord give wisdom to the simple,* that is, to little ones, both in standing and understanding. In standing, as unto little Daniel, little John the evangelist, little Timothy : to little ones in understanding ; for the great philosophers who were the wizards of the world, because they were not acquainted with God's law became fools while they professed themselves wise. Rom. i. 22. But our prophet saith, " I have more understanding than all my teachers, because thy testimonies are my meditation," and my study. Psalm cxix. 99. To conclude, whatsoever we are by corruption of nature, God's law *converteth* us, and maketh us to speak with new tongues, and to sing new songs unto the Lord, and to become new men and new creatures in Christ. 2 Cor. v. 17.—*J. Boys.*

Verse 8.—" *The statutes.*"—Many divines and critics, and Castalio in particular, have endeavoured to attach a distinct shade of meaning to the words, *law, testimony, the statutes, commandments, fear, judgments,* occurring in this context. תּוֹרָה, *the law,* has been considered to denote the perceptive part of revelation. עֵדוּת, *the testimony,* has been restricted to the doctrinal part. פִּקּוּדִים, *the statutes,* has been regarded as relating to such things as have been given in charge. מִצְוָה, *the commandment,* has been taken to express the general body of the divine law and doctrine. יִרְאָה, *religious fear.* מִשְׁפָּטִים, *the judgments,* the civil statutes of the Mosaic law, more particularly the penal sanctions.—*John Morison.*

Verse 8.—" *The statutes of the Lord are right, rejoicing the heart.*" How odious is the profaneness of those Christians who neglect the Holy Scriptures, and give themselves to reading other books ! How many precious hours do many spend, and that not only on work days, but holy days, in foolish romances, fabulous histories, lascivious poems ! And why this, but that they may be cheered and delighted, when as full joy is only to be had in these holy books. Alas ! the joy you find in those writings is perhaps pernicious, such as tickleth your lust, and promoteth contemplative wickedness. At the best it is but vain, such as only pleaseth the fancy and affecteth the wit ; whereas these holy writings (to use David's expression), are " *right, rejoicing the heart.*" Again, are there not many who more set by Plutarch's morals, Seneca's epistles, and such like books, than they do by the Holy Scriptures ? It is true, beloved, there are excellent truths in those moral writings of the heathen, but yet they are far short of these sacred books. Those may comfort against outward trouble, but not against inward fears ; they may rejoice the mind, but cannot quiet the conscience ; they may kindle some flashy sparkles of joy, but they cannot warm the soul with a lasting fire of solid consolations. And truly, brethren, if ever God give you a spiritual ear to judge of things aright, you will then acknowledge there are no bells like to those of Aaron's, no harp like to that of David's, no trumpet like to that of Isaiah's, no pipes like to those of the apostle's ; and, you will confess with Petrus Damianus, that those writings of heathen orators, philosophers, poets, which formerly were so pleasing, are now dull and harsh in comparison of the comfort of the Scriptures.—*Nathanael Hardy, D.D.*, 1618—1670.

Verse 10.—" *Sweeter than honey and the honeycomb.*" Love the word written. Psa. cxix. 97. " Oh, how love I thy law !" " Lord," said Augustine, " let the holy Scriptures be my chaste delight." Chrysostom compares the Scripture to a garden, every truth is a fragrant flower, which we should wear, not on our bosom, but in our heart. David counted the word " *sweeter than honey and the honeycomb.*" There is that in Scripture which may breed delight. It shows us the way to riches : Deut. xxviii. 5, Prov. iii. 10 ; to long life : Psa. xxxiv. 12 ; to a kingdom : Heb. xii. 28. Well, then, may we count those the *sweetest hours* which are spent in reading the holy Scriptures ; well may we say with the prophet (Jer. xv. 16), " Thy words were found and I did eat them ; and they were the joy and rejoicing of my heart."—*Thomas Watson.*

Verse 10.—" *Sweeter than honey and the honeycomb.*" There is no difference made amongst us between the delicacy of honey in the comb and that which is separated from it. From the information of Dr. Halle, concerning the diet of the Moors of Barbary, we learn that they esteem honey a very wholesome breakfast, " and the most delicious that which is in the comb with the young

bees in it, before they come out of their cases, whilst they still look milk-white."
(*Miscellanea Curiosa,* vol. iii. p. 382.) The distinction made by the psalmist is
then perfectly just and conformable to custom and practice, at least of most
modern, and probably, equally so of ancient times.—*Samuel Burder, A.M., in
" Oriental Customs,"* 1812.

Verse 11.—*" Moreover by them is thy servant warned."* A certain Jew had
formed a design to poison Luther, but was disappointed by a faithful friend,
who sent Luther a portrait of the man, with a warning against him. By this,
Luther knew the murderer and escaped his hands. Thus the word of God, O
Christian, shows thee the face of those lusts which Satan employs to destroy
thy comforts and poison thy soul.—*G. S. Bowes, B.A., in " Illustrative Gatherings for Preachers and Teachers,"* 1860.

Verse 11.—*" In keeping of them there is great reward."* This *" keeping of
them"* implies great carefulness to know, to remember, and to observe ; and the
" reward " (lit. *" the end "*), *i.e.,* the recompense, is far beyond anticipation.—
W. Wilson.

Verse 11.—*" In keeping of them there is great reward."* Not only for keeping, but in keeping of them, there is great reward. The joy, the rest, the
refreshing, the comforts, the contents, the smiles, the incomes that saints now
enjoy, in the ways of God, are so precious and glorious in their eyes, that they
would not exchange them for ten thousand worlds. Oh ! if the vails,[*]
be thus sweet and glorious before pay-day comes, what will be that glory
that Christ will crown his saints with for cleaving to his service in the face
of all difficulties, when he shall say to his Father, " Lo, here am I, and the
children which thou hast given me." Isa. viii. 18. If there be so much to be
had in the wilderness, what then shall be had in paradise !—*Thomas Brooks.*

Verse 11.—*" In keeping of them there is great reward."* Not only *for keeping*
but *in keeping* of them. As every flower hath its sweet smell, so every good
action hath its sweet reflection upon the soul : and as Cardan saith, that every
precious stone hath some egregious virtue ; so here, righteousness is its own
reward, though few men think so, and act accordingly. Howbeit, the chief
reward is not till the last cast, till we come to heaven. The word here rendered
" reward," signifieth *the heel,* and by a metaphor, the *end* of a work, and the
reward of it, which is not till the end.—*John Trapp.*

Verse 11.—*" Reward."* Though we should not serve God for a reward, yet
we shall have a reward for our service. The time is coming when ungodliness
shall be as much prosecuted by justice, as in times past godliness had been
persecuted by injustice. Though our reward be not for our good works, yet
we shall have our good works rewarded, and have a good reward for our works.
Though the best of men (they being at the best but unprofitable servants)
deserve nothing at the hands of God, yet they may deserve much at the hands
of men ; and if they have not the recompense they deserve, yet it is a kind of
recompense to have deserved. As he said, and nobly, " I had rather it should
be said, Why doth not Cato's image stand here ? than that it should be said,
Why doth it stand here ?"—*Ralph Venning.* 1620—1673.

Verse 12.—*" Who can understand his errors?"* After this survey of the
works and word of God, he comes at last to peruse the third book, his
conscience ; a book which though wicked men may keep shut up, and naturally
do not love to look into it, yet will one day be laid open before the great
tribunal in the view of the whole world, to the justifying of God when he
judges, and to impenitent sinners' eternal confusion. And what finds he here ?
A foul, blurred copy that he is puzzled how to read ; *" who,"* says he, *" can
understand his errors?"* Those notions which God had with his own hand

---

[*] Gratuities, presents.

imprinted upon conscience in legible characters, are partly defaced and slurred with scribble, and interlinings of " *secret faults ;*" partly obliterated and quite razed out with capital crimes, " presumptuous sins." And yet this *manuscript* cannot be so abused, but it will still give in evidence for God ; there being no argument in the world that can with more force extort an acknowledgment of God from any man's conscience than the conviction of guilt itself labours under. For the sinner cannot but know he has transgressed a law, and he finds within him, if he is not past all sense, such apprehensions that though at present he " walk in the ways of his heart and in the sight of his eyes" (as the wise man ironically advises the young man to do, Ecc. xi. 9), yet he knows (as the same wise man there from his own experience tells him) that " for all these things God will bring him into judgment." The *conscience* being thus convicted of sin, where there is any sense of true piety the soul will, with David, here address itself to God for pardon, that it may be " *cleansed from secret faults ;*" and for grace, that by its restraints, and preventions, and assistances, it may be " *kept back from presumptuous sins,*" and if unhappily engaged, that it may be freed at least from the " *dominion*" of them—" *Keep back thy servant also from presumptuous sins ; let them not have dominion over me,*" etc.—*Adam Littleton.*

Verse 12.—The prophet saith, " *Who can understand his own faults ?*" No man can, but God can ; therefore reason after this manner, as Saint Bernard saith : I know and am known ; I know but in part, but God knows me and knows me wholly ; but what I know, I know but in part. So the apostle reasons ; " I know nothing of myself, yet am I not hereby justified."

Admit that thou keepest thyself so free, and renewest thy repentance so daily that thou knowest nothing by thyself, yet mark what the apostle adds further ; " Notwithstanding, I do not judge myself I am not hereby justified, but he that judgeth me is the Lord." This is the condition of all men ; he that is infinite knows them ; therefore they should not dare to judge themselves, but with the prophet David, in Psalm xix., entreat the Lord that he would cleanse them from their secret sins.—*Richard Stock.*

Verse 12.—" *Who can understand his own errors?*" None can to the depth and bottom. In this question there are two considerables :—1. A concession ; 2. A confession. He makes a grant that *our life is full of errors ;* and the Scriptures say the same, while they affirm that " All we like sheep have gone astray" (Isa. liii. 6) ; " I have gone astray like a lost sheep" (Psa. cxix. 176) ; that the " house of Israel " hath " lost sheep," Matt. x. 6. I need not reckon up the particulars, as the errors of our senses, understandings, consciences, judgments, wills, affections, desires, actions, and occurrences. The whole man *in nature* is like a tree nipped at root, which brings forth worm-eaten fruits. The whole man *in life* is like an instrument out of tune, which jars at every stroke. If we cannot understand them, certainly they are very many.—*Robert Abbot,* 1646.

Verse 12.—" *Who can understand his errors ?*" If a man repent not until he have made confession of all his sins in the ear of his ghostly father, if a man cannot have absolution of his sins until his sins be told by tale and number in the priest's ear ; in that, as David saith, *none* can understand, much less, then, utter all his sins : *Delicta quis intelligat ?* " *Who can understand his sins ?*" In that David of himself complaineth elsewhere how that his " sins are overflowed his head, and as a heavy burden do depress him" (Psalm xxxviii. 4) ; alas ! shall not a man by this doctrine be utterly driven from repentance ? Though they have gone about something to make plasters for their sores, of confession or attrition to assuage their pain, bidding a man to hope well of his contrition, though it be not so full as is required, and of his confession, though he have not numbered all his sins, if so be that he do so much as in him lieth ; dearly beloved, in that there is none but that herein he is guilty (for who doth as much as he may ?) trow ye that this plaster is not like salt for sore eyes ? Yes, undoubtedly, when they have done all they can for the appeasing of consciences in these points, this is the sum, that we yet should hope well, but yet so hope that we must stand in a mammering * and doubting whether our sins be forgiven. For to believe *remissionem peccatorum*, that is to be certain of "forgiveness of sins," as our creed teacheth us, they count it a presumption. Oh, abomination! and that not only herein, but in all their penance as they paint it. *John Bradford (Martyr)*, 1510—1555.

Verse 12.—"*Who can understand his errors?*" By "*errors*" he means his unwitting and inconsiderate mistakes. There are sins, some of which are committed when the sun shines—*i.e.*, with light and knowledge ; and then, as it is with colours when the sun shines, you may see them ; so these, a man can see, and know, and confess them particularly to be transgressions. There are other sins which are committed either in the times of ignorance, or else (if there be knowledge), yet with unobservance. Either of these may be so heaped up in the particular number of them, that as a man did when he did commit them, take no notice of them ; so now, after the commission, if he should take the brightest candle to search all the records of his soul, yet many of them would escape his notice. And, indeed, this is a great part of our misery, that we cannot understand all our debts. We can easily see too many, yet many more lie, as it were, dead and out of sight. To sin is one great misery, and then to forget our sins is a misery too. If in repentance we could set the battle in array, point to every individual sin in the true and particular times of acting and re-acting, oh, how would our hearts be more broken with shame and sorrow, and how would we adore the richness of the treasure of mercy which must have a multitude in it to pardon the multitude of our infinite errors and sins. But this is the comfort ; though we cannot understand every particular sin, or time of sinning, yet if we be not idle to search and cast over the books, and if we be heartily grieved for these sins which we have found out, and can by true repentance turn from them unto God, and by faith unto the blood of Jesus Christ, I say that God, who knows our sins better than we can know them, and who understands the true intentions and dispositions of the heart—that if it did see the unknown sins it would be answerably carried against them—he will for his own mercy sake forgive them, and he, too, will not remember them. Nevertheless, though David saith, "*Who can understand his errors?*" as the prophet Jeremiah spake also, "The heart of man is desperately wicked, who can know it ?" yet must we bestir ourselves at heaven to get more and more heavenly light, to find out more and more of our sinnings. So the Lord can search the heart ; and, though we shall never be able to find out all our sins which we have committed, yet it is proper and beneficial for us to find out yet more sins than yet we do know. And you shall find these in your own experience ; that as soon as ever grace entered your hearts, you saw sin in another way than you ever saw it before ; yea, and the more grace hath traversed and increased in the soul, the more full discoveries hath it made of sins. It hath shown new sins as it were ; new sins, not for their being, not as if they were not in the heart and life before, but for their evidence and our apprehension. We do now see such wages and such inclinations to be sinful which we did not think to be so before. As physic brings those humours which had their residence before now more to the sense of the patient, or as the sun makes open the motes of dust which were in the room before, so doth the light of the word discover more corruption.—*Obadiah Sedgwick.*

Verse 12.—"*Who can understand his errors?*" Who can tell how oft he offendeth ? No man. The hairs of a man's head may be told, the stars appear in multitudes, yet some have undertaken to reckon them ; but no arithmetic can number our sins. Before we can recount a thousand we shall commit ten thousand more ; and so rather multiply by addition than divide by subtraction ; there is no possibility of numeration. Like Hydra's head, while we are cutting off twenty by repentance, we find a hundred more grown up. It is just, then, that infinite sorrows shall follow infinite sins.—*Thomas Adams.*

---

* Hesitating.

Verse 12.—" *Cleanse thou me from secret faults.*" It is the desire of a holy person to be cleansed, not only from public, but also from *private and secret sins.* Rom. vii. 24. " O wretched man (saith Paul), who shall deliver me ?" Why, O blessed apostle ! what is it that holds thee ? What is it that molests thee ? Thy life, thou sayest, was unblamable before thy conversion, and since thy conversion. Phil. iii. Thou hast exercised thyself to have always a conscience void of offence toward God and toward men. Acts xxiv. 16. And yet thou criest out, " O wretched man," and yet thou complainest, " Who shall deliver me ?" Verily, brethren, it was not sin abroad, but at home : it was not sin without, but at this time sin within ; it was not Paul's sinning with man, but Paul's sinning within Paul : oh ! that " law of his members warring (secretly within him) against the law of his mind ;" this, this made that holy man so to cry out, so to complain. As Rebekah was weary of her life, not as we read for any foreign disquietments, but because of domestic troubles : " The daughters of Heth" within the house made her " weary of her life ;" so the private and secret birth of corruption within Paul—the workings of that—that was the cause of his trouble, that was the ground of his exclamation and desires, " Who shall deliver me ?" I remember that the same Paul adviseth the Ephesians as " to put off the former conversation" so " to put on the renewed spirit of the mind " (Eph. iv.º 22, 23) ; intimating that there are sins lurking within as well as sins walking without ; and that true Christians must not only sweep the door, but wash the chamber ; my meaning is, not only come off from sins which lie open in the conversation, but also labour to be cleansed from sins and sinning which remain secret and hidden in the spirit and inward disposition.—*Obadiah Sedgwick.*

Verse 12.—" *Cleanse thou me from secret faults.*" Learn to see thy spots. Many have unknown sins, as a man may have a mole on his back and himself never know it. Lord, cleanse me from my secret faults. But have we not spots whereof we are not ignorant ? In diseases sometimes nature is strong enough to put forth spots, and there she cries to us by these outward declarations that we are sick. Sometimes she cannot do it but by the force of cordials. Sometimes conscience of herself shows us our sins ; sometimes she cannot but by medicines, arguments that convince us out of the holy word. Some can see, and will not, as Balaam ; some would see, and cannot, as the eunuch ; some neither will nor can, as Pharaoh ; some both can and will, as David. . . . . We have many spots which God does not hear from us, because we see them not in ourselves. Who will acknowledge that error, whereof he does not know himself guilty ? ·The sight of sins is a great happiness, for it causeth an ingenuous confession.—*Thomas Adams.*

Verse 12.—" *Cleanse thou me from secret faults.*"—The law of the Lord is so holy that forgiveness must be prayed for, even for hidden sins. (*Note*—This was a principal text of the Reformers against the auricular confession of the Roman Catholics.)—*T. C. Barth's " Bible Manual.*" 1865.

Verse 12.—" *Secret faults.*" Sins may be termed " *secret* " either, 1. *When they are coloured and disguised*—though they do fly abroad, yet not under that name, but apparelled with some semblance of virtues. Cyprian complains of such tricks in his second epistle, which is to Donatus. 2. *When they are kept off from the stage of the world ;* they are like fire in the chimney ; though you do not see it, yet it burns. So many a person, like those in Ezekiel, " commit abominations in secret"—that is, so as the public eye is not upon them. He is sinful, and acts it with the greatest vileness ; all the difference betwixt another sinner and him is this—that he is, and the other saith he is, a sinner. Just as 'twixt a book shut and a book opened ; that which is shut hath the same lines and words, but the other being opened every man may see and read them. 3. *When they are kept, not only from the public eye, but from any mortal eye ;* that is, the carnal eye of him who commits the sins sees them not ; he doth, indeed, see them with the eye of conscience, but not with an eye of natural sense. Even those persons with whom he doth converse, and who highly commend the frame of his ways, cannot yet see the secret discoursings and actings of sin in his mind and heart. For, brethren, all the actings of sin are not without, they are not visible ; but there are some, yea, the most dangerous actings within the soul, where corruption lies as a fountain and root. The heart of man is a scheme of wickedness ; nay, a man saith that in his heart which he dares not speak with his tongue, and his thought will do that which his hands dare not to execute. Well, then, sin may be called " *secret* " when it is sin, and acted as sin, even there, where none but God and conscience can see. Methinks sin is like a candle in a lantern, where the shining is first within and then bursting out at the windows ; or like evils and ulcerous humours, which are scabs and scurvy stuff, first within the skin, and afterwards they break out to the view on the outside. So it is with sin ; it is a malignant humour and a fretting leprosy, diffusing itself into several secret acts and workings within the mind, and then it breaks abroad and dares adventure the practice of itself to the eye of the world ; and be it that it may never see the light, that it may be like a child born and buried in the womb, yet as that child is a man, a true man there closeted in that hidden frame of nature, so sin is truly sin, though it never gets out beyond the womb which did conceive and enliven it.— *Obadiah Sedgwick.*

Verse 12.—" *Secret faults.*" " *Secret sins*" are more dangerous to the person in some respects than open sins. For *a man doth, by his art of sinning, deprive himself of the help of his sinfulness.* Like him who will carry his wound covered, or who bleeds inwardly, help comes not in because the danger is not descried nor known. If a man's sin breaks out there is a minister at hand, a friend near, and others to reprove, to warn, to direct ; but when he is the artificer of his lusts, he bars himself of all public remedy, and takes great order and care to damn his soul, by covering his " *secret sins*" with some plausible varnish which may beget a good opinion in others of his ways. *A man does by his secrecy give the reins unto corruption :* the mind is fed all the day long either with sinful contemplations or projectings, so that the very strength of the soul is wasted and corrupted. Nay, *secret actings do but heat and inflame natural corruption.* As in shouldering in a crowd, when one hath got out of the door, two or three are ready to fall out after ; so when a man hath given his heart leave to act a secret sin, this begets a present, and quick, and strong flame in corruption to repeat and multiply and throng out the acts. Sinful acts are not only fruits of sin, but helps and strengths, all sinning being more sinful by more sinning, not only in the effects but in the cause : the spring and cause of sin will grow mad and insolent hereby, and more corrupt ; this being a truth, that if the heart gives way for one sin, it will be ready for the next ; if it will yield to bring forth once at the devil's pleasure, it will bring it forth twice by its own motion. A man by " *secret sins* " doth but polish and square the hypocrisy of his heart : he doth strive to be an exact hypocrite ; and the more cunning he is in the palliating of his sinnings, the more perfect he is in his hypocrisy.— *Obadiah Sedgwick.*

Verse 12.—" *Secret faults.*" Beware of committing acts which it will be necessary to conceal. There is a singular poem by Hood, called " The Dream of Eugene Aram"—a most remarkable piece it is indeed, illustrating the point on which we are now dwelling. Aram had murdered a man, and cast his body into the river—" a sluggish water, black as ink, the depth was so extreme." The next morning he visited the scene of his guilt—

> " And sought the black accursed pool,
>   With a wild misgiving eye ;
> And he saw the dead in the river bed,
>   For the faithless stream was dry."

Next he covered the corpse with heaps of leaves, but a mighty wind swept through the wood and left the secret bare before the sun—

> " Then down I cast me on my face,
>   And first began to weep,
> For I knew my secret then was one
>   That earth refused to keep :
> On land or sea though it should be
>   Ten thousand fathoms deep.

In plaintive notes he prophesies his own discovery. He buried his victim in a cave, and trod him down with stones, but when years had run their weary round, the foul deed was discovered and the murderer put to death.

Guilt is a "grim chamberlain," even when his fingers are not bloody red. Secret sins bring fevered eyes and sleepless nights, until men burn out their consciences, and become in very deed ripe for the pit. Hypocrisy is a hard game to play at, for it is one deceiver against many observers ; and for certain it is a miserable trade, which will earn at last, as its certain climax, a tremendous bankruptcy. Ah ! ye who have sinned without discovery, "Be sure your sin will find you out ;" and bethink you, it may find you out ere long. Sin, like murder, will come out ; men will even tell tales about themselves in their dreams. God has made men to be so wretched in their consciences that they have been obliged to stand forth and confess the truth. Secret sinner ! if thou wantest the foretaste of damnation upon earth, continue in thy secret sins ; for no man is more miserable than he who sinneth secretly, and yet trieth to preserve a character. Yon stag, followed by the hungry hounds, with open mouths, is far more happy than the man who is pursued by his sins. Yon bird, taken in the fowler's net, and labouring to escape, is far more happy than he who hath weaved around himself a web of deception, and labours to escape from it, day by day making the toils more thick and the web more strong. Oh the misery of secret sins ! One may well pray, "Cleanse thou me from secret faults."—*Spurgeon's Sermon* (No. 116), on "Secret Sins."

Verse 12.—The sin through ignorance (שְׁגָגָה) is the same that David prays against in Psalm xix. 12, "Who can understand his *errors* (שְׁגִיאוֹת) ? cleanse thou me from secret things !" These are not sins of omission, but acts committed by a person, when at the time, he did not suppose that what he did was sin. Although he did the thing deliberately, yet he did not perceive the sin of it. So deceitful is sin, we may be committing that abominable thing which cast angels into an immediate and an eternal hell, and yet at the moment be totally unaware ! Want of knowledge of the truth, and too little tenderness of conscience hide it from us. Hardness of heart and a corrupt nature cause us to sin unperceived. But here again the form of the Son of Man appears ! Jehovah, God of Israel, institutes sacrifice for *sins of ignorance*, and thereby discovers the same compassionate and considerate heart that appears in our High Priest, "who can have compassion on the *ignorant !*" Heb. v. 2. Amidst the types of this tabernacle, we recognize the presence of Jesus—it is his voice that shakes the curtains, and speaks in the ear of Moses, "If a soul shall sin through ignorance !" The same yesterday, to-day, and for ever !—*Andrew A. Bonar, in "Commentary on Leviticus,"* ch. iv. v. 2.

Verse 12 (last clause).—This is a singular difference between pharisaical and real sanctity : that is curious to look abroad, but seeth nothing at home : so that Pharisee condemned the Publican, and saw nothing in himself worthy of blame ; but this careful to look at home, and searcheth into the secret corners, the very spirit of the mind. So did good David when he prayed, "*Cleanse thou me from secret faults.*"—*Nathanael Hardy.*

Verse 12.—Our corruptions have made us such combustible matter, that there is scarce a dart thrown at us in vain : when Satan tempts us, it is but like the casting of fire into tinder, that presently catcheth : our hearts kindle upon the least spark that falls ; as a vessel that is brimful of water, upon the least jog, runs over. Were we but true to ourselves, though the devil might knock by his temptations, yet he could never burst open the everlasting doors of our hearts by force or violence : but, alas ! we ourselves are not all of one heart and one mind : Satan hath got a strong party within us, that, as soon as he knocks, opens to him, and entertains him. And hence it is, that many times, small temptations and very petty occasions draw forth great corruptions : as a vessel, that is full of new liquor, upon the least vent given, works over into foam and froth ; so truly, our hearts, almost upon every slight and trivial temptation, make that inbred corruption that lodgeth there, swell and boil, and run over into abundance of scum and filth in our lives and conversations.— *Ezekiel Hopkins.*

Verse 12.—Sins are many times hid from the godly man's eye, though he commits them, because he is not diligent and accurate in making a search of himself, and in an impartial studying of his own ways. If any sin be hid, as Saul was behind the stuff, or as Rahab had hid the spies, unless a man be very careful to search, he shall think no sin is there where it is. Hence it is that the Scripture doth so often command that duty of *searching* and *trying*, of examining and communing with our hearts. Now what need were there of this duty, but that it is supposed many secret and subtle lusts lie lurking in our hearts, which we take no notice of? If then the godly would find out their hidden lusts, know the sins they not yet know, they must more impartially judge themselves ; they must take time to survey and examine themselves ; they must not in an overly and slight manner, but really and industriously look up and down as they would search for thieves ; and they must again and again look into this dark corner, and that dark corner of their hearts, as the woman sought for the lost groat. This self-scrutiny, and self-judging, this winnowing and sifting of ourselves, is the only way to see what is chaff and what is wheat, what is mere refuse and what is enduring.—*Anthony Burgess.*

Verse 12.—Sin is of a growing and advancing nature. From weakness to wilfulness, from ignorance to presumption, is its ordinary course and progress. The cloud that Elijah's man saw, was at first no bigger than a hand's-breadth, and it threatened no such thing as a general tempest ; but yet, at last, it overspread the face of the whole heavens ; so truly, a sin that at first ariseth in the soul but as a small mist, and is scarcely discernible ; yet, if it be not scattered by the breath of prayer, it will at length overspread the whole life, and become most tempestuous and raging. And therefore, David, as one experienced in the deceitfulness of sin, doth thus digest and methodise his prayer : first against secret and lesser sins ; and then against the more gross and notorious ; as knowing the one proceeds and issues from the other : Lord, *cleanse me from my secret faults ;* and this will be a most effectual means to preserve and *keep thy servant from presumptuous sins.*—*Ezekiel Hopkins.*

Verses 12, 13.—That there is a difference betwixt *infirmities* and *presumptuous sins* is not to be denied ; it is expressly in the holy Scripture. Papists say that the man who doth a mortal sin is not in the state of grace ; but for venials, a man may commit (in their divinity) who can tell how many of them, and yet be in Christ for all that ! I hope there is no such meaning in any of our divines as to tie up men's consciences, to hang on such a distinction of sins ; since it is beyond the wit of man to set down a distinct point between mortal and venial sins. Now when it is an impossible matter punctually to set down to the understanding of man which is, and which is not a venial sin, they must pardon me for giving the least way to such divinity as must needs leave the conscience of a man in a maze and labyrinth. I find that the nature of infirmities doth so depend upon circumstances, that that is an infirmity in one man which is a gross sin in another ; and some men plead for themselves that the things they do are but infirmities. He that *will* sin, and when he hath done will say—not to comfort his soul against Satan, but—to flatter himself in his sin, that it is but an infirmity ; for aught I know, he may go to hell for his infirmities. Besides, if that be good divinity, that a man who is in the state of grace may do infirmities, but not commit gross sins, then I would I could see a man that would undertake to find us out some rule out of the word, by which a sinner may find by his sin, when he is in Christ and when out of Christ ; at what degrees of sinning—where lies the mathematical point and stop—that a man may say, " Thus far may I go and yet be in grace ; but if I step a step farther, then I am none of Christ's." We all know that sins have their latitude ; and for a man to hang his conscience on such a distinction as hath no rule to define where the difference lies, is not safe divinity. The conscience on the rack will not be laid and said with forms and quiddities. The best and nearest way to quiet the heart of man is to say, that be the sin a sin of *infirmity* when we strive and strive but yield at last ; or, of *precipitancy*, when we be taken in haste, as he was who said in his haste, " All men are liars ;" or, a mere *gross* sin in the matter : ay, say it be a *presumptuous* sin, yet if we allow it not, it hinders not but we are in Christ, though we do with reluctancy act and commit it. And I say that we do resist it if we do not allow it. For let us not go about to deny that a godly man during his being a godly man may possibly commit *gross* and *presumptuous sins ;* and for infirmities, if we allow them and like them that we know to be sins, then we do not resist them ; and such a man who allows himself in one is guilty of all, and is none of Christ's as yet. Be the sin what it will, James makes no distinction ; and, where the law distinguisheth not, we must not distinguish. I speak not of *doing* a sin, but *allowing ;* for a man may do it, and yet allow it not ; as in Paul (Rom. vii. 15, 16), " That which I would not, that I do ;" and he that allows not sin doth resist it. Therefore, a man may resist it, hate it, and yet do it. All the difference that I know is this : 1. That a man may live after his conversion all his days, and yet never fall into a gross sin. By gross here I mean *presumptuous* sins also. So David saith not " *cleanse,*" but " KEEP BACK *thy servant from presumptuous sins.*" We may, then, be *kept* from them. I speak not that all are, but some be ; and, therefore, in itself all might be. 2. For lesser sins, " *secret faults,*" we cannot live without them—they are of daily and almost hourly incursion ; but yet we must be *cleansed* from them, as David speaks. Daily get your pardon ; there is a pardon, of course, for them ; they do not usually distract and plague the conscience, but yet we must not see them and allow them ; if we do our case is to be pitied, we are none of Christ's as yet. 3. Great staring sins a man cannot usually and commonly practise them, but he shall allow them. So Psalm xix. 13, " *Keep back thy servant from presumptuous sins ; let them not have dominion over me,*" implying that except we be kept back from them they will *have dominion over us.* It follows, " *then shall I be upright ;*" so that the man in whom *gross or presumptuous sin or sins* have no *dominion,* he is an *upright man.—Richard Capel.*

Verses 12, 13.—The psalmist was sensible of sin's force and power ; he was weary of sin's dominion ; he cries unto God to deliver him from the reign of all the sins he knew ; and those sins which were secret and concealed from his view, he begs that he might be convinced of them, and thoroughly cleansed from them. The Lord can turn the heart perfectly to hate the sin that was most of all beloved ; and the strength of sin is gone when once 'tis hated ; and as the hatred grows stronger and stronger, sin becomes weaker and weaker daily.—*Nathaniel Vincent,* 1695.

Verse 13.—" *Keep back thy servant also from all presumptuous sins.*" He doth desire absolutely to be kept from " *presumptuous sins ;*" but then, he adds by way of supposition and reserve, that if he could not by reason of his naughty heart be kept from them, yet that they might not have full power and dominion over him.—*Thomas Manton.*

Verse 13.—" *Keep back thy servant.*" It is an evil man's cross to be restrained, and a good man's joy to be *kept back* from sin. When sin puts forth itself, the evil man is putting forth his hand to the sin ; but when sin puts forth itself, the good man is putting forth his hand to heaven ; if he finds his heart yielding, out he cries, O *keep back thy servant.* An evil man is *kept back* from sin, as a friend from a friend, as a lover from his lover, with knit affections and projects of meeting ; but a good man is *kept back* from sin, as a man from his deadly enemy, whose presence he hates, and with desires of his ruin and destruction. It is the good man's misery that he hath yet a heart to be more tamed and mastered ; it is an evil man's vexation and discontent, that still, or at any time, he is held in by cord or bridle. And thus you see what David aims at in desiring to be *kept back from presumptuous sins,* namely, not a mere suspension, but a mortification, not a not acting only, but a subduing of the inclination ; not for a time, but for ever.—*Obadiah Sedgwick.*

Verse 13.—" *Keep back thy servant,*" etc. Even all the people of God, were they not kept by God's grace and power, they would every moment be undone both in soul and body. It is not our grace, our prayer, our watchfulness keeps us, but it is the power of God, his right arm, supports us ; we may see David praying to God that he would " *keep*" him in both these respects from temporal dangers (Psalm xvii. 8, 9 ; " *keep me,*") etc. ; where he doth not only pray to be kept, but he doth insinuate how carefully God keeps his people, and in what precious account their safety is, even as " the apple of the eye," and for spiritual preservation he often begs it. Though David be God's " *servant* " yet he will, like a wild horse, run violently, and that into " *presumptuous sins,*" if God " *keep*" him not " *back,*" yea, he prayeth that God would " *keep*" the particular parts of his body that they sin not : " keep the door of my lips" (Psalm cxli. 3) ; he entreateth God to " *keep*" his lips and to set a watch about his mouth, as if he were not able to set guard sure enough : thus much more are we to pray that God would " *keep*" our hearts, our minds, our wills, our affections, for they are more masterful.—*Anthony Burgess.*

Verse 13.—" *Keep back thy servant.*" God *keeps back* his servants from sin, 1. *By preventing grace,* which is, by infusing such a nature as is like a bias into a bowl, drawing it aside another way ; 2. *By assisting grace,* which is a further strength superadded to that first-implanted nature of holiness ; like a hand upon a child holding him in ; 3. *By quickening grace,* which is, when God doth enliven our graces to manifest themselves in actual opposition ; so that the soul shall not yield, but keep off from entertaining the sin ; 4. *By directing grace,* which is, when God confers that effectual wisdom to the mind, tenderness to the conscience, watchfulness to the heart, that his servants become greatly solicitous of his honour, scrupulously jealous of their own strength, and justly regardful of the honour of their holy profession ; 5. *By doing grace,* which is, when God effectually inclines the hearts of his servants to the places and ways of their refuge, safeties, and preservations from sin, by enlarging the spirit of supplication, and framing the heart to the reverent and affectionate use of his ordinances.—*Condensed from Obadiah Sedgwick.*

Verse 13.—" *Thy servant :*" as if he had said, " O God, thou art my Lord, I have chosen thee, to whom I will give obedience ; thou art he whom I will follow ; I bestow all that I am on thee. Now a lord will help his servant against an enemy, who for the lord's service is the servant's enemy. O my Lord, help me ! I am not able by my own strength to uphold myself, but thou art All-sufficiency"—" *Keep back thy servant from presumptuous sins.*" . . . Beloved, it is a great thing to stand in near relations to God ; and then it is a good thing to plead by them with God, forsomuch as nearer relations have strongest force with all. The servant can do more than a stranger, and the child than a servant, and the wife than a child. . . . . . . There be many reasons against sinning. . . . Now this also may come in, namely, the speciality of our relation to God, that we are his children, and he is our Father ; we are his servants, and he is our Lord : though the common obligations are many and sufficient, yet the special relations are also a further tie : the more near a person comes to God, the more careful he should be not to sin against God.—*Obadiah Sedgwick.*

Verse 13.—" *Presumptuous sins.*" The Rabbins distinguish all sins unto those committed בִּשְׁוֹגֵג *ignorantly,* and קָרִיד *presumptuously.*—*Benjamin Kennicott, D.D.,* 1718—1783.

Verse 13.—" *Presumptuous sins.*" When sin grows up from act to delight, from delight to new acts, from repetition of sinful acts to vicious indulgence, to habit and custom and a second nature, so that anything that toucheth upon it is grievous, and strikes to the man's heart ; when it is got into God's place, and requires to be loved with the whole strength, makes grace strike sail, and other vices do it homage, demands all his concerns to be sacrificed to it and to be served with his reputation, his fortunes, his parts, his body and soul, to the irreparable loss of his time and eternity both—this is the height of its *dominion*—then sin becomes "exceedingly sinful," and must needs make strange and sad alterations in the state of saints themselves, and be great hindrances to them in their way to Heaven, having brought them so near to Hell."—*Adam Littleton.*

Verse 13.—"*Presumptuous sins.*" The distribution of sins into sins of *ignorance*, of *infirmity*, and of *presumption*, is very usual and very useful, and complete enough without the addition (which some make) of a fourth sort, to wit, sins of *negligence* or *inadvertency*, all such sins being easily reducible to some of the former three. The ground of the distinction is laid in the soul of man, where there are three distinct prime faculties, from which all our actions flow—the understanding, the will, and the sensual appetite or affections. . . . . The enquiry must be, when a sin is done, where the fault lay most ; and thence it must have the right denomination. 1. If the *understanding* be most in fault, not apprehending that good it should, or not aright, the sin so done, though possibly it may have in it somewhat both of infirmity and presumption withal, is yet properly a sin of *ignorance*. 2. If the main fault be in the *affections*, through some sudden passion òr perturbation of mind, blinding, or corrupting, or but outrunning the judgment—as of fear, angèr, desire, joy, or any of the rest—the sin thence arising, though perhaps joined with some ignorance or presumption withal, is yet properly a sin of *infirmity*. But if the understanding be competently informed with knowledge, and not much blinded or transported with the incursion of any sudden, or violence of any vehement perturbation, so as the greatest blame must remain upon the untowardness of the *will*, resolvedly bent upon the evil, the sin arising from such *wilfulness*, though probably not free from all mixture of ignorance and infirmity withal, is yet properly a *wilful presumption*, such a *presumptuous sin* as we are now in treaty of. Rules are soonest learned and best remembered when illustrated with fit examples ; and of such the rich storehouse of the Scripture affordeth us in each kind variety and choice enough, whence it shall suffice us to propose but one eminent of each sort. *The men*, all of them for their holiness, of singular and worthy renown : David, St. Peter, and St. Paul. *The sins*, all of them for their matter, of the greatest magnitude : murdering of the innocent, abnegation of Christ, persecution of the church : Paul's persecution a grievous sin, yet a sin of *ignorance ;* Peter's denial a grievous sin, yet a sin of *infirmity ;* David's murder, a far more grievous sin than either of both, because a sin of *presumption.* St. Paul, before his conversion, whilst he was Saul, persecuted and wasted the church of God to the utmost of his power, making havoc of the professors of Christ, entering into their very houses, and haling thence to prison, both men and women ; and posting abroad with letters into remote quarters, to do all the mischief he could, everywhere with great fury, as if he had been mad, breathing out, wherever he came, nothing but threatenings and slaughter against the disciples of the Lord. His *affections* were not set against them through any personal provocations, but merely out of zeal to the law ; and surely his zeal had been good had it not been blind. Nor did his *will* run cross to his judgment, but was led by it, for he "verily thought in himself that he ought to do many things contrary to the name of Jesus ;" and verily his will had been good had it not been misled. But the error was in his *understanding*, his judgment being not yet actually convinced of the truth of the Christian religion. He was yet fully persuaded that Jesus was an impostor, and Christianity a pestilent sect, raised by Satan, to the disgrace and prejudice of Moses and the law. If these things had indeed been so, as he apprehended them, his *affections* and *will*, in seeking to root out such a sect, had been not only blameless but commendable. It was his erroneous judgment that poisoned all, and made that which otherwise had been zeal, to become persecution. But, however, the first discernible obliquity therein being in the *understanding*, that persecution of his was therefore a *sin of ignorance*, so called, and under that name condemned by himself. 1 Tim. i. 13. But such was not Peter's denial of his Master. He *knew* well enough who he was having conversed so long with him, and having, long before, so amply confessed him. And he *knew* also that he ought not, for anything in the world, to have denied him. That made him so confident before that he *would not* do it, because he was abundantly satisfied that he *should not* do it. Evident it is, then, that Peter wanted no *knowledge*, either of the Master's person, or of his own duty; and so no plea left him of *ignorance*, either *facti* or *juris*. Nor was the fault so much in his *will* as to make it a sin properly of *presumption*. For albeit *de facto* he did deny him when he was put to it, and that with fearful oaths and imprecations, yet was it not done with any prepensed apostacy, or out of design, yea, he came rather with a *contrary resolution*, and he still honoured his Master *in his heart*, even then when he denied him with his tongue; and as soon as ever the watchword was given him by the second cock, to prefer to his consideration what he had done, it grieved him sore that he had so done, and he wept bitterly for it. We find no circumstance, in the whole relation, that argueth any deep obstinacy in his *will*. But in his *affections*, then! Alas! there was the fail! A sudden qualm of fear surprising his soul when he saw his Master so despitefully used before his face (which made him apprehensive of what hard usage himself might fall under if he should there and then have owned him) took from him for that time the benefit and use of his reason, and so drew all his thoughts to this one point—how to decline the present danger— that he had never a thought at so much liberty as to consult his judgment, whether it were a sin or no. And this, proceeding from such a sudden distemper of passion, Peter's denial was a sin properly of *infirmity*. But David's sin, in contriving the death of Uriah, was of a yet higher pitch, and of a deeper dye than either of these. He was no such stranger in the law of God as not to know that the wilful murder of an innocent party, such as he also knew Uriah to be, was a most loud crying sin; and therefore nothing surer than that it was not merely a sin of *ignorance*. Neither yet was it a sin properly of *infirmity*, and so capable of that extenuating circumstance of being done in the heat of anger, as his uncleanness with Bathsheba was in the heat of lust, although that extenuation will not be allowed to pass there, unless *in tanto* only, and as it standeth in comparison with this fouler crime. But having time and leisure enough to bethink himself what he was about, he doth it *in cool blood*, and with much advised *deliberation*, plotting and contriving this way and that way to perfect his design. He was *resolved*, whatsoever should become of it, to have it done; in regard of which *settled resolution of his will*, this sin of David was therefore a high *presumptuous sin.—Robert Sanderson (Bishop of Lincoln)*, 1587—1662–3.

Verse 13.—" Presumptuous sins." David prays that God would keep him back from *"presumptuous sins,"* from known and evident sins, such as proceed from the choice of the perverse will against the enlightened mind, which are committed with deliberation, with design, resolution, and eagerness, against the checks of conscience, and the motions of God's spirit: such sins are direct rebellion against God, a despising of his command, and they provoke his pure eyes.—*Alexander Cruden.*

Verse 13.—" Then shall I be innocent from the great transgression." It is in the motions of a tempted soul to sin, as in the motions of a stone falling from the brow of a hill; it is easily stopped at first, but when once it is set a-going, who shall stay it? And therefore it is the greatest wisdom in the world to observe the first motions of the heart, to check and stop it there.—*G. H. Salter.*

Verse 13.—" The great transgression." Watch very diligently against all sin; but above all, take special heed of those sins that come near to the sin against the Holy Ghost; and these are, hypocrisy, taking only the outward profession of religion, and so dissembling and mocking of God; sinning wilfully against conviction of conscience, and against great light and knowledge, sinning presumptuously, with a high hand. These sins, though none of them are the direct sin against the Holy Ghost, yet they will come very near to it: therefore take special heed of them, lest they, in time, should bring you to the committing of that unpardonable sin.—*Robert Russel,* 1705.

Verse 13.—" *Let them not have dominion over me.*" Any small sin may get the upper-hand of the sinner and bring him under in time, and after that is once habituated by long custom so as he cannot easily shake off the yoke, neither redeem himself from under the tyranny thereof. We see the experiment of it but too often, and too evidently in our common swearers and drunkards. Yet do such kind of sins, for the most part, grow on by little and little, steal into the throne insensibly, and do not *exercise dominion* over the enslaved soul till they have got strength *by many and multiplied acts.* But a *presumptuous sin* worketh a great alteration in the state of the soul *at once*, and by one single act advanceth marvellously, weakening the spirit, and giving a mighty advantage to the flesh, even to the hazard of *a complete conquest.*—*Robert Sanderson.*

Verse 13.—To sin presumptuously is the highest step. So in David's account ; for first he prays, " *Lord, keep me from secret sins,*" which he maketh sins of ignorance, and then next he prays against " *presumptuous sins,*" which, as the opposition shows, are sins against knowledge ; for says he, " if they get dominion over me, I shall not be free from that great offence," that is, that unpardonable sin which shall never be forgiven : so as these are nearest it of any other, yet not so as that every one that falls into such a sin commits it, but he is nigh to it, at the next step to it. For to commit that sin, but two things are required—light in the mind, and malice in the heart ; not malice alone, unless there be light, for then that apostle had sinned it, so as knowledge is the parent of it, it is " after receiving the knowledge of the truth." Heb. x. 27, 28.— *Thomas Goodwin.*

Verse 13.—Happy souls, who, under a sense of peace through the blood of Jesus, are daily praying to be kept by the grace of the Spirit. Such truly know themselves, see their danger of falling, will not, dare not palliate or lessen the odious nature, and hateful deformity of their sin. They will not give a softer name to sin than it deserves, lest they depreciate the infinite value of that precious blood which Jesus shed to atone its guilt. Far will they be from flattering themselves into a deceitful notion that they are perfect, and have no sin in them. The spirit of truth delivers them from such errors ; he teacheth them as poor sinners to look to the Saviour, and to beseech him to " *keep back*" the headstrong passions, the unruly lusts, and evil concupiscences which dwell in their sinful natures. Alas ! the most exalted saint, the most established believer, if left to himself, how soon might the blackest crimes, the most " *presumptuous sins,*" get the " *dominion*" over him ! David had woful experience of this for a season. He prays from a heartfelt sense of past misery, and the dread of future danger, and he found the blessing of that covenant-promise : " Sin shall not have dominion over you ; for ye are not under the law, but under grace." Rom. vi. 14.—*William Mason, 1719—1791, in* "*A Spiritual Treasury for the Children of God.*"

Verse 14.—" *Let the words of my mouth, and the meditation of my heart, be acceptable in thy sight, O Lord,*" was David's prayer. David could not bear it, that a word, or a thought of his should miss acceptation with God. It did not satisfy him that his actions were well witnessed unto men on earth, unless his very thoughts were witnessed to by the Lord in heaven.—*Joseph Caryl.*

Verse 14.—" *Let the words of my mouth,*" etc. The best of men have their failing, and an honest Christian may be a weak one ; but weak as he may be, the goodness and sincerity of his heart will entitle him to put the petition of this verse, which no hypocrite or cunning deceiver can ever make use of.— *Thomas Sherlock (Bishop), 1676—1761.*

Verse 14.—" *Let the words of my mouth, and the meditation of my heart be acceptable in thy sight, O Lord, my strength, and my Redeemer.*" Fast and pray ; Lord, I do fast, and I would pray ; for to what end do I withhold sustenance from my body if it be not the more to cheer up my soul ? my hungry, my thirsty soul ? But the bread, the water of life, both which I find nowhere but in thy word, I partake not but by exercising my soul therein. This I begin to do, and fain would do it well, but in vain shall I attempt except thou do bless : bless me then, O Lord ; bless either part of me, both are thine, and I would withhold neither part from thee. Not my body ; I would set my tongue on work to speak of thee ; not my soul, I would exercise my heart in thinking on thee ; I would join them in devotion which thou hast joined in creation. Yea, Lord, as they have conspired to sin against thee, so do they now consort to do their duty to thee ; my tongue is ready, my heart is ready ; I would think, I would speak ; think upon thee, speak to thee. But, Lord, what are my *words ?* what are my *thoughts ?* Thou knowest the thoughts of men, that they are altogether vanity, and our words are but the blast of such thoughts ; both are vile. It were well it were no more ; both are wicked, my heart a corrupt fountain, and my tongue an unclean stream ; and shall I bring such a sacrifice to God ? The halt, the lame, the blind, though otherwise the beasts be clean, yet are they sacrifices abominable to God : how much more if we offer those beasts which are unclean ? And yet, Lord, my sacrifice is no better, faltering words, wandering thoughts, are neither of them presentable to thee ; how much less evil thoughts and idle words ? Yet such are the best of mine. What remedy ? If any, it is in thee, O Lord, that I must find it, and for it now do I seek unto thee. Thou only, O Lord, canst hallow my tongue, and hallow my heart that my tongue may speak, and my heart think that which may *"be acceptable unto thee,"* yea, that which may be thy delight. Do not I lavish ? Were it not enough that God should bear with, that he should not punish, the defects of my words, of my thoughts ? May I presume that God shall accept of me ? nay, delight in me ? Forget I who the Lord is ? Of what majesty ? Of what felicity ? Can it stand with his Majesty to vouchsafe acceptance ? with his felicity to take content in the words of a worm ? in the thoughts of a wretch ? And, Lord, I am too proud that vilify myself so little, and magnify thee no more. But see whither the desire of thy servant doth carry him ; how, willing to please, I consider not how hard it is for dust and ashes to please God, to do that wherein God should take content. But Lord, here is my comfort, that I may set God to give content unto God ; God is *mine*, and I cannot want access unto God, if God may approach himself. Let me be weak, yet God is strong ; O Lord, thou art *" my strength."* Let me be a slave to sin, God is a *Saviour ;* O Lord, thou art *my Saviour ;* thou hast *redeemed* me from all that woful state whereunto Adam cast me, yea, thou hast built me upon a rock, strong and sure, that the gates of hell might never prevail against me. These two things hast thou done for me, O Lord, and what may not he presume of for whom thou hast done these things ! I fear not to come before thee. I presume my devotion shall content thee ; be thine eyes never such all-seeing eyes, I will be bold to present my inward, my outward man before thee ; be thy eyes never so holy eyes, I will not fly with Adam to hide my nakedness from thee, for I am able to keep my ground ; seeing I am supported by *my Lord*, I doubt not but to prove a true Israelite, and to prevail with God. For all my woe, for all my sin, I will not shrink, nay, I will approach, approach to thee, for thou art *" My Redeemer."* The nearer I come to thee, the freer shall I be both from sin and woe. Oh, blessed state of man who is so weak, so strong ; so wretched, and so happy ; weak in himself, strong in God ; most happy in God, though in himself a sinful wretch. And now, my soul, thou wouldst be devout ; thou mayst be what thou wouldst : sacrifice to God thy words, sacrifice to God thy thoughts, make thyself a holocaust, doubt not but thou shalt be accepted, thou shalt content even the most glorious, the most holy eyes of God. Only presume not of thyself, presume on him ; build thy words, build thy thoughts upon thy *Rock*, they shall not be shaken ; free thy words, free thy thoughts (thoughts and words enthralled to sin), by thy Saviour, and thy sacrifice shall be accepted. So let me build on thee, so let me be enlarged by thee, in soul, in body, that *" The words of my mouth, and the meditation of my heart, be acceptable in thy sight, O Lord, my strength, and my Redeemer."—Arthur Lake (Bishop), in " Divine Meditations,"* 1629.

HINTS TO THE VILLAGE PREACHER.

Verse 1.—" Chalmers' Astronomical Discourses " will suggest to the preacher many ways of handling this theme. The power, wisdom, goodness, punctuality, faithfulness, greatness, and glory of God are very visible in the heavens.

Verses 1—5.—Parallel between the heavens and the revelation of Scripture, dwelling upon Christ as the central Sun of Scripture.

Verse 1.—" *The heavens declare the glory of God.*" Work in which we may unite, the nobility, pleasure, usefulness, and duty of such service.

Verse 2.—Voices of the day and of the night. Day and night thoughts.

Verse 3 —The marginal reading, coupled with verse four, suggests the eloquence of an unobtrusive life—silent, yet heard.

Verse 4.—In what sense God is revealed to all men.

Verses 4, 5, 6.—The Sun of Righteousness. I. His tabernacle. II. His appearance as a Bridegroom. III. His joy as a champion. IV. His circuit and his influence.

Verse 5.—" *Rejoiceth as a strong man,*" etc. The joy of strength, the joy of holy labour, the joy of the anticipated reward.

Verse 6.—The permeating power of the gospel.

Verse 7 (first clause).— Holy Scripture. I. What it is—" law." II. Whose it is—" of the Lord." III. What is its character—" perfect." IV. What its result—" converting the soul."

Verse 7 (second clause).—I. Scholars. II. Class-book. III. Teacher. IV. Progress.

Verses 7, 8, 9.—The Hexapla. *See Notes.*

Verse 7 (last clause).—The wisdom of a simple faith.

Verse 8 (first clause).—The heart-cheering power of the Word. I. Founded in its righteousness. II. Real in its quality. III. Constant in its operation.

Verse 8 (second clause).—Golden ointment for the eyes.

Verse 9.—The purity and permanence of true religion, and the truth and justice of the principles upon which it is founded.

Verse 10.—Two arguments for loving God's statutes—Profit and Pleasure.

Verse 10.—The inexpressible delights of meditation on Scripture.

Verse 11 (first clause).—I. What ? " Warned." II. How ? " By them." III. Who ? " Thy servant." IV. When ? " Is"—present.

Verse 11 (second clause).—Evangelical rewards—" *In,*" not *for* keeping.

Verse 12.—See " Spurgeon's Sermons," No. 116. " Secret Sins."

Verses 12, 13.—The three grades of sin—secret, presumptuous, unpardonable.

Verse 13.—See " Spurgeon's Sermons," No. 135. " Presumptuous Sins."

Verse 13 (last clause).—" *The great transgression.*" What it is not, may be, involves, and suggests.

Verse 14.—A prayer concerning our holy things.

Verse 14.—All wish to please. Some please *themselves.* Some please *men.* Some seek to please *God.* Such was David. I. The prayer shows his *humility.* II. The prayer shows his *affection.* III. The prayer shows a *consciousness of duty.* IV. The prayer shows a *regard to self-interest.—William Jay.*

Verse 14.—The harmony of heart and lips needful for acceptance.

WORKS UPON THE NINETEENTH PSALM.

" *The Works* of JOHN BOYS," 1626, folio, pp. 791—798. An Exposition of Psalm XIX.

Hulsean Lectures for 1827. On the Proofs of Divine Power and Wisdom, derived from the Study of Astronomy : and on the Evidence, Doctrines, and Pre-cepts of Revealed Religion. By the Rev. TEMPLE CHEVALIER, M.A.

[" The Nineteenth Psalm has been adopted as the model for the arrangement of the first twelve Lectures." *Extract from Preface.*]

PSALM XX.

SUBJECT.— *We have before us a National Anthem, fitted to be sung at the outbreak of war, when the monarch was girding on his sword for the fight. If David had not been vexed with wars, we might never have been favoured with such psalms as this. There is a needs be for the trials of one saint, that he may yield consolation to others. A happy people here plead for a beloved sovereign, and with loving hearts cry to Jehovah, "God save the King." We gather that this song was intended to be sung in public, not only from the matter of the song, but also from its dedication "To the Chief Musician." We know its author to have been Israel's sweet singer, from the short title, "A Psalm of David." The particular occasion which suggested it, it would be mere folly to conjecture, for Israel was almost always at war in David's day. His sword may have been hacked, but it was never rusted. Kimchi reads the title, concerning David, or, for David, and it is clear that the king is the subject as well as the composer of the song. It needs but a moment's reflection to perceive that this hymn of prayer is prophetical of our Lord Jesus, and is the cry of the ancient church on behalf of her Lord, as she sees him in vision enduring a great fight of afflictions on her behalf. The militant people of God, with the great Captain of salvation at their head, may still in earnest plead that the pleasure of the Lord may prosper in his hand. We shall endeavour to keep to this view of the subject in our brief exposition, but we cannot entirely restrict our remarks to it.*

DIVISION.— *The first four verses are a prayer for the success of the king. Verses 5, 6, and 7 express unwavering confidence in God and his Anointed; verse 8 declares the defeat of the foe, and verse 9 is a concluding appeal to Jehovah.*

EXPOSITION.

THE LORD hear thee in the day of trouble ; the name of the God of Jacob defend thee ;

2 Send thee help from the sanctuary, and strengthen thee out of Zion ;

3 Remember all thy offerings, and accept thy burnt sacrifice ; Selah.

4 Grant thee according to thine own heart, and fulfil all thy counsel.

1. " *The Lord hear thee in the day of trouble.*" All loyal subjects pray for their king, and most certainly citizens of Zion have good cause to pray for the Prince of Peace. In times of conflict loving subjects redouble their pleas, and surely in the sorrows of our Lord his church could not but be in earnest. All the Saviour's days were days of trouble, and he also made them days of prayer ; the church joins her intercession with her Lord's, and pleads that he may be heard in his cries and tears. The agony in the garden was especially a gloomy hour, but he was heard in that he feared. He knew that his Father heard him always, yet in that troublous hour no reply came until thrice he had fallen on his face in the garden ; then sufficient strength was given in answer to prayer, and he rose a victor from the conflict. On the cross also his prayer was not unheard, for in the twenty-second Psalm he tells us, " thou hast heard me from the horns of the unicorns." The church in this verse implies that her Lord would be himself much given to prayer ; in this he is our example, teaching us that if we are to receive any advantage from the prayers of others, we must first pray for ourselves. What a mercy that we *may* pray in the day of trouble, and what a still more blessed privilege that no trouble can prevent the Lord from hearing us ! Troubles roar like thunder, but the believer's voice will be heard above the storm. O Jesus, when thou pleadest for us in our hour of trouble, the Lord

Jehovah will hear thee. This is a most refreshing confidence, and it may be indulged in without fear.

"*The name of the God of Jacob defend thee;*" or, as some read it, "set thee in a high place." By "*the name*" is meant the revealed character and Word of God; we are not to worship "the unknown God," but we should seek to know the covenant God of Jacob, who has been pleased to reveal his name and attributes to his people. There may be much in a royal name, or a learned name, or a venerable name, but it will be a theme for heavenly scholarship to discover all that is contained in the divine name. The glorious power of God defended and preserved the Lord Jesus through the battle of his life and death, and exalted him above all his enemies. His warfare is now accomplished in his own proper person, but in his mystical body, the church, he is still beset with dangers, and only the eternal arm of our God in covenant can defend the soldiers of the cross, and set them on high out of the reach of their foes. The day of trouble is not over, the pleading Saviour is not silent, and the name of the God of Israel is still the defence of the faithful. The name, "*God of Jacob,*" is suggestive; Jacob had his day of trouble, he wrestled, was heard, was defended, and in due time was set on high, and his God is our God still, the same God to all his wrestling Jacobs. The whole verse is a very fitting benediction to be pronounced by a gracious heart over a child, a friend, or a minister, in prospect of trial; it includes both temporal and spiritual protection, and directs the mind to the great Source of all good. How delightful to believe that our heavenly Father has pronounced it upon our favoured heads!

2. "*Send thee help from the sanctuary.*" Out of heaven's sanctuary came the angel to strengthen our Lord, and from the precious remembrance of God's doings in his sanctuary our Lord refreshed himself when on the tree. There is no help like that which is of God's sending, and no deliverance like that which comes out of his sanctuary. The sanctuary to us is the person of our blessed Lord, who was typified by the temple, and is the true sanctuary which God has pitched, and not man: let us fly to the cross for shelter in all times of need and help will be sent to us. Men of the world despise sanctuary help, but our hearts have learned to prize it beyond all material aid. They seek help out of the armoury, or the treasury, or the buttery, but we turn to the sanctuary. "*And strengthen thee out of Zion.*" Out of the assemblies of the pleading saints who had for ages prayed for their Lord, help might well result to the despised sufferer, for praying breath is never spent in vain. To the Lord's mystical body the richest comes in answer to the pleadings of his saints assembled for holy worship as his Zion. Certain advertisers recommend a strengthening plaster, but nothing can give such strength to the loins of a saint as waiting upon God in the assemblies of his people. This verse is a benediction befitting a Sabbath morning, and may be the salutation either of a pastor to his people, or of a church to its minister. God in the sanctuary of his dear Son's person, and in the city of his chosen church is the proper object of his people's prayers, and under such a character may they confidently look to him for his promised aid.

3. "*Remember all thy offerings, and accept thy burnt sacrifice. Selah.*" Before war kings offered sacrifice, upon the acceptance of which they depended for success; our blessed Lord presented himself as a victim, and was a sweet savour unto the Most High, and then he met and routed the embattled legions of hell. Still does his burnt sacrifice perfume the courts of heaven, and through him the offerings of his people are received as *his* sacrifices and oblations. We ought in our spiritual conflicts to have an eye to the sacrifice of Jesus, and never venture to war until first the Lord has given us a token for good at the altar of the cross, where faith beholds her bleeding Lord. "*Selah.*" It is well to pause at the cross before we march onward to battle, and with the psalmist cry "Selah." We are too much in a hurry to make good haste. A little pausing might greatly help our speed. Stay, good man, there is a haste which hinders; rest awhile, meditate on the burnt sacrifice, and put thy heart right for the stern work which lieth before thee.

4. "*Grant thee according to thine own heart, and fulfil all thy counsel.*" Christ's desire and counsel were both set upon the salvation of his people ; the church of old desired for him good speed in his design, and the church in these latter days, with all her heart desires the complete fulfilment of his purpose. In Christ Jesus sanctified souls may appropriate this verse as a promise ; they shall have their desire, and their plans to glorify their Master shall succeed. We may have our own will, when our will is God's will. This was always the case with our Lord, and yet he said, " not as I will, but as thou wilt." What need for submission in our case ; if it was necessary to him, how much more for us !

5 We will rejoice in thy salvation, and in the name of our God we will set up *our* banners : the LORD fulfil all thy petitions.

6 Now know I that the LORD saveth his anointed ; he will hear him from his holy heaven with the saving strength of his right hand.

7 Some *trust* in chariots, and some in horses : but we will remember the name of the LORD our God.

5. "*We will rejoice in thy salvation.*" In Jesus there is salvation ; it is his own, and hence it is called thy *salvation ;* but it is ours to receive and ours to rejoice in. We should fixedly resolve that come what may, we will rejoice in the saving arm of the Lord Jesus. The people in this psalm, before their king went to battle, felt sure of victory, and therefore began to rejoice beforehand ; how much more ought we to do this who have seen the victory completely won ! Unbelief begins weeping for the funeral before the man is dead ; why should not faith commence piping before the dance of victory begins ? Buds are beautiful, and promises not yet fulfilled are worthy to be admired. If joy were more general among the Lord's people, God would be more glorified among men ; the happiness of the subjects is the honour of the sovereign. " *And in the name of our God we will set up our banners.*" We lift the standard of defiance in the face of the foe, and wave the flag of victory over the fallen adversary. Some proclaim war in the name of one king, and some of another, but the faithful go to war in Jesu's name, the name of the incarnate God, Immanuel, God with us. The times are evil at present, but so long as Jesus lives and reigns in his church we need not furl our banners in fear, but advance them with sacred courage.

> " Jesu's tremendous name
>   Puts all our foes to flight ;
>   Jesus, the meek, the angry Lamb
>   A lion is in fight."

The church cannot forget that Jesus is her advocate before the throne, and therefore she sums up the desires already expressed in the short sentence, " *The Lord fulfil all thy petitions.*" Be it never forgotten that among those petitions is that choice one, " Father, I will that they also whom thou hast given me be with me where I am."

6. "*Now know I that the Lord saveth his anointed.*" We live and learn, and what we learn we are not ashamed to acknowledge. He who thinks he knows everything will miss the joy of finding out new truth ; he will never be able to cry, " now know I," for he is so wise in his own conceit that he knows all that can be revealed and more. Souls conscious of ignorance shall be taught of the Lord, and rejoice as they learn. Earnest prayer frequently leads to assured confidence. The church pleaded that the Lord Jesus might win the victory in his great struggle, and now by faith she sees him saved by the omnipotent arm. She evidently finds a sweet relish in the fragrant title of " anointed ;" she thinks of him as ordained before all worlds to his great work, and then endowed with the needful qualifications by being anointed of the Spirit of the Lord ; and this is evermore the choicest solace of the believer, that Jehovah himself hath anointed Jesus to be a Prince and a Saviour, and that our shield is thus the Lord's own anointed. " *He will hear him from his holy heaven with the saving*

strength of his right hand." It is here asserted confidently that God's holiness and power would both come to the rescue of the Saviour in his conflict, and surely these two glorious attributes found congenial work in answering the sufferer's cries. Since Jesus was heard, we shall be ; God is in heaven, but our prayers can scale those glorious heights ; those heavens are holy, but Jesus purifies our prayers, and so they gain admittance ; our need is great, but the divine arm is strong, and all its strength is "saving strength ;" that strength, moreover, is in the hand which is most used and which is used most readily—the right hand. What encouragements are these for pleading saints !

7. Contrasts frequently bring out the truth vividly, and here the church sets forth the creature confidences of carnal men in contrast with her reliance upon the Prince Immanuel and the invisible Jehovah. "*Some trust in chariots, and some in horses.*" Chariots and horses make an imposing show, and with their rattling, and dust, and fine caparisons, make so great a figure that vain man is much taken with them ; yet the discerning eye of faith sees more in an invisible God than in all these. The most dreaded war-engine of David's day was the war-chariot, armed with scythes, which mowed down men like grass : this was the boast and glory of the neighbouring nations ; but the saints considered the name of Jehovah to be a far better defence. As the Israelites might not keep horses, it was natural for them to regard the enemy's cavalry with more than usual dread. It is, therefore, all the greater evidence of faith that the bold songster can here disdain even the horse of Egypt in comparison with the Lord of hosts. Alas, how many in our day who profess to be the Lord's are as abjectly dependent upon their fellow-men or upon an arm of flesh in some shape or other, as if they had never known the name of Jehovah at all. Jesus, be thou alone our rock and refuge, and never may we mar the simplicity of our faith. "*We will remember the name of the Lord our God.*" "Our God" in covenant, who has chosen us and whom we have chosen ; this God is our God. The name of our God is JEHOVAH, and this should never be forgotten ; the self-existent, independent, immutable, ever-present, all-filling I AM. Let us adore that matchless name, and never dishonour it by distrust or creature confidence. Reader, you must *know* it before you can *remember* it. May the blessed Spirit reveal it graciously to your soul !

8 They are brought down and fallen : but we are risen, and stand upright.

9 Save, LORD : let the king hear us when we call.

8. How different the end of those whose trusts are different ! The enemies of God are uppermost at first, but they ere long are brought down by force, or else fall of their own accord. Their foundation is rotten, and therefore when the time comes it gives way under them ; their chariots are burned in the fire, and their horses die of pestilence, and where is their boasted strength ? As for those who rest on Jehovah, they are often cast down at the first onset, but an Almighty arm uplifts them, and they joyfully stand upright. The victory of Jesus is the inheritance of his people. The world, death, Satan, and sin, shall all be trampled beneath the feet of the champions of faith ; while those who rely upon an arm of flesh shall be ashamed and confounded for ever.

9. The Psalm is here recapitulated. That Jesus might himself be delivered, and might then, as our King, hear us, is the two-fold desire of the Psalm. The first request is granted, and the second is sure to all the seed ; and therefore we may close the Psalm with the hearty shout, "God save the King." "God save King Jesus, and may he soon come to reign."

EXPLANATORY NOTES AND QUAINT SAYINGS.

Whole Psalm.—This Psalm is the prayer which the church might be supposed offering up, had all the redeemed stood by the cross, or in Gethsemane, in full consciousness of what was doing there. Messiah, in reading these words, would know that he had elsewhere the sympathy he longed for, when he said to the three disciples, "Tarry ye here, and watch with me." Matt. xxvi. 38. It is thus a pleasant song, of the sacred singer of Israel, to set forth the feelings of the redeemed in their Head, whether in his sufferings or in the glory that was to follow.—*Andrew A. Bonar.*

Whole Psalm.—There are traces of liturgical arrangement in many of the Psalms. There is frequently an adaptation to the circumstances of public worship. Thus, when the Jewish church wished to celebrate the great act of Messiah the High Priest making a sacrifice for the people on the day of atonement, as represented in the twenty-second Psalm, a subject so solemn, grand, and affecting, was not commenced suddenly and unpreparedly, but first a suitable occasion was sought, proper characters were introduced, and a scene in some degree appropriate to the great event was fitted for its reception. The priests and Levites endeavour to excite in the minds of the worshippers an exalted tone of reverential faith. The majesty and power of God, all the attributes which elevate the thoughts, are called in to fill the souls of the worshippers with the most intense emotion ; and when the feelings are strung to the highest pitch, an awful, astounding impression succeeds, when the words are slowly chanted, "My God, my God, why hast thou forsaken me ?" We are to suppose, then, that the series of Psalms, from the twentieth to the twenty-fourth inclusive, was used as a service or office in the public worship of the Jewish church.*—R. H. Ryland, M.A., in "The Psalms Restored to Messiah," 1853.*

Whole Psalm.—Really good wishes are good things, and should be expressed in words and deeds. The whole Psalm thus teaches. Christian sympathy is a great branch of Christian duty. There may be a great deal of obliging kindness in that which costs us little.—*William S. Plumer.*

Verse 1.—"*The Lord hear thee in the day of trouble.*" All the days of Christ were *days of trouble.* He was a brother born for adversity, a man of sorrows and acquainted with griefs. . . . But more particularly it was a "*day of trouble*" with him when he was in the garden, heavy and sore amazed, and his sweat was, as it were, drops of blood falling on the ground, and his soul was exceeding sorrowful, even unto death ; but more especially this was his case when he hung upon the cross . . . . when he bore all the sins of his people, endured the wrath of his Father, and was forsaken by him. Now, in this "*day of trouble,*" both when in the garden and on the cross, he prayed unto his Father, as he had been used to do in other cases, and at other times ; and the church here prays that God would hear and answer him, as he did.—*Condensed from John Gill.*

Verse 1.—"*The name.*" Whereas they say, "*The name of the God of Jacob,*" thereby they mean God himself ; but they thus speak of God because all the knowledge that we have of God ariseth from the knowledge of his name, and as to that end he hath given himself in the Scriptures sundry names, that thereby we might know not only what he is in himself, so far as it is meet for us to know, but especially what he is to us, so by them, and them principally, we know him to be, as he is, not only in himself, but unto us. . . . From this knowledge of the name of God ariseth confidence in prayer ! as when they know him, and here call him "*the God of Jacob,*" that is, he that hath made a covenant of mercy with him and with his posterity, that he will be their God and they shall be his people, that they may be bold to flee to him for succour, and

---

* This is a purely gratuitous statement, but is less unlikely than many other assertions of annotators who have a cause to plead.—*C. H. S.*

confidently call upon him in the day of their trouble to hear them, and to help them, as they do. And the more that they know of his name, that is, of his goodness, mercy, truth, power, wisdom, justice, etc., so may they the more boldly pray unto him, not doubting but that he will be answerable unto his name. . . . . For as among men, according to the good name that they have for liberality and pity, so will men be ready to come unto them in their need, and the poor will say, "I will go to such an house, for they have a good name, and are counted good to the poor, and merciful, all men speak well of them for their liberality;" and this name of theirs giveth the encouragement to come boldly and often. So when we know God thus by his name, it will make us bold to come unto him in prayer. . . . . Or, if a man be never so merciful, and others know it not, and so they are ignorant of his good name that he hath, and that he is worthy of, they cannot, with any good hope, come unto him, for they know not what he is ; they have heard nothing of him at all. So when, by unbelief, we hardly conceive of God and of his goodness, or for want of knowledge are ignorant of his good name, even of all his mercy, and of his truth, pity, and compassion that is in him, and so know not his great and glorious name, we can have little or no heart at all to come unto him in trouble, and seek unto him for help by prayer, as these did here ; and this maketh some so forward unto prayer, they are so well acquainted with *the name of God*, that they doubt not of speeding, and others again are so backward unto it, they are so wholly ignorant of his name.—*Nicholas Bownd*, 1604.

Verse 1.—" *The name of the God of Jacob defend thee.*" This is a beautiful allusion to the history of the patriarch Jacob. Jehovah had appeared for him, when he fled from his brother Esau, at Bethel, and Jacob said to his household, " Let us arise, and go up to Bethel ; and I will make there an altar unto God, *who answered me in the day of my distress*, and was with me in the way which I went." Gen. xxxv. 3.—*John Morison.*

Verse 1.—" *The name of the God of Jacob defend thee.*" Hebrew, " *set thee in an high place*," such as God's name is. Prov. xviii. 10. " The righteous runneth into it and is safe," as in a tower of brass, or town of war. By *the name of God* is meant, *Deus nominatissimus*, the most renowned God, saith Junius, and " worthy to be praised," as Psalm xviii. 3 ; and he is called the God of Jacob here, saith another, first, because Jacob was once in the like distress (Gen. xxxii. 6, 7) ; secondly, because he prayed to the like purpose (Gen. xxxv. 3) ; thirdly, because he prevailed with God as a prince ; " and there God spake with us" (Hosea xii. 4) ; fourthly, because *God of Jacob* is the same with " God of Israel," and so the covenant is pleaded.—*John Trapp.*

Verse 1.—" *The name of the God of Jacob defend thee.*" There is an assurance of thy protection, of thy safety, in the midst of ten thousand foes, and of thy perseverance to the end. But you will say, how will the name of the God of Jacob defend me ? Try it. I have, over and over again ; therefore I speak what I do know, and testify what I have seen. " *The name of the God of Jacob defend thee.*" I was once goaded by a poor silly Irish papist to try it, who told me, in his consummate ignorance and bigotry, that if a priest would but give him a drop of holy water, and make a circle with it around a field full of wild beasts, they would not hurt him. I retired in disgust at the abominable trickery of such villains, reflecting, what a fool I am that I cannot put such trust in my God as this poor deluded man puts in his priest and a drop of holy water ! And I resolved to try what " *the name of the God of Jacob*" would do, having the Father's fixed decrees, the Son's unalterable responsibility, and the Spirit's invincible grace and operation around me. I tried it and felt my confidence brighten. O brethren, get encircled with covenant engagements, and covenant blood, and covenant grace, and covenant promises, and covenant securities ; then will " the Lord *hear you in the time of trouble, and the name of the God of Jacob will defend you.*"—*Joseph Irons.*

Verse 1.—A sweeter wish, or a more consolatory prayer for a child of sorrow was never uttered by man, " *The Lord hear thee in the day of trouble; the name of the God of Jacob defend thee.*" And who is there of the sons of men to whom a "*day of trouble*" does not come, whose path is not darkened at times, or with whom is it unclouded sunshine from the cradle to the grave? "Few plants," says old Jacomb, "have both the morning and the evening sun;" and one far older than he said, "Man is born to trouble." A "*day of trouble,*" then, is the heritage of every child of Adam. How sweet, as I have said, how sweet the wish, "*The Lord hear thee in the day of trouble.*" It is the prayer of another in behalf of some troubled one, and yet it implies that the troubled one him-self had also prayed, "*The Lord hear thee*"—hear and answer thine own prayer! *Barton Bouchier.*

Verses 1, 2.—The scene presented in this place to the eye of faith is deeply affecting. Here is the Messiah pouring out his heart in prayer in the day of his trouble; his spouse overhears his agonising groans; she is moved with the tenderest sympathy towards him; she mingles her prayers with his; she entreats that he may be supported and defended. . . . . It may now, perhaps, be said, he is out of the reach of trouble, he is highly exalted, he does not want our sympathies or our prayers. True; yet still we may pray for him—see Matthew xxv. 40—"Inasmuch as ye have done it unto one of the least of these my brethren, ye have done it unto me." We can pray for him in his members. And thus is fulfilled what is written in Psalm lxxii. 15, "And he shall live, and to him shall be given of the gold of Sheba; *prayer* also shall be made for him continually (that is, in his suffering members); and daily shall he be praised" (that is, in his own admirable person).—*Hamilton Verschoyle,* 1843.

Verses 1—5.—These are the words of the people, which they spake unto God in the behalf of their king; and so they did as David desired them, namely, pray for him. If they did thus pray for him, being desired thereunto, and it was their bound duty so to do, and they knew it to be so, and therefore did make conscience of it, and it had been a great fault for them to have failed in it; then by consequence it followeth of necessity, that whensoever any of our brethren or sisters in Christ shall desire this duty at our hands, we must be careful to perform it; and it were a fault not to be excused in us, both against God and them, to fail in it. Therefore we must not think that when godly men and women at their parting or otherwise, desire our prayers, and say, "I pray you pray for me," or, "remember me in your prayers," that these are words of course (though I do not deny, but that many do so use them, and so doing they take the name of God in vain); but we should be persuaded, that out of the abundance of their feeling of their own wants they speak unto us, and so be willing by our prayers to help to supply them. And especially we should do it when they shall make known their estate unto us, as here David did to the people, giving them to understand that he should or might be in great danger of his enemies, and so it was "*a time of trouble*" unto him, as he called it. . . . Most of all, this duty of prayer ought to be carefully performed when we have promised it unto any upon such notice of their estate. For as all promises ought to be kept, yea, though it be to our own hindrance, so those most of all that so nearly concern them. And as if when any should desire us to speak to some great man for them, and we promise to do it, and they trust to it, hoping that we will be as good as our words; it were a great deceit in us to fail them, and so to frustrate their expectation; so when any have desired us to speak to God for them, and upon our promise they would comfort themselves over it, if we should by negligence deceive them, it were a great fault in us, and that which the Lord would require at our hands, though they should never know of it. Therefore, as we ought daily to pray one for another unasked, as our Saviour Christ hath taught us, "O our Father which art in heaven," etc., so more especially and by name should we do it for them that have desired it of us. And so parents especially should not forget their children in their prayers, which daily ask their blessing, and hope to be blessed of God by their prayers. Secondarily, if we should neglect to pray for them that have desired it at our hands, how could we have any hope that others whom we have desired to pray for us should perform that duty unto us? Nay, might not we justly fear that they would altogether neglect it, seeing we do neglect them? and should it not be just with God so to punish us? according to the saying of our Saviour Christ, "With what measure ye mete, it shall be measured to you again." Matt. vii. 2. And I remember that this was the saying of a reverend father in the church, who is now fallen asleep in the Lord, when any desired him to pray for them (as many did, and more than any that I have known), he would say unto them, "I pray you, pray for me, and pray that I may remember you, and then I hope I shall not forget you." Therefore if we would have others pray for us, let us pray for them.—*Nicholas Bownd.*

Verses 1, 5.—In the first verse the psalmist says, "*The Lord hear thee in the day of trouble;*" and in the fifth he says, "*The Lord perform all thy petitions.*" Does he in both these cases refer to one and the same time? The prayers mentioned in the first verse are offered in "*the day of trouble,*" in the days of his flesh; are the petitions to which he refers in the fourth verse also offered in the days of his flesh? Many think not. Before our blessed Saviour departed out of this world, he prayed to the Father for those whom he had given him, that he would keep them from the evil of the world, that they might be one, even as he was one with the Father. He prayed too for his murderers. After his ascension into heaven, he sat down at the right hand of the Father, where he "maketh intercession for us." "If any man sin, we have an advocate with the Father, Jesus Christ, the righteous." It is to this, as many think, that the prophet refers when he says, "*The Lord perform all thy petitions;*" to the intercession which he is continually making for us.—*F. H. Dunwell.*

Verse 2.—"*Send thee help from the sanctuary.*" Here we see the nature of true faith, that it causeth us to see *help* in *heaven,* and so to pray for it when there is none to be seen in the earth. And this is the difference between faith and unbelief; that the very unbelievers can by reason conceive of help, so long as they have any means to help them; but if they fail they can see none at all; so they are like unto those that are purblind, who can see nothing but near at hand. But faith seeth afar off, even into heaven, so that it is "the evidence of things that are not seen;" for it looketh unto the power of God, who hath all means in his hand, or can work without them, who made all of nothing, and "calleth the things that be not, as though they were." So that as the holy martyr Stephen, when his enemies were ready to burst for anger, and gnash at him with their teeth, looked steadfastly into heaven, and saw Christ standing at the right hand of God ready to defend him; so faith in the promises of the word doth see help in heaven ready for us, when there are no means in earth.—*Nicholas Bownd.*

Verse 2.—"*Send thee help from the sanctuary.*" Why "*from the sanctuary,*" but because the Lord presented himself there as upon the mercy-seat! The sanctuary was in Zion, the mercy-seat was in the sanctuary, the Lord was in the mercy-seat; he would have himself set forth as residing there. Herein they pray, and pray in faith, for help and strength.—*David Clarkson.*

Verse 2.—"*Strengthen thee out of Zion.*" That is, out of the assemblies of the saints, where they are praying hard for thy welfare.—*John Trapp.*

Verse 3.—"*Remember all thy offerings, and accept thy burnt sacrifice.*" "*All thy offerings:*" the humiliation that brought him from heaven to earth; the patient tabernacling in the womb of the holy Virgin; the poor nativity; the hard manger; ox and ass for courtiers; the weary flight into Egypt; the poor cottage in Nazareth; the doing all good, and bearing all evil; the miracles, the sermons, the teachings; the being called a man gluttonous and a wine-bibber, the friend of publicans and sinners; the attribution of his wondrous deeds to Beelzebub. "*And accept thy burnt sacrifice.*" As every part of the victim was consumed in a burnt sacrifice, so what limb, what sense of our dear Lord did not agonise in his passion? The thorny crown on his head; the nails in his hands and feet ; the reproaches that filled his ears ; the gloating multitude on whom his dying gaze rested ; the vinegar and the gall ; the evil odours of the hill of death and corruption. The ploughers ploughed upon his back, and made long furrows ; his most sacred face was smitten with the palm of the hand, his head with the reed. What could have been done more for the vineyard than he did not do in it ? Isa. v. 4. So, what more could have been borne by the vine, that this dear Vine did not bear ? " *Remember* " them now, O Father, call to mind for us sinners, for us miserable sinners, and for our salvation, " *all* " these " *offerings ;* " " *accept,* " instead of our eternal punishment, who are guilty, his " *burnt sacrifice,* " who did no sin, neither was guile found in his mouth !—*Dionysius, and Gerhohus* (1093—1169), *quoted by J. M. Neale.*

Verse 3.—" *Accept :* " Hebrew, " *turn to ashes,* " by fire from heaven, in token of his acceptance, as was usual.—*Matthew Poole.*

Verse 3.—" *That thy burnt offering may be fat.* " That is, abundant, fruitful, and full. But here we must understand this burnt offering, as we did the sacrifice, in a spiritual sense, as we have before observed. Thus Christ offered up himself wholly upon the cross to be consumed by the fire of love. And here, instead of " all thy sacrifice," it might be rendered " the whole of thy sacrifice." Even as burnt sacrifice (*holocaustum*) signifies the whole of it being burnt with fire. By which groaning of the Spirit, he shows and teaches the righteous, that they should pray and hope that none of their sufferings shall be vain, but that all shall be well-pleasing, remembered, and fully acceptable.—*Martin Luther.*

Verse 3.—" *Selah.* " * This word, in the judgment of the learned, is sometime *vox optantis,* the voice of one that wisheth, equivalent to *amen ;* or *vox admirantis,* the voice of one admiring, showing some special matter ; or *vox affirmantis,* of one affirming, avouching what is said ; or *vox meditantis,* of one meditating, requiring consideration of what is said. But withal, it is a rest in music. Jerome saith it is *commutatio metri,* or *vicissitudo canendi.—Edward Marbury.*

Verse 4.—" *Grant thee according to thine own heart, and fulfil all thy counsel.* " Let us here call to mind the zealous and earnest desire of the Redeemer to accomplish his work, " I have a baptism to be baptised with ; and how am I straitened till it be accomplished." Luke xii. 50. " With desire I have desired to eat this passover with you before I suffer" (Luke xxii. 15) ; that he might leave a memorial of his sufferings and death, for the strengthening and refreshing of their souls. These earnest desires and anticipations did the Father satisfy, as of one with whom he was well pleased.—*W. Wilson.*

Verse 4.—" *Fulfil all thy counsel ;* " whatever was agreed upon in the counsel and covenant of peace between him and his Father, relating to his own glory, and the salvation of his people.—*John Gill.*

Verse 4.—" *Fulfil all thy counsel.* " Answer thee, *ad cardinem desiderii,* as a father, Augustine, expresseth it ; let it be unto thee even as thou wilt. Sometimes God doth not only grant a man's prayer, but fulfilleth his counsel ; that is, in that very way, by that very means, which his judgment pitched upon in his thoughts.—*John Trapp.*

Verse 5 (first clause).—Whosoever do partake with Christ's subjects in trouble, shall share with them also in the joy of their deliverance ; therefore it is said, " *We will rejoice in thy salvation.* "—*David Dickson.*

Verse 5.—" *In the name of our God.* " As those cried out, Judges vii. 20, " The sword of the Lord and of Gideon ;" and as we have it in Joshua vi. 20, " And the people shouted, and the walls of Jericho fell down ;" and king Abiah, crying out with his men in the same, killed five hundred thousand of the children of Israel ; and so now also, according to the military custom in

---

* See pages 25, 29, 38.

our day, the soldiers boast in the name and glory of their general, in order to encourage themselves against their enemies. And it is just this custom that the present verse is now teaching, only in a godly and religious manner.— *Martin Luther.*

Verse 5.—*" In the name of our God we will set up our banners."* The banners formerly so much used were a part of military equipage, borne in times of war to assemble, direct, distinguish, and encourage the troops. They might possibly be used for other purposes also. Occasions of joy, splendid processions, and especially a royal habitation, might severally be distinguished in this way. The words of the psalmist may perhaps be wholly figurative : but if they should be literally understood, the allusion of erecting a banner in the name of the Lord, acknowledging his glory, and imploring his favour, might be justified from an existing practice. Certain it is that we find this custom prevalent on this very principle in other places, into which it might originally have been introduced from Judea. Thus Mr. Turner (*Embassy to Thibet,* p. 31), says, " I was told that it was a custom with the Soobah to ascend the hill every month, when he sets up a white flag, and performs some religious ceremonies, to conciliate the favour of a dewta, or invisible being, the genius of the place, who is said to hover about the summit, dispensing at his will, good and evil to every thing around him."—*Samuel Burder's " Oriental Customs,"* 1812.

Verse 5.—*" In the name of our God we will set up our banners."* In all religious as well as warlike processions the people carry banners. Hence, on the pinnacles of their sacred cars, on the domes or gateways of their temples, and on the roof of a new house, may be seen the banner of the caste or sect, floating in the air. Siva the Supreme, also, is described as having a banner in the celestial world.—*Joseph Roberts' " Oriental Illustrations."*

Verse 5.—*" In the name of our God we will set up our banners."* 1. We will wage war in his name, we will see that our cause be good, and make his glory our end in every expedition ; we will ask counsel at his mouth, and take him along with us ; we will follow his conduct, implore his aid, and depend upon it, and refer the issue to him. David went against Goliath in the name of the Lord of hosts. 1 Sam. xvii. 45. 2. We will celebrate our victories in his name. When *" we lift up our banners"* in triumph, and set up our trophies, it shall be *" in the name of our God,"* he shall have all the glory of our success, and no instrument shall have any part of the honour that is due to him.— *Matthew Henry.*

Verse 5.—*" We will set up our banners."* Confession of Christ, as the only name whereby we can be saved, is the *" banner"* which distinguishes his faithful people. O that this confession were more distinct, more pure, more zealous, in those who seem to be his followers, then would they be more united, more bold, in the profession of their religion, more successful in the cause of Christ, terrible as an army with *" banners."* Cant. vi. 4.— *W. Wilson.*

Verse 5.—*" Our banners."* Will you know the staff, the colours, and the flag or streamer of this ensign ? Why, the staff is his cross, the colours are blood and water, and the streamer the gospel, or preaching of them to the world. The staff that carried the colours, was of old time fashioned like a cross, a cross bar near the top there was, from which the flag or streamer hung ; so as it were prefiguring, that all the hosts and armies of the nations were one day to be gathered under the *banner of the cross,* to which soldiers should daily flow out of all the nations and kingdoms of the earth.—*Mark Frank,* 1613—1664.

Verse 5.—*" The Lord fulfil all thy petitions,"* for thyself and for others, now that thou sittest on the right hand of the Father, pleading for us and showing thy side and thy wounds.—*Dionysius, quoted by Isaac Williams.*

Verse 6.—*" Now know I."* A sudden change of number, speaking in the person of one, thereby to note the unity and consent of the people to this prayer, as though they had been all one, and uttered it all with one mouth. *" The Lord will help his anointed ;"* that is, his king, whom he hath established.

See Psalm ii. 2 ; xviii. 50. "*And will hear him* (see verse 1), *from his sanctuary.*" One readeth it thus—" from the heavens of his holiness ;" meaning, from heaven where his holiness dwelleth.—*Thomas Wilcocks.*

Verse 6.—"*He will hear him.*" I would be glad of the prayers of all the churches of Christ ; O that there were not a saint on earth but that I were by name in his morning and evening prayer (whosoever thou art that readest, I beseech thee pray for me) ; but above all, let me have a property in those prayers and intercessions that are proper only to *Christ ;* I am sure then I should never miscarry : Christ's prayers are heavenly, glorious, and very effectual. *Isaac Ambrose,* 1592—1674.

Verse 6.—"*His anointed.*" As priests, and sometimes kings and prophets, were among the Jews *anointed* to their offices, so our Saviour was anointed as a Prophet, to preach glad tidings to the meek ; as a Priest, to bind up the broken-hearted ; and as a King to deliver the captives. As the unction means designation and ordination, it is properly applied to the divine person of the Mediator : he is spoken of as God, who was "anointed with the oil of gladness above his fellows." Heb. i. 8, 9. As the anointing with the Holy Spirit signifies the *gifts* and *aids* of the Holy Spirit, it terminates upon his human nature only, and not his divine person, which has all the perfections in itself, and cannot properly, in the sense last mentioned, be said to be anointed with the Holy Spirit. But yet as the human nature is taken into a subsistence in his divine Person, the anointed may properly enough be predicated and affirmed of his Person. The unction of our Redeemer has a great *stress* laid upon it in Scripture. And therefore we read, "Whosoever believeth that Jesus is the Christ, is born of God." "Who is a liar but he that denieth that Jesus is the Christ ?" 1 John v. 1 ; ii. 22. Our Saviour's enemies were sensible of this, when they made an order, that if "any man did confess that he was Christ, he should be put out of the synagogue." John ix. 22. Our Saviour's anointing was *superior* to that of any other, and more excellent as to the work to which he was consecrated. The apostles and others, who are called his followers, had the Spirit *by measure,* but Christ *without measure.* He is "fairer than the sons of men" (Psalm xlv. 2) ; and had a glory as the "only begotten of the Father, full of grace and truth" (John i. 14, 16) ; and of his fulness the apostles and all others receive. Christ's anointing answers to that of Aaron his type ; the precious ointment which was "poured upon his head, ran down to the skirts of his garments." Psalm cxxxiii. 2. Our Saviour was so anointed, as to "fill all in all." Eph. i. 23. He filleth all his members, and all their faculties, with all those measures of the Spirit, which they ever receive.—*Condensed from John Hurrion,* 1675—1731.

Verse 7.—"*Some trust in chariots, and some in horses : but we will remember the name of the Lord our God.*" About Michaelmas I was in the utmost extremity, and having gone out in very fine weather, I contemplated the azure heavens, and my heart was so strengthened in faith (which I do not ascribe to my own powers, but solely to the grace of God), that I thought within myself, "What an excellent thing it is when we have nothing, and can rely upon nothing, but yet are acquainted with the living God, who made heaven and earth, and place our confidence alone in him, which enables us to be so tranquil even in necessity !" Although I was well aware that I required something that very day, yet my heart was so strong in faith that I was cheerful, and of good courage. On coming home I was immediately waited upon by the overseer of the workmen and masons, who, as it was Saturday, required money to pay their wages. He expected the money to be ready, which he wished to go and pay, but enquired, however, whether I had received anything. "Has anything arrived ?" asked he. I answered, "No, but I have faith in God." Scarcely had I uttered the words when a student was announced, who brought me thirty dollars from some one, whom he would not name. I then went into the room again, and asked the other "how much he required this time for the workmen's wages ?'' He answered, "Thirty dollars." "Here they are," said I, and enquired at the same time, "if he needed any more ?'' He said, "No," which very much strengthened the faith of both of us, since we so visibly saw the miraculous hand of God, who sent it at the very moment when it was needed.—*Augustus Herman Franké*, 1663—1727.

Verse 7.--" *Some trust in chariots*," etc.—Vain is the confidence of all wickedness. In war, chariots, horses, navies, numbers, discipline, former successes, are relied on ; but the battle is not to the strong. "Providence favours the strong battalions " may sound well in a worldling's ear, but neither Providence nor the Bible so teaches. In peace, riches, friends, ships, farms, stocks, are relied upon, yet they can neither help nor save. Let him that glorieth glory in the Lord.— *William S. Plumer.*

Verse 7.—" *We will remember the name of the Lord our God.*" By *the name of God* is generally understood, in Holy Writ, the various properties and attributes of God : these properties and attributes make up and constitute the *name* of God. As when Solomon says, "The name of the Lord is a strong tower ; the righteous runneth into it and is safe." And, by remembering, considering, meditating upon this name of God, the psalmist represents himself as comforted or strengthened, whatever might be the duties to which he was called, or the dangers to which he was exposed. Others were for looking to other sources of safety and strength. "some trusting in chariots, and some in horses ;" but the psalmist always set himself to the "remembering the name of the Lord our God ;" and always, as it would seem, with satisfaction and success. And here is the peculiarity of the passage on which we wish to dwell, and from which we hope to draw important lessons and truths—the psalmist "remembers the name of the Lord his God ;" not any one property or attribute of God ; but the whole combination of divine perfections. And he " *remembers* " this " name ;" the expression implying, not a transient thought, but meditation—consideration ; and yet the result of the recollection is gladness and confidence.— *Henry Melvill.*

Verse 7.—It is easy to persuade papists to lean on priests and saints, on old rags and painted pictures—on any idol ; but it is hard to get a Protestant to trust in the living God.—*William Arnot*, 1858.

Verse 7.—Weak man cannot choose but have some confidence without himself in case of apparent difficulties, and natural men do look first to some earthly thing wherein they confide. " *Some trust in chariots, and some in horses,*" some in one creature, some in another. The believer must quit his confidence in these things, whether he have them or want them, and must rely on what God hath promised in his word to do unto us. " *But we will remember the name of the Lord our God.*"—*David Dickson.*

Verse 7.—They that " *trust in chariots and horses*," will have no king but Cæsar ; but the " armies in heaven " which follow thee have themselves no arms, and no strength but in following thee.—*Isaac Williams.*

Verse 7.—Numa being told that his enemies were coming upon him, as he was offering sacrifices, thought it was sufficient for his safety that he could say, I am about the service of my God. When Jehoshaphat had once established a preaching ministry in all the cities of Judah, then, and not till then, the fear of the Lord fell on the neighbouring nations, and they made no war ; albeit, he had before that placed forces in all the fenced cities.—*Charles Bradbury.*

Verse 7.—

> " Some their warrior horses boast,
> Some their chariots' marshall'd host ;
> But our trust will we proclaim
> In our God Jehovah's name."
>
> *Richard Mant.*

Verse 8.—" *They are brought down*" from their horses and chariots in which they trusted. Hebrew : *they bowed down*, as being unable to stand longer because of their mortal wounds. Compare Judges v. 27. " *Stand upright.*" Standing firmly upon our legs, and keeping the field, as conquerors use to do.— *Matthew Poole.*

HINTS TO THE VILLAGE PREACHER.

This Psalm has been much used for coronation, thanksgiving, and fast sermons, and no end of nonsense and sickening flattery has been tacked thereto by the trencher-chaplains of the world's church. If kings had been devils, some of these gentry would have praised their horns and hoofs ; for although some of their royal highnesses have been very obedient servants of the prince of darkness, these false prophets have dubbed them "most gracious sovereigns," and have been as much dazzled in their presence as if they had beheld the beatific vision.—*C. H. S.*

Whole Psalm.—A loyal song and prayer for subjects of King Jesus.

Verse 1.—Two great mercies in great trouble—hearing at the throne, and defence from the throne.

Verses 1, 2.—I. The Lord's trouble in its nature and its cause. II. How the Lord exercised himself in his trouble. III. We ought not to be unmoved spectators of the trouble of Jesus.—*Hamilton Verschoyle.*

Verses 1—3.—A model of good wishes for our friends. I. *They include personal piety.* The person who is spoken of prays, goes to the sanctuary, and offers sacrifice. We must wish our friends grace. II. *They point upward.* The blessings are distinctly recognised as divine. III. *They do not exclude trouble.* IV. *They are eminently spiritual.* Acceptance, etc.

Verse 2.—Sanctuary help—a suggestive topic.

Verse 3.—God's ceaseless respect to the sacrifice of Jesus.

Verses 3, 4.—The great privilege of this fourfold acceptance in the Beloved.

Verse 5.—Joy in salvation, to be resolved on and practised.

Verse 5.—*Setting up the banner.* Open avowal of allegiance, declaration of war, index of perseverance, claim of possession, signal of triumph.

Verse 5 (last clause).—The prevalence of our Lord's intercession, and the acceptance of our prayers through him.

Verse 6.—"*His anointed.*" Our Lord as the Anointed. When ? With what unction ? How ? For what offices ? etc.

Verse 6.—"*He will hear him.*" The ever-prevalent Intercessor.

Verse 6.—God's "*saving strength ;*" the strength of his most used and most skilful hand.

Verse 6 (first clause).—"*Now know I.*" The moment when faith in Jesus fills the soul. The time when assurance is given. The period when a truth gleams into the soul, etc.

Verse 7.—*Creature confidence.* Apparently mighty, well adapted, showy, noisy, etc. *Faithful trust.* Silent, spiritual, divine, etc.

Verse 7.—"*The name of the Lord our God.*"—Comfortable reflections from the name and character of the true God.

Verse 8.—*Tables turned.*

Verse 9.—"*Save, Lord.*" One of the shortest and most pithy prayers in the Bible.

Verse 9 (last clause).—I. To whom we come, and what then. "*To a king.*" II. How we come, and what it means. "*We call.*" III. What we want, and what it implies. "*Hear us.*"

WORK UPON THE TWENTIETH PSALM.

"*Medicines for the Plague ;* that is, Godly and Fruitfull Sermons upon part of the Twentieth Psalme, full of instructions and comfort ; very fit generally for all times of affliction, but more particularly applied to this late visitation of the Plague. Preached at the same time at Norton in Suffolke, by NICHOLAS BOWND, Doctor of Divinitie. . . . . 1604." [Twenty-one Sermons on verses 1—6. 4to.]

PSALM XXI.

SUBJECT.—*The title gives us but little information ; it is simply,* To the chief Musician, a Psalm of David. *Probably written by David, sung by David, relating to David, and intended by David to refer in its fullest reach of meaning to David's Lord. It is evidently the fit companion of Psalm Twenty, and is in its proper position next to it. Psalm Twenty anticipates what this regards as realized. If we pray to-day for a benefit and receive it, we must, ere the sun goes down, praise God for that mercy, or we deserve to be denied the next time. It has been called David's triumphant song, and we may remember it as* The Royal Triumphal Ode. *" The king" is most prominent throughout, and we shall reaa it to true profit if our meditation of him shall be sweet while perusing it. We must crown him with the glory of our salvation ; singing of his love, and praising his power. The next psalm will take us to the foot of the cross, this introduces us to the steps of the throne.*

DIVISION.—*The division of the translators will answer every purpose.* A thanksgiving for victory, verses 1 to 6. Confidence of further success, verses 7 to 13.

EXPOSITION.

THE king shall joy in thy strength, O LORD ; and in thy salvation how greatly shall he rejoice !

2 Thou hast given him his heart's desire, and hast not withholden the request of his lips. Selah.

3 For thou preventest him with the blessings of goodness : thou settest a crown of pure gold on his head.

4 He asked life of thee, *and* thou gavest *it* him, *even* length of days for ever and ever.

5 His glory *is* great in thy salvation : honour and majesty hast thou laid upon him.

6 For thou hast made him most blessed for ever : thou hast made him exceeding glad with thy countenance.

1. " *The king shall joy in thy strength, O Lord.*" Jesus is a Royal Personage. The question, " Art thou a King then ?" received a full answer from the Saviour's lips : " Thou sayest that I am a King. To this end was I born, and for this purpose came I into this world, that I might bear witness unto the truth." He is not merely *a* King, but *the* King ; King over minds and hearts, reigning with a dominion of love, before which all other rule is but mere brute force. He was proclaimed King even on the cross, for there, indeed, to the eye of faith, he reigned as on a throne, blessing with more than imperial munificence the needy sons of earth. Jesus has wrought out the salvation of his people, but as a man he found his strength in Jehovah his God, to whom he addressed himself in prayer upon the lonely mountain's side, and in the garden's solitary gloom. That strength so abundantly given is here gratefully acknowledged, and made the subject of joy. The Man of Sorrows is now anointed with the oil of gladness above his fellows. Returned in triumph from the overthrow of all his foes, he offers his own rapturous *Te Deum* in the temple above, and joys in the power of the Lord. Herein let every subject of King Jesus imitate the King ; let us lean upon Jehovah's strength, let us joy in it by unstaggering faith, let us exult in it in our thankful songs. Jesus not only has thus rejoiced, but he *shall* do so as he sees the power of divine grace bringing out from their sinful hiding-places the purchase of his soul's travail ; we also shall rejoice more and more as we learn by experience more and more fully the strength of the arm of our covenant God. Our weakness unstrings our harps, but his strength tunes them anew. If we

cannot sing a note in honour of our own strength, we can at any rate rejoice in our omnipotent God.

"*And in thy salvation how greatly shall he rejoice!*" Everything is ascribed to God ; the source is *thy strength* and the stream is *thy salvation*. Jehovah planned and ordained it, works it and crowns it, and therefore it is his salvation. The joy here spoken of is described by a note of exclamation and a word of wonder : "*how greatly!*" The rejoicing of our risen Lord must, like his agony, be unutterable. If the mountains of his joy rise in proportion to the depth of the valleys of his grief, then his sacred bliss is high as the seventh heaven. For the joy which was set before him he endured the cross, despising the shame, and now that joy daily grows, for he rests in his love and rejoices over his redeemed with singing, as in due order they are brought to find their salvation in his blood. Let us with our Lord rejoice in salvation, as coming from God, as coming to us, as extending itself to others, and as soon to encompass all lands. We need not be afraid of too much rejoicing in this respect ; this solid foundation will well sustain the loftiest edifice of joy. The shoutings of the early methodists in the excitement of the joy were far more pardonable than our own lukewarmness. Our joy should have some sort of inexpressibleness in it.

2. "*Thou hast given him his heart's desire.*" That desire he ardently pursued when he was on earth, both by his prayer, his actions, and his suffering ; he manifested that his heart longed to redeem his people, and now in heaven he has his desire granted him, for he sees his beloved coming to be with him where he is. The desires of the Lord Jesus were from his heart, and the Lord heard them ; if our hearts are right with God, he will in our case also "fulfil the desire of them that fear him."

"*And hast not withholden the request of his lips.*" What is in the well of the heart is sure to come up in the bucket of the lips, and those are the only true prayers where the heart's desire is first, and the lip's request follows after. Jesus prayed vocally as well as mentally ; speech is a great assistance to thought. Some of us feel that even when alone we find it easier to collect our thoughts when we can pray aloud. The requests of the Saviour were not withheld. He was and still is a prevailing Pleader. Our Advocate on high returns not empty from the throne of grace. He asked for his elect in the eternal council-chamber, he asked for blessings for them here, he asked for glory for them hereafter, and his requests have speeded. He is ready to ask for us at the mercy-seat. Have we not at this hour some desire to send up to his Father by him ? Let us not be slack to use our willing, loving, all-prevailing Intercessor.

"*Selah.*" Here a pause is very properly inserted, that we may admire the blessed success of the king's prayers, and that we may prepare our own requests which may be presented through him. If we had a few more quiet rests, a few more Selahs in our public worship, it might be profitable.

3. "*For thou preventest him with the blessings of goodness.*" The word *prevent* formerly signified to precede or go before, and assuredly Jehovah preceded his Son with blessings. Before he died saints were saved by the anticipated merit of his death, before he came believers saw his day and were glad, and he himself had his delights with the sons of men. The Father is so willing to give blessings through his Son, that instead of his being constrained to bestow his grace, he outstrips the Mediatorial march of mercy. "I say not that I will pray the Father for you, for the Father himself loveth you." Before Jesus calls the Father answers, and while he is yet speaking he hears. Mercies may be bought with blood, but they are also freely given. The love of Jehovah is not caused by the Redeemer's sacrifice, but that love, with its blessings of goodness, preceded the great atonement, and provided it for our salvation. Reader, it will be a happy thing for thee if, like thy Lord, thou canst see both providence and grace preceding thee, forestalling thy needs, and preparing thy path. Mercy, in the case of many of us, ran before our desires and prayers, and it ever outruns our endeavours and expectancies, and even our hopes are left to lag behind. Prevenient grace deserves a song ; we may make one out of this sentence ; let us

try. All our mercies are to be viewed as "*blessings ;*" gifts of a blessed God, meant to make us blessed ; they are "*blessings of goodness,*" not of merit, but of free favour ; and they come to us in a *preventing way,* a way of prudent foresight, such as only preventing love could have arranged. In this light the verse is itself a sonnet !

"*Thou settest a crown of pure gold on his head.*" Jesus wore the thorn-crown, but now wears the glory-crown. It is a "*crown,*" indicating royal nature, imperial power, deserved honour, glorious conquest, and divine government. The crown is of the richest, rarest, most resplendent, and most lasting order— "*gold,*" and that gold of the most refined and valuable sort, "*pure gold,*" to indicate the excellence of his dominion. This crown is set upon his head most firmly, and whereas other monarchs find their diadems fitting loosely, his is fixed so that no power can move it, for Jehovah himself has set it upon his brow. Napoleon crowned himself, but Jehovah crowned the Lord Jesus ; the empire of the one melted in an hour, but the other has an abiding dominion. Some versions read, "a crown of precious stones ;" this may remind us of those beloved ones who shall be as jewels in his crown, of whom he has said, "They shall be mine in the day when I make up my jewels." May we be set in the golden circlet of the Redeemer's glory, and adorn his head for ever !

4. "*He asked life of thee, and thou gavest it him, even length of days for ever and ever.*" The first words may suit King David, but the length of days for ever and ever can only refer to the King Messiah. Jesus, as man, prayed for resurrection and he received it, and now possesses it in immortality. He died once, but being raised from the dead he dieth no more. "Because I live, ye shall live also," is the delightful intimation which the Saviour gives us, that we are partakers of his eternal life. We had never found this jewel, if he had not rolled away the stone which covered it.

5. "*His glory is great in thy salvation.*" Immanuel bears the palm ; he once bore the cross. The Father has glorified the Son, so that there is no glory like unto that which surroundeth him. See his person as it is described by John in the Revelation ; see his dominion as it stretches from sea to sea : see his splendour as he is revealed in flaming fire. Lord, who is like unto thee ? Solomon in all his glory could not be compared with thee, thou once despised Man of Nazareth ! Mark, reader : salvation is ascribed to God ; and thus the Son, as our Saviour, magnifies his Father ; but the Son's glory is also greatly seen, for the Father glorifies his Son.

"*Honour and majesty hast thou laid upon him.*" Parkhurst reads, "splendour and beauty." These are put upon Jesus, as chains of gold, and stars and tokens of honour are placed upon princes and great men. As the wood of the tabernacle was overlaid with pure gold, so is Jesus covered with glory and honour. If there be a far more exceeding and eternal weight of glory for his humble followers, what must there be for our Lord himself ? The whole weight of sin was laid upon him ; it is but meet that the full measure of the glory of bearing it away should be laid upon the same beloved person. A glory commensurate with his shame he must and will receive, for well has he earned it. It is not possible for us to honour Jesus too much ; what our God delights to do, we may certainly do to our utmost. Oh for new crowns for the lofty brow which once was marred with thorns !

> "Let him be crowned with majesty
> Who bowed his head to death,
> And be his honours sounded high
> By all things that have breath."

6. "*For thou hast made him most blessed for ever.*" He is most blessed in himself, for he is God over all, blessed for ever ; but this relates to him as our Mediator, in which capacity blessedness is given to him as a reward. The margin has it, *thou hast set him to be blessings ;* he is an overflowing wellspring of blessings to others, a sun filling the universe with light. According as the Lord sware unto Abraham, the promised seed is an everlasting source of

blessings to all the nations of the earth. He is set for this, ordained, appointed, made incarnate with this very design, that he may bless the sons of men. Oh that sinners had sense enough to use the Saviour for that end to which he is ordained, viz., to be a Saviour to lost and guilty souls.

"*Thou hast made him exceeding glad with thy countenance.*" He who is a blessing to others cannot but be glad himself ; the unbounded good-doing of Jesus ensures him unlimited joy. The loving favour of his Father, the countenance of God, gives Jesus exceeding joy. This is the purest stream to drink of, and Jesus chooses no other. His joy is full. Its source is divine. Its continuance eternal. Its degree exceeding all bounds. The countenance of God makes the Prince of Heaven glad ; how ought we to seek it, and how careful should we be lest we should provoke him by our sins to hide his face from us ! Our anticipations may cheerfully fly forward to the hour when the joy of our Lord shall be shed abroad on all the saints, and the countenance of Jehovah shall shine upon all the blood-bought. So shall we " enter into the joy of our Lord."

So far all has been " the shout of them that triumph, the song of them that feast." Let us shout and sing with them, for Jesus is our King, and in his triumphs we share a part.

7 For the king trusteth in the LORD, and through the mercy of the most High he shall not be moved.

8 Thine hand shall find out all thine enemies : thy right hand shall find out those that hate thee.

9 Thou shalt make them as a fiery oven in the time of thine anger : the LORD shall swallow them up in his wrath, and the fire shall devour them.

10 Their fruit shalt thou destroy from the earth, and their seed from among the children of men.

11 For they intended evil against thee : they imagined a mischievous device, *which* they are not able *to perform*.

12 Therefore shalt thou make them turn their back, *when* thou shalt make ready *thine arrows* upon thy strings against the face of them.

13 Be thou exalted, LORD, in thine own strength : *so* will we sing and praise thy power.

7. "*For the king trusteth in the Lord.*" Our Lord, like a true King and leader, was a master in the use of the weapons, and could handle well the shield of faith, for he has set us a brilliant example of unwavering confidence in God. He felt himself safe in his Father's care until his hour was come, he knew that he was always heard in heaven ; he committed his cause to him that judgeth right, and in his last moments he committed his spirit into the same hands. The joy expressed in the former verses was the joy of faith, and the victory achieved was due to the same precious grace. A holy confidence in Jehovah is the true mother of victories. This psalm of triumph was composed long before our Lord's conflict began, but faith overleaps the boundaries of time, and chants her " Io triumphe," while yet she sings her battle song.

"*Through the mercy of the Most High he shall not be moved.*" Eternal mercy secures the mediatorial throne of Jesus. He who is Most High in every sense, engages all his infinite perfections to maintain the throne of grace upon which our King in Zion reigns. He was not moved *from* his purpose, nor *in* his sufferings, nor *by* his enemies, nor shall he be moved *from* the completion of his designs. He is the same yesterday, to-day, and for ever. Other empires are dissolved by the lapse of years, but eternal mercy maintains his growing dominion evermore ; other kings fail because they rest upon an arm of flesh, but our monarch reigns on in splendour because he trusteth in Jehovah. It is a great display of divine mercy to men that the throne of King Jesus is still among them : nothing but divine mercy could sustain it, for human malice would overturn it to-morrow if it could. We ought to trust in God for the promotion of the Redeemer's kingdom, for in Jehovah the King himself trusts : all unbelieving methods of action, and especially all reliance upon mere human ability, should be for ever discarded from a kingdom where the monarch sets the example of walking by faith in God.

8. *" Thine hand shall find out all thine enemies : thy right hand shall find out those that hate thee."* The destruction of the wicked is a fitting subject for joy to the friends of righteousness ; hence here, and in most scriptural songs, it is noted with calm thanksgiving. " Thou hast put down the mighty from their seats," is a note of the same song which sings, " and hast exalted them of low degree." We pity the lost for they are men, but we cannot pity them as enemies of Christ. None can escape from the wrath of the victorious King, nor is it desirable that they should. Without looking for his flying foes he will find them with his hand, for his presence is about and around them. In vain shall any hope for escape, he will find out all, and be able to punish all, and that too with the ease and rapidity which belong to the warrior's right hand. The finding out relates, we think, not only to the discovery of the hiding-places of the haters of God, but to the touching of them in their tenderest parts, so as to cause the severest suffering. When he appears to judge the world hard hearts will be subdued into terror, and proud spirits humbled into shame. He who has the key of human nature can touch all its springs at his will, and find out the means of bringing the utmost confusion and terror upon those who aforetime boastfully expressed their hatred of him.

9. *" Thou shalt make them as a fiery oven in the time of thine anger."* They themselves shall be an oven to themselves, and so their own tormentors. Those who burned with anger against thee shall be burned by thine anger. The fire of sin will be followed by the fire of wrath. Even as the smoke of Sodom and Gomorrah went up to heaven, so shall the enemies of the Lord Jesus be utterly and terribly consumed. Some read it, " thou shalt put them as it were into a furnace of fire." Like faggots cast into an oven they shall burn furiously beneath the anger of the Lord ; " they shall be cast into a furnace of fire, there shall be weeping and gnashing of teeth." These are terrible words, and those teachers do not well who endeavour by their sophistical reasonings to weaken their force. Reader, never tolerate slight thoughts of hell, or you will soon have low thoughts of sin. The hell of sinners must be fearful beyond all conception, or such language as the present would not be used. Who would have the Son of God to be his enemy when such an overthrow awaits his foes ? The expression, " the time of thine anger," reminds us that as now is the time of his grace, so there will be a set time for his wrath. The judge goes upon assize at an appointed time. There is a day of vengeance of our God ; let those who despise the day of grace remember this day of wrath.

" The Lord shall swallow them up in his wrath, and the fire shall devour them." Jehovah will himself visit with his anger the enemies of his Son. The Lord Jesus will, as it were, judge by commission from God, whose solemn assent and co-operation shall be with him in his sentences upon impenitent sinners. An utter destruction of soul and body, so that both shall be swallowed up with misery, and be devoured with anguish, is here intended. Oh, the wrath to come ! The wrath to come ! Who can endure it ? Lord, save us from it, for Jesu's sake.

10. *" Their fruit shalt thou destroy from the earth."* Their life's work shall be a failure, and the result of their toil shall be disappointment. That in which they prided themselves shall be forgotten ; their very names shall be wiped out as abominable, *" and their seed from among the children of men."* Their posterity following in their footsteps shall meet with a similar overthrow, till at last the race shall come to an end. Doubtless the blessing of God is often handed down

by the righteous to their sons, as almost a heirloom in the family, while the dying sinner bequeaths a curse to his descendants. If men will hate the Son of God, they must not wonder if their own sons meet with no favour.

11. *" For they intended evil against thee."* God takes notice of intentions. He who would but' could not is as guilty as he who did. Christ's church and cause are not only attacked by those who do not understand it, but there are many who have the light and yet hate it. Intentional evil has a virus in it which is not found in sins of ignorance ; now as ungodly men with malice afore-thought attack the gospel of Christ, their crime is great, and their punishment will be proportionate. The words *" against thee "* show us that he who intends evil against the poorest believer means ill to the King himself : let persecutors beware.

" They imagined a mischievous device, which they are not able to perform." Want of power is the clog on the foot of the haters of the Lord Jesus. They have the wickedness to *imagine,* and the cunning to *devise,* and the malice to plot *mischief,* but blessed be God, they fail in ability ; yet they shall be judged as to their hearts, and the will shall be taken for the deed in the great day of account. When we read the boastful threatenings of the enemies of the gospel at the present day, we may close our reading by cheerfully repeating, *" which they are not able to perform."* The serpent may hiss, but his head is broken ; the lion may worry, but he cannot devour ; the tempest may thunder, but cannot strike. Old Giant Pope bites his nails at the pilgrims, but he cannot pick their bones as aforetime. Growling forth a hideous *" non possumus,"* the devil and all his allies retire in dismay from the walls of Zion, for the Lord is there.

12. *" Therefore shalt thou make them turn their back, when thou shalt make ready thine arrows upon thy strings against the face of them."* For a time the foes of God may make bold advances, and threaten to overthrow everything, but a few ticks of the clock will alter the face of their affairs. At first they advance impudently enough, but Jehovah meets them to their teeth, and a taste of the sharp judgments of God speedily makes them flee in dismay. The original has in it the thought of the wicked being set as a butt for God to shoot at, a target for his wrath to aim at. What a dreadful situation ! As an illustration upon a large scale, remember Jerusalem during the siege ; and for a speci-men in an individual, read the story of the death-bed of Francis Spira. God takes sure aim ; who would be his target ? His arrows are sharp and transfix the heart ; who would wish to be wounded by them ? Ah, ye enemies of God, your boastings will soon be over when once the shafts begin to fly !

13. *" Be thou exalted, Lord, in thine own strength."* A sweet concluding verse. Our hearts shall join in it. It is always right to praise the Lord when we call to remembrance his goodness to his Son, and the overthrow of his foes. The exaltation of the name of God should be the business of every Christian ; but since such poor things as we fail to honour him as he deserves, we may invoke his own power to aid us. Be high, O God, but do thou maintain thy loftiness by thine own almightiness, for no other power can worthily do it.

" So will we sing and praise thy power." For a time the saints may mourn, but the glorious appearance of their divine Helper awakens their joy. Joy should always flow in the channel of praise All the attributes of God are fitting subjects to be celebrated by the music of our hearts and voices, and when we observe a display of his *power,* we must extol it. He wrought our deliverance alone, and he alone shall have the praise.

EXPLANATORY NOTES AND QUAINT SAYINGS.

Whole Psalm.—The last Psalm was a litany before the king went forth to battle. This is apparently a *Te Deum* on his return.—*J. J. Stewart Perowne, B.D., in the "Book of Psalms: a New Translation, with Introductions and Notes,"* 1864.

Whole Psalm.—The prayer which the church offers up at the conclusion of the preceding Psalm now issues in a hymn of praise, the result of a believing view of the glory which is to follow, when Messiah's sufferings are ended. This is one of the beautiful songs of which we find many in Scripture, prepared by the Holy Spirit to awaken and enliven the hopes and expectations of the church while she waits for the Lord, and to give utterance to her joy at the time of his arrival. The theme is Messiah's exaltation and glory, and the time chosen for its delivery is just the moment when darkness covered the earth, and all nature seemed about to die with its expiring Lord. Scripture deals largely in contrasts. It seems to be suitable to the human mind to turn from one extreme to another. Man can endure any change, however violent and contradictory, but a long continuance, a sameness either of joy or sorrow, has a debilitating and depressing effect.—*R. H. Ryland.*

Whole Psalm.—" After this I looked .... and behold a throne was set in heaven, and one sat on the throne." Rev. iv. 1, 2. Such may be considered as the description of this Psalm, after the foregoing prayer. "He who in the preceding Psalm," says St. Jerome, "was prayed for as having taken the form of a servant, in this is Kings of kings, and Lord of lords."—*Isaac Williams.*

Whole Psalm.—I am persuaded that there is not one who consents to the application of the preceding Psalm to Christ in his trouble, who will fail to recognise in this, Christ in his triumph. There he was in the dark valley—the valley of Achor ; now he is on the mount of Zion ; there he was enduring sorrow and travail ; now he remembers no more the anguish, for joy that a spiritual seed is born into the world ; there he was beset with deadly enemies, who encompassed him on every side ; but here he has entered upon that which is written in Psalm lxxviii. 65, 66, "Then the Lord awaked as one out of sleep, and like a mighty man that shouteth by reason of wine. And he smote his enemies in the hinder parts : he put them to a perpetual reproach."—*Hamilton Verschoyle.*

Whole Psalm.—As you have already observed in the heading of this Psalm, it is said to have been composed by David. He wrote of himself in the third person, and as " *the king.*" He penned the Psalm, not so much for his own use, as for his people's. It is, in fact, a national anthem, celebrating the majesty and glory of David, but ascribing both to God—expressing confidence in David's future, but building that confidence upon God alone.—*Samuel Martin, in* " *Westminster Chapel Pulpit,*" 1860.

Verse 1.—" *Thy strength . . . thy salvation.*" So you have two words, " *virtus* and *salus,*" strength and salvation. Note them well ; for not *virtus* without *salus,* nor *salus* without *virtus,* neither without the other is full, nor both without *Tua Domine.* *In virtute* is well, so it have *in salute* after it. For not in strength alone is there matter of joy, every way considered. No, not in *God's strength,* if it have not *salvation* behind it. Strength, not to smite us down, but strength to deliver ; this is the joyful side. Now turn it the other way. As strength, if it end in salvation, is just cause for joy, so salvation, if it go with strength, makes joy yet more joyful ; for it becomes a strong salvation, a mighty deliverance.—*Launcelot Andrews (Bishop),* 1555—1626, *in* " *Conspiracie of the Gowries.*"

Verse 1.—" *In thy salvation how greatly shall he rejoice.*" Oh, it is good rejoicing in the strength of that arm which shall never wither, and in the shadow of those wings which shall never cast their feathers ! in him that is not there yesterday and here to-day, but the same yesterday, to-day, and for ever ! For as he is, so shall the joy be.—*Launcelot Andrews.*

Verse 2.—" *Thou hast given him the desire of his soul.*" He desired to eat the passover, and to lay down his life when he would, and again when he would to take it ; and thou hast given it to him. " *And hast not deprived him of the good pleasure of his lips.*" " My peace," saith he, " I leave with you ;" and it was done.—*Augustine, in loc.*

Verse 2 (*first clause*).—Good men are sure to have out their prayers either in money, or in money's worth, as they say—in that very thing, or a better.—*John Trapp.*

Verse 2.—" *Selah.*" See pp. 25, 29, 38, 345.

Verse 3.—" *For thou preventest him with the blessings of goodness : thou settest a crown of pure gold on his head.*" The Son of God could not be more ready to ask for the blessings of the divine goodness, than the Father was to give them ; and his disposition is the same towards all his adopted sons. Christ, as King and Priest, weareth a crown of glory, represented by the purest and most resplendent of metals—gold. He is pleased to esteem his saints, excelling in different virtues, as the rubies, the sapphires, and the emeralds, which grace and adorn that crown. Who would not be ambitious of obtaining a place therein ?—*George Horne.*

Verse 3.—" *Thou hast prevented him with the blessings of goodness.*" As if he should say, " Lord, I never asked a kingdom, I never thought of a kingdom, but thou hast prevented me with the blessings of thy goodness." . . . . . From whence I take up this note or doctrine, that it is a sweet thing and worthy of all our thankful acknowledgments, to be prevented with the blessings of God's goodness, or God's good blessings. . . . . It is no new thing for God to walk in a way of preventing love and mercy with the children of men. Thus he hath always dealt, doth deal, and will deal ; thus he hath always dealt with the world, with the nations of the world, with great towns and places, with families, and with particular souls. . . . As for particular souls, you know how it was with Matthew the publican, sitting at the receipt of custom. " Come and follow me," says Christ ; preventing of him. And you know how it was with Paul : " I was a blasphemer, and I was a persecutor, but I obtained mercy." How so ? Did he seek it first ? " No," says he, " I went breathing out threatenings against the people of God, and God met me, and unhorsed me ; God prevented me with his grace and mercy." Thus Paul. And pray tell me what do you think of that whole chapter of Luke—the fifteenth ? There are three parables : the parable of the lost groat, of the lost sheep, and of the lost son. The woman lost her groat, and swept to find it ; but did the groat make first towards the woman, or the woman make after the groat first ? The shepherd lost his sheep, but did the sheep make first after the shepherd, or the shepherd after the sheep ? Indeed, it is said concerning the lost son, that he first takes up a resolution, " I will return home to my father," but when his father saw him afar off, he ran and met him, and embraced him, and welcomed him home. Why ? But to show that the work of grace and mercy shall be all along carried on in a way of preventing love.—*Condensed from William Bridge,* 1600—1670.

Verse 3.—" *For thou hast prevented him with the blessings of sweetness.*" Because he had first quaffed the blessing of thy sweetness, the gall of our sins did not hurt him.—*Augustine.*

Verse 3.—" *Thou preventest him.*" The word " *prevent* " is now generally used to represent the idea of hindrance. " *Thou preventest him,*" would mean commonly, " Thou hinderest him." But here the word " prevent " means *to go before.* Thou goest before him with the blessings of thy goodness as a pioneer, to make crooked ways straight, and rough places smooth ; or, as one who strews flowers in the path of another, to render the way beautiful to the eye and pleasant to the tread.—*Samuel Martin.*

Verse 3 (*first clause*).—The text is an acknowledgment of God's goodness. God had anticipated David's wants ; and he writes, " *Thou preventest—thou* goest before him—*with goodness.*" The words "*blessings of goodness*" suggest that God's gifts are God's love embodied and expressed. And this greatly enhances the value of our blessings—that they are cups as full of God and of God's kindness as of happiness and blessedness.—*Samuel Martin.*

Verse 3 (first clause).—A large portion of our blessing is given us before our asking or seeking. Existence, reason, intellect, a birth in a Christian land, the calling of our nation to the knowledge of Christ, and Christ himself, with many other things, are unsought bestowed on men, as was David's right to the throne on him. No one ever asked for a Saviour till God of his own motion promised "the seed of the woman."—*William S. Plumer.*

Verse 3.—"*Thou settest a crown of pure gold on his head.*" Christ may be said to have a fourfold glory, or crown. 1. As God co-essential with the Father; "the brightness of the Father's glory, and the express image of his person." Heb. i. 2, 3. 2. He hath a crown and glory as Mediator, in respect of the power, authority, and glory wherewith he is invested as God's great deputy, and anointed upon the hill of Zion, having power, and a rod of iron, even in reference to enemies. 3. He hath a crown and glory in respect of the manifestation of his glory in the executing of his offices, when he makes his mediatory power and glory apparent in particular steps: thus sometimes he is said *to take his power to him* (Rev. xi. 17); and is said *to be crowned* when the white horse of the gospel rides in triumph. Rev. vi. 2. The last step of this glory will be in the day of judgment; in short, this consists in his exercising his former power committed to him as Mediator. 4. There is a crown and glory which is in a manner put on him by particular believers, when he is glorified by them, not by adding anything to his infinite glory, but by their acknowledging of him to be so.—*James Durham*, 1622—1658.

Verse 3.—The "*crown of pure gold*" has respect to his exaltation at the right hand of God, where he is crowned with glory and honour, and this "*crown*" being of "*pure gold,*" denotes the purity, glory, solidity, and perpetuity of his kingdom.—*John Gill.*

Verse 4.—"*He asked life of thee, and thou gavest it him, even length of days for ever and ever.*" The glory of God is concerned in Christ's living for ever— 1. The glory of his *faithfulness:* for eternal life and blessedness were pledged to Immanuel in covenant as the reward of his work (Psalm cx. 1—4; Isaiah ix. 6, 7, etc.); and it was in the anticipation and confident hope of this, that he "endured the cross, despising the shame." Heb. xii. 2; Psalm xvi. 8—11. 2. The glory of his *justice.* The justice of God was honoured and fully satisfied in all its righteous demands by the death of Christ. His subsequent life is the expression on the part of God of that satisfaction. His perpetual life is a permanent declaration that in him and his finished work the everlasting righteousness of Jehovah rests for ever satisfied. Death can "never more have dominion over him:" for to inflict the penalty again would be a violation of justice. 3. The glory of his *grace.* The glory of this grace he now lives actively to promote. John xvii. 2. By living "*ever*" at God's right hand, he appears as an eternal memorial of God's love in making him our Mediator and Substitute—our Saviour from sin and wrath; and his permanent appearance there will keep all heaven perpetually in mind that "by the grace of God they are what they are," owing all to the sovereign mercy of God through Jesus Christ. He shall appear as the blessed medium through which all the gifts and joys of salvation shall flow to the guilty for evermore. Thus the power of God and all his moral attributes secure the perpetuity of the life of the risen and exalted Saviour.—*Ralph Wardlaw, D.D.*

Verse 4.—"*He asked life of thee, and thou gavest it him.*" He asked a resurrection, saying, "Father, glorify thy Son;" and thou gavest it him, "*Length of days for ever and ever.*" The prolonged ages of this world which the church was to have, and after them an eternity, world without end.—*Augustine.*

Verse 4.—"*He asked life of thee,*" etc. Thus God is better to his people than their prayers ; and when they ask but one blessing, he answereth them as Naaman did Gehazi, with, Nay, take two. Hezekiah asked but one life, and God gave him fifteen years, which we reckon at two lives and more. He giveth liberally and like himself ; as great Alexander did when he gave the poor beggar a city ; and when he sent his schoolmaster a ship full of frankincense, and bade him sacrifice freely.—*John Trapp.*

Verses 4—8.—If David had before been without the symbol of his royal dignity, namely, the diadem, he was the more justified in praising the goodness of God, which had now transferred it from the head of an enemy to his own.— *Augustus F. Tholuck.*

Verse 5.—"*His glory is great in thy salvation.*"—I remember one dying, and hearing some discourse of Jesus Christ ; "Oh," said she, "speak more of this— —let me hear more of this—be not weary of telling his praise ; I long to see him, how should I but long to hear of him ?" Surely I cannot say too much of Jesus Christ. On this blessed subject no man can possibly hyperbolise. Had I the tongues of men and angels, I could never fully set forth Christ. It involves an eternal contradiction, that the creature can see to the bottom of the Creator. Suppose all the sands on the sea-shore, all the flowers, herbs, leaves, twigs of trees in woods and forests, all the stars of heaven, were all rational creatures ; and had they that wisdom, and tongues of angels to speak of the loveliness, beauty, glory, and excellency of Christ, as gone to heaven, and sitting at the right hand of his Father, they would, in all their expressions, stay millions of miles on this side Jesus Christ. Oh, the loveliness, beauty, and glory of his countenance ! Can I speak, or you hear of such a Christ ? And are we not all in a burning love, in a seraphical love, or at least in a conjugal love ? O my heart, how is it thou are not love sick ? How is it thou dost not charge the daughters of Jerusalem as the spouse did : "I charge you, O daughters of Jerusalem, if ye find my beloved, that ye shall tell him, that I *am* sick of love." Cant. v. 8.—*Isaac Ambrose.*

Verse 5.—"*Honour and majesty hast thou laid upon him.*" If it be demanded whether Christ were exalted unto his glory and dignity, according to both his natures, both his Godhead and his manhood, I answer, according to both. According to his Godhead, not as it is considered in itself, but inasmuch as his Godhead, which from his birth unto his death did little show itself, after his resurrection was made manifest in his manhood ; for, as the apostle saith (Rom. i. 4), "He was declared mightily to be the Son of God by the resurrection from the dead," even by the resurrection, and after his resurrection from the dead, he which was thought only to be man, was most plainly manifested likewise to be God. Now, as touching his manhood, he was therein exalted unto highest majesty in the heavenly places, not only shaking off all infirmities of man's nature, but also being beautified and adorned with all qualities of glory, both in his soul and in his body, yet so that he still retaineth the properties of a true body, for even as he was man, he was set at the right hand of the Father. to rule and reign over all, till all his enemies he destroyed, and put under his feet. To knit up all in a word, Christ, God and man, after his resurrection, was crowned with glory and honour, even such as plainly showed him to be God, and was set on the throne of God, there to rule and reign as sovereign Lord and King, till he come in the clouds to judge both quick and dead. Here, then, is both matter of comfort and consolation unto the godly, and likewise for fear and astonishment unto the wicked and ungodly.—*Henry Airay,* 1560—1616.

Verse 5 (*last clause*).—Christ was "a man of sorrows" on earth, but he is full of joy in heaven. He that "wipes away all tears from the eyes of his people," surely has none in his own. There was a *joy set before him* before he suffered, and doubtless it was given him, when he sat down at God's right hand. We may take the latter to be an actual donation of the former ; the joy he had in prospect when he suffered he had in possession when he came to his throne. This is the time of his receiving the Father's public approbation, and the tokens of his love, before the whole heavenly assembly, which must be matter of great joy to him who so much valued and delighted in his Father's love.—*John Hurrion*, 1675—1731.

Verse 5.—Happy he who hath a bone, or an arm, to put the crown upon the head of our highest King, whose chariot is paved with love. Were there ten thousand millions of heavens created above these highest heavens, and again as many above them, and as many above them, till angels were wearied with counting, it were but too low a seat to fix the princely throne of that Lord Jesus (whose ye are) above them all.—*Samuel Rutherford.*

Verse 6.—" *Thou hast made him exceeding glad :*" literally, "brightened him," possibly in allusion to the brightness of Moses' face.—*Dalman Hapstone, M.A.,* in " *The Ancient Psalms. . . . A Literal Translation and Notes,*" etc., 1867.

Verse 6.—" *Thou hast made him exceeding glad with thy countenance.*" Though this be metaphorically used for *favour*, yet is the speech not all metaphor, and that well-experienced Christians will tell you.—*Zachary Bogan, in " The Mirth of a Christian Life,*" 1653.

Verse 6 (*first clause*).—Literally, as in the Bible marginal translation, " Thou hast set him *to be* blessings for ever." Most truly said of the King in whom all the nations of the earth were to be blessed.—*Richard Mant.*

Verse 8.—" *Thine hand shall find out all thine enemies : thy right hand shall find out those that hate thee.*" By a kind of climax in the form of expression, "*hand,*" is followed by "*right hand,*" a still more emphatic sign of active strength. To "*find,*" in this connection, includes the ideas of detecting and reaching. Compare 1 Sam. xxiii. 17 ; Isaiah x. 10 ; in the latter of which places the verb is construed with a preposition (ל), as it is in the first clause of the verse before us, whereas in the other clause it governs the noun directly. If any difference of meaning was intended, it is probably not greater than that between *find* and *find out* in English.—*Joseph Addison Alexander.*

Verse 8.—" *Thine hand shall find out all thine enemies : thy right hand shall find out those that hate thee.*" Saul killed himself, for fear of falling into the hands of his enemies, and thought death less terrible than the shame that he would have endured in seeing himself in their power. What will it be then " to fall into the hands of the living God " (Heb. x. 31), of an offended God ? of God unchangeably determined to be avenged ? " Who can stand before his indignation ?" says the prophet Nahum (chap. i. 6). Who will dare look on him ? Who will dare show himself ? " *Who may abide the day of his coming*" (Mal. iii. 2) without shuddering and fainting for fear ? If Joseph's brethren were so terrified that they " could not answer him," when he said, " I am Joseph your brother," how will it be with sinners, when they shall hear the voice of the Son of God, when he shall triumph over them in his wrath, and say unto them, " I am he " whom ye despised ; " I am he " whom ye have offended ; " I am he " whom ye have crucified ? If these words, " I am he," overthrew the soldiers in the garden of Olives (John xviii. 6), though spoken with extreme gentleness, how will it be when his indignation bursts forth, when it falls upon his enemies like a thunderbolt, and reduces them into dust ? Then will they cry out in terror, and say to the mountains, " *Fall on us, and hide us from the face of him that sitteth on the throne, and from the wrath of the Lamb.*" Rev. vi. 16.—*James Nouet.*

Verse 8.—" *Thine hand shall find out,*" etc. It is not meant only of a discovery of a person (though it be a truth, that the Lord will discover all that are his enemies), but *thine hand shall find them out*, is, it shall take hold of them, grasp them, and arrest them. " Thine hand shall find out " *all* " thine enemies," though close, though covert enemies ; not only thy above-ground enemies, but thy under-ground enemies ; as well those that undermine thee, as those that assault thee.—*Joseph Caryl.*

Verse 9.—" *Thou shalt make them as a fiery oven in the time of thine anger:
the Lord shall swallow them up in his wrath, and the fire shall devour them.*"
How then shall it fare with sinners, when, after all, shall come that general fire
so often foretold, which shall either fall from heaven, or ascend out of hell, or
(according to Albertus Magnus), proceed from both, and shall devour and consume all it meets with ? Whither shall the miserable fly, when that river of
flames, or (to say better), that inundation and deluge of fire shall so encompass
them, as no place of surety shall be left ; where nothing can avail but a holy
life ; when all besides shall perish, in that universal ruin of the whole world ?
What lamentations were in Rome, when it burnt for seven days together !
What shrieks were heard in Troy, when it was wholly consumed with flames !
What howling and astonishment in Pentapolis, when those cities were destroyed
with fire from heaven ! What weeping was there in Jerusalem, when they
beheld the house of God, the glory of their kingdom, the wonder of the world,
involved in fire and smoke ! Imagine what these people felt ; they saw their
houses and goods on fire, and no possibility of saving them ; when the husband
heard the shrieks and cries of his dying wife ; the father, of his little children ;
and, unawares, perceived himself so encompassed with flames, that he could
neither relieve them, nor free himself. What shall it then profit the worldlings,
to have rich vessels of gold and silver, curious embroideries, precious tapestries,
pleasant gardens, sumptuous palaces, and all what the world now esteems, when
they shall with their own eyes, behold their costly palaces burnt, their rich and
curious pieces of gold melted, and their flourishing and pleasant orchards consumed, without power to preserve them or themselves ? All shall burn, and
with it the world, and all the memory and fame of it shall die ; and that which
mortals thought to be immortal, shall then end and perish.—*Jeremy Taylor.*

Verse 9.—" *Thou shalt make them as a fiery oven in the time of thine anger.*"
They shall not only be cast into a furnace of fire (Matt. xiii. 42), but he shall
make them themselves as a fiery oven or furnace, they shall be their own
tormentors, the reflections and terrors of their own consciences will be their
hell. Those that might have had Christ to rule and save them, but rejected
him, and fought against him, even the remembrance of that will be enough to
make them to eternity a fiery oven to themselves.—*Matthew Henry.*

Verse 9.—" *Thou shalt make them as a fiery oven :*" thou shalt make them on
fire within, by the consciousness of their ungodliness : " *In the time of thy countenance ;*" in the time of thy manifestation.—*Augustine.*

Verse 9.—" *As a fiery oven,*" where the burning is extremely hot, the heat
striking upon what is in it from all sides, above, below, and about, on all hands,
and the door closed from going out, or from suffering any cool refreshment to
come in.—*David Dickson.*

Verse 9.—" *As a fiery oven.*" Shall make them like a vault of fire, literally,
" *an oven,*" as in our translation, or " furnace of fire." Bishop Horsley remarks,
" It describes the smoke of the Messiah's enemies perishing by fire, ascending
like the smoke of a furnace. ' The smoke of their torments shall ascend for ever
and ever.' " How awfully grand is that description of the ruins of the cities of
the plain, as the prospect struck on Abraham's eye on the fatal morning of
their destruction ! " And he looked toward Sodom and Gomorrah, and toward
all the land of the plain, and beheld, and, lo, the smoke of the country went up
as the smoke of a furnace." Milton puts it—

> " Overhead the dismal hiss
> Of fiery darts in flaming volleys flew,
> And flying vaulted either host with fire."

Richard Mant.

Verse 9.—The Chaldee reads :—" The fire of Gehenna, or hell."—*John
Morison.*

Verse 9.—" *The time of thine anger.*" If God be willing to pour out his
heavy displeasure upon those that displease him, what can hinder his mighty

arm from performing? Creatures indeed may be angry, but oftentimes, like drones without stings, cannot hurt ; as cannons charged with powder without shot only make a roaring ; like the Pope's Bulls, threaten many, hurt none but those whose consciences are enslaved. Saul may be angry at David, but cannot find him out ; but from God's all-piercing eye none can hide himself. Satan may desire to kill Job, Jonah may be angry till death for Nineveh's preservation ; yet God puts a bit in both their mouths, who, if he be angry, nothing can be holden out of his reach. Princes, if they take captives, may have them rescued from them again, as Lot was from the King of Sodom ; bought with a price, as Joseph of the Ishmaelites. But no power can rescue us from God's anger, no ransom but Christ's blood redeem us. God's will being set afoot, all his attributes follow ; if his will say, Be angry, his eye seeks out the object of his anger, and finds it ; his wisdom tempers the cup, his hand whets the sword, his arm strikes the blow. Thus you see there is a time of God's anger for sin, because he will have it so.—*John Cragge.*

Verse 9.—" *The fire shall devour them.*" Being troubled by the vengeance of the Lord, after the accusation of their conscience, they shall be given up to eternal fire to be devoured.—*Augustine.*

Verse 9.—I have read that a frown of Queen Elizabeth killed Sir Christopher Hatton, the Lord Chancellor of England. What then shall the frowns of the King of nations do? If the rocks rend, the mountains melt, and the foundations of the earth tremble under his wrath ; how will the ungodly sinner appear when he comes in all his royal glory to take vengeance on all that knew him not, and that obeyed not his glorious gospel ?—*Charles Bradbury.*

Verse 10.—" *Their fruit shalt thou destroy from the earth, and their seed from among the children of men.*" A day is coming when all the "*fruits*" of sin, brought forth by sinners in their words, their writings, and their actions shall be "*destroyed ;*" yea, the tree itself, which had produced them, shall be rooted up, and cast into the fire. The "*seed*" and posterity of the wicked, if they continue in the way of their forefathers, will be punished like them. Let parents consider, that upon their principles and practices may depend the salvation or destruction of multitudes after them. The case of the Jews, daily before their eyes, should make them tremble.—*George Horne.*

Verse 11.—" *They intended,*" or warped. Hebrew, *have bent or stretched.* A similitude taken from weavers, who warp their yarn before they weave : or from archers, who, when they have bent their bow and put in their arrow, do take their aim.—*John Diodati.*

Verse 12.—" *Therefore shalt thou make them turn their back,*" or, *thou shalt set them as a butt,* " *when thou shalt make ready thine arrows upon thy strings against the face of them.*" The judgments of God are called his "*arrows,*" being sharp, swift, sure, and deadly. What a dreadful situation, to be set as a mark and "*butt*" at which these arrows are directed ! View Jerusalem encompassed by the Roman armies without, and torn to pieces by the animosity of desperate and bloody factions within ! No farther commentary is requisite upon this verse.—*George Horne.*

HINTS TO THE VILLAGE PREACHER.

Verse 1.—The joy of Jesus and of his people in the strength and salvation of God.

Verses 1, 2.—The doctrine of the resurrection of Jesus Christ contained in the text, may be considered under three heads :—I. *As an answer to prayer.* II. *His joy therein—even in the resurrection.* III. As a necessary appendage to this—*our own individual concern in his glory and in his joy.—Hamilton Verschoyle.*

Verse 2.—The successful Advocate.

Verse 3 (*first clause*).—Preventing mercies.

Verse 3 (*first clause*).—GOD GOING BEFORE US, or, God's anticipation of our necessities by his merciful dispensations. God prevents us with the blessings of his goodness :—I. When we come into the world. II. When we become personal transgressors. III. When we enter upon the duties and upon the cares of mature life. IV. When, in the general course of life, we enter upon new paths. V. In the dark "valley of the shadow of death." VI. By giving us many mercies without our asking for them ; and thus creating occasion, not for prayer, but for praise only. VII. By opening to us the gate of heaven, and by storing heaven with every provision for our blessedness.—*Samuel Martin.*

Verse 3 (*second clause*).—Jesus crowned. I. His previous labors. II. The dominion bestowed. III. The character of the crown. IV. The divine coronant.

Verse 4.—Jesus ever living.

Verse 5.—The glory of the Mediator.

Verse 6.—The blessedness of Jesus.

Verse 7.—Jesus, an example of faith and of its results.

Verse 8.—The secret sinner unearthed, and deprived of all hope of concealment.

Verses 8, 9.—The certainty and terror of the punishment of the wicked.

Verses 11, 12.—The guilt and punishment of evil intentions.

Verse 12.—The retreat of the grand army of hell.

Verse 13.—*A devout Doxology.* I. God exalted. II. God alone exalted. III. God exalted by his own strength. IV. His people singing his praise.

PSALM XXII.

TITLE.—"To the chief Musician upon Aijeleth Shahar. A Psalm of David." *This ode of singular excellence was committed to the most excellent of the temple songsters; the chief among ten thousand is worthy to be extolled by the chief Musician; no meaner singer must have charge of such a strain; we must see to it that we call up our best abilities when Jesus is the theme of praise. The words Aijeleth Shahar are enigmatical, and their meaning is uncertain; some refer them to a musical instrument used upon mournful occasions, but the majority adhere to the translation of our margin, "Concerning the kind of the morning." This last interpretation is the subject of much enquiry and conjecture. Calmet believes that the psalm was addressed to the music master who presided over the band called the "Morning Hind," and Adam Clarke thinks this to be the most likely of all the conjectural interpretations, although he himself inclines to the belief that no interpretation should be attempted, and believes that it is a merely arbitrary and unmeaning title, such as Orientals have always been in the habit of appending to their songs. Our Lord Jesus is so often compared to a hind, and his cruel huntings are so pathetically described in this most affecting psalm, that we cannot but believe that the title indicates the Lord Jesus under a well-known poetical metaphor; at any rate, Jesus is that Hind of the morning concerning whom David here sings.*

SUBJECT.—*This is beyond all others* THE PSALM OF THE CROSS. *It may have been actually repeated word by word by our Lord when hanging on the tree; it would be too bold to say that it was so, but even a casual reader may see that it might have been. It begins with, "My God, my God, why hast thou forsaken me?" and ends, according to some, in the original with "It is finished." For plaintive expressions uprising from unutterable depths of woe we may say of this psalm, "there is none like it." It is the photograph of our Lord's saddest hours, the record of his dying words, the lachrymatory of his last tears, the memorial of his expiring joys. David and his afflictions may be here in a very modified sense, but, as the star is concealed by the light of the sun, he who sees Jesus will probably neither see nor care to see David. Before us we have a description both of the darkness and of the glory of the cross, the sufferings of Christ and the glory which shall follow. Oh for grace to draw near and see this great sight! We should read reverently, putting off our shoes from off our feet, as Moses did at the burning bush, for if there be holy ground anywhere in Scripture it is in this psalm.*

DIVISION.—*From the commencement to the twenty-first verse is a most pitiful cry for help, and from verse 21 to 31 is a most precious foretaste of deliverance. The first division may be subdivided at the tenth verse, from verse 1 to 10 being an appeal based upon covenant relationship; and from verse 10 to 21 being an equally earnest plea derived from the imminence of his peril.*

EXPOSITION.

M Y God, my God, why hast thou forsaken me? *why art thou so* far from helping me, *and from* the words of my roaring?

2 O my God, I cry in the daytime, but thou hearest not ; and in the night season, and am not silent.

3 But thou *art* holy, *O thou* that inhabitest the praises of Israel.

4 Our fathers trusted in thee : they trusted, and thou didst deliver them.

5 They cried unto thee, and were delivered : they trusted in thee, and were not confounded.

6 But I *am* a worm, and no man ; a reproach of men, and despised of the people.

7 All they that see me laugh me to scorn : they shoot out the lip, they shake the head, *saying*,

8 He trusted on the LORD *that* he would deliver him : let him deliver him, seeing he delighted in him.

9 But thou *art* he that took me out of the womb : thou didst make me hope *when I was* upon my mother's breasts.

10 I was cast upon thee from the womb : thou *art* my God from my mother's belly.

1. "*My God, my God, why hast thou forsaken me?*" This was the startling cry of Golgotha : Eloi, Eloi, lama sabacthani. The Jews mocked, but the angels adored when Jesus cried this exceeding bitter cry. Nailed to the tree we behold our great Redeemer in extremities, and what see we? Having ears to hear let us hear, and having eyes to see let us see! Let us gaze with holy wonder, and mark the flashes of light amid the awful darkness of that midday-midnight. First, our Lord's faith beams forth and deserves our reverent imitation ; he keeps his hold upon his God with both hands and cries twice, "*My God, my God!*" The spirit of adoption was strong within the suffering Son of Man, and he felt no doubt about his interest in his God. Oh that we could imitate this cleaving to an afflicting God! Nor does the sufferer distrust the power of God to sustain him, for the title used—"*El*"—signifies *strength*, and is the name of the Mighty God. He knows the Lord to be the all-sufficient support and succour of his spirit, and therefore appeals to him in the agony of grief, but not in the misery of doubt. He would fain know why he is left, he raises that question and repeats it, but neither the power nor the faithfulness of God does he mistrust. What an enquiry is this before us! "*Why hast thou forsaken me?*" We must lay the emphasis on every word of this saddest of all utterances. "*Why?*" what is the great cause of such a strange fact as for God to leave his own Son at such a time and in such a plight? There was no cause in him, why then was he deserted? "*Hast:*" it is done, and the Saviour is feeling its dread effect as he asks the question ; it is surely true, but how mysterious! It was no threatening of forsaking which made the great Surety cry aloud, he endured that forsaking in very deed. "*Thou:*" I can understand why traitorous Judas and timid Peter should be gone, but *thou*, my God, my faithful friend, how canst thou leave me? This is worst of all, yea worse than all put together. Hell itself has for its fiercest flame the separation of the soul from God. "*Forsaken:*" if thou hadst chastened I might bear it, for thy face would shine ; but to forsake me utterly, ah! why is this? "*Me:*" thine innocent, obedient, suffering Son, why leavest thou *me* to perish? A sight of self seen by penitence, and of Jesus on the cross seen by faith will best expound this question. Jesus is forsaken because our sins had separated between us and our God.

"*Why art thou so far from helping me, and from the words of my roaring?*" The Man of Sorrows had prayed until his speech failed him, and he could only utter moanings and groanings as men do in severe sicknesses, like the roarings of a wounded animal. To what extremity of grief was our Master driven! What strong crying and tears were those which made him too hoarse for speech! What must have been his anguish to find his own beloved and trusted Father standing afar off, and neither granting help nor apparently hearing prayer! This was good cause to make him "roar." Yet there was reason for all this which those who rest in Jesus as their Substitute well know.

2. "*O my God, I cry in the daytime, but thou hearest not.*" For our prayers to appear to be unheard is no new trial, Jesus felt it before us, and it is observable that he still held fast his believing hold on God, and cried still, "*My God.*" On the other hand his faith did not render him less importunate, for amid the hurry and horror of that dismal day he ceased not his cry, even as in Gethsemane he had agonized all through the gloomy night. Our Lord continued to pray even

though no comfortable answer came, and in this he set us an example of obedience to his own words, "men ought always to pray, and not to faint." No daylight is too glaring, and no midnight too dark to pray in ; and no delay or apparent denial, however grievous, should tempt us to forbear from importunate pleading.

3. "*But thou art holy, O thou that inhabitest the praises of Israel.*" However ill things may look, there is no ill in thee, O God ! *We* are very apt to think and speak hardly of God when we are under his afflicting hand, but not so the obedient Son. He knows too well his Father's goodness to let outward circumstances libel his character. There is no unrighteousness with the God of Jacob, he deserves no censure ; let him do what he will, he is to be praised, and to reign enthroned amid the songs of his chosen people. If prayer be unanswered it is not because God is unfaithful, but for some other good and weighty reason. If we cannot perceive any ground for the delay, we must leave the riddle unsolved, but we must not fly in God's face in order to invent an answer. While the holiness of God is in the highest degree acknowledged and adored, the afflicted speaker in this verse seems to marvel how the holy God could forsake him, and be silent to his cries. The argument is, thou art holy, oh ! why is it that thou dost disregard thy holy One in his hour of sharpest anguish ? We may not question the holiness of God, but we may argue from it, and use it as a plea in our petitions.

4. "*Our fathers trusted in thee : they trusted, and thou didst deliver them.*" This is the rule of life with all the chosen family. Three times over is it mentioned, they *trusted*, and *trusted*, and *trusted*, and never left off trusting, for it was their very life ; and they fared well too, for *thou didst deliver them.* Out of all their straits, difficulties, and miseries faith brought them by calling their God to the rescue ; but in the case of our Lord it appeared as if faith would bring no assistance from heaven, he alone of all the trusting ones was to remain without deliverance. The experience of other saints may be a great consolation to us when in deep waters if faith can be sure that their deliverance will be ours ; but when we feel ourselves sinking, it is poor comfort to know that others are swimming. Our Lord here pleads the past dealings of God with his people as a reason why he should not be left alone ; here again he is an example to us in the skilful use of the weapon of all prayer. The use of the plural pronoun "*our*" shows how one with his people Jesus was even on the cross. We say, "Our Father which art in heaven," and he calls those "our fathers" through whom we came into the world, although he was without father as to the flesh.

5. "*They cried unto thee, and were delivered : they trusted in thee, and were not confounded.*" As if he had said, "How is it that I am now left without succour in my overwhelming griefs, while all others have been helped ?" We may remind the Lord of his former lovingkindnesses to his people, and beseech him to be still the same. This is true wrestling ; let us learn the art. Observe, that ancient saints *cried* and *trusted*, and that in trouble we must do the same ; and the invariable result was that they were not ashamed of their hope, for deliverance came in due time ; this same happy portion shall be ours. The prayer of faith can do the deed when nothing else can. Let us wonder when we see Jesus using the same pleas as ourselves, and immersed in griefs far deeper than our own.

6. "*But I am a worm, and no man.*" This verse is a miracle in language. How could the Lord of glory be brought to such abasement as to be not only lower than the angels, but even lower than men. What a contrast between "I AM" and "*I am a worm*"! yet such a double nature was found in the person of our Lord Jesus when bleeding on the tree. He felt himself to be comparable to a helpless, powerless, down-trodden worm, passive while crushed, and unnoticed and despised by those who trod upon him. He selects the weakest of creatures, which is all flesh ; and becomes, when trodden upon, writhing, quivering flesh, utterly devoid of any might except strength to suffer. This

was a true likeness of himself when his body and soul had become a mass of misery—the very essence of agony—in the dying pangs of crucifixion. Man by nature is but a worm ; but our Lord puts himself even beneath man, on account of the scorn which was heaped upon him and the weakness which he felt, and therefore he adds, *" and no man."* The privileges and blessings which belonged to the fathers he could not obtain while deserted by God, and common acts of humanity were not allowed him, for he was rejected of men ; he was outlawed from the society of earth, and shut out from the smile of heaven. How utterly did the Saviour empty himself of all glory, and become of no reputation for our sakes ! *" A reproach of men"*—their common butt and jest ; a byword and a proverb unto them : the sport of the rabble, and the scorn of the rulers. Oh the caustic power of reproach, to those who endure it with patience, yet smart under it most painfully ! *" And despised of the people."* The *vox populi* was against him. The very people who would once have crowned him then contemned him, and they who were benefited by his cures sneered at him in his woes. Sin is worthy of all reproach and contempt, and for this reason Jesus, the Sinbearer, was given up to be thus unworthily and shamefully entreated.

7, 8. *" All they that see me laugh me to scorn."* Read the evangelistic narrative of the ridicule endured by the Crucified One, and then consider, in the light of this expression, how it grieved him. The iron entered into his soul. Mockery has for its distinctive description " cruel mockings ;" those endured by our Lord were of the most cruel kind. The scornful ridicule of our Lord was universal ; all sorts of men were unanimous in the derisive laughter, and vied with each other in insulting him. Priests and people, Jews and Gentiles, soldiers and civilians, all united in the general scoff, and that at the time when he was prostrate in weakness and ready to die. Which shall we wonder at the most, the cruelty of man or the love of the bleeding Saviour ? How can we ever complain of ridicule after this ?

" They shoot out the lip, they shake the head." These were gestures of contempt. Pouting, grinning, shaking of the head, thrusting out of the tongue, and other modes of derision were endured by our patient Lord ; men made faces at him before whom angels vail their faces and adore. The basest signs of disgrace which disdain could devise were maliciously cast at him. They punned upon his prayers, they made matter for laughter of his sufferings, and set him utterly at nought. Herbert sings of our Lord as saying,—

> " Shame tears my soul, my body many a wound ;
> Sharp nails pierce this, but sharper that confound ;
> Reproaches which are free, while I am bound.
> Was ever grief like mine ? "

" Saying, He trusted on the Lord that he would deliver him : let him deliver him, seeing he delighted in him." Here the taunt is cruelly aimed at the sufferer's faith in God, which is the tenderest point in a good man's soul, the very apple of his eye. They must have learned the diabolical art from Satan himself, for they made rare proficiency in it. According to Matthew xxvii. 39—44, there were five forms of taunt hurled at the Lord Jesus ; this special piece of mockery is probably mentioned in this psalm because it is the most bitter of the whole ; it has a biting, sarcastic irony in it, which gives it a peculiar venom ; it must have stung the Man of Sorrows to the quick. When we are tormented in the same manner, let us remember him who endured such contradiction of sinners against himself, and we shall be comforted. On reading these verses one is ready, with Trapp, to ask, Is this a prophecy or a history ? for the description is so accurate. We must not lose sight of the truth which was unwittingly uttered by the Jewish scoffers. They themselves are witnesses that Jesus of Nazareth trusted in God : why then was he permitted to perish ? Jehovah had aforetime delivered those who rolled their burdens upon him : why was this man deserted ? Oh that they had understood the answer ! Note further, that their ironical jest, *" seeing he delighted in him,"* was true. The Lord did delight in his dear Son,

and when he was found in fashion as a man, and became obedient unto death, he still was well pleased with him. Strange mixture ! Jehovah delights in him, and yet bruises him ; is well pleased, and yet slays him.

9. "*But thou art he that took me out of the womb.*" Kindly providence attends with the surgery of tenderness at every human birth ; but the Son of Man, who was marvellously begotten of the Holy Ghost, was in an especial manner watched over by the Lord when brought forth by Mary. The destitute state of Joseph and Mary, far away from friends and home, led them to see the cherishing hand of God in the safe delivery of the mother, and the happy birth of the child ; that Child now fighting the great battle of his life, uses the mercy of his nativity as an argument with God. Faith finds weapons everywhere. He who wills to believe shall never lack reasons for believing. "*Thou didst make me hope when I was upon my mother's breasts.*" Was our Lord so early a believer ? Was he one of those babes and sucklings out of whose mouths strength is ordained ? So it would seem ; and if so, what a plea for help ! Early piety gives peculiar comfort in our after trials, for surely he who loved us when we were children is too faithful to cast us off in our riper years. Some give the text the sense of "gave me cause to trust, by keeping me safely," and assuredly there was a special providence which preserved our Lord's infant days from the fury of Herod, the dangers of travelling, and the ills of poverty.

10. "*I was cast upon thee from the womb.*" Into the Almighty arms he was first received, as into those of a loving parent. This is a sweet thought. God begins his care over us from the earliest hour. We are dandled upon the knee of mercy, and cherished in the lap of goodness ; our cradle is canopied by divine love, and our first totterings are guided by his care. "*Thou art my God from my mother's belly.*" The psalm begins with "*My God, my God,*" and here, not only is the claim repeated, but its early date is urged. Oh noble perseverance of faith, thus to continue pleading with holy ingenuity of argument ! Our birth was our weakest and most perilous period of existence ; if we were then secured by Omnipotent tenderness, surely we have no cause to suspect that divine goodness will fail us now. He who was our God when we left our mother, will be with us till we return to mother earth, and will keep us from perishing in the belly of hell.

11 Be not far from me ; for trouble *is* near ; for *there is* none to help.

12 Many bulls have compassed me : strong *bulls* of Bashan have beset me round.

13 They gaped upon me *with* their mouths, *as* a ravening and a roaring lion.

14 I am poured out like water, and all my bones are out of joint: my heart is like wax ; it is melted in the midst of my bowels.

15 My strength is dried up like a potsherd ; and my tongue cleaveth to my jaws ; and thou hast brought me into the dust of death.

16 For dogs have compassed me : the assembly of the wicked have inclosed me : they pierced my hands and my feet.

17 I may tell all my bones : they look *and* stare upon me.

18 They part my garments among them, and cast lots upon my vesture.

19 But be not thou far from me, O LORD : O my strength, haste thee to help me.

20 Deliver my soul from the sword ; my darling from the power of the dog.

21 Save me from the lion's mouth : for thou hast heard me from the horns of the unicorns.

The crucified Son of David continues to pour out his complaint and prayer. We need much grace that while reading we may have fellowship with his sufferings. May the blessed Spirit conduct us into a most clear and affecting sight of our Redeemer's woes.

11. *"Be not far from me."* This is the petition for which he has been using such varied and powerful pleas. His great woe was that God had forsaken him, his great prayer is that he would be near him. A lively sense of the divine presence is a mighty stay to the heart in times of distress. *"For trouble is near ; for there is none to help."* There are two *"fors,"* as though faith gave a double knock at mercy's gate ; that is a powerful prayer which is full of holy reasons and thoughtful arguments. The nearness of trouble is a weighty motive for divine help ; this moves our heavenly Father's heart, and brings down his helping hand. It is his glory to be our very present help in trouble. Our Substitute had trouble in his inmost heart, for he said, "the waters have come in, even unto my soul ;" well might he cry, *"be not far from me."* The absence of all other helpers is another telling plea. In our Lord's case none either could or would help him, it was needful that he should tread the wine-press alone ; yet was it a sore aggravation to find that all his disciples had forsaken him, and lover and friend were put far from him. There is an awfulness about absolute friendlessness which is crushing to the human mind, for man was not made to be alone, and is like a dismembered limb when he has to endure heart-loneliness.

12. *"Many bulls have compassed me : strong bulls of Bashan have beset me round."* The mighty ones in the crowd are here marked by the tearful eye of their victim. The priests, elders, scribes, Pharisees, rulers, and captains bellowed round the cross like wild cattle, fed in the fat and solitary pastures of Bashan, full of strength and fury ; they stamped and foamed around the inno-cent One, and longed to gore him to death with their cruelties. Conceive of the Lord Jesus as a helpless, unarmed, naked man, cast into the midst of a herd of infuriated wild bulls. They were brutal as bulls, many, and strong, and the Rejected One was all alone, and bound naked to the tree. His position throws great force into the earnest entreaty, "Be not far from me."

13. *"They gaped upon me with their mouths, as a ravening and a roaring lion."* Like hungry cannibals they opened their blasphemous mouths as if they were about to swallow the man whom they abhorred. They could not vomit forth their anger fast enough through the ordinary aperture of their mouths, and therefore set the doors of their lips wide open like those who gape. Like roaring lions they howled out their fury, and longed to tear the Saviour in pieces, as wild beasts raven over their prey. Our Lord's faith must have passed through a most severe conflict while he found himself abandoned to the tender mercies of the wicked, but he came off victorious by prayer ; the very dangers to which he was exposed being used to add prevalence to his entreaties.

14. Turning from his enemies, our Lord describes his own personal condition in language which should bring the tears into every loving eye. *"I am poured out like water."* He was utterly spent, like water poured upon the earth ; his heart failed him, and had no more firmness in it than running water, and his whole being was made a sacrifice, like a libation poured out before the Lord. He had long been a fountain of tears ; in Gethsemane his heart welled over in sweat, and on the cross he gushed forth with blood ; he poured out his strength and spirit, so that he was reduced to the most feeble and exhausted state. *"All my bones are out of joint,"* as if distended upon a rack. Is it not most probable that the fastenings of the hands and feet, and the jar occasioned by fixing the cross in the earth, may have dislocated the bones of the Crucified One? If this is not intended, we must refer the expression to that extreme weakness which would occasion relaxation of the muscles and a general sense of parting asunder throughout the whole system. *"My heart is like wax ; it is melted in the midst*

of my bowels." Excessive debility and intense pain made his inmost life to feel like wax melted in the heat. The Greek liturgy uses the expression, "thine unknown sufferings," and well it may. The fire of Almighty wrath would have consumed our souls for ever in hell ; it was no light work to bear as a substitute the heat of an anger so justly terrible. Dr. Gill wisely observes, "if the heart of Christ, the Lion of the tribe of Judah, melted at it, what heart can endure, or hands be strong, when God deals with them in his wrath ?"

15. "*My strength is dried up like a potsherd.*" Most complete debility is here portrayed ; Jesus likens himself to a broken piece of earthenware, or an earthen pot, baked in the fire till the last particle of moisture is driven out of the clay. No doubt a high degree of feverish burning afflicted the body of our Lord. All his strength was dried up in the tremendous flames of avenging justice, even as the paschal lamb was roasted in the fire. "*My tongue cleaveth to my jaws ;*" thirst and fever fastened his tongue to his jaws. Dryness and a horrible clamminess tormented his mouth, so that he could scarcely speak. "*Thou hast brought me into the dust of death ;*" so tormented in every single part as to feel dissolved into separate atoms, and each atom full of misery ; the full price of our redemption was paid, and no part of the Surety's body or soul escaped its share of agony. The words may set forth Jesus as having wrestled with Death until he rolled into the dust with his antagonist. Behold the humiliation of the Son of God ! The Lord of Glory stoops to the dust of death. Amid the mouldering relics of mortality Jesus condescends to lodge !

Bishop Mant's version of the two preceding verses is forcible and accurate :—

> "Pour'd forth like water is my frame ;
> My bones asunder start ;
> As wax that feels the searching flame,
> Within me melts my heart.
>
> My wither'd sinews shrink unstrung
> Like potsherd dried and dead :
> Cleaves to my jaws my burning tongue
> The dust of death my bed."

16. We are to understand every item of this sad description as being urged by the Lord Jesus as a plea for divine help ; and this will give us a high idea of his perseverance in prayer. "*For dogs have compassed me.*" Here he marks the more ignoble crowd, who, while less strong than their brutal leaders, were not less ferocious, for there they were howling and barking like unclean and hungry dogs. Hunters frequently surround their game with a circle, and gradually encompass them with an ever-narrowing ring of dogs and men. Such a picture is before us. In the centre stands, not a panting stag, but a bleeding, fainting man, and around him are the enraged and unpitying wretches who have hounded him to his doom. Here we have the "hind of the morning" of whom the psalm so plaintively sings, hunted by bloodhounds, all thirsting to devour him. *The assembly of the wicked have inclosed me :* thus the Jewish people were unchurched, and that which called itself an assembly of the righteous is justly for its sins marked upon the forehead as an assembly of the wicked. This is not the only occasion when professed churches of God have become synagogues of Satan, and have persecuted the Holy One and the Just. *They pierced my hands and my feet.* This can by no means refer to David, or to any one but Jesus of Nazareth, the once crucified but now exalted Son of God. Pause, dear reader, and view the wounds of thy Redeemer.

17. So emaciated was Jesus by his fastings and sufferings that he says, "*I may tell all my bones.*" He could count and re-count them. The posture of the body on the cross, Bishop Horne thinks, would so distend the flesh and skin as to make the bones visible, so that they might be numbered. The zeal of his Father's house had eaten him up ; like a good soldier he had endured hardness. Oh that we cared less for the body's enjoyment and ease and more for our Father's business ! It were better to count the bones of an emaciated body than to bring leanness into our souls.

"*They look and stare upon me.*" Unholy eyes gazed insultingly upon the

Saviour's nakedness, and shocked the sacred delicacy of his holy soul. The sight of the agonizing body ought to have ensured sympathy from the throng, but it only increased their savage mirth, as they gloated their cruel eyes upon his miseries. Let us blush for human nature, and mourn in sympathy with our Redeemer's shame. The first Adam made us all naked, and therefore the second Adam became naked that he might clothe our naked souls.

18. *" They part my garments among them, and cast lots upon my vesture."* The garments of the executed were the perquisites of the executioners in most cases, but it was not often that they cast lots at the division of the spoil ; this incident shows how clearly David in vision saw the day of Christ, and how surely the Man of Nazareth is he of whom the prophets spake : " these things, *therefore*, the soldiers did." He who gave his blood to cleanse us gave his garments to clothe us. As Ness says, " this precious Lamb of God gave up his golden fleece for us." How every incident of Jesus' griefs is here stored up in the treasury of inspiration, and embalmed in the amber of sacred song ; we must learn hence to be very mindful of all that concerns our Beloved, and to think much of everything which has a connection with him. It may be noted that the habit of gambling is of all others the most hardening, for men could practise it even at the cross-foot while besprinkled with the blood of the Crucified. No Christian will endure the rattle of the dice when he thinks of this.

19. *" But be not thou far from me, O Lord."* Invincible faith returns to the charge, and uses the same means, viz., importunate prayer. He repeats the petition so piteously offered before. He wants nothing but his God, even in his lowest state. He does not ask for the most comfortable or nearest presence of God, he will be content if he is not far from him ; humble requests speed at the throne. *" O my strength, haste thee to help me."* Hard cases need timely aid: when necessity justifies it we may be urgent with God as to time, and cry, " make haste ;" but we must not do this out of wilfulness. Mark how in the last degree of personal weakness he calls the Lord *" my strength ;"* after this fashion the believer can sing, " when I am weak, then am I strong."

20. *" Deliver my soul from the sword."* By the sword is probably meant entire destruction, which as a man he dreaded ; or perhaps he sought deliverance from the enemies around him, who were like a sharp and deadly sword to him. The Lord had said, " Awake, O sword," and now from the terror of that sword the Shepherd would fain be delivered as soon as justice should see fit. *" My darling from the power of the dog."* Meaning his soul, his life, which is most dear to every man. The original is, " my only one," and therefore is our soul dear, because it is our only soul. Would that all men made their souls their darlings, but many treat them as if they were not worth so much as the mire of the streets. *The dog* may mean Satan, that infernal Cerberus, that cursed and cursing cur ; or else the whole company of Christ's foes, who though many in number were as unanimous as if there were but one, and with one consent sought to rend him in pieces. If Jesus cried for help against the dog of hell, much more may we. *Cave canem*, beware of the dog, for his power is great, and only God can deliver us from him. When he fawns upon us, we must not put ourselves in his power ; and when he howls at us, we may remember that God holds him with a chain.

21. *" Save me from the lion's mouth : for thou hast heard me from the horns of the unicorns."* Having experienced deliverance in the past from great enemies, who were strong as the unicorns, the Redeemer utters his last cry for rescue from death, which is fierce and mighty as the lion. This prayer was heard, and the gloom of the cross departed. Thus faith, though sorely beaten, and even cast beneath the feet of her enemy, ultimately wins the victory. It was so in our Head, it shall be so in all the members. We have overcome the unicorn, we shall conquer the lion, and from both lion and unicorn we shall take the crown.

22 I will declare thy name unto my brethren : in the midst of the congregation will I praise thee.

23 Ye that fear the LORD, praise him ; all ye the seed of Jacob, glorify him ; and fear him, all ye the seed of Israel.

24 For he hath not despised nor abhorred the affliction of the afflicted ; neither hath he hid his face from him ; but when he cried unto him, he heard.

25 My praise *shall be* of thee in the great congregation : I will pay my vows before them that fear him.

26 The meek shall eat and be satisfied : they shall praise the LORD that seek him : your heart shall live for ever.

27 All the ends of the world shall remember and turn unto the LORD : and all the kindreds of the nations shall worship before thee.

28 For the kingdom *is* the LORD'S : and he *is* the governor among the nations.

29 All *they that be* fat upon earth shall eat and worship : all they that go down to the dust shall bow before him : and none can keep alive his own soul.

30 A seed shall serve him ; it shall be accounted to the Lord for a generation.

31 They shall come, and shall declare his righteousness unto a people that shall be born, that he hath done *this*.

The transition is very marked ; from a horrible tempest all is changed into calm. The darkness of Calvary at length passed away from the face of nature, and from the soul of the Redeemer, and beholding the light of his triumph and its future results the Saviour smiled. We have followed him through the gloom, let us attend him in the returning light. It will be well still to regard the words as a part of our Lord's soliloquy upon the cross, uttered in his mind during the last few moments before his death.

22. "*I will declare thy name unto my brethren.*" The delights of Jesus are always with his church, and hence his thoughts, after much distraction, return at the first moment of relief to their usual channel ; he forms fresh designs for the benefit of his beloved ones. He is not ashamed to call them brethren, "Saying, I will declare thy name unto my brethren, in the midst of the church will I sing praise unto thee." Among his first resurrection words were these, "Go to my brethren." In the verse before us, Jesus anticipates happiness in having communication with his people ; he purposes to be their teacher and minister, and fixes his mind upon the subject of his discourse. The *name, i.e.*, the character and conduct of God are by Jesus Christ's gospel proclaimed to all the holy brotherhood ; they behold the fulness of the Godhead dwelling bodily in him, and rejoice greatly to see all the infinite perfections manifested in one who is bone of their bone and flesh of their flesh. What a precious subject is the name of our God ! It is the only one worthy of the only Begotten, whose meat and drink it was to do the Father's will. We may learn from this resolution of our Lord, that one of the most excellent methods of showing our thankfulness for deliverances is to tell to our brethren what the Lord has done for us. We mention our sorrows readily enough ; why are we so slow in declaring our deliverances ? "*In the midst of the congregation will I praise thee.*" Not in a little household gathering merely does our Lord resolve to proclaim his Father's love, but in the great assemblies of his saints, and in the general assembly and church of the first-born. This the Lord Jesus is always doing by his representatives, who are the heralds of salvation, and labour to praise God. In the great universal church Jesus is the One authoritative teacher, and all others, so far as they are worthy to be called teachers, are nothing but echoes of his voice. Jesus, in this second sentence, reveals his object in declaring the divine

name, it is that God may be praised ; the church continually magnifies Jehovah for manifesting himself in the person of Jesus, and Jesus himself leads the song, and is both precentor and preacher in his church. Delightful are the seasons when Jesus communes with our hearts concerning divine truth ; joyful praise is the sure result.

23. *" Ye that fear the Lord praise him."* The reader must imagine the Saviour as addressing the congregation of the saints. He exhorts the faithful to unite with him in thanksgiving. The description of " fearing the Lord " is very frequent and very instructive ; it is the beginning of wisdom, and is an essential sign of grace. " I am a Hebrew and I fear God " was Jonah's confession of faith. Humble awe of God is so necessary a preparation for praising him that none are fit to sing to his honour but such as reverence his word ; but this fear is consistent with the highest joy, and is not to be confounded with legal bondage, which is a fear which perfect love casteth out. Holy fear should always keep the key of the singing pew. Where Jesus leads the tune none but holy lips may dare to sing. *" All ye the seed of Jacob glorify him."* The genius of the gospel is praise. Jew and Gentile saved by sovereign grace should be eager in the blessed work of magnifying the God of our salvation. *All* saints should unite in the song ; no tongue may be silent, no heart may be cold. Christ calls us to glorify God, and can we refuse ? *" And fear him, all ye the seed of Israel."* The spiritual Israel all do this, and we hope the day will come when Israel after the flesh will be brought to the same mind. The more we praise God the more reverently shall we fear him, and the deeper our reverence the sweeter our songs. So much does Jesus value praise that we have it here under his dying hand and seal that all the saints must glorify the Lord.

24. *" For he hath not despised nor abhorred the affliction of the afflicted."* Here is good matter and motive for praise. The experience of our covenant Head and Representative should encourage all of us to bless the God of grace. Never was man so afflicted as our Saviour in body and soul from friends and foes, by heaven and hell, in life and death ; he was the foremost in the ranks of the afflicted, but all those afflictions were sent in love, and not because his Father despised and abhorred him. 'Tis true that justice demanded that Christ should bear the burden which as a substitute he undertook to carry, but Jehovah always loved him, and in love laid that load upon him with a view to his ultimate glory and to the accomplishment of the dearest wish of his heart. Under all his woes our Lord was honourable in the Father's sight, the matchless jewel of Jehovah's heart. *" Neither hath he hid his face from him."* That is to say, the hiding was but temporary, and was soon removed ; it was not final and eternal. *" But when he cried unto him, he heard."* Jesus was heard in that he feared. He cried *in extremis* and *de profundis*, and was speedily answered ; he therefore bids his people join him in singing a *Gloria in excelsis*.

Every child of God should seek refreshment for his faith in this testimony of the Man of Sorrows. What Jesus here witnesses is as true to-day as when it was first written. It shall never be said that any man's affliction or poverty prevented his being an accepted suppliant at Jehovah's throne of grace. The meanest applicant is welcome at mercy's door :—

> " None that approach his throne shall find
> A God unfaithful or unkind."

25. *" My praise shall be of thee in the great congregation."* The one subject of our Master's song is the Lord alone. The Lord and the Lord only is the theme which the believer handleth when he gives himself to imitate Jesus in praise. The word in the original is " from thee,"—true praise is of celestial origin. The rarest harmonies of music are nothing unless they are sincerely consecrated to God by hearts sanctified by the Spirit. The clerk says, " Let us sing to the praise and glory of God ;" but the choir often sing to the praise and glory of themselves. Oh when shall our service of song be a pure offering ? Observe in this verse how Jesus loves the public praises of the saints, and thinks

with pleasure of the great congregation. It would be wicked on our part to despise the twos and threes ; but, on the other hand, let not the little companies snarl at the greater assemblies as though they were necessarily less pure and less approved, for Jesus loves the praise of the great congregation. *"I will pay my vows before them that fear him."* Jesus dedicates himself anew to the carrying out of the divine purpose in fulfilment of his vows made in anguish. Did our Lord when he ascended to the skies proclaim amid the redeemed in glory the goodness of Jehovah? And was that the vow here meant? Undoubtedly the publication of the gospel is the constant fulfilment of covenant engagements made by our Surety in the councils of eternity. Messiah vowed to build up a spiritual temple for the Lord, and he will surely keep his word.

26. *" The meek shall eat and be satisfied."* Mark how the dying Lover of our souls solaces himself with the result of his death. The spiritually poor find a feast in Jesus, they feed upon him to the satisfaction of their hearts, they were famished until he gave himself for them, but now they are filled with royal dainties. The thought of the joy of his people gave comfort to our expiring Lord. Note the characters who partake of the benefit of his passion ; *" the meek,"* the humble, and lowly. Lord, make us so. Note also the certainty that gospel provisions shall not be wasted, *" they shall eat ;"* and the sure result of such eating, *" and be satisfied."* *" They shall praise the Lord that seek him."* For a while they may keep a fast, but their thanksgiving days must and shall come. *" Your heart shall live for ever."* Your spirits shall not fail through trial, you shall not die of grief, immortal joys shall be your portion. Thus Jesus speaks even from the cross to the troubled seeker. If his dying words are so assuring, what consolation may we not find in the truth that he ever liveth to make intercession for us ! They who eat at Jesus' table receive the fulfilment of the promise, "Whosoever eateth of this bread shall live for ever."

27. In reading this verse one is struck with the Messiah's missionary spirit. It is evidently his grand consolation that Jehovah will be known throughout all places of his dominion. *" All the ends of the world shall remember and turn unto the Lord."* Out from the inner circle of the present church the blessing is to spread in growing power until the remotest parts of the earth shall be ashamed of their idols, mindful of the true God, penitent for their offences, and unanimously earnest for reconciliation with Jehovah. Then shall false worship cease, *" and all the kindreds of the nations shall worship before thee,"* O thou only living and true God. This hope which was the reward of Jesus is a stimulus to those who fight his battles.

It is well to mark the order of conversion as here set forth ; they shall *" remember"*—this is reflection, like the prodigal who came unto himself ; *" and turn unto Jehovah*—this is repentance, like Manasseh who left his idols and *" worship"*—this is holy service, as Paul adored the Christ whom once he abhorred.

28. *" For the kingdom is the Lord's."* As an obedient Son the dying Redeemer rejoiced to know that his Father's interests would prosper through his pains. " The Lord reigneth" was *his* song as it is ours. He who by his own power reigns supreme in the domains of creation and providence, has set up a kingdom of grace, and by the conquering power of the cross that kingdom will grow until all people shall own its sway and proclaim that *" he is the governor among the nations."* Amid the tumults and disasters of the present the Lord reigneth ; but in the halcyon days of peace the rich fruit of his dominion will be apparent to every eye. Great Shepherd, let thy glorious kingdom come.

29. *" All they that be fat upon earth,"* the rich and great are not shut out. Grace now finds the most of its jewels among the poor, but in the latter days the mighty of the earth *" shall eat,"* shall taste of redeeming grace and dying love, and shall *" worship"* with all their hearts the God who deals so bountifully with us in Christ Jesus. Those who are spiritually fat with inward prosperity

shall be filled with the marrow of communion, and shall worship the Lord with peculiar fervour. In the covenant of grace Jesus has provided good cheer for our high estate, and he has taken equal care to console us in our humiliation, for the next sentence is, "*all they that go down to the dust shall bow before him.*" There is relief and comfort in bowing before God when our case is at its worst ; even amid the dust of death prayer kindles the lamp of hope.

While all who come to God by Jesus Christ are thus blessed, whether they be rich or poor, none of those who despise him may hope for a blessing. "*None can keep alive his own soul.*" This is the stern counterpart of the gospel message of "look and live." There is no salvation out of Christ. We must hold life, and have life as Christ's gift, or we shall die eternally. This is very solid evangelical doctrine, and should be proclaimed in every corner of the earth, that like a great hammer it may break in pieces all self-confidence.

30. "*A seed shall serve him.*" Posterity shall perpetuate the worship of the Most High. The kingdom of truth on earth shall never fail. As one generation is called to its rest, another will arise in its stead. We need have no fear for the true apostolic succession ; that is safe enough. "*It shall be accounted to the Lord for a generation.*" He will reckon the ages by the succession of the saints, and set his accounts according to the families of the faithful. Generations of sinners come not into the genealogy of the skies. God's family register is not for strangers, but for the children only.

31. "*They shall come.*" Sovereign grace shall bring out from among men the bloodbought ones. Nothing shall thwart the divine purpose. The chosen shall come to life, to faith, to pardon, to heaven. In this the dying Saviour finds a sacred satisfaction. Toiling servant of God, be glad at the thought that the eternal purpose of God shall suffer neither let nor hindrance. "*And shall declare his righteousness unto a people that shall be born.*" None of the people who shall be brought to God by the irresistible attractions of the cross shall be dumb, they shall be able to tell forth the righteousness of the Lord, so that future generations shall know the truth. Fathers shall teach their sons, who shall hand it down to their children ; the burden of the story always being "*that he hath done this,*" or, that "It is finished." Salvation's glorious work is done, there is peace on earth, and glory in the highest. "It is finished," these were the expiring words of the Lord Jesus, as they are the last words of this Psalm. May we by living faith be enabled to see our salvation finished by the death of Jesus !

EXPLANATORY NOTES AND QUAINT SAYINGS.

Title.—Aijeleth Shahar. The title of the twenty-second Psalm is Aijeleth Shahar—*the morning hart.* The whole Psalm refers to Christ, containing much that cannot be applied to another : parting his garments, casting lots for his vesture, etc. He is described as a kindly, meek and beautiful hart, started by the huntsman at the dawn of the day. Herod began hunting him down as soon as he appeared. Poverty, the hatred of men, and the temptation of Satan, joined in the pursuit. There always was some " dog," or " bull," or " unicorn," ready to attack him. After his first sermon the huntsmen gathered about him, but he was too fleet of foot, and escaped. The church had long seen the Messiah " like a roe, or a young hart, upon the mountains," had " heard the voice of her Beloved," and had cried out, " Behold, he cometh, leaping upon the mountains, skipping upon the hills ;" sometimes he was even seen, with the dawn of the day, in the neighbourhood of the temple, and beside the enclosures of the vineyards. The church requested to see him " on the mountains of Bether," and upon " the mountains of spices." The former probably signifying the place of his sufferings, and the latter the sublime acclivities of light, glory, and honour, where the " hart " shall be hunted no more. But in the afternoon, the huntsmen who had been following the " young roe" from early day-break, had succeeded in driving him to the mountains of Bether. Christ found Calvary a craggy, jagged, and fearful hill—" a mountain of division." Here he was driven by the huntsmen to the edges of the awful precipices yawning destruction from below, while he was surrounded and held at bay by all the beasts of prey and monsters of the infernal forest. The " unicorn," and the " bulls of Bashan," gored him with their horns ; the great " lion" roared at him ; and the " dog" fastened himself upon him. But he foiled them all. In his own time he bowed his head and gave up the ghost. He was buried in a new grave ; and his assailants reckoned upon complete victory. They had not considered that he was a " morning hart." Surely enough, at the appointed time, did he escape from the hunter's net, and stand forth on the mountains of Israel ALIVE, and *never*, NEVER to die again. Now he is with Mary in the garden, giving evidence of his own resurrection ; in a moment he is at Emmaus, encouraging the too timid and bewildered disciples. Nor does it cost him any trouble to go thence to Galilee to his friends, and again to the Mount of Olives, " on the mountains of spices," *carrying with him the day-dawn*, robed in life and beauty for evermore."—*Christmas Evans*, 1766—1838.

Title.—It will be very readily admitted that the *hind* is a very appropriate emblem of the suffering and persecuted righteous man who meets us in this Psalm. . . . That the *hind* may be a figurative expression significant of suffering innocence, is put beyond a doubt by the fact, that the wicked and the persecutors in this Psalm, *whose peculiar physiognomy is marked by emblems drawn from the brute creation*, are designed by the terms *dogs, lions, bulls*, etc.—*E. W. Hengstenberg*.

Title.—" *The hind*." Much extraordinary symbolism has by old authors been conjured up and clustered around the hind. According to their curious natural history, there exists a deadly enmity between the deer and the serpent, and the deer by its warm breath draws serpents out of their holes in order to devour them. The old grammarians derived *Elaphas*, or hart, from *elaunein tous opheis*, that is, of driving away serpents. Even the burning a portion of the deer's horns was said to drive away all snakes. If a snake had escaped the hart after being drawn out by the hart by its breath, it was said to be more vehemently poisonous than before. The timidity of the deer was ascribed to the great size of its heart, in which they thought was a bone shaped like a cross.—*Condensed from Wood's " Bible Animals," by C. H. S.*

Whole Psalm.—This is a kind of gem among the Psalms, and is peculiarly excellent and remarkable. It contains those deep, sublime, and heavy sufferings of Christ, when agonising in the midst of the terrors and pangs of divine wrath and death, which surpass all human thought and comprehension. I know not whether any Psalm throughout the whole book contains matter more weighty, or from which the hearts of the godly can so truly perceive those sighs and groans, inexpressible by man, which their Lord and Head, Jesus Christ, uttered when conflicting for us in the midst of death, and in the midst of the pains and terrors of hell. Wherefore this Psalm ought to be most highly prized by all who have any acquaintance with temptations of faith and spiritual conflicts.—*Martin Luther*.

Whole Psalm.—This Psalm, as it sets out the sufferings of Christ to the full, so also his three great offices. His sufferings are copiously described from the beginning of the Psalm to verse 22. The prophetical office of Christ, from verse 22 to verse 25. That which is foretold about his vows (verse 25), hath respect to his priestly function. In the rest of the Psalm the kingly office of Christ is set forth.—*William Gouge, D.D.* (1575—1653), *in " A Commentary on the whole Epistle to the Hebrews."* *

---

* Reprinted in Nichol's Series of Commentaries.

Whole Psalm.—This Psalm seems to be less a prophecy than a history.—*Cassiodorus.*

Whole Psalm.—This Psalm must be expounded, word for word, entire and in every respect, of Christ only ; without any allegory, trope, or *anagoge.*—*Bakius, quoted by F. Delitzsch, D.D., on Hebrews,* ii. 12.

Whole Psalm.—A prophecy of the passion of Christ, and of the vocation of the *Gentiles.*—*Eusebius of Cæsarea.*

Verse 1.—"*My God, my God, why hast thou forsaken me ?*" We contrast this with John xvi. 32, "*I am not alone, because the Father is with me.*" That these words in David were notwithstanding the words of Christ, there is no true believer ignorant ; yet how cross our Lord's words in John ! Answer :—It is one thing to speak out of present sense of misery, another thing to be confident of a never-separated Deity. The condition of Christ in respect of his human state (not the divine), is in all outward appearances, like ours ; we conceive the saints' condition very lamentable at times, as if God were for ever gone. And Christ (to teach us to cry after God the Father, like children after the mother, whose very stepping but at the door, ofttimes makes the babe believe, and so saith that his father is gone for ever), presents in his own sufferings how much he is sensible of ours in that case. As for his divine nature, he and his Father can never sunder in that, and so at no time is he alone, but the Father is always with him.—*William Streat, in "The Dividing of the Hoof,"* 1654.

Verse 1.—"*My God, my God,*" etc. There is a tradition that our Lord, hanging on the cross, began, as we know from the gospel, this Psalm ; and repeating it and those that follow, gave up his most blessed spirit when he came to the sixth verse of the thirty-first Psalm. However that may be, by taking these first words on his lips, he stamped the Psalm as belonging to himself.—*Ludolph, the Carthusian (circa.* 1350), *in J. M. Neale's Commentary.*

Verse 1.—"*My God, my God,*" etc. It was so sharp, so heavy an affliction to Christ's soul, that it caused him who was meek under all other sufferings as a lamb, to roar under this like a lion. For so much those words of Christ signify, "*My God, my God, why hast thou forsaken me ? why art thou so far from helping me, and from the words of my roaring ?*" It comes from a root that signifies to howl or roar as a lion, and rather signifies the noise made by a wild beast than the voice of a man. And it is as much as if Christ had said, O my God, no words can express my anguish, I will not speak, but roar, howl out my complaints. Pour it out in volleys of groans. I roar as a lion. It's no small matter will make that majestic creature to roar. And sure so great a spirit as Christ's would not have roared under a slight burden.

Did God really forsake Jesus Christ upon the cross ? then from the desertion of Christ singular consolation springs up to the people of God ; yea, manifold consolation. Principally it's a support in these two respects, as it is *preventive* of your final desertion, and a comfortable pattern to you in your present sad desertions. 1. Christ's desertion is *preventive* of your final desertion. Because he was forsaken for a time you shall not be forsaken for ever. For he was forsaken for you. It is every way as much for the dear Son of God, the darling delight of his soul, to be forsaken of God for a time, as if such a poor inconsiderable thing as thou art shouldst be cast off to eternity. Now, this being equivalent and borne in thy room, must needs give thee the highest security in the world that God will never finally withdraw from thee. 2. Moreover, this sad desertion of Christ becomes a comfortable *pattern* to poor deserted souls in divers respects ; and the proper business of such souls, at such times, is to eye it believingly. Though God deserted Christ, yet at the same time he powerfully supported him. His omnipotent arms were under him, though his pleased face was hid from him. He had not indeed his smiles, but he had his supportations. So, Christian, just so shall it be with thee. Thy God may turn away his face, he will not pluck away his arm. When one asked of holy Mr. Baines how the case stood with his soul, he answered, " Supports I have, though suavities I want." Our Father in this deals with us as we ourselves sometimes do with a child that is stubborn and rebellious. We turn him out of doors and bid him begone out of our sight, and there he sighs and weeps ; but however for the humbling of him, we will not presently take him into house and favour ; yet we order, at least permit the servants to carry him meat and drink : here is fatherly care and support, though no former smiles or manifested delights. . . . Though God forsook Christ, yet at that time he could justify God. So you read, "O my God (saith he), I cry in the day time ; but thou hearest not, and in the night season, and am not silent ; but thou art holy." Is not thy spirit according to thy measure, framed like Christ's in this ; canst thou not, say even when he writes bitter things against thee, he is a holy, faithful and good God for all this ! I am deserted but not wronged. There is not one drop of injustice in all the sea of my sorrows. Though he condemned me I must and will justify him : this also is Christ-like.—*John Flavel.*

Verse 1.—" *My God, my God.*" The repetition is expressive of fervent desire—" *My God,*" in an especial sense, as in his words after the resurrection to Mary Magdalene, "I ascend unto my God, and your God ;" " My God," not as the Son of God only, but in that nature which he hath assumed, as the beloved Son in whom the Father is well pleased ; who is loved of the Father and who loveth the Father more than the whole universe. It is observed that this expression, " My God," is three times repeated.—*Dionysius, quoted by Isaac Williams.*

Verse 1.—" *My God.*" It was possible for Christ by *faith* to know that he was beloved of God, and he did know that he was beloved of God, when yet as to *sense* and *feeling* he tasted of God's *wrath.* Faith and the want of sense are not inconsistent ; there may be no present sense of God's love, nay, there may be a present sense of his wrath, and yet there may be faith at the same time.— *John Row's " Emmanuel,"* 1680.

Verse 1.—This word, " *My God,*" takes in more than all the philosophers in the world could draw out of it.—*Alexander Wedderburn,* 1701.

Verse 1.—That there is something of a singular force, meaning, and feeling in these words is manifest from this—the evangelists have studiously given us this verse in the very words of the Hebrew, in order to show their emphatic force. And moreover I do not remember any one other place in the Scriptures where we have this repetition, ELI, ELI.—*Martin Luther.*

Verse 1.—" *Why ?*" Not the " *why*" of impatience or despair, not the sinful questioning of one whose heart rebels against his chastening, but rather the cry of a lost child who cannot understand why his father has left him, and who longs to see his father's face again.—*J. J. Stewart Perowne.*

Verse 1.—" *My roaring.*" שׁאג, seems primarily to denote the roaring of a lion ; but, as applied to intelligent beings, it is generally expressive of profound mental anguish poured forth in audible and even vehement strains. Psalm xxxviii. 9 ; xxxiii. 3 ; Job iii. 24. Thus did the suffering Messiah pour forth strong crying and tears, to him that was able to save him from death. Heb. v. 7.—*John Morison.*

Verse 1.—When Christ complains of having been forsaken by God, we are not to understand that he was forsaken by the First Person, or that there was a dissolution of the hypostatic union, or that he lost the favour and friendship of the Father ; but he signifies to us that God permitted his human nature to undergo those dreadful torments, and to suffer an ignominious death, from which he could, if he chose, most easily deliver him. Nor did such complaints proceed either from impatience or ignorance, as if Christ were ignorant of the cause of his suffering, or was not most willing to bear such abandonment in his suffering ; such complaints were only a declaration of his most bitter sufferings. And whereas, through the whole course of his passion, with such patience did our Lord suffer, as not to let a single groan or sigh escape from him, so now, lest the bystanders may readily believe that he was rendered impassible by some superior power ; therefore, when his last moments were nigh, he protests that he is true man, truly passible ; forsaken by his Father in his sufferings, the bitterness and acuteness of which he then intimately felt. — *Robert Bellarmine (Cardinal)*, 1542—1621.

Verse 1.—Divines are wont commonly to say, that Christ, from the moment of his conception, had the sight of God, his human soul being immediately united to the Deity, Christ from the very moment of his conception had the sight of God. Now for our Saviour, who had known experimentally how sweet the comfort of his Father's face had been, and had lived all his days under the warm beams and influences of the Divinity, and had had his soul all along refreshed with the sense of the Divine presence, for him to be left in that horror and darkness, as to have no taste of comfort, no glimpse of the Divinity breaking in upon his human soul, how great an affliction must that needs be unto him ! *John Row.*

Verse 1.—Desertion is in itself no sin ; for Christ endured its bitterness, ay, he was so deep in it, that when he died, he said, " *Why hast thou forsaken me ?*" A total, a final desertion ours is not ; partial the best have had and have. God turns away his face, David himself is troubled : " *The just shall live by faith*," and not by feeling.—*Richard Capel.*

Verse 1.—Oh ! how will our very hearts melt with love, when we remember that as we have been distressed for our sins against him ; so he was in greater agonies for us ? We have had gall and wormwood, but he tasted a more bitter cup. The anger of God has dried up our spirits, but he was scorched with a more flaming wrath. He was under violent pain in the garden, and on the cross ; ineffable was the sorrow that he felt, being forsaken of his Father, deserted by his disciples, affronted and reproached by his enemies, and under a curse for us. This Sun was under a doleful eclipse, this living Lord was pleased to die, and in his death was under the frowns of an angry God. That face was then hid from him that had always smiled before ; and his soul felt that horror and that darkness which it had never felt before. So that there was no separation between the divine and human nature, yet he suffered pains equal to those which we had deserved to suffer in hell for ever. God so suspended the efficacies of his grace that it displayed in that hour none of its force and virtue on him. He had no comfort from heaven, none from his angels, none from his friends, even in that sorrowful hour when he needed comfort most. Like a lion that is hurt in the forest, so he roared and cried out, though there was no despair in him ; and when he was forsaken, yet there was trust and hope in these words, " *My God, my God.*"—*Timothy Rogers.*

Verse 1.—Here is comfort to *deserted souls ;* Christ himself was deserted ; therefore, if thou be deserted, God dealeth no otherwise with thee than he did with Christ. Thou mayst be beloved of God and not feel it ; Christ was so, he was beloved of the Father, and yet had no present sense and feeling of his love. This may be a great comfort to holy souls under the suspension of those comforts and manifestations which sometimes they have felt ; Christ himself underwent such a suspension, therefore such a suspension of divine comfort may consist with God's love. Thou mayst conclude possibly, " I am a hypocrite, and therefore God hath forsaken me ;" this is the complaint of some doubting Christians, " I am a hypocrite, and therefore God hath forsaken me ;" but thou hast no reason so to conclude : there was no failure in Christ's obedience, and yet Christ was forsaken in point of comfort ; therefore desertion, in point of comfort, may consist with truth of grace, yea, with the highest measure of grace ; so it did in our Saviour.—*John Row.*

Verse 1.—Lord, thou knowest what it is for a soul to be forsaken, it was sometime thine own case when thou complainedst, " *My God, why hast thou forsaken me ?*" not, O my Lord ! but that thou hadst a divine supportment, but thou hadst not (it seemeth) that inward joy which at other times did fill thee ; now thou art in thy glory, pity *a worm* in misery, that mourns and desires more after thee than all things : Lord, thou paidst dear for my good, let good come unto me.—*Joseph Symonds*, 1658.

Verse 1.—The first verse expresses a species of suffering that never at any other time was felt in this world, and never will be again—the vengeance of the Almighty upon his child—"My God, why hast thou forsaken me?"—*R. H. Ryland.*

Verse 2.—" *O my God, I cry in the daytime, but thou hearest not,*" etc. How like is this expostulation to that of a human child with its earthly parent! It is based on the ground of relationship—"I am thine; I cry day and night, yet I am not heard. Thou art my God, yet nothing is done to silence me. In the day-time of my life I cried; in this night season of my death I intreat. In the garden of Gethsemane I occupied the night with prayers; with continual ejaculations have I passed through this eventful morning. O my God, thou hast not yet heard me, therefore am I not yet silent; I cannot cease till thou answerest." Here Christ urges his suit in a manner which none but filial hearts adopt. The child knows that the parent yearns over him. His importunity is strengthened by confidence in paternal love. He keeps not silence, he gives him no rest because he confides in his power and willingness to grant the desired relief. This is natural. It is the argument of the heart, an appeal to the inward yearnings of our nature. It is also scriptural, and is thus stated, "If ye then being evil, know how to give good gifts unto your children, how much more shall your heavenly Father give the Holy Spirit to them that ask him?" Luke xi. 13. *John Stevenson, in " Christ on the Cross,"* 1842.

Verse 2.—The princely prophet says, " *Lord, I cry unto thee in the daytime, but thou hearest not, also in the night time, and yet this is not to be thought folly to me.*" * Some perhaps would think it a great point of folly for a man to cry and call unto him who stops his ears, and seems not to hear. Nevertheless, this folly of the faithful is wiser than all the wisdom of the world. For we know well enough, that howsoever God seem at the first not to hear, yet the Lord is a sure refuge *in due time—in affliction.* Psalm ix. 9.—*Thomas Playfere.*

Verses 2, 3.—Well, what hears God from him, now he hears nothing from God, as to the deliverance prayed for? No murmuring at God's proceedings; nay, he hears quite the contrary, for he justifies and praises God : " *But thou art holy, O thou that inhabitest the praises of Israel.*" Observe whether thou canst not gather something from the manner of God's denying the thing prayed for, which may sweeten it to thee! Haply thou shalt find he denies thee, but it is with a smiling countenance, and ushers it in with some expressions of grace and favour, that may assure thee his denial proceeds not from displeasure. As you would do with a dear friend, who, may be, comes to borrow a sum of money of you; lend it you dare not, because you see plainly it is not for his good; but in giving him the denial, lest he should misinterpret it, as proceeding from want of love and respect, you preface it with some kind of language of your hearty affection to him, as that you love him, and therefore deny him, and shall be ready to do for him more than that comes to. Thus God sometimes wraps up his denials in such sweet intimations of love, as prevents all jealousies arising in the hearts of his people.—*William Gurnall.*

Verses 2, 3.—They that have conduit-water come into their houses, if no water come they do not conclude the spring to be dry, but the pipes to be stopped or broken. If prayer speed not, we must be sure that the fault is not in God, but in ourselves; were we but ripe for mercy, he is ready to extend it to us, and even waits for the purpose.—*John Trapp.*

Verse 3.—"*But thou art holy.*" Here is the triumph of faith—the Saviour stood like a rock in the wide ocean of temptation. High as the billows rose, so did his faith, like the coral rock, wax greater and stronger till it became an island of salvation to our shipwrecked souls. It is as if he had said, " It matters not what I endure. Storms may howl upon me; men despise; devils tempt;

---

* Septuagint version.

circumstances overpower ; and God himself forsake me, still God is holy ; there is no unrighteousness in him."—*John Stevenson.*

Verse 3. —" *But thou art holy.*" Does it seem strange that the heart in its darkness and sorrow should find comfort in this attribute of God ? No, for God's holiness is but another aspect of his faithfulness and mercy. And in that remarkable name, " the Holy One *of Israel,*" we are taught that he who is the " *holy*" God is also the God who has made a covenant with his chosen. It would be impossible for an Israelite to think of God's holiness without thinking also of that covenant relationship. " Be ye holy ; for I, the Lord your God am holy," were the words in which Israel was reminded of their relation to God. See especially Lev. xix. 1. We see something of this feeling in such passages as Psalm lxxxix. 16—19 ; xcix. 5—9 ; Hosea xi. 8, 9 ; Isaiah xli. 14 ; xlvii. 4.— *J. J. Stewart Perowne.*

Verse 3.—Were temptations never so black, faith will not hearken to an ill word spoken against God, but will justify God always.—*David Dickson.*

Verses 4, 5.—Those who look upon this Psalm as having a primary reference to the King of Israel, attribute great beauty to these words, from the very pleasing conjecture that David was, at the time of composing them, sojourning at Mahanaim, where Jacob, in his distress, wrestled with the angel, and obtained such signal blessings. That, in a place so greatly hallowed by associations of the past, he should make his appeal to the God of his fathers, was alike the dictate of patriarchal feeling and religion.—*John Morison, D.D., in " Morning Meditations."*

Verse 5.—" *Thou didst deliver them,*" but thou wilt not deliver me ; nay, rather thou didst deliver them because thou wilt not deliver me.—*Gerhohus.*

Verse 6.—" *But I am a worm, and no man.*" A fisherman, when he casts his angle into the river, doth not throw the hook in bare, naked, and uncovered, for then he knows the fish will never bite, and therefore he hides the hook within a worm, or some other bait, and so, the fish, biting at the worm, is catched by the hook. Thus Christ, speaking of himself, saith, " *Ego vermis et non homo.*" He, coming to perform the great work of our redemption, did cover and hide his Godhead within the worm of his human nature. The grand water-serpent, Leviathan, the devil, thinking to swallow the worm of his humanity, was caught upon the hook of his divinity. This hook stuck in his jaws, and tore him very sore. By thinking to destroy Christ, he destroyed his own kingdom, and lost his own power for ever.—*Lancelot Andrewes.*

Verse 6.—" *I am a worm.*" Christ calls himself " *a worm*" . . . on account of the opinion that men of the world had of him. . . . The Jews esteemed Christ as a worm, and treated him as such ; he was loathsome to them and hated by them ; every one trampled upon him, and trod him under foot as men do worms. . . . . . The Chaldee paraphrase renders it here *a weak worm ;* and though Christ is the mighty God, and is also the Son of man, whom God made strong for himself ; yet there was a weakness in his human nature, and he was crucified through it, 2 Cor. xiii. 4 : and it has been observed by some, that the word תּוֹלַעַת there used signifies the scarlet worm, or the worm that is in the grain or berry with which scarlet is dyed : and like this scarlet worm did our Lord look, when by way of mockery he was clothed with a scarlet robe ; and especially when he appeared in his dyed garments, and was red in his apparel, as one that treadeth in the wine fat ; when his body was covered with blood when he hung upon the cross, which was shed to make crimson and scarlet sins as white as snow.—*John Gill.*

Verse 6.—" *I am a worm.*" An humble soul is emptied of all swelling thoughts of himself. Bernard calls humility a self-annihilation. Job xxii. 29. " Thou wilt save the humble ;" in the Hebrew it is, " Him that is of low eyes."

An humble man hath lower thoughts of himself than others can have of him ; David, though a king, yet looked upon himself as " *a worm :*" " *I am a worm, and no man.*" Bradford, a martyr, yet subscribes himself " a sinner." Job x. 15. " If I be righteous, yet will I not lift up my head :" like the violet, a sweet flower, but hangs down the head.—*Thomas Watson.*

Verse 6.—"*A worm.*" So trodden under foot, trampled on, maltreated, buffeted and spit upon, mocked and tormented, as to seem more like a worm than a man. Behold what great contempt hath the Lord of Majesty endured, that his confusion may be our glory ; his punishment our heavenly bliss ! With-out ceasing impress this spectacle, O Christian, on thy soul !—*Dionysius, quoted by Isaac Williams.*

Verse 6.—" *I am a worm.*" Among the Hindoos, when a man complains and abhors himself, he asks ; " What am I ? A worm ! a worm !" " Ah, the proud man ! he regarded me as a worm, well should I like to say to him, ' We are all worms.' " " Worm, crawl out of my presence."—*Joseph Roberts.*

Verse 7.—" *All they that see me laugh me to scorn,*" etc. Imagine this dread-ful scene. Behold this motley multitude of rich and poor, of Jews and Gentiles ! Some stand in groups and gaze. Some recline at ease and stare. Others move about in restless gratification at the event. There is a look of satisfaction on every countenance. None are silent. The velocity of speech seems tardy. The theme is far too great for one member to utter. Every lip, and head, and finger, is now a tongue. The rough soldiers, too, are busied in their coarse way. The work of blood is over. Refreshment has become necessary. Their usual beverage of vinegar and water is supplied to them. As they severally are satis-fied, they approach the cross, hold some forth to the Saviour, and bid him drink as they withdraw it. Luke xxiii. 36. They know he must be suffering an intense thirst, they therefore aggravate it with the mockery of refreshment. Cruel Romans ! and ye, O regicidal Jews ! Was not death enough ? Must mockery and scorn be added ? On this sad day Christ made you *one* indeed ! Dreadful unity—which constituted you the joint mockers and murderers of the Lord of glory !—*John Stevenson.*

Verse 7.—" *All they that see me laugh me to scorn,*" etc. There have been persons in our own days, whose crimes have excited such detestation that the populace would probably have torn them in pieces, before, and even after their trial, if they could have had them in their power. Yet when these very obnoxious persons have been executed according to their sentence, if, perhaps, there was not one spectator who wished them to escape, yet neither was one found so lost to sensibility as to insult them in their dying moments. But when Jesus suffers, *all that see him laugh him to scorn ; they shoot out the lip, they shake the head ;* they insult his character and his hope.—*John Newton.*

Verse 7.—" *They shoot out the lip.*" To protrude the lower lip is, in the East, considered a very strong indication of contempt. Its employment is chiefly confined to the lower orders.—*Illustrated Commentary.*

Verses 7, 8.—It was after his crucifixion, and during the hours that he hung upon the cross, that his sufferings in this way—the torment of beholding and hearing the scorn and mockery which was made of the truth of his person and doctrine—exceedingly abounded, and in such and so many kinds of mockery and insult that some consider this to have been the chiefest pain and sorrow which he endured in his most sacred passion. For as, generally, those things are considered the most painful to endure of which we are most sensible, so it seems to these persons, that sufferings of this kind contain in them more cause for feeling than any other sufferings. And, therefore, although all the torments of the Lord were very great, so that each one appears the greatest, and no com-parison can be made between them ; yet, nevertheless, this kind of suffering appears to be the most painful. Because in other troubles, not only the pain and suffering of them, but the troubles themselves, in themselves, may be desired by us, and such as we suffer for love's sake, in order by them to evince that love. Wherefore, the stripes, the crown of thorns, the buffetings, the cross, the gall, the vinegar, and other bodily torments, besides that they torment the body, are often a means for promoting the divine honour, which it holds in esteem above all else. But to blaspheme God, to give the lie to eternal truths, to deface the supreme demonstrations of the divinity and majesty of the Son of God (although God knoweth how to extract from these things the good which he intends), nevertheless are, in their nature, things, which, from their so greatly affecting the divine honour, although they may be, for just considerations, endured, can never be desired by any one, but must be abhorrent to all. Our Lord then, being, of all, the most zealous for the divine honour, for which he also died, found in this kind of suffering, more than in all other, much to abhor and nothing to desire. Therefore with good reason it may be held to be the greatest of all, and that in which, more than in all other, he exhibited the greatest suffering and patience.—*Fra Thomé de Jesu, in "The Sufferings of Jesus,"* 1869.

Verses 7—9.—All that see me made but a laughynge stocke on me, they mocked me wyth their lyppes, and wagged theyr heades at me. Sayenge, thys vyllayne referred all thynges to the Lord, let him now delyver hym yf he wyll, for he loveth hym well. But yet thou arte he whyche leddest me oute of my mother's wombe myne own refuge, even from my mother's teates. As sone as I came into this worlde, I was layde in thy lappe, thou art my God even from my mother's wombe.—*From " The Psalter of David in English, truly translated out of Latyn," in " Devout Psalms," etc., by E. Whitchurche,* 1547.

Verse 8.—Here are recorded some of those very words, by which the persecutors of our Lord expressed their mockery and scorn. How remarkable to find them in a Psalm written so many hundred years before !—*John Stevenson.*

Verses 9, 10.—Faith is much strengthened by constant evidences of God's favour. Herewith did he support his faith that said to God, " *Thou art he that took me out of the womb: thou didst make me hope when I was upon my mother's breasts. I was cast upon thee from the womb : thou art my God from my mother's belly.*" " Thou art my trust from my youth. By thee have I been holden up from the womb : thou art he that took me out of my mother's bowels." Psalm lxxi. 5, 6. It was not only the disposition of Obadiah towards God, but also the evidence that thereby he had of God's affection towards him, that made him with confidence say to Elijah, "I fear the Lord from my youth." 1 Kings xviii. 12. By long continuance of ancient favour, many demonstrations are given of a fast, fixed, and unremovable affection. So as if, by reason of temptations, one or more evidences should be questioned, yet others would remain to uphold faith, and to keep it from an utter languishing, and a total falling away. As when a house is supported by many pillars, though some be taken away, yet by the support of them which remain, the house will stand.—*William Gouge.*

Verses 9, 10.—David acknowledges ancient mercies, those mercies which had been cast upon him long ago, these were still fresh and new in his memory, and this is one affection and disposition of a thankful heart—to remember those mercies which another would have quite forgotten, or never thought of. Thus does David here ; the mercies of his *infancy,* and his *childhood,* and his *younger years,* which one would have imagined, that now in his age had been quite out of his mind ; yet these does he here stir up himself to remember and bring to his thoughts. " *Took me out of the womb:*" when was that ? It may have been threescore years ago, when David penned the Psalms. He thinks of those mercies which God vouchsafed him *when he was not capable of thinking,* nor considering what was bestowed upon him ; and so are we taught hence to do, in an imitation of this holy example which is here set before us : those mercies which God hath bestowed in our minority, we are to call to mind and acknowledge in our riper years.—*Thomas Horton.*

Verses 9, 10.—Here the tribulation begins to grow lighter, and hope inclines towards victory ; a support, though small, and sought out with deep anxiety, is now found. For after he had felt that he had suffered without any parallel or example, so that the wonderful works of God as displayed toward the fathers afforded him no help, he comes to the wonderful works of God toward himself, and in these he finds the goodwill of God towards him, and which was displayed towards him alone in so singular a way.—*Martin Luther.*

Verses 9, 10.—The bitter severity of the several taunts with which his enemies assailed our Lord, had no other effect than to lead the Saviour to make a direct appeal to his Father. . . . . That appeal is set before us in these two verses. It is of an unusual and remarkable nature. The argument on which it is founded is most forcible and conclusive. At the same time, it is the most seasonable and appropriate that can be urged. We may thus paraphrase it, " I am now brought as a man to my last extremity. It is said that God disowns me ; but it cannot be so. My first moment of existence he tenderly cared for. When I could not even ask for, or think of his kindness, he bestowed it upon me. If, of his mere good pleasure he brought me into life at first, he will surely not forsake me when I am departing out of it. In opposition, therefore, to all their taunts, I can and I will appeal to himself. Mine enemies declare, O God, that thou hast cast me off—*but thou art he that took me out of the womb.* They affirm that I do not, and need not trust in thee ; but *thou didst make me hope* (or, *keptest me in safety,* margin) *when I was upon my mother's breasts.* They insinuate that thou wilt not acknowledge me as thy Son ; but *I was cast upon thee from the womb ; thou art my God from my mother's belly.*"—*John Stevenson.*

Verse 10.—" *I was cast upon thee from the womb : thou art my God from my mother's belly.*" There is a noble passage in Eusebius, in which he shows the connection between our Lord's incarnation and his passion : that he might well comfort himself while hanging on the cross by the remembrance that the very same body then " marred more than any man, and his form more than the sons of men" (Isaiah lii. 14), was that which had been glorified by the Father with such singular honour, when the Holy Ghost came upon Mary, and the power of the Highest overshadowed her. That this body, therefore, though now so torn and so mangled, as it had once been the wonder, so it would for ever be the joy, of the angels ; and having put on immortality, would be the support of his faithful people to the end of time.—*J. M. Neale, in loc.*

Verse 10.—I was like one forsaken by his parent, and wholly cast upon Providence. I had no father upon earth, and my mother was poor and helpless.—*Matthew Poole.*

Verse 11.—" *Be not far from me ; for trouble is near ;*" and so it is high time for thee to put forth a helping hand. *Hominibus profanis mirabilis videtur hæc ratio,* to profane persons, this seemeth to be a strange reason, saith an interpreter ; but it is a very good one, as this prophet knew, who therefore makes it his plea.—*John Trapp.*

Verse 12.—" *Strong bulls of Bashan have beset me round.*" These animals are remarkable for the proud, fierce, and sullen manner in which they exercise their great strength. Such were the persecutors who now beset our Lord. These were first, human, and secondly, spiritual foes ; and both were alike distinguished by the proud, fierce, and sullen manner in which they assaulted him. *John Stevenson.*

Verses 12, 13.—" Bashan" was a fertile country (Numb. xxxii. 4), and the cattle there fed were fat and " strong." Deut. xxxii. 14. Like them, the Jews, in that good land, " waxed fat and kicked," grew proud and rebelled ; forsook God " that made them, and lightly esteemed the rock of their salvation."—*George Horne.*

Verse 13.—A helpless infant, or a harmless lamb, surrounded by furious bulls and hungry lions, aptly represented the Saviour encompassed by his insulting and bloody persecutors.—*Thomas Scott, 1747—1821.*

25

Verse 14.—" *I am poured out like water, and all my bones are out of joint : my heart is like wax ; it is melted in the midst of my bowels.*" He was faint. Such a feeling of languor and faintness supervened that language fails to express it, and the emblem of " water poured out" is employed to represent it. As the water falls from the vessel to the earth, see how its particles separate farther and farther from each other. Its velocity increases as it falls. It has no power to stay itself midway, much less to return to its place. It is the very picture of utter weakness. So did our Lord feel himself to be when hanging on the cross. He was faint with weakness. The sensations experienced when about to faint away are very overpowering. We appear to our own consciousness to be nothing but weakness, as water poured out. All our bones feel relaxed and out of joint ; we seem as though we had none. The strength of bone is gone, the knitting of the joints is loosened, and the muscular vigour fled. A sickly giddiness overcomes us. We have no power to bear up. All heart is lost. Our strength disappears like that of wax, of melting wax, which drops upon surrounding objects, and is lost. Daniel thus describes his sensations on beholding the great vision, " There remained no strength in me : for my vigour was turned into corruption, and I retained no strength." Dan. x. 8. In regard, however, to the faintness which our Lord experienced, we ought to notice this additional and remarkable circumstance, that he did not altogether faint away. The relief of insensibility he refused to take. When consciousness ceases, all perception of pain is necessarily and instantly terminated. But our Lord retained his full consciousness throughout this awful scene ; and patiently endured for a considerable period, those, to us, insupportable sensations which precede the actual swoon.—*John Stevenson.*

Verse 14.—" *I am poured out like water :*" that is, in the thought of my enemies I am utterly destroyed. " For we must needs die, and are as water spilt on the ground, which cannot be gathered up again." 2 Sam. xiv. 14. " What marvel," asks St. Bernard, " that the name of the Bridegroom should be as ointment poured forth, when he himself, for the greatness of his love, was poured forth like water !"—*J. M. Neale.*

Verse 14.—" *I am poured out like water,*" *i.e.*, I am almost past all recovery, as water spilt upon the ground.—*John Trapp.*

Verse 14.—" *All my bones are out of joint.*" The *rack* is devised as a most exquisite pain, even for terror. And the *cross* is a *rack*, whereon he was stretched till, saith the Psalm, " *all his bones were out of joint.*" But even to *stand*, as he *hung*, three long hours together, holding up but the arms at length, I have heard it avowed of some that have felt it, to be a pain scarce credible. But the hands and the feet being so cruelly *nailed* (part, of all other, most sensible, by reason of the texture of sinews there in them most) it could not but make his pain out of measure painful. It was not for nothing, that *dolores acerrimi dicuntur cruciatus* (saith the heathen man), that the most sharp and bitter pains of all other have their name from hence, and are called *cruciatus*— pains like those of the *cross*. It had a meaning, that *they gave him,* that he had (for his *welcome* to the cross) a cup mixed with gall or myrrh ; and (for his *farewell*) a *sponge of vinegar ;* to show by the one the *bitterness,* and by the other the *sharpness* of the pains of this painful death.—*Lancelot Andrewes.*

Verse 14.—" *All my bones are out of joint.*" We know that the greatest and most intolerable pain that the body can endure, is that arising from a bone out of its place, or dislocated joint. Now when the Lord was raised up upon the cross, and his sacred body hung in the air from the nails, all the joints began to give, so that the bones were parted the one from the other so visibly that, in very truth (as David had prophesied) *they might tell all his bones,* and thus, throughout his whole body, he endured acute torture. Whilst our Lord suffered these torments, his enemies, who had so earnestly desired to see him crucified, far from pitying him, were filled with delight, as though celebrating a victory.—*Fra Thomé de Jesu.*

Verse 15.—"*My strength is dried up*," etc. Inflammation must have commenced early and violently in the wounded parts—then been quickly imparted to those that were strained, and have terminated in a *high degree of feverish burning over the whole body.* The animal juices would be thus dried up, and the watery particles of the blood absorbed. The skin parched by the scorching sun till midday would be unable to supply or to imbibe any moisture. The loss of blood at the hands and feet would hasten the desiccation. Hence our Lord says, "My strength is dried up like a potsherd, and my tongue cleaveth to my jaws." The fever would devour his small remaining strength. And THIRST, that most intolerable of all bodily privations, must have been overpowering. His body appeared to his feeling like a potsherd that had been charred in the potter's kiln. It seemed to have neither strength nor substance left in it. So feeble had he become, so parched and dried up that CLAMMINESS OF THE MOUTH, one of the forerunners of immediate dissolution, had already seized him ; "My tongue cleaveth to my jaws, and thou hast brought me into the dust of death."—*John Stevenson.*

Verse 15.—"*My strength is dried up;*" not as in the trial of gold and silver, but "*like a potsherd,*" as the earthen vessel dried up by the heat, spoken in humiliation.—*Isaac Williams, in loc.*

Verse 15.—"*A potsherd.*" חֶרֶשׂ rendered *potsherd*, is a word which denotes a piece of earthenware, frequently in a broken state. As employed in the verse under consideration, it seems to derive considerable illustration from the corresponding word in ARABIC, which expresses roughness of skin, and might well convey to the mind an idea of the bodily appearance of one in whom the moisture of the fluids had been dried up by the excess of grief.—*John Morison.*

Verse 15.—That hour what his feelings were it is dangerous to define : we know them not ; we may be too bold to determine of them. To very good purpose it was that the ancient Fathers of the Greek church in their liturgy, after they had recounted all the particular pains, as they are set down in his passion, and by all and by everyone of them called for mercy, do, after all, shut up with this Δι αγνωστων κοπων κι βασανων ελεησον κι σωσον ημας. By thine unknown sorrows and sufferings, felt by thee, but not distinctly known by us, have mercy upon us and save us.—*Lancelot Andrewes.*

Verse 16.—"*Dogs have compassed me.*" So great and varied was the malignity exhibited by the enemies of our Lord, that the combined characteristics of two species of ferocious animals were not adequate to its representation. Another emblematical figure is therefore introduced. The assembly of the wicked is compared to that of "dogs" who haunt about the cities, prowl in every corner, snarl over the carrion, and devour it all with greediness—like "dogs," with their wild cry in full pursuit, with unfailing scent tracking their victim, with vigilant eye on all its movements, and with a determination which nothing can falter, they run it on to death. The Oriental mode of hunting, both in ancient and modern times, is murderous and merciless in the extreme. A circle of several miles in circumference is beat round ; and the men, driving all before them, and narrowing as they advance, inclose the prey on every side. Having thus made them prisoners, the cruel hunters proceed to slaughter at their own convenience. So did the enemies of our Lord : long before his crucifixion it is recorded that they used the most treacherous plans to get him into their power.—*John Stevenson.*

Verse 16.—"*Dogs have compassed me.*" At the hunting of the lion, a whole district is summoned to appear, who, forming themselves first into a circle, enclose a space of four or five miles in compass, according to the number of the people and the quality of the ground which is pitched upon for the scene of action. The footmen advance first, rushing into the thickets with their dogs and spears, to put up the game ; while the horsemen, keeping a little behind, are always ready to charge upon the first sally of the wild beast. In this manner they proceed, still contracting their circle, till they all at last close in together, or meet with some other game to divert them.—*Dr. Shaw's Travels, quoted in Paxton's " Illustrations of Scripture."*

Verse 16.—*" They pierced my hands and my feet ;"* namely, when they nailed Christ to the cross. Matt. xxvii. 35 ; John xx. 25. Where let me simulate, saith a learned man, the orator's gradation, *Facinus vincire civem Romanum,* etc. It was much for the Son of God to be bound, more to be beaten, most of all to be slain ; *Quid dicam in crucem tolle ?* but what shall I say to this, that he was crucified ? That was the most vile and ignominious ; it was also a cruel and cursed kind of death, which yet he refused not ; and here we have a clear testimony for his cross.—*John Trapp.*

Verse 16.—*" They pierced my hands and my feet."* Of all sanguinary punishments, that of crucifixion is one of the most dreadful—no vital part is immediately affected by it. The hands and feet which are furnished with the most numerous and sensitive organs, are perforated with nails, which must necessarily be of some size to suit their intended purpose. The tearing asunder of the tender fibres of the hands and feet, the lacerating of so many nerves, and bursting so many blood-vessels, must be productive of intense agony. The nerves of the hand and foot are intimately connected, through the arm and leg, with the nerves of the whole body ; their laceration therefore must be felt over the entire frame. Witness the melancholy result of even a needle's puncture in even one of the remotest nerves. A spasm is not unfrequently produced by it in the muscles of the face, which locks the jaws inseparably. When, therefore the hands and feet of our blessed Lord were transfixed with nails, he must have felt the sharpest pangs shoot through every part of his body. Supported only by his lacerated limbs, and suspended from his pierced hands, our Lord had nearly six hours' torment to endure.—*John Stevenson.*

Verse 16.—*" They pierced my hands and my feet."* That evangelical prophet testifies it, " Behold, I have graven thee upon the palms of my hands." Isaiah xlix. 16. Were we not engraven there when his hands were pierced for us ? " They digged my hands and my feet." And they digged them so deep, that the very prints remained after his resurrection, and their fingers were thrust into them for evidence sake. Some have thought that those scars remain still in his glorious body, to be showed at his second appearing : " They shall see him whom they have pierced." That is improbable, but this is certain ; there remains still an impression upon Christ's hands and his heart, the sealing and wearing of the elect there, as precious jewels.—*Thomas Adams.*

Verse 17.—*" I may tell all my bones : they look and stare upon me."* The skin and flesh were distended by the posture of the body on the cross, that the bones, as through a thin veil, became visible, and might be counted.—*George Horne.*

Verse 17.—*" I may tell all my bones."* For, as the first Adam by his fall, lost the robe of innocence, and thenceforth needed other garments, so the second Adam vouchsafed to be stripped of his earthly vestments, to the end it might hereafter be said to us, " Bring forth the first robe, and put it on him." Luke xv. 22.—*Gerhohus, quoted by J. M. Neale.*

Verse 17.—*" They look and stare upon me."* Sensitively conscious of his condition upon the cross, the delicate feelings of the holy Saviour were sorely pained by the gaze of the multitude. With impudent face they looked upon him. To view him better they halted as they walked. With deliberate insolence they collected in groups, and made their remarks to each other on his conduct and appearance. Mocking his naked, emaciated, and quivering body, they " looked and stared upon him."—*John Stevenson.*

Verse 17.—*" They look and stare upon me."* Oh, how different is that look which the awakened sinner directs to Calvary, when faith lifts up her eye to him who agonised, and bled, and died, for the guilty ! And what gratitude should perishing men feel, that from him that hangs upon the accursed tree there is heard proceeding the inviting sound, " Look unto me, and be ye saved, all ye ends of the earth, for I am God, and besides me there is none else."—*John Morison.*

Verse 18.—"*They part my garments,*" etc. Perfectly naked did the cruciarii hang upon the cross, and the executioners received their clothes. There is nothing to show that there was a cloth even round the loins. The clothes became the property of the soldiers, after Roman usage. The outer garment was divided probably into four, by ripping up the seams. Four soldiers were counted off as a guard, by the Roman code. The under garment could not be divided, being woven ; and this led the soldiers to the dice-throwing.—*J. P. Lange, D.D., on Matthew,* 27, 35.

Verse 18.—"*They part my garments,*" etc. Instruments will not be wanting to crucify Christ, if it were but for his old clothes, and those but little worth ; for these soldiers crucify him, though they got but his garments for their reward. Christ did submit to suffer naked, hereby to teach us :—1. That all flesh are really naked before God by reason of sin (Exodus xxxii. 25 ; 2 Chron. xxviii. 19), and therefore our Surety behoved to suffer naked. 2. That he offered himself a real captive in his sufferings, that so he might fully satisfy justice by being under the power of his enemies, till he redeemed himself by the strong hand, having fully paid the price ; for therefore did he submit to be stripped naked, as conquerors use to do with prisoners. 3. That by thus suffering naked he would expiate our abuse of apparel, and purchase to us a liberty to make use of suitable raiment, and such as becometh us in our station. 4. That by this suffering naked he would purchase unto them who flee to him, to be covered with righteousness and glory, and to walk with him in white for ever, and would point out the nakedness of those who, not being found clothed with his righteousness, shall not be clothed upon with immortality and glory. 2 Cor. v. 2, 3. 5. He would also by this, teach all his followers to resolve on nakedness in their following of him, as a part of their conformity with their Head (1 John iv. 17 ; Rom. viii. 35 ; Heb. xi. 37), and that therefore they should not dote much on their apparel when they have it.—*George Hutcheson,* 1657.

Verse 18.—"*And cast lots upon my vesture.*" Trifling as this act of casting the lot for our Lord's vesture may appear, it is most significant. It contains a double lesson. It teaches us how greatly that seamless shirt was valued ; how little he to whom it had belonged. It seemed to say, this garment is more valuable than its owner. As it was said of the thirty pieces of silver, " A goodly price at which I was prized at of them ;" so may we say regarding the casting of the lot, " How cheaply Christ was held !"—*John Stevenson.*

Verse 20.—"*My darling*" had better be rendered "my lonely, or solitary one." For he wishes to say that his soul was lonely and forsaken by all, and that there was no one who sought after him as a friend, or cared for him, or comforted him : as we have it, Psalm cxlii. 4, " Refuge failed me ; no one cared for my soul ; I looked on my right hand, but there was no one who would know me ;" that is, solitude is of itself a certain cross, and especially so in such great torments, in which it is most grievous to be immersed without an example and without a companion. And yet, in such a state, everyone of us must be, in some suffering or other, and especially in that of death ; and we must be brought to cry out with Psalm xxv. 16, " Turn thee unto me, and have mercy upon me, for I am desolate and afflicted."—*Martin Luther.*

Verse 20.—"*The dog.*" It is scarcely possible for a European to form an idea of the intolerable nuisance occasioned in the villages and cities of the East, by the multitudes of dogs that infest the streets. The natives, accustomed from their earliest years to the annoyance, come to be regardless of it ; but to a stranger, these creatures are the greatest plague to which he is subjected ; for as they are never allowed to enter a house, and do not constitute the property of any particular owner, they display none of those habits of which the domesticated species among us are found susceptible, and are destitute of all those social qualities which often render the dog the trusty and attached friend of man. . . . The race seems wholly to degenerate in the warm regions of the East, and to approximate to the character of beasts of prey, as in disposition they are ferocious, cunning, bloodthirsty, and possessed of the most insatiable voracity : and even in their very form there is something repulsive ; their sharp and savage features ; their wolf-like eyes ; their long hanging ears ; their straight and pointed tails ; their lank and emaciated forms, almost entirely without a belly, give them an appearance of wretchedness and degradation, that stands in sad contrast with the general condition and qualities of the breed in Europe. . . . . These hideous creatures, dreaded by the people for their ferocity, or avoided by them as useless and unclean, are obliged to prowl about everywhere in search of a precarious existence. . . . . They generally run in bands, and their natural ferocity, inflamed by hunger, and the consciousness of strength, makes them the most troublesome and dangerous visitors to the stranger who unexpectedly finds himself in their neighbourhood, as they will not scruple to seize whatever he may have about him, and even, in the event of his falling, and being otherwise defenceless, to attack and devour him. . . . These animals, driven by hunger, greedily devour everything that comes in their way ; they glut themselves with the most putrid and loathsome substances that are thrown about the cities, and of nothing are they so fond as of human flesh, a repast, with which the barbarity of the despotic countries of Asia frequently supplies them, as the bodies of criminals slain for murder, treason, or violence, are seldom buried, and lie exposed till the mangled fragments are carried off by the dogs.— *From " Illustrations of Scripture, by the late Professor George Paxton, D.D., revised and enlarged by Robert Jamieson,"* 1843.

Verse 21.—" *Save me from the lion's mouth.*" Satan is called a lion, and that fitly ; for he hath all the properties of the lion : as bold as a lion, as strong as a lion, as furious as a lion, as terrible as the roaring of a lion. Yea, worse : the lion wants subtlety and suspicion ; herein the devil is beyond the lion. The lion will spare the prostrate, the devil spares none. The lion is full and forbears, the devil is full and devours. He seeks all ; let not the simple say, He will take no notice of me ; nor the subtle, He cannot overreach me ; nor the noble say, He will not presume to meddle with me ; nor the rich, He dares not contest with me ; for he seeks to devour all. He is our common adversary, therefore let us cease all quarrels amongst ourselves, and fight with him.— *Thomas Adams.*

Verse 21.—" *Save me . . . from the horns of the unicorns.*" Those who are in great trouble from the power or cruelty of others, often cry out to their gods, " Ah ! save me from the tusk of the elephant ! from the mouth of the tiger and the tusks of the boar, deliver me, deliver me !" " Who will save me from the horn of the *Kāndam ?*" This animal is now extinct in these regions, and it is not easy to determine what it was ; the word in the Sathur—*Agarāthe*—is rendered " jungle cow."—*Joseph Roberts.*

Verse 21.—" *The horns of the unicorns.*" On turning to the Jewish Bible we find that the word רְאֵם is translated as buffalo, and there is no doubt that this rendering is nearly the correct one, and at the present day naturalists are nearly agreed that the reêm of the Old Testament must have been now the extinct urus. . . . . The presence of these horns affords a remarkable confirmation to a well-known passage in Julius Cæsar's familiar " Commentaries." " The uri are little inferior to elephants in size" (" *magnitudine paulo infra elephantos ;*") " but are bulls in their nature, color, and figure. Great is their strength, and great their swiftness ; nor do they spare man or beast when they have caught sight of them."—*J. G. Wood, M.A., F.L.S., in " Bible Animals,"* 1869.

Verse 22.—" *I will declare thy name unto my brethren.*" Having thus obtained relief from the oppressive darkness, and regained conscious possession of the joy and light of his Father's countenance, the thoughts and desires of the Redeemer flow into their accustomed channel. The glory of God in the salvation of his church.—*John Stevenson.*

Verse 22.—" *My brethren.*" This gives evidence of the low condescension of the Son of God, and also of the high exaltation of sons of men ; for the Son of God to be a brother to sons of men is a great degree of humiliation, and for sons of men to be made brethren with the Son of God is a high degree of exaltation ; for Christ's brethren are in that respect sons of God, heirs of heaven, or kings, not earthly, but heavenly ; not temporary, but everlasting kings. . . . . This respect of Christ to his brethren is a great encouragement and comfort to such as are despised and scorned by men of this world for Christ's professing of them. *William Gouge.*

Verse 24. —" *For he hath not despised nor abhorred the prayer of the poor, neither hath he hid his face from me ; but when I cried unto him, he heard me.*" Let him, therefore, that desires to be of the seed of Israel, and to rejoice in the grace of the gospel, become poor, for this is a fixed truth, our God is one that has respect unto the poor ! And observe the fulness and diligence of the prophet. He was not content with having said " will not despise," but adds, " and will not abhor ;" and, again, " will not turn away his face ;" and again, " will hear." And then he adds himself as an example, saying " When I cried," as our translation has it. As if he had said, " Behold ye, and learn by my example, who have been made the most vile of all men, and numbered among the wicked ; when I was despised, cast out, rejected, behold ! I was held in the highest esteem, and taken up, and heard. Let not this state of things, there-fore, after this, my encouraging example, frighten you ; the gospel requires a man to be such a character before it will save him." These things, I say, because our weakness requires so much exhortation, that it might not dread being humbled, nor despair when humbled, and thus might, after the bearing of the cross, receive the salvation.—*Martin Luther.*

Verse 25.—" *My praise shall be of thee in the great congregation,*" etc. The joy and gratitude of our adorable Lord rise to such a height at this great deliverance, his heart so overflows with fresh and blessed consciousness of his heavenly Father's nearness, that he again pours forth the expression of his praise. By its repetition, he teaches us that this is not a temporary burst of gratitude, but an abiding determination, a full and settled resolution.—*John Stevenson.*

Verse 25.—" *In the great congregation.*" Saints are fittest witnesses of sacred duties. That which, in Psa. cxvi. 14, is implied under this particle of restraint, " his," in " the presence of all his people," is in Psa. xxii. 25, more expressly noted by a more apparent description, thus : " *I will pay my vows before them that fear him.*" None but true saints do truly fear God. 1. This property of God's people, that they fear the Lord, showeth that they will make the best use of such sacred, solemn duties performed in their presence. They will glorify God for this your zeal ; they will join their spirits with your spirit in this open performance of duty ; they will become followers of you, and learn of you to vow and pay unto the Lord, and that openly, publicly. 2. As for others, they are no better than such hogs and dogs as are not meet to have such precious pearls and holy things cast before them, lest they trample them under their feet.—*William Gouge.*

Verse 26.—" *The meek shall eat and be satisfied : they shall praise the Lord that seek him ; your heart shall live for ever.*" A spiritual banquet is prepared in the church for the " *meek* " and lowly in heart. The death of Christ was the sacrifice for sin ; his flesh is meat indeed, and his blood is drink indeed. The poor in spirit feed on this provision, in their hearts by faith, and are *satisfied ;* and thus, whilst they " *seek* " the Lord, they " *praise*" him also, and their

" *hearts*" (or souls), are preserved unto eternal life.—"*Practical Illustrations of the Book of Psalms,*" 1826.

Verse 26.—" *The meek.*" Bonaventure engraved this sweet saying of our Lord, " Learn of me, for I am meek and lowly in heart," in his study. O that this saying was engraved upon all your foreheads, and upon all your hearts ! *Charles Bradbury.*

Verse 26.—" *They shall praise the Lord that seek him ; your heart shall live for ever.*" Now, I would fain know the man that ever went about to form such laws as should bind the *hearts* of men, or prepare such rewards as should reach the souls and consciences of men ! Truly, if any mortal man should make a law that his subjects should love him with all their hearts and souls, and not dare, upon peril of his greatest indignation, to entertain a traitorous thought against his royal person, but presently confess it to him, or else he would be avenged on him, he would deserve to be more laughed at for his pride and folly, than Xerxes for casting his fetters into the Hellespont, to chain the waves into his obedience ; or Caligula, that threatened the air, if it durst rain when he was at his pastimes, who durst not himself so much as look into the air when it thundered. Certainly a madhouse would be more fit for such a person than a throne, who should so far forfeit his reason, as to think that the thoughts and hearts of men were within his jurisdiction.— *William Gurnall.*

Verse 26.—" *Your heart,*" that is, not your outward man, but the hidden man of the heart (Ezek. xxxvi. 26) ; the new man which is created after the image of God in righteousness and true holiness, " *shall live for ever.*" The life which animates it is the life of the Spirit of God.—*John Stevenson.*

Verse 27.—" *All the ends of the world shall remember and turn unto the Lord ; and all the kindreds of the nations shall worship before him.*" This passage is a prediction of the conversion of the Gentiles. It furnishes us with two interesting ideas ; the nature of true conversion—and the extent of it under the reign of the Messiah. 1. The NATURE of true conversion :—It is to " *remember*"—to " *turn to the Lord* "—and to " *worship before him.*" This is a plain and simple process. Perhaps the first religious exercise of mind of which we are conscious is reflection. A state of unregeneracy is a state of forgetfulness. God is forgotten. Sinners have lost all just sense of his glory, authority, mercy, and judgment ; living as if there were no God, or as if they thought there was none. But if ever we are brought to be the subjects of true conversion, we shall be brought to remember these things. This divine change is fitly expressed by the case of the prodigal, who is said to have *come to himself*, or to his right mind. But further, true conversion consists not only in remembering but in " *turning to the Lord.*" This part of the passage is expressive of a cordial relinquishment of our idols, whatever they have been, and an acquiescence in the gospel way of salvation by Christ alone. Once more, true conversion to Christ will be·accompanied with the " *worship*" of him. Worship, as a religious exercise, is the homage of the heart, presented to God according to his revealed will. . . . . . . 2. The EXTENT of conversion under the kingdom or reign of the Messiah : " *All the ends of the world shall remember and turn unto the Lord ; and all the kindreds of the nations shall worship before him.*" It was fit that the accession of the Gentiles should be reserved for the gospel day, that it might grace the triumph of Christ over his enemies, and appear to be what it is, " the travail of his soul." This great and good work, begun in the apostles' days, *must* go on, and " must increase," till " *All the ends of the world shall remember and turn,*" and " *all the kindreds of the nations shall worship before him.*" Conversion work has been *individual ;* God has gathered sinners one by one. Thus it is at present with us ; but it will not be thus always. People will flock to Zion as doves to their windows. Further, conversion work has hitherto been circumscribed within certain parts of the world. But the time will come when " all the kindreds of the earth" shall worship. These hopes are not the flight of an ardent imagination ; they are founded on the true sayings of God. Finally, while we are concerned for the world, let us not forget our own souls. So the whole world be saved and we lost, what will it avail us?—*Condensed from Andrew Fuller.*

Verse 27.—"*All the ends of the world shall* REMEMBER"—this is a remarkable expression. It implies that man has forgotten God. It represents all the successive generations of the world as but *one*, and then it exhibits that one generation, as if it had been once in paradise, suddenly remembering the Lord whom it had known there, but had long forgotten. . . . . The converted nations, we learn by this verse, will not only obtain remembrance of their past loss, but will also be filled with the knowledge of present duty.—*John Stevenson.*

Verse 27.—"*All the nations of the world*" (יִזְכְּרוּ *jizkeru*, the same Hebrew root with אַזְכִּיר *azkir*) "*shall remember;*" why? what is that? or what shall they remember? Even this: they shall turn to the Lord, and worship him, in his name, in his ordinances; as is explained in the words following of the verse: "*And all the families of the nations*" (וְיִשְׁתַּחֲווּ *jishtachavu*, "*shall bow*" down themselves, or) "*worship before thee,*" etc. And so in Psalm lxxxvi. 9, "All nations whom thou hast made shall come" (וְיִשְׁתַּחֲווּ *vejishtachavu*) "and they shall worship before thee;" and how shall they do so? Even by recording, remembering, and making mention of the glory of thy name; as in the words following (וִיכַבְּדוּ שְׁמֶךָ! *vicabbedu lishmecha,*) "and shall glorify thy name." *William Strong's* "*Saint's Communion with God,*" 1656.

Verses 27, 28.—The one undeviating object of the Son all through was, the glory of the Father: he came to do his will, and he fulfilled it with all the unvarying intensity of the most heavenly affection. What, then, will not be the exuberant joy of his heart, when in his glorious kingdom, he shall see the Father beyond all measure glorified? . . . The praise and honour and blessing which will be yielded to the Father in that day through him, so that God shall be all in all, will make him feel he underwent not a sorrow too much for such a precious consummation. . . . Every note of thanksgiving which ascends to the Father, whether from the fowls of the air, or the beasts of the field, or the fishes of the sea, or the hills, or the mountains, or the trees of the forest, or the rivers of the valleys—all shall gladden his heart, as sweet in the ears of God, for the sake of him who redeemed even them from the curse, and restored to them a harmony more musical than burst from them on the birthday of their creation. And man! renewed and regenerated man! for whose soul the blood was spilt, and for the redemption of whose body death was overcome, how shall the chorus of his thanksgiving, in its intelligent and articulate hallelujahs, be the incense which that Saviour shall still love to present unto the Father, a sweet-smelling savour through himself, who, that he might sanctify his people by his own blood, suffered without the camp. How are the channels choked up or impaired in this evil world, wherein the praise and glory of our God should flow as a river! How will Christ then witness, to the delight of his soul, all cleared and restored! No chill upon the heart, no stammering in the tongue, in his Father's praises! No understanding dull, or eye feeble, in the apprehension of his glory! No hand unready, or foot stumbling, in the fulfilling of his commandments. God, the glory of his creatures: his glory their service and their love; and *all* this the reward to Jesus of once suffering himself.—*C. J. Goodhart, M.A., in* "*Bloomsbury Lent Lectures,*" 1848.

Verse 29.—"*And they shall bow that go down into the dust; their soul liveth not:*" that is, *whose soul liveth not*, by an Hebraism; it being meant, that he who is of most desperate condition, being without hope of life and salvation, his sins are so notorious, shall "eat" also of this feast, and be turned to God to "worship" and serve him; being thus plucked out of the jaws of death and everlasting destruction, as it were, being before this very hour ready to seize upon him. The new translation, "*None can keep alive his own soul,*" as it agreeth not with the Hebrew, so it makes the sense more perplexed. By "*him that goeth down to the dust, whose soul liveth not,*" some understand the most miserably poor, who have nothing to feed upon, whereby their life may be preserved, yet shall feed also of this feast as well as the rich, and praise God. Ainsworth is for either spiritually poor and miserable, because most wicked, or worldly poor ; and there is an exposition of Basil's, understanding by the rich, the rich in faith and grace, touching which, or the rich properly so called, he is indifferent. But because it is said, " *The fat of the earth*," I prefer the former, and that the close of the verse may best answer to the first part ; the latter by " *those that are going to the dust*," understand the miserably poor. So that there is a common-place of comfort for all, both richest and poorest, if they be subjects of God's kingdom of grace : their souls shall be alike fed by him and saved.—*John Mayer.*

Verse 29.—"*All they that go down to the dust ;*" either those who stand quivering on the brink of the grave, or those who occupy the humble, sequestered walks of life. As the great and opulent of the earth are intended in the first clause, it is not by any means unnatural to suppose that the image of going " *down to the dust*," is designed to represent the poor and mean of mankind, who are unable to support themselves, and to provide for their multiplied necessities. If the grave be alluded to, as is thought by many eminent divines, the beautiful sentiment of the verse will be, that multitudes of dying sinners shall be brought to worship Jehovah, and that those who cannot save or deliver themselves shall seek that shelter which none can find but those who approach the mercy-seat. " Rich and poor," as Bishop Horne observes, " are invited "—that is, to " worship God ;" " and the hour is coming when all the race of Adam, as many as sleep in the ' dust ' of the earth, unable to raise themselves from thence, quickened and called forth by the voice of the Son of Man, must bow the knee to King Messiah."—*John Morison.*

Verse 29.—To be brought to the dust, is, first, a circumlocution or description of death : " *Shall the dust praise thee, shall it declare thy truth ?*" Psalm xxx. 9. That is, shall I praise thee when I am among the dead ? "*What profit is there in my blood, when I go down to the pit ?*" Not that profit, sure, I cannot bring thee in the tribute of praise when my life's gone out. Secondly, to be brought to the dust is a description of any low and poor condition. " *All they that be fat upon the earth*" (that is, the great and mighty), "*shall eat and worship*" " *all they that go down to the dust*" (that is, the mean and base), " *shall bow before him.*" As if he had said, rich and poor, high and low, the king and the beggar, have alike need of salvation by Jesus Christ, and must submit unto him, that they may be saved, for, as it there follows, "*none can keep alive his own soul.*" The captivity of the Jews in Babylon is expressed under those notions of *death*, and of *dwelling in the dust* (Isaiah xxvi. 19) ; to show how low, that no power but his who can raise the dead, could work their deliverance.—*Joseph Caryl.*

Verse 29.—"*None can keep alive his own soul.*" And yet we look back to our conversion, and its agonies of earnestness, its feelings of deep, helpless dependence—of Christ's being absolutely our daily, hourly need—supplier—as a *past* something—a stage of spiritual life which is *over*. And we are satisfied to have it so. The Spirit of God moved over our deadness, and breathed into us the breath of life. My soul became *a living soul*. But was this enough ? God's word says, No. " None can *keep alive* his own soul." My heart says, No. Truth must ever answer to truth. I cannot (ah ! have I not tried, and failed ?) I cannot *keep alive* my own soul. We cannot live upon ourselves. Our physical life is kept up by supply from without—air, food, warmth. So must the spiritual life. Jesus gives, Jesus feeds us day by day, else must the life fade out and die. " None can *keep alive* his own soul." It is not enough to be made alive. I must be fed, and guided, and taught, and kept in life. Mother, who hast brought a living babe into the world, is your work done ? Will you not nurse it, and feed it, and care for it, that it may be *kept alive ?* Lord, I am this babe. I live indeed, for I can crave and cry. Leave me not, O my Saviour. Forsake not the work of thine own hands. In thee I live. Hold me, carry me, feed me, let me abide in thee. " For thy kingdom is the Lord's : and he is the governor among the nations. All they that be fat upon earth shall eat and worship : all they that go down to the dust shall bow before him : and none can keep alive his own soul." In our work for God, we need to remember this. Is not the conversion, the arousing of sinners, the great, and with many, the sole aim in working for God? Should it be so? Let us think of this other work. Let us help to *keep alive*. Perhaps it is less distinguished, as it may be less distinguished to feed a starving child than to rescue a drowning man. But let us walk less by sight, more by faith. Let us not indeed neglect to call to life those who are spiritually dead. But oh! let us watch for the more hidden needs of the living—the fading, starving, fainting souls, which yet can walk and speak, and cover their want and sorrow. Let us be fellow-workers with God in *all* his work. And with a deep heart-feeling of the need of *constant* life supplies from above, let us try how often, how freely, we may be made the channels of those streams of the " water of life,"—for " none can keep alive his own soul." *Mary B. M. Duncan, in " Bible Hours,"* 1866.

Verse 29.—Having considered the vastness and glory of the prospect, our Lord next contemplates the reality and minuteness of its accomplishment. He sets before his mind individual cases and particular facts. He appears to look upon this picture of the future as we do upon a grand historical painting of the past. It seems natural to gaze with silent admiration on the picture as a whole, then to fix the attention on particular groups, and testify our sense of the general excellence, by expatiating on the truth and beauty of the several parts. *John Stevenson.*

Verse 30.—" *A seed shall serve him.*" This figurative expression signifies Christ and his people, who yield true obedience to God—they are called by this name in a spiritual and figurative, but most appropriate sense. The idea is taken from the operations of the husbandman who carefully reserves every year a portion of his grain for seed. Though it be small, compared with all the produce of his harvest, yet he prizes it very highly and estimates it by the value of that crop which it may yield in the succeeding autumn. Nor does he look only to the quantity, he pays particular regard to the quality of the seed. He reserves only the best, nay, he will put away his own if spoiled, that he may procure better. The very smallest quantity of really good seed, is, to him, an object of great desire, and if by grievous failure of crops, he should not be able to procure more than a single grain, yet would he accept it thankfully, preserve it carefully, and plant it in the most favourable soil. Such is the source from which the metaphor is taken.—*John Stevenson.*

Verse 31.—" *And shall declare his righteousness.*" The occupation of the seed is to " *declare*," to testify from their own experience, from their own knowledge and convictions, that grand subject, theme, or lesson, which they have learned. . . . . . . They will declare the righteousness of God the Holy Ghost in his convictions of sin, in his reproofs of conscience, in his forsaking of the impenitent, and in his abiding with the believer. And in a special manner, they will declare the righteousness of God the Son, during his human life, in his sufferings, and death, as man's surety, by which he " magnified the law, and made it honourable" (Isa. xlii. 21), and on account of which they are able to address him by this name, " The Lord our Righteousness." (Jer. xxiii. 6.)—*John Stevenson.*

Verse 31.—" *A people that shall be born.*" What is this? What people is there that is not born? According to my apprehensions I think this is said for this reason—because the people of other kings are formed by laws, by customs, and by manners ; by which, however, you can never move a man to true righteousness : it is only a fable of righteousness, and a mere theatrical scene or representation. For even the law of Moses could form the people of the Jews unto nothing but unto hypocrisy. But the people of this King are not formed by laws to make up an external appearance, but they are begotten by water and by the Spirit unto a new creature of truth.—*Martin Luther.*

HINTS TO THE VILLAGE PREACHER.

Whole Psalm.—The volume entitled "Christ on the Cross," by Rev. J. Stevenson, has a sermon upon every verse. We give the headings, they are suggestive. *Verse* 1. The Cry. 2. The Complaint. 3. The Acknowledgment. 4—6. The Contrast. 6. The Reproach. 7. The Mockery. 8. The Taunt. 9, 10. The Appeal. 11. The Entreaty. 12, 13. The Assault. 14. The Faintness. 15. The Exhaustion. 16. The Piercing. 17. The Emaciation. 17. The Insulting Gaze. 18. The Partition of the Garments and Casting Lots. 19—21. The Importunity. 21. The Deliverance. 22. The Gratitude. 23. The Invitation. 24. The Testimony. 25. The Vow. 26. The Satisfaction of the Meek ; the Seekers of the Lord Praising Him ; the Eternal Life. 27. The Conversion of the World. 28. The Enthronement. 29. The Author of the Faith. 30. The Seed. 31. The Everlasting Theme and Occupation. The Finish of the Faith.

Verse 1.—The Saviour's dying cry.

Verse 2.—*Unanswered prayer.* Enquire the reasons for it ; encourage our hope concerning it ; urge to continue in importunity.

Verse 3.—Whatever God may do, we must settle it in our minds that he is holy and to be praised.

Verse 4.—God's faithfulness in past ages a plea for the present.

Verses 4, 5.—Ancient saints. I. Their life. "*They trusted.*" II. Their practice. "*They cried.*" III. Their experience. "*Were not confounded.*" IV. Their voice to us.

Verses 6—18.—Full of striking sentences upon our Lord's sufferings.

Verse 11.—A saint's troubles, his arguments in prayer.

Verse 20.—"*My darling.*" A man's soul to be very dear to him.

Verse 21 (*first clause*).—"*Lion's mouth.*" Men of cruelty. The devil. Sin. Death. Hell.

Verse 22.—Christ as a brother, a preacher, and a precentor.

Verse 22.—A sweet subject, a glorious preacher, a loving relationship, a heavenly exercise.

Verse 23.—*A threefold duty*, " praise him," " glorify him ;" " fear him ;" *towards one object*, " the Lord ;" *for three characters*, " ye that fear him, seed of Jacob, seed of Israel," *which are but one person.*

Verse 23.—Glory to God the fruit of the tree on which Jesus died.

Verse 24.—A consoling fact in history attested by universal experience.

Verse 24 (*first clause*).—A common fear dispelled.

Verse 25.—Public praise. I. A delightful exercise—" praise." II. A personal participation—" My praise." III. A fitting object—" of thee." IV. A special source—" from thee." V. An appropriate place—" in the great congregation."

Verse 25 (*second clause*).—*Vows.* What vows to make, when and how to make them, and the importance of paying them.

Verse 26.—*Spiritual feasting.* The guests, the food, the host, and the satisfaction.

Verse 26 (*second clause*).—*Seekers who shall be singers.* Who they are ? What they shall do ? When ? and what is the reason for expecting that they shall ?

Verse 27 (*last clause*). — *Life everlasting.* What lives ? Source of life. Manner of life. Why for ever ? What occupation ? What comfort to be derived from it ?

Verse 27.—Nature of true conversion, and extent of it under the reign of the Messiah.—*Andrew Fuller.*

Verse 27.—The universal triumph of Christianity certain.

Verse 27.—The order of conversion. See the Exposition.

Verse 28.—The empire of the King of kings as it is, and as it shall be.

Verse 29.—Grace for the rich, grace for the poor, but all lost without it.

Verse 29 (*last clause*).—A weighty text upon the vanity of self-confidence.

Verse 30.—The perpetuity of the church.

Verse 30 (*last clause*).—Church history, the marrow of all history.

Verse 31.—Future prospects for the church. I. Conversions certain. II. Preachers promised. III. Succeeding generations blest. IV. Gospel published. V. Christ exalted.

WORK UPON THE TWENTY-SECOND PSALM.

Christ on the Cross: An Exposition of the Twenty-second Psalm. By the Rev. JOHN STEVENSON, Perpetual Curate of Curry and Gunwalloe, Cornwall. 1842.

PSALM XXIII.

There is no inspired title to this psalm, and none is needed, for it records no special event, and needs no other key than that which every Christian may find in his own bosom. It is David's Heavenly Pastoral ; a surpassing ode, which none of the daughters of music can excel. The clarion of war here gives place to the pipe of peace, and he who so lately bewailed the woes of the Shepherd tunefully rehearses the joys of the flock. Sitting under a spreading tree, with his flock around him, like Bunyan's shepherd-boy in the Valley of Humiliation, we picture David singing this unrivalled pastoral with a heart as full of gladness as it could hold ; or, if the psalm be the product of his after years, we are sure that his soul returned in contemplation to the lonely water-brooks which rippled among the pastures of the wilderness, where in early day she had been wont to dwell. This is the pearl of psalms whose soft and pure radiance delights every eye ; a pearl of which Helicon need not be ashamed, though Jordan claims it. Of this delightful song it may be affirmed that its piety and its poetry are equal, its sweetness and its spirituality are unsurpassed.

The position of this psalm is worthy of notice. It follows the twenty-second, which is peculiarly the Psalm of the Cross. There are no green pastures, no still waters on the other side of the twenty-second psalm. It is only after we have read, "My God, my God, why hast thou forsaken me?" that we come to "The Lord is my Shepherd." We must by experience know the value of the blood-shedding, and see the sword awakened against the Shepherd, before we shall be able truly to know the sweetness of the good Shepherd's care.

It has been said that what the nightingale is among birds, that is this divine ode among the psalms, for it has sung sweetly in the ear of many a mourner in his night of weeping, and has bidden him hope for a morning of joy. I will venture to compare it also to the lark, which sings as it mounts, and mounts as it sings, until it is out of sight, and even then is not out of hearing. Note the last words of the psalm—"I will dwell in the house of the Lord for ever;" these are celestial notes, more fitted for the eternal mansions than for these dwelling places below the clouds. Oh that we may enter into the spirit of the psalm as we read it, and then we shall experience the days of heaven upon the earth!

EXPOSITION.

THE Lord *is* my shepherd ; I shall not want.

2 He maketh me to lie down in green pastures : he leadeth me beside the still waters.

3 He restoreth my soul : he leadeth me in the paths of righteousness for his name's sake.

4 Yea, though I walk through the valley of the shadow of death, I will fear no evil : for thou *art* with me ; thy rod and thy staff they comfort me.

5 Thou preparest a table before me in the presence of mine enemies : thou anointest my head with oil ; my cup runneth over.

6 Surely goodness and mercy shall follow me all the days of my life : and I will dwell in the house of the LORD for ever.

1. " *The Lord is my shepherd.*" What condescension is this, that the Infinite Lord assumes towards his people the office and character of a Shepherd ! It should be the subject of grateful admiration that the great God allows himself to be compared to anything which will set forth his great love and care for his own people. David had himself been a keeper of sheep, and understood both

the needs of the sheep and the many cares of a shepherd.   He compares himself
to a creature weak, defenceless, and foolish, and he takes God to be his Provider,
Preserver, Director, and, indeed, his everything.   No man has a right to consider himself the Lord's sheep unless his nature has been renewed, for the
scriptural description of unconverted men does not picture them as sheep, but
as wolves or goats.   A sheep is an object of property, not a wild animal ; its
owner sets great store by it, and frequently it is bought with a great price.   It is
well to know, as certainly as David did, that we belong to the Lord.   There
is a noble tone of confidence about this sentence.   There is no " if " nor " but,"
nor even " I hope so ;" but he says, " The Lord *is* my shepherd."   We must
cultivate the spirit of assured dependence upon our heavenly Father.   The
sweetest word of the whole is that monosyllable, " *My*."   He does not say, " The
Lord is the shepherd of the world at large, and leadeth forth the multitude as
his flock," but " The Lord is *my* shepherd ; " if he be a Shepherd to no one else,
he is a Shepherd to *me ;* he cares for *me*, watches over *me*, and preserves *me*.
The words are in the present tense.   Whatever be the believer's position, he is
even now under the pastoral care of Jehovah.

The next words are a sort of inference from the first statement—they are
sententious and positive—" *I shall not want*."   I might want otherwise, but
when the Lord is my Shepherd he is able to supply my needs, and he is certainly
willing to do so, for his heart is full of love, and therefore " *I shall not want*."   I
shall not lack for *temporal things*.   Does he not feed the ravens, and cause the
lilies to grow ?   How, then, can he leave his children to starve ?   I shall not
want *for spirituals*, I know that his grace will be sufficient for me.   Resting in
him he will say to me, " As thy day so shall thy strength be."   I may not
possess all that I wish for, but " I shall not *want*."   Others, far wealthier and
wiser than I, may want, but " *I shall not*."   " The young lions *do* lack, and
suffer hunger : but they that seek the Lord shall not want any good thing."   It
is not only " I do not want," but " I *shall not* want."   Come what may, if famine
should devastate the land, or calamity destroy the city, " *I shall not want*."   Old
age with its feebleness shall not bring me any lack, and even death with its
gloom shall not find me destitute.   I have all things and abound ; not because
I have a good store of money in the bank, not because I have skill and wit with
which to win my bread, but because " *The Lord is my shepherd*."   The wicked
always want, but the righteous never ; a sinner's heart is far from satisfaction,
but a gracious spirit dwells in the palace of content.

2.   " *He maketh me to lie down in green pastures : he leadeth me beside the still
waters*."   The Christian life has two elements in it, the contemplative and the
active, and both of these are richly provided for.   First, the contemplative.
" *He maketh me to lie down in green pastures*."   What are these " *green pastures*"
but the Scriptures of truth—always fresh, always rich, and never exhausted ?
There is no fear of biting the bare ground where the grass is long enough for
the flock to lie down in it.   Sweet and full are the doctrines of the gospel ;
fit food for souls, as tender grass is natural nutriment for sheep.   When by faith
we are enabled to find rest in the promises, we are like the sheep that lie down
in the midst of the pasture ; we find at the same moment both provender and
peace, rest and refreshment, serenity and satisfaction.   But observe : " *He
maketh* me to lie down."   It is the Lord who graciously enables us to perceive
the preciousness of his truth, and to feed upon it.   How grateful ought we to
be for the power to appropriate the promises !   There are some distracted souls
who would give worlds if they could but do this.   They know the blessedness
of it, but they cannot say that this blessedness is theirs.   They know the
" *green pastures*," but they are not made to " *lie down*" in them.   Those believers who have for years enjoyed a " full assurance of faith" should greatly
bless their gracious God.

The second part of a vigorous Christian's life consists in gracious activity.
We not only think, but we act.   We are not always lying down to feed, but are
journeying onward toward perfection ; hence we read, " *he leadeth me beside the*

still waters." What are these *" still waters"* but the influences and graces of his blessed Spirit? His Spirit attends us in various operations, like waters—in the plural—to cleanse, to refresh, to fertilise, to cherish. They are *" still waters,"* for the Holy Ghost loves peace, and sounds no trumpet of ostentation in his operations. He may flow into our soul, but not into our neighbour's, and therefore our neighbour may not perceive the divine presence; and though the blessed Spirit may be pouring his floods into one heart, yet he that sitteth next to the favoured one may know nothing of it.

> "In sacred silence of the mind
> My heaven, and there my God I find."

Still waters run deep. Nothing more noisy than an empty drum. That silence is golden indeed in which the Holy Spirit meets with the souls of his saints. Not to raging waves of strife, but to peaceful streams of holy love does the Spirit of God conduct the chosen sheep. He is a dove, not an eagle; the dew, not the hurricane. Our Lord leads us beside these *" still waters;"* we could not go there of ourselves, we need his guidance, therefore it is said, *" he leadeth me."* He does not drive us. Moses drives us by the law, but Jesus leads us by his example, and the gentle drawings of his love.

3. *" He restoreth my soul."* When the soul grows sorrowful he revives it; when it is sinful he sanctifies it; when it is weak he strengthens it. *" He"* does it. His ministers could not do it if he did not. His Word would not avail by itself. *" He restoreth my soul."* Are any of us low in grace? Do we feel that our spirituality is at its lowest ebb? He who turns the ebb into the flood can soon restore our soul. Pray to him, then, for the blessing—" Restore thou me, thou Shepherd of my soul!"

" He leadeth me in the paths of righteousness for his name's sake." The Christian delights to be obedient, but it is the obedience of love, to which he is constrained by the example of his Master. *" He leadeth me."* The Christian is not obedient to some commandments and neglectful of others; he does not pick and choose, but yields to all. Observe, that the plural is used—" the *paths* of righteousness." Whatever God may give us to do we would do it, led by his love. Some Christians overlook the blessing of sanctification, and yet to a thoroughly renewed heart this is one of the sweetest gifts of the covenant. If we could be saved from wrath, and yet remain unregenerate, impenitent sinners, we should not be saved as we desire, for we mainly and chiefly pant to be saved *from* sin and led in the way of holiness. All this is done out of pure free grace; *" for his name's sake."* It is to the honour of our great Shepherd that we should be a holy people, walking in the narrow way of righteousness. If we be so led and guided we must not fail to adore our heavenly Shepherd's care.

4. *" Yea, though I walk through the valley of the shadow of death, I will fear no evil: for thou art with me; thy rod and thy staff they comfort me."* This unspeakably delightful verse has been sung on many a dying bed, and has helped to make the dark valley bright times out of mind. Every word in it has a wealth of meaning. *" Yea, though I walk,"* as if the believer did not quicken his pace when he came to die, but still calmly *walked* with God. To walk indicates the steady advance of a soul which knows its road, knows its end, resolves to follow the path, feels quite safe, and is therefore perfectly calm and composed. The dying saint is not in a flurry, he does not run as though he were alarmed, nor stand still as though he would go no further, he is not confounded nor ashamed, and therefore keeps to his old pace. Observe that it is not walking *in* the valley, but *through* the valley. We go through the dark tunnel of death and emerge into the light of immortality. We do not die, we do but sleep to wake in glory. Death is not the house but the porch, not the goal but the passage to it. The dying article is called a *valley*. The storm breaks on the mountain, but the valley is the place of quietude, and thus full often the last days of the Christian are the most peaceful in his whole career; the mountain is bleak and bare, but the valley is rich with golden sheaves, and many a saint

has reaped more joy and knowledge when he came to die than he ever knew while he lived. And, then, it is not "the valley of death," but "the valley *of the shadow* of death," for death in its substance has been removed, and only the shadow of it remains. Some one has said that when there is a shadow there must be light somewhere, and so there is. Death stands by the side of the highway in which we have to travel, and the light of heaven shining upon him throws a shadow across our path ; let us then rejoice that there is a light beyond. Nobody is afraid of a shadow, for a shadow cannot stop a man's pathway even for a moment. The shadow of a dog cannot bite ; the shadow of a sword cannot kill ; the shadow of death cannot destroy us. Let us not, therefore, be afraid. "*I will fear no evil.*" He does not say there shall not be any evil ; he had got beyond even that high assurance, and knew that Jesus had put all evil away ; but "I will *fear* no evil ;" as if even his fears, those shadows of evil, were gone for ever. The worst evils of life are those which do not exist except in our imagination. If we had no troubles but real troubles, we should not have a tenth part of our present sorrows. We feel a thousand deaths in fearing one, but the psalmist was cured of the disease of fearing. "I will fear *no evil,*" not even the Evil One himself ; I will not dread the last enemy, I will look upon him as a conquered foe, an enemy to be destroyed, "*For thou art with me.*" This is the joy of the Christian ! "*Thou* art with me." The little child out at sea in the storm is not frightened like all the other passengers on board the vessel, it is asleep in its mother's bosom ; it is enough for it that its mother is with it ; and it should be enough for the believer to know that Christ is with him. "*Thou* art with me ; I have, in having thee, all that I can crave : I have perfect comfort and absolute security, for *thou* art with me." "*Thy rod and thy staff,*" by which thou governest and rulest thy flock, the ensigns of thy sovereignty and of thy gracious care—"*they comfort me.*" I will believe that thou reignest still. The rod of Jesse shall still be over me as the sovereign succour of my soul.

Many persons profess to receive much comfort from the hope that they shall not die. Certainly there will be some who will be "alive and remain" at the coming of the Lord, but is there so very much of advantage in such an escape from death as to make it the object of Christian desire ? A wise man might prefer of the two to die, for those who shall not die, but who "shall be caught up together with the Lord in the air," will be losers rather than gainers. They will lose that actual fellowship with Christ in the tomb which dying saints will have, and we are expressly told they shall have no preference beyond those who are asleep. Let us be of Paul's mind when he said that "To die is gain," and think of "departing to be with Christ, which is far better." This twenty-third psalm is not worn out, and it is as sweet in a believer's ear now as it was in David's time, let novelty-hunters say what they will.

5. "*Thou preparest a table before me in the presence of mine enemies.*" The good man has his enemies. He would not be like his Lord if he had not. If we were without enemies we might fear that we were not the friends of God, for the friendship of the world is enmity to God. Yet see the quietude of the godly man in spite of, and in the sight of, his enemies. How refreshing is his calm bravery ! "*Thou preparest a table before me.*" When a soldier is in the presence of his enemies, if he eats at all he snatches a hasty meal, and away he hastens to the fight. But observe : "Thou *preparest* a table," just as a servant does when she unfolds the damask cloth and displays the ornaments of the feast on an ordinary peaceful occasion. Nothing is hurried, there is no confusion, no disturbance, the enemy is at the door, and yet God prepares a table, and the Christian sits down and eats as if everything were in perfect peace. Oh ! the peace which Jehovah gives to his people, even in the midst of the most trying circumstances !

> "Let earth be all in arms abroad,
> They dwell in perfect peace."

"*Thou anointest my head with oil.*" May we live in the daily enjoyment of this blessing, receiving a fresh anointing for every day's duties. Every Christian is a priest, but he cannot execute the priestly office without unction, and hence we must go day by day to God the Holy Ghost, that we may have our heads anointed with oil. A priest without oil misses the chief qualification for his office, and the Christian priest lacks his chief fitness for service when he is devoid of new grace from on high. " *My cup runneth over.*" He had not only enough, a cup full, but more than enough, a cup which overflowed. A poor man may say this as well as those in higher circumstances. "What, all this, and Jesus Christ too ?" said a poor cottager as she broke a piece of bread and filled a glass with cold water. Whereas a man may be ever so wealthy, but if he be discontented his cup cannot run over ; it is cracked and leaks. Content is the philosopher's stone which turns all it touches into gold ; happy is he who has found it. Content is more than a kingdom, it is another word for happiness.

6. " *Surely goodness and mercy shall follow me all the days of my life.*" This is a fact as indisputable as it is encouraging, and therefore a heavenly *verily,* or " *surely*" is set as a seal upon it. This sentence may be read, " *only* goodness and mercy," for there shall be unmingled mercy in our history. These twin guardian angels will always be with me at my back and my beck. Just as when great princes go abroad they must not go unattended, so is it with the believer. Goodness and mercy follow him always—" *all the days of his life*"—the black days as well as the bright days, the days of fasting as well as the days of feasting, the dreary days of winter as well as the bright days of summer. Goodness supplies our needs, and mercy blots out our sins. " *And I will dwell in the house of the Lord for ever.*" " A servant abideth not in the house for ever, but the son abideth ever." While I am here I will be a child at home with my God ; the whole world shall be his house to me ; and when I ascend into the upper chamber I shall not change my company, nor even change the house ; I shall only go to dwell in the upper storey of the house of the Lord for ever.

May God grant us grace to dwell in the serene atmosphere of this most blessed Psalm !

EXPLANATORY NOTES AND QUAINT SAYINGS.

Whole Psalm.—David has left no sweeter Psalm than the short twenty-third. It is but a moment's opening of his soul ; but, as when one, walking the winter street sees the door opened for some one to enter, and the red light streams a moment forth, and the forms of gay children are running to greet the comer, and genial music sounds, though the door shuts and leaves the night black, yet it cannot shut back again all that the eyes, the ear, the heart, and the imagination have seen—so in this Psalm, though it is but a moment's opening of the soul, are emitted truths of peace and consolation that will never be absent from the world. The twenty-third Psalm is the nightingale of the Psalms. It is small, of a homely feather, singing shyly out of obscurity ; but, oh ! it has filled the air of the whole world with melodious joy, greater than the heart can conceive. Blessed be the day on which that Psalm was born ! What would you say of a pilgrim commissioned of God to travel up and down the earth singing a strange melody, which, when one heard, caused him to forget whatever sorrow he had ? And so the singing angel goes on his way through all lands, singing in the language of every nation, driving away trouble by the pulses of the air which his tongue moves with divine power. Behold just such an one ! This pilgrim God has sent to speak in every language on the globe. It has charmed more griefs to rest than all the philosophy of the world. It has remanded to their dungeon more felon thoughts, more black doubts, more thieving sorrows, than there are sands on the sea-shore. It has comforted the noble host of the poor. It has sung courage to the army of the disappointed. It has poured balm and consolation into the heart of the sick, of captives in dungeons, of widows in their pinching griefs, of orphans in their loneliness. Dying soldiers have died easier as it was read to them ; ghastly hospitals have been illuminated ; it has visited the prisoner, and broken his chains, and, like Peter's angel, led him forth in imagination, and sung him back to his home again. It has made the dying Christian slave freer than his master, and consoled those whom, dying, he left behind mourning, not so much that he was gone, as because they were left behind, and could not go too. Nor is its work done. It will go singing to your children and my children, and to their children, through all the generations of time ; nor will it fold its wings till the last pilgrim is safe, and time ended ; and then it shall fly back to the bosom of God, whence it issued, and sound on, mingled with all those sounds of celestial joy which make heaven musical for ever.—*Henry Ward Beecher, in " Life Thoughts."*

Whole Psalm.—This Psalm may well be called David's *bucolicon*, or pastoral, so daintily hath he struck upon the whole string, through the whole hymn. *Est Psalmus honorabilis*, saith Aben-Ezra ; it is a noble Psalm, written and sung by David, not when he fled into the forest of Hareth (1 Sam. xxii. 5), as some Hebrews will have it ; but when as having overcome all his enemies, and settled his kingdom, he enjoyed great peace and quiet, and had one foot, as it were, upon the battlements of heaven. The Jews at this day use for most part to repeat this Psalm after they are sat down to meat.—*John Trapp.*

Whole Psalm.—Augustine is said to have beheld, in a dream, the one hundred and nineteenth Psalm rising before him as a tree of life in the midst of the paradise of God. This twenty-third may be compared to the fairest flowers that grew around it. The former has even been likened to the sun amidst the stars—surely this is like the richest of the constellations, even the Pleiades themselves !—*John Stoughton, in " The Songs of Christ's Flock,"* 1860.

Whole Psalm.—Some pious souls are troubled because they cannot at all times, or often, use, in its joyous import, the language of this Psalm. Such should remember that David, though he lived long, never wrote but one twenty-third Psalm. Some of his odes do indeed express as lively a faith as this, and faith can walk in darkness. But where else do we find a whole Psalm expressive of personal confidence, joy, and triumph, from beginning to end ? God's people have their seasons of darkness and their times of rejoicing.—*William S. Plumer.*

Verse 1.—" *The Lord is my shepherd ; I shall not want.*" Let them say that will, " My lands shall keep me, I shall have no want, my merchandise shall be my help, I shall have no want ;" let the soldier trust unto his weapons, and the husbandman unto his labour ; let the artificer say unto his art, and the tradesman unto his trade, and the scholar unto his books, " These shall maintain me, I shall not want." Let *us* say with the church, as we both say and sing, " The Lord is my keeper, I shall not want." He that can truly say so, contemns the rest, and he that desires more than God, cannot truly say, the Lord is his, the Lord is this shepherd, governor and commander, and therefore I shall not want.—*John Hull, B.D., in " Lectures on Lamentations,"* 1617.

Verse 1.—" *The Lord is my shepherd ; I want nothing :*" thus it may be equally well rendered, though in our version it is in the future tense.—*J. R. Macduff, D.D., in " The Shepherd and his Flock,"* 1866.

Verse 1.—" *The Lord is my shepherd.*" We may learn in general from the metaphor, that it is the property of a gracious heart to draw some spiritual use or other from his former condition. David himself having sometimes been a shepherd, as himself confesseth when he saith, " he took David from the sheepfold from following the sheep," etc., himself having been a shepherd, he beholds the Lord the same to him. Whatsoever David was to his flock—watchful over them, careful to defend them from the lion and the bear, and whatsoever thing else might annoy them, careful of their pasturage and watering, etc., the same and much more he beholds the Lord to himself. So Paul : " I was a persecutor, and an oppressor : but the Lord had mercy on me." This we may see in good old Jacob : " With this staff," saith he. " I passed over Jordan ;" and that now God had blessed him and multiplied him exceedingly. The doctrine is plain ;

the reasons are, first, because true grace makes no object amiss to gather some gracious instruction : it skills not what the object be, so that the heart be gracious ; for that never wants matter to work upon. And secondly, it must needs be so, for such are guided by God's Spirit, and therefore are directed to a spiritual use of all things.—*Samuel Smith's " Chiefe Shepheard,"* 1625.

Verse 1.—*" Shepherd."* May this sweet title persuade Japhet to dwell in the tents of Shem : my meaning is, that those who as yet never knew what it was to be enfolded in the bosom of Jesus, who as yet were never lambs nor ewes in Christ's fold, consider the sweetness of this Shepherd, and come in to him. Satan deals seemingly sweet, that he may draw you into sin, but in the end he will be really bitter to you. Christ, indeed, is seemingly bitter to keep you from sin, hedging up your way with thorns. But he will be really sweet if you come into his flock, even notwithstanding your sins. Thou lookest into Christ's fold, and thou seest it hedged and fenced all about to keep you in from sin, and this keeps thee from entering ; but, oh ! let it not. Christ, indeed, is unwilling that any of his should wander, and if they be unwilling too, it's well. And if they wander he'll fetch them in, it may be with his shepherd's *dog* (some affliction) ; but he'll not be, as we say, *dogged* himself. No, he is and will be sweet. It may be, now Satan smiles, and is pleasant to you while you sin ; but know, he'll be bitter in the end. He that sings syren-like now, will devour lion-like at last. He'll torment you and vex you, and be burning and bitterness to you. O come in therefore to Jesus Christ ; let him be now the shepherd of thy soul. And know then, he'll be sweet in endeavouring to keep thee from sin before thou commit it ; and he'll be sweet in delivering thee from sin after thou hast committed it. O that this thought—that Jesus Christ is sweet in his carriage unto all his members, unto all his flock, especially the sinning ones, might persuade the hearts of some sinners to come in unto his fold. *John Durant,* 1652.

Verse 1 (*first clause*).—*Feedeth me,* or, is *my feeder, my pastor.* The word comprehendeth all duties of a good herd, as together feeding, guiding, governing, and defending his flock.—*Henry Ainsworth.*

Verse 1.—*" The Lord is my shepherd."* Now the reasons of this resemblance I take to be these :—First, one property of a good shepherd is, skill to know and judge aright of his sheep, and hence is it that it is a usual thing to set mark upon sheep, to the end that if they go astray (as of all creatures they are most subject to wander), the shepherd may seek them up and bring them home again. The same thing is affirmed of Christ, or rather indeed Christ affirmeth the same thing of himself, " I know them, and they follow me." John x. 27. Yea, doubtless, he that hath numbered the stars, and calleth them all by their names, yea, the very hairs of our head, taketh special notice of his own children, " the sheep of his pasture," that they may be provided for and protected from all danger. Secondly, a good shepherd must have skill in the pasturing of his sheep, and in bringing them into such fruitful ground, as they may battle and thrive upon : a good shepherd will not suffer his sheep to feed upon rotten soil, but in wholesome pastures. . . . Thirdly, a good shepherd, knowing the straying nature of his sheep, is so much the more diligent to watch over them, and if at any time they go astray, he brings them back again. This is the Lord's merciful dealing towards poor wandering souls. . . . Fourthly, a good shepherd must have will to feed his sheep according to his skill : the Lord of all others is most willing to provide for his sheep. How earnest is Christ with Peter, to " feed his sheep," urging him unto it three several times ! Fifthly, a good shepherd is provided to defend his flock. . . . The Lord is every way provided for the safety and defence of his sheep, as David confesseth in this Psalm (verse 4), " *Thy rod and thy staff they comfort me.*" And again, " I took unto me two staves" (saith the Lord), " the one I called Beauty, and the other I called Bands ; and I fed the flock." Zech. xi. 7. Sixthly, it is the property of a good shepherd, that if any of his sheep be weak and feeble, or his lambs young, for their safety and recovery he will bear them in his arms. The Lord is not wanting to us herein. Isa. xl. 11. And lastly, it is the property of a good shepherd to rejoice when the strayed sheep is brought home. The Lord doth thus rejoice at the conversion of a sinner. Luke xv. 7.—*Samuel Smith.*

Verse 1.—" *The Lord is my shepherd.*" I notice that some of the flock keep near the shepherd, and follow whithersover he goes without the least hesitation, while others stray about on either side, or loiter far behind ; and he often turns round and scolds them in a sharp, stern cry, or sends a stone after them. I saw him lame one just now. Not altogether unlike the good Shepherd. Indeed, I never ride over these hills, clothed with flocks, without meditating upon this delightful theme. Our Saviour says that the good shepherd, when he putteth forth his own sheep, goeth before them, and they follow. John x. 4. This is true to the letter. They are so tame and so trained that they *follow* their keeper with the utmost docility. He leads them forth from the fold, or from their houses in the villages, just where he pleases. As there are many flocks in such a place as this, each one takes a different path, and it is his business to find pasture for them. It is necessary, therefore, that they should be taught to follow, and not to stray away into the unfenced fields of corn which lie so temptingly on either side. Any one that thus wanders is sure to get into trouble. The shepherd calls sharply from time to time to remind them of his presence. They know his voice, and follow on ; but, if a stranger call, they stop short, lift up their heads in alarm, and, if it is repeated, they turn and flee, because they know not the voice of a stranger. This is not the fanciful costume of a parable, it is simple fact. I have made the experiment repeatedly. The shepherd goes before, not merely to point out the way, but to see that it is practicable and safe. He is armed in order to defend his charge, and in this he is very courageous. Many adventures with wild beasts occur, not unlike that recounted by David (1 Sam. xvii. 34—36), and in these very mountains ; for though there are now no lions here, there are wolves in abundance ; and leopards and panthers, exceeding fierce, prowl about the wild wadies. They not unfrequently attack the flock in the very presence of the shepherd, and he must be ready to do battle at a moment's warning. I have listened with intense interest to their graphic descriptions of downright and desperate fights with these savage beasts. And when the thief and the robber come (and come they do), the faithful shepherd has often to put his life in his hand to defend his flock. I have known more than one case in which he had literally to lay it down in the contest. A poor faithful fellow last spring, between Tiberias and Tabor, instead of fleeing, actually fought three Bedawin robbers until he was hacked to pieces with their khanjars, and died among the sheep he was defending. Some sheep always keep near the shepherd, and are his special favorites. Each of them has a name, to which it answers joyfully, and the kind shepherd is ever distributing to such, choice portions which he gathers for that purpose. These are the contented and happy ones. They are in no danger of getting lost or into mischief, nor do wild beasts or thieves come near them. The great body, however, are mere worldings, intent upon their mere pleasures or selfish interests. They run from bush to bush, searching for variety or delicacies, and only now and then lift their heads to see where the shepherd is, or, rather where the general flock is, lest they get so far away as to occasion a remark in their little community, or rebuke from their keeper. Others, again, are restless and discontented, jumping into everybody's field, climbing into bushes, and even into leaning trees, whence they often fall and break their limbs. These cost the good shepherd incessant trouble.—*W. M. Thomson, D.D., in " The Land and the Book."*

Verse 1.—" *Shepherd.*" As we sat the silent hillsides around us were in a moment filled with life and sound. The shepherds led their flocks forth from the gates of the city. They were in full view, and we watched them and listened to them with no little interest. Thousands of sheep and goats were there, grouped in dense, confused masses. The shepherds stood together until all came out. Then they separated, each shepherd taking a different path, and uttering as he advanced a shrill peculiar call. The sheep heard them. At first the masses swayed and moved, as if shaken by some internal convulsion ; then points struck out in the direction taken by the shepherds ; these became longer and longer until the confused masses were resolved into long, living streams, flowing after their leaders. Such a sight was not new to me, still it had lost none of its interest. It was perhaps one of the most vivid illustrations which human eyes could witness of that beautiful discourse of our Lord recorded by John, "And the sheep hear the shepherd's voice : and he calleth his own sheep by name, and leadeth them out. And when he putteth forth his own sheep, he goeth before them, and the sheep follow him : for they know his voice. And a stranger will they not follow, but will flee from him : for they know not the voice of strangers," chap. x. 3—5. The shepherds themselves had none of that peaceful and placid aspect which is generally associated with pastoral life and habits. They looked more like warriors marching to the battle-field— a long gun slung from the shoulder, a dagger and heavy pistols in the belt, a light battle-axe or ironheaded club in the hand. Such were the equipments ; and their fierce flashing eyes and scowling countenances showed but too plainly that they were prepared to use their weapons at any moment.—*J. L. Porter, A.M., in "The Giant Cities of Bashan,"* 1867.

Verse 1.—"*I shall not want.*" You must distinguish 'twixt *absence*, and 'twixt *indigence*. *Absence* is when something is not present ; *indigence* or *want*, is when a needful good is not present. If a man were to walk, and had not a staff, here were something absent. If a man were to walk, and had but one leg, here were something whereof he were indigent. It is confessed that there are many good things which are absent from a good person, but no good thing which he wants or is indigent of. If the good be absent and I need it not, this is no want ; he that walks without his cloak, walks well enough, for he needs it not. As long as I can walk carefully and cheerfully in my general or particular calling, though I have not such a load of accessories as other men have, yet I *want* nothing, for my little is enough and serves the turn. . . . . Our corruptions are still craving, and they are always inordinate, they can find more wants than God needs to supply. As they say of fools, they can propose more questions than twenty wise men need to answer. They in James iv. 3, did *ask*, but *received not ;* and he gives two reasons for it :—1. This *asking* was but a *lusting :* "ye lust and have not" (verse 4): another, they did ask *to consume it upon their lusts* (verse 3). God will see that his people shall not want ; but withal, he will never engage himself to the satisfying of their corruptions, though he doth to the supply of their conditions. It is one thing what the sick man wants, another what his disease wants. Your ignorance, your discontents, your pride, your unthankful hearts, may make you to believe that you dwell in a barren land, far from mercies (as melancholy makes a person to imagine that he is drowning, or killing, etc.) ; whereas if God did open your eyes as he did Hagar's, you might see fountains and streams, mercies and blessings sufficient ; though not many, yet enough, though not so rich, yet proper, and every way convenient for your good and comfort ; and thus you have the genuine sense, so far as I can judge of David's assertion, "*I shall not want.*"—*Obadiah Sedgwick.*

Verse 1.—"*I shall not want.*" Only he that can want does not want ; and he that cannot, does. You tell me that a godly man wants these and these things, which the wicked man hath ; but I tell you he can no more be said to "*want*" them than a butcher may be said to want Homer, or such another thing, because his disposition is such, that he makes no use of those things which you usually mean. 'Tis but only necessary things that he cares for, and those are not many. But *one* thing is necessary, and that he hath chosen, namely, *the better part.* And therefore if he have nothing at all of all other things, he does not *want*, neither is there anything *wanting* which might make him rich enough, or by absence whereof, his riches should be said to be deficient. A body is not *maimed* unless it have lost a principal part : only *privative* defects discommend a thing, and not those that are *negative*. When we say, there is nothing *wanting* to such-and-such a creature or thing that a man hath made, we mean that it hath all that belongs necessarily to it. We speak not of such things as may be added for compliments or ornaments or the like, such as are those things usually wherein wicked men excel the godly. Even so it is when we say that a godly man *wanteth nothing*. For though in regard of unnecessary goods he be "as having nothing," yet in regard of others he is as if he possessed all things. He wants nothing that is necessary either for his glorifying of God (being able to do that best in and by his afflictions), or for God's glorifying of him, and making him happy, having God himself for his portion and supply of his wants, who is abundantly sufficient at all times, for all persons, in all conditions.—*Zachary Bogan.*

Verse 1.—"*I shall not want.*" To be raised above the fear of want by committing ourselves to the care of the Good Shepherd, or by placing our confidence in worldly property, are two distinct and very opposite things. The confidence in the former case, appears to the natural man to be hard and difficult, if not unreasonable and impossible : in the latter it appears to be natural, easy, and consistent. It requires, however, no lengthened argument to prove that he who relies on the promise of God for the supply of his temporal wants, possesses an infinitely greater security than the individual who confides in his accumulated wealth. The ablest financiers admit that there must be appended to their most choice investments, this felt or expressed proviso—"So far as human affairs can be secure.". . . . Since then no absolute security against want can be found on earth, it necessarily follows, that he who trusts in God is the most wise and prudent man. Who dare deny that the promise of the living God is an absolute security ?—*John Stevenson.*

Verse 1.—"*I shall not want.*" The sheep of Christ may change their pasture, but they shall never want a pasture. "Is not the life more than meat, and the body than raiment ?" Matt. vi. 25. If he grant unto us great things, shall we distrust him for small things ? He who has given us heavenly beings, will also give us earthly blessings. The great Husbandman never overstocked his own commons.—*William Secker.*

Verse 1.—"*I shall not want.*" Ever since I heard of your illness, and the Lord's mercy in sustaining and restoring, I have been intending to write, to bless the Lord with my very dear sister, and ask for some words to strengthen my faith, in detail of your cup having run over in the hour of need. Is it not, indeed, the bleating of Messiah's sheep, "*I shall not want*" ? "shall not want," because the Lord is our Shepherd ! Our Shepherd the All-sufficient ! nothing can unite itself to him ; nothing mingle with him ; nothing add to his satisfying nature ; nothing diminish from his fulness. There is a peace and fulness of expression in this little sentence, known only to the sheep. The remainder of the Psalm is a drawing out of this, "*I shall not want.*" In the unfolding we find repose, refreshment, restoring mercies, guidance, peace in death, triumph, an overflowing of blessings ; future confidence, eternal security in life or death, spiritual or temporal, prosperity or adversity, for time or eternity. May we not say, "*The Lord is my Shepherd*" ? for we stand on the sure foundation of the twenty-third Psalm. How can we want, when united to him ! we have a right to use all his riches. Our wealth is his riches and glory. With him nothing can be withheld. Eternal life *is* ours, with the promise that *all* shall be added ; all *he* knows we want. Our Shepherd has learned the wants of his sheep by experience, for he was himself "led as a sheep to the slaughter." Does not this expression, dictated by the Spirit, imply a promise, and a full promise, when connected with his own words, "*I know my sheep,*" by what painful discipline he was instructed in this knowledge, subjected himself to the wants of every sheep, every lamb of his fold, that he might be able to be touched with a feeling of their infirmities ? The timid sheep has nothing to fear ; fear not want, fear not affliction, fear not pain ; "*fear not ;*" according to your want shall be your supply, "The Lord is my portion, saith my soul ; *therefore* will I trust in him."—*Theodosia A. Howard, Viscountess Powerscourt* (1830), *in* " *Letters,*" etc., *edited by Robert Daly, D.D.*, 1861.

Verse 1.—"*I shall not want.*" One of the poor members of the flock of Christ was reduced to circumstances of the greatest poverty in his old age, and yet he never murmured. "You must be badly off," said a kind-hearted neighbour to him one day as they met upon the road, "you must be badly off ; and I don't know how an old man like you can maintain yourself and your wife ; yet you are always cheerful !" "Oh, no !" he replied, "we are not badly off, I have a rich Father, and he does not suffer me to want." "What ! your father not dead yet ? he must be very old indeed !" "Oh !" said he, "my Father never dies, and he always takes care of me !" This aged Christian was a daily pensioner on the providence of his God. His struggles and his poverty were known to all ; but his own declaration was, that he never wanted what was absolutely necessary. The days of his greatest straits were the days of his most signal and timely deliverances. When old age benumbed the hand of his industry, the Lord extended to him the hand of charity. And often has he gone forth from his scanty breakfast, not knowing from what earthly source his next meal was to be obtained. But yet with David he could rely on his Shepherd's care, and say, " I shall not want ;" and as certainly as he trusted in God, so surely, in some unexpected manner was his necessity supplied.— *John Stevenson.*

Verse 1.—In the tenth chapter of John's gospel, you will find six marks of Christ sheep :—1. They *know their Shepherd ;* 2. *They know his voice ;* 3. They *hear him* calling them each by name ; 4. They *love* him ; 5. They *trust* him ; 6. They *follow* him.—*In " The Shepherd King," by the Authoress of " The folded Lamb"* [*Mrs. Rogers*], 1856.

Verses 1—4.—Come down to the river ; there is something going forward worth seeing. Yon shepherd is about to lead his flock across ; and as our Lord says of the good shepherd—you observe that he goes before, and the sheep follow. Not all in the same manner, however. Some enter boldly, and come straight across. These are the loved ones of the flock, who keep hard by the footsteps of the shepherd, whether sauntering through green meadows by the still waters, feeding upon the mountains, or resting at noon beneath the shadow of great rocks. And now others enter, but in doubt and alarm. Far from their guide, they miss the ford, and are carried down the river, some more, some less ; and yet, one by one, they all struggle over and make good their landing. Notice those little lambs. They refuse to enter, and must be driven into the stream by the shepherd's dog, mentioned by Job in his "parable." Poor things ! how they leap, and plunge, and bleat in terror ! That weak one yonder will be swept quite away, and perish in the sea. But no ; the shepherd himself leaps into the stream, lifts it into his bosom, and bears it trembling to the shore. All safely over, how happy they appear ! The lambs frisk and gambol about in high spirits, while the older ones gather round their faithful guide, and look up to him in subdued but expressive thankfulness. Now, can you watch such a scene, and not think of that Shepherd who leadeth Joseph like a flock ; and of another river, which all his sheep must cross ? He, too, goes before, and, as in the case of this flock, they who keep near him " fear no evil." They hear his sweet voice, saying, " When thou passest through the waters, I will be with thee ; and through the rivers, they shall not overflow thee." Isaiah xliii. 2. With eye fastened on him, they scarcely see the stream, or feel its cold and threatening waves.— *W. M. Thomson.*

Verse 2.—"*He maketh me to lie down in green pastures,*" etc. Not only he hath "*green pastures*" to lead me into, which shows his ability, but he *leads me into them*, which shows his goodness. He leads me not into pastures that are withered and dry, that would distaste me before I taste them ; but he leads me into "*green* pastures," as well to please my eye with the verdure as my stomach with the herbage ; and inviting me, as it were, to eat by setting out the meat in the best colour. A meat though never so good, yet if it look not handsomely, it dulls the appetite ; but when besides the goodness, it hath also a good look, this gives the appetite another edge, and makes a joy before enjoying. But yet the goodness is not altogether in the greenness. Alas ! green is but a colour, and colours are but deceitful things ; they might be green leaves, or they might be green flags or rushes ; and what good were to me in such a greenness ? No, my soul ; the goodness is in being " green *pastures*," for now they perform as much as they promise ; and as in being *green* they were a comfort to me as soon as I saw them, so in being green " *pastures*" they are a refreshing to me now as soon as I taste them. As they are pleasant to look on, so they are wholesome to feed on : as they are sweet to be tasted, so they are easy to be digested ; that I am now, methinks, in a kind of paradise and seem not to want anything, unless perhaps a little water with which now and then to wash my mouth, at most to take sometimes a sip : for though sheep be no great drinkers, and though their pastures being green, and full of sap, make drink the less needful ; yet some drink they must have besides. And now see the great goodness of this Shepherd, and what just cause there is to depend upon his providence ; for he lets not his sheep want this neither, but " *he leadeth them besides still waters*," not waters that roar and make a noise, enough to fright a fearful sheep, but waters " *still* " and quiet ; that though they drink but little, yet they may drink that little without fear. And may I not justly say now, " *The Lord is my Shepherd ; I shall not want*" ? And yet perhaps there will be *want* for all this ; for is it enough that he lead them into green pastures and beside still waters ? May he not lead them in, and presently take them out again before their bellies be half full ; and so instead of making them happy, make them more miserable ? set them in a longing with the sight, and then frustrate them of their expectation ? No, my soul ; the measure of this Shepherd's goodness is more than so. He not only leadeth them into green pastures, but " *he makes them to lie down* " in *them*—he leads them not in to post over their meat as if they were to eat a passover, and to take it *in transitu*, as dogs drink Nylus ; but, " *he makes them to lie down in green pastures*," that they may eat their fill and feed at leisure ; and when they have done, " *lie down*" and take their ease, that their after-reckoning may be as pleasing as their repast.—*Sir Richard Baker.*

Verse 2.—" *He leadeth me.*" Our guiding must be mild and gentle, else it is not *duxisti*, but *traxisti*—drawing and driving, and no *leading. Leni spiritu non durâ manu*—rather by an inward sweet influence to be *led*, than by an outward extreme violence to be forced forward. . . . . Touching what kind of cattle, to very good purpose, Jacob, a skilful shepherd, answereth Esau (who would have had Jacob and his flocks have kept company with him in his *hunting* pace), Nay, not so, sir, said Jacob, it is a tender cattle that is under my hands, and must be softly driven, as they may endure : if one " should over drive them but one day," they would all die or be laid up for many days after. Gen. xxxiii. 13.—*Lancelot Andrewes.*

Verse 2.—" *He leadeth me*," etc. In ordinary circumstances the shepherd does not *feed* his flock, except by leading and guiding them where they may gather for themselves ; but there are times when it is otherwise. Late in autumn, when the pastures are dried up, and in winter, in places covered with snow, he must furnish them food or they die. In the vast oak woods along the eastern sides of Lebanon, between Baalbek and the cedars, there are there gathered innumerable flocks, and the shepherds are all day long in the bushy trees, cutting down the branches, upon whose green leaves and tender twigs the sheep and goats are entirely supported. The same is true in all mountain districts, and large forests are preserved on purpose.—*W. M. Thomson.*

Verse 2.—" *Lie down*"—" *leadeth.*" Sitting Mary and stirring Martha are emblems of contemplation and action, and as they dwell in one house, so must these in one heart.—*Nathanael Hardy.*

Verse 2.—This short but touching epitaph is frequently seen in the catacombs at Rome, " *In Christo, in pace*"—(In Christ, in peace). Realise the constant presence of the Shepherd of peace. "HE maketh me to lie down!" "HE leadeth me."—*J. R. Macduff, D.D.*

Verse 2 (last clause.—"Easily leadeth," or *"comfortably guideth me:"* it noteth a soft and gentle leading, with sustaining of infirmity.—*H. Ainsworth.*

Verse 2.—"Green pastures." Here are many pastures, and every pasture rich so that it can never be eaten bare; here are many streams, and every stream so deep and wide that it can never be drawn dry. The sheep have been eating in these pastures ever since Christ had a church on earth, and yet they are as full of grass as ever. The sheep have been drinking at these streams ever since Adam, and yet they are brim full to this very day, and they will so continue till the sheep are above the use of them in heaven!—*Ralph Robinson,* 1656.

Verse 2.—"Green pastures. . . . beside the still waters." From the top of the mound [of Arban on the Khabour] the eye ranged over a level country bright with flowers, and spotted with black tents, and innumerable flocks of sheep and camels. During our stay at Arban, the color of these great plains was undergoing a continual change. After being for some days of a golden yellow, a new family of flowers would spring up, and it would turn almost in a night to a bright scarlet, which would again as suddenly give way to the deepest blue. Then the meadows would be mottled with various hues, or would put on the emerald green of the most luxuriant of pastures. The glowing descriptions I had so frequently received from the Bedouins of the beauty and fertility of the banks of the Khabour were more than realised. The Arabs boast that its meadows bear three distinct crops of grass during the year, and the wandering tribes look upon its wooded banks and constant greensward as a paradise during the summer months, where man can enjoy a cool shade, and beast can find fresh and tender herbs, whilst all around is yellow, parched, and sapless.—*Austin H. Layard,* 1853.

*Verse 2.—*With guidance to *"green pastures,"* the psalmist has, with good reason, associated guardianship beside *"still waters:"* for as we can only appropriate the word through the Spirit, so we shall ordinarily receive the Spirit through the word; not indeed only by hearing it, not only by reading it, not only by reflecting upon it. The Spirit of God, who is a most free agent, and who is himself the source of liberty, will come into the heart of the believer when he will, and how he will, and as he will. But the effect of his coming will ever be the realisation of some promise, the recognition of some principle, the attainment of some grace, the understanding of some mystery, which is already in the word, and which we shall thus find, with a deeper impression, and with a fuller development, brought home with power to the heart. —*Thomas Dale, M.A., in " The Good Shepherd,"* 1847.

Verse 2.—" Still waters;" which are opposed to great rivers, which both affright the sheep with their noise, and expose them to the danger of being carried away by their swift and violent streams, whilst they are drinking at them.—*Matthew Poole.*

Verse 2.—" Still waters;" Hebrew, "Waters of rests," *ex quibus diligunt oves bibere,* saith Kimchi, such as sheep love to drink of, because void of danger, and yielding a refreshing air. Popish clergymen are called the "inhabitants of the sea," Rev. xii. 12, because they set abroach gross, troubled, brackish, and sourish doctrine, which rather bringeth barrenness to their hearers, and gnaweth their entrails than quencheth their thirst, or cooleth their heat. The doctrine of the gospel, like the waters of Siloe (Isa. viii. 8), run gently, but taste pleasantly.—*John Trapp.*

Verse 3.—" He restoreth my soul," etc. The subjects experimentally treated in this verse are, first, the believer's liability to fall, or deviate even within the fold of the church, else wherefore should he need to be *" restored"?* Next, the promptitude of the Good Shepherd to interpose for his rescue. *" He restoreth my soul."* Then, Christ's subsequent care to *" lead him in the paths of righteousness;*" and lastly, the reason assigned wherefore he will do this—resolving all into the spontaneousness, the supremacy, the omnipotence of grace. He will do all "*for his own name's sake.*"—*Thomas Dale.*

Verse 3.—"*He restoreth my soul.*" The same hand which first rescued us from ruin, reclaims us from all our subsequent aberrations. Chastisement itself is blended with tenderness ; and the voice which speaks reproof, saying, " They have perverted their way, and they have forsaken the Lord their God," utters the kindest invitation, " Return, ye backsliding children, and I will heal your backslidings." Nor is the voice unheard, and the call unanswered or unfelt. " Behold, we come unto thee ; for thou art the Lord our God." Jer. iii. 22. " When thou saidst. Seek my face ; my heart said unto thee, Thy face, Lord, will I seek."—*J. Thornton's " Shepherd of Israel,*" 1826.

Verse 3.—" *He restoreth my soul.*" He restores it to its original purity, that was now grown foul and black with sin ; for also, what good were it to have " *green*" pastures and a *black* soul ! He " *restores*" it to its natural temper in affections, that was grown distempered with violence of passions ; for alas ! what good were it to have " *still* " waters and *turbulent* spirits ! He " *restores*" it indeed to life, that was grown before in a manner quite dead ; and who could " *restore my soul* " to life, but he only that is the Good Shepherd and gave his life for his sheep ?—*Sir Richard Baker.*

Verse 3.—" *He shall convert my soul ;*" turn me not only from sin and ignorance, but from every false confidence, and every deceitful refuge. " *He shall bring me forth in paths of righteousness ;*" in those paths of imputed righteousness which are always adorned with the trees of holiness, are always watered with the fountains of consolation, and always terminate in everlasting rest. Some, perhaps, may ask, why I give this sense to the passage ? Why may it not signify the paths of duty, and the way of our own obedience ? Because such effects are here mentioned as never have resulted, and never can result, from any duties of our own. These are not " *green pastures,*" but a parched and blasted heath. These are not " *still waters,*" but a troubled and disorderly stream. Neither can these speak peace or administer comfort when we pass through the valley and shadow of death. To yield these blessings, is the exalted office of Christ, and the sole prerogative of his obedience.—*James Hervey.*

Verse 3.—" *He restoreth my soul :*" Hebrew, " He bringeth it back ;" either, 1. From its errors or wandering ; or, 2. Into the body, out of which it was even departing and fainting away. He reviveth or comforteth me.—*Matthew Poole.*

Verse 3.—" *Paths of righteousness.*" Alas! O Lord, these " *paths of righteousness,*" have a long time so little been frequented, that prints of a *path* are almost clean worn out ; that it is a hard matter now, but to find where the *paths* lie, and if we can find them, yet they are so narrow and so full of ruts, that without special assistance it is an impossible thing not to fall or go astray. Even so angels, and those no mean ones, were not able to go right in these " *paths of righteousness,*" but for want of leading, went away and perished. O, therefore, thou the Great Shepherd of my soul, as thou art pleased of thy grace to lead me *into* them, so vouchsafe with thy grace to lead me *in* them ; for though in themselves they be " paths of *righteousness,*" yet to me they will be but paths of *error* if thou vouchsafe not, as well to lead me *in* them, as *into* them.—*Sir Richard Baker.*

Verse 3.—" *Paths.*" In the wilderness and in the desert there are no raised paths, the paths being merely tracks ; and sometimes there are six or eight paths running unevenly along side each other. No doubt this is what is figuratively referred to in Psalm xxiii. 3, " *He leadeth me in the paths of righteousness,*" all leading to one point.—*John Gadsby.*

Verse 3.—" *For his name's sake.*" Seeing he hath taken upon him the *name* of a " *Good Shepherd,*" he will discharge his part, whatever his sheep be. It is not their being *bad sheep* that can make him leave being a " *Good Shepherd,*" but he will be " *good,*" and maintain the credit of " his name" in spite of all their badness ; and though no benefit come to them of it, yet there shall glory accrue to him by it, and *" his name"* shall nevertheless be magnified and extolled.— *Sir Richard Baker*

Verse 4.—" Yea, though I walk through the valley of the shadow of death, I will fear no evil." To " fear no evil," then, " in the valley of the shadow of death," is a blessed privilege open to every true believer ! For death shall be to him no death at all, but a very deliverance from death, from all pains, cares, and sorrows, miseries and wretchedness of this world, and the very entry into rest, and a beginning of everlasting joy : a tasting of heavenly pleasures, so great, that neither tongue is able to express, neither eyes to see, nor ear to hear them, no, nor any earthly man's heart to conceive them. . . . And to comfort all Christian persons herein, holy Scripture calleth this bodily death a sleep, wherein man's senses be, as it were, taken from him for a season, and yet, when he waketh, he is more fresh than when he went to bed ! . . . . Thus is this bodily death a door or entering into life, and therefore not so much dreadful, if it be rightly considered, as it is comfortable ; not a mischief, but a remedy for all mischief ; no enemy, but a friend ; not a cruel tyrant, but a gentle guide ; leading us not to mortality, but to immortality ! not to sorrow and pain, but to joy and pleasure, and that to endure for ever !—*Homily against the Fear of Death,* 1547.

Verse 4.—" Yea, though I walk through the valley of the shadow of death, I will fear no evil." Though I were called to such a sight as Ezekiel's vision, a valley full of dead men's bones ; though the king of terrors should ride in awful pomp through the streets, slaying heaps upon heaps, and thousands should fall at my side, and ten thousands at my right hand, I will fear no evil. Though he should level his fatal arrows at the little circle of my associates, and put lover and friend far from me, and mine acquaintance into darkness, I will fear no evil. Yea, though I myself should feel his arrow sticking fast in me, the poison drinking up my spirits ; though I should in consequence of that fatal seizure, sicken and languish, and have all the symptoms of approaching disso-lution, still I will fear no evil. Nature, indeed, may start back and tremble, but I trust that he who knows the flesh to be weak, will pity and pardon these struggles. However I may be afraid of the agonies of dying, I will fear no evil in death. The venom of his sting is taken away. The point of his arrow is blunted, so that it can pierce no deeper than the body. My soul is invulnerable. I can smile at the shaking of his spear ; look unmoved on the ravages which the unrelenting destroyer is making on my tabernacle ; and long for the happy period when he shall have made a breach wide enough for my heaven-aspiring spirit to fly away and be at rest.—*Samuel Lavington.*

Verse 4.—" Yea, though I walk through the valley of the shadow of death, I will fear no evil." " I want to talk to you about heaven," said a dying parent * to a member of his family. " We may not be spared to each other long. May we meet around the throne of glory, one family in heaven !" Overpowered at the thought, his beloved daughter exclaimed, " Surely you do not think there is any danger ?" Calmly and beautifully he replied, " Danger, my darling ! Oh, do not use that word! There can be no danger to the Christian, whatever may happen ! All is right ! All is well ! God is love ! All is well ! Everlastingly well ! Everlastingly well !"—*John Stevenson.*

Verse 4.—" Though I walk through the valley of the shadow of death, I will fear no evil." What not fear then ? Why, what friend is it that keeps up your spirits, that bears you company in that black and dismal region ? He will soon tell you God was with him, and in those slippery ways he leaned upon his staff, and these were the cordials that kept his heart from fainting. I challenge all the gallants in the world, out of all their merry, jovial clubs, to find such a company of merry cheerful creatures as the friends of God are. It is not the company of God, but the want of it, that makes sad. Alas ! you know not what

---

* The late Rev. Hugh Stowell, Rector of Ballaugh, Isle of Man.

their comforts be, and strangers intermeddle not with their joy. You think they cannot be merry when their countenance is so grave ; but they are sure you cannot be truly merry when you smile with a curse upon your souls. They know that he spoke that sentence which could not be mistaken, "Even in laughter the heart is sorrowful ; and the end of that mirth is heaviness." Prov. xiv. 13. Then call your roaring, and your singing, and laughter, mirth ; but the Spirit of God calls it madness. Eccl. ii. 2. When a carnal man's heart is ready to die within him, and, with Nabal, to become like a stone, how cheerfully then can those look that have God for their friend ! Which of the valiant ones of the world can outface death, look joyfully into eternity ? Which of them can hug a fagot, embrace the flames ? This the saint can do, and more too ; for he can look infinite justice in the face with a cheerful heart ; he can hear of hell with joy and thankfulness ; he can think of the day of judgment with great delight and comfort. I again challenge all the world to produce one out of all their merry companies, one that can do all this. Come, muster up all your jovial blades together ; call for your harps and viols ; add what you will to make the concert complete ; bring in your richest wines ; come, lay your heads together, and study what may still add to your comfort. Well, is it done ? Now, come away, sinner, this night thy soul must appear before God. Well now, what say you, man ? What ! doth your courage fail you ? Now call for your merry companions, and let them cheer thy heart. Now call for a cup, a whore ; never be daunted, man. Shall one of thy courage quail, that could make a mock at the threatenings of the Almighty God ? What, so boon and jolly but now, and now down in the mouth ! Here's a sudden change indeed ! Where are thy merry companions, I say again ? All fled ? Where are thy darling pleasures ? Have all forsaken thee ? Why shouldst thou be dejected ; there's a poor man in rags that's smiling ? What ! art thou quite bereft of all comfort ? What's the matter, man ? What's the matter ? There's a question with all my heart, to ask a man that must appear before God to-morrow morning. Well, then, it seems your heart misgives you. What then did you mean to talk of joys and pleasures ? Are they all come to this ? Why, there stands one that now hath his heart as full of comfort as ever it can hold, and the very thoughts of eternity, which do so daunt your soul, raise his ! And would you know the reason ? He knows he is going to his Friend ; nay, his Friend bears him company through that dirty lane. Behold how good and how pleasant a thing it is for God and the soul to dwell together in unity ! This it is to have God for a friend. "Oh, blessed is the soul that is in such a case ; yea, blessed is the soul whose God is the Lord." Psa. cxliv. 15.—*James Janeway.*

Verse 4.—" *Though I walk through the valley of the shadow of death.*" Any darkness is evil, but *darkness and the shadow of death* is the utmost of evils. David put the worst of his case and the best of his faith when he said, " *Though I walk in the valley of the shadow of death, I will fear no evil;*" that is, in the greatest evil I will fear no evil. . . . . . Again, to be under the shadow of a thing, is to be under the power of a thing. . . . . . Thus to be under the shadow of death, is to be so under the power or reach of death, that death may take a man and seize upon him when it pleaseth. " *Though I walk in the valley of the shadow of death,*" that is, though I be so near death, that it seems to others death may catch me every moment, though I be under so many appearances and probabilities of extreme danger, that there appears an impossibility, in sense, to escape death, " *yet I will not fear.*"—*Joseph Caryl.*

Verse 4.—" *Valley of the shadow of death.*" A valley is a low place, with mountains on either side. Enemies may be posted on those mountains to shoot their arrows at the traveller, as ever was the case in the East ; but he *must* pass through it. The psalmist, however, said he would fear no evil, not even the fiery darts of Satan, for the Lord was with him. The figure is not *primarily*, as is sometimes supposed, our dying moments, though it will beautifully bear that explanation ; but it is the valley beset with enemies, posted on the hills. David was not only protected in that valley, but even in the presence of those enemies, his table was bountifully spread (verse 5). The Bedouin, at the present day often post themselves on the hills to harass travellers, as they pass along the valleys.—*John Gadsby.*

Verse 4.—"*I will fear no evil.*" It hath been an ancient proverb, when a man had done some great matter, he was said to have "plucked a lion by the beard;" when a lion is dead, even to little children it hath been an easy matter. As boys, when they see a bear, a lion, or a wolf dead in the streets, they will pull off their hair, insult over them, and deal with them as they please; they will trample upon their bodies, and do that unto them being *dead*, which they durst not in the least measure venture upon whilst they are *alive*. Such a thing is *death*, a furious beast, a ramping lion, a devouring wolf, the *helluo generis humani* (eater up of mankind), yet Christ hath laid him at his length, hath been the *death of death*, so that *God's children* triumph over him, such as those refined ones in the ore of the church, those martyrs of the primitive times, who cheerfully offered themselves to the fire, and to the sword, and to all the violence of this hungry beast; and have played upon him, scorned and derided him, by the faith that they had in the life of Christ, who hath subdued him to himself. 1 Cor. xv.—*Martin Day*, 1660.

Verse 4.—"*Thou art with me.*" Do you know the sweetness, the security, the strength of "*Thou art with me*"? When anticipating the solemn hour of death, when the soul is ready to halt and ask, How shall it then be? can you turn in soul-affection to your God any say, "There is nothing in death to harm me, while thy love is left to me"? Can you say, "O death, where is thy sting"? It is said, when a bee has left its sting in any one, it has no more power to hurt. Death has left its sting in the humanity of Christ, and has no more power to harm his child. Christ's victory over the grave is his people's. "At that moment I am with you," whispers Christ; "the same arm you have proved strong and faithful all the way up through the wilderness, which has never failed, though you have been often forced to lean on it all your weakness." "On this arm," answers the believer, "*I feel at home;* with soul-confidence, I repose on my Beloved; for he has supported through so many difficulties, from the contemplation of which I shuddered. He has carried over so many depths, that I know his arm to be the arm of love." How can that be dark, in which God's child is to have the accomplishment of the longing desire of his life? How can it be dark to come in contact with the light of life? It is "*his rod,*" "*his staff;*" therefore they "*comfort.*" Prove him—prove him now, believer! it is your privilege to do so. It will be precious to him to support your weakness; prove that when weak, then are you strong; that you may be secure, his strength shall be perfected in your perfect weakness. Omnipotent love must fail before one of his sheep can perish; for, says Christ, "none shall pluck my sheep out of my hand." "I and my Father are one;" therefore we may boldly say, "*Yea, though I walk through the valley of the shadow of death, I will fear no evil: for thou art with me.*"—*Viscountess Powerscourt.*

Verse 4.—"*Thy rod.*" Of the *virga pastoralis* there are three uses:—
1. *Numerare oves*—to reckon up or count the sheep; and in this sense they are said "to pass under the rod" (Lev. xxvii. 32), the shepherd tells them one by one. And even so are the people of God called the rod of his inheritance (Jer. x. 16), such as he takes special notice or account of. And take the words in this sense—"*Thy rod doth comfort me*"—it holds well; *q.d.* "Though I am in such eminent dangers by reason of evil men, yet this is my comfort—I am not neglected of thee; thou dost not suffer me to perish; thou takest notice of me; thou dost take and make an account of me; thy special care looks after me." 2. *Provocare oves:* when the sheep are negligent and remiss in following or driving, the shepherd doth, with his rod, put them on, quicken their pace. And in this sense also David saith well, "*Thy rod doth comfort me;*" for it is a work which doth breed much joy and comfort in the hearts of God's people, when God doth put them out of a lazy, cold, formal walking, and doth, some

way or other, cause them to mend their pace, to grow more active and fervent in his service and worship. 3. *Revocare oves:* the sheep sometimes are *petulante divagantes,* idly and inconsiderately straying from the flock, grazing alone, and wandering after other pastures, not considering the dangers which attend them by such a separation and wandering ; and, therefore, the shepherd doth with his rod strike and fetch them in again, and so preserve them. In this sense also David might well say, " *Thy rod doth comfort me ;*" for it is a great comfort that the Lord will not leave his sheep to the ways of discomfort, but brings them off from sinful errings and wanderings, which always do expose them to their greatest dangers and troubles. So that the words do intimate a singular part of God's gubernation or careful providence of his flock.—*Obadiah Sedgwick.*

Verse 4.—" *Rod and staff.*" The shepherd invariably carries a staff or rod with him when he goes forth to feed his flock. It is often bent or hooked at one end, which gave rise to the shepherd's crook in the hand of the Christian bishop. With this staff he rules and guides the flock to their green pastures, and defends them from their enemies. With it also he corrects them when disobedient, and brings them back when wandering. This staff is associated as inseparably with the shepherd as the goad is with the ploughman.—*W. M. Thomson.*

Verse 4.—The psalmist will trust, *even though all be unknown.* We find him doing this in Psalm xxiii. 4 : " *Yea, though I walk through the valley of the shadow of death, I will fear no evil.*" Here, surely, there is trust the most complete. We dread the unknown far above anything that we can see ; a little noise in the dark will terrify, when even great dangers which are visible do not affright : the unknown, with its mystery and uncertainty often fills the heart with anxiety, if not with foreboding and gloom. Here, the psalmist takes the highest form of the unknown, the aspect which is most terrible to man, and says, that even in the midst of it he will trust. What could be so wholly beyond the reach of human experience or speculation, or even imagination, as " *the valley of the shadow of death,*" with all that belonged to it ? but the psalmist makes no reservation against it ; he will trust where he cannot see. How often are we terrified at the unknown ; even as the disciples were, " who feared as they entered the cloud ;" how often is the uncertainty of the future a harder trial to our faith than the pressure of some present ill ! Many dear children of God can trust him in all *known* evils ; but why those fears and forebodings, and sinkings of heart, if they trust him equally for the *unknown?* How much, alas ! do we fall short of the true character of the children of God, in this matter of the unknown ! A child practically acts upon the declaration of Christ that " sufficient unto the day is the evil thereof," we, in this respect far less wise than he, people the unknown with phantoms and speculations, and too often forget our simple trust in God.—*Philip Bennett Power.*

Verse 4.—" *For thou art with me ; thy rod and thy staff comfort me. Thou shalt prepare a table before me, against them that trouble me. Thou hast anointed my head with oil, and my cup shall be full.*" Seeing thou art with me, at whose power and will all troubles go and come, I doubt not but to have the victory and upper hand of them, how many and dangerous soever they are ; for thy rod chasteneth me when I go astray, and thy staff stayeth me when I should fall—two things most necessary for me, good Lord ; the one to call me from my fault and error, and the other to keep me in thy truth and verity. What can be more blessed than to be sustained and kept from falling by the staff and strength of the Most High ? And what can be more profitable than to be beaten with his merciful rod when we go astray ? For he chasteneth as many as he loveth, and beateth as many as he receiveth into his holy profession. Notwithstanding, while we are here in this life, he feeds us with the sweet pastures of the wholesome herbs of his holy word, until we come to eternal life ; and when we put off these bodies, and come into heaven, and know the blessed fruition and riches of his kingdom, then shall we not only be his sheep, but also the guests of his everlasting banquet ; which, Lord, thou settest before all them that love thee in this world, and dost so anoint and make glad our minds with thine Holy Spirit, that no adversities nor troubles can make us sorry. In this sixth part, the prophet declares the old saying amongst wise men, " It is no less mastery to keep the thing that is won, than it was to win it." King David perceives right well the same ; and, therefore, as before in the Psalm he said, the Lord turned his soul, and led him into the pleasant pastures, where virtue and justice reigned, *for his name's sake*, and not for any righteousness of his own ; so saith he now, that being brought into the pastures of truth, and into the favour of the Almighty, and accounted and taken for one of his sheep, it is only God that keeps and maintains him, in the same state, condition, and grace. For he could not pass through the troubles and shadow of death, as he and all God's elect people must do, but only by the assistance of God, and, therefore, he saith, he passes through all peril because he was with him.—*John Hooper (martyr),* 1495—1555.

Verse 4.—By the way, I note that David amidst his green pastures, where he wanted nothing, and in his greatest ease and highest excellency, recordeth the valley of misery and shade of death which might ensue, if God so would ; and therewithal reckoneth of his safest harbour and firm repose, even in God alone. And this is true wisdom indeed, in fair weather to provide for a tempest ; in health to think of sickness ; in prosperity, peace, and quietness, to forecast the worst, and with the wise emmet, in summer to lay up for the winter following. The state of man is full of trouble, the condition of the godly man more. Sinners must be corrected, and sons chastised, there is no question. The ark was framed for the waters, the ship for the sea ; and happy is the mariner that knoweth where to cast anchor ; but, oh ! blessed is the man that can take a right sanctuary, and knoweth whereupon to rely, and in whom to trust in the day of his need. "*I will not fear, for thou art with me.*" In this Psalm, I take it, is rather vouched not what the prophet always performed, but what in duty must be performed, and what David's purpose was to endeavour unto for the time to come. For after so many pledges of God's infinite goodness, and by the guidance of his rod and stay of his sheep-hook, God willing, he would not fear, and this is the groundwork of his affiance. Peter in the gospel by our Saviour, in consideration of infirmity through fear denying his Master, is willed after his conversion by that favourable aspect of our Saviour, to confirm his brethren, and to train them in constancy ; for verily God requireth settled minds, resolute men, and confirmed brethren. So upon occasions past, David found it true that he should not have been heretofore at any time, and therefore professeth, that for the time to come he would be no marigold-servant of the Lord, to open with the sun and shut with the dew—to serve him in calmer times only, and at a need, to shoot neck out of collar, fearfully and faithlessly to slip aside or shrink away. Good people, in all heartless imperfections, mark, I pray you, that they who fear every mist that ariseth, or cloud that appeareth—who are like the mulberry tree, that never shooteth forth or showeth itself till all hard weather be past—who, like standers-by and lookers on, neuters and internimists—who, like Metius Suffetius, dare not venture upon, nor enter into, nor endeavour any good action of greatest duty to God, prince, or country, till all be sure in one side—are utterly reproved by this ensample.—*John Prime,* 1588.

Verse 4.—The death of those that are under sin, is like a malefactor's execution : when he is panelled and justly convicted, one pulleth the hat doggedly from him, another his band, a third bindeth his hands behind his back ; and the poor man, overcome with grief and fear, is dead before he die. But I look for the death of the righteous, and a peaceable end, that it shall be as a going to bed of an honest man : his servants with respect take off his clothes and lay them down in order ; a good conscience then playing the page ordereth all, so that it confirmeth and increaseth his peace ; it biddeth good night to Faith, Hope, and such other attending graces and gifts in the way—when we are come home to heaven there is no use of them—but it directeth Love, Peace, Joy, and other *home graces*, that as they conveyed us in the way, so they attend at death, and enter into the heavens with us.—*William Struther.*

Verse 4.—The Lord willeth us in the day of our troubles to call upon him, adding this promise—that he will deliver us. Whereunto the prophet David did so trust, feeling the comfortable truth thereof at sundry times in many and dangerous perils, that he persuaded himself (all fear set ,apart), to undergo one painful danger or other whatsoever ; yea, if it were to "*walk in the valley of the shadow of death,*" that he should not have cause to fear ; comforting himself with this saying (which was God's promise made unto all), "*For thou art with me ; thy rod and thy staff they comfort me.*" Is God's "*staff*" waxen so weak, that we dare not now lean too much thereon, lest it should break ? or is he now such a changeling, that he will not be with us in our trouble according to his promise ? Will he not give us his "*staff*" to stay us by, and reach us his hand to hold us up, as he hath been wont to do ? No doubt but that he will be most ready in all extremity to help, according to his promise. The Lord that created thee, O Jacob, and he that formed thee, O Israel, saith thus ; Fear not, for I will defend thee," etc. Isaiah xliii.—*Thomas Tymme.*

Verse 4.—Not long before he died, he blessed God for the assurance of his love, and said, He could now as easily die as shut his eyes ; and added, Here am I longing to be silent in the dust, and enjoying Christ in glory. I long to be in the arms of Jesus. It is not worth while to weep for me. Then, remembering how busy the devil had been about him, he was exceedingly thankful to God for his goodness in rebuking him.—*Memoir of James Janeway.*

Verse 4.—When Mrs. Hervey, the wife of a missionary in Bombay, was dying, a friend said to her, that he hoped the Saviour would be with her as she walked through the dark valley of the shadow of death. "If this," said she, " is the dark valley, it has not a dark spot in it ; all is light." She had, during most of her sickness, bright views of the perfections of God. " His awful holiness," she said, " appeared the most lovely of all his attributes." At one time she said she wanted words to express her views of the glory and majesty of Christ. "It seems," said she, " that if all other glory were annihilated and nothing left but his bare self, it would be enough ; it would be a universe of glory !"

Verses 4, 5.—A readiness of spirit to suffer gives the Christian the true enjoyment of life. . . . The Christian, that hath this preparation of heart, never tastes more sweetness in the enjoyments of this life, than when he dips these morsels in the meditation of death and eternity. It is no more grief to his heart to think of the remove of these, which makes way for those far sweeter enjoyments, than it would be to one at a feast, to have the first course taken off, when he hath fed well on it, that the second course of all rare sweetmeats and banqueting stuff may come on, which it cannot till the other be gone. Holy David, in this place, brings in, as it were, a death's head with his feast. In the same breath almost, he speaks of his dying (verse 4), and of the rich feast he at present sat at through the bounty of God (verse 5), to which he was not so tied by the teeth, but if God, that gave him this cheer, should call him from it, to look death in the face, he could do it, and *fear no evil* when *in the valley of the shadow of it.* And what think you of the blessed apostle Peter ? Had not he, think you, the true enjoyment of his life, when he could sleep so sweetly in a prison (no desirable place), fast bound between two soldiers (no comfortable posture), and this the very night before Herod would have brought him forth, in all probability, to his execution ? no likely time, one would think, to get any rest ; yet we find him, even there, thus, and then, so sound asleep, that the angel, who was sent to give him his gaol deliverance, smote him on the side to awake him. Acts xii. 6, 7. I question whether Herod himself slept so well that night, as this his prisoner did. And what was the potion that brought this holy man so quietly to rest ? No doubt this preparation of the gospel of peace—*he was ready to die,* and that made him able to sleep. Why should that break his rest in this world, which if it had been effected, would have brought him to his eternal rest in the other ?—*William Gurnall.*

Verses 4, 6.—The psalmist expresseth an exceeding confidence in the midst

27

of most inexpressible troubles and pressures. He supposes himself "*walking through the valley of the shadow of death*." As "*death*" is the worst of evils, and comprehensive of them all, so the "*shadow*" of death is the most dismal and dark representation of those evils into the soul, and the "*valley*" of that shadow the most dreadful bottom and depth of that representation. This, then, the prophet supposed that he might be brought into. A condition wherein he may be overwhelmed with sad apprehensions of the coming of a confluence of all manner of evils upon him—and that not for a short season, but he may be necessitated to "*walk*" in them, which denotes a state of some continuance, a conflicting with most dismal evils, and in their own nature tending to death—is in the supposal. What, then, would he do if he should be brought into this estate? Saith he, "Even in that condition, in such distress, wherein I am, to my own and the eyes of others, hopeless, helpless, gone, and lost, 'I will fear no evil.'" A noble resolution, if there be a sufficient bottom and foundation for it, that it may not be accounted rashness and groundless confidence, but true spiritual courage and holy resolution. Saith he, "It is because the Lord is with me." But, alas! what if the Lord should now forsake thee in this condition, and give thee up to the power of thine enemies, and suffer thee, by the strength of thy temptations, wherewith thou art beset, to fall utterly from him? Surely then thou wouldst be swallowed up for ever; the waters would go over thy soul, and thou must for ever lie down in the shades of death. "Yea," saith he, "but I have an assurance to the contrary; '*Goodness and mercy shall follow me all the days of my life.*"—*John Owen.*

Verse 5.—"*Thou preparest a table before me in the presence of mine enemies.*" God doth not at all depend upon wicked men in the benediction of his servant; they concur not with him, neither *per modum principii*, for he alone is the cause; nor *per modum auxilii*, for he without them can bless his all: their malicious renitency of spirit, or attempt against God's blessing of his people, is too impotent to frustrate God's intention and pleasure. An effectual impediment must not only have contrariety in it, but superiority: a drop of water cannot put out the fire, for though it hath a contrary nature, yet it hath not greater power. Now the malice and contrivances of evil men are too short and weak for the divine intention of blessing, which is accompanied with an almighty arm. Evil men are but men, and God is a God; and being but men, they can do no more than men. The Lord will clear it to all the world, that he rules the earth, and that "his counsel shall stand;" and where he blesseth, that man shall be blessed; and whom he curseth, that man shall be cursed; that the creatures can do neither good nor evil; that his people are the generation of his care and love, though living in the midst of deadly enemies.—*Condensed from Obadiah Sedgwick.*

Verse 5.—"*In the presence of mine enemies:*" they seeing and envying and fretting at it, but not being able to hinder it.—*Matthew Poole.*

Verse 5.—"*Thou anointest my head with oil; my cup runneth over.*" In the East the people frequently anoint their visitors with some very fragrant perfume; and give them a cup or glass of some choice wine, which they are careful to fill till it runs over. The first was designed to show their love and respect; the latter to imply that while they remained there, they should have an abundance of everything. To something of this kind the psalmist probably alludes in this passage.—*Samuel Burder.*

Verse 5.—"*Thou anointest my head with oil.*" Anointing the head with oil is a great refreshment. There are three qualities of oil—*lævor, nitor, odor,* a smoothness to the touch, brightness to the sight, fragrancy to the smell, and so, gratifying the senses, it must needs cause delight to those anointed with it. To this Solomon alludes when persuading to a cheerful life, he saith, "Let thy head lack no ointment." How fully doth this represent the Spirit's unction which alone rejoices and exhilarates the soul! It is called the "oil of gladness," and the "joy of the Holy Ghost."—*Nathanael Hardy.*

Verse 5.—" *Thou anointest my head with oil.*" It is an act of great respect to pour perfumed oil on the head of a distinguished guest ; the woman in the gospel thus manifested her respect for the Saviour by pouring " precious ointment" on his head. An English lady went on board an Arabian ship which touched at Trincomalee, for the purpose of seeing the equipment of the vessel, and to make some little purchases. After she had been seated some time in the cabin, an Arabian female came and poured perfumed oil on her head.—*Joseph Roberts.*

Verse 5.—" *Thou anointest my head with oil.*" In the East no entertainment could be without this, and it served, as elsewhere a bath does, for (bodily) refreshment. Here, however, it is naturally to be understood of the spiritual oil of gladness.—*T. C. Barth.*

Verse 5.—" *Thou anointest my head with oil.*" Thou hast not confined thy bounty merely to the necessaries of life, but thou hast supplied me also with its luxuries.—*In* " *A plain Explanation of Difficult Passages in the Psalms,*" 1831.

Verse 5.—" *Thou anointest my head with oil.*" The unguents of Egypt may preserve our bodies from corruption, ensuring them a long duration in the dreary shades of the sepulchre, but, O Lord, the precious perfumed oil of thy grace which thou dost mysteriously pour upon our souls, purifies them, adorns them, strengthens them, sows in them the germs of immortality, and thus it not only secures them from a transitory corruption, but uplifts them from this house of bondage into eternal blessedness in thy bosom.—*Jean Baptiste Massillon,* 1663—1742.

Verse 5.—" *My cup runneth over.*" He had not only a fulness of *abundance,* but of *redundance.* Those that have this happiness must carry their cup upright, and see that it overflow into their poor brethren's emptier vessels.—*John Trapp.*

Verse 5.—" *My cup runneth over.*" Wherefore doth the Lord make your cup run over, but that other men's lips might taste the liquor ? The showers that fall upon the highest mountains, should glide into the lowest valleys. " Give, and it shall be given you," is a maxim little believed. Luke vi. 38.—*William Secker.*

Verse 5.—" *My cup runneth over.*" Or as it is in the Vulgate : *And my inebriating chalice, how excellent it is !* With this cup were the martyrs inebriated, when, going forth to their passion, they recognised not those that belonged to them ; not their weeping wife, not their children, not their relations ; while they gave thanks and said, " I will take the cup of salvation !"—*Augustine.*

Verse 6.—" *I will dwell in the house of the Lord for ever.*" A wicked man, it may be, will turn into God's house, and say a prayer, etc., but the prophet would (and so all godly men must) *dwell* there *for ever ;* his soul lieth always at the throne of grace, begging for grace. A wicked man prayeth as the cock croweth ; the cock crows and ceaseth, and crows again, and ceaseth again, and thinks not of crowing till he crows again : so a wicked man prays and ceaseth, prays and ceaseth again ; his mind is never busied to think whether his prayers speed or no ; he thinks it is good religion for him to pray, and therefore he takes for granted that his prayers speed, though in very deed God never hears his prayers, nor no more respects them than he respects the lowing of oxen, or the gruntling of hogs.—*William Fenner, B.D.* (1600—1640), *in* " *The Sacrifice of the Faithful.*"

Verse 6.—" *I will dwell in the house of the Lord for ever.*" This should be at once the crown of all our hopes for the future, and the one great lesson taught us by all the vicissitudes of life. The sorrows and the joys, the journeying and the rest, the temporary repose and the frequent struggles, all these should make us sure that there is an end which will interpret them all, to which they all point, for which they all prepare. We get the table in the wilderness here. It is as when the son of some great king comes back from foreign soil to his father's dominions, and is welcomed at every stage in his journey to the capital with pomp of festival and messengers from the throne, until at last he enters his palace home, where the travel-stained robe is laid aside, and he sits down with his father at his table.—*Alexander Maclaren*, 1863.

Verse 6.—Mark David's resolute persuasion, and consider how he came unto it, namely, by experience of God's favour at sundry times, and after sundry manners. For before he set down this resolution, he numbered up divers benefits received of the Lord ; that *he fed him in green pastures, and led him by the refreshing waters* of God's word ; that he *restores him and leads him in the paths of righteousness ;* that he strengthened him in great dangers, even of death, and preserveth him ; that in despite of his enemies, he enricheth him with many benefits. By means of all these mercies of God bestowed on him, he came to be persuaded of the continuance of the favour of God towards him.—*William Perkins.*

HINTS TO THE VILLAGE PREACHER.

Verse 1.—Work out the similitude of a shepherd and his sheep. He rules, guides, feeds, and protects them ; and they follow, obey, love and trust him. Examine as to whether we are sheep ; show the lot of the goats who feed side by side with the sheep.

Verse 1 (*second clause*).—The man who is beyond the reach of want for time and eternity.

Verse 2 (*first clause*).—Believing rest. I. Comes from God—"*He maketh.*" II. Is deep and profound—"*lie down.*" III. Has solid sustenance—"*in green pastures.*" IV. Is subject for constant praise.

Verse 2.—The contemplative and the active element provided for.

Verse 2.—The freshness and richness of Holy Scripture.

Verse 2 (*second clause*).—Onward. The Leader, the way, the comforts of the road, and the traveller in it.

Verse 3.—Gracious restoration, holy guidance, and divine motives.

Verse 4.—The soft silence of the Spirit's work.

Verse 4.—God's presence the only sure support in death.

Verse 4.—Life in death and light in darkness.

Verse 4 (*second clause*).—The calm and quiet of the good man's end.

Verse 4 (*last clause*).—The tokens of divine government—the consolation of the obedient.

Verse 5.—The warrior feasted, the priest anointed, the guest satisfied.

Verse 5 (*last clause*). The means and uses of the continued anointings of the Holy Spirit.

Verse 5.—Providential super-aboundings, and what is our duty concerning them.

Verse 6 (*first clause*).—The blessedness of content.

Verse 6.—On the road and at home, or heavenly attendants and heavenly mansions.

WORKS UPON THE TWENTY-THIRD PSALM.

Certain Comfortable Expositions of the Constant Martyrs of Christ. JOHN HOOPER, Bishop of Gloucester and Worcester, 1555, written in the time of his Tribulation and Imprisonment, upon the Twenty-third, Sixty-second, Seventy-third, and Seventy-seventh Psalm of the prophet David. [In Parker Society's publications, and also in the "British Reformers" series of the Religious Tract Society.] '

The Chiefe Shepheard ; or, an Exposition upon ye Twenty-third Psalme. . . . . By SAMUEL SMITH, Minister of ye Word of God, at Prittlewell, in Essex. 1625. 8vo.

Meditations and Disquisitions upon Seven Consolatorie Psalmes of David. By Sir RICHARD BAKER. 1640. [See "WORKS," p. 10.]

The Shepherd of Israel ; or, God's pastoral care over his people. Delivered in divers Sermons on the whole Twenty-third Psalme. . . . . By that Reverend and Faithful Minister of the Gospel, Mr. OBADIAH SEDGWICK, B.D. 1658. 4to.

The Shepherd of Israel : a practical Exposition and Improvement of the Twenty-third Psalm. By J. THORNTON. 1826. 12mo.

The Lord our Shepherd : an Exposition of the Twenty-third Psalm. By the Rev. JOHN STEVENSON, perpetual Curate of Cury and Gunwalloe, Cornwall. 1845. 8vo.

The Good Shepherd and the Chosen Flock : shewing the progress of the sheep of Christ through the wilderness of this world to the pastures of the Heavenly Zion. An Exposition of the Twenty-third Psalm. By THOMAS DALE, M.A., Canon Residentiary of St. Paul's, London. 1847. 12mo.

The Shepherd King ; or, Jesus seen in the Life of David. Designed for the Young. By the Authoress of "The Folded Lamb." [Mrs. ROGERS.] 1856. 12mo.

The Song of Christ's Flock in the Twenty-third Psalm. By JOHN STOUGHTON. 1860. 12mo.

PSALM XXIV.

TITLE.—A Psalm of David. *From the title we learn nothing but the authorship : but this is interesting, and leads us to observe the wondrous operations of the Spirit upon the mind of Israel's sweet singer, enabling him to touch the mournful string in Psalm twenty-two, to pour forth gentle notes of peace in Psalm twenty-three, and here to utter majestic and triumphant strains. We can do or sing all things when the Lord strengtheneth us.*

This sacred hymn was probably written to be sung when the ark of the covenant was taken up from the house of Obed-edom, to remain within curtains upon the hill of Zion. The words are not unsuitable for the sacred dance of joy in which David led the way upon that joyful occasion. The eye of the psalmist looked, however, beyond the typical upgoing of the ark to the sublime ascension of the King of glory. We will call it The Song of the Ascension.

DIVISION.—*The Psalm makes a pair with the fifteenth Psalm. It consists of three parts. The first glorifies the true God, and sings of his universal dominion ; the second describes the true Israel, who are able to commune with him ; and the third pictures the ascent of the true Redeemer, who has opened heaven's gates for the entrance of his elect.*

EXPOSITION.

THE earth *is* the LORD'S, and the fulness thereof ; the world, and they that dwell therein.

2 For he hath founded it upon the seas, and established it upon the floods.

1. How very different is this from the ignorant Jewish notion of God which prevailed in our Saviour's day ? The Jews said, " The holy land is God's, and the seed of Abraham are his only people ;" but their great Monarch had long before instructed them, —" *The earth is the Lord's, and the fulness thereof.*" The whole round world is claimed for Jehovah, " *and they that dwell therein*" are declared to be his subjects. When we consider the bigotry of the Jewish people at the time of Christ, and how angry they were with our Lord for saying that many widows were in Israel, but unto none of them was the prophet sent, save only to the widow of Sarepta, and that there were many lepers in Israel, but none of them was healed except Naaman the Syrian,—when we recollect, too, how angry they were at the mention of Paul's being sent to the Gentiles, we are amazed that they should have remained in such blindness, and yet have sung this psalm, which shows so clearly that God is not the God of the Jews only, but of the Gentiles also. What a rebuke is this to those wiseacres who speak of the negro and other despised races as though they were not cared for by the God of heaven ! If a man be but a man the Lord claims him, and who dares to brand him as a mere piece of merchandise ! The meanest of men is a dweller in the world, and therefore belongs to Jehovah. Jesus Christ has made an end of the exclusiveness of nationalities. There is neither barbarian, Scythian, bond nor free ; but we all are one in Christ Jesus.

Man lives upon " *the earth*," and parcels out its soil among his mimic kings and autocrats ; but the earth is not man's. He is but a tenant at will, a leaseholder upon most precarious tenure, liable to instantaneous ejectment. The great Landowner and true Proprietor holds his court above the clouds, and laughs at the title-deeds of worms of the dust. The fee-simple is not with the lord of the manor nor the freeholder, but with the Creator. The " *fulness*" of the earth may mean its harvests, its wealth, its life, or its worship ; in all these senses the Most High God is Possessor of all. The earth is full of God ; he made it full and he keeps it full, notwithstanding all the demands which living creatures make upon its stores. The sea is full, despite all the clouds which rise from it ; the air is full, notwithstanding all the lives which breathe it ; the soil is full, though millions of plants derive their nourishment from it. Under man's tutored hand the world is coming to a greater fulness than ever, but it is all the Lord's ; the field and the fruit, the earth and all earth's wonders are Jehovah's. We look also for a sublimer fulness when the true ideal of a world for God shall have been reached in millennial glories, and then most clearly the earth will be the Lord's and the fulness thereof. These words are now upon London's Royal Exchange, they shall one day be written in letters of light across the sky.

The term "*world*" indicates the habitable regions, wherein Jehovah is especially to be acknowledged as Sovereign. He who rules the fish of the sea and the fowl of the air should not be disobeyed by man, his noblest creature. Jehovah is the Universal King, all nations are beneath his sway : true Autocrat of all the nations, emperors and czars are but his slaves. Men are not their own, nor may they call their lips, their hearts, or their substance their own ; they are Jehovah's rightful servants. This claim especially applies to us who are born from heaven. We do not belong to the world or to Satan, but by creation and redemption we are the peculiar portion of the Lord.

Paul uses this verse twice, to show that no food is unclean, and that nothing is really the property of false gods. All things are God's ; no ban is on the face of nature, nothing is common or unclean. The world is all God's world, and the food which is sold in the shambles is sanctified by being my Father's, and I need not scruple to eat thereof.

2. In the second verse we have the reason why the world belongs to God, namely, because he has created it, which is a title beyond all dispute. "*For he hath founded it upon the seas.*" It is God who lifts up the earth from out of the sea, so that the dry land, which otherwise might in a moment be submerged, as in the days of Noah, is kept from the floods. The hungry jaws of ocean would devour the dry land if a constant fiat of Omnipotence did not protect it. "*He hath established it upon the floods.*" The world is Jehovah's, because from generation to generation he preserves and upholds it, having settled its foundations. Providence and Creation are the two legal seals upon the title-deeds of the great Owner of all things. He who built the house and bears up its foundation has surely a first claim upon it. Let it be noted, however, upon what insecure foundations all terrestrial things are founded. Founded on the seas ! Established on the floods ! Blessed be God the Christian has another world to look forward to, and rests his hopes upon a more stable foundation than this poor world affords. They who trust in worldly things build upon the sea ; but we have laid our hopes, by God's grace, upon the Rock of Ages ; we are resting upon the promise of an immutable God, we are depending upon the constancy of a faithful Redeemer. Oh ! ye worldlings, who have built your castles of confidence, your palaces of wealth, and your bowers of pleasure upon the seas, and established them upon the floods ; how soon will your baseless fabrics melt, like foam upon the waters ! Sand is treacherous enough, but what shall be said of the yet more unstable seas ?

3 Who shall ascend into the hill of the LORD? or who shall stand in his holy place ?

4 He that hath clean hands, and a pure heart ; who hath not lifted up his soul unto vanity, nor sworn deceitfully.

5 He shall receive the blessing from the LORD, and righteousness from the God of his salvation.

6 This *is* the generation of them that seek him, that seek thy face, O Jacob. Selah.

Here we have the true Israel described. The men who shall stand as courtiers in the palace of the living God are not distinguished by race, but by character ; they are not Jews only, nor Gentiles only, nor any one branch of mankind peculiarly, but a people purified and made meet to dwell in the holy hill of the Lord.

3. " *Who shall ascend into the hill of the Lord ?*" It is uphill work for the creature to reach the Creator. Where is the mighty climber who can scale the towering heights ? Nor is it height alone ; it is glory too. Whose eye shall see the King in his beauty and dwell in his palace ? In heaven he reigns most gloriously, who shall be permitted to enter into his royal presence ? God has made all, but he will not save all ; there is a chosen company who shall have the singular honour of dwelling with him in his high abode. These choice spirits desire to commune with God, and their wish shall be granted them. The solemn enquiry of the text is repeated in another form. Who shall be able to " *stand* " or continue there ? He casteth away the wicked, who then can abide in his house ? Who is he that can gaze upon the Holy One, and can abide in the blaze of his glory ? Certainly none may venture to commune with God upon the footing of the law, but grace can make us meet to behold the vision of the divine presence. The question before us is one which all should ask for themselves, and none should be at ease till they receive an answer of peace. With careful self-examination let us enquire, " Lord, is it I ?"

4. " *He that hath clean hands.*" Outward, practical holiness is a very precious mark of grace. To wash in water with Pilate is nothing, but to wash in inno-cency is all-important. It is to be feared that many professors have perverted the doctrine of justification by faith in such a way as to treat good works with contempt ; if so, they will receive everlasting contempt at the last great day. It is vain to prate of inward experience unless the daily life is free from impurity, dishonesty, violence, and oppression. Those who draw near to God must have " *clean hands.*" What monarch would have servants with filthy hands to wait at his table ? They who were ceremonially unclean could not enter into the Lord's house which was made with hands, much less shall the morally defiled be allowed to enjoy spiritual fellowship with a holy God. If our hands are now unclean, let us wash them in Jesu's precious blood, and so let us pray unto God, lifting up pure hands. But " *clean hands* " would not suffice, unless they were connected with " *a pure heart.*" True religion is heart-work. We may wash the outside of the cup and the platter as long as we please, but if the inward parts be filthy, we are filthy altogether in the sight of God, for our hearts are more truly ourselves than our hands are. We may lose our hands and yet live, but we could not lose our heart and still live ; the very life of our being lies in the inner nature, and hence the imperative need of purity within. There must be a work of grace in the core of the heart as well as in the palm of the hand, or our religion is a delusion. May God grant that our inward powers may be cleansed by the sanctifying Spirit, so that we may love holiness and abhor all sin. The pure in heart shall see God, all others are but blind bats ; stone-blindness in the eyes arises from stone in the heart. Dirt in the heart throws dust in the eyes.

The soul must be delivered from delighting in the grovelling toys of earth ; the man who is born for heaven " *hath not lifted up his soul unto vanity.*" All men have their joys, by which their souls are lifted up ; the worldling lifts up his soul in carnal delights, which are mere empty vanities ; but the saint loves more substantial things ; like Jehoshaphat, he is lifted up in the ways of the Lord. He who is content with the husks will be reckoned with the swine. If we suck our consolation from the breasts of the world, we prove ourselves to be its home-born children. Does the world satisfy thee ? Then thou hast thy reward and thy portion in this life ; make much of it, for thou shalt know no other joy.

" *Nor sworn deceitfully.*" The saints are men of honour still. The Christian man's word is his only oath ; but that is as good as twenty oaths of other men. False speaking will shut any man out of heaven, for a liar shall not enter into God's house, whatever may be his professions or doings. God will have nothing to do with liars, except to cast them into the lake of fire. Every liar is a child of the devil, and will be sent home to his father. A false declaration, a fraudulent statement, a cooked account, a slander, a lie—all these may suit the assembly of the ungodly, but are detested among true saints : how could they have fellowship with the God of truth, if they did not hate every false way ?

5. It must not be supposed that the persons who are thus described by their inward and outward holiness are saved by the merit of their works ; but their works are the evidences by which they are known. The present verse shows that in the saints grace reigns and grace alone. Such men wear the holy livery of the Great King because he has of his own free love clothed them therewith. The true saint wears the wedding garment, but he owns that the Lord of the feast provided it for him, without money and without price. *" He shall receive the blessing from the Lord, and righteousness from the God of his salvation."* So that the saints need salvation ; they receive righteousness, and *" the blessing"* is a boon from God their Saviour. They do not ascend the hill of the Lord as givers but as receivers, and they do not wear their own merits, but a righteousness which they have received. Holy living ensures a blessing as its reward from the thrice Holy God, but it is itself a blessing of the New Covenant and a delightful fruit of the Spirit. God first gives us good works, and then rewards us for them. Grace is not obscured by God's demand for holiness, but is highly exalted as we see it decking the saint with jewels, and clothing him in fair white linen ; all this sumptuous array being a free gift of mercy.

6. *" This is the generation of them that seek him, that seek thy face, O Jacob."* These are the regeneration, these are in the line of grace ; these are the legitimate seed. Yet they are only seekers ; hence learn that true seekers are very dear in God's esteem, and are entered upon his register. Even *seeking* has a sanctifying influence ; what a consecrating power must lie in finding and enjoying the Lord's face and favour ! To desire communion with God is a purifying thing. Oh to hunger and thirst more and more after a clear vision of the face of God ; this will lead us to purge ourselves from all filthiness, and to walk with heavenly circumspection. He who longs to see his friend when he passes takes care to clear the mist from the window, lest by any means his friend should go by unobserved. Really awakened souls seek the Lord above everything, and as this is not the usual desire of mankind, they constitute a generation by themselves ; a people despised of men but beloved of God. The expression *" O Jacob"* is a very difficult one, unless it be indeed true that the God of Jacob here condescends to be called Jacob, and takes upon himself the name of his chosen people.

The preceding verses correct the inordinate boastings of those Jews who vaunted themselves as the favourites of heaven ; they are told that their God is the God of all the earth, and that he is holy, and will admit none but holy ones into his presence. Let the mere professor as he reads these verses listen to the voice which saith, " without holiness no man shall see the Lord."

" Selah." Lift up the harp and voice, for a nobler song is coming ; a song of our Well-beloved.

7 Lift up your heads, O ye gates ; and be ye lift up, ye everlasting doors ; and the King of glory shall côme in.

8 Who *is* this King of glory? The Lord strong and mighty, the Lord mighty in battle.

9 Lift up your heads, O ye gates ; even lift *them* up, ye everlasting doors ; and the King of glory shall come in.

10 Who is this King of glory? The Lord of hosts, he *is* the King of glory. Selah.

7. These last verses reveal to us the great representative man, who answered to the full character laid down, and therefore by his own right ascended the holy hill of Zion. Our Lord Jesus Christ could ascend into the hill of the Lord because his hands were clean and his heart was pure, and if we by faith in him are con-

formed to his image we shall enter too. We have here a picture of our Lord's glorious ascent. We see him rising from amidst the little group upon Olivet, and as the cloud receives him, angels reverently escort him to the gates of heaven.

The ancient gates of the eternal temple are personified and addressed in song by the attending cohort of rejoicing spirits.

> " Lo his triumphal chariot waits,
>   And angels chant the solemn lay.
> ' Lift up your heads, ye heavenly gates ;
>   Ye everlasting doors, give way.' "

They are called upon " *to lift up their heads,*" as though with all their glory they were not great enough for the Allglorious King. Let all things do their utmost to honour so great a Prince ; let the highest heaven put on unusual loftiness in honour of " *the King of Glory.*" He who, fresh from the cross and the tomb, now rides through the gates of the New Jerusalem is higher than the heavens ; great and everlasting as they are, those gates of pearl are all unworthy of him before whom the heavens are not pure, and who chargeth his angels with folly. " *Lift up your heads, O ye gates.*"

8. The watchers at the gate hearing the song look over the battlements and ask, " *Who is this King of glory ?*" A question full of meaning and worthy of the meditations of eternity. Who is he in person, nature, character, office and work ? What is his pedigree ? What his rank and what his race ? The answer given in a mighty wave of music is, " *The Lord strong and mighty, the Lord mighty in battle.*" We know the might of Jesus by the battles which he has fought, the victories which he has won over sin, and death, and hell, and we clap our hands as we see him leading captivity captive in the majesty of his strength. Oh for a heart to sing his praises ! Mighty hero, be thou crowned for ever King of kings and Lord of lords.

9. " *Lift up your heads, O ye gates ; even lift them up, ye everlasting doors ; and the King of glory shall come in.*" The words are repeated with a pleasing variation. There are times of deep earnest feeling when repetitions are not vain but full of force. Doors were often taken from their hinges when Easterns would show welcome to a guest, and some doors were drawn up and down like a portcullis, and may possibly have protruded from the top ; thus literally lifting up their heads. The picture is highly poetical, and shows how wide heaven's gate is set by the ascension of our Lord. Blessed be God, the gates have never been shut since. The opened gates of heaven invite the weakest believer to enter.

Dear reader, it is possible that you are saying, " I shall never enter into the heaven of God, for I have neither clean hands nor a pure heart." Look then to Christ, who has already climbed the holy hill. He has entered as the forerunner of those who trust him. Follow in his footsteps, and repose upon his merit. He rides triumphantly into heaven, and you shall ride there too if you trust him. " But how can I get the character described ?" say you. The Spirit of God will give you that. He will create in you a new heart and a right spirit. Faith in Jesus is the work of the Holy Spirit, and has all virtues wrapped up in it. Faith stands by the fountain filled with blood, and as she washes therein, clean hands and a pure heart, a holy soul and a truthful tongue are given to her.

10. The closing note is inexpressibly grand. Jehovah of hosts, Lord of men and angels, Lord of the universe, Lord of the worlds, is the King of glory. All true glory is concentrated upon the true God, for all other glory is but a passing pageant, the painted pomp of an hour. The ascended Saviour is here declared to be the Head and Crown of the universe, the King of Glory. Our Immanuel is hymned in sublimest strains. Jesus of Nazareth is Jehovah Sabaoth.

EXPLANATORY NOTES AND QUAINT SAYINGS.

Whole Psalm—It will be seen that this Psalm was written to be chanted in responsive parts, with two choruses. To comprehend it fully, it should be understood that Jerusalem, as the city of God, was by the Jews regarded as a type of heaven. It so occurs in the Apocalypse, whence we have adopted it in our poetical and devotional aspirations. The court of the tabernacle was the scene of the Lord's more immediate residence—the tabernacle his palace, and the ark his throne. With this leading idea in his mind, the most cursory reader —if there be cursory readers of the Bible—cannot fail to be struck with the beauty and sublimity of this composition, and its exquisite suitableness to the occasion. The chief musician, who was probably in this case the king himself, appears to have begun the sacred lay with a solemn and sonorous recital of these sentences :—

> " The earth is the Lord's, and the fulness thereof ;
> The world, and they that dwell therein.
> For he hath founded it upon the seas,
> And established it upon the floods."

The chorus of vocal music appears to have then taken up the song, and sung the same words in a more tuneful and elaborate harmony ; and the instruments and the whole chorus of the people fell in with them, raising the mighty declaration to heaven. There is much reason to think that the people, or a large body of them, were qualified or instructed to take their part in this great ceremonial. The historical text says, " David, and *all the house of Israel played before the Lord*, upon all manner of instruments," etc. We may presume that the chorus then divided, each singing in their turns, and both joining at the close—

> " For he hath founded it upon the seas,
> And established it upon the floods."

This part of the music may be supposed to have lasted until the procession reached the foot of Zion, or came in view of it, which, from the nature of the enclosed site, cannot be till one comes quite near to it. Then the king must be supposed to have stepped forth, and begun again, in a solemn and earnest tone—

> " Who shall ascend into the hill of the Lord ?
> Or who shall stand in his holy place ? "

To which the first chorus responds—

> " He that hath clean hands, and a pure heart ;
> Who hath not lifted up his soul unto vanity, nor sworn deceitfully."

And then the second chorus—

> " He shall receive the blessing from the Lord,
> And righteousness from the God of his salvation."

This part of the sacred song may, in like manner, be supposed to have lasted till they reached the gate of the city, when the king began again in this grand and exalted strain :—

> " Lift up your heads, O ye gates ;
> And be ye lift up, ye everlasting doors,
> And the King of glory shall come in ! "

repeated then, in the same way as before, by the general chorus.
The persons having charge of the gates on this high occasion ask—

> " Who is the King of glory ? "

To which the first chorus answers—

> " It is Jehovah, strong and mighty—
> Jehovah mighty in battle."

which the second chorus then repeats in like manner as before, closing it with the grand universal chorus,

"He is the King of glory ! He is the King of glory !"

We must now suppose the instruments to take up the same notes, and continue them to the entrance to the court of the tabernacle. There the king again begins—

"Lift up your heads, O ye gates ;
And be ye lift up, ye everlasting doors ;
And the King of glory shall come in."

This is followed and answered as before—all closing, the instruments sounding, the chorus singing, the people shouting—

"He is the King of glory !"

John Kitto's " Daily Bible Illustrations."

Whole Psalm.—The coming of the Lord of glory, the high demands upon his people proceeding from this, the absolute necessity to prepare worthily for his arrival, form the subject-matter of this Psalm.—*E. W. Hengstenberg.*

Whole Psalm.—We learn from the rabbins, that this was one of certain Psalms which were sung in the performance of Jewish worship on each day in the week :—

The 24th Psalm on the 1st, the Lord's-day, our Sunday.

48th	"	2nd	"
82nd	"	3rd	"
94th	"	4th	"
81st	"	5th	"
93rd	"	6th	"
92nd	"	7th, the Jewish Sabbath.	

This Psalm, then, appropriated to the Lord's-day, our Sunday, was intended to celebrate the resurrection of Messiah, and his ascension into heaven, there to sit as a priest upon God's throne, and from thence to come down bringing blessings and mercies to his people.—*R. H. Ryland.*

Whole Psalm.—Anthem of praise, performed when the heads of the gates of Jerusalem were lifted up to receive the ark ; and those of the Israelites who were ceremoniously clean, were alone permitted to accompany it into the court of the tabernacle: A Psalm of David. Verses 1, 2, chorus. 3. First voice. 4, 5. Second voice. 6. Chorus. 7. Semi-chorus accompanying the ark. 8. Voice from within the gates. 8. Chorus of priests accompanying the ark. 9. Chorus of priests and people with the ark. 10. Voice within the gates. 10. Grand chorus.—*From " The Psalms, with Prefatory Titles, etc., from the Port Royal Authors," by Mary Anne Schimmelpenninck,* 1825.

Whole Psalm.—How others may think upon this point, I cannot say, nor pretend to describe, but for my own part, I have no notion of hearing, or of any man's ever having seen or heard, anything so great, so solemn, so celestial, on this side the gates of heaven.—*Patrick Delany, D.D.,* 1686—1768.

Verse 1.—" *The earth is the Lord's,*" that is, Christ's, who is the " Lord of lords" (Rev. xix. 16) ; for the whole world and all the things therein are his by a twofold title. First, by donation of God his Father, having " all power given unto him in heaven and in earth" (Matt. xxviii. 18), even whatsoever things the Father hath are his (John xvi. 15) ; and so consequently " made heir of all things." Heb. i. 2. Secondly, the earth is Christ's and all that therein is, by right of creation, for " *he founded it,*" saith our prophet, and that after a wonderful manner, " *upon the seas and floods.*" . . . . . All things then are Christ's, in respect of *creation,* " by whom all things were made" (John i. 3) ; in respect of *sustentation,* as upholding all things by his mighty word (Heb. i. 3) ; in respect of *administration,* as reaching from one end to another, and ordering all things sweetly (Wis. viii. 1) : in one word—" Of him, and through him, and to him, are all things." Rom. xi. 36. From hence we may learn (1), That Christ is "the King of glory," "Lord of Hosts," even Almighty God. For he that made all, is "Lord over all ;" he that is the Creator of heaven and earth is Almighty (saith our Creed) ; able to do whatsoever he will, and more than he will too—more by his absolute power, than he will by his actual—"able to raise up children unto Abraham" out of the very stones of the street, though he doth not actually produce such a generation. His almightiness evidently proves him to be God, and his *founding of the world* his almightiness ; for "The gods that have not made the heaven and earth shall perish from the earth, and from under these heavens." Jer. x. 11. (2.) Seeing the compass of the world and all they that dwell therein are the Lord's, it is plain that the church is not confined within the limits of one region, or glued, as it were, to one seat only. The Donatists in old time, would tie the church only to Cartenna in Africa, the Papists in our time to Rome in Italy ; but the Scriptures plainly affirm that the golden candlesticks are removed from one place to another, and that the kingdom of God is taken away from one nation and given unto another country that brings forth the fruit thereof ; in every region he that feareth God and worketh righteousness is accepted of him. Acts x. 35.—*John Boys.*

Verse 1.—" *The earth is Jehovah's.*"—The object of the beginning of the Psalm is to show that the Jews had nothing of themselves which could entitle them to approach nearer or more familiarly to God than the Gentiles. As God by his providence preserves the world, the power of his government is alike extended to all, so that he ought to be worshipped by all, even as he also shows to all men, without exception, the fatherly care he has about them.—*J. Calvin.*

Verse 1.—" *The earth is the Lord's.*" It is Christ's, by creation (verse 2 ; John i. 1, 2), and it is his by resurrection (Matt. xxviii. 18), and by his glorious ascension into heaven, where he is enthroned King of the world in his human nature. This Psalm takes up the language of the first Ascension Psalm (Psalm viii.)—*Christopher Wordsworth, D.D., in loc.*

Verse 1.—St. Chrysostom, suffering under the Empress Eudoxia, tells his friend Cyriacus how he armed himself before hand : εἰ μέ᾽ βούλεται ἡ βασίλισσα ἐ ξορίσαι μέ, etc. "I thought, will she banish me ? ' *The earth is the Lord's and the fulness thereof.*' Take away my goods ? ' *Naked came I into the world, and naked must I return.*' Will she stone me ? I remembered Stephen. Behead me ? John Baptist came into my mind," etc. Thus it should be with every one that intends to live and die comfortably : they must, as we say, lay up something for a rainy day ; they must stock themselves with graces, store up promises, and furnish themselves with experiences of God's lovingkindness to others and themselves too, that so, when the evil day comes, they may have much good coming thereby.—*John Spencer.*

Verse 1.—" *The earth is the Lord's.*" As David, in his youthful days, was tending his flocks on Bethlehem's fertile plains, the spirit of the Lord descended upon him, and his senses were opened, and his understanding enlightened, so that he could understand the songs of the night. The heavens proclaimed the glory of God, and glittering stars formed the general chorus, their harmonious melody resounded upon earth, and the sweet fulness of their voices vibrated to its utmost bounds.

" *Light* is the countenance of the Eternal," sung the setting sun : "I am the hem of his garment," responded the soft and rosy twilight. The clouds gathered themselves together and said, "We are his nocturnal tent." And the waters in the clouds, and the hollow voices of the thunders, joined in the lofty chorus, "The voice of the Eternal is upon the waters, the God of glory thundereth in the heavens, the Lord is upon many waters."

"He flieth upon my wings," whispered the winds, and the gentle air added, "I am the breath of God, the aspirations of his benign presence." "We hear the songs of praise," said the parched earth ; "all around is praise ; I alone am sad and silent." Then the falling dew replied, "I will nourish thee, so that thou shalt be refreshed and rejoice, and thy infants shall bloom like the young rose." " Joyfully we bloom," sang the refreshed meads ; the full ears of corn waved as they sang, " We are the blessing of God, the hosts of God against famine."

" We bless thee from above," said the gentle moon ; " We, too, bless thee," responded the stars ; and the lightsome grasshopper chirped, " Me, too, he blesses in the pearly dew-drop." " He quenched my thirst," said the roe ; " And refreshed me," continued the stag ; " And grants us our food," said the beasts of the forest ; " And clothes my lambs," gratefully added the sheep.

"He heard me," croaked the raven, " when I was forsaken and alone ;" " He heard me," said the wild goat of the rocks, " when my time came, and I brought forth." And the turtle-dove cooed, and the swallow and other birds joined the song, " We have found our nests, our houses, we dwell upon the altar of the Lord, and sleep under the shadow of his wing in tranquillity and peace." " And peace," replied the night, and echo prolonged the sound, when chanticleer awoke the dawn, and crowed with joy, " Open the portals, set wide the gates of the world ! The King of glory approaches. Awake ! Arise, ye sons of men, give praises and thanks unto the Lord, for the King of glory approaches."

The sun arose, and David awoke from his melodious rapture. But as long as he lived the strains of creation's harmony remained in his soul, and daily he recalled them from the strings of his harp.—*From the " Legend of the Songs of the Night," in the Talmud, quoted in " Biblical Antiquities." By F. A. Cox, D.D., LL.D.*, 1852.

Verse 1.—The pious mind views all things in God, and God in all things.— *Ingram Cobbin*, 1839.

Verse 2.—" *He hath founded it upon the seas, and established it upon the floods."* This *founding the land upon the seas*, and preparing it *upon the floods*, is so wonderfully wonderful, that Almighty God asked his servant Job, " Whereupon are the foundations thereof fastened ?" Job xxxviii. 6. Xerxes commanded his soldiers to fetter the waters of Hellispontus ; and so God bindeth, as it were, the floods in fetters, at St. Basil plainly, *Ligatum est mare præcepto Creatoris quasi compedibus ;* he saith unto the sea, " Hitherto shalt thou come, but no further, there shall it stay thy proud waves." " He gathereth the waters of the sea together as an heap ; he layeth up the depth in storehouses" (Job xxxviii. 11 ; Psalm xxxiii. 7) ; so that without his leave not so much as one drop can overflow the land.—*John Boys.*

Verse 2.—(*New Translation.*) " *For he hath founded it upon the seas, and upon streams doth he make it fast."* The reference is no doubt to the account of the Creation, in Genesis, the dry land having emerged from the water, and seeming to rest upon it. (Comp. cxxxvi. 6 ; Prov. viii. 29.) It would, however, be quite out of place to suppose that in such language we have the expression of any theory, whether popular or scientific, as to the structure of the earth's surface : Job says (xxvi. 7), " He hangeth the earth upon nothing." Such expressions are manifestly poetical. See Job xxxviii. 6.—*J. J. Stewart Perowne.*

Verse 2.—" *Upon the seas :"* that is, upon the great abyss of waters which is under the earth, enclosed in great hollow places, whence the heads of rivers do spring, and other waters bubble out upon the earth.—*John Diodati.*

Verse 2.—" *Above the floods he hath established it."* Both the words עָל (Al) in the two clauses of this verse mean either " above" as we have rendered it, and refer to Gen. i. 9, 10, denoting that Jehovah hath called forth dry land from the midst of the seas, and established it above the floods, and hath set a boundary to the latter never to turn and overflow it (see Job xxxviii. 8 ; Psalm civ. chronologically Psalm vii. 9) ; or " by, or at," as they often denote, and refer to the same subject of the omnipotence of God in relation to the same quoted passages, *i.e.*, that though our globe is situated at or by the floods—is surrounded with mighty waters whose single wave could bury it for ever, still the Lord has so established it that this never can happen. This is a mighty reason why the earth and all its fulness and inhabitants belong to Jehovah.—*Benjamin Weiss.*

Verse 2.—Hereby is mystically meant, that he hath set his church above the waters of adversities, so that how high soever they arise, it is kept still above them in safety, and so shall be for evermore ; or it may agree thus—he will take in all nations to be his in grace, because all be his creatures ; he made them so admirable an habitation at the first, and upholds it still, showing hereby how much he regards them ; therefore he will now extend his favour further towards them, by taking them in to be his people.—*Augustine, quoted by Mayer.*

Verse 3.—" *Who shall ascend ?*" Indeed, if none must ascend but he that is clean and pure, and without vanity and deceit, the question is quickly answered, None shall, for there is none *so :* dust is our matter, so not clean ; defiled is our nature, so not pure ; lighter, the heaviest of us, than vanity, and deceitful upon the balance the best of us ; so no ascending so high for any of us. Yet there is One we hear of, or might have heard of to-day, that rose and ascended up on high, was thus qualified as the psalmist speaks of, all clean and pure, no chaff at all, no guile found in his mouth. 1 Pet. ii. 22. Yea, but it was but One that was so ; what's that to all the rest ? Yes, somewhat 'tis. *He* was our *Head,* and if the Head be once risen and ascended, the members will all follow after in their time.—*Mark Frank.*

Verse 3.—" *The hill of the Lord,*" can be no other than a hill of glory. His holy place is no less than the very place and seat of glory. And being such, you cannot imagine it but *hard to come by,* the very petty glories of the world are so. This is a *hill* of glory, hard to climb, difficult to ascend, craggy to pass up, steep to clamber, no plain campagnia to it, the broad easy way leads some whither else (Matt. vii. 13) ; the way to this is narrow (verse 14) ; 'tis rough and troublesome. To be of the number of Christ's true faithful servants is no slight work ; 'tis a fight, 'tis a race, 'tis a continual warfare ; fastings and watchings, and cold and nakedness, and hunger and thirst, bonds, imprisonments, dangers and distresses, ignominy and reproach, afflictions and persecutions, the world's hatred and our friends' neglect, all that we call hard or difficult is to be found in the way we are to go. A man cannot leave a lust, shake off bad company, quit a course of sin, enter upon a way of virtue, profess his religion, or stand to it, cannot ascend the spiritual *hill,* but he will meet some or other of these to contest and strive with. But not only to ascend, but to *stand* there, as the word signifies ; to continue at so high a pitch, to be constant in truth and piety, that will be hard indeed, and bring more difficulties to contest with. *Mark Frank.*

Verses 3, 4.—The Psalm begins with a solicitous enquiry, subjoins a satisfactory answer, and closes with a most pertinent but rapturous apostrophe. This is the enquiry, " *Who shall ascend into the hill of the Lord ? or who shall stand in his holy place ?*" This is the answer, " *He that hath clean hands, and a pure heart ;*" " *he shall receive the blessing*" of plenary remission " *from the Lord, and righteousness also from the God of his salvation :*" even that perfect righteousness which is not acquired by man, but bestowed by Jehovah ; which is not performed by the saint, but received by the sinner ; which is the only solid basis to support our hopes of happiness, the only valid plea for an admission into the mansions of joy. Then follows the apostrophe : the prophet foresees the ascension of Christ and his saints into the kingdom of heaven. He sees his Lord marching at the head of the redeemed world, and conducting them into regions of honour and joy. Suitably to such a view, and in a most beautiful strain of poetry, he addresses himself to the heavenly portals. " *Lift up your heads, O ye gates ; and be ye lift up, ye everlasting doors ; and the King of glory,*" with all the heirs of his grace and righteousness, shall make their triumphant entry ; " *shall enter in,*" and go out no more.—*James Hervey.*

Verses 3, 4.—It is not he who sings so well or so many Psalms, nor he who fasts or watches so many days, nor he who divides his own among the poor, nor he who preaches to others, nor he who lives quietly, kindly, and friendly ; nor, in fine, is it he who knows all sciences and languages, nor he who works all virtuous and all good works that ever any man spoke or read of, but it is he alone, who is pure within and without.—*Martin Luther.*

Verse 4.—" *He that hath clean hands, and a pure heart.*" Shall I tell you, then, who is a moral man in the sight of God ? It is he that bows to the divine law as the supreme rule of right ; he that is influenced by a governing regard to God in all his actions ; he that obeys other commands spontaneously, because he has obeyed the first and great command, " Give me thy *heart.*" His conduct is not conformed to custom or expediency, but to one consistent, immutable standard of duty. Take this man into a court of justice, and call on him to testify, and he will not bear false witness. Give him the charge of untold treasures, he will not steal. Trust him with the dearest interests of yourself or family, you are safe, because he has a living principle of truth and integrity in his bosom. He is as worthy of confidence in the dark as at noonday ; for he is a moral man, not because reputation or interest demands it, not because the eye of public observation is fixed upon him, but because the love and fear of God have predominant ascendency in his heart.—*Ebenezer Porter, D.D.*, 1834.

Verse 4.—Conditions that suit none but Christ. [Bellarmine.] " *He that hath clean hands ;*" " the clean of hands," Marg. :—those hands from which went forth virtue and healing ; hands ever lifted up in prayer to God, or in blessing to man ; hands stretched forth on the cross for the cleansing of the whole world.—*Isaac Williams, in loc.*

Verse 4.—" *Who hath not lifted up his soul unto vanity,*" is read by Arius Montanus, " He that hath not received his soul in vain." Oh ! how many receive their souls in vain, making no more use of them than the swine, of whom the philosopher observes, *cujus anima pro sale,* their souls are only for salt to keep their bodies from stinking. Who would not grieve to think that so choice a piece should be employed about so vain a use !—*George Swinnock.*

Verse 4.—" *Nor sworn deceitfully ;*" or inured his tongue to any other kind of the language of hell's rotten communication, to the dishonouring of God, or deceiving of others. Perjury is here instanced for the rest, as one of the most heinous. But Peraldus reckoneth up four-and-twenty several sins of the tongue, all which every burgess of the New Jerusalem is careful to avoid, as the devil's drivel, no way becoming his pure lip.—*John Trapp.*

Verse 4.—Now we come to the four conditions requisite to render such an ascent possible. 1. Abstinence from evil doing : " *He that hath clean hands.*" 2. Abstinence from evil thought : " *and a pure heart.*" 3. Who does that duty which he is sent into the world to do : " *That hath not lift up his mind unto vanity ;*" or, as it is in the Vulgate, " *Who hath not received his soul in vain.*" And, 4. Remembers the vows by which he is bound to God : " *nor sworn to deceive.*" And in the fullest sense, there was but One in whom all these things were fulfilled ; so that in reply to the question, " Who shall ascend into the hill of the Lord ?" He might well answer, " No man hath ascended up to heaven, but he that came down from heaven, even the Son of man which is in heaven." John iii. 13. " Therefore it is well written," says St. Bernard, " that such an High Priest became us, because he knows the difficulty of that ascent to the celestial mountain, he knows the weakness of us that have to ascend."—*Lorinus and Bernard, quoted by J. M. Neale.*

Verse 4.—Heaven is not won with good words and a fair profession. The doing Christian is the man that shall stand, when the empty boaster of his faith shall fall. The great talkers of religion are often the least doers. His religion is in vain whose profession brings not letters testimonial from a holy life.—*William Gurnall.*

Verse 5.—" *He shall receive the blessing ;*" as before, " Thou shalt set him to be a blessing." Psalm xxi. 6. His name is never without blessing. In him shall all the nations of the earth be blessed. On the mount of his beatitudes, on the heavenly Mount Sion, crowned as " the Son of the Blessed." " *From the Lord ;*" even " the God and father of our Lord Jesus Christ." Eph. i. 3.—*Isaac Williams.*

Verse 5.—" *He shall receive . . . righteousness.*" As for our own righteousness which we have without him, Esay telleth us, " it is a defiled cloth ;" and St. Paul, that it is but " dung." Two very homely comparisons, but they be the Holy Ghost's own ; yet nothing so homely as in the original, where they be so odious, as what manner of defiled cloth, or what kind of dung we have not dared to translate. Our own then being no better, we are driven to seek for it elsewhere. " *He shall receive his righteousness,*" saith the prophet ; and " *the gift of righteousness,*" saith the apostle. Phil. iii. 8, 9 ; Rom. v. 17. It is then another, to be *given us,* and to be *received* by us, which we must seek for. And whither shall we go for it ? Job alone dispatcheth this point (chap. xv. 15 ; iv. 18 ; xxv. 5.) Not to *the heavens* or *stars,* they are *unclean in his sight.* Not to the *saints,* for in them *he found folly.* Not to the *angels,* for neither in them found he *steadfastness.* Now, if none of these will serve, we see a necessary reason why Jehovah must be a part of this name, " the LORD our righteousness." Jer. xxiii. 6.—*Lancelot Andrewes.*

Verse 6.—" *This is the generation of them that seek him, that seek thy face.*" Christians must be seekers. This is *the generation of seekers.* All mankind, if ever they will come to heaven, they must be a generation of seekers. Heaven is a generation of finders, of possessors, of enjoyers, seekers of God. But here we are a generation of seekers. We want somewhat that we must seek. When we are at best, we want the accomplishment of our happiness. It is a state of seeking here, because it is a state of want ; we want something alway. But to come more particularly to this *seeking the face of God,* or the presence of God. . . . The presence of God meant here is, that presence that he shows *in the time of need, and in his ordinances.* He shows a presence in need and necessity, that is, a gracious presence to his children, a gracious face. As in want of direction, he shows his presence of light to direct them ; in weakness he shows his strength ; in trouble and perplexity he will show his gracious and comfortable presence to comfort them. In perplexity he shows his presence to set the heart at large, answerable to the necessity. So in need God is present with his children, to direct them, to comfort them, to strengthen them, if they need that.—*Richard Sibbes.*

Verse 6.—" *This is the generation.*" By the demonstrative pronoun " *this,*" the psalmist erases from the catalogue of the servants of God all counterfeit Israelites, who, trusting only to their circumcision and the sacrifice of beasts, have no concern about offering themselves to God ; and yet, at the same time, they rashly thrust themselves into the church.—*John Calvin.*

Verse 6.—" *That seek thy face, O Jacob.*" In Prov vii. 15, and xxix. 26, we have " *seeking the face of*" in the sense of seeking the favour of, or showing delight in. Their delight is not in Esau, who got " the fatness of earth " (Gen. xxvii. 39) as his portion. And those writers may be right who consider Jacob as a name for Messiah, to whom belong the true birthright and blessing.—*Andrew A. Bonar.*

Verse 6.—" *That seek thy face, O Jacob.*" He is " the seed of Jacob ;" he is " the Holy One of Israel ;" " the face of thine Anointed " is the face of him who is both God and man ; for " we shall see him as he is."—*Isaac Williams.*

Verse 6.—" *O Jacob,*" or, O God of Jacob. As the church is called *Christ* (1 Cor. xii. 12), so God is here called " *Jacob ;*" such a near union there is betwixt him and his people. Or, *this is* Jacob. So the true *seekers* are fitly called, first, because Israelites indeed (John i. 47 ; Rom. ix. 6) ; secondly, because they see God face to face, as Jacob did at Peniel (Gen. xxxii. 24—30) ;

28

thirdly, because they also, as he, do bear away a blessing (Hos. xii. 4), even "righteousness from the God of their salvation," as in the verse aforegoing.—*John Trapp.*

Verse 7.—"*Lift up your heads, O ye gates.*" The gates of the temple were indeed as described, very lofty and magnificent, in proportion to the gigantic dimensions of that extraordinary edifice. But the phrase, "*Lift up your heads,*" refers not so much to their loftiness, as to the upper part being formed so as to be lifted up; while the under portion opened in folding doors.—*Robert Jamieson, in "Paxton's Illustrations of Scriptures."*

Verse 7.—"*Lift up your heads, O ye gates.*" At the castle of Banias, in Syria, are the remains of an ancient gate which was drawn up, like a blind, the gate fitting in grooves. This will fully explain the term.—*John Gadsby.*

Verse 7.—"*Lift up.*" A phrase or term taken from triumphal arches, or great porticoes, set up, or beautified and adorned for the coming in of great, victorious, and triumphant captains.—*John Diodati.*

Verse 7.—"*Be ye lift up, ye everlasting doors; and the King of glory shall come in.*" Some interpret this of the doors of our heart, according to that (Rev. iii. 20), "Behold, I stand at the door, and knock: if any man hear my voice, and open the door, I will come in to him," etc. In the gospel history, we find that Christ had a fourfold entertainment among men. Some received him into house, not into heart, as Simon the Pharisee (Luke vii. 44), who gave him no kiss nor water to his feet; some into heart, but not into house, as the faithful centurion (Matt. viii. 8), esteeming himself unworthy that Christ should come under his roof; some neither into house nor heart, as the graceless Gergesites (Matt. viii. 34); some both into house and heart, as Lazarus, Mary, Martha. John iii. 15; Luke x. 38. Now that Christ may dwell in our hearts by faith, and that our bodies may be temples of his Holy Spirit, we must as our prophet exhorts here, *lift up our souls,* that is, in the words of St. Paul (Col. iii. 2), our affections must be set on things which are above, and not on things which are on earth: if we desire to lift up our hearts unto Christ's verity, we may not lift them up unto the world's vanity; that is, we must not fasten our love too much upon the things of this life, but on those pleasures at God's right hand which are evermore; that as we have borne the image of the first Adam, who was earthly, so we should bear the image of the second Adam, which is heavenly. 1 Cor. xv. 49. The prophane worldling sings a *Nunc dimittis* unto Christ, and saith as the devils, "Ah! what have we to do with thee, thou Jesus of Nazareth?" (Mark i. 24); and as Job reports his words, "Depart from us, for we desire not the knowledge of thy ways." Job xxi. 14. On the contrary, the religious soul, enjoying the possession of the Saviour, chanteth a merry *Magnificat,* and a pleasant *Te Deum:* she saith unto Christ, as Ruth unto Naomi (Ruth i. 16), "Intreat me not to leave thee, or to return from following after thee." Nay, death itself shall not part us, for when I am loosed out of my body's prison, I hope to be with Christ; as Ittai then unto David, I say unto Jesus, "As the Lord liveth, and as my lord the king liveth, surely in what place my lord the king shall be, whether in death, or life, even there also will thy servant be." 2 Sam. xv. 21. O Lord, which art the God of my salvation, I lift my heart to thee, desirous to seek thee, both in the right *ubi*—where thou mayest be found, and in the right *quando*—while thou mayest be found. Psalm xviii. 47; xxv. 1. Open my dull ears and hard heart, that thy Son my Saviour may come in and dwell with me. Grant me grace that I may still hear while he calleth, open while he knocketh, and hold him also when I have him; that I may both *ascend thine hill,* and *stand in thine holy place;* that I may not only sojourn in thy tabernacle, but also rest and dwell upon the mountain of thine holiness.—*John Boys.*

Verse 7.—"*Everlasting doors.*" Heaven's gates are called "*everlasting,*" because they shall endure for ever, or because they be the doors unto the life which is everlasting.—*John Boys.*

Verse 7.—Whatever we may think of these things, David thought it high time for him to bid such a messenger welcome, and to open his heart for the receiving his God. Hear what he saith to his own heart and others : " *Lift up your heads, O ye gates ; and be ye lift up, ye everlasting doors ; and the King of glory shall come in.*" And because the door of men's hearts is locked, and barred, and bolted, and men are in a deep sleep, and will not hear the knocking that is at the gate, though it be loud, though it be a king ; therefore David knocks again, " *Lift up, ye everlasting doors.*" Why, what haste, saith the sinner? What haste? Why, here's the King at your gates ; and that not an ordinary king neither ; he is a glorious King, that will honour you so far, if you open quickly, as to lodge within, to take up his abode in your house, to dwell with you. But the soul for all this doth not yet open, but stands still questioning, as if it were an enemy rather than a friend that stood there, and asks, " *Who is this King of glory?*" Who? He answers again, " *It is the Lord of Hosts ;*" he, that if you will not open quickly and thankfully too, can easily pull your house down about your ears ; he is the Lord of hosts, that King who hath a mighty army always at his command, who stand ready for their commission, and then you should know who it is you might have had for your friend ; "Lift up, therefore, your heads, O ye gates." Open quickly, ye that had rather have God for your friend than for your enemy. Oh, why should not the soul of every sinner cry out, Lord, the door is locked, and thou hast the key ; I have been trying what I can do, but the wards are so rusty that I cannot possibly turn the key? But, Lord, throw the door off the hinges, anything in the world, so thou wilt but come in and dwell here. Come, O mighty God, break through doors of iron, and bars of brass, and make way for thyself by thy love and power. Come, Lord, and make thyself welcome ; all that I have is at thy service ; O fit my soul to entertain thee !—*James Janeway.*

Verse 7.—He hath left with us the earnest of the Spirit, and taken from us the earnest of our flesh, which he hath carried into heaven as a pledge that the whole shall follow after.—*Tertullian.*

Verse 7.—Christ is gone to heaven as a victor ; leading sin, Satan, death, hell, and all his enemies, in triumph at his chariot wheels. He has not only overcome his enemies for himself, but for all his people, whom he will make conquerors, yea, "more than conquerors." As he has overcome, so shall they also overcome ; and as he is gone to heaven a victor, they shall follow in triumph. He is in heaven as a Saviour. When he came from heaven it was in the character of a Saviour ; when on earth he obtained eternal salvation ; in heaven he lives as a Saviour ; when he comes again from heaven he will come as a Saviour ; and when he will return, he will return as a Saviour. He is also gone to heaven as the rightful heir. He is not gone to heaven as a sojourner, but as " the heir of all things." He is the heir of heavenly glory and happiness, and believers are " heirs of God, and joint heirs with Christ."—*Henry Pendlebury*, 1626—1695.

Verse 7.—" O clap your hands together, all ye people ; sing unto God with the voice of melody. God is gone up with a merry noise, and the Lord with the sound of the trump." Psalm xlvii. 1, 5. This Ark, which has saved the world from destruction, after floating on a deluge of blood, rests at length on the mountain. This innocent Joseph, whose virtue had been oppressed by the synagogue, is brought out of the dungeon to receive a crown. This invincible Samson has carried away the gates of hell, and goes in triumph to the everlasting hills. This victorious Joshua has passed over Jordan with the ark of the covenant, and takes possession of the land of the living. This Sun of righteousness, which had gone down ten degrees, returns backward to the place which it had left. He who was " a worm " at his birth, a Lamb in his passion, and a Lion in his resurrection, now ascends as an Eagle to heaven, and encourages us to follow him thither. This day heaven learns to endure man's presence, and men to walk above the stars ; the heavenly Jerusalem receives its rightful King, the church its High Priest, the house of God its Heritor, the whole world its Ruler. " O sing praises, sing praises unto our God : O sing praises, sing praises unto our King.'' Psalm xlvii. 6—8. '' God reigneth over the heathen, God sitteth upon his holy seat.'' '' The princes of the people are joined unto '' him ; '' he is very highly exalted '' above them.—*From '' The Life of Jesus Christ in Glory,''* translated from the French of James Nouet.

Verses 7, 8.—Christ being now arrived at heaven's doors, those heavenly spirits that accompanied him began to say, '' *Lift up your heads, O ye gates ; and be ye lift up, ye everlasting doors ; and the King of glory shall come in !*'' to whom some of the angels that were within, not ignorant of his person, but admiring his majesty and glory, said again, ''*Who is the King of glory ?*'' and then they answered '' *The Lord strong and mighty, the Lord mighty in battle,*'' and there-upon those twelve gates of the holy city, of new Jerusalem, opened of their own accord, and Jesus Christ with all his ministering spirits entered in. O my soul, how should this heighten thy joy and enlarge thy comforts, in that Christ is now received up into glory ? Every sight of Christ is glorious, and in every sight thou shouldst wait on the Lord Jesus Christ for some glorious manifestations of himself. Come, live up to the rate of this great mystery ; view Christ as entering into glory, and thou wilt find the same sparkles of glory on thy heart. O ! this sight is a transforming sight : '' We all, with open face beholding as in a glass the glory of the Lord, are changed into the same image from glory to glory, even as by the Spirit of the Lord.'' 2 Cor. iii. 18.—*Isaac Ambrose.*

Verses 7, 8.—Ye that are thus the living temples of the Lord, and have already entertained his sanctifying Spirit into you, do you lift up your hearts in the use of holy ordinances through faith, in joyful desires and assured expec-tation of him ; yea, be you abundantly lift up by faith in the use of holy means who are the everlasting habitation of an everlasting God, with a joyful and assured welcome of him ; for so shall you invite and undoubtedly entertain the high and mighty Potentate the Lord Christ into your souls, with the glorious manifestation and ravishing operation of his love, benefits, and graces. And know, O all ye faithful and obedient ones, for your courage and comfort, who, and of what quality this glorious King, the Lord Jesus is, whom the world despises but you honour. Why, he is the Almighty God, of power all-sufficient to preserve and defend his people and church, that in trust of him do love and serve him, against all the strength and power of men and devils that do or shall malign or oppose themselves against them, and to put them to the foil, as we his Israel in the letter have found by experience for your instruction and cor-roboration that are his people in spirit.—*George Abbot, in '' Brief notes upon the whole Book of Psalms,''* 1651.

Verses 7.—10.—Oh, what tongue of the highest archangel of heaven can express the welcome of thee, the King of glory, into these blessed regions of immortality ? Surely the empyreal heaven never resounded with so much joy : God ascended with jubilation, and the Lord with the sound of the trumpet. It is not for us, weak and finite creatures, to wish to conceive those incomprehensible, spiritual, divine gratulations, that the glorious Trinity gave to the victorious and now glorified human nature. Certainly, if, when he brought his only-begotten Son into the world, he said, '' Let all the angels worship him ;'' much more now that he ''ascends on high, and hath led captivity captive, hath he given him a name above all names, that at the name of Jesus all knees should bow.'' And if the holy angels did so carol at his birth, in the very entrance into that state of humiliation and infirmity, with what triumph did they receive him now re-turning from the perfect achievement of man's redemption ? and if, when his type had vanquished Goliath, and carried his head into Jerusalem, the damsels came forth to meet him with dances and timbrels, how shall we think those angelical spirits triumphed, in meeting of the great Conqueror of hell and death ? How did they sing, ''*Lift up your heads, ye gates! and be lifted up, ye everlast-ing doors ; and the King of glory shall come in.*'' Surely, as he shall come, so he went ; and, '' Behold, he shall come with thousands of his holy ones ; thousand thousands ministered unto him, and ten thousand thousands stood before him ; '' from all whom, methinks I hear that blessed applause, '' Worthy is the Lamb that was killed, to receive power, and riches, and wisdom, and strength, and honour, and glory, and praise : praise and honour, and glory, and power, be to him that sitteth upon the throne, and to the Lamb for evermore." And why dost not thou, O my soul, help to bear thy part with that happy choir of heaven? Why art not thou rapt out of my bosom, with an ecstacy of joy, to see this human nature of ours exalted above all the powers of heaven, adored of angels, archangels, cherubim, seraphim, and all those mighty and glorious spirits, and sitting there crowned with infinite glory and majesty?—*Joseph Hall.*

Verses 7—10.—In the twenty-fourth Psalm, we have an account of the actual entrance of Christ into heaven. When the King of England wishes to enter the city of London, through Temple Bar, the gate being closed against him, the herald demands entrance. "Open the gate." From within a voice is heard, "Who is there?" The herald answers, "The King of England!" The gate is at once opened, and the king passes, amidst the joyful acclamations of his people. This is an ancient custom, and the allusion is to it in this Psalm. "The Lord ascended with a shout;" he approached the heavenly portal—the herald in his escort demanded an entrance, "*Lift up your heads, O ye gates; and be ye lift up, ye everlasting doors; and the King of glory shall come in.*" The celestial watchers within ask, "*Who is the King of glory?*" The heralds answer, "*The Lord strong and mighty, the Lord mighty in battle.*" The question and answer being repeated once more, the gates lift up their heads, and the everlasting doors are lifted up. The Prince enters his Father's palace, greeted with the acclamations of heaven, all whose inhabitants unite in one shout of joy ineffable : "*The Lord of Hosts, he is the King of glory!*"—*Christmas Evans.*

Verses 7—10.—If we follow our Redeemer in his ascension and session at the right hand of God, where he is constituted Lord of all, angels, principalities, and powers being made subject to him, and where he sits till his enemies are made his footstool, we shall observe the tide of celestial blessedness rise higher and higher still. The return of a great and beloved prince, who should by only hazarding his life, have saved his country, would fill a nation with ecstacy. Their conversation in every company would turn upon him, and all their thoughts and joys concentrate in him. See then the King of kings, after having by death abolished death, and brought life and immortality to light; after spoiling the powers of darkness, and ruining all their schemes; see him return in triumph! There was something like triumph when he entered into Jerusalem. All the city was moved, saying, "Who is this?" And the multitude answered, It is Jesus, the prophet of Nazareth; and the very children sung, Hosannah to the Son of David : blessed be he that cometh in the name of the Lord; hosannah in the highest! How much greater then must be the triumph of his entry into the heavenly Jerusalem! Would not all the city be "moved" in this case, saying, "*Who is this?*" See thousands of angels attending him, and ten thousand times ten thousand come forth to meet him! The entrance of the ark into the city of David was but a shadow of this, and the responsive strains which were sung on that occasion would on this be much more applicable.—*Andrew Fuller.*

Verses 7—10.—Why is the song repeated? Why are the everlasting gates invited to lift up their heads a second time? We may not pretend here, or in any place, to know all the meaning of the divine Psalms. But what if the repetition of the verse was meant to put us in mind that our Saviour's ascension will be repeated also? He will not indeed die any more; death can no more have any dominion over him; "there remaineth no more sacrifice for sin." Neither of course can he rise again any more. But as he will come again at the end of the world, to judge the quick and the dead, so after that descent he will have to ascend again. And I say, this second ascension may be signified by the psalmist, calling on the everlasting doors to lift up their heads a second time, and make way for the King of glory. Now observe the answer made this second time, "*Who is the King of glory? The Lord strong and mighty, the Lord mighty in battle. Lift up your heads, O ye gates; even lift them up, ye everlasting doors; and the King of glory shall come in. Who is this King of glory? The Lord of hosts, he is the King of glory."* Before, it was, *"the Lord strong and mighty, the Lord mighty in battle;"* now it is *" The Lord of hosts."* Christ ascending the first time, to intercede for us at his Father's right hand, is called *" The Lord mighty in battle."* But Christ, ascending the second time, after the world hath been judged, and the good and bad separated for ever, is called *"the Lord of hosts."* Why this difference in his divine titles? We may reverently take it, that it signifies to us the difference between his first and second coming down to earth, his first and second ascension into heaven. As in other respects his first coming was in great humility, so in this, that he came, in all appearance, alone. The angels were indeed waiting round him, but not visibly, not in glory. "He trode the winepress alone, and of the people there was none with him." He wrestled with death, hell, and Satan, alone. Alone he rose from the dead: alone, as far as man could see, he went up to heaven. Thus he showed himself "the Lord mighty in battle," mighty in that single combat which he, as our champion, our David, victoriously maintained against our great enemy. But when he shall come down and go up the second time, he will show himself "the Lord of hosts." Instead of coming down alone in mysterious silence, as in his wonderful incarnation, he will be followed by all the armies of heaven. "The Lord my God will come, and all his saints with him." "The Lord cometh with ten thousand of his saints." "The Son of Man will come in the glory of his Father, and all the holy angels with him." "Thousand thousands will stand around him, and ten thousand times ten thousand will minister unto him." Instead of the silence of that quiet chamber at Nazareth, and of the holy Virgin's womb, there will be the voice of the archangel, and the trump of God accompanying him. Thus he will come down as the Lord of hosts, and as the Lord of hosts he will ascend again to his Father. After the judgment, he will pass again through the everlasting doors, with a greater company than before; for he will lead along with him, into the heavenly habitation, all those who shall have been raised from their graves and found worthy. Hear how the awful sight is described by one who will doubtless have a high place in that day near the Judge. The great apostle and prophet, St. Paul, says, "The Lord himself shall descend from heaven with a shout; and the dead in Christ shall rise first: then we which are alive and remain shall be caught up together with them in the clouds, to meet the Lord in the air, and so shall we ever be with the Lord."—*John Keble, M.A.*

Verses 7—10.—

In his blessed life
I see the path, and in his death the price,
And in his great ascent the proof supreme
Of immortality. And did he rise?
Hear, O ye nations! hear it, O ye dead!
He rose! He rose! He burst the bars of death.
Lift up your heads, ye everlasting gates!
And give the King of glory to come in.
Who is the King of glory? He who left
His throne of glory for the pangs of death.

Lift up your heads, ye everlasting gates!
And give the King of glory to come in.
Who is the King of glory? He who slew
The ravenous foe that gorged all human race.
The King of glory, he whose glory filled
Heaven with amazement at his love to man,
And with divine complacency beheld
Powers most illumined 'wildered in the theme.

Edward Young.

Verses 7—10.—

Lift up your heads, ye gates, and, O prepare,
Ye living orbs, your everlasting doors,
The King of glory comes!
What King of glory? He whose puissant might
Subdued Abaddon, and the infernal powers
Of darkness bound in adamantine chains:
Who, wrapp'd in glory, with the Father reigns,
Omnipotent, immortal, infinite!

James Scott.

Verse 8.—"*Who is the King of glory?*" Christ in two respects is "*the King of glory.*" 1. For that all honour and glory belongs properly to him—his is "the kingdom, the power, and the glory" (Matt. vi. 13), called in this regard, "The Lord of glory." 1 Cor. ii. 8. 2. For that Christ maketh us partakers of his glory, termed in this respect our glorious Lord Jesus. James ii. 1. If the Lord of hosts, strong and mighty in battle, be the king of glory, then Christ (having conquered all his enemies, and made them his footstool, triumphing over death, and the devil which is the founder of death, and sin which is the sting of death, and the grave which is the prison of death, and hell itself which is the proper dominion of the devil and death) is doubtless in himself, "*the King of glory.*" And for as much as he died for our sins, and is risen again for our justification, and is ascended on high to give gifts unto men—in this life grace, in the next glory—what is he less than a "*King of glory*" towards us, of whom and through whom alone we that fight his battles are delivered from the hands of all that hate us, and so made victors (1 Cor. xv. 57), yea, "more than conquerors." Rom. viii. 37.—*John Boys.*

Verse 8.—"*The Lord strong and mighty.*" "*Strong and mighty*" in subduing all adversaries; and overcoming death and the devil who had the power of death.—*Ludolphus, quoted by Isaac Williams.*

Verse 10.—"*Jehovah of hosts,*" or, as the Hebrew is, *Jehovah Tsebaoth,* for so the word is used by the apostles, untranslated in the Greek, *Sabaoth.* Rom. ix. 29. It signifieth *hosts* or *armies* standing ready in martial order, and in battle array, and comprehendeth all creatures in heaven and in earth, which are pressed to do the will of God.—*Henry Ainsworth.*

HINTS TO THE VILLAGE PREACHER.

Verse 1.—The great Proprietor, his estates and his servants, his rights and wrongs.

Verse 1.—"*The earth is the Lord's.*" I. *Mention other claimants*—idols: pope, man, devil, etc. II. *Try the suit.* III. *Carry out the verdict.* Use our substance, preach everywhere, claim all things for God. IV. *See how glorious the earth looks when she bears her Master's name.*

Verse 1 (*last clause*).—All men belong to God. His sons or his subjects, his servants or his serfs, his sheep or his goats, etc.

Verse 2.—Divine purposes acomplished by singular means.

Verse 2.—*Founded on the seas.* Instability of terrestrial things.

Verse 3.—The all-important question.

Verse 4 (*first clause*).—Connection between outward morality and inward purity.

Verse 4 (*second clause*).—Men judged by their delights.

Verse 4.—"*Clean hands.*" I. How to get them clean. II. How to keep them clean. III. How to defile them. IV. How to get them clean again.

Verses 4, 5.—Character manifested and favour received.

Verse 5. (*second clause*).—The good man receiving righteousness and needing salvation, or the evangelical meaning of apparently legal passages.

Verse 6.—Those who truly seek fellowship with God.

Verse 7.—Accommodate the text to the entrance of Jesus Christ into our hearts. I. There are obstacles, "*gates,*" "*doors.*" II. We must will to remove them: "*lift up.*" III. Grace must enable us: "*be ye lift up.*" IV. Our Lord will enter. V. He enters as "*King,*" and "*King of glory.*"

Verse 7.—The ascension and its teachings.

Verses 7—10.—I. His title—the Lord of hosts. II. His victories, implied in the expression. The Lord strong and mighty in battle. III. His mediatorial title, The King of glory. IV. His authoritative entrance into the holy place. - *John Newton's " Messiah."*

Verse 8.—The mighty Hero. His pedigree, his power, his battles, his victories.

Verse 10.—The sovereignty and glory of God in Christ.

WORK UPON THE TWENTY-FOURTH PSALM.

In the "Works" of John Boys, 1626, folio, pp. 908—913, there is an Exposition of this Psalm.

PSALM XXV.

TITLE.—A Psalm of David. *David is pictured in this Psalm as in a faithful miniature. His holy trust, his many conflicts, his great transgression, his bitter repentance, and his deep distresses are all here; so that we see the very heart of "the man after God's own heart." It is evidently a composition of David's later days, for he mentions the sins of his youth, and from its painful references to the craft and cruelty of his many foes, it will not be too speculative a theory to refer it to the period when Absalom was heading the great rebellion against him. This has been styled the second of the seven Penitential Psalms. It is the mark of a true saint that his sorrows remind him of his sins, and his sorrow for sin drives him to his God.*

SUBJECT AND DIVISION.—*The twenty-two verses of this Psalm begin in the original with the letters of the Hebrew alphabet in their proper order. It is the first instance we have had of an inspired acrostic or alphabetical song. This method may have been adopted by the writer to assist the memory; and the Holy Spirit may have employed it to show us that the graces of style and the arts of poetry may lawfully be used in his service. Why should not all the wit and ingenuity of man be sanctified to noblest ends by being laid upon the altar of God? From the singularity of the structure of the Psalm, it is not easy to discover any marked divisions; there are great changes of thought, but there is no variation of subject; the moods of the writer's mind are twofold—prayer and meditation; and as these appear in turns, we shall thus divide the verses. Prayer from verses 1 to 7; meditation, verses 8, 9, 10; prayer, verse 11; meditation, verses 12—15; prayer, verses 16 to end.*

EXPOSITION.

UNTO thee, O LORD, do I lift up my soul.

2 O my God, I trust in thee : let me not be ashamed, let not mine enemies triumph over me.

3 Yea, let none that wait on thee be ashamed : let them be ashamed which transgress without cause.

4 Shew me thy ways, O LORD ; teach me thy paths.

5 Lead me in thy truth, and teach me : for thou *art* the God of my salvation ; on thee do I wait all the day.

6 Remember, O LORD, thy tender mercies and thy loving-kindnesses ; for they *have been* ever of old.

7 Remember not the sins of my youth, nor my transgressions : according to thy mercy remember thou me for thy goodness' sake, O LORD.

1. "*Unto thee, O Lord.*"—See how the holy soul flies to its God like a dove to its cote. When the storm-winds are out, the Lord's vessels put about and make for their well-remembered harbour of refuge. What a mercy that the Lord will condescend to hear our cries in time of trouble, although we may have almost forgotten him in our hours of fancied prosperity. "*Unto thee, O Jehovah, do I lift up my soul.*" It is but mockery to uplift the hands and the eyes unless we also bring our souls into our devotions. True prayer may be described as the soul rising from earth to have fellowship with heaven; it is taking a journey upon Jacob's ladder, leaving our cares and fears at the foot, and meeting with a covenant God at the top. Very often the soul cannot rise, she has lost her wings, and is heavy and earth-bound ; more like a burrowing mole than a soaring eagle. At such dull seasons we must not give over prayer, but must, by God's assistance, exert all our powers to lift up our hearts. Let faith be the lever and

grace be the arm, and the dead lump will yet be stirred.   But what a lift it has sometimes proved !   With all our tugging and straining we have been utterly defeated, until the heavenly loadstone of our Saviour's love has displayed its omnipotent attractions, and then our hearts have gone up to our Beloved like mounting flames of fire.

2. " *O my God.* "   This title is more dear and near than the name Jehovah, which is used in the first sentence.   Already the sweet singer has drawn nearer to his heavenly helper, for he makes bold to grasp him with the hand of assured possession, calling him, my God.   Oh the more than celestial music of that word—" *My God !* "   It is to be observed that the psalmist does not deny expression to those gracious feelings with which God had favoured him ; he does not fall into loathsome mock modesty, but finding in his soul a desire to seek the Lord he avows it ; believing that he had a rightful interest in Jehovah he declares it, and knowing that he had confidence in his God he professes it ; " *O my God, I trust in thee.* "   Faith is the cable which binds our boat to the shore, and by pulling at it we draw ourselves to the land ; faith unites us to God, and then draws us near to him.   As long as the anchor of faith holds there is no fear in the worst tempest ; if that should fail us there would be no hope left.   We must see to it that our faith is sound and strong, for otherwise prayer cannot prevail with God.   Woe to the warrior who throws away his shield ; what defence can be found for him who finds no defence in his God ?   " *Let me not be ashamed.* "   Let not my disappointed hopes make me feel ashamed of my former testimonies to thy faithfulness.   Many were on the watch for this.   The best of men have their enemies, and should pray against them that they may not see their wicked desires accomplished.   " *Let not mine enemies triumph over me.* "   Suffer no wicked mouth to make blasphemous mirth out of my distresses by asking, " Where is thy God ?"   There is a great jealousy in believers for the honour of God, and they cannot endure that unbelievers should taunt them with the failure of their expectations from the God of their salvation.   All other trusts will end in disappointment and eternal shame, but our confidence shall never be confounded.

3. " *Yea, let none that wait on thee be ashamed.* "   Suffering enlarges the heart by creating the power to sympathize.   If we pray eagerly for ourselves, we shall not long be able to forget our fellow-sufferers.   None pity the poor like those who have been or are still poor, none have such tenderness for the sick as those who have been long in ill health themselves.   We ought to be grateful for occasional griefs if they preserve us from chronic hard-heartedness ; for of all afflictions, an unkind heart is the worst, it is a plague to its possessor, and a torment to those around him.   Prayer when it is of the Holy Ghost's teaching is never selfish ; the believer does not sue for monopolies for himself, but would have all in like case to partake of divine mercy with him.   The prayer may be viewed as a promise ; our Heavenly Father will never let his trustful children find him untrue or unkind.   He will ever be mindful of his covenant.   " *Let them be ashamed which transgress without cause.* "   David had given his enemies no provocation ; their hatred was wanton.   Sinners have no justifiable reason or valid excuse for transgressing ; they benefit no one, not even themselves by their sins ; the law against which they transgress is not harsh or unjust ; God is not a tyrannical ruler, providence is not a bondage : men sin because they will sin, not because it is either profitable or reasonable to do so.   Hence shame is their fitting reward.   May they blush with penitential shame now, or else they will not be able to escape the everlasting contempt and the bitter shame which is the promotion of fools in the world to come.

4. " *Shew me thy ways, O Lord.* "   Unsanctified natures clamour for their own way, but gracious spirits cry, " Not my will, but thine be done."   We cannot at all times discern the path of duty, and at such times it is our wisdom to apply to the Lord himself.   Frequently the dealings of God with us are mysterious, and then also we may appeal to him as his own interpreter, and in due time he will make all things plain.   Moral, providential and mental forms of guidance

are all precious gifts of a gracious God to a teachable people. The second petition, "*teach me thy paths*," appears to mean more than the first, and may be illustrated by the case of a little child who should say to his father, "Father, first tell me which is the way, and then teach my little trembling feet to walk in it." What weak dependent creatures we are! How constantly should we cry to the Strong for strength!

5. "*Lead me in thy truth, and teach me.*" The same request as in the last verse. The little child having begun to walk, asks to be still led onward by its parent's helping hand, and to be further instructed in the alphabet of truth. Experimental teaching is the burden of this prayer. Lead me according to thy truth, and prove thyself faithful; lead me into truth that I may know its preciousness, lead me by the way of truth that I may manifest its spirit. David knew much, but he felt his ignorance, and desired to be still in the Lord's school; four times over in these two verses he applies for a scholarship in the college of grace. It were well for many professors if instead of following their own devices, and cutting out new paths of thought for themselves, they would enquire for the good old ways of God's own truth, and beseech the Holy Ghost to give them sanctified understandings and teachable spirits. "*For thou art the God of my salvation.*" The Three-One Jehovah is the Author and Perfecter of salvation to his people. Reader, is he the God of *your* salvation? Do you find in the Father's election, in the Son's atonement, and in the Spirit's quickening all the grounds of your eternal hopes? If so, you may use this as an argument for obtaining further blessings; if the Lord has ordained to save you, surely he will not refuse to instruct you in his ways. It is a happy thing when we can address the Lord with the confidence which David here manifests, it gives us great power in prayer, and comfort in trial. "*On thee do I wait all the day.*" Patience is the fair handmaid and daughter of faith; we cheerfully wait when we are certain that we shall not wait in vain. It is our duty and our privilege to wait upon the Lord in service, in worship, in expectancy, in trust all the days of our life. Our faith will be tried faith, and if it be of the true kind, it will bear continued trial without yielding. We shall not grow weary of waiting upon God if we remember how long and how graciously he once waited for us.

6. "*Remember, O Lord, thy tender mercies and thy loving-kindnesses.*" We are usually tempted in seasons of affliction to fear that our God has forgotten us, or forgotten his usual kindness towards us; hence the soul doth as it were put the Lord in remembrance, and beseech him to recollect those deeds of love which once he wrought towards it. There is a holy boldness which ventures thus to deal with the Most High, let us cultivate it; but there is also an unholy unbelief which suggests our fears, let us strive against it with all our might. What gems are those two expressions, "*tender mercies and loving-kindnesses*"! They are the virgin honey of language; for sweetness no words can excel them; but as for the gracious favours which are intended by them, language fails to describe them.

> "When all thy mercies, O my God,
>   My rising soul surveys,
> Transported with the view, I'm lost
>   In wonder, love and praise."

If the Lord will only do unto us in the future as in the past, we shall be well content. We seek no change in the divine action, we only crave that the river of grace may never cease to flow.

"*For they have been ever of old.*" A more correct translation would be "from eternity." David was a sound believer in the doctrine of God's eternal love. The Lord's loving-kindnesses are no novelties. When we plead with him to bestow them upon us, we can urge use and custom of the most ancient kind. In courts of law men make much of precedents, and we may plead them at the throne of grace. "Faith," saith Dickson, "must make use of experiences and read them over unto God, out of the register of a sanctified memory, as a recorder to him who cannot forget." With an unchangeable God it is a most effectual argument to remind him of his ancient mercies and his eternal love. By tracing all that we enjoy to the fountain-head of everlasting love we shall greatly cheer our hearts, and those do us but sorry service who try to dissuade us from meditating upon election and its kindred topics.

7. "*Remember not the sins of my youth.*" Sin is *the* stumbling-block. This is the thing to be removed. Lord, pass an act of oblivion for all my sins, and especially for the hot-blooded wanton follies of my younger years. Those offences which we remember with repentance God forgets, but if we forget them, justice will bring them forth to punishment. The world winks at the sins of young men, and yet they are none so little after all ; the bones of our youthful feastings at Satan's table will stick painfully in our throats when we are old men. He who presumes upon his youth is poisoning his old age. How large a tear may wet this page as some of us reflect upon the past ! "*Nor my transgressions.*" Another word for the same evils. Sincere penitents cannot get through their confessions at a gallop ; they are constrained to use many bemoanings, for their swarming sins smite them with so innumerable griefs. A painful sense of any one sin provokes the believer to repentance for the whole mass of his iniquities. Nothing but the fullest and clearest pardon will satisfy a thoroughly awakened conscience. David would have his sins not only forgiven, but forgotten.

"*According to thy mercy remember thou me for thy goodness' sake, O Lord.*" David and the dying thief breathe the same prayer, and doubtless they grounded it upon the same plea, viz., the free grace and unmerited goodness of Jehovah. we dare not ask to have our portion measured from the balances of justice, but we pray to be dealt with by the hand of mercy.

8 Good and upright *is* the LORD : therefore will he teach sinners in the way.

9 The meek will he guide in judgment : and the meek will he teach his way.

10 All the paths of the LORD *are* mercy and truth unto such as keep his covenant and his testimonies.

These three verses are a meditation upon the attributes and acts of the Lord. He who toils in the harvest field of prayer should occasionally pause awhile and refresh himself with a meal of meditation.

8. "*Good and upright is the Lord : therefore will he teach sinners in the way.*" Here the goodness and the rectitude of the divine character are beheld in friendly union ; he who would see them thus united in bonds of perfect amity must stand at the foot of the cross and view them blended in the sacrifice of the Lord Jesus. It is no less true than wonderful that through the atonement the justice of God pleads as strongly as his grace for the salvation of the sinners whom Jesus died to save. Moreover, as a good man naturally endeavours to make others like himself, so will the Lord our God in his compassion bring sinners into the way of holiness and conform them to his own image ; thus the goodness of our God leads us to expect the reclaiming of sinful men. We may not conclude from God's goodness that he will save those sinners who continue to wander in their own ways, but we may be assured that he will renew transgressors' hearts and guide them into the way of holiness. Let those who desire to be delivered from sin take comfort from this. God himself will condescend to be the teacher of sinners. What a ragged school is this for God to teach in ! God's teaching is practical ; he teaches sinners not only the doctrine, but *the way*.

9. "*The meek will he guide in judgment.*" Meek spirits are in high favour with the Father of the meek and lowly Jesus, for he sees in them the image of his only-begotten Son. They know their need of guidance, and are willing to submit their own understandings to the divine will, and therefore the Lord condescends to be their guide. Humble spirits are in this verse endowed with a rich inheritance ; let them be of good cheer. Trouble puts gentle spirits to their wits' ends, and drives them to act without discretion, but grace comes to

the rescue, enlightens their mind to follow that which is just, and helps them to discern the way in which the Lord would have them to go. Proud of their own wisdom fools will not learn, and therefore miss their road to heaven, but lowly hearts sit at Jesu's feet, and find the gate of glory, for "*the meek will he teach his way.*" Blessed teacher! Favoured scholar! Divine lesson! My soul, be thou familiar with the whole.

10. This is a rule without an exception. God is good to those that be good. Mercy and faithfulness shall abound towards those who through mercy are made faithful. Whatever outward appearances may threaten we should settle it steadfastly in our minds that while grace enables us to obey the Lord's will we need not fear that Providence will cause us any real loss. There shall be mercy in every unsavoury morsel, and faithfulness in every bitter drop; let not our hearts be troubled, but let us rest by faith in the immutable covenant of Jehovah, which is ordered in all things and sure. Yet this is not a general truth to be trampled upon by swine, it is a pearl for a child's neck. Gracious souls, by faith resting upon the finished work of the Lord Jesus, *keep* the *covenant* of the Lord, and, being sanctified by the Holy Spirit, they walk in *his testimonies;* these will find all things co-working for their good, but to the sinner there is no such promise. Keepers of the covenant shall be kept by the covenant; those who follow the Lord's commands shall find the Lord's mercy following them.

11 For thy name's sake, O LORD, pardon mine iniquity; for it *is* great.

This sentence of prayer would seem out of place were it not that prayer is always in its place, whether in season or out of season. Meditation having refreshed the Psalmist, he falls to his weighty work again, and wrestles with God for the remission of his sin. "*For thy name's sake, O Lord.*" Here is a blessed, never-failing plea. Not for our sakes or our merits' sake, but to glorify thy mercy, and to show forth the glory of thy divine attributes. "*Pardon mine iniquity.*" It is confessed, it is abhorred, it is consuming my heart with grief; Lord forgive it; let thine own lips pronounce my absolution. "*For it is great.*" It weighs so heavily upon me that I pray thee remove it. Its greatness is no difficulty with thee, for thou art a great God, but the misery which it causes to me is my argument with thee for speedy pardon. Lord, the patient is sore sick, therefore heal him. To pardon a great sinner will bring thee great glory, therefore for thy name's sake pardon me. Observe how this verse illustrates the logic of faith, which is clean contrary to that of a legal spirit; faith looks not for merit in the creature, but hath regard to the goodness of the Creator; and instead of being staggered by the demerits of sin it looks to the precious blood, and pleads all the more vigorously because of the urgency of the case.

12 What man *is* he that feareth the LORD? him shall he teach in the way *that* he shall choose.

13 His soul shall dwell at ease; and his seed shall inherit the earth.

14 The secret of the LORD *is* with them that fear him; and he will shew them his covenant.

15 Mine eyes *are* ever toward the LORD; for he shall pluck my feet out of the net.

12. "*What man is he that feareth the Lord?*" Let the question provoke self-examination. Gospel privileges are not for every pretender. Art thou of the seed royal or no? "*Him shall he teach in the way that he shall choose.*" Those whose hearts are right shall not err for want of heavenly direction. Where God sanctifies the heart he enlightens the head. We all wish to choose our way; but what a mercy is it when the Lord directs that choice, and makes free-will to be good-will! If we make our will God's will, God will let us have our will.

God does not violate our will, but leaves much to our choice ; nevertheless, he instructs our wills, and so we choose that which is well-pleasing in his sight. The will should be subject to law ; there is a way which we should choose, but so ignorant are we that we need to be taught, and so wilful that none but God himself can teach us effectually.

13. He who fears God has nothing else to fear. "*His soul shall dwell at ease.*" He shall lodge in the chamber of content. One may sleep as soundly in the little bed in the corner as in the Great Bed of Ware ; it is not abundance but content that gives true ease. Even here, having learned by grace both to abound and to be empty, the believer dwells at ease ; but how profound will be the ease of his soul for ever ! There he will enjoy the "*otium cum dignitate ;*" ease and glory shall go together. Like a warrior whose battles are over, or a husbandman whose barns are full, his soul shall take its ease, and be merry for ever. "*His seed shall inherit the earth.*" God remembers Isaac for the sake of Abraham, and Jacob for the sake of Isaac. Good men's sons have a goodly portion to begin the world with, but many of them, alas ! turn a father's blessing into a curse. The promise is not broken because in some instances men wilfully refuse to receive it ; moreover, it is in its spiritual meaning that it now holds good ; our spiritual seed do inherit all that was meant by "*the earth,*" or Canaan ; they receive the blessing of the new covenant. May the Lord make us the joyful parents of many spiritual children, and we shall have no fears about their maintenance, for the Lord will make each one of them princes in all the earth.

14. "*The secret of the Lord is with them that fear him.*" Some read it "the friendship :" it signifies familiar intercourse, confidential intimacy, and select fellowship. This is a great secret. Carnal minds cannot guess what is intended by it, and even believers cannot explain it in words, for it must be felt to be known. The higher spiritual life is necessarily a path which the eagle's eye hath not known, and which the lion's whelp has not travelled ; neither natural wisdom nor strength can force a door into this inner chamber. Saints have the key of heaven's hieroglyphics ; they can unriddle celestial enigmas. They are initiated into the fellowship of the skies ; they have heard words which it is not possible for them to repeat to their fellows. "*And he will shew them his covenant.*" Its antiquity, security, righteousness, fulness, graciousness and excellence, shall be revealed to their hearts and understandings, and above all, their own part in it shall be sealed to their souls by the witness of the Holy Spirit. The designs of love which the Lord has to his people in the covenant of grace, he has been pleased to show to believers in the Book of Inspiration, and by his Spirit he leads us into the mystery, even the hidden mystery of redemption. He who does not know the meaning of this verse, will never learn it from a commentary ; let him look to the cross, for the secret lies there.

15. "*Mine eyes are ever toward the Lord.*" The writer claims to be fixed in his trust, and constant in his expectation ; he looks in confidence, and waits in hope. We may add to this look of faith and hope the obedient look of service, the humble look of reverence, the admiring look of wonder, the studious look of meditation, and the tender look of affection. Happy are those whose eyes are never removed from their God. "The eye," says Solomon, "is never satisfied with seeing," but this sight is the most satisfying in the world. "*For he shall pluck my feet out of the net.*" Observe the conflicting condition in which a gracious soul may be placed, his eyes are in heaven and yet his feet are sometimes in a net ; his nobler nature ceases not to behold the glories of God, while his baser parts are enduring the miseries of the world. A net is the common metaphor for temptation. The Lord often keeps his people from falling into it, and if they have fallen he rescues them. The word "*pluck*" is a rough word, and saints who have fallen into sin find that the means of their restoration are not always easy to the flesh ; the Lord plucks at us sharply to let us feel that sin is an exceeding bitter thing. But what a mercy is here : Believer, be very grateful for it. The Lord will deliver us from the cunning devices of our cruel enemy, and even if through infirmity we have fallen into sin, he will not leave us to be utterly

destroyed but will pluck us out of our dangerous state ; though our feet are in the net, if our eyes are up unto God, mercy certainly will interpose.

16 Turn thee unto me, and have mercy upon me ; for I *am* desolate and afflicted.

17 The troubles of my heart are enlarged : *O* bring thou me out of my distresses.

18 Look upon mine affliction and my pain ; and forgive all my sins.

19 Consider mine enemies ; for they are many ; and they hate me with cruel hatred.

20 O keep my soul, and deliver me : let me not be ashamed ; for I put my trust in thee.

21 Let integrity and uprightness preserve me ; for I wait on thee.

22 Redeem Israel, O God, out of all his troubles.

16. His own eyes were fixed upon God, but he feared that the Lord had averted his face from him in anger. Oftentimes unbelief suggests that God has turned his back upon us. If we know that we turn to God we need not fear that he will turn from us, but may boldly cry, " *Turn thee unto me.*" The ground of quarrel is always in ourselves, and when that is removed there is nothing to prevent our full enjoyment of communion with God. " *Have mercy upon me.*" Saints still must stand upon the footing of mercy ; notwithstanding all their experience they cannot get beyond the publican's prayer, " Have mercy upon me." " *For I am desolate and afflicted.*" He was lonely and bowed down. Jesus was in the days of his flesh in just such a condition ; none could enter into the secret depths of his sorrows, he trod the winepress alone, and hence he is able to succour in the fullest sense those who tread the solitary path.

> " Christ leads me through no darker rooms
> Than he went through before;
> He that into God's kingdom comes,
> Must enter by this door."

17. " *The troubles of my heart are enlarged.*" When trouble penetrates the heart it is trouble indeed. In the case before us, the heart was swollen with grief like a lake surcharged with water by enormous floods ; this is used as an argument for deliverance, and it is a potent one. When the darkest hour of the night arrives we may expect the dawn ; when the sea is at its lowest ebb the tide must surely turn ; and when our troubles are enlarged to the greatest degree, then may we hopefully pray, " *O bring thou me out of my distresses.*"

18. " *Look upon mine affliction and my pain.*" Note the many trials of the saints ; here we have no less than six words all descriptive of woe. " Desolate, and afflicted, troubles enlarged, distresses, affliction, and pain." But note yet more the submissive and believing spirit of a true saint ; all he asks for is, " Lord, look upon my evil plight ;" he does not dictate, or even express a complaint ; a look from God will content him, and that being granted he asks no more. Even more noteworthy is the way in which the believer under affliction discovers the true source of all the mischief, and lays the axe at the root of it. " *Forgive all my sins,*" is the cry of a soul that is more sick of sin than of pain, and would sooner be forgiven than healed. Blessed is the man to whom sin is more unbearable than disease, he shall not be long before the Lord shall both forgive his iniquity and heal his diseases. Men are slow to see the intimate connection between sin and sorrow, a grace-taught heart alone feels it.

19. " *Consider mine enemies.*" Watch them, weigh them, check them, defeat them. " *For they are many.*" They need the eyes of Argus to watch them, and the arms of Hercules to match them, but the Lord is more than sufficient to

defeat them. The devils of hell and the evils of earth are all vanquished when the Lord makes bare his arm. "*They hate me with cruel hatred.*" It is the breath of the serpent's seed to hate ; their progenitor was a hater, and they themselves must needs imitate him. No hate so cruel as that which is unreasonable and unjust. A man can forgive one who has injured him, but one whom he has injured he hates implacably. "Behold, I send you forth as sheep in the midst of wolves," is still our Master's word to us.

20. "*O keep my soul*" out of evil, "*and deliver me*" when I fall into it. This is another version of the prayer, "Lead us not into temptation, but deliver us from evil."

"*Let me not be ashamed.*" This is the one fear which like a ghost haunted the psalmist's mind. He trembled lest his faith should become the subject of ridicule through the extremity of his affliction. Noble hearts can brook anything but shame. David was of such a chivalrous spirit, that he could endure any torment rather than to be put to dishonour. "*For I put my trust in thee.*" And therefore the name of God would be compromised if his servants were deserted ; this the believing heart can by no means endure.

21. "*Let integrity and uprightness preserve me.*" What better practical safeguards can a man require ? If we do not prosper with these as our guides, it is better for us to suffer adversity. Even the ungodly world admits that "honesty is the best policy." The heir of heaven makes assurance doubly sure, for apart from the rectitude of his public life, he enlists the guardian care of heaven in secret prayer : "*for I wait on thee.*" To pretend to wait on God without holiness of life is religious hypocrisy, and to trust to our own integrity without calling upon God is presumptuous atheism. Perhaps the integrity and uprightness referred to are those righteous attributes of God, which faith rests upon as a guarantee that the Lord will not forfeit his word.

22. "*Redeem Israel, O God, out of all his troubles.*" This is a very comprehensive prayer, including all the faithful and all their trials. Sorrow had taught the psalmist sympathy, and given him communion with the tried people of God ; he therefore remembers them in his prayers. *Israel*, the tried, the wrestling, the conquering hero, fit representative of all the saints. Israel in Egypt, in the wilderness, in wars with Canaanites, in captivity, fit type of the church militant on earth. Jesus is the Redeemer from trouble as well as sin, he is a complete Redeemer, and from every evil he will rescue every saint. Redemption by blood is finished : O God, send us redemption by power. Amen and Amen.

EXPLANATORY NOTES AND QUAINT SAYINGS.

Whole Psalm.—This is the first of the seven alphabetical Psalms, the others being the 34th, 37th, 111th, 112th, 119th, and 145th. They are specimens of that acrostic mode of writing which seems to have been once so fashionable among the Jews, as is testified by numerous instances of such composition, which are to be met with in their works. Other poetic artifices were likewise adopted. We find many instances of poems being so constructed, that a proper name, or some particular sentiment, would be not unfrequently expressed by the initial letters of the verses. See Bartolocci's "Bibliotheca Rabbinica," vol. ii. p. 260, where examples of such artifices are cited.—*George Phillips, B.D., in "The Psalms in Hebrew, with a Commentary,"* 1846.

Whole Psalm.—This is the first fully *alphabetic* Psalm. . . . The only lesson which the use of the *alphabetic* form may teach is this :—that the Holy Spirit was willing to throw his words into all the moulds of human thought and speech ;

and whatever ingenuity man may exhibit in intellectual efforts, he should consecrate these to his Lord, making him the "*Alpha and Omega*" of his pursuits. *Andrew A. Bonar.*

Whole Psalm.—Saving grace is a secret that no man knows but the elect, and the elect cannot know it neither without special illumination :—1. Special showing—"*Shew me thy ways, O Lord,*" saith David. 2. Barely showing will not serve the turn, but there must be a special teaching—"*Teach me thy paths,*" ver. 4. 3. Bare teaching will not avail neither, but there must be a special inculcative teaching—"*Teach me in thy ways,*" to ver. 8. 4. Inculcative teaching will not do the deed neither, but there must be a special directive teaching—"*Guide in judgment and teach,*" ver. 9. 5. Directive teaching will not be sufficient neither, but there must be a special manu-ductive teaching—"*Lead me forth in thy truth, and teach me,*" ver. 5. 6. Manu-ductive teaching will not be effectual, but there must be also a special, choice teaching, a determinating of the very will, an elective teaching—"*Him shall he teach in the way that he shall choose,*" verse 12. And what secret is this? not common grace, for that is not the secret of the elect, but special and peculiar grace. 1. The special grace of prayer—"*Unto thee, O Lord, do I lift up my soul,*" verse 1. 2. A special grace of faith—"*My God, I trust in thee,*" ver. 2. 3. A special grace of repentance—"*Remember not the sins of my youth,*" etc., verse 7. 4. A special grace of hope—"*My hope is in thee,*" verse 21. 5. A special grace of continual living in God's sight, and dependence upon God—"*Mine eyes are ever toward the Lord,*" verse 15. 6. Which is the root of all God's special and eternal favour and mercy—"*Remember, O Lord, thy tender mercies and thy lovingkindnesses; for they have been ever of old,*" verse 6; even God's special mercy to him in particular, verse 11.—*William Fenner, in "Hidden Manna,"* 1626.

Whole Psalm —In these four Psalms which immediately follow one another, we may find the soul of David presented in all the several postures of piety—*lying, standing, sitting, kneeling.* In the twenty-second Psalm, he is lying all along, falling flat on his face, low grovelling on the ground, even almost entering into a degree of despair. Speaking of himself in the history of Christ in the mystery, "My God, why hast thou forsaken me?" In the twenty-third Psalm, he is *standing*, and through God's favour, in despite of his foes, trampling and triumphing over all opposition; "The Lord is my shepherd, therefore shall I lack nothing." In the twenty-fourth Psalm he is *sitting*, like a doctor in his chair, or a professor in his place, reading a lecture of divinity, and describing the character of that man—how he must be accomplished—"who shall ascend into the holy hill," and hereafter be partaker of happiness. In this twenty-fifth Psalm, he is *kneeling*, with hands and voice lifted up to God, and on these two hinges the whole Psalm turneth; the one is a hearty beseeching of God's mercy, the other a humble bemoaning of his own misery.—*Thomas Fuller.*

Verse 1.—"*Unto thee, O Lord, do I lift up my soul.*" *The lifting up of the heart* presupposeth a former dejection of his soul. The soul of man is pressed down with sin and with the cares of this world, which, as lead doth the net, draweth it so down, that it cannot mount above till God send spiritual prayers, as cork to the net, to exalt it; which arise out of faith, as the flame doth out of the fire, and which must be free of secular cares, and all things pressing down, which showeth unto us that worldlings can no more pray than a mole is able to fly. But Christians are as eagles which mount upward. Seeing then the heart of man by nature is fixed to the earth, and of itself is no more able to rise therefrom than a stone which is fixed in the ground, till God raises it by his power, word, and workmen; it should be our principal petition to the Lord that it would please him to draw us, that we might run after him; that he would exalt and lift up our hearts to heaven, that they may not lie still in the puddle of this earth.—*Archibald Symson.*

Verse 1.—"*Unto thee, O Lord, do I lift up my soul.*" A godly man prays as a builder builds. Now a builder first layeth a foundation, and because he cannot finish in one day, he comes the second day, and finds the frame standing that he made the first day, and then he adds a second day's work ; and then he comes a third day and finds his two former days' work standing ; then he proceeds to a third day's work, and makes walls to it, and so he goes on till his building be finished. So prayer is the building of the soul till it reach up to heaven ; therefore a godly heart prays, and reacheth higher and higher in prayer, till at last his prayers reach up to God.—*William Fenner.*

Verse 1.—" *Unto thee, O Lord, do I lift up my soul :*" *unto thee* in the fulness of thy merits, *unto thee* in the riches of thy grace ; *unto thee* in the embraces of thy love and comforts of thy Spirit ; *unto thee,* that thy thorns may be my crown, thy blood my balsam, thy curse my blessing, thy death my life, thy cross my triumph. Thus is my "life hid with Christ in God ;" and if so, then where should be my soul, but where is my life ? And, therefore, "*unto thee, O Lord, do I lift up my soul.*" . . . . O make good thy name of Lord unto me ; as Lord, rebuke Satan and restrain all earthly and carnal affections, that they do not once dare to whisper a temptation to my soul, a distraction to my thoughts, whilst I am in communion with thee, in prayer at thy holy ordinance. Do thou as Lord, rule me by thy grace, govern me by thy Spirit, defend me by thy power, and crown me with thy salvation. Thou Lord, the preserver of heaven and earth, "thou openest thy hand, and satisfiest the desire of every living thing." Psalm cxlv. 16. O open now thine hand, thy bosom, thy bounty, thy love, and satisfy the desires of my longing soul, which I here "*lift up unto thee.*"—*Robert Mossom,* 1657.

Verse 1.—"*Unto thee, O Lord, do I lift up my soul.*" Cyprian saith, that in the primitive times the minister was wont to prepare the people's minds to pray, by prefacing, *Sursum corda,* lift up your hearts. The Jews at this day write upon the walls of their synagogues these words, *Tephillah belo cavannah ceguph belo neshamah ;* that is, A prayer without the intention of the affection is like a body without a soul. And yet their devotion is a mere outside, saith one—a brainless head and a soulless body : "This people draweth nigh to me with their lips, but their heart is far from me." Isaiah xxix. 13. A carnal man can as little *lift up his heart* in prayer, as a mole can fly. A David finds it a hard task ; since the best heart is lumpish, and naturally beareth downwards, as the poise of a clock, as the lead of a net. Let us therefore "lay aside every weight, and the sin that doth so easily beset us ;" and pray to God to draw us up to himself, as the loadstone doth the iron.—*John Trapp.*

Verse 1.—"*Unto thee,* I lift up my *soul.*" This follows by a natural consequence after the sublime appeal in the foregoing Psalm to the gates of heaven to *lift up* their heads to receive Christ, the Lord of hosts and the King of glory, ascending into heaven. As the Collect for Ascension day expresses it, "Grant, O Lord, that like as we do believe thy only-begotten Son, our Lord Jesus Christ, to have ascended into the heavens, so we may also, in *heart* and *mind* thither *ascend ;*" and for the Sunday after Ascension, "O God, who hast *exalted* thine only Son with great triumph to thy kingdom in heaven, send thy Holy Ghost to comfort us, and *exalt us* to the same place, whither our Saviour Christ is gone before."—*Christopher Wordsworth, in loc.*

Verse 1.—"*I lift up my soul,* alluding to the sacrifices, which were wont to be *lifted up.* Hence prayers not answered, not accepted, are said to be stopped from ascending. Lam. iii. 44. When you meet with such expressions in the Old Testament concerning prayer, you must still understand them to be allusions to the sacrifices, because the sacrifices were *lifted up and did* ascend.—*Joseph Caryl.*

Verse 1.—"*My soul.*" But how shall I call it mine, seeing it is thine, thine by purchase, thine, having bought it with thy blood ? Yea, is it not thy spouse, whom thou hast wedded to thyself by thy Spirit through faith ? And is not this holy sacrament the marriage feast ? If so, sure then, my Jesus, I was lost in myself, till found in thee ; and therefore my soul is now, and not

till now, truly mine, in being wholly thine ; so that I can say with confidence,
" *I lift up my soul unto thee."—Robert Mossom.*

Verses 2, 3.—When David had prayed, " *O my God, I trust in thee ; let me
not be ashamed !* " In the next verse, as if conscious to himself that his prayers
were too restrictive, narrow, and niggardly, he enlargeth the bounds thereof,
and builds them on a broader bottom, "*Yea, let none that wait on thee be
ashamed.*" Thus it is that charity in the midst of our religious devotions must
have *rehoboth* (room enough to expatiate in). Our petitions must not be pent
or confined to our own private good, but extended to the benefit of all God's
servants, in what condition soever.—*Thomas Fuller.*

Verse 3.—" *Yea, let none that wait on thee be ashamed.*" To wit, neither by
their own disappointments, nor mine. For this last some add because if he
should fail of his hopes, he knew this would be a great discouragement to others.—
Arthur Jackson, M.A., 1593—1666.
Verse 3.—"*Let them be ashamed which transgress without cause.*" All persons who transgress, do it, in some sense, without cause ; since they cannot
excuse or justify their conduct. God is so amiable and excellent in every part
of his great name, that he deserves our constant reverence and love. His law
is so holy, just, and good, and all his precepts concerning all things so righteous
and calculated to make us happy, that the mouth of every transgressor must
be stopped. Hence we must all be covered with shame, if dealt with according
to our deserts, for all have sinned. But since God has promised to be merciful
to those who truly repent, and unfeignedly believe his holy gospel, shame will
be the portion of those only who wilfully persist in their wickedness, and refuse
to return to God by Jesus Christ. These then are the persons whom the
psalmist speaks of as transgressing without cause, and doubtless these have no
cloak for their sin.—*William Richardson,* 1825.
Verse 3.—"*Let them be ashamed which transgress without cause.*" Let shame
be sent to the right owner, even to those that deal disloyally, unprovoked on
my part. And so it was ; for Achitophel hanged himself ; Absalom was trussed
up by the hand of God, and dispatched by Joab ; the people that conspired with
him, partly perished by the sword, and partly fled home, much ashamed of their
enterprise. Oh, the power of prayer ! What may not the saints have for asking ?
John Trapp.

Verse 4.—" *Shew me thy ways, O Lord,*" etc. There are the "*ways*" of men,
and the "*ways*" of God ; the "*paths*" of sin, and the "*paths*" of righteousness : there are "*thy* ways," and there are *my* ways ; *thine* the ways of truth,
mine the ways of error ; *thine* which are good in thine eyes, and *mine* which are
good in mine eyes ; *thine* which lead to heaven, *mine* which lead to hell. Wherefore, " *Shew me thy ways, O Lord ; teach me thy paths,*" lest I mistake mine own
ways for thine ; yea, lead me in the truth, and teach me, lest I turn out of thy
ways into mine own : " *shew me thy ways,*" by the ministry of thy word ; "*teach
me thy paths,*" in the guidance of thy Spirit, " *lead me in thy truth,*" by the assistance of thy grace.—*Robert Mossom.*
Verses 4, 5, 9.—Do what you know, and God will teach you what to do. Do
what you know to be your *present* duty and God will acquaint you with your
future duty as it comes to be *present.* Make it your business to avoid
known omissions, and God will keep you from feared commissions. This rule is
of great moment, and therefore I will charge it upon you by express Scripture.
"*Shew me thy ways, O Lord,*" i.e., those ways wherein I cannot err. "*Teach
me thy paths,*" i.e., that narrow path which is too commonly unknown, those
commands that are most strict and difficult, verse 5. " *Lead me in thy
truth, and teach me,*" i.e., teach me evidently, that I may not be deceived;
so teach me, that I may not only know thy will, but do it. Here's his
prayer, but what grounds hath he to expect audience ? " *For thou art the*

God of my salvation," q.d., thou Lord, wilt save me, and therefore do not refuse to teach me. *" On thee do I wait all the day,"* i.e., the whole day, and every day. Other arguments are couched in the following verses, but *what* answer? verse 9, *"The meek will he guide in judgment: and the meek will he teach his way,"* i.e., those that submit their neck to his yoke, those that are not conceited that they can guide themselves; in necessary, great and weighty matters they shall not err.—*Samuel Annesley, D.D.* (1620—1696), *in " Morning Exercises at Cripplegate."*

Verse 5.—"Lead me in thy truth, and teach me." The soul that is unsatiable in prayer, he proceeds, he gets near to God, he gains something, he winds up his heart higher. As a child that seeth the mother have an apple in her hand, and it would fain have it, it will come and pull at the mother's hand for it : now she lets go one finger, and yet she holds it, and then he pulls again; and then she lets go another finger, and yet she keeps it, and then the child pulls again, and will never leave pulling and crying till it hath got it from its mother. So a child of God, seeing all graces to be in God, he draws near to the throne of grace begging for it, and by his earnest and faithful prayers he opens the hands of God to him; God dealing as parents to their children, holds them off for awhile; not that he is unwilling to give, but to make them more earnest with God ; to draw them the nearer to himself.—*William Fenner.*

Verse 5.—"On thee do I wait all the day." We must *"wait all the day."* 1. Though it be a *long* day, though we be kept waiting a great while, quite beyond our own reckoning ; though when we have waited long, we are still put to wait longer, and are bid, with the prophet's servant, to go yet seven times (1 Kings xviii. 43), before we perceive the least sign of mercy coming. . . . . . 2. Though it be a *dark* day, yet let us wait upon God *" all the day."* Though while we are kept waiting for what God will do, we are kept in the dark concerning what he is doing, and what is best for us to do, yet let us be content to wait in the dark. Though we see not our signs, though there is none to tell us how long, yet let us resolve to wait, how long soever it may be ; for though what God doth we know not now, yet we shall know hereafter when the mystery of God shall be finished. . . . . 3. Though it be a *stormy* day, yet we must wait upon God *" all the day."* Though we are not only becalmed, and do not get forward, but though the wind be contrary, and drive us back ; nay, though it be boisterous, and the church be tossed with tempests, and ready to sink, yet we must hope the best, yet we must wait, and weather the storm by patience. It is some comfort that Christ is in the ship ; the church's cause is Christ's own cause, he has espoused it, and he will own it ; he is embarked in the same bottom with his people, and therefore why are you fearful? . . . . *To wait on God,* is— 1. To live a life of desire towards God; to wait on him as the beggar waits on his benefactor, with earnest desire to receive supplies from him, as the sick and sore at Bethesda's pool waited for the stirring of the water, and attended in the porches with desire to be helped in and healed. . . . . 2. It is to live a life of delight in God, as the lover waits on his beloved. Desire is love in motion, as a bird upon the wing ; delight is love at rest, as a bird upon the nest ; now, though our desire must still be so towards God, as that we must be wishing for more of God, yet our delight must be so in God, as that we must never wish for more than God. . . . . 3. It is to live a life of dependence on God, as the child waits on his father, whom he has confidence in, and on whom he casts all his care. To wait on God is to expect all good to come to us from him, as the worker of all good for us and in us, the giver of all good to us, and the protector of us from all evil. Thus David explains himself (Psalm lxii. 5), "My soul, wait thou only upon God," and continue still to do so, for "my expectation is from him." . . . . 4. It is to live a life of devotedness to God, as the servant waits on his master, ready to observe his will, and to do his work, and in everything to consult his honour and interest. To wait on God is entirely and unreservedly to refer ourselves to his wise and holy directions and disposals, and cheerfully to acquiesce in them, and comply with them. The servant that waits on his master, chooseth not his own way, but follows his master step by step. Thus must we wait on God, as those that have no will of our own but what is wholly resolved into his, and must therefore study to accommodate ourselves to his.—*Condensed from Matthew Henry, on "Communion with God."*

Verse 5.—"*On thee do I wait all the day.*" "*On thee,*" whose hand of bounty, whose bosom of love, yea, whose bowels of mercy are not only opened, but enlarged to all humble penitents. "*On thee do I wait,*" *wait* to hear the secret voice of thy Spirit, speaking peace unto my conscience, *wait* to feel the reviving vigour of thy grace, quickening mine obedience ; *wait* to see the subduing power of thy Holy Spirit quelling my rebellious sin ; *wait* to feel the cheering virtue of thy heavenly comforts, refreshing my fainting soul ; for all these thy blessings, "*O thou God of my salvation, on thee do I wait all the day.*" "*All the day :*" being never so satisfied with thy goodness, as not more eagerly to long after thy heavenly fulness ; wherefore now refresh my faintings, quench not my desires ; but the more freely thou givest, let me the more eagerly covet ; the more sweet is thy mercy, let be the more eager my longings, that so my whole life on earth may be a continual breathing after that eternal fellowship and communion with thee in heaven ; thus, thus, *let me wait,* even all my life, *all the day.—Robert Mossom.*

Verse 6.—"*Thy tender mercies.*" O how does one deep call upon another ! The depth of my multiplied miseries, calls, loudly calls, upon the depth of thy manifold mercies ; even *that mercy* whereby thou dost pardon my sin and help mine infirmities ; *that mercy* whereby thou dost sanctify me by thy grace, and comfort me by thy Spirit ; *that mercy* whereby thou dost deliver me from hell, and possess me of heaven. "*Remember, O Lord,*" all those thy mercies, *thy tender mercies,* which have been "*of old*" unto thy saints.—*Robert Mossom.*

Verse 6.—"*Thy tender mercies and thy lovingkindnesses. . . . have been ever of old.*" Let the ancientness of divine love draw up our hearts to a very dear and honourable esteem of it. Pieces of antiquity, though of base metal, and otherwise of little use or value, how venerable are they with learned men ! and ancient charters, how careful are men to preserve them ; although they contain but temporary privileges, and sometimes but of trivial moment ! How then should the great charter of heaven, so much older than the world, be had in everlasting remembrance, and the thoughts thereof be very precious to us ; lying down, rising up, and all the day long accompanying of us ! . . . That which is from everlasting shall be to everlasting ; if the root be eternal, so are the branches. . . . Divine love is an eternal fountain that never leaves running while a vessel is empty or capable of holding more ; and it stands open to all comers : therefore, come ; and if ye have not sufficient of your own, go and borrow vessels, empty vessels, not a few ; "pay your debts out of it, and live on the rest " (2 Kings iv. 7), to eternity.—*Elisha Coles on " God's Sovereignty,"* 1678.

Verse 7.—"*Remember not the sins of my youth, nor my trangressions.*" In the first place, considering that he had not begun only of late to commit sin, but that he had for a long time heaped up sin upon sin, he bows himself, if we may so speak, under the accumulated load ; and, in the second place, he intimates, that if God should deal with him according to the rigour of the law, not only the sins of yesterday, or of a few days, would come into judgment against him, but all the instances in which he had offended, even from his infancy, might now with justice be laid to his charge. As often, therefore, as God terrifies us by his judgments and the tokens of his wrath, let us call to our remembrance, not only the sins which we have lately committed, but also all the transgressions of our past life, proving to us the ground of renewed shame and renewed lamentation.—*John Calvin.*

Verse 7.—"*Remember not the sins of my youth.*" This may seem but a superfluous prayer of David ; for whereas in charity it may and must be presumed that David long since had begged pardon for his youthful sins, that upon his begging God hath granted it, that upon his granting God never revoked it. What need now had David to prefer this petition for pardon of antiquated sin, time out of mind committed by him, time out of mind remitted by God ? To this objection I shape a fourfold answer. *First,* though David no doubt long since had been truly sorrowful for his youthful sins, yet he was sensible in himself that if God would be extreme to mark what was done amiss, though he had repented of those sins, yet he had sinned in that his repentance. *Secondly,* though God had forgiven David's sins so far forth as to pardon him eternal damnation, yet he had not remitted unto him temporal afflictions which perchance pressing upon him at this present, he prayeth in this Psalm for the removing or mitigating of them. So then the sense of his words sound thus, "*Remember not, Lord, the sins of my youth,*" that is, Lord, lighten and lessen the afflictions which lie upon me in this mine old age, justly inflicted on me for my youthful sins. *Thirdly,* God's pardon for sins past, is ever granted with this condition, that the party so pardoned is bound to his good behaviour for the time to come, which if he breaks, he deserves in the strictness of justice to forfeit the benefit of his pardon. Now David was guilty afterward in that grand transgression of Bathsheba and Uriah, which might in the extremity of justice have made all his youthful sins to be punished afresh upon him. *Lastly,* grant David certainly assured of the pardon of his youthful sins, yet God's servants may pray for those blessings they have in possession, not for the obtaining of that they have—that is needless—but for the keeping of what they have obtained, that is necessary. Yea, God is well pleased with such prayers of his saints, and interprets them to be praises unto him, and then these words, "*Remember not the sins of my youth,*" amount to this effect : blessed be thy gracious goodness, who hast forgiven me the sins of my youth.— *Thomas Fuller.*

Verse 7.—"*Remember not the sins of my youth.*" David, after he was called by the power of the word, cries out, "*Lord, remember not,*" etc.; that gravelled and galled his conscience, the *sins* of his *youth* before his call. O beloved, the sins of your youth, though you should be Jobs converted, yet they will bring great disquietness and great horror when you come to age. The lusts of youth, and the vanities of youth, and the sensual pleasures of your youthful days, they will lay a foundation of sorrow when you come to grey hairs to be near your graves. So Job. xx. 11.—*Christopher Love,* 1654.

Verse 7.—"*Remember not the sins of my youth ;*" let them not move thee to punish or be avenged on me for them ; as men, when they remember injuries, seek to be avenged on those who have done them.—*William Greenhill.*

Verse 7.—"*Remember not the sins of my youth.*" It is not safe to be at odds with the "Ancient of days."—*John Trapp.*

Verse 7.—"*The sins of my youth.*" Before we come to the principal point we must first clear the text from the incumbrance of a double objection. The first is this :—It may seem (may some say) very improbable that David should have any sins of his youth, if we consider the principals whereupon his youth was past. The first was *poverty.* We read that his father Jesse passed for an *old* man, we read not that he passed for a *rich* man ; and probably his seven sons were the principal part of his wealth. Secondly, *painfulness.* David, though the youngest, was not made a darling, but a drudge ; sent by his father to follow the ewes big with young ; where he may seem to have learned innocence and simplicity from the sheep he kept. Thirdly, *piety* (Psalm lxxi. 5), "For thou art my hope, O Lord God ; thou art my trust from my youth." And again in the seventeenth verse of the same Psalm, "O God, thou hast taught me from my youth :" David began to be good betimes, *a young saint,* and yet crossed that pestilent proverb, was no *old devil*. And what is more still, he was constantly in the furnace of affliction. Psalm lxxxviii. 15. "Even from my youth up, thy terrors have I suffered with a troubled mind." The question then will be this, How could that water be corrupted which was daily clarified? How could that steel gather rust which was duly filed? How could David's soul in his *youth* be sooty with sin, which was constantly scoured with suffering? But the answer is easy; for though David for the main were a man after God's own heart (the best transcript of the best copy), yet he, especially in his youth, had his faults and infirmities, yea, his sins and transgressions. Though the Scripture maketh mention of ♦ no eminent sin in his youth, the business with Bathsheba being justly to be referred to David's reduced and elder age. I will not conclude that David was of a wanton constitution because of a reddy complexion. It is as injurious an inference to conclude all bad which are beautiful, as it is a false and flattering consequence to say all are honest who are deformed. Rather we may collect David's youth guilty of wantonness from his having so many wives and concubines. But what go I about to do? Expect not that I should tell you the particular sins, when he could not tell his own. Psalm xix. "Who can tell how oft he offendeth?" Or how can David's sins be known to me, which he confesseth were unknown to himself, which made him say, "O Lord, cleanse me from secret sins"? But to silence our curiosity, that our conscience may speak:—If David's youth, which was poor, painful, and pious, was guilty of sins, what shall we say, of such whose education hath been wealthy, wanton, and wicked? And I report the rest to be acted with shame, sorrow, and silence in every man's conscience.—*Thomas Fuller.*

Verse 7.—"*The sins of my youth.*" Two aged disciples, one eighty-seven years old, one day met. "Well," enquired the younger, of his fellow pilgrim, "how long have you been interested in religion?" "Fifty years," was the old man's reply. "Well, have you ever regretted that you began when young to devote yourself to religion?" "Oh, no!" said he, and the tears trickled down his furrowed cheeks; "I weep when I think of the sins of my youth; it is this which makes me weep now."—*From K. Arvine's "Cyclopædia of Moral and Religious Anecdotes,"* 1859.

Verse 7.—"*According to* THY *mercy,*" not *mine;* for I have forsaken those *mercies* thou madest *mine own* (Jonah ii. 8; Psalm lix. 10, 17), in being cruel to myself by my sin, through distrust of thy promise, and upon presumption in thy mercy; yea, let it be, "*for* THY *goodness' sake,*" not *mine*, for in me, that is, in my flesh, dwelleth no manner of thing that is good. Let thy goodness, then, be the motive, thy mercy the rule of all that grace, and of all those blessings thou vouchsafest unto my soul.—*Robert Mossom.*

Verse 7.—"*According to thy mercy.*" Moses was the first that brought up this happy expression, "*According to thy mercy*" (I know not where it is used by any other man), that is, according to the infinite mercy that is in thy heart and nature. David did next use it (Psalm xxv.), and in the great case of his sin and adultery (Psalm li. 1), "that he would be merciful to him, according to the multitude of his mercies." And as he needed all the mercies in God, so he confessed the sin of his nature, and hath recourse to the mercies in God's nature. But it is Psalm xxv. 7, I pitch on; there he doth not content himself only with this expression, "*According to thy mercy,*" but he adds another phrase, "For thy mercy's sake," and "*goodness' sake.*" Muis observes in this coherence, "*Good and upright is the Lord*" (verse 8), that he centres in his nature. Thou hast a merciful nature; deal with me according to that, and for the sake of that, "according to thy mercy," "for thy goodness' sake." The meditation of that attribute was the foundation of his faith and prayer herein. When he hath done, he referreth himself to Moses: verse 11, "*For thy name's sake, O Lord, pardon mine iniquity; for it is great.*" He refers to that name proclaimed before Moses. Exodus xxxiv. 6, 7. But you will say, how do these expressions, "for thy name's sake," "for thy goodness' sake," "for thy mercy's sake," imply the same as "for himself," "for his own sake"? how do they involve the Godhead? Look to Isaiah xliii. 25, "I, even I, am he that blotteth out thy transgressions for mine own sake," that is, for myself. Isaiah xlviii. 11. "For mine own sake, even for mine own sake, will I do it." You have it twice in one verse; and that which is "for mercy's sake" in one place, is "for mine own sake" in another, and behold it is I, I am he, as I am God, who doth it. What is this, but Jehovah, Jehovah, God merciful"?—*Thomas Goodwin.*

Verse 8.—"*Good and upright is the Lord: therefore will he teach sinners in the way.*" As election is the effect of God's sovereignty, our pardon the fruit of his mercy, our knowledge a stream from his wisdom, our strength an impression of his power; so our purity is a beam from his holiness. As the rectitude of the creature at the first creation was the effect of his holiness, so the purity of the creature by a new creation, is a draught of the same perfection. He is called the Holy One of Israel more in Isaiah, that evangelical prophet, in erecting Zion, and forming a people for himself, than in the whole Scripture besides.—*Stephen Charnock.*

Verse 8.—"*Good and upright is the Lord: therefore will he teach sinners in the way.*" Will not the Lord, who is good, be as gracious to his enemies as he requires us to be to ours? It is his own law, "If thou meet thine enemy's ox or his ass going astray, thou shalt surely bring it back to him again." Exodus xxiii. 4. Now God meets us sinners, and all sinners as such are his enemies; he meets us straying like the beast without understanding; and what? will he not bring us again unto himself, the sole proprietary, by that first right of creation, and that more firm right of redemption?—*Robert Mossom.*

Verse 9.—"*The meek will he guide in judgment;*" or, *the poor* (namely, in spirit), will he make to tread in judgment, to foot it aright, to walk judiciously, to behave themselves wisely, as David did (1 Sam. xxiv.), so that Saul feared him. Natural conscience cannot but stoop to the image of God, shining in the hearts and lives of the really religious.—*John Trapp.*

Verse 9.—"*The meek will he guide in judgment.*" They have been made meek, *i.e.*, desirous of being taught, and praying to be so; but, being now sensible of unworthiness, they are afraid that God will not teach them. This may be done to other sinners but not to them. Therefore they are told who may expect teaching, even they who desire and pray for teaching.—*John Berridge, 1716—1793.*

Verse 9.—"*He will guide the poor in judgment.*" Never will this docility be found in any man, until the heart, which is naturally elated and filled with pride, has been humbled and subdued. As the Hebrew word denotes the *poor* or *afflicted*, and is employed in a metaphorical sense, to denote *the meek and humble*, it is probable that David, under this term, includes the afflictions which serve to restrain and subdue the frowardness of the flesh, as well as the grace of humility itself; as if he had said, When God has first humbled them, then he kindly stretches forth his hand to them, and leads and guides them throughout the whole course of their life.—*John Calvin.*

Verse 9.—"*The meek,*" etc. Pride and anger have no place in the school of Christ. The Master himself is "meek and lowly of heart;" much more, surely, ought the scholars to be so. He who hath no sense of his ignorance, can have no desire, or capability of knowledge, human or divine.—*George Horne.*

Verse 9 (last clause).—The Lord will teach the humble his secrets, he will not teach proud scholars.—*Thomas Goodwin.*

Verse 9 (last clause).—Such as lie at his feet and say, "Speak, Lord, for thy servant heareth," such whose hearts are *supple* and *soluble*, tractable, and teachable, so that a *little child* may *lead them.* (Isaiah xi. 6.) Austin was such an one. Saith he, "I am here an old man ready to learn of a young man, my coadjutor in the ministry, who hath scarce been one year in the service."—*John Trapp.*

Verse 10.—"*All the paths of the Lord,*" אָרְחוֹת *orchoth* signifies the tracks or ruts made by the wheels of wagons by often passing over the same ground. Mercy and truth are the paths in which God constantly walks in reference to the children of men ; and so frequently does he show them mercy, and so frequently does he fulfil his truth, that his paths are easily discerned. How frequent, how deeply indented, and how multiplied are those tracks to every family and individual ! Wherever we go, we see that God's mercy and truth have been there by the deep tracks they have left behind them. But he is more abundantly merciful to those who keep his covenant and his testimonies ; *i. e.*, those who are conformed, not only to the letter, but to the spirit of his pure religion.—*Adam Clarke.*

Verse 10.—"*All the paths of the Lord are mercy and truth.*" As his *nature* is *love and truth,* so all his *ways* are *mercy and truth.* They are "*mercy*" in respect of aiming at our good, and "*truth*" in respect of fulfilling his promises and faithful carriage to us ; therefore, whatsoever befalls thee, though it be clean contrary to thy expectation, interpret it in love. Many actions of men are such as a good interpretation cannot be put upon them, nor a good construction made of them ; therefore interpreters restrain those sayings of love, that it believes all, etc. ; that is, *credibilia,* all things believable, otherwise to put all upon charity, will eat out charity. But none of God's ways are such, but love and faith may pick a good meaning out of these. *A bono Deo nil nisi bonum,* from a good God there comes nothing but what is good ; and therefore says Job, "Though he kill me, I will trust in him. Endeavour to spy out some end of his for good at the present, and if none ariseth to thy conjecture, resolve it into faith, and make the best of it.—*Thomas Goodwin.*

Verse 10.—"*Unto such as keep,*" etc. : he is never out of the road of mercy unto them.—*Thomas Goodwin.*

Verse 11.—"*For thy name's sake, O Lord, pardon mine iniquity ; for it is great.*" I cannot do better than quote one of those beautiful passages of the great Vieyra, which gave him the character of the first preacher of his age :— "I confess, my God, that it is so ; that we are all sinners in the highest degree." He is preaching on a fast on occasion of the threatened destruction of the Portuguese dominion in Brazil by the Dutch. "But so far am I from considering this any reason why I should cease from my petition, that I behold in it a new and convincing argument which may influence thy goodness. All that I have said before is based on no other foundation than the glory and honour of thy most holy Name. *Propter nomen tuum.* And what motive can I offer more glorious to that same Name, than that our sins are many and great? *For thy name's sake, O Lord, be merciful unto my sin, for it is great.* I ask thee, saith David, to pardon, not every-day sins, but numerous sins, but great sins : *multum est enim.* O motive worthy of the breast of God ! Oh, consequence which can have force only when it bears on supreme goodness ! So that in order to obtain remission of his sins, the sinner alleges to God that they are many and great. Verily so ; and that not for love of the sinner nor for the love of sin, but for the love of the honour and glory of God ; which glory, by how much the sins he forgives are greater and more numerous, by so much the more ennobles and exalts itself. The same David distinguishes in the mercy of God greatness and multitude : greatness, *secundum magnam misericordiam tuam ;* multitude, *et secundum multitudinem miserationum tuarum.* And as the greatness of the divine mercy is immense, and the multitude of his lovingkindnesses infinite ; and forasmuch as the immense cannot be measured, nor the infinite counted, in order that the one and the other may in a certain manner have a proportionate material of glory, it is necessary to the very greatness of mercy that the sins to be pardoned should be great, and necessary to the very multitude of lovingkindnesses that they should be many. *Multum est enim.* Reason have I then, O Lord, not to be dismayed because our sins are many and great. Reason have I also to demand the reason from thee, why thou dost not make haste to pardon them?"—*Vieyra, quoted by J. M. Neale.*

Verse 11.—"*For thy name's sake, O Lord, pardon mine iniquity.*" It is a very usual notion by "*name*" to understand honour and glory. When God saith to David, "I have made thee a name like the name of men that are in the earth;" when the church saith to God, "Thou didst get thee a name as it is this day;" it is manifest that by name glory is intended. Suitable to this it is that famous men are called by the Hebrews, אַנְשֵׁי הַשֵּׁם (Gen. vi. 4), and by the Latins, *viri nominum,* men of name, in which sense the poet adorneth it with these epithets—

"Magnum et memorabile nomen,"

or great and memorable. Thus, when God forgiveth sin, he doth it *for his name's sake,* that is, for his own honour and glory. Indeed, God's own glory is the ultimate end of all his actions. As he is the first, so is he the last, the efficient, and the final cause; nor is there anything done by him which is not for him. The end of our actions must be his glory, because both our being and working are from him; but the end of his work is his own glory, because his being and acting are of and from himself. Among all divine works, there is none which more setteth forth his glory than this of remission. Sin, by committing it, brings God a great deal of dishonour, and yet, by forgiving it, God raiseth to himself a great deal of honour. "It is the glory of a man," and much more of God, "to pass by an offence;" as acts of power, so acts of grace, are exceeding honourable. The attributes of God's grace, mercy, goodness, clemency, shine forth in nothing so much as in pardoning sins. Paul speaks of riches of goodness which attend God's forbearance; how much greater riches must there needs be in forgiveness? Nay, indeed, God hath so ordered the way of pardon, that not only the glory of his mercy, but justice, yea, of his wisdom in the wonderful contemporation of both these, is very illustrious. *Nomen quasi notamen, quia notificat,* the name is that which maketh one known; and by remission of sins, God maketh known his choice and glorious attributes; and for this end it is that he vouchsafeth it. It is a consideration that may be our consolation. Since God forgiveth sins *for his name's sake,* he will be ready to forgive many sins as well as few, great as small; indeed, the more and greater our sins are, the greater is the forgiveness, and, consequently, the greater is God's glory; and therefore David, upon this consideration of God's name and glory, maketh the *greatness of his iniquity* a motive of forgiveness. Indeed, to run into gross sins, that God may glorify himself by forgiving them, is an odious presumption, but to hope that those gross sins we have run into may, and will, be forgiven by God to us, being truly penitent, *for his name's sake,* is a well grounded expectation, and such as may support our spirits against the strongest temptations to despair.—*Nathanael Hardy.*

Verse 11.—"*Pardon mine iniquity; for it is great.*" He pleads the greatness of his sin, and not the smallness of it: he enforces his prayer with this consideration, that his sins are very heinous. But how could he make this a plea for pardon? I answer, Because the greater his iniquity was, the more *need* he had of pardon. It is as much as if he had said, Pardon mine iniquity, for it is so great that I cannot bear the punishment; my sin is so great that I am in necessity of pardon; my case will be exceedingly miserable, unless thou be pleased to pardon me. He makes use of the greatness of his sin, to enforce his plea for pardon, as a man would make use of the greatness of calamity in begging for relief. When a beggar begs for bread, he will plead the greatness of his poverty and necessity. When a man in distress cries for pity, what more suitable plea can be urged than the extremity of his case? And God allows such a plea as this: for he is moved to mercy towards us by nothing in us, but the miserableness of our case. He doth not pity sinners because they are worthy, but because they need his pity. . . . Herein doth the *glory of grace* by the redemption of Christ much consist; namely, in its sufficiency for the pardon of the *greatest* sinners. The whole contrivance of the way of salvation is for this end, to glorify the free grace of God. God had it on his heart from all eternity to glorify this attribute; and therefore it is, that the device of saving sinners by Christ was conceived. The greatness of divine grace appears very much in this, that God by Christ saves the *greatest* offenders. The *greater* the guilt of any sinner is, the more glorious and wonderful is the grace manifested in his pardon. Rom. v. 20: "Where sin abounded, grace did much more abound." The apostle, when telling how great a sinner he had been, takes notice of the abounding of grace in his pardon, of which his great guilt was the occasion. 1 Tim. i. 13, 14. "Who was before a blasphemer, and a persecutor, and injurious: but I obtained mercy, because I did it ignorantly in unbelief. And the grace of our Lord was exceeding abundant with faith and love which is in Christ Jesus." The Redeemer is glorified, in that he proves sufficient to redeem those who are exceeding sinful, in that his blood proves sufficient to wash away the greatest guilt, in that he is able to save men to the uttermost, and in that he redeems even from the greatest misery. It is the honour of Christ to save the greatest sinners, when they come to him, as it is the honour of a physician that he cures the most desperate diseases or wounds. Therefore, no doubt, Christ will be willing to save the greatest sinners, if they come to him; for he will not be backward to glorify himself, and to commend the value and virtue of his own blood. Seeing he hath so laid out himself to redeem sinners, he will not be unwilling to show that he is able to redeem to the uttermost.—*Jonathan Edwards.*

Verse 11.—"*Pardon mine iniquity; for it is great.*" Is any man miserable, are his miseries great, are they spiritual, are they temporal? Undoubtedly, if he be humbled in the sense of them, and see himself unworthy of any mercy, he may still be assured of mercy. Though there be spiritual evils, yet if a man see himself wretched, and miserable, the more heavy he finds his iniquity to be, the more hope of mercy there is for him: the Lord's mercy is over all his works, therefore is he much more merciful to such. If a man hath a feeling of his miseries and unworthiness, then he may use this argument for mercy, *my miseries are great:* even as David did, "*O Lord, be merciful to me, and pardon my iniquity, for it is great.*" And the more miserable men are in their own sense, the fitter objects they are for God to show mercy unto. Thus it was with the publican, and so with the prodigal; therefore never doubt, though thy iniquities be never so great, there is a sea of mercy in God. Bernard well observes the difference between justice and mercy; justice requires that there should be desert, but mercy looks upon them that are miserable; and, saith the father, true mercy doth affect misery; mercy doth not stand upon inquisition, but it is glad to find occasion of exercising itself.—*Richard Stock.*

Verse 11.—"*Mine iniquity . . . is great.*" Such who come to God to have their sins pardoned, they look upon them as great sins. "*Pardon mine iniquity, for it is great.*" The original word as well signifies *many* as great—"My sins are great and many," many great sins lie upon me, pardon, oh! pardon them, O Lord, &c. . . . . In the opening of this point, I would show *why* such as come in a right way for pardon do look upon their sins as *great* sins 1 Sinners that come to God for pardon and find it, do look upon their sins as *great sins,* because against a *great* God, great in power, great in justice, great in holiness. I am *a worm,* and yet sin, and that boldly against a God so *great;* for a worm to lift up himself against a great and infinite God; oh! this makes every little sin *great,* and calls for *great* vengeance from so *great* a God. 2. Because *they have sinned against great patience,* despising the goodness, forbearance, and long-suffering of God, which is called, "treasuring up wrath." Rom. ii. 4, 5. . . . . 3. Sins do appear *great* because *against great mercies.* Oh! against how many mercies and kindnesses do sinners sin, and turn all the mercies of God into sin! . . . . 4. That which *greatens* sin in the eyes of poor sinners that cry for pardon, is, that *they have sinned against great light*—light in the conscience; this heightens sin exceedingly, especially to such as are under gospel means; and is indeed the sin of all in this nation; there's nothing more abaseth a soul than this, nothing makes it more difficult to believe pardon, when humbled for it. . . . 5. *Continuance in sin* much *greatens* sin to a poor soul that is after pardon; especially such as are not very early converted. Psalm lxviii. 21. Oh! I added sin unto sin, saith a poor soul, spending the choice time of my youth in sin, when I might have been getting the knowledge of Jesus Christ, and honouring of God. This lay close upon David's spirit, as appears from the seventh verse: "Oh! remember not the sins of my youth." Yet we do not find that David's youth was notoriously sinful; but inasmuch as he spent not his youth to get knowledge, and to serve the Lord fully, 'twas his burden and complaint before the Lord ; much more such whose youth was spent in nothing but vanity, profaneness, lying, swearing, profaning of the Sabbath, sports, pastimes, excess of riot, and the like, when God lays it in upon their consciences, must be grievous and abominable to their souls. . . . 6. *Multitudes of sins* do make sin appear great ; this made David cry out for "multitude of mercies." Psalm li., and xl. 12. . . . . 7. Another thing that *greatens* sin is, that it was *against purposes and resolutions of forsaking such and such sins;* and yet all broken, sometimes against solemn vows, against prayers. . . . 8. Sin appears *great* when seen by a poor soul, because it was *reigning* sin. Rom. v. 6. "Sin reigned unto death," etc. Oh! saith a poor humbled sinner, I did not only *commit* sin, but I was the *servant* and *slave* of sin. . . . . 9. Sin *in the fountain makes it great.* As it may be said, there is more water in the fountain than in the pools and streams it makes. . . . . So in the nature, in the heart, is there, as in the fountain, and therefore 'tis more there than in the breakings forth of it in the outward man. . . . . 10. A sinner drawing nigh to God for pardon sees his sin as *great,* because thereby he was *led captive by the devil* at his will. . . 11. Sin appears *great* because *great is the wrath of God against sin.* Rom. ii. 12. The way of any sinner's deliverance from such wrath shows sin to be exceeding great *in the price and ransom that is paid for the salvation of him from his sins*—the price of the blood of the eternal Son of God. . . . 13. Lastly, this consideration also *greatens* sin, inasmuch as a poor creature *hath drawn and tempted others* to sin with him, especially such as have lived more vainly and loosely, and it lies hard upon many a poor soul after thorough conviction.—*Anthony Palmer* (——1678), *in " The Gospel New-creature."*

Verse 11.—I plead not, Lord, my merits, who am less than the least of thy mercies ; and as I look not upon my merit, so nor do thou look upon my demerit ; as I do not view my worthiness, so nor do thou view my unworthiness ; but thou who art called *the God of mercy* be unto me what thou art called ; make good the glory of thine own name in being merciful unto my sin, of which I cannot say as Lot of Zoar, "Is it not a little one?" No, it is *great,* for that it is against thee so great a God and so good to me : *great,* for that my place, my calling, my office is great. The sun the higher it is, the less it seems ; but my sins, the higher I am the greater they are, even in thine and others' eyes.—*Robert Mossom.*

Verse 11.—Plead we the greatness of our sins not to keep us from mercy, but to prevail for it : " *Pardon mine iniquity ;* " why so? " *for it is great.*" "Heal my soul, for I have sinned against thee." Psalm xli. 4. "Do thou it for thy name's sake : for our backslidings are many ; we have sinned against thee." Jer. xiv. 7. This is a strong plea, when sincerely urged by an humble and contrite spirit. It glorifieth God as one that is abundant in goodness, rich in mercy, and one with whom are forgivenesses and plenteous redemption ; and it honoureth Christ as infinite in mercy. Hence also the Lord himself, when he would stir up himself to choice acts of mercy to his poor people, he first aggravateth their sin against him to the highest, and then he expresseth his royal act of grace to them. So Isaiah xliii. 22—25. Thou hast not called upon me, O Jacob, but thou hast been weary of me, O Israel ; thou hast not honoured me with thy sacrifices, but thou hast wearied me with thine iniquities. I, even I, am he that blotteth out thy transgressions for mine own sake, and will not remember thy sins."—*Thomas Cobbet,* 1608—1686.

Verse 11.—"Oh," says Pharaoh, "take away these filthy frogs, this dreadful thunder!" But what says holy David? " Lord, take away the iniquity of thy servant!" The one would be freed from punishment, the effect of sin; the other from sin, the cause of punishment. And it is most true that a true Christian man is more troubled at sin than at frogs and thunder; he sees more filthiness in sin than in frogs and toads, more horror than in thunder and lightning. —*Jeremiah Dyke's " Worthy Communicant,"* 1645.

Verse 11.—Pharaoh more lamented the hard strokes that were upon him, than the hard heart which was within him. Esau mourned not because he sold the birthright, which was his sin, but because he lost the blessing, which was his punishment. This is like weeping with an onion; the eye sheds tears because it smarts. A mariner casts overboard that cargo in a tempest, which he courts the return of when the winds are silenced. Many complain more of the sorrows to which they are born, than of the sins with which they were born; they tremble more at the vengeance of sin, than at the venom of sin; one delights them, the other affrights them.—*William Secker.*

Verse 12.—"*What man is he that feareth the Lord?*" Blessed shall he be—1. In the sacred knowledge of Christ's will; "*Him shall he teach in the way that he shall choose.*" 2. Blessed shall he be in the quiet peace of a good conscience; "*His soul shall dwell at ease.*" 3. Blessed he shall be in the present comfort of a hopeful progeny; "*His seed shall inherit the earth.*" *Robert Mossom.*

Verse 12.—"*What man is he that feareth the Lord?*" There is nothing so effectual to obtain grace, to retain grace, as always to be found before God not over wise, but *to fear:* happy art thou, if thy heart be replenished with three fears; a fear for received grace, a greater fear for lost grace, a greatest fear to recover grace.—*Bernard.*

Verse 12.—"*He that feareth the Lord.*" Present fear begetteth eternal security: fear God, which is above all, and no need to fear man at all.—*Augustine.*

Verse 12.—"*Him shall he teach in the way that he shall choose,*" *i.e.*, that the good man shall pitch upon. God will direct him in all dealings to make a good choice, and will give good success. This is not in a man's own power to do. Jer. x. 23. *John Trapp.*

Verse 13.—"*His soul shall dwell at ease; and his seed shall inherit the earth.*" The holy fear of God shall destroy all sinful fears of men, even as Moses' serpent devoured all those serpents of the magicians. The fear of God hath this good effect, that it makes other things not to be feared; so that the soul of him who feareth the Lord doth dwell, as *in rest*, so in goodness; as *in peace*, so in patience, till this moment of time be swallowed up in the fulness of eternity, and he change his earthly dwelling for an heavenly mansion, and his spiritual peace for an everlasting blessedness.—*Robert Mossom.*

Verse 13.—"*His soul shall dwell at ease.*" Shall tarry in good things, as it is in the Vulgate. Unlike the soul of Adam, who, being put into possession of the delights of paradise, tarried there but a few days or hours.—*Gerhohus, quoted by J. M. Neale.*

Verse 13.—"*His soul shall dwell at ease.*" He expresses with great sweetness spiritual delectation, when he says, "*His soul shall tarry in good things.*" For whatever is carnally sweet yields without doubt a delectation for the time to such as enjoy it, but cannot tarry long with them; because, while by its taste it provokes appetite, by its transit it cheats desire. But spiritual delights, which neither pass away as they are tasted, nor decrease while they refresh, nor cloy while they satiate, can tarry for ever with their possessors.—*Hugo Victorinus* (1130), *quoted by J. M. Neale.*

Verse 13 *(first clause).*—In the reception of the gifts of God, they do not devour them without feeling a sense of their sweetness, but really relish them, so that the smallest competency is of more avail to satisfy them than the greatest abundance is to satisfy the ungodly. Thus, according as every man is contented with his condition, and cheerfully cherishes a spirit of patience and tranquillity, his soul is said *to dwell in good.—John Calvin.*

Verse 13.—" *The earth*," *or the land,* to wit Canaan ; which was promised and given, as an earnest of the whole covenant of grace and all its promises, and therefore it is synecdochically put for all of them. The sense is, his seed shall be blessed.—*Matthew Pool.*

Verse 14.—" *The secret of the Lord is with them that fear him,*" etc. It is the righteous that is God's friend, it is to him that God is joined in a loving familiarity, it is to him that God revealeth his secret, telling him what misery and torments he hath reserved for them who by wickedness flourish in this world. And indeed the Lord doth not more hate the wicked than he loves the godly: if he keeps far from the froward, as being an abomination unto him, his very secret shall be with the righteous, as with his dearest friend. It is an honour to him to whom a secret is committed by another, a greater honour to him to whom the king shall commit his own secret ; but how is he honoured to whom God committed his secret ? for where the secret of God is, there is his heart and there is himself. Thus was his secret with St. John, of whom St. Bernard saith, by occasion of the beginning of his gospel, "Doth he not seem unto thee to have dived into the bowels of the divine Word, and from the secrets of his breast, to have drawn a sacred pith of concealed wisdom ?" Thus was his secret with St. Paul, who saith, "We speak the wisdom of God in a mystery, even the hidden wisdom, which none of the princes of this world knew." 1 Cor. ii. 7, 8. St. Gregory reads, for the secret of God, as the Vulgar Latin doth, *sermocinatio Dei,* the communication of God is with the righteous ; but then addeth, *Dei sermocinari est per illustrationem suæ præsentiæ humanis mentibus arcana revelare,* God's communication is, by the illustration of his presence, to reveal secrets to the minds of men. But to consider the words somewhat more generally. There is no less a secret of godliness, than there is of any other trade or profession. Many profess an art or a trade, but thrive not by it, because they have not the secret and mystery of it ; and many profess godliness, but are little the better for it, because they have not the true secret of it : he hath that, with whom God is in secret in his heart ; and he that is righteous in secret, where no man sees him, he is the righteous man with whom the secret of the Lord is.—*Michael Jermin, D.D.,* 1591—1659.

Verse 14.—" *The secret of the Lord is with them that fear him,*" etc. There is a vital sense in which "the natural man discerneth not the things of the Spirit of God ;" and in which all the realities of Christian experience are utterly hid from his perceptions. To speak to him of communion with God, of the sense of pardon, of the lively expectation of heaven, of the witness of the Holy Ghost, of the struggles of the spiritual life, would be like reasoning with a blind man about colours, or with one deaf about musical harmony.—*John Morison.*

Verse 14.—" *The secret of the Lord is with them that fear him,*" etc. Albeit the Lord's covenant with the visible church be open, and plain in itself to all men in all the articles thereof, yet it is a mystery to know the inward sweet fellowship which a soul may have with God by virtue of this covenant ; and a man fearing God shall know this mystery, when such as are covenanters only in the letter do remain ignorant thereof ; for to *the fearers of God* only is this promise made—that to *them* the Lord *will show his covenant.—David Dickson.*

Verse 14.—" *The secret of the Lord is with them that fear him.*" The gospel, though published to all the world, yet it is entitled a mystery, and a mystery hid, for none know it but the saints, who are taught of God, and are his scholars. John vi. 45. That place shows that there must be a secret teaching by God, and a secret learning. "If they have heard, and been taught of God." Now God teacheth none but saints, for all that are so taught come unto him : "Every one who hath heard, and learned of the Father, cometh unto me." Ay, but you will say, Do not many carnal men know the gospel, and discourse of things in it, through strength of learning, etc. ? I answer out of the text (Col. i. 26, 27), that though they may know the things which the gospel reveals, yet not the riches and glory of them, that same rich knowledge spoken of in the word, they want, and therefore know them not ; as a child and a jeweller looking upon a pearl, both look upon it, and call it by the same name ; but the child yet knows it not as a pearl in the worth and riches of it as the jeweller doth, and therefore cannot be said to know it. Now in Matt. xiii. 45, a Christian only is likened to a merchantman, that finds a pearl of great price, that is, discovered to be so, and sells all he hath for it, for he knows the worth of it. But you will say, Do not carnal men know the worth of the things in the gospel, and can they not discourse of the rich grace of Christ, and of his worth ? I answer, yes, as a man who hath gotten an inventory by heart, and the prices also, and so may know it ; yet never was he led into the exchequer and treasury, to see all the jewels themselves, the wardrobe of grace, and Christ's righteousness, to see the glory of them ; for these are all " spiritually discerned," as the apostle says expressly, 1 Cor. ii. 14.—*Thomas Goodwin.*

Verse 14.—" *The secret of the Lord is with them that fear him.*" The truth and sincerity of God to his people appears in the openness and plainness of his heart to them. A friend that is close and reserved, deservedly comes under a cloud in the thoughts of his friends ; but he who carries, as it were, a window of crystal in his breast, through which his friend may read what thoughts are writ in his very heart, delivers himself from the least suspicion of unfaithfulness. Truly, thus open-hearted is God to his saints : " *The secret of the Lord is with them that fear him.*" He gives us his key, that will let us into his very heart, and acquaint us what his thoughts are, yea, were, towards us, before a stone was laid in the world's foundation ; and this is no other than his Spirit (1 Cor. ii. 10, 11), " One who knows the deep things of God ;" for he was at the council-table in heaven, where all was transacted. This, his Spirit, he employed to put forth and publish in the Scriptures, indited by him, the substance of those counsels of love which had passed between the Trinity of Persons for our salvation ; and that nothing may be wanting for our satisfaction, he hath appointed the same Holy Spirit to abide in his saints, that as Christ in heaven presents our desires to him, so he may interpret his mind out of his word to us ; which word answers the heart of God, as face answers face in the glass.—*William Gurnall.*

Verse 14.—" *The secret of the Lord.*" This " *secret* " is called a *secret* three ways. 1. *Secret* to the eye of sole nature, and thus it is not meant ; for so the grace of Christ is a *secret* only to heathens and such as are blind as they, for common Christians know it—the rind of it. 2. *Secret* to the eye of taught nature, nor thus is it meant ; for so the grace of Christ is a *secret* only to the ignorant sort of Christians ; many carnal gospellers that sit under a good ministry know it and the bark of it. 3. *Secret* to the eye of enlightened nature, and thus it is meant ; for so the grace of Christ is a *secret* to all unsanctified professors, whether learned or unlearned, namely, the pith of it ; for though great doctors and profound clerks, and deep studied divines unconverted, know the doctrine of grace, and the truth of grace ; though they can dispute of grace and talk of the glory of grace, yea, and taste a little the good word of grace, yea, and understand it generally, it may be as well as St. Paul and St. Peter, as Judas did, yet the special and the spiritual knowledge thereof, for all their dogmatical illumination, is a *secret* unto them.—*William Fenner.*

Verse 14.—" *The secret.*" Arminius and his company ransack all God's *secrets*, divulge and communicate them to the seed of the woman, and of the serpent all alike ; they make God's eternal love of election no *secret*, but a vulgar idea ; they make the mystery of Christ, and him crucified, no *secret*, but like an apothecary's drug, catholical ; they make the especial grace of God no *secret*, but a common quality ; faith no *secret*, but a general virtue ; repentance and the new creature no *secret*, but an universal gift ; no *secret* favour to St. Peter, but make God a party *ante*, not to love St. Peter more than Judas ; no *secret* intent to any one person more than another ; but that Christ might have died for all him, and never a man saved ; no *secret* working of the Lord in any more than other ; but for anything that either God the Father hath done by creating, God the Son by redeeming, or God the Holy Ghost by sanctifying, all the world were left to their scrambling—take it if you will, if you will not, refuse. They say God would have men to be saved, but that he will not work it for his own part, rather for this man or that man determinatively that he be saved.—*William Fenner.*

Verse 14.—" *He will shew them his covenant,*" or, *and he will make them to know* (for the infinitive is here thought to be put for the future tense of the indicative, as it is Eccles. iii. 14, 15, 18 ; Hos. ix. 13 ; xii. 3), *his covenant, i. e.,* he will make them clearly to understand it, both its duties or conditions, and its blessings or privileges ; neither of which ungodly men rightly understand. Or, he will make them to know it by experience, or by God's making it good to them ; as, on the contrary, God threatens to make ungodly men to *know his breach of promise.* Numb. xiv. 34. Or, as it is in the margins of our Bibles, *and his covenant,* (is, *i. e.,* he hath engaged himself by his promise or covenant) *to make them know* it, to wit, his secret, *i. e.,* that he will manifest either his word or his favour to them.—*Matthew Pool.*

Verse 14.—It is neither learning nor labour that can give insight into God's secrets, those *Arcana imperii,* " The mysteries of the kingdom of heaven." Matt. xiii. 11. " The mind of Christ." 1 Cor. ii. 16. These things come by revelation rather than by discourse of reason, and must therefore be obtained by prayer. Those that diligently seek him shall be of his *Cabinet Council,* shall know his soul secrets, and be admitted into a gracious familiarity and friendship. " Henceforth I call you not servants ; for the servant knoweth not what his lord doeth ; but I have called you friends ; for all things that I have heard of my Father I have made known unto you." John xv. 15.—*John Trapp.*

Verse 14.—Walking with God is the best way to know the mind of God ; friends who walk together impart their secrets one to another : " *The secret of the Lord is with them that fear him.*" Noah walked with God, and the Lord revealed a great *secret* to him, of destroying the old world, and having him in the ark. Abraham walked with God, and God made him one of his privy council : " Shall I hide from Abraham that thing which I do ?" Gen. xxiv. 40, and xviii. 17. God doth sometimes sweetly unbosom himself to the soul in prayer, and in the holy supper, as Christ made himself known to the disciples in the breaking of bread. Luke xxiv. 35.—*Thomas Watson.*

Verse 15.—" *Mine eyes are ever toward the Lord.*" Though we cannot see him by reason of our present distance and darkness, yet we must look towards him, towards the place where his honour dwells, as those that desire the knowledge of him and his will, and direct all to his honour as the mark we aim at, labouring in this, that " whether present or absent, we may be accepted of him." *Matthew Henry*

Verse 15.—" *Mine eyes.*" As the sense of sight is very quick, and exercises an entire influence over the whole frame, it is no uncommon thing to find all the affections denoted by the term " *eyes.*"—*John Calvin.*

Verse 15.—" *He shall pluck my feet out of the net.*" An unfortunate dove, whose feet are taken in the snare of the fowler, is a fine emblem of the soul, entangled in the cares or pleasures of the world ; from which she desires, through the power of grace, to fly away, and to be at rest, with her glorified Redeemer. *George Horne.*

Verse 17.—" *The troubles of my heart are enlarged.*" Let no good man be surprised that his affliction is great, and to him of an unaccountable character. It has always been so with God's people. The road to heaven is soaked with the tears and blood of the saints.—*William S. Plumer.*

Verse 17.—" *O bring thou me out of my distresses.*" We may not complain of God, but we may complain to God. With submission to his holy will we may earnestly cry for help and deliverance.—*William S. Plumer.*

Verse 18.—*"Look upon mine affliction and my pain; and forgive all my sins."* We may observe here, that *sickness and weakness of the body come from sin, and is a fruit of sin.* Some are weak, and some are sick, "for this cause." I shall not need to be long in the proof of that, which you have whole chapters for, as Deut. xxviii. 27, *seq;* and many Psalms, cvii., and others. It is for the sickness of the soul that God visits with the sickness of the body. He aims at the cure of the soul in the touch of the body. And therefore in this case, when God visits with sickness, we should think our work is more in heaven with God than with men or physic. Begin first with the soul. So David (Psa. xxxii. 5), till he dealt roundly with God, without all kind of guile, and confessed his sins, he roared; his moisture was turned into the drought of summer. But when he dealt directly and plainly with God, and confessed his sins, then God forgave him them, and healed his body too. And therefore the best method, when God visits us in this kind, is to think that we are to deal with God. Begin the cure there with the soul. When he visits the body, it is for the soul's sake: "Many are weak and sickly among you."—*Richard Sibbes.*

Verse 18.—*"Look upon mine affliction and my pain."* In sickness of body trust to Jesus, he is as powerful and as willing to help us now as he was to help others in the days of his flesh. All things are possible to us if we believe. It is but a word for him to rebuke all storms and tempests whatsoever. Let us not do like Asa, trust only in the physician, or in subordinate means, but know that all physic is but dead means without him. 2 Chron. xvi. 12. Therefore, with the means, run to Christ, that he may work with them, and know that virtue and strength comes from him to bless or curse all sort of means.—*Richard Sibbes.*

Verse 19.—*" Consider mine enemies,"* etc. Or *look* upon them; but with another kind of look; so as he looked through the pillar of fire upon the Egyptians, and troubled them (Exod. xiv. 24), with a look of wrath and vengeance. The arguments he uses are taken both from the quantity and quality of his enemies, their number and their nature, *"For they are many;"* the hearts of the people of Israel, in general, being after Absalom (2 Sam. xv. 12, 13); and so the spiritual enemies of the Lord's people are many; their sins and corruptions, Satan, and his principalities and powers, and the men of this world. *"And they hate me with cruel hatred;"* like that of Simeon and Levi (Gen. xlix. 7); their hatred broke out in a cruel manner, in acts of force and cruelty; and it was the more cruel, inasmuch as it was without cause; and such is the hatred of Satan and his emissaries against the followers of Christ; who breathe out cruelty, thirst after their blood, and make themselves drunk with it; even their tender mercies are cruel, and much more their hatred.—*John Gill.*

Verse 19.—*"Consider mine enemies."* God needeth not hound out many creatures to punish man, he doeth that on himself. There is no kind of creature so hurtful to itself as he. Some hurt other kinds and spare their own, but mankind in all sorts of injuries destroyeth itself. Man to man is more crafty than a fox, more cruel than the tiger, and more fierce then a lion, and in a word, if he be left to himself man unto man is a devil.—*William Struther's "Christian Observations,"* 1629.

Verse 19, 20.—*"Consider mine enemies. . . . . O keep my soul and deliver me."* We may say of original concupiscence, strengthened and heightened by customary transgressions, its name is legion, for it is many. Hydra-like, it is a body with many heads; and when we cut off one head, one enormous impiety, there presently sprouts up another of like monstrous nature, like venomous guilt. From the womb then it is of original sin and sinful custom, as from the belly of the Trojan horse, there does issue forth a whole army of unclean lusts, to surround the soul in all its faculties, and the body too in all its members.— *Robert Mossom.*

Verse 20.—*"Let me be not ashamed; for I put my trust in thee."* When David reaches verse 20, we are reminded of Coriolanus betaking himself to the hall of Attius Tullus, and sitting as a helpless stranger there, claiming the king's hospitality, though aware of his having deserved to die at his hands. The psalmist throws himself on the compassions of an injured God with similar feelings; *"I trust in thee!"*—*Andrew A. Bonar.*

Verse 21.—*"For I trust in, or wait on thee."* As preservation is a continued creation, so is *waiting* a continued trusting; for, what trust believes by faith, it *waits for* by hope; and thus is trust a compound of both.—*Robert Mossom.*

Verse 22.—*"Redeem Israel, O God, out of all his troubles."* If thou wilt not pity and help me, yet spare thy people, who suffer for my sake, and in my sufferings.—*Matthew Pool.*

Verse 22.—*" Redeem Israel,"* etc. *In vita vel post mortem meam,*[*] either whiles I live, or after my death. This is every good man's care and prayer. None is in case to pray for the church, that hath not first made his own peace with God.— *John Trapp.*

Verse 22.—This most beautiful of "Psalms and hymns and spiritual songs" closes with a sweet petition—such an one, as every one of the true Israel of God would wish to depart with on his lips. *"Redeem Israel, O God, out of all his troubles."* It breathes the same holy aspiration as the aged Simeon's "Lord! now lettest thy servant depart in peace, for mine eyes have seen thy salvation." *Barton Bouchier.*

HINTS TO THE VILLAGE PREACHER.

Verse 1.—Heavenly machinery for uplifting an earthbound soul.

Verse 1.—Genuine devotion described and commended.

Verse 2.—The soul at anchor, and the two rocks from which it would be delivered.

Verse 3.—Shame out of place and in place.

Verse 4.—Practical divinity the best study; God the best teacher; Prayer the mode of entrance into the school.

Verses 4, 5.—"*Shew.*" "*Teach.*" "*Lead.*" Three classes in the school of grace.

Verse 5.—I. Sanctification desired. II. Knowledge sought. III. Assurance enjoyed. IV. Patience exercised.

Verse 5.—"*Thou art the God of my salvation.*" A rich and overflowing text.

Verse 5 (last clause).—How to spend the day with God.—*Matthew Henry.*

Verse 6.—The antiquity of mercy.

Verses 6, 7.—The three Remembers.

Verse 7 (first clause).—The best Act of Oblivion.—*Thomas Fuller.*

Verse 7.—Oblivion desired and remembrance entreated. Note "*my,*" and "*thy.*"

Verse 8.—Opposing attributes co-working. God teaching sinners—a great wonder.

---

[*] Rabbi David.

Verse 9.—" *The meek.*" Who they are? What are their privileges? How to be like them?

Verse 9 (*first clause*).—Moral purity needful to a well-balanced judgment.

Verse 10.—God's mercy and faithfulness in providence, and the persons who may derive comfort therefrom.

Verse 11.—A model prayer. Confession, argument, entreaty, etc.

Verse 11.—Great guilt no obstacle to the pardon of the returning sinner.— *Jonathan Edwards.*

Verse 12.—Holiness the best security for a well ordered life. Free-will at school, questioned and instructed.

Verse 13.—A man at ease for time and eternity.

Verse 14.—I. A secret, and who know it. II. A wonder, and who see it.

Verse 15. I. What we are like. A silly bird. II. What is our danger? "Net." III. Who is our friend? "The Lord." IV. What is our wisdom? "Mine eyes," etc.

Verse 16.—A desolate soul seeking heavenly company, and an afflicted spirit crying for divine mercy. Our God the balm of all our wounds.

Verses 16—18.—David is a petitioner as well as a sufferer; and those sorrows will never injure us that bring us near to God. Three things he prays for:— I. *Deliverance.* This we are called to desire, consistently with resignation to the divine will. II. *Notice.* A kind look from God is desirable at any time, in any circumstances; but in affliction and pain, it is like life from the dead. III. *Pardon.* Trials are apt to revive a sense of guilt.—*William Jay.*

Verse 17.—Special seasons of trouble and special resort to prayer for special deliverance.

Verse 18.—Two things are here taught us :—I. That a kind look from God is very desirable in affliction. II. That the sweetest cordial under trouble would be an assurance of divine forgiveness. I. That a kind look, etc. (subdivisions), 1. It is a look of special observation. 2. It is a look of tender compassion. 3. It is a look of support and assistance (with God, power and compassion go together). II. That the sweetest cordial, etc. (subdivisions), 1. Because trouble is very apt to bring our sins to remembrance. 2. Because a sense of pardon will in great measure remove all distressing fears of death and judgment. *Improvement.* 1. Let us adore the goodness of God, that one so great and glorious should bestow a favourable look upon any of our sinful race. 2. Let the benefit we have received from the Lord's looking upon us in *former* afflictions, engage us to *pray*, and encourage us to *hope*, that he will now look upon us again. 3. If a kind look from God be so comfortable, what must *heaven* be !—*Samuel Lavington.*

Verse 18.—I. It is well when our sorrows remind us of our sins. II. When we are as earnest to be forgiven as to be delivered. III. When we bring both to the right place in prayer. IV. When we are submissive about our sorrows—" *Look,*" etc.—but very explicit about our sins—" *Forgive,*" etc.

Verse 19.—The spiritual enemies of the saint. Their number, malice, craft, power, etc.

Verse 20.—Soul preservation. I. Its twofold character, " Keep," and " deliver." II. Its dreadful alternative, " Let me not be ashamed." III. Its effectual guarantee, " I put my trust in thee."

Verse 20.—A superhuman keeping, a natural fear, a spiritual trust.

Verse 21.—The open way of safety in action, and the secret way of safety in devotion.

Verse 22.—Jacob's life, as typical of ours, may illustrate this prayer.

Verse 22.—A prayer for the church militant.

WORKS ON THE TWENTY-FIFTH PSALM.

A Godly and Fruitful Exposition on the Twenty-fifth Psalme, the second of the Penitentials; (in "A Sacred Septenarie.") By ARCHIBALD SYMSON. 1638. [See p. 74.]

The Preacher's Tripartite, in Three Books. The First, to raise Devotion in Divine Meditations upon Psalm XXV. By R. MOSSOM, Preacher of God's Word, late at St. Peter's, Paul's Wharf, London, 1657. Folio.

Six Sermons in "Expository Discourses," by the late Rev. WILLIAM RICHARDSON, Subchanter of York Cathedral. 1825.

PSALM XXVI.

TITLE.—A Psalm of David. *The sweet singer of Israel appears before us in this Psalm as one enduring reproach ; in this he was the type of the great Son of David, and is an encouraging example to us to carry the burden of slander to the throne of grace. It is an ingenious surmise that this appeal to heaven was written by David at the time of the assassination of Ish-bosheth, by Baanah and Rechab, to protest his innocence of all participation in that treacherous murder ; the tenor of the Psalm certainly agrees with the supposed occasion, but it is not possible with such a slender clue to go beyond conjecture.*

DIVISION.—*Unity of subject is so distinctly maintained, that there are no sharp divisions. David Dickson has given an admirable summary in these words :—"He appealeth to God, the supreme Judge, in the testimony of a good conscience, bearing him witness ; first, of his endeavour to walk uprightly as a believer, verses, 1, 2, 3 ; secondly, of his keeping himself from the contagion of the evil counsel, sinful causes, and example of the wicked, verses, 4, 5 ; thirdly, of his purpose still to behave himself holily and righteously, out of love to be partaker of the public privileges of the Lord's people in the congregation, verses, 6, 7, 8. Whereupon he prayeth to be free of the judgment coming upon the wicked, verses, 9, 10, according as he had purposed to eschew their sins, verse 11 ; and he closeth his prayer with comfort and assurance of being heard, verse 12.*

EXPOSITION.

JUDGE me, O LORD ; for I have walked in mine integrity : I have trusted also in the LORD ; *therefore* I shall not slide.

2 Examine me, O LORD, and prove me ; try my reins and my heart.

3 For thy lovingkindness *is* before mine eyes : and I have walked in thy truth.

1. "*Judge me, O Jehovah.*"—A solemn appeal to the just tribunal of the heart-searching God, warranted by the circumstances of the writer, so far as regarded the particular offences with which he was wrongly charged. Worried and worn out by the injustice of men, the innocent spirit flies from its false accusers to the throne of Eternal Right. He had need have a clear case who dares to carry his suit into the King's Bench of heaven. Such an appeal as this is not to be rashly made on any occasion ; and as to the whole of our walk and conversation, it should never be made at all, except as we are justified in Christ Jesus : a far more fitting prayer for a sinful mortal is the petition, "Enter not into judgment with thy servant." "*For I have walked in mine integrity.*" He held integrity as his principle, and walked in it as his practice. David had not used any traitorous or unrighteous means to gain the crown, or to keep it ; he was conscious of having been guided by the noblest principles of honour in all his actions with regard to Saul and his family. What a comfort it is to have the approbation of one's own conscience ! If there be peace within the soul, the blustering storms of slander which howl around us are of little consideration. When the little bird in my bosom sings a merry song, it is no matter to me if a thousand owls hoot at me from without. "*I have trusted also in the Lord.*" Faith is the root and sap of integrity. He who leans upon the Lord is sure to walk in righteousness. David knew that God's covenant had given him the crown, and therefore he took no indirect or unlawful means to secure it ; he would not slay his enemy in the cave, nor suffer his men-at-arms to smite him when he slept unguarded on the plain. Faith will work hard for the Lord, and in the Lord's way, but she refuses so much as to lift a finger to fulfil the devices of unrighteous cunning. Rebecca acted out a great falsehood in order to fulfil the Lord's decree in favour of Jacob—this was unbelief ; but Abraham left the

Lord to fulfil his own purposes, and took the knife to slay his son—this was faith. Faith trusts God to accomplish his own decrees. Why should I steal when God has promised to supply my need? Why should I avenge myself when I know that the Lord has espoused my cause? Confidence in God is a most effectual security against sin. "*Therefore I shall not slide.*" Slippery as the way is, so that I walk like a man upon ice, yet faith keeps my heels from tripping, and will continue to do so. The doubtful ways of policy are sure sooner or later to give a fall to those who run therein, but the ways of honesty, though often rough, are always safe. We cannot trust in God if we walk crookedly; but straight paths and simple faith bring the pilgrim happily to his journey's end.

2. There are three modes of trial here challenged, which are said in the original to refer to trial by touch, trial by smell, and trial by fire. The psalmist was so clear from the charge laid against him, that he submitted himself unconditionally to any form of examination which the Lord might see fit to employ. "*Examine me, O Lord.*" Look me through and through; make a minute survey; put me to the question, cross-examine my evidence. "*And prove me.*" Put me again to trial; and see if I would follow such wicked designs as my enemies impute to me. "*Try my reins and my heart.*" Assay me as metals are assayed in the furnace, and do this to my most secret parts, where my affections hold their court; see, O God, whether or no I love murder, and treason, and deceit. All this is a very bold appeal, and made by a man like David, who feared the Lord exceedingly, it manifests a most solemn and complete conviction of innocence. The expressions here used should teach us the thoroughness of the divine judgment, and the necessity of being in all things profoundly sincere, lest we be found wanting at the last. Our enemies are severe with us with the severity of spite, and this a brave man endures without a fear; but God's severity is that of unswerving right. Who shall stand against such a trial? The sweet singer asks, "Who can stand before his cold?" and we may well enquire, "Who can stand before the heat of his justice?"

3. "*For thy lovingkindness is before mine eyes.*"—An object of memory and a ground of hope. A sense of mercy received sets a fair prospect before the faithful mind in its gloomiest condition, for it yields visions of mercies yet to come, visions not visionary but real. Dwell, dear reader, upon that celestial word *lovingkindness*. It has a heavenly savour. Is it not an unmatchable word, unexcelled, unrivalled? The goodness of the Lord to us should be before our eyes as a motive actuating our conduct; we are not under the bondage of the law, but we are under the sweet constraints of grace, which are far more mighty, although far more gentle. Men sin with the law before their eyes, but divine love, when clearly seen, sanctifies the conversation. If we were not so forgetful of the way of mercy in which God walks towards us, we should be more careful to walk in the ways of obedience toward him. "*And I have walked in thy truth.*" The psalmist was preserved from sin by his assurance of the truthfulness of God's promise, which truth he endeavoured to imitate as well as to believe. Observe from this verse that an experience of divine love will show itself in a practical following of divine truth; those who neglect either the doctrinal or practical parts of truth must not wonder if they lose the experimental enjoyment of it. Some *talk of* truth, it is better to *walk in* it. Some vow to do well in future, but their resolutions come to nothing; only the regenerate man can say "*I have walked* in thy truth."

4 I have not sat with vain persons, neither will I go in with dissemblers.

5 I have hated the congregation of evil doers; and will not sit with the wicked.

So far from being himself an open offender against the laws of God, the psalmist had not even associated with the lovers of evil. He had kept aloof from the men of Belial. A man is known by his company, and if we have kept ourselves apart from the wicked, it will always be evidence in our favour should our character be impugned. He who was never in the parish is not likely to have stolen the corn. He who never went to sea is clearly not the man who scuttled the ship.

4. " *I have not sat with vain persons.*"—True citizens have no dealings with traitors. David had no seat in the parliament of triflers. They were not his boon companions at feasts, nor his advisers in council, nor his associates in conversation. We must needs see, and speak, and trade, with men of the world, but we must on no account take our rest and solace in their empty society. Not only the profane, but the vain are to be shunned by us. All those who live for this life only are vain, chaffy, frothy men, quite unworthy of a Christian's friendship. Moreover as this vanity is often allied with falsehood, it is well to save ourselves altogether from this untoward generation, lest we should be led from bad to worse and from tolerating the vain should come to admire the wicked. "*Neither will I go in with dissemblers.*" Since I know that hypocritical piety is double iniquity, I will cease all acquaintance with pretenders. If I must needs walk the same street, I will not enter the same door and spend my time in their society. The congregation of the hypocrites is not one with which we should cultivate communion ; their ultimate rendezvous will be the lowest pit of hell, let us drop their acquaintance now ! for we shall not desire it soon. They hang their beads around their necks and carry the devil in their hearts. This clause is in the future tense, to indicate that the writer felt no desire to begin an acquaintance with characters whom up till then he had shunned. We must maintain the separated path with more and more circumspection as we see the great redemption day approaching. Those who would be transfigured with Jesus, must not be disfigured by conformity to the world. The resolution of the psalmist suggests, that even among professed followers of truth we must make distinctions, for as there are vain persons out of the church, so there are dissemblers in it and both are to be shunned with scrupulous decision.

5. " *I have hated the congregation of evil doers.*"—A severe sentence, but not too severe. A man who does not hate evil terribly, does not love good heartily. Men, as men, we must always love, for they are our neighbours, and therefore to be loved as ourselves ; but evil doers, as such, are traitors to the Great King, and no loyal subject can love traitors. What God hates we must hate. The congregation or assembly of evil doers, signifies violent men in alliance and conclave for the overthrow of the innocent ; such synagogues of Satan are to be held in abhorrence. What a sad reflection it is that there should be a congregation of evil doers as well as a congregation of the upright, a church of Satan as well as a church of God; a seed of the serpent as well as a seed of the woman; an old Babylon as well as a new Jerusalem ; a great whore sitting upon many waters, to be judged in wrath, as well as a chaste bride of the Lamb to be crowned at his coming. " *And will not sit with the wicked.*" Saints have a seat at another table, and will never leave the King's dainties for the husks of the swine-trough. Better to sit with the blind, and the halt, and the lame, at the table of mercy, than with the wicked in their feasts of ungodliness, yea, better to sit on Job's dunghill than on Pharaoh's throne. Let each reader see well to his company, for such as we keep in this world, we are likely to keep in the next.

6 I will wash mine hands in innocency : so will I compass thine altar, O LORD :

7 That I may publish with the voice of thanksgiving, and tell of all thy wondrous works.

8 LORD, I have loved the habitation of thy house, and the place where thine honour dwelleth.

6. " *I will wash mine hands in innocency.*"—He would publicly avow himself to be altogether clear of the accusations laid against him, and if any fault in other

matters could be truthfully alleged against him, he would for the future abstain from it. The washing of the hands is a significant action to set forth our having no connection with a deed, as we still say, "I wash my hands of the whole business." As to perfect innocence, David does not here claim it, but he avows his innocence of the crimes whereof he was slanderously accused ; there is, however, a sense in which we may be washed in absolute innocence, for the atoning blood makes us clean every whit. We ought never to rest satisfied short of a full persuasion of our complete cleansing by Jesus' precious blood. "*So will I compass thine altar, O Lord.*" Priests unto God must take great care to be personally cleansed ; the brazen laver was as needful as the golden altar ; God's worship requires us to be holy in life. He who is unjust to man cannot be acceptably religious towards God. We must not bring our thank offerings with hands defiled with guilt. To love justice and purity is far more acceptable to God, than ten thousands of the fat of fed beasts. We see from this verse that holy minds delight in the worship of the Lord, and find their sweetest solace at his altar ; and that it is their deepest concern never to enter upon any course of action which would unfit them for the most sacred communion with God. Our eye must be upon the altar which sanctifieth both the giver and the gift, yet we must never draw from the atoning sacrifice an excuse for sin, but rather find in it a most convincing argument for holiness.

7. "*That I may publish with the voice of thanksgiving.*" David was so far instructed that he does not mention the typical offering, but discerns the spiritual offering which was intended thereby, not the groans of bullocks, but songs of gratitude the spiritual worshipper presents. To sound abroad the worthy praises of the God of all grace should be the every-day business of a pardoned sinner. Let men slander us as they will, let us not defraud the Lord of his praises ; let dogs bark, but let us like the moon shine on. "*And tell of all thy wondrous works.*" God's people should not be tongue-tied. The wonders of divine grace are enough to make the tongue of the dumb sing. God's works of love are wondrous if we consider the unworthiness of their objects, the costliness of their method, and the glory of their result. And as men find great pleasure in discoursing upon things remarkable and astonishing, so the saints rejoice to tell of the great things which the Lord hath done for them.

8. "*Lord, I have loved the habitation of thy house.*" Into the abodes of sin he would not enter, but the house of God he had long loved, and loved it still. We were sad children if we did not love our Father's dwelling-place. Though we own no sacred buildings, yet the church of the living God is the house of God, and true Christians delight in her ordinances, services, and assemblies. O that all our days were Sabbaths ! "*And the place where thine honour dwelleth.*" In his church where God is had in honour at all times, where he reveals himself in the glory of his grace, and is proclaimed by his people as the Lord of all. We come not together as the Lord's people to honour the preacher, but to give glory to God ; such an occupation is most pleasant to the saints of the Most High. What are those gatherings where God is not honoured, are they not an offence to his pure and holy eyes, and are they not a sad stumbling-block to the people of God ? It brings the scalding-tear upon our cheek to hear sermons in which the honour of God is so far from being the preacher's object, that one might almost imagine that the preacher worshipped the dignity of manhood, and thought more of it than of the Infinite Majesty of God.

9 Gather not my soul with sinners, nor my life with bloody men : 10 In whose hand *is* mischief, and their right hand is full of bribes.

9. "*Gather not my soul with sinners.*"—Lord, when, like fruit, I must be gathered, put me not in the same basket with the best of sinners, much less with the worst of them. The company of sinners is so distasteful to us here, that we cannot endure the thought of being bound up in the same bundle with them to all eternity. Our comfort is, that the Great Husbandman discerns the tares from

the wheat, and will find a separate place for distinct characters. In the former verses we see that the psalmist kept himself clear of profane persons, and this is to be understood as a reason why he should not be thrust into their company at the last. Let us think of the doom of the wicked, and the prayer of the text will forcibly rise to our lips; meanwhile, as we see the rule of judgment by which like is gathered to its like, we who have passed from death unto life have nothing to fear. *"Nor my life with bloody men."* Our soul sickens to hear them speak; their cruel dispatches, in which they treat the shooting of their fellow-men as rare sport, are horrifying to us; Lord, let us not be shut up in the same prison with them; nay, the same paradise with such men would be a hell, if they remained as they now are.

10. *"In whose hands is mischief."*—They have both hands full of it, plotting it and carrying it out. *"And their right hand,"* with which they are most dexterous, *"is full of bribes;"* like thieves who would steal with impunity, they carry a sop for the dogs of justice. He who gives bribes is every way as guilty as the man who takes them, and in the matter of our parliamentary elections the rich villain who gives the bribe is by far the worse. Bribery, in any form or shape, should be as detestable to a Christian as carrion to a dove, or garbage to a lamb. Let those whose dirty hands are fond of bribes remember that neither death nor the devil can be bribed to let them escape their well-earned doom.

11 But as for me, I will walk in mine integrity : redeem me, and be merciful unto me.

Here is the lover of godliness entering his personal protest against unright-eous gain. He is a Nonconformist, and is ready to stand alone in his Noncon-formity. Like a live fish, he swims against the stream. Trusting in God, the psalmist resolves that the plain way of righteousness shall be his choice, and those who will, may prefer the tortuous paths of violence and deceit. Yet, he is by no means a boaster, or a self-righteous vaunter of his own strength, for he cries for redemption and pleads for mercy. Our integrity is not absolute nor inherent, it is a work of grace in us, and is marred by human infirmity ; we must, therefore, resort to the redeeming blood and to the throne of mercy, confessing that though we are saints among men, we must still bow as sinners before God.

12 My foot standeth in an even place : in the congregations will I bless the LORD.

The song began in the minor, but it has now reached the major key. Saints often sing themselves into happiness. The *even place* upon which our foot stands is the sure, covenant faithfulness, eternal promise and immutable oath of the Lord of Hosts ; there is no fear of falling from this solid basis, or of its being removed from under us. Established in Christ Jesus, by being vitally united to him, we have nothing left to occupy our thoughts but the praises of our God. Let us not forsake the assembling of ourselves together, and when assembled, let us not be slow to contribute our portion of thanksgiving. Each saint is a witness to divine faithfulness, and should be ready with his testimony. As for the slanderers, let them howl outside the door while the children sing within.

EXPLANATORY NOTES AND QUAINT SAYINGS.

Whole Psalm.—This Psalm is coupled on to the foregoing by thoughts and words. At the close of the foregoing the psalmist had prayed for *integrity* (verse 1). Unless this Psalm is regarded as a sequel to the preceding one, it will seem vainglorious; but being combined with the penitential acknowledgments of sin, and with the earnest supplications for pardon and grace, and with the earnest profession of faith that God has heard his prayer, which breathe forth in the foregoing Psalm, it will be seen that the declarations which the psalmist now makes of integrity, are not assertions of human merit, but acknowledgments of divine mercy. As Augustine says, "*Non merita mea, sed misericordia tua, ante oculos meos est.*"—*Christopher Wordsworth.*

Verse 1.—"*Judge me, O Lord; for I have walked in mine integrity.*"—A good cause, a good conscience, and a good deportment, are good grounds of appeal to God.—*Ingram Cobbin.*

Verse 1.—"*Judge me, O Lord.*" Nothing is so pleasing to him that is upright as to know that God knoweth he is so. As it is a small matter with those who are sincere to be condemned by men, so it is not much with them to be condemned or approved by them; for indeed neither "he that commendeth himself," as the apostle speaks (2 Cor. x. 18), nor he that is commended by others, "is approved, but whom the Lord commendeth." The testimony, or letters commendatory of all the men in the world will do us no good, unless God give us his also.—*Joseph Caryl.*

Verse 1.—"*Judge me, O Lord.*" As an instance of appeal to heaven, we quote that mighty preacher of the Word, George Whitfield. "However some may account me a mountebank and an enthusiast, one that is only going to make you methodically mad; they may breathe out their invectives against me, yet Christ knows all; he takes notice of it, and I shall leave it to him to plead my cause, for he is a gracious Master. I have already found him so, and am sure he will continue so. Vengeance is his, and he will repay it."—*George Whitfield*, 1714—1770.

Verse 1.—"*Integrity.*" הֹם, or תֻּמִּים is used of whatever is uninjured, or is free from any spot or blemish; and hence we find the term applied to an unblemished animal offered in sacrifice. Lev. i. 3; iii. 9.—*George Phillips.*

Verse 1.—"*Mine integrity.*" There is a force in the possessive pronoun "my," which must be attended to. The psalmist intimates that he had proceeded in one uniform course, notwithstanding all the devices of his enemies. *W. Wilson, D.D.*

Verse 1.—"*I have trusted in the Lord.*" Trust in God is the *fountain* of "integrity." Whoever places his hope in God need not seek to advance his worldly interests by violating his duty towards his neighbour: he waits for everything *from above*, and is, at the same time, always determined that he will not be deprived of the favour of his heavenly Father through violating his commandments.—*E. W. Hengstenberg.*

Verse 1.—"*I shall not slide.*" It is a striking word, as fully expressive of the completeness of God's protection and the security of his upholding hand as the psalmist's language of the integrity of his walk and trust in God. It is not, as in our Prayer-book version, "I shall not fall," but it is, "*I shall not even slide;*" not even make a false step or stumble.—*Barton Bouchier.*

Verse 2.—The psalmist uses three words, "*examine,*" "*prove,*" "*try.*" These words are designed to include all the modes in which the reality of anything is tested; and they imply together that he wished the most *thorough* investigation to be made; he did not shrink from any test.—*Albert Barnes.*

Verse 2.—" *Examine* "—" *prove* "—" *try*." **As** gold, by fire, is severed and parted from dross, so singleness of heart and true Christian simplicity is best seen and made most evident in troubles and afflictions. In prosperity every man will seem godly, but afflictions do draw out of the heart whatsoever is there, whether it be good or bad.—*Robert Cawdray.*

Verse 2. —" *Prove me.*" The work of conscience within us doth *prove* us. God hath set up a light within us, and when this is enlightened by the Word, then it makes a man's breast full of light. Now a faithful godly man loveth that this should be tender, active, speaking out of God's Word for every duty, and against every sin. You see the quickness of it in David, when it is said, " His heart smote him ;" and 1 John iii., " If thy heart condemn thee, God is greater than thy heart." Alas! if thou within thine own self judgest thyself to sin thus and thus, God doth much more. Try thy integrity ; art thou willing to have a tender conscience, and an informed conscience? Dost thou love to hear what that speaks out of God's Word? whether peace or duty? this is comfort- able. But on the other side, if thou art a man that rebellest against the light of it, wouldst fain put out the sting of it, wouldst be glad to feel no such living thing in thy breast, then thou hast c use to suspect thyself. Oh, it is to be feared that there are many that give themselves to lusts, and carnal pleasures, that so they may put a foggy mist between their conscience and themselves. Others dig into the world, labouring to become senseless, that so there may be an eclipse of this light by the interposition of the earth. Others run to damnable heresies, denying Scriptures, God, heaven, hell ; pleading for an universal salvation of all. What are these but refuges of guilty consciences? We must distinguish between our carnal concupiscence, and conscience ; between deluded imagina- tions, and conscience ; between an erroneous and scrupulous conscience, and a well-grounded and truly informed conscience ; and when we have done so, we must follow conscience as far as that follows the Word.—*Anthony Burgess.*

Verse 2.—" *Reins* . . . . . *heart.*"—The " *reins*," as the seat of the lower animal passions ; the " *heart*," as comprising not only the higher affections, but also the will and the conscience. He thus desires to keep nothing back ; he will submit himself to the searching flame of the Great Refiner, that all dross of self-deception may be purged away.—*J. J. Stewart Perowne.*

Verse 3.—The practical effect of divine goodness is seen in this text. As the chief thing communicated from God is the divine nature, whereby we are made to resemble him, so the promises of God set home upon the soul are the means of communication ; they are the milk and honey of the Scripture, which do not cherish the old man, but support the new ; they are not pillows for sinful sloth, but spurs to holy diligence. The promises of grace animate the soul to duty ; and when we thus see the goodness of the Lord, it encourages our subjection to his government.—*Timothy Cruso.*

Verses 3, 4.—" *I have walked in thy truth, I have not sat with vain persons.*" Be as careful as thou canst, that the persons thou choosest for thy companions be such as fear God. The man in the gospel was possessed with the devil, who dwelt among the tombs, and conversed with graves and carcasses. Thou art far from walking after the good Spirit, if thou choosest to converse with open sepulchres, and such as are dead in sins and trespasses. God will not shake the wicked by the hand, as the Vulgate reads (Job viii. 20), neither must the godly man. David proves the sincerity of his course, by his care to avoid such society : " *I have walked in thy truth ; I have not sat with vain persons.*" There is a twofold " *truth.*" 1. Truth of doctrine. Thy law is the truth, free from all dross of corruption and falsehood of error. 2. Truth of affection, or of the inward parts. This may be called " *thy truth*," or God's truth, though man be the subject of it, partly because it proceedeth from him, partly because it is so pleasant to him ; in which respect a broken heart is called the " sacrifice of God." Psalm li. 6. As if he had said, I could not have walked in the power of religion, and in integrity, if I had associated with vile and vain company; I could never have walked in thy precepts if I had "*sat with vain persons.*" Observe the phrase, "*I have not sat with vain persons.*" 1. Sitting is a posture of choice. It is at a man's liberty, whether he will sit or stand. 2. Sitting is a posture of pleasure. Men sit for their ease, and with delight; therefore, the glorified are said to "sit in heavenly places." Eph. ii. 6. 3. Sitting is a posture of staying or abiding. 2 Kings v. 3. Standing is a posture of going, but sitting of staying. The blessed, who shall forever be with the Lord and his chosen, are mentioned "to sit down with Abraham, Isaac, and Jacob, in the kingdom of heaven." Matt. viii. 11. David in neither of these senses durst *sit with vain persons.*" He might, as his occasions required, use their company, but durst not knowingly choose such company. They could not be the object of his election who were not the object of his affection. "*I hate the congregation of evil doers,*" saith he. As sitting is a posture of pleasure, he did not sit with vain persons. He was sometimes amongst them to his sorrow, but not to his solace. They were to him, as the Canaanites to the Israelites, pricks in his eyes, and thorns in his sides. "Woe is me, that I sojourn in Mesech, that I dwell in the tents of Kedar!" Psalm cxx. 5. It caused grief, not gladness, that he was forced to be amongst the profane.—*George Swinnock.*

Verse 4.—"*I have not sat with vain persons.*" There is a necessary commerce with men in buying and selling, or as the apostle says, "We must needs go out of the world," but do not voluntarily choose the company of the wicked. 1 Cor. v. 10. "I have written unto you not to keep company," etc. 1 Cor. v. 11. Do not be too familiar with them. What do Christ's doves among birds of prey? What do virgins among harlots? The company of the wicked is very defiling, it is like going among them that have the plague. "They were mingled among the heathen and learned their works." If you mingle bright armor with rusty, the bright armor will not brighten the rusty, but the rusty armor will spoil the bright. Pharaoh taught Joseph to swear, but Joseph did not teach Pharaoh to pray.—*Thomas Watson.*

Verse 4.—"*Neither will I go with dissemblers.*" Chaldee: "I will not go in with those that hide themselves to do evil." Wickedness is uncandid, and loves concealment, while truth and righteousness are open, and seek scrutiny. Job xxiv. 13—17; John iii. 20, 21. None will deny that the candid man has far fewer troubles with his own conduct than the tortuous and deceitful. The righteous shun the wicked both for the *sin* and for the misery that are in their ways.—*William S. Plumer.*

Verse 4.—"*Dissemblers.*" The hypocrite has much angel without, more devil within. He fries in words, freezes in works; speaks by ells, doth good by inches. He is a stinking dunghill, covered over with snow; a loose-hung mill that keeps great clacking, but grinds no grist; a lying hen that cackles when she hath not laid.—*Thomas Adams.*

Verse 4.—"*Dissemblers.*" Perhaps when the bright sunbeams of an early spring have robed all nature in a smiling garb, you have taken your little baskets, and gone in quest of a bank of sweet-smelling modest violets, and you may have found flowers so like them, in form and color, that you have been deceived, and eagerly grasped your prize; but alas! the sweet odour which should have scented the gale, was found wanting, and betrayed the dog violet. An apt emblem this of those, who, "having the form of godliness, deny the power thereof." 2 Tim. iii. 5.—*Mrs. Rogers, in "The Shepherd King."*

Verses 4, 5.—As rotten apples corrupt those sound ones that do touch them and lie close to them, even so the evil manners and bad conditions of the ungodly do infect those that keep them company.—*Robert Cawdray.*

Verses 4, 5.—"It is difficult (saith a late ingenious writer) even to a miracle to keep God's commandments and evil company too." How suddenly after your soul-refreshments in your closet communion have you lost all your heats and spiritual fervencies, which you had in secret, and have instantly cooled by going forth into cold and corrupt air! When a saint hath been in private ravished with the love of God and the joys of heaven, and afterwards meets with company, which neither doth nor can speak one word of such matters, what a damp is it to him! What a quenching, as it were, of the Spirit of God in him! Nay, is not that true which one saith, that "the people of God do generally lose more by worldly men, that are of a blameless conversation before men, than they lose by wicked and profane men"?—*Lewis Stuckley.*

Verses 4, 5, 9.—He that would not be found amongst sinners in the other world, must take heed that he do not frequent their company in this. Those whom the constable finds wandering with vagrants, may be sent with them to the house of correction. "Lord," said a good woman, on her death bed, when in some doubt of her salvation, "send me not to hell amongst wicked men, for thou knowest I never loved their company all my life long." David deprecates their future doom upon the like ground, and argueth it as a sign of his sincerity: *"I have not sat with vain persons, neither will I go in with dissemblers. I have hated the congregation of evil doers; and will not sit with the wicked. . . O gather not my soul with sinners."* Lord, I have not loved the wicked so well as to sit with them for a little time, and shall I live with them for ever? I have not lain amongst them rotting on the earth; and wilt thou gather my soul with those sticks for the unquenchable fire of hell? Lord, I have been so far from liking, that thou knowest I have loathed the congregation of evil doers. Do not I hate them that hate thee? Yea, I hate them with perfect hatred; and shall thy friends fare as thy foes? I appeal to thy Majesty, that my great comfort is in thy chosen. I rejoice only to be amongst thy children here, and shall I be excluded their company hereafter? "*O do not gather my soul with sinners,*" for the wine-press of thine eternal anger! Marcion, the heretic, seeing Polycarp, wondered that he would not own him. Do you not know me, Polycarp? Yea, saith Polycarp, "*Scio te esse primogenitum diaboli;*" "I know thee to be the firstborn of the devil," and so despised him.—*George Swinnock.*

Verse 5.—"*I have hated the congregation of evil doers,*" etc. The hatred of God's enemies, *quâ* his enemies—"yea, I hate them right sore" so entirely opposed to the indifferentism of the present day, has always been one distinguishing mark of his ancient servants. Witness Phinehas (Psalm cvi. 41); "And that was counted unto him for righteousness unto all generations for evermore;" Samuel with Agag; Elias with the priests of Baal. And notice the commendation of the angel of Ephesus, "Thou canst not bear them that are evil." Rev. ii. 2.—*J. M. Neale.*

Verse 5.—"*I have hated the congregation of evil doers.*" We consider them as God's enemies, so we hate them; not their persons, but their vices; for that, as Augustine defineth it, is *odium perfectum*, a perfect hatred. And indeed it is the hatred that God beareth to his enemies; for "the wrath of God is revealed from heaven against all ungodliness and unrighteousness of men" (Rom. i. 18); not against their persons—they are his workmanship, and carry his image in some sort, though much disfigured; but against the unrighteousness and ungodliness of men, by which their persons do stand obnoxious to his displeasure. And thus I find the saints of God have triumphed over the wicked, as Israel over Pharaoh, and the Gileadites over the children of Ammon; not rejoicing in the destruction of God's creatures, but of God's enemies; and wishing with Deborah and Barak, "So let all thine enemies perish, O Lord." This is no more but an applauding of the judgment of God, and a celebration of his justice.—*Edward Marbury.*

Verse 5.—"*I have hated,*" etc. Consider that there can be no true friendship betwixt a godly and a wicked person; therefore it concerneth thee to be the more wary in thy choice. He that in factions hath an eye to power, in friendship will have an eye to virtue. Friendship, according to the philosopher, is one soul in two bodies. But how can they ever be of one soul that are as different as air and earth, and as contrary as fire and water? All true love is, *motus animi ad fruendum Deo propter ipsum; se et proximo propter Deum*—a motion of the soul towards the enjoyment of God for himself, and his neighbours for God's sake; so that he can never truly love man who doth not love his Maker. God is the only foundation upon which we can build friendship; therefore such as live without him, cannot love us in him. That building which is loose, without this foundation can never stand long. A wicked man may call that profession he maketh to his brother by the name of love, but heathens can tell us that virtue alone is the hand which can twist the cords of love; that other combinations are but a confederacy, and all other but conjunctions in hypocrisy.—*George Swinnock.*

Verse 5.—Wheresoever we perceive any people to worship God truly after his word, there we may be certain the church of Christ to be, unto the which we ought to associate ourselves, and to desire, with the prophet David, to praise God in the midst of this church. But if we behold, through the iniquity of time, congregations to be made with counterfeit religion, otherwise than the word of God doth teach, we ought then, if we be required to be companions thereof, to say again with David, "*I have hated the synagogue of the malignant, and will not sit with the wicked.*" In the Apocalypse, the church of Ephesus is highly commended, because she tried such as said they were apostles and were not in deed, and therefore would not abide the company of them. Further, God commanded his people that they should not seek Bethel, neither enter into Galgala, where idolatry was used, by the mouth of his prophet Amos.—*John Philpot (Martyr). Burnt at Smithfield, 1555.*

Verse 5.—How few consider how they harden wicked men by an intimacy with them, whereas withdrawment from them might be a means to make them ashamed! Whilst we are merry and jovial with them, we make them believe their condition is not deplorable, their danger is not great; whereas if we shunned them, as we would a bowed wall, whilst they remain enemies to the Lord, this might do them good, for the startling of them, and rousing of them out of their unhappy security and strong delusions wherein they are held.—*Lewis Stuckley.*

Verse 6.—"*I will wash mine hands in innocency.*" There are two eminent lavers in the gospel; the first, Christ's bath, a hot bath, *lavacrum sanguinis*, the laver of Christ's blood; the second, our bath, a cold bath, *lavacrum lachrimarum*, the laver of repentance. These two mixed together will prove a sovereign composition, wrought first by Christ himself when he sweat water and blood. The first is as that pool of Bethesda into which whosoever enters with *faith*, is healed; the blood of Christ is the true laver of regeneration, a fountain set open for Judah and Jerusalem to wash in. "The blood of Christ purgeth us from all sins." 1 John i. 7. We account it charity in mothers to feed their children with their own milk: how dear is the love of Christ, that both washeth and feeds us with his own blood! No sooner are we born in Christ, but just as our mother's, so Christ's blood is turned into milk, nourishing us to everlasting salvation. What is *calamus benjamini*, or storax, or a thousand rivers of oil, to make us clean, except the Lord purge and cleanse us? No; 'tis his blood "that speaks better things than the blood of Abel." "Unto him, therefore, that loved us and washed us from our sins in his own blood, and hath made us kings and priests to God and his Father: to him be glory and dominion for ever." Rev. i. 5. 6. But yet 'tis the second bath, the laver of repentance, that must apply and make the first operative. This bath of Mary Magdalene's repentance, it is a kind of rebaptisation, giving strength and effect to the first washing. And it implies a three-fold act: first, to bruise our hearts by *contrition;* secondly, to lay our wounds open by *confession* to God; thirdly, to *wash our hands in innocency*, by *satisfaction* to men. . . . Wash now and wash all; from the crown of the head to the sole of the foot there is nothing in us but wounds and sores; yet above all there is something here in it that David washeth his "*hands.*" Indeed it is not enough to come with wet eyes, if we come with foul hands to offer with unwashen hands; the Gentiles would not do it. Contrition and confession to God make not up complete repentance without satisfaction to men. *Non remittitur peccatum nisi restituatur ablatum:** it is as true as old, and in old father Latimer's English it is, "Either there must be restitution, open or secret, or else hell." Whoever repairs not the wrong, rejoiceth in the sin. Prov. ii. 14. Where there is no satisfaction, "*Non agitur sed fingitur pœnitentia,*" saith St. Augustine; and those who restore not all, wash not their whole hands, they dip only the tips of their fingers. Extortion, rapine, bribery, these are the sins of the hands (sins so proper to the Jews, that they may well conceive as they do that the devil lies all night on their hands, and that is it makes them so diligent in washing); but as for us Christians, unless these vipers be shaken off our hands, though ye cover the altar of the Lord with tears, with weeping, and with crying out, yet if you continue in your pollutions, God regards not your offering any more, nor will he receive it with good will at your hands. Matt. ii. 13. *Isaac Bargrave's Sermon before the House of Commons,* 1623.

Verse 6.—"*I will wash mine hands in innocency: so will I compass thine altar, O Lord.*" If *greatness* might have privileged this person from impurity, David was a king; if the *grace of his soul* might have freed him from the soil of sin, he was "a man after God's own heart." But let not great men put too much trust in their greatness; the longer the robe is, the more soil it contracts: great power may prove the mother of great damnation. And as for purity, there is a generation that say there's no sin in them, but they deceive themselves; there is no truth in them. Whatever Rome's φυσιόλογοι pretend for the power of nature, and of free will, we wretched sinners are taught to conceive more truly of our own infirmity. Christ's own apostle, stout Thomas, failed in the faith of his resurrection; Peter (whose chair is now the pretended seat of infallibility) denied his Master; David, "a man after God's own heart," hath need of *washing;* and who can say, I am pure in the sight of the Lord? Certainly, O Lord, no flesh is righteous in thy sight. No; this is the best ground of Christian felicity, if with David we fall to a sight of our own sins; if with the Publican we strike our own breasts, and not with the Pharisee, cast our eye so much upon other men's faults. Why should we, like tailors, measure all men but ourselves? as if the best of us had not sin enough of his own to think on. See how David calls himself to account for his own sins; "O Lord, I know mine iniquity, and my sin is ever before me." Oh, the powerful effect of Christian devotion, when by the reflective act of the understanding, science is turned into conscience, and our knowledge is but the glass of our imperfection, the glass wherein the sight of our sins sends us presently to God, as it did David here, who makes this account only betwixt God and his own soul, "*I, O Lord.*" First, he takes his rise from humility and the sight of his own sins, and he soars up by the wings of faith to the throne of God's mercy: "*I, O Lord.*" He sees with his own eyes, and not only with the church, or the priest's spectacles; he is his own penitentiary and confessor; here's no intercession by saints, no masses, merits, indulgences, trentals, dirges: all's done betwixt God and him: "*I, O Lord.*" With the eye of *humility* he looks to himself and his own misery; then with the eye of *faith* to God and his mercy, and from both these results a third virtue of *repentance* in the act of preparation, washing the soil of sin in the bath of sorrow: "*I will wash mine hands,*" etc.—*Isaac Bargrave.*

Verse 6.—"*I will wash my hands in purity.*" Referring in these words, to the ordinary use of the sacrifices, he makes a distinction between himself and those who professed to offer the same divine worship, and thrust themselves forward in the services of the sanctuary, as if they alone had the sole right to perform them. As David, therefore, and these hypocrites were one in this respect, that they entered the sanctuary, and surrounded the sacred altar together, he proceeds to show that he was a true worshipper, declaring that he not only diligently attended to the external rites, but came to worship God

---

* Augustine.

with unfeigned devotion. It is obvious that he alludes to the solemn rite of washing which was practised under the law. He, accordingly, reproves the gross superstition of hypocrites, who, in seeking only the purification of water, neglected true purification; whereas it was God's design, in the appointment of the outward sign, to put men in mind of their inward pollution, and thus to encourage them to repentance. The outward washing alone, instead of profiting hypocrites, kept them at a greater distance from God. When the psalmist, therefore, says, "*I will wash my hands in innocence*," he intimates that they only gather more pollution and filth by their washings. The Hebrew word, נִקָּיוֹן *nikkayon*, signifies the cleanness of anything, and is figuratively used for *innocence*. We thus see, that as hypocrites derive no moral purity whatever from their washings, David mocks at the labour with which they vainly toil and torment themselves in such rites.—*John Calvin*.

Verse 6.—"*I will wash mine hands*," etc. David willing to express his coming with a pure heart to pray to God, doth it by this similitude of a priest; that as a priest *washes his hands*, and *then offers oblation*, so had he constantly joined *purity* and *devotion* together.—*Henry Hammond*.

Verse 6.—"*In innocency*." The very ἀκμή and crown of all our preparation, the purest water we can wash in, is *innocency;* and *innocency* is a virtue of the heart as well as of the hand. "Cleanse your hands, ye sinners; and purify your hearts, ye double minded." James iv. 8. I could wish our washing might be like Cyprian's baptising, *ad tincturam*, even till we were dyed in repentance and the blood of Christ. Let the quantity of thy sins be the measure of thy repentance. First offer thine *innocency*, then thy sacrifice. It is not enough that you come this day by order, you must come with *innocency*. God requires the duty of the second table, as well as of the first; he abhors the outward act of piety where he finds no conscience and practice of *innocency*.—*Isaac Bargrave*.

Verse 6 (*first clause*).—One morning, as Gotthold was pouring water into a basin, he recollected the words of Scripture: "*I will wash my hands in innocency*," a text which shows how diligently the royal prophet had endeavoured to lead a blameless life, and walk habitually in the fear of God. Upon this he mused, and said, Henceforth, my God, every time I pour out water to wash with, I will call to mind that it is my duty to cleanse my hands from wicked actions, my mouth from wicked words, and my heart from wicked lusts and desires, that so I may be enabled to lift holy hands unto thee, and with unspotted lips and heart worship thee, to the best of my ability. What will it profit me to strive after outward purity, if my heart is filthy and abominable in thy sight? Can the food nourish me which I have earned with polluted hands, or seized with violence and injustice, or eaten with insensibility and ingratitude? Ah! no, my God; far from me be food like this. My first care shall be to maintain a blameless walk; my next, when I have thoughtlessly defiled myself, to cleanse and wash away the stain, and remove mine iniquity from thine eyes. "*Purge me, O my God, and I shall be clean: wash me, and I shall be whiter than snow.*" Psalm li. 7.—*Christian Scriver* (1629—1693), in "*Gotthold's Emblems.*"

Verse 6.—"*I will compass thine altar, O Lord.*" On the next day after this feast [the Feast of Tabernacles], the people compassed the altar seven times, with palm boughs in their hands, in the remembrance of the overthrow of Jericho. . . . Not only the boughs, but the days of this whole Feast of Tabernacles, were termed *Hosannoth*, from the usual acclamation of the people whilst they carried the boughs up and down.—*Thomas Godwyn, B.D.* (1587—1643), in "*Moses and Aaron.*"

Verse 6.—By the phrase *compassing the altar*, either he alludes to some Levitical custom of going about the altar, as the priests did in the oblation of their sacrifices; and the people, especially those of them who were more devout and zealous, who possibly moved from place to place, but still within their own court, that they might discern what was done on the several sides of the altar, and so be the more affected with it; or rather he implies that he would offer many sacrifices together, which would employ the priests round about the altar.—*Matthew Pool.*

Verse 8.—"*Lord, I have loved the habitation of thy house,*" etc. "I have in my congregation," said a venerable minister of the gospel, "a worthy, aged woman, who has for many years been so deaf as not to distinguish the loudest sound, and yet she is always one of the first in the meeting. On asking the reason of her constant attendance (as it was impossible for her to hear my voice), she answered, 'Though I cannot hear you, I come to God's house because I love it, and would be found in his ways; and he gives me many a sweet thought upon the text when it is pointed out to me: another reason is, because there I am in the best company, in the more immediate presence of God, and among his saints, the honourable of the earth. I am not satisfied with serving God in private; it is my duty and privilege to honour him regularly in public.'" What a reproof this is to those who have their hearing, and yet always come to a place of worship late, or not at all!—*K. Arvine.*

Verse 9.—"*Gather not my soul with sinners.*" Now is the time that people should be in care and concern, that their souls be not gathered with sinners in the other world. In discoursing from this doctrine we shall—1. Consider some things implied in it. 2. Show who are the sinners, that we are to have a horror of our souls being gathered with in the other world. 3. What it is for one's soul to be gathered with sinners in the other world. 4. Consider this care and concern, or show what is implied in this earnest request, "Gather not my soul with sinners." 5. Give the reasons why we should be in such care and concern. 6. Make application.

Death is the gathering time, which the psalmist has in view in the text. Ye have a time here that ye call the gathering time, about the term when the servants are going away, wherein ye gather your strayed sheep, that every one may get their own again. Death is God's gathering time wherein he gets the souls belonging to him, and the devil those belonging to him. They did go long together, but then they are parted; and saints are taken home to the congregation of saints, and sinners to the congregation of sinners. And it concerns us to say, "Gather not my soul with sinners." Whoever be our people here, God's people or the devil's, death will gather our souls to them.

It is a horrible thing to be gathered with sinners in the other world. To think of our souls being gathered with them there, may make the hair of one's head stand up. Many now like no gathering like the gathering with sinners; it is the very delight of their hearts, it makes a brave jovial life in their eyes. And it is a pain to them to be gathered with saints, to be detained before the Lord on a Sabbath-day. But to be gathered with them in the other world, is a horror to all sorts. 1. The saints have a horror of it, as in the text. To think to be staked down in their company in the other world would be a hell of itself to the godly. David never had such a horror of the society of the diseased, the persecuted, etc., as of sinners. He is content to be gathered with saints of whatever condition; but, "Lord," says he, "Gather not my soul with sinners." 2. The wicked themselves have a horror of it. Numb. xxiii. 10. "Let me die the death of the righteous," said the wicked Balaam, "and let my last end be like his." Though they would be content to live with them, or be with them in life, their consciences bear witness that they have a horror of being with them in death. They would live with sinners, but they would die with saints. A poor, unreasonable, self-condemning thought.—*Thomas Boston.*

Verse 9.—"*Gather not my soul with sinners.*" Bind me not up in the same bundle with them, like the tares for the fire. Matt. xiii. 30. The contrast to this is seen in the following Psalm (verse 10), "When my father and my mother forsake me, then the Lord will take me up;" literally, will *gather me* to his fold. *Christopher Wordsworth.*

Verse 9.—"*Gather not my soul with sinners.*" The Lord hath a harvest and a gleaning time also, set for cutting down and binding together, in the fellow-ship of judgments, God's enemies, who have followed the same course of sinning : for here we are given to understand that God will "*gather their souls*," and so will let none escape.—*David Dickson.*

Verse 9.—"*Gather not my soul with sinners.*" After all, it may be objected that this concern seems to be common to saints and sinners. Even a wicked Balaam said, "Let me die the death of the righteous, and let my last end be like his." Numb. xxiii. 10. Take a few differences between them in this matter. 1. It is separation from Christ that makes the saints to have a horror at being gathered with sinners hereafter. Separation from Christ is the main ground of the believer's horror : but if other things were to be right with the sinner in the other world, he would be easy under separation from Christ. 2. The believer has a horror at being gathered with sinners on account of their filthiness ; but the thing that makes the sinner concerned is the prospect of punishment. No doubt, a principle of self-preservation must make punishment frightful to all ; but abstracted from that, the saints have a concern not to be gathered with sinners in the other world, upon account of their unholiness and filthiness. "He who is filthy, let him be filthy still," is enough to make a saint abhor the lot of sinners in the life to come. 3. The concern of the saints has a mighty influence upon them, to make them study holiness here ; but sinners live unholy for all their concern. "And every man that hath this hope in him purifieth himself, even as he is pure." 1 John iii. 3. What hope ? The hope of seeing Christ as he is, and of being perfectly like him, of being separated from sinners. 4. Lastly, the concern of the saints is such, that they do with purpose of heart come out from among sinners more and more in this world ; but sinners are not concerned to be separated from sinners here. Balaam wished to die the death of the righteous ; but he had no concern to live the life of the righteous, and to be separated from sinners here.—*James Scot*, 1773.

Verses 9—12.—David prays that God would not "gather his soul with sinners, whose right hand is full of bribes ;" such as, for advantage, would be bribed to sin, to which wicked gang he opposeth himself, verse 11 : "*But as for me, I will walk in mine integrity ;*" where he tells us what kept him from being corrupted and enticed, as they were, from God—it was his *integrity*. A soul walking in its integrity will take bribes neither from men, nor sin itself : and therefore he saith (verse 12), "His foot stood in an even place ;" or, as some read it, "My foot standeth in righteouness."— *William Gurnall.*

Verse 10.—"*Their right hand is full of bribes.*" If the great men in Turkey should use their religion of Mahomet to sell, as our patrons commonly sell benefices here (the office of preaching, the office of salvation), it should be taken as an intolerable thing ; the Turk would not suffer it in his common-wealth. Patrons be charged to see the office done, and not to seek a lucre and a gain by their patronship. There was a patron in England that had a benefice fallen into his hand, and a good brother of mine came unto him, and brought him thirty apples in a dish, and gave them to his man to carry them to his master. It is like he gave one to his man for his labour, to make up the gain, and so there was thirty-one. This man cometh to his master, and presented him with the dish of apples, saying, " Sir, such a man hath sent you a dish of fruit, and desireth you to be good unto him for such a benefice." "Tush, tush," quoth he, "this is no apple matter, I will none of his apples, I have as good as these (or any he hath) in mine own orchard." The man came to the priest again, and told him what his master said. "Then," quoth the priest, "desire him yet to prove one of them for my sake, he shall find them much better than they look for." He cut one of them, and found ten pieces of gold in it. "Marry," quoth he, "this is a good apple." The priest standing not far off, hearing what the gentleman said, cried out and answered, "they are all one apples, I warrant you, sir ; they grew all on one tree, and have all one taste." "Well, he is a good fellow, let him have it," quoth the patron, etc. Get you a graft of this same tree, and I warrant you it shall stand you in better stead than all St. Paul's learning.—*Hugh Latimer.*

Verse 10.—*" Bribes.''* They that see furthest into the law, and most clearly discern the cause of justice, if they suffer the dust of bribes to be thrown into their sight, their eyes will water and twinkle, and fall at last to blind connivance. It is a wretched thing when justice is made a hackney that may be backed for money, and put on with golden spurs, even to the desired journey's end of injury and iniquity. Far be from our souls this wickedness, that the ear which should be open to complaints should be stopped with the earwax of partiality. Alas! poor truth, that she must now be put to the charges of a golden earpick, or she cannot be heard!—*Thomas Adams.*

Verse 10.—

> What makes all doctrines plain and clear?
> About two hundred pounds a-year,
> And that which was proved true before
> Proved false again? Two hundred more.

Samuel Butler (1600 —1680), *in " Hudibras."* Part III. Canto I.

Verse 12 (*first clause*).—The upright man's *"foot,"* is said to *" stand in an even place;''* he walks not haltingly and uncomely, as those who go in unequal ways, which are hobbling, and up and down, or those whose feet and legs are not even (as Solomon saith), '' The legs of the lame are not equal,'' and so cannot *stand in an even place,* because one is long and the other short; the sincere man's feet are *even,* and legs of a length, as I may say; his care alike conscientious to the whole will of God. The hypocrite, like the badger, hath one foot shorter than another; or, like a foundered horse, he doth not stand, as we say, right of all four; one foot at least you shall perceive he favours, loth to put it down.—*William Gurnall.*

Verse 12.—*" On an even place."* As a man whose feet are firmly fixed upon even ground is apprehensive of no fall, so the pious worshippers of Jehovah feel no dread lest their adversaries should finally triumph over them.—*William Walford.*

HINTS TO THE VILLAGE PREACHER.

Verse 1.—*I. Two inseparable companions*—faith and holiness. II. *The blessedness of the man who possesses them.* He needs not fear the judgment, nor the danger of the way. III. *The only means of procuring them.*

Verse 1 (*last sentence*).—The upholding power of trust in God.

Verse 2.—*Divine examinations.* Their variety, severity, searching nature, accuracy, certainty: when to be desired, and when to be dreaded.

Verse 3.—Delight for the eyes and safety for the feet; or the good man's sweet contemplation and holy practice; or the heavenly compound of godliness—motive, and motion, enjoying and acting, love and truth, free grace and good works.

Verse 3.—*" Thy lovingkindness is before mine eyes."* It might be well to follow David and to keep the lovingkindness of God before *our* eyes. This should be done in four ways:—I. As a subject of contemplation. II. As the source of encouragement. III. As an incitement to praise. IV. As an example for imitation.—*William Jay.*

Verse 4.—*" Vain persons."* Who they are. Why they are to be avoided. What will become of them. *" Dissemblers."* Describe this numerous family. Show what their objects are. The mischief done to believers by their craftiness. The need of shunning them, and their fearful end.

Verse 5.—*Bad company.* Cases of its evil results, excuses for it answered, warnings given, motives urged for relinquishing.

Verse 6.—The necessity of personal holiness in order to acceptable worship.

Verse 7.—I. The believer's calling—a publisher. II. The author selected, and the quality of his works. "*Thy wondrous works*." III. The mode of advertising—"*voice of thanksgiving*," "*tell*," etc.

Verse 8.—God's house. Why we love it. What we love in it. How we show our love. How our love will be rewarded.

Verse 9.—See "Spurgeon's Sermons," No. 524. "The Saints' Horror at the Sinners' Hell."

Verse 11.—The best men needing redemption and mercy; or the outward walk before men, and the secret walk with God.

Verse 12.—Secure standing, honoured position, grateful praise.

Verse 12 (*last clause*).—Congregational Psalmody, and our personal share in it.